Java™ 2 Enterprise Edition Bible

Justin Couch and Daniel H. Steinberg

Best-Selling Books • Digital Downloads • e-Books • Answer Networks • e-Newsletters • Branded Web Sites • e-Learning

New York, NY ✦ Cleveland, OH ✦ Indianapolis, IN

Java™ 2 Enterprise Edition Bible

Published by
Hungry Minds, Inc.
909 Third Avenue
New York, NY 10022
www.hungryminds.com

Library of Congress Catalog Card Number: 2001093855

ISBN: 0-7645-0882-2

Printed in the United States of America

10 9 8 7 6 5 4 3 2 1

1B/SY/QT/QS/IN

Distributed in the United States by Hungry Minds, Inc.

Distributed by CDG Books Canada Inc. for Canada; by Transworld Publishers Limited in the United Kingdom; by IDG Norge Books for Norway; by IDG Sweden Books for Sweden; by IDG Books Australia Publishing Corporation Pty. Ltd. for Australia and New Zealand; by TransQuest Publishers Pte Ltd. for Singapore, Malaysia, Thailand, Indonesia, and Hong Kong; by Gotop Information Inc. for Taiwan; by ICG Muse, Inc. for Japan; by Intersoft for South Africa; by Eyrolles for France; by International Thomson Publishing for Germany, Austria, and Switzerland; by Distribuidora Cuspide for Argentina; by LR International for Brazil; by Galileo Libros for Chile; by Ediciones ZETA S.C.R. Ltda. for Peru; by WS Computer Publishing Corporation, Inc., for the Philippines; by Contemporanea de Ediciones for Venezuela; by Express Computer Distributors for the Caribbean and West Indies; by Micronesia Media Distributor, Inc. for Micronesia; by Chips Computadoras S.A. de C.V. for Mexico; by Editorial Norma de Panama S.A. for Panama; by American Bookshops for Finland.

For general information on Hungry Minds' products and services please contact our Customer Care department within the U.S. at 800-762-2974, outside the U.S. at 317-572-3993 or fax 317-572-4002.

For sales inquiries and reseller information, including discounts, premium and bulk quantity sales, and foreign-language translations, please contact our Customer Care department at 800-434-3422, fax 317-572-4002 or write to Hungry Minds, Inc., Attn: Customer Care Department, 10475 Crosspoint Boulevard, Indianapolis, IN 46256.

For information on licensing foreign or domestic rights, please contact our Sub-Rights Customer Care department at 212-884-5000.

For information on using Hungry Minds' products and services in the classroom or for ordering examination copies, please contact our Educational Sales department at 800-434-2086 or fax 317-572-4005.

For press review copies, author interviews, or other publicity information, please contact our Public Relations department at 317-572-3168 or fax 317-572-4168.

For authorization to photocopy items for corporate, personal, or educational use, please contact Copyright Clearance Center, 222 Rosewood Drive, Danvers, MA 01923, or fax 978-750-4470.

Credits

Acquisitions Editors
Greg Croy
Grace Buechlein

Project Editor
Michael Koch

Technical Editors
David M. Williams
Ramesh Krishnaswamy

Copy Editor
S. B. Kleinman

Editorial Manager
Mary Beth Wakefield

Vice President and Executive Group Publisher
Richard Swadley

Vice President and Executive Publisher
Bob Ipsen

Vice President and Publisher
Joseph B. Wikert

Editorial Director
Mary Bednarek

Project Coordinator
Regina Snyder

Graphics and Production Specialists
Beth Brooks, Sean Decker,
Joyce Haughey, Gabriele McCann,
Barry Offringa, Heather Pope,
Betty Schulte, Rashell Smith,
Ron Terry, Jeremey Unger, Erin Zeltner

Quality Control Technician
Laura Albert, John Greenough,
Andy Hollandbeck, Angel Perez,
Marianne Santy,

Proofreading and Indexing
TECHBOOKS Production Services

About the Authors

Justin Couch has been a professional Java programmer since early 1996 and hasn't looked back since. His travels have taken him through all realms of the Java world — from writing parts for the VRML specification (leading working groups and authoring the External Authoring Interface) to the IETF — working on the URN specifications. The applications realm he has worked on has gone through a similar wide variety — from mobile distributed applications to large-scale Web site hosting and electronic display systems. His main programming interests are virtual reality and the distributed systems required to run them. He currently runs the Java 3D community site (`http://www.j3d.org/`) and the Java 3D Programmers FAQ (`http://www.j3d.org/faq/`). When not programming Justin's interests are music (classical and electronic), gliding, and attempting to shorten his life by riding motorcycles.

Daniel H. Steinberg is the director of Java Offerings at Dim Sum Thinking. A trainer and consultant, he has been teaching and writing about Java since 1996. Daniel has covered Java on the Macintosh for *JavaWorld* magazine and the O'Reilly Network's Mac DevCenter. He managed the Mac FAQ at jGuru and served as editor of developerWorks Java Technology Zone and of the CodeMasters Challenge for *JavaWorld* magazine. Although he does Java development for and on platforms other than Mac OS X, he's happier on his Mac. Daniel has been working with Colleges and Universities to help their faculty and students keep up with the quickly changing technology. His current interests have led him to lead sessions in refactoring and extreme programming. Mostly Daniel enjoys being a dad and hanging out with his wife, two daughters, and black Lab.

Uma Veeramani, author of Chapters 18 and 19, is a software programmer and member of the technical staff at a security software company in Austin, TX. Her prior experience was as a Java developer in the financial services industry. She has experience working on a number of platforms and languages, including Java, ASP, C++, etc. Uma was a gold medallist at the University of Madras, India, and graduated with degrees in physics and computer applications.

Bruce Beyeler, author of Chapter 22, is the owner of Arizona Software Insights, a Java consulting and training company. Bruce has been consulting and training (corporate and collegiate) in Java for over four years and has 15+ years of experience developing software systems. He specializes in embedded systems, communications, and application integration. Bruce has led numerous projects ranging from embedded applications to J2EE projects in a variety of industries such as aerospace, automotive, telephony, and e-commerce. Bruce is currently working on his Ph.D. in computer science at Arizona State University, where his emphasis is embedded systems and communications.

Mike Jasnowski, author of Chapter 23, is a senior software engineer at eXcelon Corporation in Burlington, MA, and has XML and Java coming out of his ears. He works as leader of the project that develops Web-based tools for administering eXcelon's Business Process Manager. He has been involved with computers and software for over 18 years, dating back to the days before Java and XML, when he wrote some of his first programs on a TRS-80 and Apple IIe. Mike has worked on a variety of operating systems, including Multiple Virtual Storage (MVS), Linux, Windows, and Virtual Machine (VM), in addition to a variety of programming languages. He worked for Sprint for over nine years as a systems programmer and moved on to work in the healthcare and finance industries as a software engineer before finally landing at eXcelon. He is the lead author of *Java, XML, and Web Services Bible* (Hungry Minds, Inc., 2002), and he contributed three chapters to the book *Developing Dynamic WAP Applications* (Manning Press, 2001). He's also written articles for *Java Developers Journal* and *XML Journal.* He lives in Amherst, New Hampshire, with his wife Tracy, his daughter Emmeline, and a host of pets.

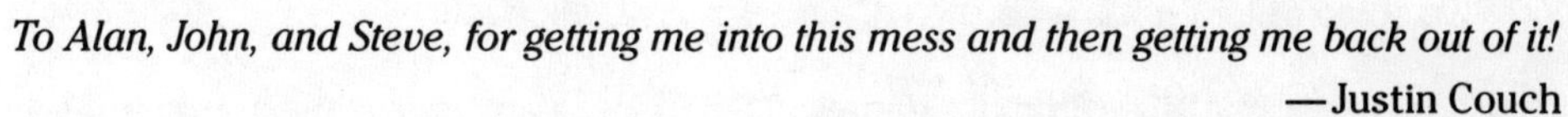

To Alan, John, and Steve, for getting me into this mess and then getting me back out of it!

—Justin Couch

To Stephen Wong, for arguing with me every day for two years until I began to get it.

—Daniel H. Steinberg

Preface

Welcome to *Java 2 Enterprise Edition Bible*. This book, which is a follow-up to *Java 2 Bible*, is for readers who wish to know more about the enterprise market. Enterprise programming is a hot topic these days, as more and more companies decide they need an online presence to complement their existing bricks-and-mortar version. This online presence is more than just a couple of Web pages; it extends to a complete electronic catalogue and purchasing system.

XML is one of the biggest drivers of the enterprise market. As companies are starting to realize they need to work together to smooth out the supply-chain management, they are building their second- or third-generation systems. They are doing this in collaboration with their suppliers and partners. To build these systems they need interoperability, and whole industries are springing up around this need alone. Need to add a new partner or supplier? Just ask for the XML DTD. Very quickly you can now include the new functionality in your system.

Throughout this book we will reference various commercial sites that you will be familiar with as examples of how large-scale businesses are integrating not only their own Web sites, but also those of partners and suppliers, into one single system. Order your computer from Dell and you can track it through every stage of the build process. Then, once it has hit the courier, you can use the Dell site to trace the courier's information about its progress. Dell doesn't use just one courier, either — yet your experience is identical regardless of which one is used.

What this Book Aims to Do

The aim of this book is to introduce you to all the enterprise Java APIs. Many books are floating around that deal with specific elements of the J2EE specification — Enterprise Java Beans and XML being the most prevalent. Yet what these titles fail to address is the whole collection of other interfaces that you as a Java programmer might find useful. For example, did you know that an API exists for e-mail and newsgroup handling as part of J2EE?

As a programmer, I like to stay informed about all of the possible options. If I know about them, I can investigate them further if they sound useful. If I don't know about them, I might be missing some very important information that might have made my life much easier. Therefore, the aim of this book is to give you as broad an understanding as possible of the APIs that can be useful in creating an enterprise-level application. The primary focus is on the J2EE specification, but we also introduce other libraries where we feel they will benefit your application.

We do not try to cover every topic in great depth. We leave that for other books. What we do is cover each topic in sufficient detail that you can get started with simple programs and then *know* the right questions to ask next. J2EE is a huge specification. If we were to cover it all in depth, you would need to cart the volumes of the book on a trolley. No doubt you already have a bookshelf full of programming books and don't need a lot more. Use this book as the introduction to all the parts of J2EE, and then consult other books that treat specific areas of knowledge in depth.

Who this Book Is For

This book is aimed at the intermediate to advanced programmer. We assume that you already have some Java programming under your belt. We don't spend any time introducing the programming language, and we assume you know how to compile and debug a Java application in your favorite development environment.

If you are looking for a beginner-level Java book then we can recommend the *Java 2 Bible* (ISBN 0-7645-4632-5) written by Aaron Walsh, Justin Couch, and Daniel H. Steinberg.

For the intermediate programmer, this book will introduce all the various technologies available to you as a J2EE programmer. Perhaps you have never used J2EE before, so this book will show you where to start and what order to approach your learning in.

For the more advanced programmer, this book can serve as a guide to expanding your horizon over the more concentrated areas of programming. Use it as a guide to exploring more possibilities within the area that you have already been working on, or new ways to address a problem. Finally, you can use it to learn about new areas that you have not heard of before. Because of the breadth of J2EE, it is always possible that new topics exist that you haven't heard of. Even after six-plus years of Java programming experience, I am constantly finding new items popping up to learn about.

How to Use this Book

This book is divided into a number of parts. Each part is a self-contained area that focuses on just one piece of the enterprise puzzle. Within each part, each chapter will stand alone if you know the underlying technology.

Our approach is to cover all the parts of developing an enterprise application. That is, we don't follow just the Java APIs, but introduce the fundamentals of the technology that Java operates on. We believe that for you to be the best developer, you must have a solid understanding of the foundations. In fact, many of the enterprise APIs demand it. If you don't understand how an XML document is structured, and the terms involved, you will find it very hard to use the XML-parsing APIs, or to define how to load Enterprise Java Beans on your Web server.

We recommend reading the parts of the book that are useful for what you need to do now. There is no need to read it from cover to cover. If you haven't written an enterprise application before then we highly recommend you look at Part I of the book. After that, feel free to roam to the sections that best suit your needs. If we need another part of the book to help explain a piece of technology, we'll give you a cross reference to the appropriate chapter.

This book is comprised of six parts that lead you from the front end of the system to the back end. Each part covers a number of topics. We can summarize these parts as follows.

Part I: Getting Started

The introductory parts show you around the enterprise space and the various parts of the J2EE specification: why you would want to use it, what constitutes an "enterprise" application, and some examples. The advanced user can skip this part and head into the more specific chapters.

Part II: Delivering Content

Here we focus on the APIs that are used to deal with an external user — receiving input and sending output back. It is all about presentation. Rarely is there application logic in these parts. They are more about assembling pieces of pre-built logic into some correct order and then presenting the output to the user. More often than not, the output is presented in a Web page, but (as you will see) there is more to this part than just making a pretty Web site.

Part III: Finding Things with Databases and Searches

At the heart of every enterprise system is a database. In that database is a lot of information. In fact, so much, that without having some form of search capability, you would find it almost impossible to do in anything else with your application. The database has many forms other than the Oracle or MS Access that you are used to. Specialized databases exist for many different purposes, and sometimes using Oracle alone is the wrong solution.

Part IV: Communicating Between Systems with XML

As e-commerce systems become more and more complex, the ability to seamlessly talk between systems becomes more important. It will be an extremely rare situation when you as the developer have to build the complete end-to-end system. It is almost guaranteed that you will need to integrate third-party software into the end product. The technology most commonly used for this purpose is XML. As a text-based structured data format, it works wonderfully well for this. However, to make the most out of XML requires an awful lot of knowledge, and so we devote an entire part of the book to learning everything about XML.

Part V: Abstracting the System

When system complexity or load grow high enough, a simple two-tier application will no longer handle your demands. To help alleviate this problem, a range of different technologies have been introduced over the years to allow you to abstract the raw data sources into collections of business logic. These collections can be used in many different forms to present a range of applications to the end user.

Part VI: Building Big Systems

Moving up to the really huge systems that you might see in a site like Amazon.com demands even more of your application. The skills and knowledge needed to implement these solutions is often very specialized. How often will you get a complete system failure today? Most likely never, so you have to know how to build applications that can deal with partial failures and still continue to operate normally. This part is devoted to the Java technologies needed to deal with such applications.

Appendixes

While code and examples are extremely useful, there are many other pieces of information that you need to know. The appendices cover Sun's Reference Implementation of the J2EE specification, listings of products and vendors of J2EE systems, and also a glossary of terms to help you through all those acronyms.

Companion Web Site

Be sure to visit the companion Web site for this book at `http://www.hungryminds.com/extras`. Here you can download all of the code listings and program examples covered in the chapters.

Acknowledgments

Writing any book is time consuming at the best of times. When you then have to track and rewrite large sections of the book as specifications change so dramatically like the EJB 2.0 spec did, then it can get rather frustrating. So, my first big thanks go to Grace and Michael for managing to stick with us as we had to go back over and completely re-edit so much of this book. To Alan and Steve, my sometimes business partners and collaborators in coding – thanks for keeping me sane. Weird and wonderful these times certainly are, and I hope to keep working with you for some time yet.

—Justin Couch

The people on this project made this an enjoyable experience. Michael Koch has once again taught me a lot about writing and worked hard to make my writing say what I thought that I meant. Grace Buechlein has been kind and patient and made sure the book was completed while understanding the requirements of real life. Justin has done an amazing job in a year that presented him with challenges that would have beaten a lesser man. This book became a larger project than any of us anticipated. Thank you all for your help and encouragement.

Kimmy the wonderwife continues to know just when I need her to be supportive and when, instead, I need her to be critical. I can't imagine taking on one of these projects without her permission and help. I have traveled a lot less this year than last. It means that most days I'm able to walk my eldest daughter to and from Kindergarten and that the family gets to spend more time cooking together and hanging out. It's nice to see that there can be upsides to an economic correction.

—Daniel H. Steinberg

Contents

Getting Started

PART I

✦ ✦ ✦ ✦

In This Part

✦ ✦ ✦ ✦

CHAPTER

Defining the Enterprise

In This Chapter

Introducing J2EE, the enterprise version of the Java environment

Identifying how J2EE fits into the Java framework

Defining the various parts of an enterprise application

A lot of hype has surrounded the Java language and platform since they were first introduced in 1995. With the growth of e-commerce Web sites and other "enterprise" applications, Java has really found its niche. So what is it all about, and why is it good for you?

When it comes to building large-scale Web sites that involve e-commerce, the most frequently used language is Java. In fact, most of the time the question is "Why should we use anything other than Java?" By the time you have finished this book, you will be able to understand why that question would be asked. There are many great reasons to use the Java environment. From the very design of the Java APIs to the other technologies that Java integrates, it just makes the development process feel "right." For almost every task in the enterprise level there is a Java API to make it quick and simple to perform.

Introducing Enterprise Applications

There's an old cliché, "Ask 10 lawyers a question, and you will get 11 different answers." That about sums up how people define an "enterprise" application. Probably the best way to define an enterprise application is to show you a number of examples. It might surprise you to learn what can be classified as an enterprise application. As a programmer, you've probably wondered what goes on down the back of that Web site.

Within all applications that could be classified under the enterprise label there is a common set of features that you could expect to find:

- A database that contains a lot of information critical to the company's success.
- A set of (possibly hundreds) of small applications to access parts of the database.

✦ A number of different applications from different parts of the company integrated to look like a cohesive whole.

✦ A handful of developers madly maintaining the applications and providing new features on an ad-hoc basis.

✦ Some form of Web site for accessing information and services within the company, if the company is Internet-based or deals a lot with other companies.

Many other forms of applications can be called enterprise applications. However, these tend to become specialized to a particular product or technology area.

Chapter 2 will expand on the different classes of enterprise applications. These examples are brief, to illustrate the various ways you can think of an application as being one that is used in an enterprise setting.

Not just a pretty Web site

So what goes into an average enterprise application? From the preceding description you can imagine that almost any enterprise application is going to be a serious affair — no sitting down for a couple of hours and just churning out a thousand-line application. Although you might end up doing that for the little report generators, the system as a whole is a very large piece of software that requires you to have a good design and an understanding of the principles involved.

Before going into the details of the pieces of an enterprise application, take a look at a very typical example: the e-commerce Web site. You can find these everywhere, from Amazon.com to Buy.com. Chances are that if you are building an enterprise application, at least somewhere in it you will have to build a Web front end to it.

A quick look through one of these Web sites reveals a number of necessary features:

✦ A search engine to enable you to find the page you need from among the hundreds or thousands available.

✦ A shopping basket to enable you to purchase things.

✦ Pages that tailor themselves to your individual needs, such as by keeping track of your recent purchases.

✦ Links to third-party providers, such as the courier companies delivering your orders and the credit providers that debit your credit card.

To the end user, this might look a bit like Figure 1-1 — you have these collections of functionality behind the site doing useful stuff.

Now how does this same system appear to the guy in the warehouse packing boxes to send out to the customer? He takes a very different view, as you can see in Figure 1-2. He sees a set of forms detailing the next order he must fill, a handler for the courier company (or companies), and a way to order more parts from suppliers.

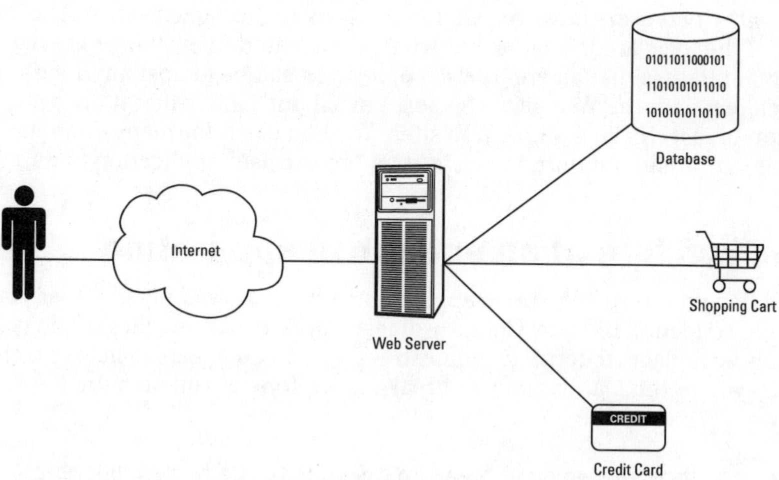

Figure 1-1: How a typical user would think of the structure of an e-commerce Web site – search engines, shopping baskets, and a payment system

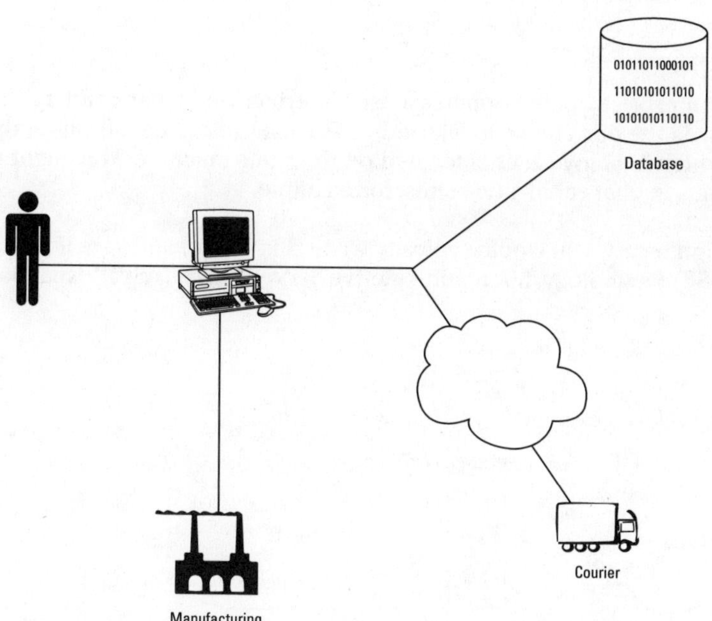

Figure 1-2: How a worker in a warehouse would think of the e-commerce system – a database of the orders to be filed, and interfaces to the courier company and to suppliers

Notice how the two users have very different views of the same system. The data and most of the logic are the same, but what is presented to each user is very different. The point here is that an enterprise application can be almost anything—don't just associate it with the Web site. The best part about J2EE is that it does not restrict you to just thinking about Web sites. You can use it for many different things that you would not normally expect an "enterprise" application to do.

The architecture of an enterprise application

When building your own enterprise application, you will generally find that you need a large collection of code. Unlike ordinary applications, in which code is all in the one physical place, enterprise applications spread code across many machines. This forces you to think about how to break up the code to run on more than one computer.

In industry parlance, the way you break up the code to run across different machines is by using what is called a tiered design. Think of all the different layers of code a piece of information passes through to get from the user to the database and back again: Each of these layers is a tier. Enterprise systems are generally classed as either 2-tier, 3-tier, or *n*-tier.

2-tier applications

A typical 2-tier enterprise application has a user interface and a back end, typically a database such as the one shown in Figure 1-3. The user interface talks directly to the database, which in many cases is located on the same machine. You might find these applications in chat room–style sites, for example.

In implementation terms, you would typically write this sort of software using Java Server Pages (JSP) technology, Microsoft's Active Server Pages (ASP)/Visual Basic, PHP, or Perl.

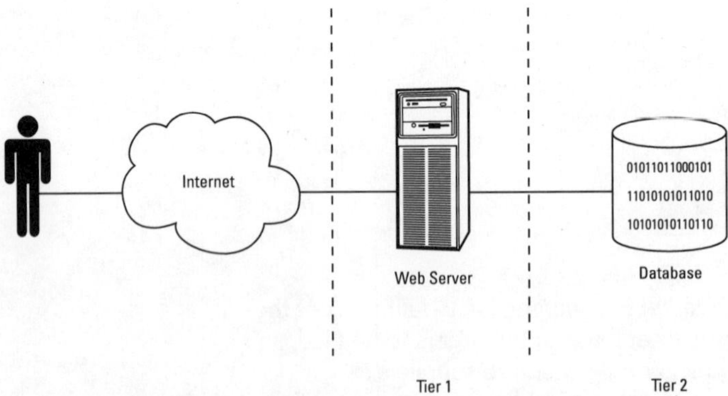

Figure 1-3: A simple 2-tier application that has a user interface (a Web browser/server) and a database

3-tier applications

In a 2-tier application, the application talks directly to the database. 3-tier applications add an extra layer of logic between the user-interface code and the database, as shown in Figure 1-4. Typically this layer is called "business logic;" it represents an abstraction of the functionality. You no longer need to worry about the database implementation, because your user-interface code now talks to this abstract representation.

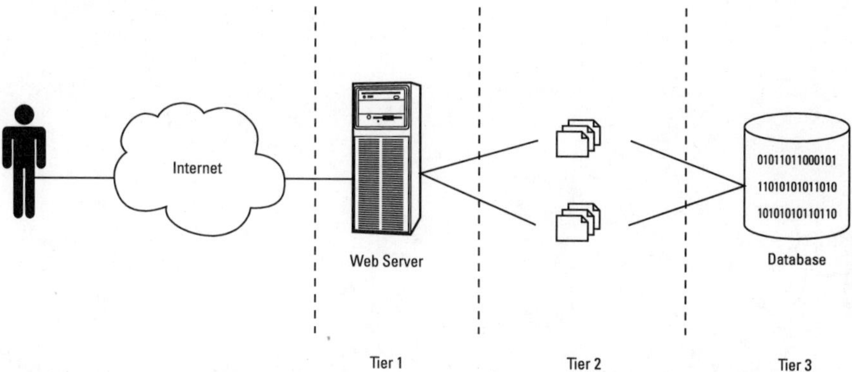

Figure 1-4: A 3-tier application inserts a layer of abstraction between the user-interface code and the database at the back.

In this middle tier, you normally use a technology that provides a level of abstraction so that you now see the functionality as a collection of objects rather than SQL calls. The most commonly used of these technology options are Enterprise Java Beans (EJB), Common Object Request Broker Architecture (CORBA), and Microsoft's Distributed Component Object Model (DCOM). The reason for using this type of architecture is that it enables you to easily increase the number of first-tier servers and services. If you need another application that needs a similar sort of logic but a different presentation (say an internal application rather than a Web site), you can quickly add the new functionality without needing to copy old code, modify it and hope it works. Of course, following good software engineering practices, you would minimize the exposure to the next level down and add extra security (for example, by limiting access to a database to only certain functions and using firewalls at each level).

n-tier applications

Once you get beyond three separate tiers of code you come to the open class where anything goes. No longer do you use the term 4-tier, 5-tier, and so on, but instead the more generic term *n*-tier. Applications that reach this size are typically much more complex and have many different layers, such as those shown in Figure 1-5. Some parts of the system might use only three while others might use six or more. Of course, the interesting thing here is that once you get to this class of design, you are only talking about one company — the interface to an external company may itself have even more tiers that you don't see in the design.

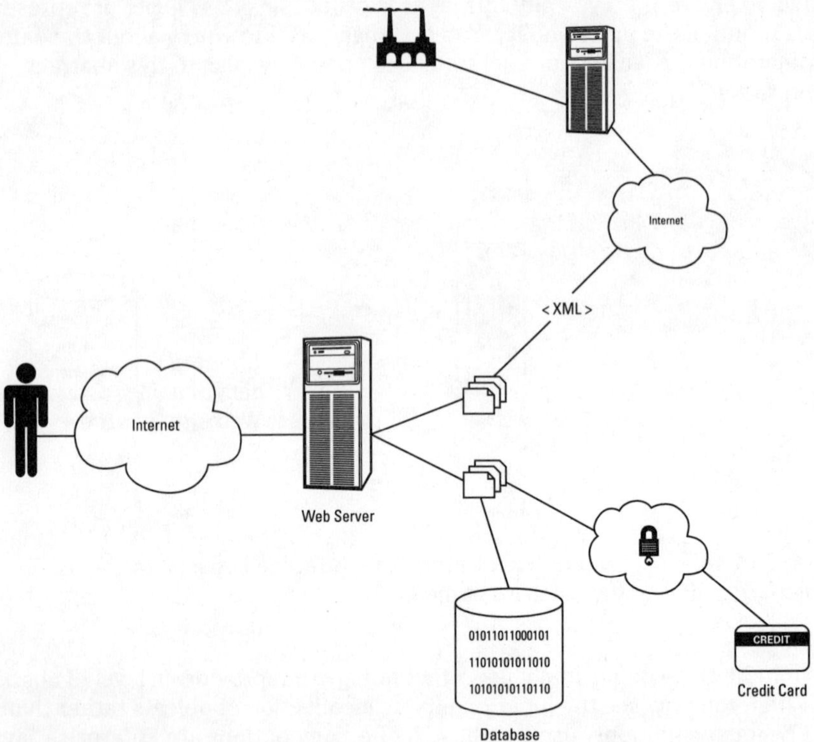

Figure 1-5: A multi-tiered application that provides services to many different systems

The middle tier is more than just an abstraction layer: It also acts as a switch to direct queries and updates to various different underlying systems. For example, to extract information about a user, you can go to an SQL database to find out the purchases he or she has made, to an LDAP database for his or her contact details, and to an extranet link to the courier company for delivery progress reports. This information is all neatly packaged and hidden inside a single application object available to the various presentation-code modules.

You now face the problem that each of these third-party systems is different, and your job as a programmer becomes that much more difficult. You have to make sure that communications always work well among disparate systems. And this is where XML enters the fray as the *lingua franca* of enterprise systems.

The building blocks of an enterprise application

When you look at these tiered application types you can see a nice pattern formed by the various items of functionality. Each of the preceding figures has one more block of functionality than the one that preceded it. Each block is self-contained and is not always appropriate for your application.

When analyzing an enterprise application you can break the code down into a series of blocks of functionality. The previous section introduced you to the definitions of these blocks. Essentially you can take each tier as the basis of that definition. If you did so, you would end up with the collection presented in the following sections. Interestingly, each of these sections also maps to a subset of the J2EE APIs; we will use these as the basis for our presentation in this book.

User presentation

We start with the thing that everyone sees — the block about user presentation. Here you take all of your underlying data and present them in a form your average user can understand. The majority of the time this is a Web site, but there are other ways of presenting user data.

If you look at some of the most popular tools within a "standard" company, you will come up with a list that contains Visual Basic, Delphi, PowerBuilder, and friends. These are also user-presentation tools. Although they won't help you build Web sites, they do provide a quick and simple way to present a complex set of underlying data with a simple user interface and a quick-to-build GUI application. In the Java realm, equivalents would be Borland's JBuilder and IBM's VisualAge. Although these are not as popular as the non-Java tools, the rise of J2EE is certainly presenting a pressing case for starting to use them.

Note

In the case of Java tools, the user interface is usually constructed with Swing components. Swing is not part of the J2EE APIs, but is part of the core Java 2 Standard Edition that you have most likely already programmed with.

Another form of presentation that you will be familiar with is e-mail. Yes, even those simple reminder and confirmation e-mails are part of an enterprise system. Just like a Web page, they take a collection of data and massage it into something you can make sense of. They operate on the same data abstraction layer and build something useful.

Note

As an example of how e-mail is just another presentation system, consider this real-world example: To maintain the Java 3D FAQ, we keep the contents in a database. Then, when we need to generate an updated page, we create an XML representation and then turn that representation into a Web page and a text file for e-mail at the same time.

Data storage and retrieval

The underlying data is the most important part of any enterprise system. Without data, all the rest is meaningless. The most popular way to store data is in a relational database, as typified by Oracle and Sybase. However, many other forms of databases are available. This is where the rubber meets the road in the application implementation. If you choose the right data-storage system, the rest becomes a relatively simple affair.

One thing you can be sure of is that for any type of data storage there will be many different vendors providing something to do the task—from open-source solutions to very expensive proprietary databases. Because there have been so many different vendors, there is a lot of pressure to conform to a set of standards for each type so that access is simple for the application writer. So what we now have is a simple collection of APIs and a vast variety of implementers of those APIs. You can use whatever data storage suits your needs and not have to rewrite the code each time it changes.

From the application perspective, at this tier you have to decide how to store data (the relational database is *not* always the best choice). Once you know how the data are going to be stored, you can then look at the available API sets. These APIs provide the programmer abstraction that you need to get the job done. Where possible, APIs should be independent of the database, but allow as much low-level access to the raw system as possible. For example, when talking to a relational database management system (RDBMS) you really want to use SQL to give you the most power and flexibility.

Communicating between different systems

An increasingly important aspect of enterprise systems is the ability to integrate with existing systems and also with systems from third-party sources—other businesses your code is interacting with. Quite often you cannot change these other applications (you don't own them, you don't have the source code, or they are just too old to modify) even though they are not completely compatible with what your code does. However, business demands mean that you must make them cooperate.

In trying to make disparate applications cooperate, you need to provide a layer of abstraction over them. Often the only way to do this is to make sure they both understand the same data. With PCs, UNIX boxes, and mainframes all potentially sharing the same data, you end up being reduced to using files. In the old days, these might have been comma-delimited files or similarly archaic, hard-to-read, and usually poorly documented systems. Over the last few years the best choice has become using a well-defined meta-language that enables particular application providers to build their own protocols. The result is that you no longer need to worry about how to parse the file and can instead concentrate on the data contained in the file. Unambiguous communications means that application developers can spend their time dealing with application logic rather than debugging their file readers.

Building components to use

Once you start building an enterprise application, you find that people would like to start using it for all sorts of things that you didn't originally envisage. In bigger companies, programmers from other groups may also want to use your system. Suddenly they start putting strange data into your database in ways that you didn't want them to, and it causes bugs in your code. This is not a healthy situation. Similarly, your Web site has suddenly grown from a thousand users to a million. You need a pile of extra hardware to support this. What are you going to do?

Creating abstract representations of your data that sit between the databases and user-presentation code has many advantages. You can:

- Implement functionality only once and have many different users take advantage of it.
- Scale any single part of the system without affecting the other parts.
- Protect vital business assets held in the database by preventing unauthorized access and manipulation of data in their raw form.
- Deal with a single source of all information regardless of whether the information came from local or remote sources (or a combination of the two).

Growing with the times

As your applications become larger and have more users, an extra set of conditions comes into play. A system that has a couple of thousand users accessing functionality every minute, requires making sure *all* the updates occur correctly and don't lead you into an unrecoverable state with some items changed and others not. Similarly, as your enterprise applications encompass more systems, the odds of any one part falling over increases. With the chance of something critical dying, you need to take more care to protect your software from creating inconsistent data.

Although the database interface enables you to change items, the typical interface only allows one interaction at a time. As applications grow you might need to make changes to two separate tables at the same time. If one fails, you don't want the other one to go ahead. Traditional API sets don't include this level of control of the transactions because many cases don't require it. To provide these capabilities you can include another independent set of controls and in this way form an extra tier in the system.

Introducing J2EE

So far we have kept discussions on a purely abstract level, staying away from Java-specific references. In this section, you'll see how these abstract concepts correspond to what Java in general, and Enterprise Java in particular, deliver.

A brief history of Enterprise Java

The Java environment has not always catered to the enterprise market. When Java was first released, the hype was about its ability to provide interactive content on Web sites. Unfortunately the delivery didn't live up to the hype, and Java suffered some bad credibility setbacks. However, some adventurous types decided to give it a try on the server side. Slowly, under the radar of the press, the tide turned in favor of these developers, and the Java environment really found a niche that has turned it into quite a market winner.

The Java editions

As you wander around the Java Web site you may become confused as to what is happening. There are just so many different products, APIs, and projects that it is easy to get confused. Most of this revolves around the way the various standard class libraries are packaged together to form what Sun calls editions of Java.

The home of Java is located at `http://java.sun.com/`. Here you can find all the information you need about APIs, download examples, and get links to external sites.

Three editions of the Java core class libraries exist: Micro, Standard, and Enterprise. These editions can be summarized as follows:

- ✦ **Micro (J2ME):** This is a heavily restricted version designed to run on embedded devices such as Palm Pilots, pagers, and mobile phones. These machines have very restricted hardware and processing power, as well as limited display capabilities.
- ✦ **Standard (J2SE):** This version includes the original core set of libraries designed to enable you to write a desktop application or applet in a Web browser. J2SE mostly consists of GUI frameworks, some networking, and I/O processing libraries.
- ✦ **Enterprise (J2EE):** This is the everything-but-the-kitchen-sink version. It contains libraries for finding and interfacing with almost any form of computerized data source. In short, J2EE is a superset of the J2SE libraries but with the main expansion being directed at the data processing and behind-the-scenes market.

J2SE is what you are introduced to in introductory texts. In this book we introduce all the new items presented by the J2EE extensions.

Integration of existing and new technologies

One of the greatest strengths of Java in the enterprise environment is the way it has gone about introducing new technologies while integrating existing technologies at the same time. In doing so it has adhered to the philosophy established in the core Java environment: provide a very consistent set of APIs that observe the 80/20 rule to speed application development.

One of the complexities of writing native code applications used to be dealing with the enormous range of options. Making a simple socket connection was typically a two-page exercise in code. With the elimination of most of these options, which are only used in 20 percent of cases, that socket connection became only five lines of code. While this eliminated a certain class of applications, the remaining 80 percent suddenly took a third or a quarter of the time to develop. For big companies, that meant realizing more requirements with less effort — a major plus in any environment, and the reason systems like Visual Basic, Delphi, and PowerBuilder became so popular.

Realizing that Java developers diligently work in environments that also include a lot of legacy code, a lot of work has gone into developing APIs that make these capabilities easier to use. For example, there is no reason to create a new database system, but it makes sense to create an abstract API to enable any developer to feed SQL statements to an existing one. Similarly, there were a lot of pre-existing mainframe applications that needed to be integrated and many military applications that used CORBA, so all of these have been integrated into the J2EE toolkit for application developers.

Navigating J2EE

From the preceding simple introduction you can see that J2EE has a lot of different capabilities. It is a very large toolkit for enterprise application developers and rivals the size of the core Java specification in size and spread of coverage. The J2EE APIs can be separated into the same categories as the building blocks of an enterprise application.

User presentation

Once you have gathered data from the various abstract objects, you need to return them to the user. The goal of the presentation layer is to facilitate this, normally by means of a Web browser using server-side Servlet or JSP technologies. There are other API sets provided, however, as documented in Table 1-1.

A common assumption made by programmers is that Servlets or JSPs are really only useful to someone dealing with Web browsers — that is, a person sitting in front of a machine looking at a Web page. They can be used for so much more than this. You can have two parts of the application talking together through an HTTP protocol passing binary data in each direction. This might be useful in situations in which you want to firewall off a certain piece of functionality behind other systems (for example, in an electronic-payment gateway system).

User presentation capabilities of the J2EE specification can be found in Part II, "Delivering Content," where you'll find chapters on Servlet and JavaServer Pages technologies and JavaMail.

Table 1-1
APIs that provide user-presentation capabilities

API	*Description*
Servlets	Used to provide dynamic Web site support for the Java language. Plugs straight into the back of the Web server to process queries for dynamic services for which you need complex capabilities.
JSP	Used for simpler, dynamic Web-server capabilities wherein Java code is intermingled with the raw HTML and processed inline.
JavaMail	Interface to the mail and newsgroups capabilities. Used to interact with any form of mail system to either receive or send e-mail.

Data storage

As we have been hinting throughout this chapter, the data-storage APIs provide a level of abstraction beyond that of the individual protocols. Two main APIs are available here, both of which are documented in Table 1-2. Both of these APIs abstract you from the low-level connection details and provide an abstract representation of the data contained in the data source.

To enable this abstraction between the data source and your code, both of these APIs use a service provider–implementation interface. This effectively enables a vendor to write an implementation without having to provide your code with the access to the vendor's internal code, while allowing the internals of the abstract API to get at the fundamental details. To configure a different provider, all you need is a string describing the name of the startup class. From there you can use and make queries on the underlying data source through the normal interfaces.

Data storage APIs are presented in Part III, "Finding Things with Databases and Searches," where we cover JDBC and JNDI. We also heavily cover the underlying technologies with separate chapters on SQL and LDAP.

Table 1-2
APIs that provide abstracted data-storage capabilities

API	*Description*
JDBC	Java DataBase Connectivity, an abstract representation of SQL interactions with a database. Enables you to create queries and to interact with the results in a Java-oriented manner rather than forcing you to use raw text processing.
JNDI	Java Naming and Directory Interface, an abstract representation of many different types of directory services, but most commonly used with LDAP databases. May also be used with DNS, file systems, and property systems (for example, Microsoft's Windows Registry).

Inter-system communications

J2EE only provides one set of inter-system communications based on XML. As XML is rapidly becoming the de facto standard for this type of work, we don't consider it much of an issue. Within the XML sphere, there is a lot of variety and many different groups all working to achieve some form of a standard—whether it be an industry standard, formal standard through one of the various bodies like ISO or W3C, or some other form. As there is no telling what will eventually become accepted, the J2EE specification is only adopting the most accepted of these proposed standards into the specification at this point. Although only four specifications are supported through J2EE, many others are working their way through the Java Community Process at the time of this writing. The standards that are covered by J2EE (and J2SE) are shown in Table 1-3.

There is an interesting set of issues here. Currently the XML-processing capabilities are defined within the J2EE specification. However, the latest version of the J2SE (v1.4) also defines the same API sets. This could lead to some interesting clashes in the current versions. (For example, it is already known that J2EE 1.3 does not play well with J2SE 1.4 betas.)

Part IV, "Communicating between Systems with XML," is devoted to exploring XML and all of the capabilities surrounding it, including some of the upcoming standards not in the current specification. Work on the future J2EE XML specifications is taking place at a very rapid pace. From the business perspective, ebXML and JAXM are the current flavors that look to be promising.

Table 1-3
APIs that provide communications capabilities

API	*Description*
JAXP	Java API for XML Processing, the highest level APIs for processing XML documents and related technologies. Enables you to create parsers without knowing the implementation. The latest version also supports XML Schemas and stylesheets (XSLT).
SAX	Simple API for XML, a representation of an XML parser that presents information in a serial format as the document is read. The interface is defined by the XML development community.
DOM	Document Object Model, an in-memory representation of an XML document after it has been parsed.

Abstract objects

A major push behind EJBs and CORBA are the principles of abstraction. This middle layer provides you with a number of different ways to abstract details of your system away. Which one you use depends on the type of application you have to write. Are you going into a system that consists of a lot of legacy code? Are you adding just another application to an existing enterprise Java environment? These are the sorts of questions you will need to ask when deciding which of these technologies to use (see Table 1-4).

Part V, "Abstracting the System," is dedicated to covering the various distributed object abstraction APIs.

Table 1-4
APIs that provide abstract object capabilities

API	*Description*
RMI	Remote Method Invocation, a simple representation of a remote object that is Java-specific. Contains its own network protocol and infrastructure.
EJB	Enterprise Java Beans, a high-level framework for the management of abstract objects. The underlying communications between the abstract representation and its server may use RMI.
CORBA	Common Object Request Broker Architecture, the predecessor of RMI and EJBs, which operates in a multi-language environment. For example, a C application may provide services to an Ada application. CORBA provides a different set of capabilities to RMI where it does some things better, and some things not as well.

Large systems

To enable the delivery of the largest of the enterprise applications with J2EE, two API sets are available (outlined in Table 1-5). These are combined with the other enterprise APIs to provide the most reliable systems.

Design principles for building large-scale systems and the APIs available to do this work are covered in Part VI, "Building Big Systems."

Table 1-5
APIs that provide robust and reliable systems

API	*Description*
JTA	Java Transaction API, robust and reliable systems that conform to ACID principles.
JMS	Java Messaging Service, interfaces to message-based systems such as mainframes.

Connecting the dots

In the latest revision of the J2EE specification, a collection of new features has been added that can best be described as Glue APIs. These are mainly focused at helping J2EE applications fit into existing environments and also enable the disparate parts of the existing J2EE APIs to work in a more cohesive and consistent manner. These new APIs are introduced in Table 1-6.

Table 1-6
APIs used to connect J2EE to other applications

API	*Description*
Activation	This is actually one of the oldest APIs around, dating back to the time that JDBC was first introduced. Activation is about locating and running external applications, as well as describing file and networking concepts using MIME types.
JAAS	Java Authentication and Authorization Service, a pluggable API for providing security services such as authenticating users of the system. For those familiar with UNIX systems, this is very similar to PAM. JAAS is part of the core J2SE 1.4 specification.
J2EE Connector Architecture	Architecture and APIs for integrating J2EE applications with existing enterprise applications like ERP and CRM systems (for example, SAP R/3).

Not just for the enterprise application

All of the APIs presented in the previous sections can also be used as standard extensions to the normal JDK. Although the focus of this book is on the use of J2EE in the enterprise application, there is nothing to stop you from using these APIs in an ordinary application. For example, XML is such a huge topic within the programming world that it is being found everywhere. Desktop applications and even little advertising applets are using XML to define their data – not to mention the fact that XML is becoming a part of the core J2SE standard from v1.4 and onwards. JNDI arrived as part of the core specification in J2SE v1.3, which has been out since summer 2000.

Deciding which parts to use

With so much to choose from it is often hard to decide where to start and what will be most useful for your application. It is often easy to take on too many new parts rather than limit what you are using to something manageable. The following sections will help you decide the best parts to start with for your project.

By programmer

If you are an experienced programmer moving to J2EE, the design of your project will automatically point out which parts of the J2EE environment you will need to use. Are you starting in an environment where you need to integrate with and/or replace existing technologies?

Beginner programmers either moving to Java or just beginning in an enterprise application will ideally be directed by the more senior members of their projects. However, some requirements will still be pretty obvious. If you need to send an e-mail there is only one API: JavaMail. Where you don't have a set direction, we suggest you start with the core protocol APIs and move upwards as you find necessary. For example, to use Enterprise Java Beans effectively you really need to know about RMI, JNDI, and JDBC (and of course SQL). It always pays to understand the lowest level first as a basis for other projects.

By project

An alternate guide to deciding which part or parts of J2EE to use is the goal of the project. The options for an all-new project are quite different from those for a project wherein you are building on a legacy system.

If you are starting a completely fresh project, then we recommend going for the complete J2EE environment. That is, don't use any of the older technologies like CORBA for your middleware infrastructure. Staying within an all-Java environment has significant advantages both in system capabilities and future migration paths for both hardware and software. As a grossly simplified taster, CORBA is not capable of passing complete abstract objects around remotely the way EJBs are. Naturally these considerations also depend on what other software projects you expect to be integrating with in the future. If you know that you will need to integrate applications that do not use Java, then you may be better off using CORBA.

Note

As an interesting aside, the reason that RMI started in the first place was due to these limitations in CORBA (only allowing primitives). Since then, the latest changes in the CORBA specification have been to bring those RMI capabilities back into CORBA, thus driving it to be more Java-like. Definitely a case of swings and roundabouts in the various specifications driving both communities forward as there is now RMI-IIOP that allows RMI objects to be made available over the IIOP protocol to CORBA-capable systems.

For an existing project, unless it is already working in a completely J2EE environment, it is most likely that you will be using CORBA APIs or JMS. The former is the middleware environment mostly used by non-Java languages such as C and Ada. If you have to integrate with existing mainframe environments such as the IBM AS/400, then you will be using the Java Messaging Service (JMS). You may also need to look around for other third-party APIs such as IBM's MQSeries libraries.

Getting Started

Now that we've introduced the J2EE specification, you need to know how to get up and running. First you will need to get J2EE installed on your computer. After installing the environment you will need to decide on a starter project to introduce the new capabilities.

Downloading and installing J2EE

Before you start coding, you need some code to start with. From the basic text editor (vi, emacs, or Notepad) to the grand development graphical development environment, each developer is different. The J2EE environment will work with all of these. In order to accommodate both camps, we will present both a basic and an all-encompassing setup that will be needed to work with J2EE.

Some incompatibility exists between the standard extensions provided by the J2EE and J2SE environments. If you are installing both on your machine, then please read the advice included in the J2EE documentation.

If you choose to use the J2EE reference implementation from Sun, please refer to Appendix A, where you'll find a very detailed set of instructions on how to install, configure, and then use the reference implementation.

The basic setup

Java is everywhere, but how do you get started? Well, first you need a copy of the Java Development Kit (JDK) for your platform. If you visit Sun's Java Web site at `http://java.sun.com/` you will find either an implementation for your platform or a link to a site from which you can download an independently supplied version. The JDK provides the basic needs for your development — compiler, documentation, and core class libraries for the J2SE environment.

You can find the homepage for the J2EE environment at `http://java.sun.com/j2ee/`.

The next thing you need will be an implementation of the J2EE specification. A sample environment is provided on Sun's Web site in the J2EE area. If you are just kicking the tires, then this should be satisfactory. For a real-world environment, it is definitely not recommended. Instead, you are going to have to look for a commercial package that implements the J2EE specification.

As far as we are aware, no complete open-source J2EE environments exist. The Tomcat/Jakarta project at the Apache foundation is close, but is not a complete J2EE environment and is missing several key API sets. The Jakarta project can be found at `http://jakarta.apache.org/`.

Once you have downloaded these packages (and don't forget the accompanying documentation!) you will need to install them. Use the suggested directories from the installation routines, making sure that you install the software before the documentation.

Basic installation is very simple, and there's not much that can go wrong if you follow all the hints. Once you're done with installation you can start writing J2EE code. Some of this code you can even run without any extra work. Code that uses XML, the Mail APIs, and JNDI will work fine. For Enterprise Java Beans (EJB) and some of the other APIs you must run through a setup (deployment is the J2EE term) process before you can execute the code. You will run through this process when you get to the EJB introduction in Chapters 16 and Chapter 17.

The grand setup

If your corporate environment is keen on going for the gold-plated option with development environments, then there are several tools worth looking into.

One of the first questions is usually, "What IDEs support J2EE?" There are several, and they cater to all tastes although each has some major pitfall. IBM has VisualAge, a good IDE but one that suffers in its debugging capabilities with libraries that use native code. Forte from Sun is a good environment but chews up excessive amounts of memory. CodeWarrior from Metroworks is also good, but supports a limited number of platforms.

If you are developing commercial applications, then an optimizer/profiler is also a much-needed tool. OptimizeIt! seems to be the one most commonly used, and it provides all the necessary capabilities. (OptimizeIt! can be found at `http://www.optimizeit.com/` where you can download free trial versions.)

On top of this you will also need a tool for design and implementation. This might be RationalRose (`http://www.rational.com/`) on the high end, or a simple UML drawing tool like MagicDraw UML (`http://www.nomagic.com/magicdrawuml/`), or even Visio with the right stencils (we recommend replacing the standard UML stencil with one provided by the UML group at `http://www.rational.com/uml/`). Code generation/reverse engineering is not a requirement, but may be useful for the way you like to work.

Deciding on a project

Now that you have a development environment that you are comfortable with and all of the right libraries, you will need to decide on a starter project. If you have been directed to use J2EE for a project, then the choice of starter project should match the requirements of your work. It is a fairly safe bet that your project will require either XML or EJBs, so you should first attempt a project using one of these topics. For newcomers, one of the following projects would be a good introduction.

The XML project

For XML projects, it is best to start with an already known XML DTD, particularly if you are not familiar with XML itself. This will eliminate one point where you might get something wrong. A good place to look for sample DTDs is at the W3C site (`http://www.w3c.org/`) and the XML sites (`http://www.xml.org/` and `http://www.xmlhack.com/`).

A whole part of this book is devoted to understanding XML as a document as well as the APIs used to read and write it. Check out Part IV, "Communicating Between Systems with XML," for all the XML information.

When building an XML project it is best to start by implementing a DOM parser. After you get the hang of implementing DOM you can move to a SAX model. Once you feel confident in your ability to interpret an XML document you can move on to code to create one.

The EJB project

Enterprise Java Beans are a fairly complex standard. They belong as a wrapper over a number of other Java technologies. Before starting on EJBs, make sure you feel fairly confident about RMI, XML, and possibly even JNDI. All of these APIs are used to build an EJB system.

Information on defining and working with EJBs is included in Chapters 16 and 17.

A simple EJB project to start with is building an abstraction of the business organization. This is analogous to the beginner database system wherein you build tables to represent employees, departments, customers, and so on. This will get you used to building standard data style objects. Next, move up in complexity by expanding the business to include items in an inventory and the ability to buy and sell them.

The directory project

JNDI projects are most useful when you are going to be seriously working with LDAP databases. However, as you will see throughout this book, JNDI is also used all over the place to store and retrieve setup information for most of the J2EE APIs. JNDI is relatively simple to learn, so the project won't be very complex. Probably the best way to start is to have an example LDAP schema and data already in place. What you learn by interfacing with LDAP databases is equally applicable to all the other uses of JNDI.

A good place to start with LDAP and the server is to use the OpenLDAP server. The setup examples that come with it also include a collection of data to populate the database.

You'll find information on LDAP in Chapter 8. We mention the JNDI API in almost every chapter, but the introduction is in Chapter 9.

First, make sure you can connect to an LDAP server (which is a little more tricky than you might expect!). Next, make sure that you can walk up and down the hierarchy and that you will be able to read attributes as required. Deleting attributes should be the next step. Finish off with modifying attributes. Once you have mastered all of these steps, you will know just about everything there is to know about JNDI.

The kitchen-sink project

J2EE is so large that we do not recommend that you attempt to use every single API in your first project. However, if you feel that you need to know how it all fits together then have a look at the J2EE specification homepage, which includes a very good example project. This project presents a store that sells pet supplies and includes all the pieces necessary to building a full application, as well as an excellent collection of documentation.

Summary

This completes our introduction to the Java 2 Enterprise Environment. The environment is extensive and covers almost every part of the enterprise space. At the same time, the capabilities are not limited to the enterprise application; you can use them in any type of application.

We have covered the following areas of J2EE in this chapter:

- An introduction to the concepts involved in developing an enterprise application.
- The new capabilities the J2EE specification introduces to the Java programming environment.
- How to set up your own programming environment to start programming with J2EE.

✦ ✦ ✦

CHAPTER 2

Introducing Enterprise Applications

✦ ✦ ✦ ✦

In This Chapter

Outlining the standard types of enterprise applications

Identifying the types of application architectures you can use

Considering the parts of the J2EE that might be useful in each application

✦ ✦ ✦ ✦

To complement Chapter 1, we will now take an extended look at the types of applications you will find in an enterprise setting. Specifically for the newcomer to enterprise programming, this chapter will outline the basic structure and architecture of a number of standard application types. This should enable you to decide on the right approach early on, and then focus on tweaking the standard model to fit your particular needs.

It is often hard to classify an application as belonging to a single design style. When you look at the goal of your project, you will probably find that you need more than one application to do the job. Not all the applications will belong to the same classification we discuss in this chapter. When building a new system, you will probably need to build a number of applications — with at least one from each of these classifications. And, depending on your perspective, that application will fall into one of two categories: business-to-consumer or business-to-business.

Something else to keep in mind is that what we are calling an "application" here is probably not what you are used to thinking of as an application in traditional software engineering. An application may in fact be a number of identifiably individual processes all occurring simultaneously in the traditional sense. For example, a Web site that offers a catalogue and online purchasing system would have two separate servlets running inside the Web server. These are two separate processes not linked in the traditional application sense, but they use a common internal middleware piece. Building enterprise-type applications requires you to rethink your traditional guidelines and terminology.

In this chapter, we will introduce the basic architectures used by each of the application types. While these should be taken as a good guide on the highest level of architecture design, you should also consider how you could modify these architectures to deal with your own particular situation. Once you feel comfortable with these breakdowns, you may wish to wander off to Chapter 24 for further discussions.

As you read through these examples, you will notice a single recurring theme—almost without fail, there is a database at the center of every enterprise application. Why? Well, an enterprise has to keep a lot of information. This information has to be accessed quickly, sorted, examined, and used to keep track of what the business is doing in every fundamental way. When someone places an order online, you need to know that he or she has placed the order and how much the order was for (so you can work out how much profit you're making), and then you need to send on the relevant information to downstream systems. You need a permanent store of information about every single thing the business does. The best method of doing this is with a database.

In most cases, a database is really a relational database such as Oracle or Informix. Here we try not to treat them as specifically relational but instead to be more open-minded about the correct solution for any given problem. However, that said, by far the majority of database-driven applications are relational and use SQL to interface with the databases, so we spend quite some time dealing with them in Part III, "Finding Things with Databases and Searches."

Business-to-Consumer Applications

Business-to-consumer (B2C) applications are defined by the need for some outsider to use the application. The most common example is the e-commerce Web site of the type made famous by the likes of Amazon.com and friends.

B2C applications come in two basic varieties:

✦ A Web browser used for the consumer interface

✦ A custom interface, typically within a fixed system with only a single task

For the purposes of this definition, "consumer" will mean the general public. A company such as Dell Corporation, which needs to have people internally read the order information and generate physical goods, needs to have a system written for it. These applications are not considered "consumers" in the software-design sense. They are internal to the company and not considered part of the general public.

Example 1: E-commerce Web site

Like it or not, the e-commerce Web site is the poster child for enterprise applications. E-commerce Web sites are the ones that get the most notice from both the general public and the press. Unfortunately, this is for both good (Dell allowing you to track the order of your new computer right to your front door) and bad reasons (like certain sites failing periodically). In general programming experience, their popularity also means that they are the kind of enterprise application you are most likely to run across when looking for jobs.

As a general rule, an e-commerce Web site will possess the following traits:

- ✦ Online catalogue of items for sale
- ✦ Shopping-basket metaphor to collect items wishing to be purchased
- ✦ Option to purchase online and have the order shipped to a given address
- ✦ All interfaces presented through a Web browser

You can augment an e-commerce Web site with other interfaces, such as phone dial-in systems for getting order information, but this is not required.

Architecture

E-commerce applications all tend to use a standard system architecture, which is outlined in Figure 2-1. This is the classical *n*-tier design, consisting of a client tier (the Web browser), a middle tier (the Web server and associated software), a third tier (the middleware components), and a final tier (the database and external components).

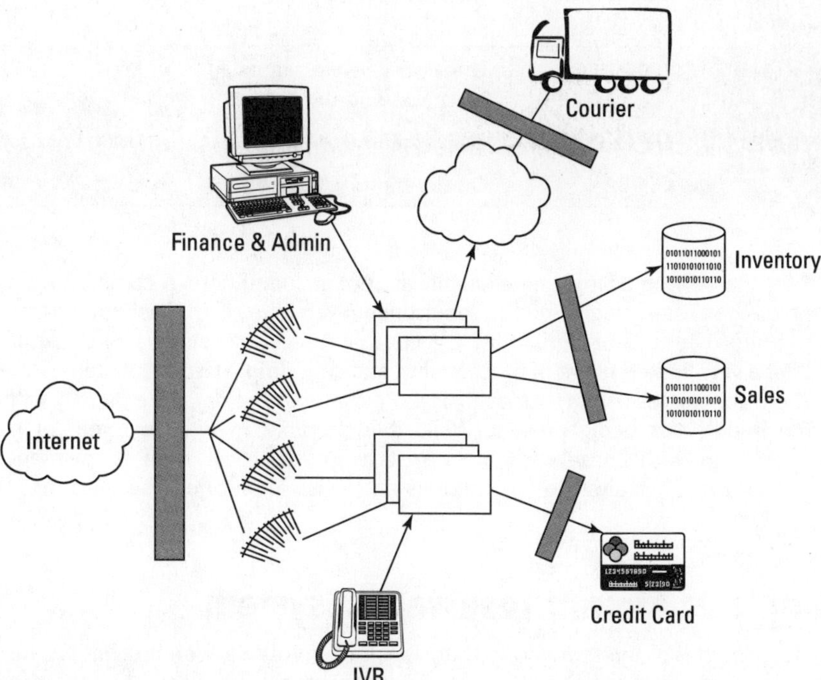

Figure 2-1: A common architecture of an e-commerce Web site

As far as you the developer are concerned, these are the only parts of the system that you need to implement. An e-commerce site has to sell something, and probably also get that something delivered. This means interacting with business-to-business systems to talk with the courier or order-fulfillment service. However, these are external entities that may use some other pre-existing software.

One point to notice, which will be a feature of many of these systems, is the firewall. Notice how almost every part of the application is protected from the rest by a firewall. This is a standard security procedure to make sure your system is as safe as possible. It may seem like overkill, but if someone compromises your Web server, do you really want to give that person access to the electronic payment gateway with no effort required?

Technologies used

Several different technologies are used for e-commerce Web sites. The most important is that there is a middle-tier layer. As you can see by looking at Table 2-1, the collection of technologies is very much determined by the operating system in use.

Table 2-1
Technologies used in E-commerce sites

Web-Page Generation	*Middleware*	*Database Server*	*Operating System*
ASP	COM/DCOM	Usually SQLServer, but could be Oracle/Informix/Sybase	Microsoft
Servlet/JSP	EJB or CORBA	Oracle/Informix/Sybase	UNIX/Microsoft
CGI	CORBA	Oracle/Informix/Sybase	UNIX

Sites that rely on a single functionality are not included here. A common example of such a site might be a community Web site like Slashdot (`http://slashdot.org/`) or LinuxToday (`http://linuxtoday.com/`). Sites like these offer a very limited range of functionality, and so a simple two-tier system is useful. The technologies used (such as PHP or Perl) access the database directly without the middle tier being present. While it is possible to write a three- or *n*-tier application with these technologies, it is not practical from a maintenance perspective. Such sites do not count as enterprise applications because they only use two tiers.

Example 2: Aircraft reservation system

Another form of B2C system is one that does not involve a Web interface. The example we are going to use here is an airline reservation system. Many airlines today enable users to book tickets through Web sites, but there is quite a large system that complements this option. Here are a few other ways in which you may need to access the same application:

✦ Travel agent to modify the booking

✦ Phones to confirm or change the flight

✦ E-ticket check-in

Architecture

A reservation system like this gives users many different ways to access the functionality. The previous short list, shows three completely different ways of extracting the same information—PC application, dial-up phone system, and fixed-function terminal. What this suggests is that there is a core system with all of the functionality resident there. Then, as shown in Figure 2-2, surrounding this core is a collection of veneer applications that perform that functionality on the specific output device.

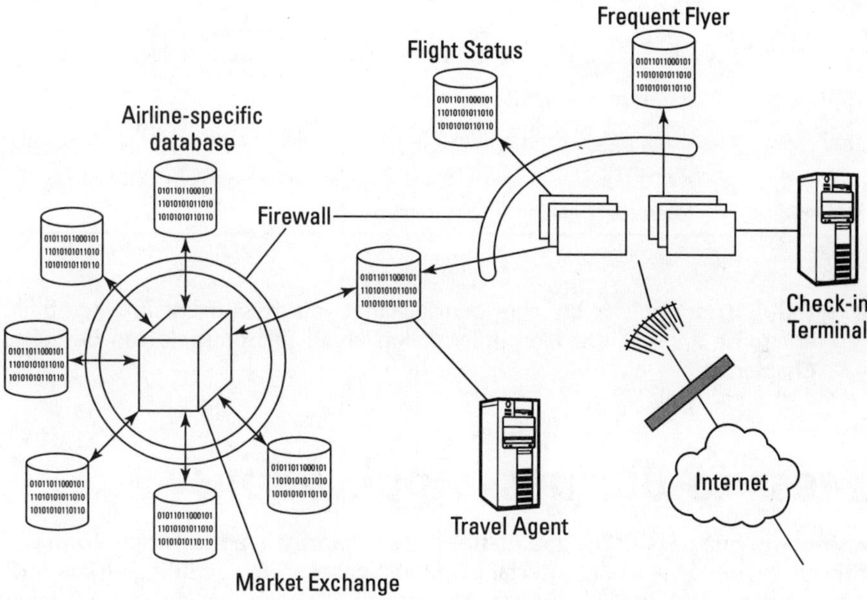

Figure 2-2: A common architecture for an airline reservation system

Technologies used

The reservation system is a large collection of systems used by airlines around the world. It is a good example of a pre-existing system that you would need to make your application work with. The majority of the system is based on IBM AS/400 mainframes. Around that functionality is a layer of abstraction that uses CORBA. Each of the outputs will then use the appropriate technology. The embedded system for the e-ticket check-in might use Java, the dialup might use the IVR (Interactive

Voice Response system)–specific language (usually a derivative of C), and the travel agent might use a 3270 terminal emulator or custom-written application for PCs. Where airlines are adding Web site information you will find a mix of technologies like the mix you might find on an e-commerce Web site. Table 2-2 shows the Java technologies you might want to use in an aircraft reservation system.

It is very unlikely that you will ever be writing a core system for an airline reservation application. The airlines have spent billions of dollars over the previous couple of decades developing a standard system that works. The airline reservation system is a good example of how a J2EE application would have to work within an existing system, as there is no hope of making any changes to the core application. J2EE would just be another veneer over the core functionality.

Table 2-2
Java technologies used in the aircraft reservation system

API	***Use***
CORBA	Abstraction of the airline reservation system for use with multiple systems.
JTAPI	Interface to the IVR system.
JTA	Ensuring fully correct functioning of bookings and payments (the ACID principle).
JMS	Interface to mainframe systems.

The ACID principle is the core principle that you must maintain when building enterprise applications. More information about this principle can be found in Chapter 24.

Business-to-Business Applications

Business-to-business (B2B) applications are primarily used to swap information without the need for a user interface. In most cases, they are fully automated. That is, one business decides it is low on stock and so automatically sends off a request to a supplier for more. There is most likely no human in the loop. If there is, he or she is using the local system to look at inventory levels and make the request through that interface rather than directly to the supplier.

Example 1: Inventory system

The inventory system monitors a user's level of consumption and makes orders from a supplier when stocks run low. For specialty parts the inventory system might order directly from the supplier. Look at your local auto-parts store, for example. You walk in looking for a specific part, say a new set of pistons. The store does not keep pistons in stock because they are rarely ordered, so the clerk brings up the order page, types in the appropriate part numbers, and tells you it will take four days to get your pistons.

In inventory systems, the idea is to replace the old paper-shuffling and phone calls with an automated system. The auto-parts store is one place where this system is slowly taking over. When the clerk brings up the order screen, he or she can tell you whether parts are in the local warehouse, in the importer's warehouse, or only in the factory in Japan — all from a single screen. Here, one interface has interacted with four different systems to find out how long it will take your order to arrive.

Architecture

The architecture of most B2B inventory applications is relatively simple. Depending on the style, there may or may not be a user interface. However, what the application will feature is a connection to one or more external systems — the suppliers. As illustrated in Figure 2-3, these systems may be unidirectional or bi-directional. Unidirectional systems will send out requests for information and make orders of the supplier. Bi-directional systems may also enable the supplier to request information (stock levels, for example) from the consuming business.

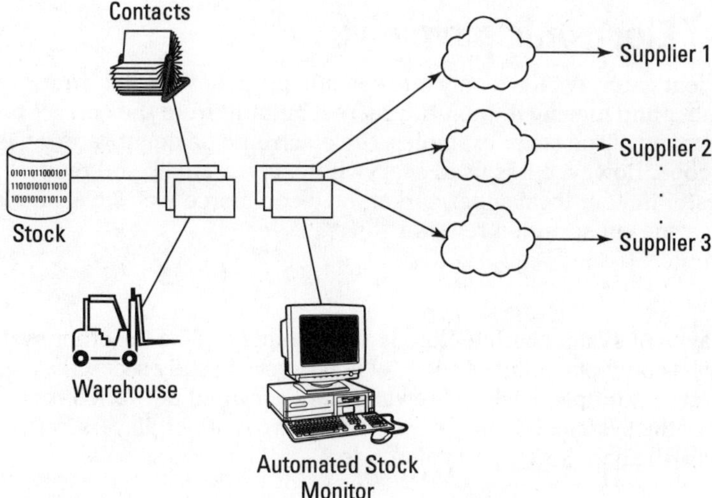

Figure 2-3: An example architecture for an inventory system

Technologies used

In the current market, it is hard to pin down a specific set of technologies used. The applications for many smaller businesses, such as the auto-parts store, are typically written with Visual Basic and an Access database. However, these sorts of applications don't tend to be networked to the suppliers. It is only when you go to larger organizations that you find more automated systems. This will change over time, but in today's market, low-end systems don't require much automated supply chain management.

For high-end systems, there is still no real clear technology being used. As an information-exchange protocol, XML is starting to make inroads; it is not there yet, though. Some companies are using the built-in capabilities of applications like SAP R/3 and PowerBuilder, but the market is still open. Naturally, a database must be involved: Almost everyone prefers Oracle. Table 2-3 shows the Java technologies you may want to use when implementing an inventory system.

Table 2-3
Java technologies used in an inventory system

API	*Use*
EJB	Abstraction of business logic.
XML	Exchange of parts information and orders.
JNDI	Customer and supplier directory handling.

Example 2: Electronic payments

Electronic payment gateways have only one specific purpose—taking your credit-card number and making it debit the correct amount from the correct bank account. Unlike many of the other examples, the electronic payment gateway is fairly small in scope. However, it is used everywhere, in the small card readers next to the cash register in your local supermarket, on e-commerce Web sites, and in your yearly magazine-subscription renewal.

Architecture

An electronic payment system architecture is very simple. Unlike the other systems, this one usually has only one point of entry, which is very heavily secured. As Figure 2-4 illustrates, multiple levels of firewalls and encrypted network links are commonly part of the system. Usually there are also two distinct players in the developed code—the bank's side and your code.

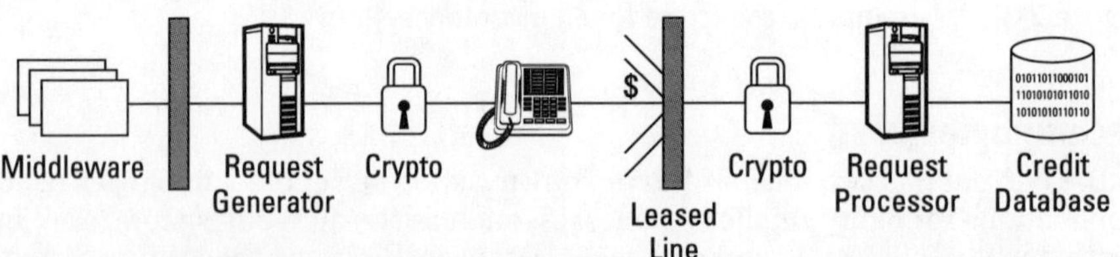

Figure 2-4: A common architecture for an electronic payment gateway system

Technologies used

Payment gateways all use similar sets of technologies, even though these technologies may be implemented in different languages. For example, each set must be able to make a secure network connection to the financial institution. They almost invariably do this through a dedicated dial-up phone line, so you need an API to find a modem, dial a number, and manage the call.

Table 2-4 lists the APIs that you might want to use if you were to implement a payment gateway in Java.

Table 2-4
APIs used in an electronic payment system

API	*Use*
JTAPI	Establishing and managing the dedicated phone links to the financial institution.
JSSEL	Creating secure socket connections and managing digital certificates.
Servlet	Processing requests through a firewall for payments.

We have included the Servlet API in this table. It seems to be quite common for gateways to take their input from the rest of the system using HTTP requests. That way a standard firewall can be in place and all an intruder would see is that port 80 is open; the intruder would not know the protocol or what requests to make. At the same time, the connection enables you to use HTTPS connections for the extra security of an encrypted link without any extra work on the programmer's part.

Back-End Applications

Back-end applications are those that tend to be placed on a server and run periodically without any direct input. The two most common uses that we've outlined here are the telco field (almost any application here would do!) and the e-zine/news site that might want to send out a periodic publication or broadcast an event.

Example 1: Telco applications

Within the telecommunications industry, many different applications could be considered back-end. For example, you could go as far back as 1996 and find companies that were using Java inside their call-monitoring section. Huge Sun machines with native compiled Java code were processing incoming-call requests, monitoring them, and then making sure the billing was correctly organized.

Today a number of standard examples exist where Java is being used in the telco industry—in wireless networking for pagers and phones, for example. The WAP market in particular is quite heavy on the use of Java-based technologies, and the latest mobile phones are including Java capabilities, using the J2ME specification to run code directly on the phone.

Example 2: Monthly electronic newsletter

Regular electronic postings, according to some, are better known as spam. However, many people regularly rely on systems with exactly the same e-mail setup to keep them in touch with the world. Every major news site and many other sites enable you to sign up for a regular e-mail service. When some significant event happens, an application kicks into life, assembles the appropriate e-mail message, and sends it out to the list of recipients.

Architecture

Batch mailing systems are quite simple in architecture. Ignoring the signup section (which is really just a form of the e-commerce Web site), you need only the four parts shown in Figure 2-5. The two most important items are the text of the message and the list of recipients. How these are stored doesn't really matter.

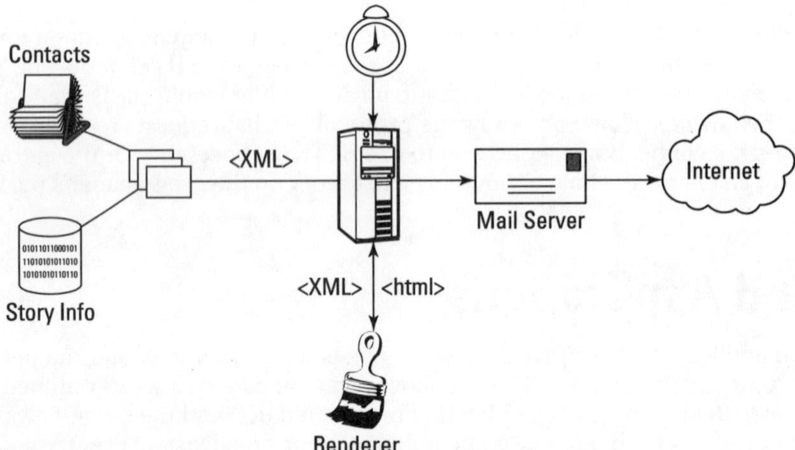

Figure 2-5: A common batch-mailing–system architecture

Technologies used

In the most simple of cases, you could use a text file for the message and an e-mail list processor such as majordomo for sending out the message. However, this being a book about Java, we need to tell you how to do it in Java! (Well, we'll ignore whether it really is a good idea or not to support the spammers of the world by giving them yet another way of stuffing our inboxes). So how would you build a Java version of the mail processor? Table 2-5 gives you a clue as to where to start looking.

First, you would start by storing all the e-mail addresses in a database. This is important because you may include other information here to enable yourself to filter out the e-mail addresses to which you want to send information. Next, you want to pre-format the message as an XML document. Using XSL, you can then send the recipient either an HTML or plain text-formatted version of the message, according to the recipient's preferences. Finally, you need to directly interact with the SMTP mail server, so JavaMail does this for you.

Table 2-5
Java technologies used in a monthly newsletter service

API	*Use*
JavaMail	Interface to e-mail system.
XML	Stores formatted message information.
JDBC	Extracts address information directly from the database.

Summary

In this chapter, we have introduced various types of applications that might be considered enterprise applications. This chapter has given you a look at the types of architectures and technologies used in each circumstance. The types of applications we examined were:

- ✦ Business-to-consumer (B2C) applications
- ✦ Business-to-business (B2B) applications
- ✦ Back-end applications

✦ ✦ ✦

Delivering Content

P A R T

✦ ✦ ✦ ✦

In This Part

✦ ✦ ✦ ✦

CHAPTER 3

Creating Dynamic Content with Servlets

In This Chapter

Creating dynamic content with servlets

Modifying the deployment descriptor

Handling requests and generating responses

Tracking sessions and sharing information

Adding functionality to servlets with filters

Getting servlets to work together

In a typical Java enterprise application, the first object the client talks to is often a servlet or a Java Server Page (JSP). In this chapter, we'll introduce you to servlets and describe their role in a J2EE solution. We'll then introduce you to the API by creating a simple `HttpServlet` and then adding dynamic elements to it. The examples in this chapter are kept simple so you can focus on the concept being explained. With that background you can take a more in-depth look at the core servlet classes and interfaces. We'll finish with a look at session tracking, sharing information, and sharing the workload.

What Is a Servlet?

Servlets are objects running in a Java Virtual Machine (JVM) on the server that generate responses to client requests. Often in a J2EE application the client will contact a JSP that communicates with a servlet. The servlet in turn will call a session bean that interacts with one or more entity beans. Each entity bean will use Java DataBase Connectivity (JDBC) to communicate with a database. You don't need all of these steps. A servlet can make a call directly into a database. You can even write your own custom file in which to keep your data. You can eliminate JSPs and just write a servlet that stands on the front line communicating with the client. In fact, JSPs are compiled into servlets before they are accessed. Chapter 4 deals with JSPs; for now you can think of them as servlets written in a more Web designer–friendly way.

Servlets are the second baseman of an enterprise system. When they get a request, they can sometimes handle it themselves and send a response back to the client. More often than not, however, they receive a request, transform it, and toss it over to another part of the system that performs the next step. If you're familiar with the Model-View-Controller (MVC) enterprise architecture, you'll recognize servlets as in the role of the controller. Another way of describing their function is to say that servlets are in the middle tier. You don't want your client thinking about how the database is organized. The client should be making requests that have to do with your business. The servlet can be built around the business logic and make the method calls of the components that make the actual calls into the database.

Servlets are often seen as an alternative to CGI (Common Gateway Interface) scripts. A CGI program, often written in Perl, has been a popular way of adding dynamic content to Web pages. In addition to the language limitations, a lot of overhead is involved in working with CGI scripts. Each request requires a new process to handle it. This presents problems for servers handling a large volume of requests. If two users want to access the same CGI script (or the same user wants to access it twice), a separate process is spawned.

In contrast, servlets are written in Java. A single instance can handle requests from different users. You don't have the CGI overhead of creating a servlet every time one is requested. Servlets are initialized once using their `init()` method and then persist. You can take advantage of their persistence to reaccess them, share information, and to connect to other resources. When you are dealing with HTTP, the `javax.servlet.http` package provides a lot of support for common tasks. You won't have to use Perl to step through long strings in order to parse and reassemble the client request. Library support exists for methods to set and get attributes, for adding and retrieving cookies, and for interacting with the client using intuitive methods and typed data. Also, because a servlet is a Java solution, you can write ordinary Java objects that work with your servlet on the server.

A servlet runs inside a JVM on a server. Before you shudder in memory of your early experience with applets, let us assure you that you won't have the same problems here. The servlet is sending back HTML or other formats that the browser (or other custom client) can render. Actually, a more accurate description is that a servlet runs inside an application called a servlet container inside a JVM on the server. You will need to test your servlets against the containers you'll be running in. The servlet container will take care of some of the life-cycle functions for you. We'll talk more about this later in this chapter in the section "Introducing the Servlet APIs." Since you're running within this servlet container you don't care about the operating system of the server, and your servlets should port easily to different Web and application servers.

We don't know which application server you do or should use and can't tell you how to set it up. Things change. Different servers add support for different versions of the J2EE release. The manufacturers change the way their servers are configured and the extras that they provide. Often you won't have a choice—you'll have to learn how to use the Web or application server that your employer has chosen.

That being said, we are covering Servlet API 2.3 and are using the reference implementation Tomcat 4.0, available from The Jakarta Project at `http://www.jakarta.apache.org`. Installation is very easy, and the documentation has greatly improved. All of our examples have been tested in this environment. If you are not seeing the results we describe and are sure you have checked your configuration, you may have to shut Tomcat down and start it back up again. If you have edited the deployment descriptor file, you will definitely need to restart Tomcat.

Creating a Basic HttpServlet

The easiest way to see what a servlet can do is to create one. In this section you will create a servlet that greets you by name and tells you what time it is at the server location. This isn't a tremendously exciting servlet, but it will introduce you to the API and to some of the nuts and bolts of running a servlet on the Tomcat server.

Using a servlet to create a static page

There is no reason to use a servlet to create a static page. If you want to create a page that simply says "Hello" you could just create a file called `Hello.html` that consists of the following code:

```
<html>
  <body>
    <h1> Hello </h1>
  </body>
</html>
```

Whether `Hello.html` is on your machine or on another, pointing your browser at the file brings up a page that reads "Hello" in large bold type. In this section we will create a servlet called `Hello.java` that does the same thing. After looking at the code, you'll see where to place the compiled `Hello.class` file and how to access the page.

Creating a servlet that says "Hello"

Here's the code for `Hello.java`, the servlet that performs the same task:

```
// Hello.java
import java.io.*;
import javax.servlet.*;
import javax.servlet.http.*;

public class Hello extends HttpServlet {

  public void doGet(HttpServletRequest request,
    HttpServletResponse response)
    throws IOException, ServletException {
```

```
        response.setContentType("text/html");
        PrintWriter out = response.getWriter();

        out.println("<html>");
        out.println("<body>");
        out.println("<h1>  Hello  </h1>");
        out.println("</body>");
        out.println("</html>");
    }
}
```

The Hello class extends HttpServlet instead of the parent Servlet class because you need to define the behavior of the doGet() method. This method takes two arguments. The first argument implements the HttpServletRequest interface, and the second implements the HttpServletResponse interface. We'll talk more about these interfaces in the next section. For now, keep in mind that a servlet processes a request and generates a response. The servlet container creates the request and the response objects, and passes them as arguments to doGet() and the other service methods. You need to import the package java.io because it includes the class IOException, and the package java.servlet because it includes the class ServletException. Everything else is contained in the package java.servlet.http.

You can see that you never use your request object. In fact, you never use the HttpServletResponse capabilities of the response object. The two methods that it uses, setContentType() and getWriter(), are specified in the ServletResponse interface. The first sets the MIME type of the response to that specified un the String parameter passed in as a String, and the second returns the PrintWriter used to send the output back to the client. Finally, the five out.println() statements contain the HTML to be sent back to the client. Although it looks as if you have complicated a simple HTML document, you have put yourself in a position to add a lot of functionality easily.

Compiling, saving, and running the servlet

You compile a servlet the same way you would any other Java source file. If this is your first servlet, you need to remember to add the location of the latest servlet.jar to your CLASSPATH. You then need to save the class file where the servlet engine can see it. For Tomcat 4, create a new folder inside the webapps directory and name it J2EEBible. At this point the J2EEBible directory should contain a further subdirectory called WEB-INF. This in turn should contain a directory named classes and an XML file that is the Web application deployment descriptor, web.xml.

Place Hello.java and Hello.class inside the classes directory. For now the web.xml file can simply contain the following code:

```
<?xml version="1.0" encoding="ISO-8859-1"?>

<!DOCTYPE web-app PUBLIC
```

```
  "-//Sun Microsystems, Inc.//DTD Web Application 2.3//EN"
  "http://java.sun.com/j2ee/dtds/web-app_2_3.dtd">

<web-app>
</web-app>
```

You will modify this file in the next section.

Check out the webapps/examples directory for an idea of how the file structure should look. Also, if you check out the file web.xml inside webapps/examples/WEB-INF, you can get a feel for the structure of this file. As you may have guessed from the previous code example, the DTD should be available at `http://java.sun.com/j2ee/dtds/web-app_2_3.dtd`. As of the time of this writing, version 2.3 is not publicly posted. You can, however, view version 2.2 at `http://java.sun.com/j2ee/dtds/web-app_2_2.dtd`.

Now you're ready to run your servlet. You can't just navigate to the appropriate directory and invoke `java Hello`. There is no `main()` method and so you would get the error `NoSuchMethodError` at runtime. You also can't just navigate the browser to your class file and expect "Hello" to display as it did for your HTML file. You have to start up Tomcat and then point your browser to the following URL:

```
http://localhost:8080/J2EEBible/servlet/Hello
```

Of course, you should replace `localhost:8080` with the appropriate information for your server configuration. If everything has been set up correctly, you should see the image shown in Figure 3-1 on your screen.

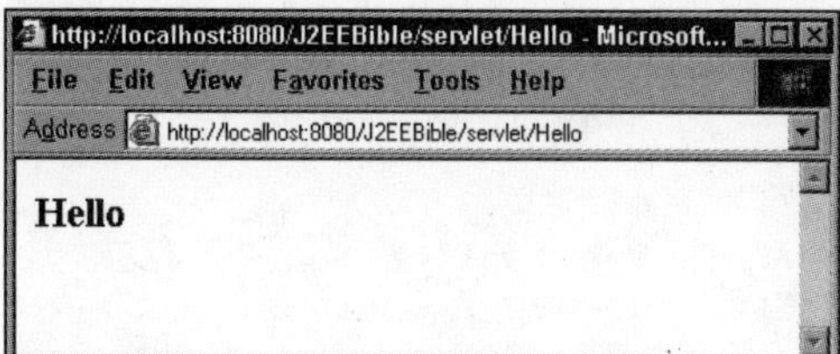

Figure 3-1: The results of running the Hello servlet

Tidying up – where to put your servlets

You don't want to put all your applications directly into the classes subdirectory. You'd soon have a mess of class files that you'd have to untangle any time you wanted to update a particular Web application. You could create lots of top-level directories in addition to the examples and J2EEBible directories, but this doesn't solve the problem of organizing all the servlets that will be placed in the J2EEBible directory either. You could put servlets that go together in the same package, but this may make the URLs long and complicated. You can fix this naming problem by adding the appropriate entry to the web.xml file. In this section, we'll quickly discuss each of these techniques.

Using packages

Suppose you want to make the Hello file part of the `Greetings` package. Create a subdirectory of classes named Greeting and place Hello.java inside it. As usual you will have to add the following package declaration to the beginning of your source code:

```
package Greetings;
```

Then compile the file from outside the Greetings directory with the following command:

```
javac Greetings/Hello.java
```

So far this is exactly the same as working with packages in any other area of Java programming. The difference is that you call the servlet by directing your browser to the following URL:

```
http://localhost:8080/J2EEBible/servlet/Greetings.Hello
```

Editing the web.xml file

Already your URL is getting a bit long for a client to type in. Also, you are confusing your clients a bit. They may reason, incorrectly, that if Hello is in the Greetings directory that they should just type `http://localhost:8080/J2EEBible/servlet/Greetings/Hello`. You can edit the web.xml file so that the mapping from a URL to a servlet is more natural. For example, consider the following changes:

```
<?xml version="1.0" encoding="ISO-8859-1"?>

<!DOCTYPE web-app PUBLIC
  "-//Sun Microsystems, Inc.//DTD Web Application 2.3//EN"
  "http://java.sun.com/j2ee/dtds/web-app_2_3.dtd">

<web-app>
  <servlet>
    <servlet-name>
      Hello
    </servlet-name>
    <servlet-class>
      Greetings.Hello
    </servlet-class>
  </servlet>

  <servlet-mapping>
    <servlet-name>
      Hello
```

```
    </servlet-name>
    <url-pattern>
      /Hi
    </url-pattern>
  </servlet-mapping>
</web-app>
```

As you can see from the XML file, you are mapping the name Hello to the Java class file Hello.class in the package `Greetings`. You are mapping the URL pattern `/Hi` to this servlet. In other words, a client can now access this servlet at the following address:

```
http://localhost:8080/J2EEBible/Hi
```

This address is much cleaner and more compact. It also doesn't contain the additional information that this file is being generated by a servlet. This technique means that the information on how you create Web documents remains private.

Adding dynamic elements

So far you've learned a lot from the simplest of servlets. Now let's add some dynamic content. In this section, you will first learn how to display the current time at the server. The point is not that you can add the time to your Web page; you can do that without using servlets. The point is that it is easy to add functionality to your servlet using Java code that you write or acquire. Later on in the section you'll take information included in the `request` object and use it in the `response`.

Including the date

With two small changes to the code, you can add the date and time at the server to the Web page, making it dynamic in a fairly uninteresting way. You'll also change the name of the class to `Hello1` and place it in the package `Greetings`. For convenience, you may want to edit the web.xml file to point to this new class. The following code shows the modifications to the original servlet:

```
package Greetings;

import java.io.*;
import javax.servlet.*;
import javax.servlet.http.*;
import java.util.*;

public class Hello1 extends HttpServlet {

  public void doGet(HttpServletRequest request,
    HttpServletResponse response)
    throws IOException, ServletException {

    response.setContentType("text/html");
    PrintWriter out = response.getWriter();
```

```
        out.println("<html>");
        out.println("<body>");
        out.println("<h1>" );
        out.println("Hello, here at the server it's <br>" );
        out.println( new Date());
        out.println("</h1>");
        out.println("</body>");
        out.println("</html>");
    }
}
```

It really is that easy to access a Java library function. You simply `import` the appropriate package and call the constructor. Because you are writing Java code, you may have been tempted to use `\n` to generate the new line before the `Date` is output. If you do, you will not get a new line in the browser output. If this puzzles you, view the source. You'll see that there is an extra line in your HTML source code. This, however, wasn't your goal. You wanted to generate an extra line in the HTML output, not in the source. To do this, you need to use the HTML command `<br>`. Figure 3-2 shows the corresponding browser output.

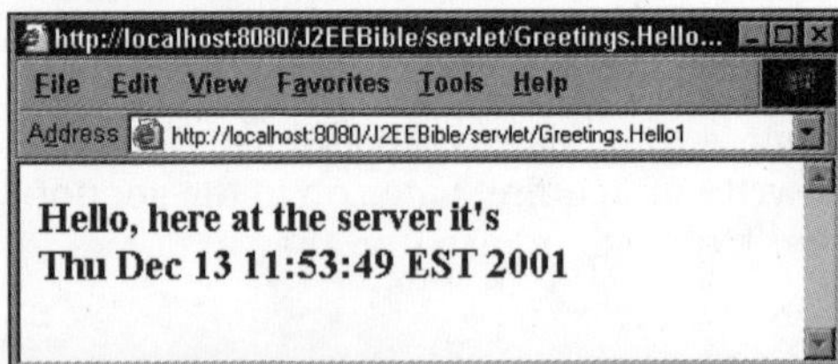

Figure 3-2: Your first dynamic Web page

You still don't need servlets to generate a page like this. If you would like to use Java technology, you could generate this simple Web page with a JSP. You'll learn about JavaServer Pages in the next chapter, but in this chapter you'll continue to add functionality to your servlet.

Using contents of the request object

In the preceding version of `Hello` the page was no longer static, but it still wasn't responding to user input. Now let's add the ability to greet the user by name. If the name isn't known, the program will respond as in the preceding example. If the name, say Elena, is known, the program will respond "Hello Elena..." For now, pass the name in the URL. After you've once again edited the web.xml file appropriately, your URL should look something like the following:

```
http://localhost:8080/J2EEBible/Hi?name=Elena
```

The additional information included in this URL is that the property `name` has the value `Elena`. This value will be part of the `request` object, and the value of the `name` property can be accessed with the following call:

```
request.getParameter("name");
```

This call returns a `String` that you can manipulate and add to the HTML being returned to the client, as shown in the following code:

```
package Greetings;

import java.io.*;
import javax.servlet.*;
import javax.servlet.http.*;
import java.util.*;

public class Hello2 extends HttpServlet {

  public void doGet(HttpServletRequest request,
    HttpServletResponse response)
    throws IOException, ServletException {

    response.setContentType("text/html");
    PrintWriter out = response.getWriter();

    String name = request.getParameter("name");
    if (name == null) name = "";
    else name = " " + name;

    out.println("<html>");
    out.println("<body>");
    out.println("<h1>" );
    out.println("Hello" + name + ",");
    out.println("here at the server it's <br>" );
    out.println( new Date());
    out.println("</h1>");
    out.println("</body>");
    out.println("</html>");
  }
}
```

You don't actually expect users to add fields like that to the URL, of course. For the most part this will be done for them when they click an address in an e-mail they've been sent, or when they respond to a prompt on a form on a Web page. Your next task will be to create a simple form that passes the information on to the servlet.

Responding to information contained in a form

Rather than have users add name-value pairs to the URL, have them input their names in a form that passes this information on to the servlet. To be consistent with your existing servlet, use the GET method to pass the information from the form to the servlet. A minimalist version of the file HelloForm.html could be the following:

```
<html>
  <body>
    <form METHOD= GET
      ACTION ="/J2EEBible/servlet/Greetings.Hello2">

      <p>If you would like to be referred to by name on
         this site, please enter your first name.
      </p>
      <p>
         <input TYPE = text NAME="name"> <br>
         <input TYPE = SUBMIT>
      </p>
    </form>
  </body>
</html>
```

Put this form in the directory ...\webapps\J2EEBible. When a user navigates to the URL http://localhost:8080/J2EEBible/HelloForm.html, he or she is prompted to enter a name by the screen shown in Figure 3-3.

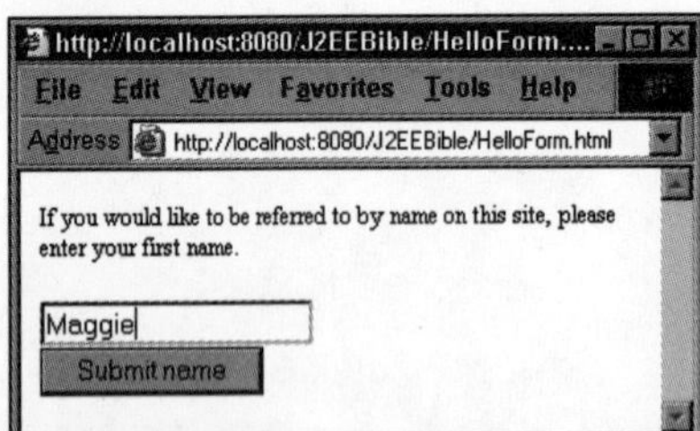

Figure 3-3: The HTML form for name entry

When the user presses the submit button, the name entered is appended to the URL http://localhost:8080/J2EEBible/servlet/Greetings.Hello2. In this case we've entered the name "Maggie" and so ?name=Maggie has been added to the URL. Our servlet Greetings.Hello2 knows how to pull that name off of the request object and handle it appropriately. This feels a little silly. The URL contains ?name=Maggie, so it isn't much of a surprise that the servlet has this information, but that's the way GET works. The data sit inside of the URL for all to see. An advantage is that you can now bookmark the page, and the bookmark will contain the additional information because it is part of the address. Clearly, you wouldn't want to do this for secure information.

You can specify the method as POST instead of GET. In that case the information is still available to be accessed with the request object. You need to make a small modification to your current servlet, or you will get a warning that the page doesn't support `POST`. To change the servlet, you would either change the name of the `doGet()` method to `doPost()` or add a `doPost()` method that calls the existing `doGet()` method so that your servlet could be accessed with a `GET` or a `POST`. To choose the second approach, add the following lines after the `doGet()` method in `Hello2`:

```
public void doPost(HttpServletRequest request,
  HttpServletResponse response)
  throws IOException, ServletException {

        doGet(request,response);
}
```

Introducing the Servlet APIs

We've said that, fundamentally, the job of a servlet is to process a request and to return a response. Let's look at the APIs for manipulating the requests that the servlets are receiving and for generating the response that the servlets are sending. We'll begin by looking at the `Servlet` and `HttpServlet` interfaces to understand the basic structure of a servlet.

The Servlet family

Part of what makes servlets so easy to work with is that the container handles many functions for you. You saw in the previous section that the container is responsible for creating the `request` and `response` objects used by methods such as `doGet()` and `doPost()`. The container also controls the life cycle of a servlet using methods declared in the `Servlet` interface. `GenericServlet` implements the `Servlet` interface as well as the `ServletConfig` interface. The `service()` method is its only abstract method. Finally, the `HttpServlet` abstract class extends `GenericServlet` and adds methods for dealing with HTTP-specific requests. It has no abstract methods, but if you don't override one of the basic methods it won't have any useful functionality and so is declared to be an abstract class. In this section, we'll provide an overview of these APIs.

The Servlet interface

When a user makes a request for a servlet, the container creates an instance on the servlet if one doesn't already exist. If there is an `init()` method, it will be called and must complete successfully before the servlet sees any client requests. After the `init()` method returns, the container may or may not call the `service()` method one or more times, passing in `ServletRequest` and `ServletResponse` objects as arguments. Finally, the container can call the `destroy()` method to finalize the servlet and clean up various resources.

You can use the web.xml file to pass in parameters used to initialize the servlet. The parameters are passed in as name-value pairs. For example, you could add the following lines to your existing file:

```
<servlet>
  <servlet-name>
    Hello2
  </servlet-name>
  <servlet-class>
    Greetings.Hello2
  </servlet-class>
  <init-param>
    <param-name>
      name
    </param-name>
    <param-value>
      Elena
    </param-value>
  </init-param>
</servlet>
```

The corresponding `init()` method would be the following:

```
String name;
public void init() throws ServletException{
  name = getInitParameter("name");
}
```

The `Servlet` interface provides the signature of the `init()`, `service()`, and `destroy()` methods. These methods give you the feel of a servlet being a server-side applet. In addition to declaring the life-cycle methods, the interface declares the methods `getServletConfig()` and `getServletInfo()`. The second method is designed to return non-technical information about the servlet: You can use it to return a `String` that contains, for example, the author's name and contact information. The `getServletConfig()` method returns a `ServletConfig` object that defines methods to return information on the various servlet-initialization parameters.

The GenericServlet abstract class

As we mentioned in the first section of this chapter, for the most part you will be creating a servlet by extending the `HttpServlet` class and overriding one of its methods. That being said, you can also create a servlet by extending `GenericServlet` and overriding the `service()` method. The `GenericServlet` class provides implementations of all of the methods in the interfaces `Servlet` and `ServletConfig` except for `service()`.

Now that you've seen what is specified by the `Servlet` interface, take a look at the four methods in the `ServletConfig` interface. The methods `getInitParameterNames()` and `getInitParameter()` provide information about initialization parameters for the servlet. GenericServlet provides an implementation for these methods. You can get an Enumeration of the initialization parameters by invoking getInitParameterNames(). To get a String containing the value of a specific parameter, use the getInitParameter() and pass in the name of the parameter as a String. You can query the name of this particular instance of the servlet with getServletName(). Finally, you can get a handle to ServletContext using getServletContext().

GenericServlet also contains two log() methods not specified in either the Servlet or the ServletConfig interface. The first takes a String as its argument that will be the message to be written to a servlet log file. The message will be tagged with the particular servlet's name so you will be able to figure out which message belongs to which servlet. You may want to use this version of log() in the various life-cycle methods so that when init() or destroy() is called a log entry is generated. The second version of the log() method takes an instance of Throwable as its second argument. This signature of log() is implemented in GenericServlet to write the message you specify as the first argument and to write a stack trace for the specified exception into the log file.

The HttpServlet abstract class

HttpServlet extends GenericServlet by adding methods to handle HTTP requests. You saw examples of handling GET and POST requests using the HttpServlet methods doGet() and doPost(). The service methods doDelete(), doHead(), doOptions(), doPut(), and doTrace() are also available to handle DELETE, HEAD, OPTIONS, PUT, and TRACE respectively. Each of these methods takes an HttpServletRequest object and an HttpServletResponse object as arguments, and can throw a ServletException or an IOException.

There are no abstract methods in the HttpServlet class. The service() method, which was abstract in the parent class, is no longer abstract in HttpServlet. Nevertheless, HttpServlet is an abstract class, so you can create servlets by extending it (as in the Hello examples) and overriding one of the service methods. The final method that has been added in HttpServlet is getLastModified(). It can help the client to not reload a page that hasn't changed since the last time he or she accessed it.

The ServletRequest family

The servlet's job is to take a request and generate a response. This means that the servlet must be able to read all the information from the request. Remember that for an HttpServlet the container passes in the handle to the HttpServletRequest and HttpServletResponse objects to the service methods. The HttpServletRequest interface extends the ServletRequest interface. The API also includes the wrapper classes ServletRequestWrapper and HttpServletRequestWrapper that you can extend rather than having to implement all the methods in the interfaces.

The ServletRequest interface consists mainly of accessor methods. get...() methods exist for anything you might want to determine from the request of a generic servlet. You can determine the character encoding, content length, and type as well as the names and values of attributes and parameters. You can determine the name and address of the client sending the request as well as the name and port of the server receiving it. In addition, you can determine whether or not the request was made on a secure channel. Three methods are available for making changes to the request. The method removeAttribute() removes the specified attribute from the request, setAttribute() sets the specified attribute to a given value in the request, and setCharacterEncoding() sets the name of the character encoding used in the request.

The HttpServletRequest interface adds four constants and 25 accessors. Each of the constants supports basic authentication. For the most part, the methods return the HTTP-related information. You can get information about sessions, cookies, the query string (the part in the previous example that followed the question mark), the path, and the header. If you are new to working with the Web, this may be a bit confusing. You may not be aware of the amount of information being passed between the client and the server that is never displayed.

Included in the Tomcat distribution are several examples that show you the information transmitted in the request. Figures 3-4 and 3-5 are the results of running the RequestInfo and RequestHeader servlets on our machine. You'll find the source code for these servlets in the examples directory of the distribution.

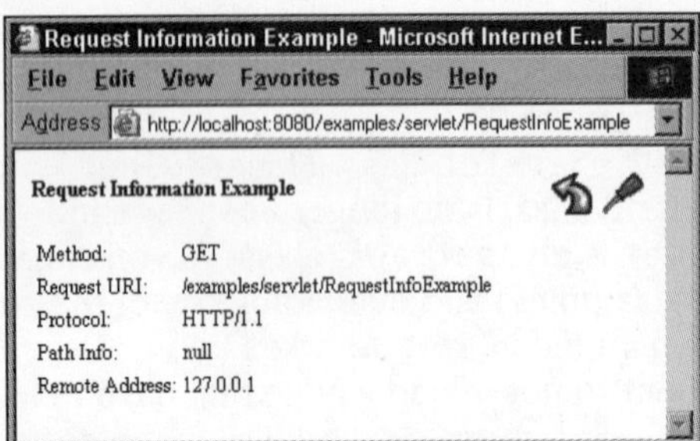

Figure 3-4: An example of RequestInfo

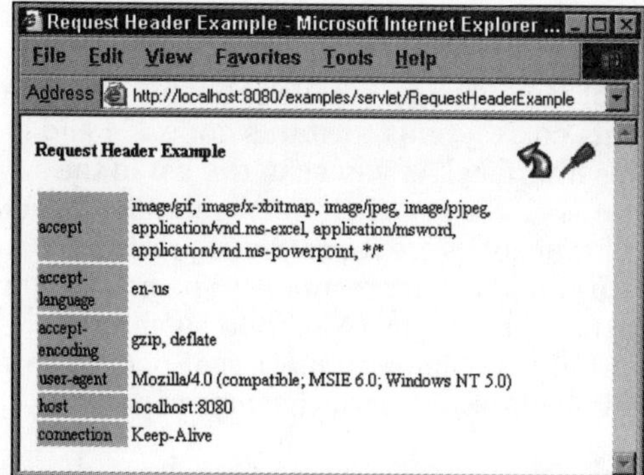

Figure 3-5: An example of RequestHeader

The ServletResponse family

Just as the API provided classes for manipulating and reading from a request, interfaces and classes are also available for working with a response. The `ServletResponse` interface outlines the functionality that should be present in sending a response to the client. The `HttpServletResponse` adds methods for handling HTTP-specific tasks as well as constants that represent the various status codes. As with the request, there are wrapper classes — `ServletResponseWrapper` and `HttpServletResponseWrapper` — for each of these.

The Hello example included some of the calls specified in the `ServletResponse` interface. The command `response.getWriter()` returned the `PrintWriter` object that you used to send the HTML back to the client. This is the standard method you'll use to send text data back to the client. If you want to send binary data use `response.getOutputStream()` to get a `ServletOutputStream`. Before getting a `PrintWriter`, you should specify the content type being sent. In Hello2 you used the command `response.setContentType("text/html")` to indicate that you were sending HTML.

The interface provides 10 more methods for handling responses. Other getters are `getBufferSize()`, `getCharacterEncoding()`, and `getLocale()`. Other setters are `setBufferSize()`, `setContentLength()`, and `setLocale()`. You can use `isCommitted()` to determine whether or not the response has been committed. You can clear the buffer in two ways: The method `resetBuffer()` will clear the buffer without clearing headers or a status code, while `reset()` will just clear the buffer. The method `flushBuffer()` forces the buffer to be sent to the client.

The HttpServletResponse interface extends the ServletResponse interface. First you'll notice almost 40 constants used to handle the various status codes. Although it never happens on a site that you manage, you've probably visited a site and gotten the message Not Found. This corresponds to status code 404 and is the constant SC_NOT_FOUND defined in this interface. As you scan the list in the javadocs you'll see a list of familiar status codes and their corresponding constant names. Several methods are included in the interface for returning status codes. The simple setStatus() sets the status code for the response. The only argument it should take is the int representing the status code. (A second signature is available, but its use has been deprecated.) You can also use sendError() to send an error response to the client that may include a descriptive message.

Seven methods deal with the response header. You can add or set the response header with a given name and value using the methods addHeader() and setHeader(). Use addDateHeader() or setDateHeader() to add or set the response header with a specified name and date. Instead of specifying the date, you can add or set a response header with a specified integer value with the methods addIntHeader() and setIntHeader(). You can use the method containsHeader() to indicate that you have already set a specified response header.

Methods are also available for adding a cookie, encoding URLs, and redirecting the client. The method addCookie() will add the Cookie object you specify to the response. We will look more at these methods in the next section. Using encodeURL() you can encode a specified URL to include the session ID if encoding is needed. You can redirect the client to a specified URL using sendRedirect(). You can also encode the redirect URL using encodeRedirectURL().

Saving and Sharing Information

There will be some information that you would like to make available to more than one servlet, to more than one user, or to the same user at different times. For servlets operating within the same context you can do this by sharing attributes. To understand context you can think of servlets that operate within the same JVM and that are in the same subdirectory of the webapps directory. You can also keep information by writing to a customized file on the server or to a database. Check out Chapter 7 on JDBC for information on interacting with a database. We'll begin this section with a look at session tracking. With many applications, you'll find it important to be able to share information about and keep track of who is accessing your resources.

Session tracking

One of the most important pieces of information is session tracking. Because HTTP is a stateless protocol, each contact from a client is like the first time you've ever heard from that client. You can't remember who is who without help. You can spend a lot of effort gathering information about your users; this does you no good if the next time they access a resource, you can't match the information to the client making the new contact. Three of your favorite techniques, hidden form fields, URL rewriting, and cookies, are still useful.

If you use `POST` as the method associated with a form, and tag some of the elements as `TYPE=hidden`, then you are effectively passing information from one resource to another. Your syntax will look something like the following form element:

```
<INPUT TYPE=hidden NAME = "secret" VALUE = "squirrel">
```

At the other end, the receiving servlet accesses the properties with a call to the method `getParameter()`, as follows:

```
request.getParameter("secret");
```

You can also rewrite URLs to pass information or to track sessions. You saw earlier in this chapter how to use the query to pass an added parameter in the HelloForm.html example. Direct support for URL rewriting is included in `HttpServletResponse`. The method `encodeURL()` takes the URL as a `String` and includes the session ID in it if it is needed. The API documentation recommends that you use this method for all URLs you send from a servlet. If the client's browser supports cookies, this method does not encode the URL. If the client's browser doesn't support cookies, or if session tracking is turned off, you will need URL encoding for session tracking.

The servlet API includes support for cookies. The `addCookie()` method in `HttpServletResponse` takes a `Cookie` object as an argument. The corresponding `getCookies()` method is in `HttpServletRequest`. This isn't like getting and setting other objects in the servlet API. In the case of attributes you can get and set a particular attribute or get an array (or list) of all of the attributes. Here you can add a particular cookie but you can only get an array of all of the `Cookie` objects sent by the client in the request. This means that you have to process this array to find the information you want.

The `Cookie` class has methods for working with cookies. The constructor takes two `String` classes: the name of the cookie and the value. You can use the method `getName()` to find the name of a cookie as you look through the array returned by `getCookies()`. Other than that, there are get and set methods for the comment, domain, maximum age of the cookie, path, whether or not the browser is sending cookies over a secure protocol, value, and version. You cannot set the name of an existing cookie.

Using the ServletContext

You saw methods that set and get attributes when you were looking at the `ServletRequest` family. You can use these methods to share information among servlets. All of your servlets within the J2EEBible directory share a common ServletContext. This means that you can use the ServletContext to get and set attributes to pass information within that world. If you are using many servers to serve up your application, then the information can only be shared within each local JVM.

The following code snippet shows how to set an attribute:

```
public void doGet(...){ ...
  ServletContext context = getServletContext();
  context.setAttribute("com.hungryminds.J2EEBible.thisCh",
    "3:Servlets");
}
```

Here you have obtained a handle to the ServletContext and set the attribute that keeps track of the current chapter in this book. In this case, the value you are setting is of type String. The second argument, however, is declared to be of type Object. This means that you can pass in a reference to any type of object. It also means that when you are retrieving the value of a named attribute, you will need to cast it to its type. In this example you would do that as follows:

```
public void doGet(...) {...
  ServletContext context = getServletContext();
  String currentChapter = (String)
    context.getAttribute("com.hungryminds.J2EEBible.thisCh");
}
```

Adding Functionality with filter(), forward(), and include()

In ordinary Java programming, when a class does too much, you want to refactor it into smaller objects that collaborate to achieve the same result in a more flexible way. The hope is that you can then use the components in other applications as well. In this section we'll introduce you to three ways to add functionality when dealing with servlets. This means that when you need to split up responsibility, you can reach for the appropriate technique. In addition, a servlet is running within a JVM so it has access to your usual bag of tricks. Here you'll see how to create filters that work with the request before it gets to the servlet and then alter the response once it leaves. We'll also discuss forwarding the results of one servlet to another resource. Finally, we'll show you how to use an include() method to combine the output of two servlets.

Using filters with servlets

The interfaces Filter, FilterChain, and FilterConfig are new with the Servlet 2.3 release. Classes that implement Filter are used to either preprocess or postprocess servlets. They can change requests before a servlet is invoked or a response after a servlet generates it. You can chain as many filters as you want together on either or both sides of the servlet you want to affect. This means that you can write filters with very specific functionality and reuse them with different servlets. You will need to modify the web.xml deployment descriptor to register the filters and to map where they are being used. You can specify the mapping by providing either the URL or the servlet name(s) the filter will be working with. The former option will enable you to apply filters to static content as well as servlets if you want.

The documentation for the Filter interface suggests that filters can be used for authentication, logging and auditing, image conversion, data compression, encryption, tokenizing, triggering resource access events, XSLT, and MIME-type chains. To demonstrate how filters work, we'll use a very simple (and utterly useless) example.

This example will work with a servlet to return an error code instead of the usual content of the servlet. The Filter interface specifies the three methods init(), destroy(), and doFilter(). The following code provides functionality only for the doFilter() method:

```
package Greetings;

import java.io.*;
import javax.servlet.*;
import javax.servlet.http.*;

public class PostFilter implements Filter {

  public void doFilter(ServletRequest request,
    ServletResponse response,FilterChain chain)
    throws IOException, ServletException  {
      int sc = ((int)(Math.random()*5)+1)*100+1;
      ((HttpServletResponse)  (response)).sendError(sc,
        "something's up");
  }

  public void init(FilterConfig filterConfig)
    throws ServletException {}
  public void destroy() {}
}
```

The doFilter() method selects one of the status codes (101, 201, 301, 401, or 501) at random. You then alter the response to sendError() with this status code and the additional message "something's up." Place PostFilter.java in the Greetings directory and compile it. Run your existing servlet and note that nothing changes: You still need to change the deployment descriptor. Make the following changes so that the filter will work when Greetings.Hello1 is accessed with the shortcut address.

Register the filter and map it to work with the servlet `Hello1` by making the following changes to web.xml:

```
<web-app>
<filter>
  <filter-name>
    PostFilter
  </filter-name>
  <filter-class>
    Greetings.PostFilter
  </filter-class>
</filter>
<filter-mapping>
  <filter-name>
    PostFilter
  </filter-name>
  <servlet-name>
    Hello1
  </servlet-name>
</filter-mapping>
<servlet>
        <servlet-name>
            Hello1
        </servlet-name>
        <servlet-class>
            Greetings.Hello1
        </servlet-class>
    </servlet>
<servlet-mapping>
        <servlet-name>
            Hello1
        </servlet-name>
        <url-pattern>
            /Hi
        </url-pattern>
    </servlet-mapping>
</web-app>
```

Now cycle the server (shut it down and bring it back up) and access the filtered servlet at the following URL:

```
http://localhost:8080/J2EEBible/Hi
```

If you still see no changes, your browser may be caching the page. Click the refresh button, and you will see a screen similar to the one shown in Figure 3-6.

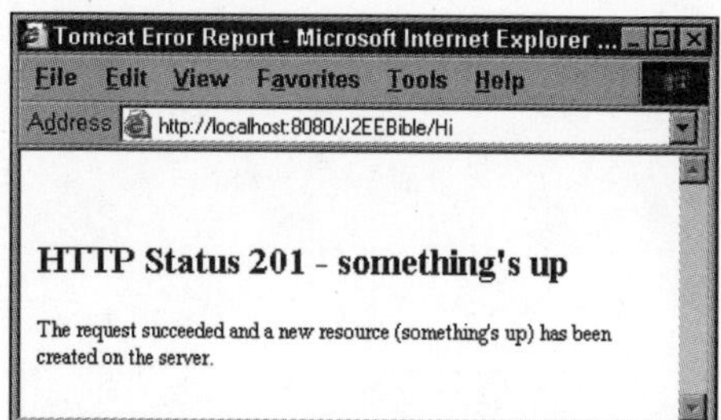

Figure 3-6: The filtered servlet

In addition to getting a handle to the current `ServletRequest` and `ServletResponse`, the `doFilter()` method also receives a handle to the `FilterChain`. The `FilterChain` interface has a single method `doFilter()` that takes a `ServletRequest` object and a `ServletResponse` object as arguments. If your filter is one in a chain of filters, then you call `chain.doFilter()` to pass control on to the next filter. You may think that this causes a problem if you don't know whether your filter will be part of a chain or not. Remember that the point of a filter is to do a specific task that could potentially be used with many different servlets. In some situations it will need to call the next filter, and in some cases there won't be a next filter. If your filter is the last filter in the chain, then `chain.doFilter()` will invoke the resource at the end of the chain. Calls that you make before the `chain.doFilter()` call are made on the way into the servlet; calls that follow `chain.doFilter()` are made on the way out.

Passing control between servlets using forward()

With filtering, you have a single servlet working along with Java objects on the server. With forwarding, your first servlet does some amount of processing on a request and then forwards the request on to another servlet or resource. You will use forwarding for sites in which you are using a servlet as a controller and a JSP for the view.

You cannot start generating the body of the response in one servlet and then forward to another. For example, you can't use the first servlet to generate part of the HTML to be returned and the second servlet to generate the rest. You can, however, set or add headers, and also set status codes and attributes. In this code example, we set the attribute `myName` in the servlet `Hello4` and then pass it on to `Hello5`. `Hello5` is the same as `Hello4` except that we've replaced the following line:

```
String name = request.getParameter("name");
```

with this line:

```
String name = request.getAttribute("myName");
```

The code for Hello4 is fairly straightforward. The relevant lines are shown in bold.

```
package Greetings;

import java.io.*;
import javax.servlet.*;
import javax.servlet.http.*;

public class Hello4 extends HttpServlet {

  public void doGet(HttpServletRequest request,
    HttpServletResponse response)
    throws IOException, ServletException {

    request.setAttribute("myName", "you've been forwarded");
    RequestDispatcher dispatcher =
     request.getRequestDispatcher("/servlet/Greetings.Hello5");
    dispatcher.forward(request, response);
  }
}
```

You set the attribute myName using the method request.setAttribute(). Now you are ready to call the Hello5 servlet. First you need a RequestDispatcher to wrap the servlet being called. The fact that your path begins with a slash (/) indicates that it is a relative path. Once you have a RequestDispatcher, you can use it either to forward a request from the first servlet to the specified servlet, or for an include. The target of a forward doesn't need to be a servlet; it could also be a JSP or an HTML file. The dispatcher knows the target and source so you need only to pass in the ServletRequest and ServletResponse as arguments to dispatcher.forward().

Figure 3-7 shows a screen shot of what the user sees. The user has no idea that the request has been forwarded. Notice that the URL is the initial servlet called, but that the attribute has been successfully set by the first servlet and read by the second.

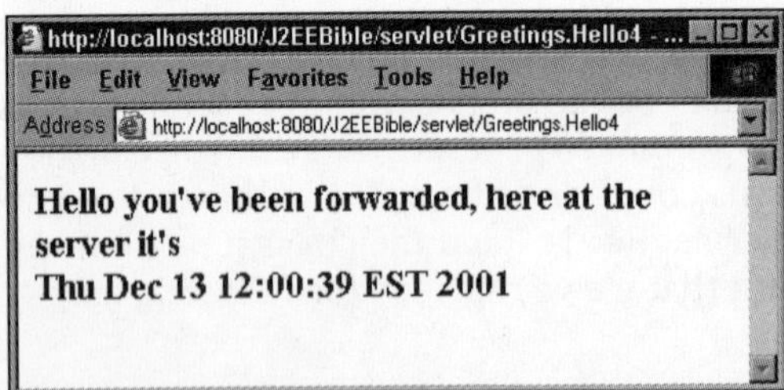

Figure 3-7: A forwarded servlet request

Including content from one resource in another

You can't use `forward()` to combine the body of the response from two different servlets. If you'd like to include the output of one resource in the output of your servlet, then you should use `include()`. You begin the same way you did with `forward()`: by creating a `RequestDispatcher` and using `request.getRequestDispatcher()` to tell it the location of the resource that you will be including. In the following example you will again set an attribute that the target servlet will use:

```
package Greetings;

import java.io.*;
import javax.servlet.*;
import javax.servlet.http.*;

public class Hello6 extends HttpServlet {

  public void doGet(HttpServletRequest request,
    HttpServletResponse response)
    throws IOException, ServletException {

    response.setContentType("text/html");
    PrintWriter out = response.getWriter();
    request.setAttribute("myName", "you've been
    included");
    RequestDispatcher dispatcher =
      request.getRequestDispatcher(
      "/servlet/Greetings.HelloInclude");

    out.println("<html>");
    out.println("<body>");
    out.println("<h1>" );
    dispatcher.include(request, response);
    out.println("here at the server it's <br>" );
    out.println( new Date());
    out.println("</h1>");
    out.println("</body>");
    out.println("</html>");
  }
}
```

Look at where the HTML is being returned to the client. In the middle you made the following call:

```
dispatcher.include(request, response);
```

To see what is placed here you need to check out the file HelloInclude as shown in the following example:

```
package Greetings;

import java.io.*;
import javax.servlet.*;
import javax.servlet.http.*;

public class HelloInclude extends HttpServlet {

  public void doGet(HttpServletRequest request,
    HttpServletResponse response)
    throws IOException, ServletException {

    PrintWriter out = response.getWriter();
    String name = (String)request.getAttribute("myName");
    out.println("Hello " + name );
  }
}
```

If you check out the boldfaced text, it is interesting to note what isn't there as well as what is. You have not set the content type of what is being returned. This servlet is called by another servlet for which the content type has already been set. You do have to call `response.getWriter()`, however. The output from this servlet is included in the output from the calling servlet. You do need a handle to the `PrintWriter` to send the output back to the client. The final line is just the HTML that returns the message "Hello you've been included" to the client.

We have purposefully created a very simple example so that the implementation of `include()` will be clear. You can imagine more useful applications of this technique. You can build a table in which the rows include information being returned by calls to a database. You could include standard top matter (such as banner ads or navigational aids) on all the pages of your site. Remember, the target of your `include()` can be an HTML page, a JSP, or a servlet.

Summary

You can find eight-hundred-page books devoted entirely to servlets. We've taken you on a quick tour that introduced you to the power and flexibility of using servlets to interact with the client in your enterprise application. You learned the following:

✦ In order to create a servlet for a Web application, you will most often begin by extending `HttpServlet` and overriding one of the service methods. If you want to respond to the `GET` method, you will override `doGet()`. Similarly, if you want to respond to the `POST` method, you will override `doPost()`.

- You can process requests using methods defined in `HttpServletRequest` and related classes and interfaces. This enables you to use information included in the header that you don't see as well as information included in the URL. You can determine the HTTP method used to make the request and the cookies that the client has sent as well as information about the user, session, and path.
- You can generate responses using methods defined in `HttpServletResponse` and related classes and interfaces. You can use these methods to create a cookie, send error messages, and set status codes. You can rewrite the URL and manipulate the contents of the buffer. Also, `HttpServletResponse` inherits from `ServletResponse` which contains the `getWriter()` and `setContentType()` methods that enable you to set the type of the content you are returning to the client and provide you with a handle to the `PrintWriter` that you use to do it.
- You can pass information among servlets within the same context by setting and getting attributes. You can also write information to a file or database that can be accessed by other servlets.
- Filters are new with the Servlet API 2.3. They enable you to pre- and post-process servlets. You can change a request before the servlet handles it or change the response (just not the body) after the servlet generates it. You can also include content from another resource using `include()` and forward the results of one servlet to another resource using `forward()`.

✦ ✦ ✦

Using JavaServer Pages

✦ ✦ ✦ ✦

In This Chapter

Creating dynamic content with JSP

Understanding the life cycle of JSPs

Introducing Java code to your JSP page in scriptlets

Using JSP expressions to display results in your page

Interacting with JavaBeans from your JSP page

Designing and implementing custom tags to give your Web designers more power

✦ ✦ ✦ ✦

In Chapter 3, we introduced servlets as a powerful way of responding to client requests. Unfortunately, they are not the best tools for generating content destined for a Web browser. Web designers can use JavaServer Pages (JSP) technology to add a lot of functionality to an HTML page. In this chapter we'll show how JSP page designers can directly add Java code and the results of Java expressions to their pages. We'll then turn to the more robust approach of having programmers design JavaBeans and custom tags that give Web designers the ability to achieve their goals without having to learn Java syntax or the various Java APIs. Finally, we'll discuss how you might use servlets and JSPs together to build your Web application.

Actually, a JSP page is compiled into a servlet the first time it is requested. This means that there's really nothing a JSP page can do that a servlet can't. As you learn about the various JSP tags you may find it useful to view the servlet source code created by the JSP container. This code shows you where your page commands end up.

Both JSPs and servlets are used as a front end for large-scale enterprise applications like e-commerce Web sites. Typically the back end that interacts with the database is handled by Enterprise JavaBeans (EJBs). To learn more about EJBs and how to integrate them with both JSP pages and servlets, read Chapter 16.

Even though a JSP "becomes" a servlet, you'll see that tasks such as presentation are better handled by a JSP page, while programming and business logic are better handled by a servlet. You are able to program in a JSP page, but it is difficult to read and maintain any but the most basic programming in this format. If you've ever debugged JavaScript you'll understand why debugging is also a problem with JSP pages. The line numbers referred to in the error messages are seldom helpful, and the cause of the error is seldom clear from these messages.

Creating a Basic JSP Page

In Chapter 3 you created a servlet that greets you by name and tells you what time it is at the server location. We'll begin our look at JSP pages by telling you how to create the JSP equivalent. You'll follow the same three steps and take a look at what's going on along the way. The rest of the chapter will provide the details of embedding Java in your JSP. For now you'll look at how to create and run a basic JSP page. You'll look at where you save your JSP page and examine its conversion into a servlet. As before, this is a toy example that is purposefully simplistic to help you focus on what we're demonstrating.

Creating, saving, and accessing a page

It is quite clunky to create a static HTML page with a servlet. You have to import some packages and create a class that extends `HttpServlet`. This class has to contain a `doGet()` method that declares its content type and obtains a `PrintWriter` object. The actual HTML has to be encased in a sequence of `out.println()` statements. This is a lot of work considering that you end up with output equivalent to the following HTML file:

```
<html>
  <body>
    <h1> Hello </h1>
  </body>
</html>
```

How much work do you need to do to encode this page as a JSP page? None. Just save it as Hello.jsp. Using Tomcat 4.0 as the reference implementation, save it in the directory *tomcatdirectory*\webapps\J2EEBible\jsp\Greetings. If you skipped Chapter 3 you will need to create a J2EEBible directory with the same structure as the existing examples directory. In either case, you will have to create a Greetings directory inside the jsp directory.

If you also have the J2EE reference implementation downloaded, then you can use that as a Web server too as it will enable you to access EJBs and other enterprise APIs. See Appendix A for how to set up and deploy the reference implementation to serve JSP pages in combination with the other enterprise code that you will develop throughout this book.

Now run the page. Make sure that your Web server is running, and use your browser to navigate to the following URL:

```
http://localhost:8080/J2EEBible/jsp/Greetings/Hello.jsp
```

Replace `localhost:8080` with whatever is appropriate for your particular setup. You will encounter a bit of a wait, and then you will see the word "Hello" proudly displayed in your browser. If you created and ran servlets, you may notice that there is a step missing here: You didn't explicitly compile your servlet. Take a minute now to find out what is going on behind the scenes.

The JSP life cycle

We said before that a JSP is compiled into and then run as a servlet. Once you have a servlet, the usual servlet life cycle (as we explained in Chapter 3) applies. Remember that the servlet life cycle was managed by the servlet container, and that as a result you still need the servlet container to run JSPs. The JSP life cycle has some convenient additions. As you will see later in this chapter, a JSP page can have many JSP-specific elements along with the HTML elements. This means that the JSP page must be processed before anyone sees it.

The role of the JSP container

The first time a JSP page is requested, it is converted into a servlet and compiled by a JSP container. The JSP container is an application (often a servlet) that performs these JSP-specific translation tasks. When a user requests a JSP page, the JSP container will check to see if the current compiled version needs to be updated. If the JSP page is new or has been modified since the last time it was converted and compiled, the container will perform the translation. One benefit of this is that you don't have to cycle the Web server when you update a JSP.

As an example, consider your Hello.jsp running under Tomcat 4.0. The setup may be different on other Web services, but the ideas are the same. That pause that you noticed before "Hello" appeared on your screen was the time it took to parse the JSP page into a servlet source file and to compile it. If you go back to the top level within the Tomcat directory you will notice the works subdirectory at the same level as the webapps and bin directories. Inside of the work/localhost/ directory, you'll find a directory structure similar to that which was inside of the webapps folder. For this example, navigate to work/localhost/J2EEBible/jsp/Greetings. There you will find the compiled servlet `Hello_jsp.class` and the `Hello_jsp.java` Java source file generated by the JSP container.

The servlet generated by the JSP container

Different Web servers will process JSPs differently. The package `javax.servlet.jsp` contains classes, interfaces, and exceptions used by the JSP container and the servlets it generates.

A lot of information is contained in the following servlet source file. We will come back to it several times throughout this chapter. When trying to understand a new JSP tag, you might find it helpful to view the generated servlet. Your training as a programmer and your experience with servlets may shed light on a tag you aren't quite certain about.

Tomcat 4.0 took the simple JSP file that contains nothing more than five lines of HTML and processed it into the servlet shown in Listing 4-1.

Listing 4-1: Sample servlet generated by the JSP container

```
package org.apache.jsp;

import javax.servlet.*;
import javax.servlet.http.*;
import javax.servlet.jsp.*;
import javax.servlet.jsp.tagext.*;
import org.apache.jasper.runtime.*;

public class Hello_jsp extends HttpJspBase {
  static {}
  public Hello_jsp( ) {}
  private static boolean _jspx_inited = false;
  public final void _jspx_init() throws
    org.apache.jasper.JasperException {}
  public void _jspService(HttpServletRequest request,
    HttpServletResponse  response)
    throws java.io.IOException, ServletException {

    JspFactory _jspxFactory = null;
    PageContext pageContext = null;
    HttpSession session = null;
    ServletContext application = null;
    ServletConfig config = null;
    JspWriter out = null;
    Object page = this;
    String  _value = null;
    try {
      if (_jspx_inited == false) {
        synchronized (this) {
          if (_jspx_inited == false) {
            _jspx_init();
            _jspx_inited = true;
          }
        }
      }
      _jspxFactory = JspFactory.getDefaultFactory();
      response.setContentType("text/html;charset=8859_1");
      pageContext = _jspxFactory.getPageContext(this, request,
        response, "", true, 8192, true);
      application = pageContext.getServletContext();
```

```
        config = pageContext.getServletConfig();
        session = pageContext.getSession();
        out = pageContext.getOut();
     // HTML // begin [file="C:\\Java\\jakarta-tomcat-4.0-b3...
     // \\webapps\\J2EEBible\\jsp\\Greetings\\Hello.jsp";...
     // from=(0,0);to=(5,0)]
        out.write("<html>\r\n  <body>\r\n    <h1> Hello </h1>\r\n
          </body>\r\n</html>\r\n");   // end
      }
      catch (Throwable t) {
        if (out != null && out.getBufferSize() != 0)
          out.clearBuffer();
        if (pageContext != null)
          pageContext.handlePageException(t);
      }
      finally {
        if (_jspxFactory != null)
          _jspxFactory.releasePageContext(pageContext);
      }
    }
  }
```

The bold portion is equivalent to the five lines of HTML from the original JSP page. Your experience with servlets should make it easy for you to figure out what is going on with the rest of this code. You can see variables such as `ServletContext` and `ServletConfig` being declared and initialized. You will also notice that you didn't do most of this when you wrote your version of the `Hello` servlet. All you did was import the appropriate packages, set the content type, obtain a handle to a `PrintWriter` and send back the HTML. You did this by extending an `HttpServlet` and implementing the `doGet()` method.

In the generated servlet you are extending the class `HttpJspBase` and implementing the method `_jspService()`. Again, the implementation in other Web servers will differ. Here `HttpJspBase` is in the package `org.apache.jasper.runtime`. The `HttpJspBase` class both extends `javax.servlet.http.HttpServlet` and implements `javax.servlet.jsp.HttpJspPage`. You can check out the classes and interfaces in the `javax.servlet.jsp` package, but they are intended to be used only by the implementers of the JSP container.

Adding dynamic elements to the JSP

With two small changes to the code you can add the date and time at the server to the Web page as you did in Chapter 3. We will explain what these elements mean in the next section, but be warned that there is a slight problem with the following code:

```
<html>
  <body>
    <h1>
      Hello <%= request.getParameter("name") %>,
```

```
      here at the server, it's <%= new Date() %>
    </h1>
  </body>
</html>
```

If you look back at the generated servlet for the previous example you'll see that the packages loaded include the one containing `HttpServletRequest`. The variable `request` is an argument of the `_jspService()` method that handles the body of the JSP page. This means that the method call

```
request.getParameter("name")
```

executes as expected. In the next section we'll explain the JSP syntax of enclosing this Java code inside of `<%=...%>` and not including a semicolon.

You'll find the problem with the code in the second method call in which you are creating and displaying a new `Date` object. If you load and run this JSP on Tomcat you will get a stack trace and an error message similar to the following:

```
A Servlet Exception Has Occurred
org.apache.jasper.JasperException: Unable to compile class for
JSPC:\Java\jakarta-tomcat-4.0-b3\bin\..
\work\localhost\J2EEBible\jsp\Greetings\Hello_jsp.java:66: C
lass org.apache.jsp.Date not found.
                out.print( new Date() );
                               ^
1 error
```

In this case, the error message is surprisingly informative. You can quickly determine that the JSP container is trying to place the `Date` class in the wrong package. You need to either import the `java.util` package or use a fully qualified name when creating a new `Date` object. You'll learn the syntax for import in the next section; for now, make the following change to the code, and it will run fine:

```
<html>
  <body>
    <h1>
      Hello <%= request.getParameter("name") %>,
      here at the server, it's <%= new java.util.Date() %>
    </h1>
  </body>
</html>
```

Navigate to the page and supply a name as a query string. For example, use the URL `http://localhost:8080/J2EEBible/jsp/Greetings/Hello.jsp?name=Kim`. You will wait while the JSP is translated and loaded, and then you will see the personalized greeting. Change the name and reload the page. As no changes have been made to the JSP, it doesn't have to be converted into a servlet or recompiled. It should load immediately with the name replaced.

Notice that you were able to change the JSP page and that the JSP container took care of delivering a compiled class file loaded by the Web server. With JSPs, you don't usually have to worry about cycling the Web server.

As a final experiment, navigate your browser directly to the `Hello.jsp` file stored in the ...\webapps\J2EEBible\jsp\Greetings directory. The page will load, and you will see "Hello , here at the server, it's". Where is the personalized greeting or the date? If you view the source, you will see that the browser is ignoring the two Java calls between `<%=` and `%>`. The browser assumes that these are unknown tags and just ignores them. This should help you see that the work really is being done on the server side. When you access the JSP page using the Web server, the server fills in the name and the date and sends them back to the browser as HTML.

Putting the "J" in JSP

So far you've used a fairly innocuous example of including Java code in a JSP page. Basically it appears that you've included code that produces output that is then returned to the client as a `String`. In this section we'll discuss JSP support that could enable you to do pretty sophisticated programming in the middle of a JSP page. We beg you not to do this. Things can get messy quickly, and debugging is very difficult. Essentially you'll be turning the Java programming experience into a JavaScript session.

The best way to use JSP technology is as a means of helping you divide the responsibilities in a development team. The Web designers should do the Web design, and the programmers should do the programming. For the most part, this should mean that the programmers set up a framework in which the Web designers can best do their work and then stay out of the way. Web designers should not be writing complex business logic within a Web page. Even if you are playing both roles yourself, there are benefits to dividing your tasks according to the technology that supports it.

In the following three subsections, we'll discuss how business logic and presentation logic can remain separated in ways that best serve the designers and the programmers. In this section we'll tell you about comments, declarations, expressions, and scriptlets. We'll also tell you about page directives and objects automatically available to you. But first we include the following warning for those people who skip introductions to sections.

The Java programming language goes to great pains to protect you from yourself. For the most part, you aren't allowed to do many of the things that could end up hurting you—even if you know what you're doing. This isn't true with JSP. Here you are given a six-pack and the keys to a smooth-riding car. Yes, you can turn the key, but you might be paying for it for a long time. Think twice before putting complex Java code inside a JSP page. Friends don't let friends write scriptlets.

Embedding Java code in a JSP page

Scripting elements fall between an opening tag that begins with <% and a closing tag that ends with %>. The default scripting language for JSPs is Java.

Comments

A comment in HTML is included between <!-- and -->. A JSP comment is placed between <%-- and --%>. To see the difference you can save the following code as Comment.jsp:

```
<html>
  <!-- This is an HTML comment -->
  <%-- This is a JSP comment --%>
  Comment page
</html>
```

Neither comment will appear on the page. The only words visible in your browser will be "Comment page". To see the difference, view the source code. The JSP comment won't appear in the source code, but the HTML comment will.

You can also include Java-style comments in scriptlets and declarations. Because you can't ordinarily be sure what the JSP container will add when it is processing your page, you should be careful about doing this. It would be a shame to use the comment delimiter // only to have the translator break the line in an unexpected place.

Expressions

The two expressions that contain Java code in Hello.jsp are examples of the JSP expression element. Its purpose is to add some piece of dynamic content to the output. The format is the following:

```
<%= theExpression %>
```

You are using Java as your scripting language, but you can use other scripting languages such as JavaScript. In the example introduced in the section "Adding dynamic elements to the JSP" earlier in this chapter, the expressions are `request.getParameter("name")` and `new java.util.Date()`. In the first case the method returns a `String` object, and in the second it returns a `Date` object. Whether an expression returns a `String`, an object, or a primitive type, the expression is converted to a `String` by various `toString()` methods.

A JSP expression is not terminated with a semicolon. You write

```
<%= new java.util.Date() %>
```

and not

```
<%= new java.util.Date(); %>
```

Declarations

You can declare variables or methods using the following syntax:

```
<%! theDeclaration %>
```

A variable introduced this way will be translated into an instance variable in the corresponding servlet. Similarly, you can call a method introduced with a JSP declaration anywhere in the JSP page. In the following code snippet we have used one declaration to declare and initialize the instance variables x and y. We've used a second declaration to define the method add(). We can then add x and y by calling add(x,y), which we do from inside an expression.

```
<html>
  <%! public int x = 3, y = 9; %>
  <%! public int add(int x, int y){
        return x+y;
      } %>
  The sum of x = <%= x %> and y = <%= y %> is <%= add(x,y) %>.
</html>
```

As a result you see the following in the browser:

```
The sum of x = 3 and y = 9 is 12.
```

In general, you should be careful about creating instance variables in a servlet or JSP page. The page can be accessed by more than one client at once. Unless you've taken care to make your page thread safe, you can end up with unexpected results when one client alters the value of a variable being used by another client.

The generated servlet in the Hello example included the _jspService() method. The other life-cycle methods that correspond to servlet init() and destroy() methods are also available to you. Using a JSP declaration for the methods _jspInit() and _jspDestroy(), you can specify what happens when the servlet is created or destroyed. The signatures of these methods are declared in the JspPage and HttpJspPage interfaces in the javax.servlet.jsp package.

Scriptlets

When you want to use Java code to perform some task in the middle of a JSP page, you use a scriptlet. The syntax for a scriptlet is the following:

```
<% theScriptlet %>
```

As an illustration, consider this JSP page:

```
<html>
  This is a
  <% for (int x = 0;x<5; x++){ %>
    very
    <% if (x <4 ) %>,
```

```
    <% } %>
    trivial example of using a scriptlet in a JSP page.
  </html>
```

Forget that there are easier ways of printing out the static page that says, "This is a very, very, very, very, very trivial example of using a scriptlet in a JSP page." You can see that we have an `if` statement inside a `for` loop. We've highlighted the beginning and end of the `for` loop so you can see how the scriptlet elements and the ordinary HTML are intermixed. Code like this quickly becomes hard to read and hard to debug.

There are times when a scriptlet seems to be the right answer. Even in those cases we encourage you to look at the next few sections and consider using a JavaBean or a custom tag instead.

Using JSP directives

The three JSP directives are `page`, `include` and `taglib`. They help set some parameters for the entire page. For example, the `page` directive enables the programmer to set various attributes, such as the scripting language of the page, the content type, and the size of the buffer. The syntax is as follows:

```
<%@ page attribute="valueOfAttribute" %>
```

Using the page directive

You can set one or more attributes in a single `page` directive. Your choices are `autoflush`, `buffer`, `contentType`, `errorPage`, `extends`, `import`, `info`, `isErrorPage`, `isThreadSafe`, `language`, and `session`. Your automatically generated servlet shows that the default for `contentType` is `text/html`, and we've already noted that the default value for `language` is `"java"`. You can specify XML, plain, or other MIME types with a page directive like the following:

```
<%@ page contentType="text/xml" %>
```

You can set the size of the buffer with the `buffer` attribute and set a Boolean to indicate whether to `autoflush` the buffer or not. If you want to restrict access to the JSP page to one user at a time, you can set the `isThreadSafe` flag to `"false"`. This, however, is usually an indication that you need to do more work to make the JSP (or more accurately, the resulting servlet) thread safe by synchronizing various blocks of code.

Recall that when Hello.jsp was turned into a servlet, the created class extended the class `HttpJspBase`. It in turn extended `javax.servlet.http.HttpServlet` and implemented the interface `javax.servlet.jsp.HttpJspPage`. You can extend your own custom class if you'd like. Specify the class you are extending with the `extend` attribute of the `page` directive. You should have a very compelling reason for doing this. In most cases you're better off working within the constraints set by the classes created by the various JSP containers.

In the Hello.jsp example you created a `Date` object by requesting a `new java.util.Date()` object. Although you could have done the same thing in an ordinary Java application, you are more likely to have imported the `java.util` package with an `import` statement. You can import one or more classes and/or packages with the `import` attribute of a `page` directive. Here is the rewritten Hello.jsp example:

```
<html>
  <body>
    <%@ page import="java.util.*" %>
    <h1> Hello <%= request.getParameter("name") %>,
    here at the server, it's <%= new Date() %></h1>
  </body>
</html>
```

Specifying tag libraries

The `taglib` directive is similar to the `import` attribute of the `page` directive. This will become important to you when you learn about custom tags later in this chapter. In this case, you are specifying a particular tag library and so the tags defined in that library are now available to be used by that JSP page. When using `taglib` you have to use the shortcut name that you define as the `prefix` to refer to the particular tags on the page.

For example, suppose you built a custom tag library for this book that you want to refer to as jb. Then you use the following tag format:

```
<%@ taglib uri="whereverItIs" prefix="jb" %>
```

You now have all of the tags defined in the jb library available to you on the page. Suppose you have a tag in that library that is called `takeANap` that takes no attributes. You will be able to call it anywhere on the page using the following tag:

```
<jb:takeANap />
```

Notice that you won't get name collisions for two reasons. First, when you use a tag you have to include a reference to the tag library in the tag. Second, this tag prefix is a name you have chosen to refer to its tag library on that specific page. You can use different tag prefixes on different pages to refer to the same library. You do, however, need to stay away from the reserved prefixes, such as `jsp`, `jspx`, `java`, `javax`, `servlet`, `sun`, and `sunw`.

Including other files

You use the `include` directive to include the contents of a specified file in the current file. The syntax is as follows:

```
<%@ include file="URL of file" %>
```

The result is the same as if you cut the contents of the file and pasted them in place of the `include` directive tag. Consider the following JSP page:

```
<html>
  <body>
    I'm thinking of including another file here.
    <%@ include file="Hello.jsp" %>
    I wonder what happened.
  </body>
</html>
```

In the middle of musing about the results of including another file, the file itself is pasted in place by the `include` directive. It's as if you now have the following new JSP page:

```
<html>
  <body>
    I'm thinking of including another file here.
      <html>
        <body>
          <%@ page import="java.util.*" %>
            <h1> Hello <%= request.getParameter("name") %>,
            here at the server, it's <%= new Date() %></h1>
        </body>
      </html>
      I wonder what happened.
  </body>
</html>
```

If instead you want to include the results of executing a JSP page, you need to look at the `include` action detailed in the next subsection.

Transferring control with actions

So far you've used the JSP tags that look a lot like Active Server Pages (ASP) tags. Each of them has a corresponding XML version. For example, the following two tags are equivalent:

```
<%@ page import="java.util.*" %>
<jsp:directive.page import="java.util.*" />
```

Note that in the second version you need to make sure that the XML tag is well formed, and so you include the closing slash (/). Potential problems exist with using the XML version when including Java code. For example, the greater-than sign (>) can be misinterpreted in an expression such as `x>5 ? x : y`.

Actions include tags for using JavaBeans, for forwarding the control to another resource, and for including another resource. We will cover the bean tags later. In this chapter we'll start by showing you the `include` action tag. First, alter the example you considered when looking at the `include` attribute for the `page` directive. Note that for some Web servers, the `<jsp:include>` tag must include the attribute `flush`, and its value must be `true`. Nevertheless, the following code runs correctly on Tomcat 4.0:

```
<html>
  <body>
    I'm thinking of including another file here.
    <jsp:include page="Hello.jsp" />
    I wonder what happened.
  </body>
</html>
```

In the section "Including other files" earlier in this chapter, the highlighted line is `<%@ include file="Hello.jsp" %>`. The effect of using these two similar-looking tags is strikingly different. Remember that in the case of the `include` attribute you just pasted the contents of the file being referred to in place of the tag. The `include` action is translated in the servlet to a `javax.servlet.jsp.PageContext.include()` method call much like the `RequestDispather.include()` that we describe in Chapter 3. You can include a JSP page or a servlet. In this particular case, Tomcat 4.0 translates the `<jsp:include>` tag into the following call (with a minor detail omitted):

```
pageContext.include("Hello.jsp");
```

Similarly, the `<jsp:forward >` tag is converted to a `javax.servlet.jsp.PageContext.forward()` call, as follows:

```
pageContext.forward("Hello.jsp");
```

The Hello.jsp page has been modified to greet the user by name. You are passing this name on as part of the query string in the URL. With an `include` directive or a `forward` directive you can pass the name on as a parameter. Replace the line `<jsp:include page = "Hello.jsp" />` with the following three lines:

```
<jsp:include page="Hello.jsp">
  <jsp:param name="name" value="Maggie" />
</jsp:include>
```

In order to pass one or more parameters to the included page you need an opening tag and a closing tag for the `<jsp:include>` directive. Other than that, you don't need to make many changes.

Accessing implicit Java objects

Although Hello.jsp seemed to be a trivial example, you've learned a lot from it and the corresponding servlet. Even for the first example with static content, the servlet contained the following code that set up a bunch of servlet objects:

```
public void _jspService(HttpServletRequest request,
    HttpServletResponse  response)
    throws java.io.IOException, ServletException {
    JspFactory _jspxFactory = null;
    PageContext pageContext = null;
    HttpSession session = null;
```

```
        ServletContext application = null;
        ServletConfig config = null;
        JspWriter out = null;
        Object page = this;
        String  _value = null;
        ...
    }
```

Here's a cool idea. If every JSP is going to be translated into a servlet that has this set of objects, why not enable JSP programmers to interact with them? For example, you can see that you have a `request` and `response` object. There is a `JspWriter` called `out` as well as a handle to the `session`, `page`, `config`, `pageContext`, and `application` (a `ServletContext`). The final implicit object is an `exception`.

You used the `request` object when you first added dynamic content to Hello.jsp. Your first expression displayed a name passed on as a parameter:

```
<%= request.getParameter("name") %>
```

These implicit objects have types that you learned about in Chapter 3. You can make the appropriate calls from the APIs from within the JSP page. Once again, we stress that just because you can do this doesn't mean you should. But if you just need to get the value of a parameter or cookie, having a `request` object is quite handy. You may want to use the `response` object for setting header information.

You can see why this is an attractive feature for those people responsible for designing JSPs. The recommendation, however, is that the JSP page should concentrate on the presentation logic. If you want access to these servlet features, then you should consider using an actual servlet.

Adding JavaBeans

In Chapter 3, we mentioned that part of the power of servlets is that they can work with filters and ordinary Java objects. For JSPs, you'll find that JavaBeans are one useful mechanism for dividing up business logic. Beans are Java classes with special conventions that allow other elements to figure out what they can do and to make appropriate requests of them. JSP technology takes advantage of this to enable a Web designer to use your beans as workhorses without getting into trouble.

Although using JavaBeans in a Web page may seem a little odd at first glance, this is the preferred method of accessing Java code. For example, in an enterprise setting, JavaBeans are used as wrappers around Enterprise JavaBeans to access databases and other enterprise data sources to provide services like shopping carts. EJBs cannot be accessed directly by a JSP so the JavaBean approach is the recommended way to do this.

Bean property conventions

JavaBeans just follow a few rules. They have no parent class to extend or bean interface to implement. They have to have a no argument constructor. In other words, the class `MySampleBean` should have a constructor like this

```
public MySampleBean(){ ... }
```

Bean properties are attributes that other Java objects can read and possibly write. Properties generally correspond to instance variables, usually with `private` access. The accessors follow a simple naming convention, illustrated by the following code snippet:

```
public class MySampleBean implements java.io.Serializable {
...
  private boolean enabled;
  private int highTemperature;
  private int[] hourlyReading;
...
}
```

For `boolean` properties, you see if they are `true` or `false` with the following getter:

```
public boolean isEnabled(){
  return enabled;
}
```

You can set them with the following setter:

```
public void setEnabled( boolean enabled) {
  this.enabled = enabled;
}
```

The convention is to get the value of a `boolean` *`property`* with a method called `isProperty()` and to set the value of *`property`* with a method called `setProperty()`.

For non-`boolean` properties the set method is exactly the same, but the get method is called `getProperty()`. In your example the methods to get and set `highTemperature` would be the following:

```
public int getHighTemperature(){
  return highTemperature;
}
public void setHighTemperature( int highTemperature){
  this.highTemperature = highTemperature;
}
```

You can access an indexed property by getting or setting the entire array:

```
public int[] getHourlyReading(){
  return hourlyReading;
}
public void setHourlyReading( int[] hourlyReading ){
  this.hourlyReading = hourlyReading;
}
```

You can also access a specified element in an array using the following methods:

```
public int getHourlyReading( int whichOne ){
  return hourlyReading[ whichOne ];
}
public void setHourlyReading(int whichOne, int hourlyReading ){
  this.hourlyReading[ whichOne ] = hourlyReading;
}
```

A bean should also implement `java.io.Serializable`. This is just a marker interface. `Serializable` doesn't force you to implement any methods; it just indicates that this object can be serialized. In this example you'll simplify `MySampleBean` and place it the package `temperature`. The entire code for the bean is as follows:

```
package temperature;

public class MySampleBean implements java.io.Serializable {

  private int highTemperature;
  private boolean enabled;

  public MySampleBean(){}

  public boolean isEnabled(){
    return enabled;
  }
  public void setEnabled( boolean enabled) {
    this.enabled = enabled;
  }
  public int getHighTemperature(){
    return highTemperature;
  }
  public void setHighTemperature( int highTemperature){
    this.highTemperature = highTemperature;
  }
}
```

Save this file as MySampleBean.java inside the ...\webapps\J2EEBible\WEB-INF\classes\temperature directory.

Compile the source code into the `MySampleBean.class`, and you are ready to use it from a JSP page.

JSP bean tags

Just three basic JSP bean tags exist, enabling you to perform three basic tasks. `<jsp:useBean>` enables you to set up the connection to the bean you're going to use, and `<jsp:setProperty>` and `<jsp:getProperty>` enable you to set and get bean properties in a few different ways.

Making the bean available with useBean

The `<jsp:useBean>` tag enables you to use the specified JavaBean on that JSP page. The main responsibility of this tag is to match what you are calling the bean on this page to the appropriate class file. The name of this instance of the bean is its `id`. You shouldn't use the same name for two different beans on the same page. The general syntax is as follows:

```
<jsp:useBean id ="bean instance name" class = "class name" />
```

In this case you can refer to an instance of the `MySampleBean` class as `temps` by using the following tag:

```
<jsp:useBean id="temps" class="temperature.MySampleBean" />
```

Other attributes that you can specify are `scope`, `type`, and `beanName`. We'll discuss `scope` later in this section. The attribute `type` is for setting the type of the bean. If you don't specify something here—such as a superclass or an interface—then the type is assumed to be the same as that of the class. Use `beanName` if you are using a serialized version of your bean to create new instances.

You may want to do some initialization once you have instantiated your bean. For this you need a start and end tag. You could, for example, set the value of the `highTemperature` property using the following code snippet:

```
<jsp:useBean id="temps" class="temperature.MySampleBean">
   <jsp:setProperty name="temps"
     property="highTemperature" value="10" />
</jsp:useBean>
```

We'll discuss `<jsp:setProperty>` in a moment. For now, the point is that you can set one or more properties between the start and end of the `<jsp:useBean>` tag.

Setting bean properties with setProperty

As shown in the previous example, you can set a property within the `<jsp:useBean>` tags:

```
<jsp:setProperty name="temps" property="highTemperature" value="10" />
```

Refer to the bean `MySampleBean` by the name that you set using the `id` property in the `<jsp:useBean>` tag. Yes, it was called `id` before, and now you call it `name`. So `name="temps"` lets you know that you are using `MySampleBean`. You then specify the `property` you are setting and the `value` you are setting it to. In this case you are setting `highTemperature` to 10.

You won't always know the values for the various properties when writing the JSP page. There are two ways to deal with this. If the value is calculated at runtime from other values, you can pass in the result of an expression as follows:

```
<jsp:setProperty name="temps" property="highTemperature"
  value="<%= someExpression %>" />
```

You may, instead, want the value of various properties to be passed in by the page's `request` object. If you would like the property `highTemperatures` to be set by the `request`, then you can leave the `value` attribute out, changing the `<jsp:setProperty>` tag to the following:

```
<jsp:setProperty name="temps" property="highTemperature" />
```

The client could set the `highTemperature` by requesting the JSP page with a query string. You've seen this before. In this case, the code would look like this:

```
http://localhost:8080/J2EEBible/jsp/Greetings/Temperature.jsp?highTemperature=40
```

If you want to do this for many or even all properties, you can either specify them or set the `value` to the wildcard * as follows:

```
<jsp:setProperty name="temps" property="highTemperature" value="*" />
```

In this case, this code would allow the client to set the value of `highTemperature` and `enabled` as long as the client knows these properties exist. You can see that you shouldn't use this approach if you don't want to allow a client request to set a property for security or other reasons.

Getting the value of bean properties with getProperty

Getting the value of a bean property is even easier than setting it. What you get back is a `String` representation of the value of the specified property. This means that you can display what is returned as part of the HTML or use it in an HTML tag to retrieve the value of a property or attribute. In this example you would retrieve the `highTemperature` by using the following call:

```
<jsp:getProperty name="temps" property="highTemperature" />
```

When the JSP page is executed, the `int` value of `highTemperature` will be converted to a `String` and appear in its place. The client browser isn't aware of all of your hard work. When the user accesses the JSP page with the following code, he or she is unaware that you have sent information to and retrieved information from a bean:

```
<html>
  <jsp:useBean id="temps" class="temperature.MySampleBean">
```

```
      <jsp:setProperty name="temps" property="highTemperature"
        value="27" />
    </jsp:useBean>
    Here in Frostbite Falls the high temperature is
    <jsp:getProperty name="temps" property="highTemperature" /> .
  </html>
```

In fact, if the user views the source of the resulting Web page, he or she will see the following simple HTML code:

```
<html>
  Here in Frostbite Falls the high temperature is
  27.
</html>
```

How you perform the magic on your site remains your business. You can also display the value of a property in your JSP page using an expression. In this example, the syntax would be as follows:

```
<%= temps.getHighTemperature() %>
```

You actually have to use this second method to get the value of a specific item in an indexed property.

Setting the scope of a bean

One of the `<jsp:useBean>` tag attributes that you haven't yet used is `scope`. You can use this attribute to specify the life and accessibility of a particular bean. If, as in all of these examples, nothing is specified, the default value is `page`. The syntax for using `scope` is as follows:

```
<jsp:useBean id="myName" class="className" scope="myScope" />
```

Your choices for *myScope* are `page`, `request`, `session`, and `application`. If the scope is `page`, then the bean is created each time the page is requested. No information persists between visits. A `request` scope enables you to pass beans on to other JSP pages and servlets when you use `<jsp:include>` and `<jsp:forward>`. This is a nice way to store information that is local to one particular request but that will be used in other parts of your Web application.

In Chapter 3, we talk about different techniques for session tracking. A `session` scope allows the bean to be accessible from other JSPs and servlets accessed during the same session. Here, if another JSP page refers to the same bean, *myName* will point to the existing bean, and a new one will not be created. If none has been created yet, then the first `<jsp:useBean>` to use that `id` will create a new instance of the particular bean. Finally, the `application` scope makes the bean available to other JSPs in the same designated Web application. It doesn't matter if more than one user is accessing the JSPs or if a session has timed out.

Using Custom Tags

Custom tags help you provide the best support for your Web designers. If the designers need a certain specific functionality, you can create it and provide them with an XML tag that they can use in the page to safely invoke it. Remember what you had to do to include something simple like the current time at the server. As a programmer you may have found this pretty straightforward, but it required that the Web designer create a `Date` object. The designer had to know what package it came from and either specify `java.util.Date` or use an `import` statement. Now you can provide that designer with a tag that gets the current time and call it `time`. You can place it in a library called `sample`, and designers can display the current time with the tag `<sample:time />`.

You've seen that your Web designers can get pretty far using the three JavaBeans tags together with the custom beans you write for them. Custom tags enable you to extend this model and create tags that they can use to get more functionality with less Java code in their JSP pages. You can create your own tag libraries in addition to using the ones that are publicly available. An open-source tag library can be found at `http://jakarta.apache.org/taglibs`. You can also find links to various JSP tag libraries at `http://jsptags.com` and at `http://java.sun.com/products/jsp/taglibraries.html`.

The process of developing and using a tag library has three basic parts. First, the programmer creates and compiles a Java class that often extends either the `TagSupport` class or the `BodyTagSupport` class in the package `javax.servlet.jsp.tagext`. This class specifies what is done at the beginning and end of the tag with the `doStartTag()` and `doEndTag()` methods. Second, the programmer places an entry, called a tag library descriptor file (TLD), in an XML file. The entry includes the name that will be used to refer to this tag, the Java class that it refers to and other information used to specify the format of the tag. Third, the Web designer writes the JSP page that uses this tag. He or she first has to use the `taglib` directive to point to the TLD created in the second step. He or she then follows the usage rules specified in the TLD to actually use the tag.

We'll walk you through these steps as you create several examples of using custom tags. First you'll create an empty tag that returns the date. Then you'll create a tag that changes the formatting of the code that comes before the opening and closing tag, which you'll see can include what is returned by another tag. You'll also see bean-like behavior as you pass the value of attributes to the class associated with the custom tag.

A class that returns the current time

Let's return to the example of displaying the current time at the server. Create a simple class with the following code:

```
package ourtags;

import javax.servlet.jsp.tagext.*;
import javax.servlet.jsp.*;
import java.io.*;
import java.util.*;

public class CurrentTime extends TagSupport{

  public int doStartTag(){
    try {
      JspWriter out = pageContext.getOut();
      out.print("Here at the server it's" + (new Date()) );
    }
    catch(IOException e){//foolishly do nothing
    }
    return(SKIP_BODY);
  }
}
```

Create a new folder, ourtags, inside the ...\webapps\J2EEBible\WEB-INF\classes\ directory, and save the file CurrentTime.java inside it. The `CurrentTime` class extends the class `TagSupport`, so you've had to `import` the `javax.servlet.jsp.tagext` package. You will override the method `doStartTag()` to specify what you want to happen when the tag you are supporting begins.

You are going to send back a simple message that includes the current time. Because you're using the `JspWriter`, you `import javax.servlet.jsp` as well. Getting the `JspWriter` forces you to catch an `IOException` so you have to `import java.io`. (You should at least send yourself a useful message in the `catch` block.) Finally, return an `int` that tells you to skip the body of the tag if there is one. (You'll see a different constant used here in the next example.) Compile CurrentTime.java, and you are ready to specify the mapping from the tag to the class.

The tag library descriptor

In Chapter 3, we discuss how the web.xml file specifies various mappings used in setting up servlets, JSPs, and filters in your Web application. The deployment descriptor enabled you to map more user-friendly URLs to your servlets. The TLD, similarly, helps you map user-friendly names for your tags to the Java classes that support them. For this example, create a folder called TagExamples inside the ...\webapps\J2EEBible\jsp\ directory, and save your TLD in this new folder.

The easiest way to get started is to use the example distributed with Tomcat 4.0 as a template. (You'll find it in the directory ...\ webapps\examples\WEB-INF\jsp\.) You are just going to create a single tag that you'll call `time`. The only part of the following TLD that is specific to this example is bolded:

```
<?xml version="1.0" encoding="ISO-8859-1" ?>
<!DOCTYPE taglib
        PUBLIC "-//Sun Microsystems, Inc.//DTD JSP Tag Library
1.1//EN"
   "http://java.sun.com/j2ee/dtds/web-jsptaglibrary_1_1.dtd">

<!-- a tag library descriptor -->

<taglib>
  <!-- after this the default space is
   "http://java.sun.com/j2ee/dtds/jsptaglibrary_1_2.dtd"
   -->

  <tlibversion>1.0</tlibversion>
  <jspversion>1.1</jspversion>
  <shortname>simple</shortname>
  <uri></uri>
  <info>
   A simple tag library for the J2EE Bible examples
  </info>

  <tag>
    <name>time</name>
    <tagclass>ourtags.CurrentTime</tagclass>
    <info> Gets the current time at the server </info>
  </tag>

</taglib>
```

You've set the name of your tag to `time` and referenced the Java class file `CurrentTime` in the package `ourtags`. Save this file as J2EEBible-taglib.tld inside `TagExamples`. That's all there is to it. You are now ready to use the tag in a JSP page.

A JSP page that uses a custom tag

Before you can use the tag, you have to point to the tag library that contains it. In this case, you need to point to the TLD file you just created. Suppose you are creating the file FirstTag.jsp and saving inside the directory TagExamples. You can then use the `taglib` directive and assign the shortcut name `sample` to refer to the tag library. Then you can access the tag with the syntax `<prefixName:tagName>`. The following is the entire FirstTag.jsp file:

```
<html>
  <%@ taglib uri="J2EEBible-taglib.tld" prefix="sample" %>
  Hello let's see what happens when we use a tag.
  <sample:time />
</html>
```

Start up your Web server and access the page at the following URL:

```
http://localhost:8080/J2EEBible/jsp/TagExamples/FirstTag.jsp
```

You will see the message from your JSP page in the browser followed by the words "Here at the server it's" and the current time. If you were actually building a `time` tag, you wouldn't have included the text, "Here at the server it's"—but it helps us make a point in the following example.

Putting one tag inside another

In the previous example you used the empty tag `<sample: tag />` because nobody needed to be enclosed between a start and end tags. Now you'll create a second tag that makes everything between the start and end tags big and bold by enclosing it in an `<H1>` block.

The Java file for handling a start and an end tag

A couple of differences exist between the following example and the previous one. First, you need to specify behavior for both the start and end tags. Second, you don't want to skip the body of the tag after you've processed the open tag. The file ChangeFont.java includes these changes:

```
package ourtags;

import javax.servlet.jsp.tagext.*;
import javax.servlet.jsp.*;
import java.io.*;
import java.util.*;

public class ChangeFont extends TagSupport{

  public int doStartTag(){
    try {
      JspWriter out = pageContext.getOut();
      out.print("<H1>" );
    }
    catch(IOException e){//foolishly do nothing
    }
    return(EVAL_BODY_INCLUDE);
  }
  public int doEndTag(){
    try {
      JspWriter out = pageContext.getOut();
      out.print("</H1>" );
    }
    catch(IOException e){//foolishly do nothing
    }
    return(SKIP_BODY);
  }
}
```

Now you have a `doStartTag()` and a `doEndTag()` method that start and end the `<H1>` environment. Notice that you've changed the return value from `doStartTag()` from `SKIP_BODY` to `EVAL_BODY_INCLUDE`. For kicks, you may want to see what happens if you keep the return value as SKIP_BODY. Nothing between the start and end tag will be executed.

Running the nested tags

Before you can have access to your new tag you have to create a new entry in the TLD. Edit J2EEBible-taglib.tld by adding the following tag definition:

```
<tag>
  <name>bigNBold</name>
  <tagclass>ourtags.ChangeFont</tagclass>
  <info> Makes the body big and bold </info>
</tag>
```

Now you are ready to use bigNBold in a JSP page. Create the file SecondTag.jsp in the TagExamples directory with the following code:

```
<html>
<%@ taglib uri="J2EEBible-taglib.tld" prefix="sample" %>

Hello let's see what happens when we use a tag.
<sample:bigNBold>
  Inside of another.
  <sample:time />
</sample:bigNBold>
What did you think?
</html>
```

It feels as if you are using bigNBold as a filter. This time the only text on your screen that isn't "big 'n bold" is the two phrases outside the bigNBold begin and end tags. Everything except "Hello let's see what happens when we use a tag." and "What did you think?" are set as H1 headings.

Attributes in custom tags

You can pass extra information to the classes handling the custom tags as attributes. For example, you can personalize the greeting by passing in the name of the person being greeted. So that you don't have to create a form for entering this information, you'll do this in a fairly uninteresting way. Your attribute will be called firstName. To record and retrieve this information you use the same convention you used with JavaBeans. You will have setFirstName() and getFirstName() methods in the corresponding GreetByName class.

A Java class that uses tag attributes

The resulting Java class looks like a combination of what you've seen so far with custom tags and what you saw in the last section when working with beans. The following code has a doStartTag() method together with the accessor methods for the attribute:

```
package ourtags;

import javax.servlet.jsp.tagext.*;
import javax.servlet.jsp.*;
import java.io.*;

public class GreetByName extends TagSupport{
  private String firstName;
  public int doStartTag(){
    try {
      JspWriter out = pageContext.getOut();
      out.print("Hello "+ firstName );
    }
    catch(IOException e){//foolishly do nothing
    }
    return(SKIP_BODY);
  }
  public void setFirstName(String firstName){
    this.firstName = firstName;
  }
  public String getFirstName(){
    return firstName;
  }
}
```

The next step is to edit the TLD file.

Specifying attributes in the TLD and using them in a JSP page

The entry that corresponds to the `GreetByName` class has a little more information than past entries. As the bolded changes show, you have to specify the name of your attribute. You can expand this section to include as many attributes as you will allow with your tag. You must also indicate whether or not the attribute is required. The following is the appropriate tag entry for this example:

```
<tag>
   <name>hello</name>
   <tagclass>ourtags.GreetByName</tagclass>
   <info> Greets user by attribute value.</info>
   <attribute>
     <name>firstName</name>
     <required>true</required>
   </attribute>
</tag>
```

Once again, you're ready to use the tag in a page. A simple example is the following, called ThirdTag.jsp:

```
<html>
<%@ taglib uri="J2EEBible-taglib.tld" prefix="sample" %>
```

```
  Excuse me.
  <sample:hello firstName="Toots" />
</html>
```

You'll see "Excuse me. Hello Toots." in your browser.

Bringing JSPs and Servlets Together

As you've seen in this chapter and in Chapter 3, when you use a `forward` or `include` directive from a servlet or JSP page, your target can be another servlet, a JSP page, or another resource. You should have a feel for what each technology is best at. You don't want to do a lot of presentation from a servlet or a lot of programming in a JSP page.

One solution is to use the Model-View-Controller (MVC) architecture with both JSP pages and servlets in what's known as model 2 architecture. The servlet plays the role of the controller, the JSP pages are the view, and JavaBeans and Enterprise JavaBeans are the model. You'll get a better idea of what you can do with EJBs in Chapters 16 and Chapter 17; for now just think about how you might mix JSPs and servlets.

The servlet controller receives the request. It may do some processing on the request before passing it on. In order to do some of the initial processing, it may use filters or other Java objects. Part of the initial processing may include setting up JavaBeans for acting on or just storing the data. The servlet then decides which JSP page can best render the results of the request and forwards the results of the preprocessing on to that page. The JSP page then uses the JavaBeans and other JSPs, servlets, and static pages to generate the result that the client will see in the browser.

As a simple example, you can imagine users being greeted by a page that asks them for their names and U.S. ZIP codes. The results of this form are sent to a servlet as a `GET` request and handled by the `doGet()` method. If the ZIP code is legitimate, the user is passed on to a JSP that displays news headlines with the weather forecast for the given ZIP code. If the ZIP code is not recognized, the request is sent to a JSP page that asks the user to reenter the ZIP code.

Summary

You can do an awful lot with JSP technology. You can start with a simple HTML page and add dynamic elements without much work. JSPs enable a programmer and a Web designer, working together, to turn out impressive Web pages. In this chapter, we've covered the following:

✦ You can create custom tags for mapping XML style tags to Java classes that can give you abilities that would be too messy to code directly into the JSP page. You learned to collect these tags into tag libraries and then to use the tags on the JSP page.

✦ You can interact with JavaBeans in a way that makes saving, processing, and retrieving information pretty easy. This is even true when you are saving with one JSP page or servlet and retrieving with another.

✦ You can write Java code in place in a servlet. You can write conditionals and loops to determine which content to display on a page. These scriptlets can be fragments of Java code interspersed among the HTML content on the page.

✦ You can use expressions to return content to the page. The argument of an expression returns a value that is converted to a `String` and displayed on the page.

✦ Actions enable you to include other JSP pages or to forward the control to those pages. Various directives enable you to specify tag libraries and various properties of the page.

✦ By using servlets and JSPs together you can take advantage of the strengths of each. You use a servlet as a controller to help steer the request to the appropriate handler. Information can be saved in JavaBeans, and the output that the client sees can then be generated and formatted by the appropriate JSP page.

✦ ✦ ✦

Sending and Receiving Mail with JavaMail

✦ ✦ ✦ ✦

In This Chapter

Introducing the JavaMail API

Understanding the format of a standard Internet-compliant e-mail message

Sending and receiving simple e-mails

Building complex filtering rules for incoming e-mails

✦ ✦ ✦ ✦

E-mail was one of the first tools available on the Internet. To the ordinary businessperson, it is an indispensable tool. For the business application, e-mail is also indispensable — be it that simple order confirmation or a mass mailing telling customers of the latest specials. Within the J2EE environment, JavaMail provides both e-mail and newsgroup capabilities.

What Is E-mail?

From being almost non-existent to being the heart of every business, e-mail has come a long way since the mid 1990s. Did you know that the first e-mails existed more than 20 years earlier than that? Ironically, they have barely changed in that time (apart from those annoying users who insist on using HTML for the body text). Of course, the most interesting part of this recent change is that all of the hard work is hidden from the user. So long as you know your recipient's e-mail address, the rest is taken care of for you by "the system." Magically it all just seems to work.

Well, we're about to lift the cover off that magic. If you are going to write an application that requires the ability to send an e-mail message, then you are going to need to know a lot more about the fundamentals of e-mail. Over the course of this section, we are going to introduce you to the whole system of e-mail — what it is, how it works, and how your application will fit into the general scheme of things. Some of this may not be of direct value to your programming, but understanding the entire system end to end will improve your general knowledge, particularly if you have to debug some odd "feature" of your e-mail system.

A day in the life of an e-mail

One day Joe Hacker wakes up. He, being the geek type of guy, wanders off to his computer to check the overnight delivery of e-mail. This is far more important than food! Dialing up his ISP, he starts up MS Outlook and downloads the mail. He has received a few interesting mails, so he decides to send a reply to some of them. Firing up Microsoft Word he writes replies to a couple of e-mails and sends them off. Satisfied with the morning's work he shuts down the modem and wanders off to the kitchen to fetch breakfast.

During this process, did you ever think of how the messages got to and from your machine? The process involves quite a number of steps that all have to work in order for your mail to be received.

Composing the message

It all starts on your computer. A mail message includes a lot of information that is not strictly related to the text that you write with your mail package. As you will see in the upcoming section, "The format of a mail message," a number of headers and ancillary information must be provided with your mail message in order for it to reach its destination.

When you press the Send button your editor takes your text, the addressing information, and a couple of other fields, and assembles them into a complete message. With the full message, it then contacts a mail server. Generally speaking, this is an SMTP (Simple Mail Transport Protocol) mail server, although other proprietary options do exist (Lotus cc:Mail being the main offender here). The mail program contacts the SMTP server and sends it the mail message, and that is the last you see of the message.

All mail is sent over the Internet using SMTP. Where software does not use SMTP internally, the message must be transformed into an SMTP message at the point where it reaches the outside world of the Internet. Similarly, incoming mail to that system will be in SMTP form so there must be a gateway to munge the mail between the internal and Internet forms.

Routing the message

Once your mail arrives on the greater Internet, the SMTP server has to find a way to deliver it. It does this by taking the destination e-mail address, stripping the domain name from it, and then attempting to locate the appropriate server for this domain. If there is no explicit mail server for a domain, the SMTP server may look to the parent domain(s) until it finds one. This server may act as a gateway to the internal network for all mail of a particular domain.

The SMTP server locates the appropriate server to send information to using the DNS system. DNS does more than just resolve domain names to IP addresses. Within the system is a set of records known as MX records. These define a list of machines, in order of priority, that are willing to receive mail for that domain. The SMTP server, when deciding how to send the mail, consults DNS for the appropriate MX record and uses the information contained there to contact the correct machine using the SMTP protocol to send the message.

Once mail has arrived at the gateway machine, the gateway is now responsible for managing the message in the internal network. On the simplest of systems, the mail will sit on the gateway machine until the receiver picks it up. However, in the more complex world of huge corporate conglomerates and firewalls, that machine really does just act as a gateway. Another machine sitting inside the firewall will pick the mail up from the gateway and then haul it to the inside network. Inside the firewall a similar routing process takes place. The internal SMTP (or other protocol) server looks up the right sub-domain mail server and sends the message on its way. Depending on the structure of the internal network, the message may go through this process a number of times before ending up at the final destination server.

Reading the mail

With the mail now sitting on the destination server, the last step is for the user to actually read it. Here the user has a wide variety of options.

The majority of users download the mail to a mail client on their local machine using the Post Office Protocol (POP). This protocol usually copies the mail from the server to the local machine and then deletes it from the server—a very simple system, but one that works for the majority of users.

There are two common variants of the POP system. Version 2 (POP2) is older than Version 3 (POP3) and much less secure. Today it is rare to find POP2 systems available.

UNIX users take a different approach—particularly if they are working full time on UNIX machines. These people use a local mail client that grabs the mail directly from the directory where incoming mail is spooled. Mail clients like PINE, ELM and emacs work this way.

High-powered, mobile users, or those with a number of separate e-mail accounts, tend to use the IMAP (Internet Mail Application Protocol) system. IMAP enables you to create all your mail folders on the mail server. This enables you to store, sort, and manage mail on each individual server without needing to move it all to your local machine. This is very useful for road-warrior types using dial-up connections from remote sites, as it saves a lot of time downloading and many messages can be pre-filtered before the user even has to read them.

The format of a mail message

The mail sent over an SMTP connection has a very specific format. It must follow the rules set down by a standard known as RFC 822. RFCs are the standards that govern all of the low-level workings of the Internet. RFC 822 specifically pertains to the contents of e-mail messages.

You can download copies of RFCs by visiting `http://www.rfc-editor.org/`. At the time of this writing there were some 2800 certified RFCs and many hundreds more in the draft stage. Not all of them are serious. Every year an RFC is released on April 1. Usually it is very, very humorous. Among the classics are the Coffee Pot Transport Protocol and IP messaging by Carrier Pigeon.

You may be wondering why we are covering the format of a mail message in depth. JavaMail is supposed to take care of all this for you, right? Well, not really. At the level we are talking about here, it is possible to stuff things up because you don't understand the correct format. If you understand the format of a mail message, you will know how to check the format of the messages that are being sent out.

Structure

A mail message is treated one line at a time. Each line is read and parsed looking for specific pieces of information. The upshot of this is that the order in which items are declared in an e-mail is not necessarily important, although everyone tends to follow the same guidelines.

Generally speaking, mail clients will put all the headers at the top of a mail message and then follow them with the body. Even more specifically, they tend to put routing information at the very start, informational headers next (subject, from, organization, and so on), followed by the body of the message. This is not a hard and fast rule, but it is the general convention.

A mail message is terminated by a single period character (`.`) at the start of a line by itself.

Headers

Despite being hidden from ordinary users, headers contain a lot of interesting information. You can tell so much about users just by looking at the information contained in their headers. Headers also look completely foreign if you are not used to seeing them, and most mailers will automatically hide them from you.

Listing 5-1 contains the full list of headers from one of our e-mail messages. We'll point out the interesting pieces shortly, but first we want to point out some of the more important features. The first line you will recognize immediately—this is the received date, the time that the message arrived at the destination server. Other familiar headers are the `Subject`, `To` and `From` lines.

These header fields belong to the mail message itself and are useful in the routing of that message. SMTP exists one level below this message and includes its own protocol, such as defining who the sender is. That is why you can get spam delivered to your e-mail address even though the To field in your mail reader does not include your e-mail address.

Listing 5-1: A full set of mail headers from a message sent to a mailing list

```
From - Thu Nov 09 23:25:03 2000
Return-Path: <wetleather@micapeak.com>
Received: from moto.micapeak.com (moto.micapeak.com
[207.53.128.12])
by case.vlc.com.au (8.9.3/8.9.3) with ESMTP id XAA05034
for <justin@vlc.com.au>; Thu, 9 Nov 2000 23:18:34 +0800
Received: from moto.micapeak.com (localhost [127.0.0.1])
by moto.micapeak.com (8.9.3/8.9.3) with SMTP id HAA02552;
Thu, 9 Nov 2000 07:19:22 -0800
Date: Thu, 9 Nov 2000 07:19:22 -0800
Message-Id: <01C04A1D.F3458360@ppphr196-39.gorge.net>
Errors-To: wetleather-owner@micapeak.com
Reply-To: wetleather@micapeak.com
Originator: wetleather@micapeak.com
Sender: wetleather@micapeak.com
Precedence: bulk
From: Vernon Wade <blah@nospam.net>
To: Northwest Bikers Social Mailing List
<wetleather@micapeak.com>
Subject: Re: Bike Licensing in WA etc
X-Listprocessor-Version: 6.0 -- ListProcessor by Anastasios
Kotsikonas
X-Comment: Northwest Bikers Social Mailing List
Status:
X-Mozilla-Status: 8011
X-Mozilla-Status2: 00000000
X-UIDL: 365419f300005da2

You might try Fernet. They are a brokerage that Triumph uses. I
think they....
```

Each line of a header starts with a single word followed by a colon (:). Headers that might use two words are hyphenated. After the header field, the value of that field is declared.

RFC 822 defines a number of standard fields that all mailers should understand. A list of the most common ones is included in Table 5-1. The RFC also allows room for mailers to make their own special fields, called extension fields. These must be registered but nobody is required to implement them. Extension fields start with "X-", and you can see a number of them at the bottom of Listing 5-1. In this case they come from the Netscape mail client.

Table 5-1
A listing of commonly used header fields

Field Name	*Explanation*
`To`	The primary destination address (there should only be one).
`Cc`	*Carbon copy*—Indicates that copies of this mail will be sent to the specified addresses in addition to the primary address.
`Bcc`	*Blind carbon copy*—The same as `Cc` except that it does not include this in the headers or anywhere that would normally make this address show up on the real receivers list.
`From`	The sender of the e-mail (not necessarily a legitimate address!).
`Date`	The date the message was composed and sent on the local system.
`Subject`	What you talkin' 'bout Willis?
`Comments`	Any arbitrary text, footnotes, and so on.
`Reply-To`	Use this address when replying, rather than the From field.
`Resent-From`	If the e-mail gets held up or needs to be resent because of system errors, this is the host.
`In-Reply-To`	The message ID that this message replied to.
`Return-Path`	A series of hosts that this mail was sent along and along which the reply should go. Useful for debugging errors and tracking the source of spam, but easy to forge.
`References`	A set of message IDs that this message is in reply to. For mail clients that do thread tracking, this is very useful for getting the right tree.
`Keywords`	A list of words for use in searching through a large volume of mail.
`Encrypted`	A flag indicating that this message is encrypted.
`Received`	A list of times that the mail message was received at each host along its transmission path. One header item exists per host (that is, multiple `Received` headers will appear in a single mail). Includes all the information about who sent the message and what IP address/domain name and IDs are associated with it.
`Message-ID`	A unique ID generated by the sending mail server for tracking.

Body

The body of the message is generally free-form text. The text must consist of seven-bit ASCII characters, which prohibits binary information or most internationalized text. To send a binary file in the earlier days of the Internet meant using a program like UUencode to turn eight-bit binary into seven-bit ASCII. The resulting fun of piecing together multiple mail messages in the right order and then decoding them was part of daily life for Internet users.

It is rare these days to see UUencoded messages. Between e-mails and newsgroups, inventive schemes appeared to make sending binary files easier to deal with. The most commonly used invention was the SHAR file, a self-executing file that would collate all the parts, decode them, and give the file the right name. (SHAR stands for SHell ARchive and only runs on UNIX-based machines.) You still occasionally see these floating around in the newsgroups, but they have generally gone out of fashion with the advent of modern mail clients that can send and receive binary files easily.

The problems of sending attachments led to the invention of the MIME (Multipurpose Internet Mail Extension) system. By putting a certain set of text at the start of the message it allowed the mail handler to change its interpretation of the body. Thanks to MIME, users could now put multiple parts of different file types into the body of the message and not have to worry about encoding and decoding messages. MIME types, the string used to determine how to interpret the file data, have become an essential part of Internet life. They are used everywhere, from e-mail to Web servers to the core of most operating systems. When you start composing mail messages later in the chapter you will see how essential they are to your application.

We mentioned earlier that the header fields could appear anywhere within the message. This can make for some interesting problems. Think of what happens when a sentence starts with the word "To" or "From" or any of the others in the list presented in Table 5-1. If one of these words happens to start a line, then the mailer at the other end will automatically interpret it to mean the start of another header field. Suddenly you get a bunch of error messages about badly formatted mail and partial message bodies and a lot of other weird stuff. To avoid this, mail clients will check the contents of your messages and automatically insert a > character at the start of any lines that may be a problem. When sending out automated mail services like newsletters or confirmation e-mails, make sure that you have your software perform checks on the messages.

Attachments can be both a blessing and curse. They enable you to include a picture of your latest vacation to send to your parents, but they also enable people to send you HTML with embedded JavaScript to cause virus-like problems (and the reason for so many problems with the Microsoft Outlook client being the source of so many prolific PC viruses).

Types of servers

What good is e-mail if you cannot read it? Once the e-mail has arrived on your local mail server, you need to read it. Ignoring the people who read e-mail directly using UNIX-based mail clients, three types of mail servers exist for handling mail over the Internet. We've touched on these briefly in this chapter, but now we will examine them in much more detail.

For the purposes of these discussions we are assuming a fully Internet-compliant mail system. Mail servers such as MS Exchange and Lotus cc:Mail/Notes that do not use standards-compliant mail protocols by default are not considered.

SMTP

An SMTP server performs the job of routing mail messages over the Internet. It is the first point of contact for your mail client after you've clicked the Send button.

The actions of an SMTP server are the same whether you are trying to send an outgoing message or are processing an incoming message from the Internet. When the SMTP server first receives the message, it strips the message into the component parts. It then applies a collection of rules to these parts to determine what to do next. With some servers, these rules can get extremely complex. You can block mail messages from any one host name or IP address, a whole collection, or automatically virus-filter the contents. Really, the sky's the limit—you can do anything your server is capable of.

By far the most common SMTP server on the Internet is Sendmail. This multipurpose mail router has been around since the early 1980s and is still the de facto standard, used by over 80 percent of sites. Sendmail is an open-source program that can be found at `http://www.sendmail.org/`. Be warned, configuring Sendmail is not for the faint of heart. Cryptic hardly describes it!

Where possible, the SMTP server tries to send mail directly to the destination server. If it cannot, it will perform what is called a relay operation. That is, one server on another domain has agreed to act as a mail server for the destination domain. An SMTP server always relays in some form, either for outgoing or incoming mail. Relaying for other hosts is also the core of Web hosting. Web-hosting companies set up a single machine that takes mail for all of the Web sites they host and then enables the user to send out mail under the address for that machine.

Improperly configured machines allowing relaying are the cause of a lot of spam. Unscrupulous spammers look for machines that allow global relaying from any host and then use that machine to act as the source for their messages. A properly configured mail server will enable you to relay from machines within the domain and any that it might virtual-host, but nothing from the outside world.

Part of the SMTP protocol includes a number of error conditions. Like the infamous 404 Not Found messages of the Web world, mail errors use a numbered system of error conditions. Part of the filtering rules enable you to respond with different messages or conditions dependent on the incoming source. A number of retry rules also exist if the destination server cannot be contacted. You usually will see the filtering rules and retry rules in combination when you get a series of error messages about mail not being sent for a given time period (four hours, three days, one week, and so on).

POP

For years the most common way to receive mail on a remote client was to use the POP server. This enabled you to log into a remote machine and download the mail to your local machine. POP allowed you to leave the messages on the server, but it meant having to download the headers every time you connected. For most users, this ends up with them downloading the entire message to the local machine.

A POP account is very limited in its capabilities. Unlike a local mail client or IMAP account, you only had a single folder to store messages in — the inbox. If you wanted anything more than that, you need to download the messages locally and then apply any filtering rules that your particular mail software provided. If you used a number of different mail clients, you had to write those same rules in each one.

IMAP

On the client side, mail readers enable you to sort of messages into different folders. The POP server just couldn't handle the requirements of users jumping between machines around the globe and even within the same office. Thus, the IMAP server was born.

Unlike POP, which only has one folder, the Inbox, IMAP enables users to create and store all their mail folders on the server. Thus, no matter where they are, users can always have their mail stored and filtered according to their own preferences. Another advantage of IMAP is the ability to keep everything secure. Both the connections and the mail folders can be encrypted, allowing for more safety when transporting messages across the open Internet to be read.

IMAP servers are commonly used in conjunction with LDAP directories for storing address information. This gives the user the advantage of having both contact information and e-mail available wherever they travel.

Webmail

No discussion about e-mail is complete without something on Webmail. Since Hotmail went online with free e-mail accounts, the face of the public e-mail for consumers has never looked the same. So what is behind a Webmail server?

Really a Webmail system is just a Web server and an e-mail server combined with some executable code in the middle. It doesn't really matter which of the POP or IMAP servers is used to retrieve mail messages down the back. Some even just use the old-style UNIX convention and grab the mail directly from the spool directory.

Setting up your own personal Webmail system is a trivial task if you have access to your own mail or Web server. Go to Freshmeat (`http://www.freshmeat.net/`) and search for Webmail. At least 10 different Open Source efforts are available from that one site alone.

Introducing JavaMail

Enough talk! Now, on to the real task of building e-mail capabilities. As we have already mentioned several times, JavaMail is the standardized e-mail API for Java. It provides a collection of abstractions so that you don't need to worry about the low-level protocols of sending mail and news items.

The JavaMail package

JavaMail consists of four packages to provide news and e-mail functionality. Although the API is capable of handling non-Internet mail and news services, the default implementation only includes Internet capabilities. JavaMail, like all of the J2EE specification, belongs to the Optional Packages extensions to the Java APIs. This means that the packages all start with the prefix javax.mail. Table 5-2 lists the four packages.

Table 5-2
The packages of the JavaMail API

Package	*Description*
`javax.mail`	A basic outline of mail capabilities.
`javax..mail.event`	Event classes and interfaces for listening to dynamic updates to the mail system, such as new mail arriving.
`javax.mail.internet`	Internet-specific mail options such as MIME types, headers, and so on.
`javax.mail.search`	Classes for building mail filters and search capabilities.

JavaMail requirements

JavaMail is a pure Java API and therefore does not depend on any given system setup. It does not even require a Java 2 system and will happily run on JDK 1.1 (though running it inside an applet is bound to cause security exceptions).

When running, JavaMail does not require any particular setup. You provide it with all the information it needs to connect to a mail server to send and receive messages at runtime.

Downloading JavaMail

If you don't already have a full version of the J2EE system on your machine, then you will need to download the JavaMail library, which can be found at `http://java.sun.com/products/javamail/`.

If you are downloading JavaMail and don't have a J2EE environment installed, you will also require a copy of the Java Activation Framework (JAF). You may already have this if you have done JavaBeans programming before, but if you don't have it you can download it from `http://java.sun.com/products/jaf/`. JAF is also included in the standard J2EE environment, so you won't need to download it separately if you already have the full setup.

JavaMail terminology

As a multipurpose, multiprotocol API, JavaMail has to abstract many things and create an appropriate set of terminologies for each abstraction. Most of these terms should feel straightforward, but we will cover them in order to make the rest of the chapter more understandable.

Session

The session is everything about your application using the mail interface. If you have multiple applications running in the same JVM instance (for example, servlets in a Web server or EJBs in a middleware server), it is possible for each to have its own environment to work in. A session defines the environment that the mail will run. This environment can be shared across many applications, or each application can have its own individual setup.

Transport

Transport is the protocol used for sending and/or receiving e-mail. For a system that will be sending out e-mail, the transport will be SMTP. For a receiving system, it will be either POP or IMAP. Naturally, you can set up a single session with a number of different transports — one for the sending side and one for the receiving side.

Message

The message is all the information that has to be sent, including the body, headers, and addressing information. You will need to create a single message for each time you need to send something to a user. Multiple recipients may be specified in the message, within the limits imposed by the mail server and Internet standards.

Store

The store is a collection of messages, just as in a mail client. A store consists of a number of folders and messages. Within each folder you can contain other folders and messages ad infinitum.

Sending an E-mail

Constructing and sending a message is a three-part process. First you need to establish all of the application-wide information. Then you need to construct each particular message with all the relevant details. Finally you have to contact the server, send the message, and check for any errors.

Setting up e-mail

To establish e-mail capabilities for your application, you first need to construct a session and the appropriate transport mechanisms. These are encapsulated in the classes with the same names: `Session` and `Transport` of the `javax.mail` package.

Step 1: Create a session

Sessions come in two flavors: the system default and a customized session built to your specific requirements. For the majority of applications, the default will be sufficient, particularly if you only have one application running per JVM instance.

Creating a session requires that the system also know what services it needs to provide. So the first step to creating a session is to create an instance of `java.util.Properties` and fill it with the appropriate information (you will notice that this step is quite common among the J2EE APIs). Table 5-3 outlines the most important properties. However, if you are just sending e-mail, you need only a small subset of these.

Table 5-3
Properties used to create a JavaMail session

Property Name	*Description*
`mail.host`	The name or address of the host that will be used for all mail interactions, unless overridden.
`mail.transport.protocol`	The protocol(s) to be loaded for this session, either smtp, pop3 or imap.
`mail.user`	The user name used to log into the mail server. This is not required at this point, as it can be supplied during message-sending.
`mail.from`	The e-mail address of the user sending this e-mail. Not required at this point as it can be supplied during mail-message construction.
`mail.smtp.host`	If you're using the SMTP transport protocol, this is the name of the host to send outgoing e-mails to.

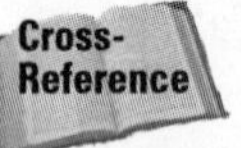

You can find a full listing of the allowed properties in Appendix A to the JavaMail specification. A link to the specification can be found on the Web site for this book.

There are two static methods in the `Session` class that you can use to initialize and create a session: `getInstance()` and `getDefaultInstance()`. Both of these have the option of providing a class called `Authenticator`. Use the `Authenticator` class if you have to securely provide a user name and password to access the mail server. We'll get to an example showing this shortly, but for the moment we show a simple startup call to get a session established:

```
Properties props = new Properties();
String mailhost = "mail.mydomain.com";

props.put("mail.host", mailhost);
props.put("mail.transport.protocol", "smtp");
props.put("mail.smtp.host", mailhost);

Session mail_session = Session.getDefaultInstance(props);
```

Your site might be set up with a lot of security, so the mail server may require a password. This is provided with the `Authenticator` class. To provide a custom password and user name, you need to extend the class and provide it with all of the basic information. Although you can use the `Authenicator` class directly, there is no way of providing it with basic information, so you must extend the class with your own implementation.

Step 2: Select a transport mechanism

After establishing the session you need to work with the transport handler. The transport handler enables you to connect to a particular host with a given protocol. In the previous code snippet, we registered that we wanted to use SMTP as the default protocol for this session.

To gain an instance of the `Transport` class that you will use to send and receive e-mail, you use one of the `getTransport()` methods:

```
Transport smtp_service;

try {
  smtp_service = mail_session.getTransport();
}
catch(MessagingException nspe) {
  // SMTP is one of the defaults. If we get this there is
  // a serious problem!
  System.err.println("Danger, Danger! No SMTP mail provider!");
}
```

Here you are using the method that returns the transport implementation for the default protocol that you nominated back when you created the session. If you are setting up an application that needs to both send and receive e-mail, then you can always ask for a particular transport type. For example:

```
smtp_service = mail_session.getTransport("imap");
```

The protocol types are always provided in lower case. Uppercase protocol names will not be found by the system, so you will get errors.

Now, if you are building a large-scale mail system (perhaps even a mail reader), you will probably want to register an instance of `TransportListener` with the `Transport` class that you've just received. This listener will give you information about how the mail system is functioning with the message(s) that you have just sent or received. For example, it will tell you if the message was successfully sent or not.

Constructing a message

With the basic system setup now complete, your application is ready to send e-mails. So far, the steps have been relatively trivial; constructing a message takes quite a bit of extra work compared to the first few steps. To send a message, you need to follow these steps:

1. Create a `Message` object to represent your complete message.
2. Create and register the address of the receivers and the sender (your application).
3. Set the subject and any other headers.
4. Build the body of the message, including any attachments.
5. Save all the changes you've made so far.
6. Send the message.

For this first part, you will just send a message containing plain text. In a short time you will come back to adding attachments to your message.

Step 1: Start a new message

You start by creating the shell of the message using the `MimeMessage` class from the package `javax.mail.internet`. You do this because you are sending an e-mail message over the Internet; if you were providing a proprietary mail system, then you would use another subclass of the `Message` class.

```
MimeMessage message = new MimeMessage(mail_session);
```

Note that you also have to use the `mail_session` object that you created earlier. Many other options for creating instances of the message object are available to you, but for purely outgoing e-mail, this is likely to be the most common way.

Step 2: Set the sender and recipients

Adding address information is the next step. You use the `InternetAddress` class from the `javax.mail.internet` package for the same reason that you use the `MimeMessage` class, as shown in this example:

```
InternetAddress sender =
  new InternetAddress("justin@vlc.com.au", "Justin Couch");
```

```
message.setFrom(sender);

InternetAddress[] to_list = {
  new InternetAddress("recipient@myplace.com") };

InternetAddress[] cc_list = {
  new InternetAddress("person1@myplace.com"),
  new InternetAddress("person2@myplace.com")
 };
message.setRecipients(Message.RecipientType.TO, to_list);
message.setRecipients(Message.RecipientType.CC, cc_list);
```

When setting the recipient information, you need to create an array of addresses, too. For the `To` list, there should only be one item in the list at any given time. It is actually illegal to have more than one item in the `To` list, but most mail servers are forgiving and will handle it if there is.

Step 3: Set the Subject and Headers

Next on your agenda is setting up all the header information. You can ignore most of the items we mentioned in Table 5-1: They are set either by the various mail servers the code passes through, through the specialized API call, or through the preceding steps.

Setting the subject is a simple call. You should already know the text string that will be used, so this

```
message.setSubject("Hello world");
```

will be all you need to set the subject on your e-mail.

All headers can be set with the generalized method `setHeader()`. This method takes two strings — one for the field name and one for the value. For example, if you want to set the Keywords field, you can use the following code:

```
message.setHeader("Keywords", "Java,J2EE,email");
```

and JavaMail will make sure that the header is correctly formatted for your message.

Step 4: Set the message body

To set the message body requires only a single call in most cases (we'll discuss adding attachments and non-text bodies shortly). Using the `setText()` method, you can place the message body in plain text:

```
String body = "Mary had a little lamb, its fleece was " +
              "white as snow.\n And everywhere that Mary " +
              "went the lamb was sure to go.";

message.setText(body);
```

Calling `setText()` more than once will replace the previous text with the new text. If you need to combine pieces of message, use `StringBuffer` to build the message string first and then set the whole lot with a single call to `setText()`.

If you examine the text string closely, you will see that we've added the newline character `\n`. This is because the message body does not automatically recognize an end-of-line character in your text (particularly if it has been taken from a `TextArea`/`JTextArea` GUI component). You will need to make sure that the string you are using already contains all the formatting required.

Sending a message

With the message construction now complete, you need to send the message. One of the features of the JavaMail API is its ability to be used for bulk mail. Before you write this off as being valuable only to spammers, think about your typical large corporate environment like Dell. How many copies of the same message do you think its employees send off in a typical day? Probably thousands. Is it really necessary to construct that same message over and over again, when all the user really needs to do is change a couple of items in the body and the recipient?

The feature that we mentioned is that none of the changes that the previous sections have made to the message actually take effect until you commit them to the message. This way you can keep a template of the message around, use it to send a message, and then immediately grab it back and start making more changes. Once you have completed the changes for the next copy, you commit those and send the message out. For large-scale corporate systems in which users need to send thousands of copies of essentially the same message, this is a great advantage. Just change the recipient name and a few details in the body and fire off the message. This handy feature has other benefits as well — reusing the same object saves on garbage being generated, which in turn results in fewer system resources being used.

Your final two steps, then, are to save the changes and send the e-mail, as follows:

```
message.saveChanges();
smtp_service.send(message);
```

As your message object already contains the sender and recipient information, there is nothing left to do. From here on, it is up to the mail system and the JavaMail API to make sure everything is done correctly.

Remember that you can listen for progress updates by registering a `TransportListener` instance with the `smtp_service` object.

Sending to newsgroups

JavaMail is not just for e-mail. E-mail and newsgroup capabilities are very similar. The only differences lie in how they are addressed initially and in what protocol they use to communicate with the server. All of the other concepts — such as folders, searches, and messages — remain the same.

Connecting to a news source is a little different from connecting to a mail server. For news services, you substitute a different protocol type for your transport type. This time, you use `nntp`, as follows:

```
Properties props = new Properties();
String mailhost = "news.mydomain.com";

props.put("mail.host", mailhost);
props.put("mail.transport.protocol", "nntp");
props.put("mail.nntp.host", mailhost);

Session mail_session = Session.getDefaultInstance(props);
```

The second change you need to make to your code is to use a different address format. Unlike with e-mail, wherein you nominate a particular person, with news you define a group name. To define a group name, you use a different form of the `Address` class, the `NewsAddress` class:

```
InternetAddress sender =
  new InternetAddress("justin@vlc.com.au", "Justin Couch");

message.setFrom(sender);

NewAddress[] to_list = {
  new NewsAddress("comp.lang.java.programmer") };

message.setRecipients(Message.RecipientType.TO, to_list);
```

From this point on, sending a message to a newsgroup is no different from sending one to an e-mail address. You construct the message, add attachments, and send it in exactly the same way.

As the `message` object is the same for both newsgroups and e-mail, you can construct a single message containing both e-mail addresses and newsgroups in the recipient list. It does take a little extra work setting up the host and protocol information, but the typical dual-protocol response that you are used to from your newsgroup reader is possible with JavaMail.

Messages with attachments

Most business e-mails are plain text. However, for more consumer-oriented applications, you may want to send out HTML mail or other attachments such as a digital signature, or even an encrypted message. To do this you need to use MIME attachments.

In adding the body text previously, you made use of the convenience method `setText()`. Adding attachments requires more work because you have to set up all the information about the attachment as well as the bytes of the attachment itself.

These processes only work with fully Internet-compliant mail systems. If you must use proprietary mail systems such as Microsoft or Lotus mail servers, then you will have to use their proprietary software interfaces. JavaMail assumes that you are using standards-compliant systems, which Microsoft and Lotus mail are not.

Messages with a single content type

Building messages with non-plain-text bodies requires delving into parts of the Java Activation Framework (JAF). Two classes are of importance here—`DataSource` and `DataHandler` from the package `javax.activation`. You will use these a lot over the next few pages, as they form the basis of dealing with MIME-encoded messages.

In earlier dealings with mail messages you used the `setText()` method to set the body of your e-mail. To use non-text bodies, such as HTML, you swap this method for the `setContent()` method. All the other setup and sending procedures stay the same.

Two variations on the `setContent()` method exist. One takes only a `Multipart` object as the parameter, while the other takes an `Object` and a `String`. You are most interested in the former. In the latter, you pass any Java object instance and a string describing its MIME type and then let the system deal with the appropriate encoding. While potentially simpler, this means you need a lot of extra third-party code responsible for dealing with these objects correctly. These libraries generally don't exist at the time of this writing. At this point in time, it is far easier just to do everything yourself.

A much better way to approach adding a single attachment is to use the `setDataHandler()` method. Don't give up on the `setContent()` method yet; it will be of more use to you in the next section, but this option actually makes it easier to attach a single item to a message. The `DataHandler` class is part of JAF. To construct an instance of it, you will need to provide either an `Object/String` combo or a `DataSource` implementation (`DataSource` is an interface).

For most attachments you will be adding some file on disk to the system. To do this you can use the `FileDataSource` class from JAF to do most of the hard work for you. To attach a file to an e-mail, use the following code:

```
String my_file = "/home/justin/.signature";
DataSource fds = new FileDataSource(my_file);
DataHandler dh = new DataHandler(fds);
message.setDataHandler(dh);
```

That's it. Very clean and simple. However, what if you want to get the attachment from another source, such as an XML document? The XML has to be processed into usable text. You really don't want to have to save the output to file and then read it in. Instead, you will need to build your own `DataSource`.

A pre-built, custom `DataSource` for dealing with `String` and generic `InputStreams` is available from the Web site.

Tips for building a custom DataSource

A custom data source is used to provide a `DataHandler` with all of the details about the raw bytes on disk. When you implement a new `DataSource`, because it is an interface, you have to do all of the basic legwork yourself, such as determining what the MIME type is, stream handling and more.

Implementing the `DataSource` interface requires you to supply four methods:

- `getInputStream()`: This method supplies a stream that represents the data you are reading. For example, if you are translating an XML stream into plain text for an e-mail, this stream contains the translated text.
- `getOutpuStream()`: This method supplies a stream that enables the end user to write data back to your underlying source. For implementations designed for use in JavaMail, you can ignore this method.
- `getContentType()`: Returns the MIME type of the underlying stream. This MIME type should reflect the content of the stream returned by `getInputStream()` rather than the item you are processing. For example, when processing the XML file to a plain text stream, this method should return `text/plain`, not `application/xml`.
- `getName()`: Return a descriptive name of the underlying object. For example, if the underlying object was a file, it might return the file name. Processing an XML document, it might return a "title" attribute value.

How you source the underlying data is dependent on what that data is. Typically you will supply a hint for this as part of the constructors for your implementing class. For example, if the data source is fetching information from a database, the constructor would provide the primary key of the row that it wants to fetch data from. As always, work out what you need to provide and write the appropriate code to handle your particular situation.

Multipart messages

On the next level of complexity, you have to assemble a message consisting of a collection of attachments. Here you can go back to the `setContent()` method that we mentioned earlier. The version that will be of most interest to you is the single parameter that takes a `Multipart` instance. Again, as in the rest of this chapter, you are not interested in the generic base class, but the Internet-specific version called `MimeMultipart` sitting in the `javax.mail.internet` package.

Start by creating an instance of `MimeMultipart` using the default constructor. This allows the class to act as a container for all the attachments that you will be adding shortly:

```
MimeMultipart body = new MimeMultipart();
```

Examining the documentation reveals that the only way to add items to this class is to use the `addBodyPart()` method. Once again you are more interested in the Internet-specific version, and so you make instances of `MimeBodyPart` to place pieces in the mail message. To add the actual data to the body part, use the `setDataHandler()` method just as you did in the single-attachment example earlier:

```
String my_file = "/home/justin/.signature";
DataSource fds = new FileDataSource(my_file);
DataHandler dh = new DataHandler(fds);

MimeBodyPart part = new MimeBodyPart();
part.setDataHandler(dh);

body.addBodyPart(dh);
```

Of course, when dealing with multiple attachments, you will probably want to roll this all up into a little loop, as shown in the following example:

```
String[] attachments = {
  "/home/justin/books/ebible/chapter5.doc",
  "/home/justin/books/ebible/pics/ch05-1.jpg",
  "/home/justin/books/ebible/pics/ch05-2.jpg",
  "/home/justin/books/ebible/pics/ch05-3.jpg",
  "/home/justin/.signature"
};

for(int i = 0; i < attachments.length; i++) {
  DataSource ds = new FileDataSource(attachments[i]);
  DataHandler dh = new DataHandler(ds);

  MimeBodyPart part = new MimeBodyPart();
  part.setDataHandler(dh);

  body.addBodyPart(dh);
}
```

An alternative to the previous method for a single attachment is to use the `MimeMultipart` class as follows:

```
String my_file = "/home/justin/.signature";
DataSource fds = new FileDataSource(my_file);
MimeMultipart content = new MimeMultipart(fds);
message.setContent(content);
```

Non-English-language handling

Your final stopping point on the way to sending e-mail is dealing with non-English-language e-mail. Despite the American view of the world, not everyone speaks English, and the number of Internet users who speak other languages is growing rapidly. For large businesses it is important to cater to these markets.

English, as far as computer usage goes, is generally defined to be the US-ASCII character set. Late in 2000, the ability to create domain names in non-ASCII characters added a new dimension, as most of the headers will now also contain non-ASCII characters for information more important than just the body and subject. Fortunately, the designers of the JavaMail libraries had this in mind.

Providing multi-language support is the job of the `MimeUtility` class.

Tip

Multi-lingual support in e-mail is defined in RFC 2047 *MIME Part Three: Message Header Extensions for Non-ASCII Text.*

Encoding messages

When sending a message, you need to encode the text into something acceptable according to mail standards. At the point when you send an e-mail, we expect that you already have the text encoding in the correct language using Java's built-in Unicode support. The problem is that Unicode is not a capability supported by Internet mail standards, so you need to encode the text differently in order to make it acceptable.

You have a number of options. If you know that you only need to handle a few words, then you should use the `encodeWord()` method. However, you are more likely to have to deal with the whole message body or header; in this case, use the `encodeText()` method:

```
String foreign_str = ".....";
String usable_str = MimeUtility.encodeText(foreign_str);
message.setText(usable_str);
```

Decoding messages

Decoding a message is just the opposite approach. First, extract the body or header item, and then run it through the decoder. Finally, display it to the user:

```
String msg_str = message.getText();
String foreign_str = MimeUtility.decodeText(msg_str);
textfield.setText(foreign_str);
```

Receiving an E-mail

For the enterprise application, receiving e-mail is not as important as sending it. However, not all applications that you will be writing will be used within the enterprise. In fact, e-mail is used for all sorts of things other than discussing the latest sports results with your mates.

Preparing to receive mail

Receiving e-mails requires the same code to get you established as sending them. You need to establish sessions and transports to receive an e-mail, just as you needed them to send it.

Step 1: Set up receiving services

Start by establishing the mail session and transport information:

```
Properties props = new Properties();
String mailhost = "mail.mydomain.com";

props.put("mail.host", mailhost);
props.put("mail.store.protocol", "pop3");
props.put("mail.smtp.host", mailhost);

Session mail_session = Session.getDefaultInstance(props);
```

The only difference between this and the earlier version for sending e-mail is the change from a transport protocol to a store protocol. To return to terminology we defined earlier, stores are how we look at incoming messages, and transports are how we look at outgoing messages. SMTP is only used to send an e-mail. If you want to receive one, you need to use a different transport mechanism. For standard Internet e-mail, you will generally use either POP3 or IMAP as your protocol. Most users only use POP, as shown in the previous sample code.

Step 2: Provide authentication information

For the vast majority of users, reading e-mail from the server means providing some form of login information. That is, you have to provide a user name and password to the server before you can properly connect. The previous sample code will attempt to connect to the server and get bounced because it cannot provide any information about the user. Somehow you need to provide this information to the system.

In the section, "Step 1: Creating a session," we talked about providing an instance of the `Authenticator` class. `Authenticator` enables you to provide the mail system with sensitive information like user names and passwords. Remember that in a big system, it is quite possible that many applications will all be using the same instance of the mail APIs, and that you don't want user names and passwords leaking from one application to another.

For this simple application, you will find the following class useful:

```
public class SimpleAuthenticator extends Authenticator {
  private PasswordAuthentication pwAuth;

  public SimpleAuthenticator(String user, String passwd)
  {
```

```
        pwAuth = new PasswordAuthentication(user, passwd);
    }

    protected PasswordAuthentication getPasswordAuthentication()
    {
        return pwAuth;
    }
}
```

This simple implementation provides just enough information to be useful. Also note that you override the `getPasswordAuthentication()` method but keep the access `protected`. This ensures that security stays as tight as possible.

The next step is to register the `Authenticator` with the system. To do this you need to make one more modification to the connection code in the previous section. The `getInstance()` and `getDefaultInstance()` methods can also take an instance of your `Authenticator` class. This is how you pass the password-connection information into the mail system in a secure way. The new code becomes:

```
...
props.put("mail.smtp.host", mailhost);

Authenicator auth =
    new SimpleAuthenticator("justin", "mypasswd");

Session mail_session = Session.getDefaultInstance(props, auth);
```

Managing incoming mail

With the setup information established, you need to connect to the mail server. Unlike with sending e-mails, you need to contact the server first to get the information before you can do anything. With the password information in hand, you now have to access stored information from the mail service.

Step 1: Connect to the server

At the moment, the transport code shown in the previous example is sitting dormant. There is no active connection to the server. You need to be active before you can ask it about any messages that may be waiting for you.

To establish a connection, you first need to request a `Store` object that represents the server. Then you use one of the `connect()` methods to create a live connection. The `Store` object represents the details of the server. Once you're done with this step, you can go on to ask for the individual mail folders such as the Inbox to look at various messages:

```
try {
    Store pop_store = mail_session.getStore();
    pop_store.connect();
}
```

```
catch(MessagingException me) {
}
```

Various options exist in the session for fetching a `Store`. As with the `Transport` class, if you want to fetch multiple `Stores` for different protocol types on the server, you can use a variant of the `getStore()` method:

```
Store pop_store = mail_session.getStore("pop3");
Store imap_store = mail_session.getStore("imap");
```

With a `Store` instance on hand and connected, you can now start examining the mail contents.

Step 2: Look at messages

Mail is represented on a server as a collection of folders. These folders are no different than what you see in your ordinary e-mail reader today. Folders contain a collection of e-mail messages and may be nested with further subfolders. To read an individual mail message, you must first access the folder it is contained in.

The Inbox is the folder you are most likely to want to read—particularly when checking for new messages:

```
Folder inbox = pop_store.getFolder("Inbox");
```

The folder name Inbox is a reserved name to represent the place where all mail first arrives at the system. The name is case-insensitive, so it doesn't matter if you ask for INBOX, inbox, or Inbox. There are no other reserved folder names, so any other folder you might be after is application-specific.

An alternate way to look for folders is to ask for the root folder and then traverse its subfolders until you find the folder you want. You can access the root folder using the `getDefaultFolder()` method. For server-based applications, this method is not particularly useful. In this environment, it is easier to find the folder if you ask for it by name. If you were to write a GUI client for managing e-mail, then the best way would be to present the default folder in a Swing `JTree`–style component.

POP3 mail protocol always has a single folder at any given time. Calling `getDefaultFolder()` or `getFolder("INBOX")` will return the same thing.

To access the content of the folder, you need to open the folder. Once it has been opened, you can view the list of contained messages and subfolders. Reading messages and subfolders is as simple as using the `getMessages()` method for messages and the `list()` method for folders. The following piece of code shows the contents of your Inbox:

```
Folder inbox = pop_store.getFolder("inbox");
inbox.open();

System.out.println("Messages");
```

```
Messages[] messages = inbox.getMessages();
for(int i = 0; i < messages.length; i++)
  System.out.println(messages[i].getSubject());

System.out.println("Folders");
Folders[] children = inbox.list();
For(int i = 0; i < children.length; i++)
  System.out.println(children[i].getName());
```

Step 3: Fetch new messages

One of the points of opening a folder to read e-mail is to determine whether you have new messages. For example, you might want to check for new messages, download any new ones, do some processing, and then delete them. If there are no messages, then you don't want to do anything.

On contact with the server, you will want to find out whether you have any new messages:

```
Folder inbox = pop_store.getFolder("inbox");
inbox.open();

if(inbox.hasNewMessages())
  // do some processing here....
```

A typical action of a mail client is to download header information without downloading the rest of the message. This enables you to quickly get a feel for what is available without having to spend a lot of time and bandwidth fetching all the e-mail. If you are like me and receive a couple of hundred e-mails in a day, then this can be a good thing.

JavaMail uses the concept of a profile to define just what information should be downloaded locally for the message and profiles are embodied in the `FetchProfile` class. This class enables you to specify a combination of header information, the current flags, and content. You can request any or all of these. For example, to ask the system to fetch header and flag information for messages, you would use the following code:

```
If(inbox.hasNewMessages()) {
    FetchProfile profile = new FetchProfile();
    profile.add(FetchProfile.Item.ENVELOPE);
    profile.add(FetchProfile.Item.FLAGS);

    Message[] msgs = inbox.getMessages();

    inbox.fetch(msgs, profile);
}
```

Building E-mail Filters

For an e-mail user, building a set of message filters is an important part of the process. It enables users to filter out spam, quickly and automatically sort e-mail from various mailing lists into smaller and more manageable areas, and provide a simple way of rating important information. To make all this possible, the JavaMail API provides a very flexible set of capabilities in the `javax.mail.search` package.

Constructing a search

The search classes from the JavaMail search package work as a set of Boolean conditions. These enable you to build anything as simple as checking for a word in the message body to creating a complex pattern looking for sender name, source information, and keywords in the body.

All the search classes extend the base class `SearchTerm`. This class has one abstract method, `search()`, that takes a `Message` object and returns a `boolean` indicating a matching condition or not. Because it is abstract, you must then build a set of classes that provide a particular search match.

Single-item comparisons

When trying to build a set of filtering rules, you don't necessarily want to search an entire message for information. You might want to search just the body for a particular keyword (great for spam!) or the subject for a particular piece of text (normal practice on most developer mailing lists).

The following four basic classes provide comparisons for a single part of the message:

- `AddressTerm`: This class looks at the address field of the mail message— either from or recipient.
- `FlagTerm`: This class looks at the flags associated with a message: Has the message been read yet, marked with a flag, or answered?
- `StringTerm`: This class provides a generalized comparison that does substring searching for a particular string. Note that it cannot do regular-expression searches.
- `ComparisonTerm`: This class provides more specific matching capabilities for numerical values such as dates and message lengths.

Each of these base classes is then extended with more specific search capabilities. For example, `AddressTerm` is then subclassed with `RecipientTerm` and `FromTerm` classes.

Boolean search classes

Even for the most simple of searches, there is the need to use Boolean conditions. These enable you to combine a number of comparisons into a single search. A typical e-mail filtering rule might be to look for the To or Cc field to be equal to a particular string. Combining the two smaller searches requires a Boolean OR operation.

The classes provided for Boolean operations follow the normal Boolean operations, AND (AndTerm), OR (OrTerm) and NOT (NotTerm). Like all Boolean operators, these can be combined into a tree structure as deep as you care to make it.

Combining classes is just like playing with Legos. Construct the classes in the order in which you want them combined. You build the expression from the bottom up. You can express the following term:

```
(a || !b) && c
```

as this:

```
NotTerm not_b = new NotTerm(b);
OrTerm a_or_b = new OrTerm(a, not_b);
AndTerm ab_and c = new AndTerm(a_or_b, c);
```

Executing a search

Now that you know the basics of the search classes, you can construct a full search of all the messages. A filter is really just a search followed by some action to be performed on the results of the search. So to build a filter you first need to search the messages for some particular set of qualities.

One common use of the filter is to put mail messages from a given list server into a separate folder. Most commonly that is done by looking at who sent the e-mail. Let's say you want to filter the messages from the XML-DEV mailing list. You will want to construct a search for the To field being from the address xml-dev@lists.xml.org:

```
SearchTerm to =
  new RecipientStringTerm(Message.RecipientType.TO,
                          "xml-dev@lists.xml.org");
```

Another way to do this is to pass Address objects rather than a string:

```
Address to_addr = new InternetAddress("xml-dev@lists.xml.org");
SearchTerm to =
    new RecipientTerm(Message.RecipientType.TO, to_addr);
```

Of course, software being software, when someone replies to a list message you don't really know whether this list message is going to be in the To field or not. Just as often as not, the mail client will put the list address in the Cc field and the user in the To field. So to be robust, your search must look at both the To and Cc fields for the net address. The first of the previous two examples now becomes the following:

```
SearchTerm to =
  new RecipientStringTerm(Message.RecipientType.TO,
                          "xml-dev@lists.xml.org");

SearchTerm cc =
  new RecipientStringTerm(Message.RecipientType.CC,
                          "xml-dev@lists.xml.org");

SearchTerm xml_search = new OrTerm(to, cc);
```

After constructing the final variant of the search term, you now need to use it. Searches can be applied to Folders only. Within the folder, the search can be applied either to the entire folder or to a nominated subset of messages only. For example, to find all the messages to the XML-DEV list in your Inbox, you need to build the previous search and then ask the folder to find the messages:

```
Messages[] xml_msgs = inbox.search(xml_search);
```

The result is a list of messages that meets the criteria.

Building Complex Search Terms

If you want to create more complex terms, both AndTerm and OrTerm can take an array of search terms. If you have a search condition like the following,

```
!(a && b) && c
```

the standard programmer would build a set of terms like this:

```
AndTerm a_and_b = new AndTerm(a, b);
NotTerm not_ab = new NotTerm(a_and_b);
AndTerm search = new AndTerm(a_or_b, c);
```

As you can see, this is a lot of class creation. You can apply De Morgan's Theorem to this expression and use a different constructor for the AndTerm. The result will be the following code:

```
NotTerm not_a = new NotTerm(a);
NotTerm not_b = new NotTerm(b);
SearchTerm[] all_terms = { not_a, not_b, c };
AndTerm search = new AndTerm(all_terms);
```

This example leads to an extra line of code, but the search will be much more efficient now. The benefits really show through when you build very complex terms involving a lot of nested Boolean conditions. The more the Boolean conditions can be simplified into a set of flatter conditional checks, the quicker your search will be. This is really important if you have a lot of e-mails to check.

Caution

The specification does not define what should happen if no messages match the search criteria. It appears that implementations are free to return either a null reference or a zero-length array. For robustness reasons you should check for both before proceeding any further with the results.

Managing messages

Once you have obtained a list of mail messages from a search, you can then do many things with them — shift them to new folders, delete them, or reply to them. Methods in the `Folder` and `Message` classes let you do all of these.

Deleting unwanted messages

Let's say you have a killfile — a file of people you don't like. You start by building a search that will find all these people in your inbox:

```
String[] killfile = ....
int size = killfile.length;
SearchTerm[] source_list = new SearchTerm[size];

for(int i = 0; i < size; i++)
    source_list[i] = new FromStringTerm(killfile[i]);

kill_search = new OrTerm(source_list);

Messages[] kill_msgs = inbox.search(kill_search);

// now mark them deleted and get rid of them
Flags delete_flag = new Flag(Flags.Flag.DELETED);
inbox.setFlags(kill_msgs, delete_flag, true);
inbox.expunge();
```

To delete a message, you must first set the flag of that message to delete and then instruct the mail system to physically delete the message from the underlying storage. Mail messages have a number of flags associated with them — including flags that mark them for deletion. If you have ever used a text-based mail reader like ELM or PINE, you will be used to seeing this. It enables you to delete things without really deleting them, just in case you accidentally marked the wrong one — the original Trash Bin.

Moving messages to other folders

Within JavaMail there are two ways of moving a message between folders. The first is to use a copy method and then delete the source e-mail, and the second is to delete the message and then append it to the new folder. While either method will work, the first method is preferable, and so it is the only one we will demonstrate here.

Copying messages to move them is the preferred method of transferring messages between files because, in situations where the server- or client-side system supports direct copies, it is much faster to use that. If the server supports it (as it does with IMAP systems), copying messages between two folders on the server side is much faster than copying the entire contents over the network connection to your client and then copying them back to the server to the new folder.

Start with your mail-list filter example again. For this example, you have a second folder represented by the variable `xml_dev`:

```
SearchTerm xml_search = new OrTerm(to, cc);
Messages[] xml_msgs = inbox.search(xml_search);

inbox.copyMessages(xml_msgs, xml_dev);
```

After you have copied the messages, you now want to remove them from the source folder. This is, after all, a filter to shuffle new messages to make your standard Inbox more manageable. The process of deletion follows the same steps as the previous example:

```
Flags delete_flag = new Flags(Flags.Flag.DELETED);
inbox.setFlags(xml_msgs, delete_flag, true);
inbox.expunge();
```

Replying to messages

As part of a business server, one function that you may need is the automatic acknowledgement of incoming e-mails. You know, those annoying messages that thank us for our business, and our e-mail will be handled by the next available operator and so on.

To build this sort of system, instead of searching on a particular recipient you want to search based on the unread flag. If you find a new unread message, send an auto reply, mark the message read, and move it to some pending folder. You can imagine this code as being some part of an automatic thread that checks the Inbox every five minutes, as shown in this example:

```
while(true) {
    if(inbox.hasNewMessages()) {
        Flags unread = new Flags(Flags.Flag.RECENT);
        unread_search = new FlagsTerm(unread);

        Messages[] unread_msgs = inbox.search(unread_search);
        For(int i = 0; i < unread_msgs.length; i++) {
            Message reply = unread_msgs[i].reply(true);

            // fill in the message here
            reply.setText(ANNOYING_MSG);
            reply.saveChanges();

            smtpService.send(reply);
        }

        // now move them to another folder
```

```
            inbox.copyMessages(unread_msgs, pending);
            Flags delete_flag = new Flags(Flags.Flag.DELETED);
            inbox.setFlags(unread_msgs, delete_flag, true);
            inbox.expunge();
        }

        thread.sleep(one_minute);
    }
```

This piece of code completes the auto-reply system. On the second line it checks to see if any new messages have turned up since the last time you checked. If so, you search the Inbox for any unread messages. You only ask for unread messages as they will be the only ones with the flag set.

In JavaMail, unread messages are indicated by two different flags. A `RECENT` message is one that has arrived in the mail folder since the last time it was checked with the `hasNewMessages()` method. However, if the message has not been downloaded or copied or otherwise looked at, the `SEEN` flag will also be set to false. As soon as you request information about the message particulars, such as a header or the body text, this flag will be set to true.

Summary

This concludes our introduction to e-mail and newsgroup capabilities in the J2EE environment. The ability to send e-mails is an essential part of any enterprise application. Whether it sends an e-mail to confirm a purchase or automatically filters support requests, almost any application will need to support e-mail.

In this chapter, we introduced you to e-mail and to JavaMail as the implementation of mail capabilities in the Java environment. The topics we covered included:

- ✦ An introduction to the parts of an e-mail message.
- ✦ Constructing and sending a basic e-mail message.
- ✦ Constructing e-mails that contain attachments.
- ✦ Reading e-mails from a server for both POP and IMAP protocols.
- ✦ Building filters and searches to find e-mails.

✦ ✦ ✦

P A R T

Finding Things with Databases and Searches

✦ ✦ ✦ ✦

In This Part

✦ ✦ ✦ ✦

Interacting with Relational Databases

✦ ✦ ✦ ✦

In This Chapter

Introduction to relational databases and SQL

Inserting, updating, and deleting data in your database

Managing database structures

Building complex queries for fast information access

✦ ✦ ✦ ✦

With the majority of enterprise applications, storing data means using a database. When people talk about databases, they almost invariably mean the relational database as typified by Oracle, Sybase, Ingress and friends. To access information in a database you need some form of query language, and SQL has risen to become the lingua franca of relational databases.

Relational databases are not the only form of database software. Other forms of database exist, such as object-relational and object-oriented databases. However, with the huge power of the current relational products, and the number of developers using them, these other forms are finding it hard to gain a large developer mind share. This results in a lack of standards for querying these forms of database, and so the relational database has gone from strength to strength in the enterprise world.

In this chapter, we are going to take our first departure from the purely Java-oriented view of the world to introduce you to relational databases and SQL. SQL is extremely important to the world of Java programmers accessing databases because it is what you use to talk to databases using the JDBC API.

We introduce JDBC in Chapter 7. JDBC is the core of most remote-object technologies, so you will see a collection of examples using JDBC in all the chapters presented in Part V, "Abstracting the System."

What Is a Relational Database?

In the early days of computing, a database consisted of a big collection of files stored on disk. Each programmer had to write his or her own code to manipulate these files. As data storage file sizes started becoming huge, this overhead became too much (not to mention the constant re-writing of applications every time a small change in format was made). A number of companies, thanks to the increasing amount of computing horsepower, started to provide off-the-shelf software for managing these growing collections of data.

As software grew in complexity, programmers found that much of the data being stored was relatively trivial — collections of names, addresses, prices, and so on. And the same piece of nearly identical information was often repeated over and over, millions of times in many cases. There grew to be lists of collections, and these collections often had trivial links among them. It wasn't necessary for the exact item of data to form the link, but there was a pattern from which one could determine that an item of data in one collection could be used to look up an item of data in another collection. Thus was born the relational database.

How data is structured in a relational database

If you wanted to create a collection of the same type of data in a normal programming language like Java, you would build a class to hold it and a collection of getter and setter methods, and then link them all together. This implies a lot of extra overhead for each piece of information stored. You have the definition of the class, all the pointers to various bits of data, some code to check that values are in range, and countless other pieces of code. Really all you want to do is put in a definition of values, and then say "store lots of this, please." That is how a relational database works.

Defining one piece of data with tables

A relational database defines its main data structure as a table. The table defines the series of attributes that it must use as columns. Each column is exactly one piece of data — a person's first name, for example. You now need to define a particular piece of information in that table — a real user. This is termed a row. You can picture tables, rows, and columns using a conceptual diagram as shown in Table 6-1. This kind of conceptual diagram is a bit like your table in a document or Web page. Across the top of the table are the names of the data stored in that column, then each row contains a piece of data.

Table 6-1
An abstract representation of a database table

First Name	*Last Name*	*Country*	*E-mail*
Justin	Couch	Australia	justin@vlc.com.au
Daniel	Steinberg	USA	dsteinberg@core.com
...	...	...	...

When you search for information in a table, it is nice to know that you have provided some unique way to access each row. Databases do not specify this unique key for you, and it is up to you to define one of the columns to provide this unique key. In database lingo, this unique identifier is known as a primary key. A table does not need to define a primary key, but it certainly makes life much easier for the programmer if there is one.

A primary key does not have to be a single column. It may be a combination of two columns, such as the first name and last name columns in Table 6-1. Whatever way the design process is defined, we highly recommend that it be a very small subset of your columns, for performance reasons. The smaller the number of columns, the faster the lookup for a particular piece of data.

Linking pieces of data together between tables

For most useful applications you are not going to want to use a single table. Databases, like code, do benefit from good software-engineering practices, and breaking common pieces of data down from one table into several smaller tables will make your application much easier to understand and maintain.

Once you have broken your data down into several tables, you need to provide some form of linking among tables. This is where your primary key becomes very important. In one table you have a primary key to define information. Another table can now make reference to that table by including a column with the matching primary key value. Consider, for example, an online store with a collection of orders linked to a certain customer. As Figure 6-1 illustrates, the store has two tables — one for the customer contact information and another for the orders. The orders make reference to the customer it is for by using the customer ID as the link between the two tables.

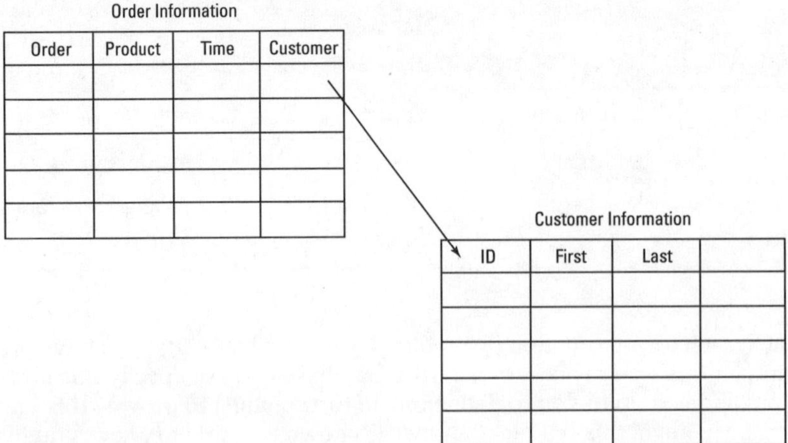

Figure 6-1: Two tables linked in a store database system by the customer ID

Now, when your outside user comes in, he or she asks for the order information. Internally your application searches through the database for the order, finds the customer number, and then looks up the customer-information table. The completed set of information is returned to the user as a single item. From this example you can see that instead of storing customer information with every order, you now need only one copy—thus saving yourself a lot of extra storage space.

The next step is to take this process to the logical conclusion. You can break your order information down into what is basically a set of references to other tables. Product ID, purchase price, customer data, and any other form of common information can be held in individual tables and collated to form an order. The sum total of all these tables and their relationships is known as a database schema.

Agreeing on a language to communicate

Databases are not much good if you cannot access the data in them or make changes to those data. Like most software, access methods started as proprietary solutions. Pressure from programmers lead to the lingua franca of relational databases: the Structured Query Language, better known as SQL.

SQL is not a programming language. You cannot combine blocks of statements into functions and functions into full applications. It is a query language, which means that there is only one statement, and that everything you need to do has to be in that one statement. Think of it as that single string you enter into a search engine to find a Web page.

Some databases do support collecting a group of SQL statements into a block of code. This block of code is typically called stored procedures. How the databases support stored procedures varies greatly from vendor to vendor, and for this reason they will not be covered in this book. In our experience, stored procedures sometimes help with speed, but often make many transactions slower once you combine SQL with JDBC. Test your applications using both methods to determine which is the faster way of accessing the database contents.

To be useful, SQL is generally used in the context of another application or development environment. You need some container that connects with the database, issues your query, and returns the results. The only time you might see SQL statements in their raw form is as a dump of the database contents to enable you to recover from a problem or as a backup. In general, all the examples you see here will involve using some form of SQL prompt to your database, or as the commands issued by JDBC.

Although SQL is an ANSI standard, every vendor seems to add its own flavor to it. Some companies seeking to build very light database implementations have taken a small subset of the full specification, while big companies like Oracle and IBM have extended the specification. For the purposes of sanity, we've stuck to the ANSI standard specification in this book. We highly recommend checking the documentation of your database for the exact version it supports and any modifications to the concepts introduced here.

Finding a database to use

Which database you choose is very heavily dependent on the requirements of your project. Heavy hitters like Oracle and SQL Server are not very appropriate for writing Palm Pilot software. Similarly, the requirements of the project may dictate a certain minimum set of capabilities, such as transaction processing. Other times, these requirements may not be needed, and so a simpler database will be more acceptable (not to mention the much lower licensing costs!).

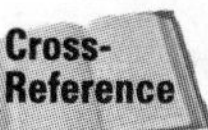

Transaction processing and the high-end features of enterprise systems are introduced in Part VI, "Building Big Systems."

You are no doubt aware of the large commercial database players such as Oracle, Sybase, Ingress, and Microsoft. However, there are many equivalent systems in the open-source realms as well. For example, PostgreSQL (`http://www.postgresql.org/`) provides almost all the full capabilities of Oracle servers and yet is an open-source product. Other products that we often use are MySQL (`http://www.mysql.com/`) and MiniSQL (`http://www.hughes.com.au/`).

It is far from our place to recommend a database solution for your needs. Databases can be anything from tiny-footprint devices for embedded devices to large distributed-transaction databases for huge Web sites. You will need to evaluate just what needs your project has.

If you just need a database to test and play with SQL, then the reference implementation of J2EE comes with a small, Java-based database. This will be suitable for testing most of the examples in this chapter.

Defining Information in an RDBMS

For many projects that you start with, you will have to define a database from scratch. The first step is to decide how you are going to organize the data. When you have the design in mind you need to tell your database software what that design is. Normally you do this through either a direct command prompt into the database or with a text file.

Before we introduce you to installing a database, you also need to know a little bit about SQL. Like every other language, it has its set of rules and conventions.

An introduction to SQL

SQL is very simple compared to Java. Only one command is issued at a time. This command must contain all of the information needed to process it. For example, if you want to enter data in the database, then you must supply the complete set of data.

Syntax fundamentals

As there are no such concepts as functions and procedures in SQL, the rules of use are quite easy to remember:

- All of the keywords in SQL are case-insensitive.
- Column and table names are case-insensitive.
- Strings are quoted with the single-quote character (`'`).
- The asterisk character (`*`) acts as a wildcard when specifying the subject of a command. (String literal matches use % although many databases seem to support both.)
- Collections of items are delimited by round brackets (`(` and `)`).

The language itself defines primitive data types and also the operators you use to work with those types. Most of the time the data type is implied by the way the data is used and combined with the operators. Once you've defined the table definitions, the operators know what sort of data you are using and how to do the appropriate comparisons. These operators are similar to the ones you are familiar with from Java— `>`, `<`, `<=`, and `==` all have the same meanings. Some operators are also in text form. Logical actions may use word forms such as `AND`, `OR`, and `NOT` to describe actions, or the Java/C style of `&&`, `||`, and `!` respectively.

SQL does not define a character that terminates a statement: The character depends on the database software. These terminators are only used when entering a text file to the database command line or in a console window. The two most common forms of terminators are the semicolon (`;`), used in DB2, PostgreSQL, and MySQL, and the backslash g (`\g`), used in Oracle, MiniSQL, and SQLServer. Check your database documentation to find out which character you need to use. Interfaces like JDBC and ODBC do not require the use of terminators for a command.

SQL coding conventions

Like all programming languages, SQL uses a common set of conventions in its syntax. Before we start describing pieces of SQL, we should cover these conventions, as they differ quite substantially from what you are used to in Java programming. All our examples will use the following conventions:

✦ Keywords from SQL are presented in upper case. This makes them easy to distinguish from the information you are defining or requesting in the table.

✦ Table names and column names are all presented in lower case. If the name contains more than one word they are separated by underscore characters (_).

✦ If one table has a column referring to the primary key of another table, these have the same name.

✦ When creating long running statements, wrap them over multiple lines. Also, indent them using the standard conventions that you are used to with Java programming. These make it easier to debug invalid commands during development as most databases will issue line numbers for errors.

Designing a new database

You can approach designing a new database just as you approach designing software. First work out what sort of data you need to store, and then build the relationships among the different collections of data. Finally, write it all down so you can remember what you just thought of!

A simple approach to designing a database is to look at what sort of data collections you need to store and to create a table for each collection. For each piece of data within a collection, define a column in that table. Remember that you also need to include columns that link to other tables.

Designing an efficient database for a large project is not a simple task. We often see databases designed by Java programmers, who unfortunately (in this case) have an object-oriented view of life. While the design looks right according to that worldview, it is often not the best way to store data. If your project is a large software project, we highly recommend using a professional database designer to do the real design work. Provide the designer with information about what you want stored and let him or her come up with the most efficient representation.

We'll start with a simple example that we'll use to illustrate the concepts in this chapter. Consider a store where users can purchase things . This store uses the typical shopping-basket approach for registered clients. The table structure you need for this store is outlined in Figure 6-2. As we'll come back to this example later in the chapter, we will leave out most of the details and just put the useful and interesting pieces in.

To start with, you need some structures to represent your customers. When a customer registers, you enter his or her details in the customer table. Each customer has an internal unique identifier. As a separate table from the customer table, you have the employee table. This is the list of the employees of the store and is used to identify who is fulfilling a request. Next you have a series of products to define. Like the customer, you need a unique product identifier. Finally, you have an order table that binds all these tables together. The order table contains a unique order identifier, customer ID, product ID, status, and price paid. This means that when an order is made, you will know the price the customer paid. Stores offer specials from time to time, which means that prices change, and stock might not be available at the time the order is made. For these orders, you don't charge the customer until the item has arrived, and you can send it out. So, in the event that the price has gone up since the order was made, you need to keep the original price information in the order so that the customer is treated fairly.

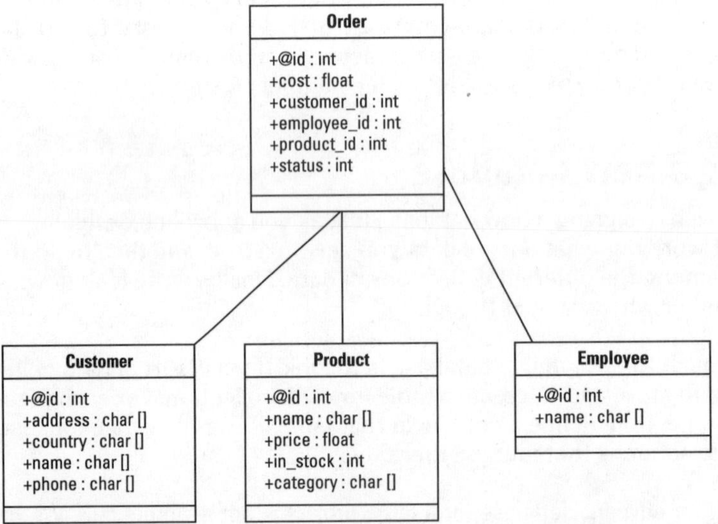

Figure 6-2: A UML description of the tables used in the online store examples

Using data types to represent data

Like many programming languages, SQL has a built-in set of data-type primitives. These primitives are used in the definition of columns of tables. Once you have a table defined, manipulating the data in the table uses these values to check any request or new data.

Built-in data types provided by SQL

Table 6-2 describes the standard data types available in SQL. Most of these will seem familiar to you. Aside from the standard integer, string, and floating-point types, some are particularly useful for a database — date and time information are considered primitives in a database. Also included is the BLOB, or binary large object. This data type is used to store large pieces of data in raw binary form in the database. You might use a BLOB to store an image directly in the database, for example.

Table 6-2
The standard primitive data types of SQL

Primitive Type	*Description*	*Java Equivalent*
`SMALLINT`	An integer type that uses two bytes for storage.	`short`
`INTEGER`	An integer type that uses four bytes for storage.	`int`
`BIGINT`	An integer type that uses eight bytes for storage.	`long`
`REAL`	A floating-point type that uses four bytes for storage.	`float`
`DOUBLE`	A floating point type that uses eight bytes for storage.	`double`
`DECIMAL`	A number that contains a fraction and whole part of fixed accuracy, such as currency values. The closest Java type is `java.math.BigDecimal`.	n/a
`NUMERIC`	A synonym for the `DECIMAL` type.	n/a
`CHAR`	A single character or fixed-length array of characters. This amount of memory is always used for this data.]	`char`, `char[`
`VARCHAR`	A variable-length array of characters. The size in memory used is dependent on the amount of data.	`String`
`DATE`	A representation of a date value holding day, month, and year information.	`java.util.Date`
`TIMESTAMP`	A representation of a time value in hours, minutes, and seconds.	n/a
`DATETIME`	A representation of both data and time information together.	n/a
`BLOB`	Storage of raw binary data.	`byte[]`

Declaring arrays of data

You can elect to have the basic primitive types as a single value or as an array of values. To declare an array of the data type you use the type name and then follow it with a set of round brackets containing the number of items to have in that array. For example, an array of 256 integer values would be represented by `INTEGER(256)`.

All of the primitive types, such as `INTEGER` and `REAL`, can be declared as arrays. Complex types such as `BLOB` and `DATE` cannot be used as an array of data because internally they are already stored as an array. SQL does not permit arrays of more than one dimension.

Empty values

SQL also enables you to declare that a value is not set by using the `NULL` keyword. `NULL` will work for any data type—even integer or floating-point values. It is simply a way of saying "I have no value to set here," instead of telling it to have a default value.

Managing tables

Tables are the most fundamental part of the database. For that reason it is rare to do much with them once they have been set. With SQL you can create, alter, and delete tables. The most common of these actions is creating a table. You can alter a table during the development process, and it is rare to delete a table. Deleting a table removes all the data in the database, so it is not wise to do it without a lot of consideration.

Creating new tables

The first step in setting up a database is to define the tables. When you define a table you include the table name and define the columns to be used. Each column has a name and data type.

To create a new table, you start with the keyword `CREATE`. This keyword may be used for a number of tasks, but in this case you want a table, and so you follow it with the word `TABLE` and the name of the table. After the name of the table you have to declare the list of columns. This is a comma-separated list of definitions, surrounded by a pair of parentheses.

In order to create the customer table from Figure 6-2, you use the following declaration:

```
CREATE TABLE customer (
    customer_id INTEGER,
    address     VARCHAR(256),
    country     CHAR(2),
```

```
        name          VARCHAR(64),
        phone         CHAR(12)
    )
```

This creates a basic table with the given structure. The numbers in parentheses after the data type define how many of the given type you want. VARCHAR(256) indicates that you want a variable-length character array that can contain up to 256 characters.

For the country information we have used a two-character fixed-size array. A typical approach in database design is to use the two-letter country code to define the name of the country rather than the full string. This is very efficient because the country codes are fixed, and two characters use a lot less memory than a whole string. For a database with a million or more entries, that can be a significant savings in space.

Having empty data in a row is not much use. If you want to send your customers information, you must have at least an address. You can make sure that someone gives you this information by appending the keywords NOT NULL to the end of a column definition. For example, to set the address column to require a value you would use the following code:

```
address VARCHAR(256) NOT NULL
```

When we specified the table earlier we said that the customer ID must be unique. SQL gives you a way of ensuring this is the case. Consider a large site that may have multiple applications interacting with the database. Having the user code keep the uniqueness contract is asking for trouble. It is much better to have the database do it.

Ensuring the uniqueness of a column's data

You can ensure the uniqueness of a column's data by using the KEY keyword and preceding it by a qualifier of the type of key. Four common types of keys are available for use in a table:

- **Unique key:** If a value is supplied in this cell, this value must be unique for all rows in this column.
- **Primary key:** This is a special kind of unique key and a guaranteed identifier for this row. A value must always be supplied for this cell.
- **Composite key:** This is a key that uses two or more columns to calculate its value.
- **Foreign key:** This column references a primary or unique key of another table. When set it will check the referred table for the existence of that key.

As the customer ID is something that you must always have and must be unique, it makes sense to define it as a primary key. The definitions of keys are included separately from the column definition. Traditionally, the declaration of primary keys is kept until the end of all column declarations. If you want to use the customer ID as a primary key, the table create command now becomes this:

```
CREATE TABLE customer (
    customer_id INTEGER NOT NULL,
    ...
    PRIMARY KEY (customer_id)
)
```

Note that we have also included the NOT NULL statement for the ID value, so that it forces the user to provide us with that information.

The last step in defining your customer database is to have the database automatically generate the customer identifier. Just as you don't want to trust the uniqueness of the key to outside applications, you don't want to trust the generating of the identifier to outside applications either. For the majority of applications, identifiers like this can be just a simple serial number incremented by one for each new entry. You can have the database generate a serial number like this for the identifier by specifying the AUTO_INCREMENT keyword after another definition for that column, like this:

```
customer_id INTEGER NOT NULL AUTO_INCREMENT
```

Not all databases support auto-increment of column values. Auto increment is part of the SQL99 standard that many database vendors have yet to fully implement. If your database does not support this keyword, then you may need to use alternatives, such as creating a small table in combination with a stored procedure that generates new unique keys on each request.

Providing default values

If a column should have data in it, but you really don't want to require the user to supply it all the time, you can use the DEFAULT keyword. This keyword is then followed with the value that should be used as a default. For example, to use the default value of 0.0 for the price of the product in the product table, you can use the following declaration:

```
price DECIMAL(6,2) DEFAULT 0.00
```

The value that you specify must follow the standard syntax rules. If it is a string or date value, then it must be quoted properly; numerical values need not be quoted.

Altering an existing table

During the development process you will probably need to alter a table. Typically this alteration consists of adding or removing a column, but it may involve any of the definitions you used to create a table, such as changing the type of a column or modifying the key settings.

To alter a table, start with the ALTER TABLE keywords followed by the name of the table you are going to play with. Then list a series of commands that declare what you are going to do. These are one of ADD, ALTER, CHANGE, MODIFY, or DROP. For example, if you want to add a new column to your employee table containing each employee's Social Security Number, you could use the following command:

```
ALTER TABLE employee ADD COLUMN ssn CHAR(16) NOT NULL
```

You can put two or more actions into one request by separating the commands with a comma. If you want to add both the SSN and address details to your employee table, the command becomes the following:

```
ALTER TABLE employee ADD COLUMN ssn CHAR(16) NOT NULL,
                     ADD COLUMN address VARCHAR(256) NOT NULL
```

Deleting a table

If something really bad happens to your database, or you decide during the development process that you no longer need a table, you can delete a table with the DROP command. Say you no longer want your employee table: You can delete it with the following code:

```
DROP TABLE employee
```

Be warned, though. Dropping a table will delete all the data in that table. None of the databases that we've used have ever offered a confirmation option for the deletion process when using an SQL prompt. If you get the syntax wrong when deleting a table, the results can be disastrous.

Improving performance of a database

You can make a number of performance improvements to a database using SQL commands. Normally we don't talk about performance until we've covered the entire introduction to a topic. In this case, however, we make an exception, because the most important performance tweaks can be applied during the setup of the database tables.

Two of the most common ways to improve performance are to allow the database to build fast indexes into itself for searching, and to restrict the view of complex tables into a series of smaller tables.

Indexing values for fast lookups

Indexing is the process whereby a database can optimize its search patterns through a table before you make requests of it. What you do is nominate to the table the columns you are going to be using for the majority of your searches. The cost of this extra speed is extra disk space consumed to hold the index values.

Most interactions with a database will be of the form "find all users who live in this area." This form of interaction doesn't find a specific row in the database but instead finds a collection of them. If you know that this is going to be a very common query, you can tell the database to build a fast lookup table based on the contents of the "area" column.

To create an index, you start again with the CREATE keyword. Follow it with either INDEX or UNIQUE INDEX, depending on whether you know that the column will contain unique values or not. Say your company wants some statistics about the countries customers are coming from. This is not a unique index, as many people will share the same country code. If you were to create an index on the customer ID, that would be unique. These two situations can be executed with the following commands:

```
CREATE INDEX country_idx ON customer(country)
CREATE UNIQUE INDEX customer_idx ON customer(customer_id)
```

One more qualifier you can add to this command is a list of other columns to include in the index value. You might use this qualifier if you know you want to search for a collection of products from a particular category and price range. You set the primary index to be the category, but tell the indexing to include the price as well to add further information for faster lookups. You define the extra information with the INCLUDE keyword and then the extra column names from that table:

```
CREATE INDEX prod_search_idx ON product(category)
    INCLUDE (price)
```

Virtual tables with views

Another way to improve performance is to create a list of virtual tables that take information from a bigger table. This automatically filters some of the table content so that when you do a search on the virtual table, the database only has to find items in your smaller virtual table. Virtual tables are known as *views*.

To create a new view, you start with the CREATE keyword, followed by the VIEW keyword. Next, you make a bracketed, comma-separated list in parentheses to define the name of the view and the names of the columns you would like to present in that view. The second half of the command defines the source of the data. To provide the source, you use a search query. We'll introduce the search query shortly, so for the moment you'll have to take the second part for granted.

In the following example, we create a view wherein we provide a table that only contains books:

```
CREATE VIEW books_view (id, name, price, in_stock)
AS SELECT id, name, price, in_stock
FROM product WHERE category='book'
```

Creating and Managing Virtual Databases

Many database applications support the concept of virtual databases. Instead of having only one area that the tables belong in, you can create a virtual database to keep different sets of tables away from each other. The advantage of this is that you only have one application running in memory, while at the same time you have a number of separate databases to prevent clashes or data from one area from spilling into another area.

The process of creating virtual databases depends on the database application. Some enable you to use an SQL-like command (for example, `CREATE DATABASE`), while others require you to use a command-line tool to initialize a new virtual database. Because of this, we won't give you any examples of setting one up; instead, we refer you to your database documentation.

The SQL syntax enables you to address a particular table within a virtual database if you have not explicitly connected to one. Nominating the virtual database in a command is in the form *database name*'.' *table name*. To create a new table in a database named test_db, you would use the following syntax:

```
CREATE TABLE test_db.customer (
    ...
)
```

This syntax form is available to all the commands in this chapter that name a column or table. You can even use it to refer to a specific column in a table, such as `test_db.customer.name`.

This view contains all the information from the product table that pertains to books. Notice that we don't supply the product's category in the list of columns that are available in this view. That is because we can make the assumption that their value will always be the string "book".

The view presented here will act like a normal table. You can issue commands on the view just as though it were a table. If you need to, you can create views that are read-only or not updatable.

Managing Data

A database without data in it is not very useful at all! So your next step is to add some data. With the tables constructed, you can add data such as information about a new customer. If the customer wants to change their address, it is an update.

The process of adding and updating data in a database assumes that you have collected data from somewhere to insert. Typically this comes from a user interface such as a form or a network communication with data stored in an XML file. If you don't nominate a piece of data, then it will go unset in the database (if you haven't specified default values when creating the table). However, sometimes you need to derive information for one table based on information in another table—the foreign keys that the example product table contains, for example. In cases like these, you cannot just have the database automagically fill the data in; you must first query for the values and then use those in the next update.

Creating a new entry

You create a new entry (row) in the database by first using the `INSERT` command. This instructs the database that you want to create a new row rather than update an existing one.

Inserting information into the database requires specifying where the values are to go (which table) and then the list of values for each column in that table. Sometimes, as in the case of our automatically incrementing ID values, these never need to be specified by the user. The database will provide them. Even then you can opt to create a new row with some or all of the values specified.

Specifying a complete new entry

The first, and most commonly used, form of the `INSERT` command is the addition of all information into the database. The syntax you use to do this is as follows:

```
INSERT INTO my_table VALUES (val1, val2, val3, ...)
```

The values are specified in the order in which you declared the table columns. For each column specified, you must provide a value here (except for columns that use auto-incremented values), even if the value is `NULL`. If you don't provide a value the database will generate an error, usually when the first value it reads doesn't match the declared column type.

You enter a new customer record into your database by using the following declaration:

```
INSERT INTO customer VALUES ('555 Mystreet Ave', 'AU',
    'Justin Couch', '+61 2 1234 5678')
```

Because each value is a string, you must quote the values used. Also notice that you don't declare the first column of the table, as it is automatically incremented by the database and set for you.

Specifying only parts of a new entry

Sometimes your application only has part of the data needed to create a new row. Instead of sending `NULL` values, you can opt to tell the database exactly which columns you are inserting values for and then their values. To do this, place the name of the columns to use after the table name. The values you supply must match the order declared in this column list.

Say you want to create an entry for a new customer, but that customer has only supplied a name and address, without specifying a phone number or country. The command now looks like this:

```
INSERT INTO customer (name, address) VALUES
  ('Justin Couch', '555 Mystreet Ave')
```

You don't need to follow the same order in the command's column as the table columns are declared when you created the table. You can re-order the column declarations in whatever way suits you. Any unspecified columns will have whatever default value is described. Automatic increment values have the next one assigned, default values are set if declared, otherwise the value is left as `NULL`. However, you must be careful with this form. Some columns are declared `NOT NULL`. If you insert a new row without giving these columns values, then the database will generate an error.

Updating an existing entry

Updating an existing entry in the database is a common task. To perform an update, you need to nominate a table, the new values to be used, and some way of defining the row or rows to be updated.

Consider the following example. A customer comes along and wants to change his or her address. The customer has given you a name:

```
UPDATE customer SET address='10 new st'
  WHERE name='Justin Couch'
```

This command says to update the customer table and look for rows that contain the column that has the value "Justin Couch." When you find one, set the address to this new value. That matches all rows that have the same name.

On a large database, chances are that there will be more than one person with a given name. (This is why we never used the customer's name as the unique key in the table.) In order to make sure you only update the right row, you should make sure the user supplies you with a customer ID rather than a name.

You do not always need to include the `WHERE` statement. For example, if you want to have a sale on all products and take 20 percent off everything, you can use the following statement:

```
UPDATE product SET price=price*0.8
```

This sets the price on every item in the Product table to 80 percent of its original value.

To change more than one value, create a comma-separated list of columns and their values after the SET keyword. Changing my name and address modifies the command to the following:

```
UPDATE customer SET address='10 new st', name='Something New'
  WHERE customer_id=1034532
```

Deleting entries

Over time, customers and products come and go. If you didn't do maintenance on your database, then the data would grow enormous. As in any good system, over time you want to trim out any dead information. Customers who have disappeared should be deleted.

Deleting data serves two purposes. First, it keeps down the amount of disk space required. Every piece of data must be stored to disk so that if you shut the database down it can start again with all the right information. Second, it makes your searches quicker. With fewer items in the table, there are fewer possibilities to check. It also means that you can store more of that table in memory rather than on disk, which speeds up your searches.

Deleting a record means starting with the DELETE FROM keywords and the name of the table. Then you specify a set of criteria about what you want to delete using a WHERE clause, just as you do when making an update. Say your store has decided to stop selling books, and that you want to delete all the books from the database. To do this, you issue the following command:

```
DELETE FROM product WHERE category='book'
```

If you don't specify the WHERE part of the command, it will automatically delete the entire contents of the specified table.

Searching for Information

Having a database full of data and then not using it is a waste! Why store all that data in the first place? The purpose of the database is to help you look up information, so searching is the next command we want to introduce.

Searching a database for information is one of the most important tasks you can do. Because you might want to search for so many different things, it is also one of the most complex. Searches can be as simple or complex as your application requires.

Creating simple searches

A simple search looks in one table and returns a collection of information. Generally, it uses a single condition to nominate the data it is looking for and returns one or two answers.

Asking for everything

The first and most simple form of search is just to ask for everything in a table. A search request always starts with the `SELECT` command. Follow this with a list of what you want to get as an answer and then the table you want to search in. To list all the contents of the table, such as all the products, you use the wildcard character (*) for the contents. For example:

```
SELECT * FROM product
```

This returns every entry in the product table. This is a useful search if you want to put a list of available options on a Web page or screen somewhere, but it is not particularly useful if you list every one of your million-plus users.

Filtering for specific columns

Say you don't want to see all the product information. When you are generating a Web page, you really want to enter just the product name and category. In order to know what product the user selected, you also use the product's ID in a hidden field. To do this, change the selection criteria to nominate the list of columns that you want returned from the query.

Select the columns to be returned by exchanging the wildcard selection criteria for a parenthetical, comma-delimited list of the column names. The order in which the columns are listed will be the order in which you get information back, rather than the order declared in the table:

```
SELECT (product_id, category, name) FROM product
```

Your query will now return only these pieces of information. It will still list every single row in the table, but this time with the unwanted data already filtered out.

Filtering for specific rows

Your store is really huge with lots of different departments. When creating a page of products, you really don't want to give the user all 10,000 products in the database. This number of products needs to be filtered down to just the products in the user's area of interest.

One way of filtering the data is to get everything and then do your own filtering in the Java code. This is a waste when you can just tell the database to do everything for you. Doing this requires the use of row-level selection.

In previous sections you saw the use of the WHERE statement. You can make use of it here with SELECT to by specifying the rows that you want. Say you want to display all the books in the product list. This requires the following search:

```
SELECT * FROM product WHERE category='book'
```

Like the first search, this one returns all the columns for those books. You can also combine the per-column filtering of text with per-row filtering to generate a list of book names and IDs:

```
SELECT (product_id, name) FROM product
    WHERE category='book'
```

Sorting the output

You can also order the output according to specific rules. This means using the database to sort the output according to a certain rule, and might be something simple such as alphabetically sorting the book names. You perform sorting by adding keywords to the end of the SELECT statement after the WHERE and then listing the conditions to sort with.

You might want to group outputs if you want to list all the products while keeping all the products in the same category together. This is useful for your end-processing code (say the return result from a JDBC query execution), and makes life simpler because you always know that everything of the same type will be located together rather than randomly distributed. Grouping requires the GROUP BY keywords. To build a sorted product list by category, use the following command:

```
SELECT * FROM product GROUP BY category
```

Applying a more specific ordering to the output is the job of the ORDER BY keywords. Like GROUP BY, they take a list of conditions to apply to the output. This time the output is more rigorous in checking the values — for example, the alphabetical sorting of customer names:

```
SELECT (name, address) FROM Customer ORDER BY name
```

You can use ordering to apply to more than one column. Say you want to list all the products in a given category and then order them by name within each group:

```
SELECT * FROM product ORDER BY group,name
```

The output results in the product category being sorted alphabetically and then, within each product category, with the rows being sorted in alphabetical order by name.

A distinction exists between ordering and grouping. Grouping puts like-minded ideas together sequentially, but the order in which you will encounter these groups is not specified. So, even though you may order the results by their product category, you cannot guarantee that the category names will be sorted alphabetically. If you require that level of sorting, then you should use the `ORDER BY` request instead.

Sorting commands are appended to any `SELECT` statement, so you can combine all the preceding examples to produce the output you want:

```
SELECT (product_id, name, category) FROM product
  WHERE in_stock > 0
  GROUP BY category
```

Facilitating complex interactions

For some environments, you want to have much more complex queries that involve more than just the values of one table. A typical query might be "find me all the book orders that are currently pending and give me the names of those books." This would require retrieving information from more than one table, collating it, and sending the value back to the caller.

Joining two tables together for a single result

When you combine the results of two table searches, it is called a *join*. Many forms of joins are available in SQL, enabling you to organize the result in many different ways. You can return the entire contents of two tables at once, match a single row with values in another table, or return only common columns among two or more tables. Although we speak of two tables here, you can generalize these actions to as many tables as you want (and your database supports!).

You join two or more tables using the normal `SELECT` command. Most of the time you will need to use the `JOIN` keyword in place of the `WHERE` section, although even that is optional!

Say you want to merge the results of two tables. In the following example you get all the orders and the products they refer to as a single return result.

```
SELECT * FROM Order,Product WHERE
Order.product_id=product.product_id
```

As you can see, this looks almost like a normal simple `SELECT`t. The result gives you all the values as a list of all the columns for both tables. The rows are returned with the first declared table and then the second declared table. If you want to reverse the order, you can use the `JOIN` keyword:

```
SELECT * FROM order RIGHT JOIN product
  ON Order.product_id=product.product_id
```

This will place the columns from the Product table before the columns from the Order table in the returned result.

Adding an extra table means using an extra `JOIN` statement. So if you want the result to include the product information, order information, and customer information columns, in that order, you use the following code:

```
SELECT * FROM order RIGHT JOIN product
    ON order.product_id=product.product_id
    LEFT JOIN customer ON
     order.customer_id=customer.customer_id
```

If the order of returned values is not important, you can use the following simpler query:

```
SELECT * FROM order,product,customer
  WHERE order.product_id=product.product_id
    AND order.customer_id=customer.customer_id
```

Listing all the orders is possibly not what you want to do. The next example filters the rows for only the results that you want. You would use it for the order example we've just mentioned — listing all the orders pending and the names of the books. To do this you want to check (assuming the status value 1 means order pending processing):

```
SELECT * FROM order,product,customer
  WHERE order.product_id=product.product_id
    AND order.customer_id=customer.customer_id
    AND order.status=1
```

You can further restrict the result by adding more conditions onto the end of the `WHERE` declaration. Note that these are standard Boolean-type conditions, so you can use `OR`, `AND`, and `NOT`, just as you would in Java programming. Think of it as a big `if` statement in Java, and you can't go too wrong.

Chaining selection requests together

Joining tables together may not produce the output that you really want. An alternative to `JOIN`s is called sub-selects or sub-queries. These use nested `SELECT` commands to feed the result from one query into another; the intermediate results are never seen by the caller.

Sub-selections are used principally when you are looking for an unknown or partially known quantity as the search criterion for a larger search. Say you want to look for all orders pending for a particular customer. JOINs won't work in this situation because you only need the partial value from the customer table of the customer ID that is then used to find the rows in the order table. You might use this sort of query in a call–center–type application wherein someone calls up and gives you a name but can't remember his or her customer ID.

Sub-selects are indicated by the use of the IN keyword in the WHERE section. Following this, you then list another full SELECT request, enclosed in a set of round brackets. The query "find all orders for Justin Couch" is expressed as follows:

```
SELECT * FROM Order WHERE customer_id IN
  (SELECT id FROM Customer WHERE name="Justin Couch")
```

In this selection, the query in the brackets is executed first. This query finds the customer ID for my name and stores it in a temporary value. The main query is then performed, and it matches the customer_id in the order table with the list of return values from the sub-select.

A difference exists between sub-selections and sub-queries. Sub-selections do not allow UPDATE or ORDER BY in their results. As this implies, you can use the sub-request format outlined here to issue commands other than just SELECT. Many people use the terms interchangeably, but you should understand that there is a technical difference in their capabilities.

A final refinement of the query is to filter out only the pending orders. Just as you did in earlier examples, here you can use AND to build a larger condition:

```
SELECT * FROM Order WHERE customer_id IN
  (SELECT id FROM Customer WHERE name="Justin Couch")
  AND status=1
```

As in the example before it, in this example the sub-select is executed first, and the results from it along with the check for the value in the status column are used to generate the result.

Summary

This concludes our introduction to SQL. SQL is a huge language with as many variations as there are database vendors. All of them will support the core ANSI standard that we've described in this chapter.

We have only just scratched the surface of what is available within SQL. For complex systems, we highly recommend that you have a database expert help you build the most efficient set of queries. However, this chapter is enough to enable you to work on small to mid-scale applications, and to help you understand what your DBA is providing if you have a larger one.

To recap what we've covered in this chapter:

- An introduction to SQL.
- Instructions for creating the major data structures in a database with tables and indices.
- Managing data in the table to insert, update, and delete entries in tables.
- Searching the database for information with simple and complex requests.

✦ ✦ ✦

CHAPTER 7

Using JDBC to Interact with SQL Databases

✦ ✦ ✦ ✦

In This Chapter

Communicating with SQL databases using JDBC

Establishing and maintaining connections to arbitrary databases

Mapping SQL datatypes to Java datatypes

Making queries of a database

Using the optimization capabilities of JDBC for faster queries

✦ ✦ ✦ ✦

In the previous chapter, we introduced SQL for querying relational databases. While a useful language, it is not much good unless it can interact with some other form of application. You need an awful lot of monkeys making queries at a console prompt to run that million-user Web site! To make it really useful, you need to combine it with some other API to allow applications to make requests of the database and process the results into something meaningful. In Java, the standardized API for doing this is the Java DataBase Connectivity API, or JDBC for short.

The precursor book to this book, the *Java 2 Bible* (Hungry Minds, 2000), also includes an introductory chapter on JDBC. That chapter is aimed at the beginning programmer. This chapter does not use the same material; here we prefer to introduce concepts more likely to be needed by the advanced and enterprise programmer. We also cover some of the more elementary steps, so feel free to skip those sections if you feel you already know the basics.

Java Abstractions of a Database

Despite what the language advocates may tell you, no one programming language will solve all the world's problems. Some are better at one form of task than others, so it makes sense to try to combine their strengths. In this way, you can get the best of both worlds.

A bit of history about the introduction of JDBC

Even back in the early days of JDK 1.0 there was a huge interest in having Java talk to a database. Various discussions ran around the Internet newsgroups about the best way of bringing this about: Should we use Java's `Socket` classes and write all the low-level interfaces ourselves? Should we try to build a Java wrapper around existing proprietary native interfaces? Was there some other way? Heated discussions raged across newsgroups and mailing lists. Native code wrappers were ruled out because this was before the existence of the standardized Java Native Interface (JNI). Socket programming was OK, but Java 1.0 sockets were fairly limited compared to their current incarnation. Many people wanted to make use of the highly optimized native interfaces, provided by the database vendors, that used proprietary, closed protocols. In general, the situation was not a happy one for the end-user programmer.

On the other side of the fence, the database companies realized that there was some demand for this abstracted view of a database, and, corralled into a working group by Sun, set about building a standardized interface between Java and databases that we now know as JDBC. Intended to maximize the strength of the existing SQL capabilities, the new specification provided a way to connect to a database, issue standard SQL queries, and present the results in a Java-centric way. We should also mention that this working group was very heavily influenced by the Open DataBase Connectivity (ODBC) standard for abstracting database interfaces. In fact, the first version of JDBC almost looked like a direct copy of the then-current ODBC standard. JDBC has since diverged from ODBC, but its core concepts remain almost identical, and the two standards remain interoperable thanks to JDBC-ODBC bridges.

The JDBC specification talks about data sources, rather than databases. It tries to allow data to come from a source other than your traditional database application like Oracle. For example, the old-style flat file is just as valid a representation of JDBC data storage as the database application. During this chapter, we will use the term *database* to mean that you can use any form of data storage, even though JDBC is rarely used with anything other than a relational database.

Hiding the implementation

One of the key successes to JDBC acceptance is the way it provides a layered structure for different levels of implementations to be provided. Many of the lessons learned in the work done on JDBC have been carried over into many other Java APIs. Although many of the techniques were originally introduced in the JDK 1.0 release, the JDBC work really brought these concepts to the fore and made them a central part of the specification.

Early on in the process, it was recognized that database vendors wanted to provide functionality at different levels. Also, a key point was that it was unlikely that every known database vendor would be able to or permitted to supply its code to the standard JDK download from Sun's Web site. Work by the specification team then proceeded to build a layered specification wherein the user code did not need to import any specific library (the same code running on different machines was able to talk to two completely different databases), but could still use objects just as if they had come directly from the database.

Factories for managing abstract definitions

For the first part of the flexibility requirements, the JDBC API divided the code into three separate areas:

1. Interfaces that user code needed to interact with the database.
2. Some form of factory-management code to handle all the different database types.
3. A standard set of interfaces that database vendors would have to implement in order to provide a JDBC interface.

The core to fulfill this flexibility was that the library needed to provide some form of mapping between the vendor-specific code and the abstract representation needed by the user-land code. Taking a lead from the then-emerging design patterns craze, a global driver-manager system was established (designers call this a Factory pattern). This pattern allows a driver to be registered with the system without having to know or import the libraries for a specific implementation. For example, a text string representing the name of the driver class file is good enough to describe the driver to use.

Once the driver name was established, it was then a simple matter to ask the global manager for a connection to "the database" and receive an abstract representation of the connection. Once you have the connection representation, all the rest of the classes that your user code deals with are also abstract without your knowing the real implementation classes.

Different driver types

Realizing that at the time not all developers, or even database vendors, were sold on the Java language, the specification enabled the vendors to provide different types of drivers. These could range from 100% pure Java to a thin wrapper over an existing library, or, in the case of ODBC, a bridge to a completely different database-interface API altogether.

As the factory concept gained greater popularity, it was possible to provide different levels of drivers even for the same database product. Users could choose which one they preferred for the given application, and even among different implementations for the same database from third-party sources. For example, if the Java code is running on the same machine as the database, a thin wrapper over the native shared memory libraries is much faster than the 100% Pure Java version that uses sockets. Yet if the applications are on separate machines, a shared memory driver will not work, and so network-aware drivers are more appropriate.

Standard APIs for driver implementers

An important factor in getting the database vendors to sign up was the internal API used to provide a consistent interface. The JDBC team did a lot of the hard work, ensuring that the top-level behavior would remain consistent so long as the minimal requirements of the internal API scheme were maintained.

This public API meant that all forms of third-party writers could build their own drivers if they wished. As a result, it helped speed the adoption of Java as hackers everywhere went to town creating drivers for every database known to man. No longer were they required to wait for the vendor to release the next version of its product in another 12 months' time when they could build it themselves and put it within a standard API for everyone to use.

Since then almost all important APIs, and in particular the enterprise APIs, have included this dual level of public APIs available to be implemented. The infrastructure has become known as the Service Provider Interface (SPI). If you look through the Javadoc for the J2EE libraries, you will notice that they all have a `.spi` package or packages. These are the internal, public interfaces that a driver manager must implement.

With the release of J2EE 1.3, the APIs are now starting to move away from the service-provider model. The Java Connector Architecture, which promises an even more abstract way of defining and locating driver implementations for the various APIs, is starting to take its place. Don't expect this to change the system overnight, but it is a big move within the enterprise space.

Getting Started

Using JDBC requires a little bit of setup. The first and most important step is to decide whether your application is going to be a simple, standalone application or a more complex one requiring the enterprise features. JDBC exists on two levels — a simple level, which is derived from the original JDBC code, and an enterprise-capable level, which encompasses all of the newest capabilities added in JDBC.

This chapter is going to deal with both levels, because they share many capabilities. The biggest difference is how you initially establish the connection to the database and the classes you use to do that.

JDBC 2.0 capabilities are provided in the J2SE 1.3*x* and J2EE 1.2*x* specifications. The most recent JDBC 3.0 specification is in J2EE 1.3 and the upcoming J2SE 1.4 specification, sometimes known as Merlin. At the time of this writing, J2SE is still in beta.

If you downloaded the J2EE environment from Sun, or have an implementation from some middleware vendor already, then these environments will provide most of the requirements of this section. However, you still need to know where to find all the pieces and just what they all do — so read on...

Finding the JDBC classes

JDBC exists across two separate packages. The core of JDBC is provided in the package `java.sql`. For the enterprise-level application, an extension set of classes is provided in the `javax.sql` package. The extension package uses the classes and interfaces from the base package but provides a different way of accessing them.

Within the core package are the classes you need to drive a standard user-level application. Simple applications might be the desktop application that does not have very high load requirements on a database. You can have a lot of people connected, none of whom is requesting much information from the database. The distinguishing factor is that your application will not be running within any other sort of application-server environment. All the code is written and used locally within the application.

Designers of enterprise applications, such as middleware systems and Web sites, will want to use the features of the extension package. These sorts of applications will define a shell user interface and then connect to some form of application logic middleware that is already running. The JDBC features will be pre-loaded by the middleware software system rather than your code. In contrast to the core system, these interfaces do not provide a standard factory for creating and managing drivers, but do offer high-end features like network load-balancing and transaction capabilities.

Current and future Java releases

The current J2SE release is version 1.3. In it you will find the core package provided by JDBC 2.1. Although the extension packages were defined as part of JDBC 2.0, they were not included in the standard edition of the Java development environment. It was only in the enterprise edition of 1.2, you that you would find the extension classes of the `javax.sql` package.

With the release of JDBC 3.0 in mid-2001, these capabilities were slotted into the next release of both major API sets. J2EE 1.3 arrived before the next major release of J2SE and so became the first to use the newest features. J2SE 1.4, which was in beta during the time of this writing, will also include the full JDBC 3.0 feature set, including, for the first time, the extension APIs. This means that everything you read about in this chapter you should be able to do in all code that uses J2SE 1.4 or later.

Downloading classes

As we mentioned in the previous section, the JDBC API set is part of one of the two major standards. Because this book concentrates on the J2EE specification, we are going to assume that you have both the core and extension packages available for use, even if you are only writing a simple desktop application.

You can get the classes you need for JDBC in two ways: You can install it with the middleware software environment or download the reference implementation of J2EE from Sun. If you just want the JDBC code without the rest of the J2EE environment, you can get it by itself. However, we don't recommend this. As you will see throughout this chapter, you are going to need some of the other J2EE APIs anyway if you want to use more than the simplest features.

The reference implementation of J2EE can be found at `http://java.sun.com/j2ee/`.

For instructions on how to download and install Sun's reference implementation, please read Appendix A, "Installing the J2EE Reference Implementation."

Introducing JDBC drivers

In the introduction to this chapter, we talked about the way the JDBC implementation has been split into a number of layers. While your application code always uses the same standard public API, internally each database you connect to will have its own custom set of implementation classes. These are known as *drivers*. A driver can be implemented in many different ways. JDBC defines four categories of drivers that we will introduce in the following sections.

Type 1 drivers

Depending on your view of life, Type 1 drivers are either the simplest or hardest to implement. These drivers map the JDBC calls to those of another data-access API, such as ODBC, and are typically called bridge drivers. While this type of driver requires minimal new implementation, the calls from one API to the other must be mapped. The JDBC-ODBC bridge driver is the most common Type 1 driver.

Figure 7-1 illustrates the layers involved in the implementation. At the top is the Java code that performs the translation between Java and the local driver. Next is the local driver and what it implements, which may require either local direct connections or a network connection.

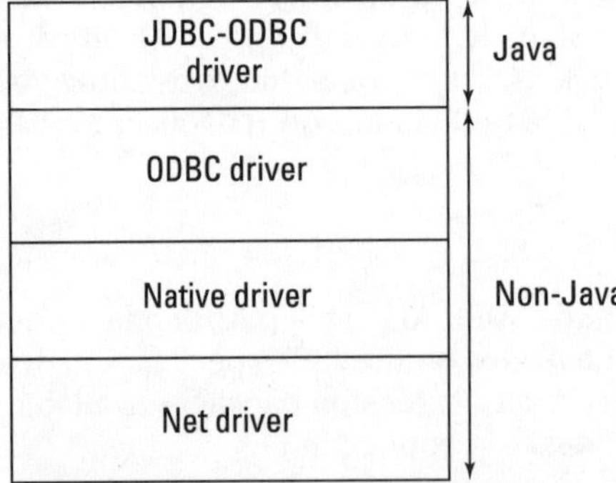

Figure 7-1: A typical layering of a Type 1 JDBC driver, as represented by the JDBC-ODBC bridge

Type 2 drivers

In our discussion of an earlier example, we mentioned the JDBC code using a driver that used shared memory segments to talk with a local database. As Java does not provide the concept of shared memory, this is an example of the JDBC calls being layered directly onto a native library specific for that database. Type 2 drivers distinguish themselves from Type 1 drivers by virtue of the fact that they use a native library specific to the data source they connect to. Type 1 drivers are written to another abstract API set that itself is agnostic of the data source connected to.

Figure 7-2 shows how the JDBC driver is a layer directly implemented over the native code driver on the system. Typically, this will mean using JNI to talk to the local libraries. The native driver may also use a network connection if the database is on a remote machine.

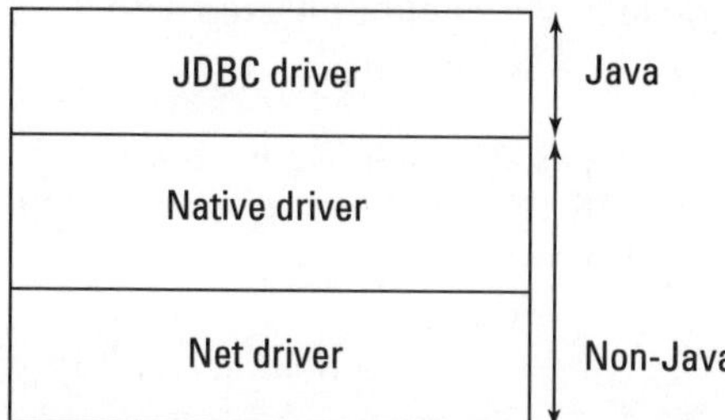

Figure 7-2: Type 2 drivers layer Java code directly over native code and sometimes use lower-level native drivers for shared memory or networking.

Type 3 drivers

For maximum flexibility Type 3 drivers are implemented completely in Java and use a database-independent networking protocol. The middleware server then acts as an intermediary by converting the independent protocol into a direct request onto the data source. You can use these drivers to talk to any database you like, because they are only dependent on the network protocol spoken between the driver and the middleware. The middleware, rather than JDBC, provides the abstraction between the database and your software.

Pure Java drivers, such as those represented in Figure 7-3, typically use the Java networking provided in the `java.net` package. They have two layers that represent the driver portion and the underlying protocol handler.

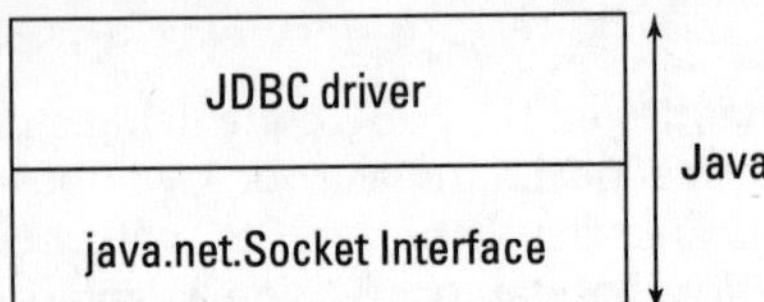

Figure 7-3: Database-independent, all Java drivers for Type 3 code usually layer over standard Java sockets.

Type 4 drivers

When you're looking for maximum speed over a network, Type 4 drivers are the best option. These are all Java drivers, but they talk the native protocol of the data source. Each driver is therefore dependent on the data source being used. They are fully portable among platforms, but an Oracle driver cannot be used with a SQLServer database.

Type 4 drivers usually end up with three layers, as shown in Figure 7-4. The driver uses a proprietary interface (usually supplied by the database vendor), which in turn is layered over the standard `java.net` drivers.

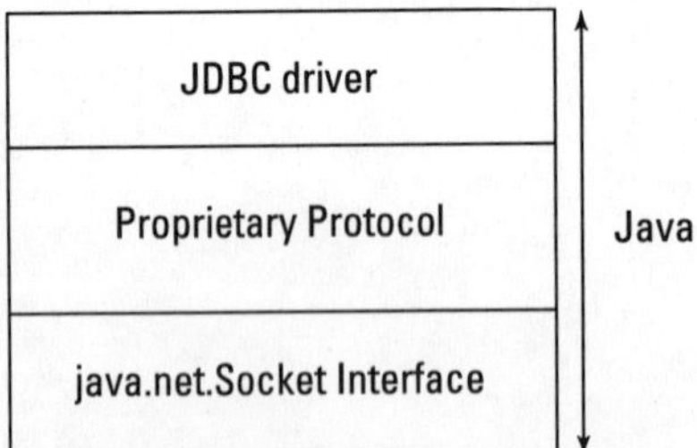

Figure 7-4: Type 4 drivers provide an interface between JDBC and the vendor's pure Java, but proprietary, API.

Finding drivers for your database

Drivers for data-source connection will be provided in a number of different ways, according to how you originally set up your environment. A number of sources of drivers exist:

✦ J2SE users will not have any standard drivers installed. You can get these standard drivers either online or from a database vendor.

✦ Application middleware implementations supply their own large collection of drivers for the most popular databases. Chances are that the database you are using will have the drivers already available for you.

✦ Database vendors include drivers on their software downloads or CDs. These are usually out-of-date, so you should try their Web sites for updates.

✦ Sun maintains a registry of known drivers at `http://industry.java.sun.com/products/jdbc/drivers`. You can search these by database vendor, driver type, and more.

Connecting to a Database

The connection process varies widely according to your application requirements. Not only are two sets of classes used, but even the method of finding and creating the basic drivers changes. Once you have established the connection, the common capabilities are available and usable within either environment.

Representing a single database connection

Before we get into how to load a database driver and establish a connection, we need to take a step back and see what the end goal is. The end goal is the representation of a single connection to the database that enables you to directly issue commands to the database and have results returned.

A single database connection is represented by the `Connection` interface and is found in the core package. Regardless of how you connect to the underlying database, this will be the end product. The `Connection` interface is the core of the JDBC API. Almost everything during the normal working life of a set of queries is performed through this interface. For this reason we won't introduce all of the methods of this class now as they will be introduced in a more coherent fashion later.

Understanding the lifespan of a connection

Let's assume that somehow you have been handed an instance of the `Connection` object. What can you do with it?

At the point that you fetch this instance, it is considered a live connection. A database driver cannot hand you a connection that does not already have an open link to the database. As soon as you have this connection, you can start making queries to the database and queries about the database. You can continue to make queries until you either have an error or deliberately close the connection.

Closing a connection is as simple as calling the `close()` method. Once you have called this method, the underlying implementation frees all its resources. Any subsequent calls to this connection will result in an `SQLException` being thrown. After you close your connection, there is nothing else for you to do—you are free to release the reference, because the connection does not have to be returned to the driver that created it.

Although JDBC specifies that the implementation should release the resources when the connection is garbage-collected, it is good practice to explicitly call the `close()` method. In this way, you make it known that you have really released the resources. Sometimes you think that the garbage collector has cleaned things up, while in reality dangling references in your code are keeping the connection information around. This can lead to difficult-to-detect problems down the track—particularly in applications that run for hours or days.

If at some stage during the life of your code you suspect that the connection has been closed on you, you can check with the `isClosed()` method. A closed connection will return `true` for this call.

Dealing with errors

Sometimes errors occur during calls to the database. These might be as simple as the network connection disappearing, or as complex as the returned data being too big for the available capabilities.

More immediate errors, such as the network connection dropping, will be indicated by a direct exception. For example, if your code is waiting to create a new request and the network fails, the method will throw an `SQLException`. These errors are serious.

Exceptions generate a number of values that will help in your debugging. For a start, there is the standard message that all exceptions may have. To complement the warning are an error code and the type of SQL standard being used. The error code is always vendor-specific, so you will need to have your database documentation handy if you want to look it up in detail. The state information tells you what version of the SQL standard this connection believes it is using. This is important if you pass SQL99 syntax or commands to a database that only accepts SQL92. You can use this extra information to determine why your perfectly valid SQL request has died unexpectedly.

An interesting feature of all SQL errors is that they can be chained together. What looks like one error might actually be four or five grouped together. For example, the request to insert data into two columns might generate two errors—one for each column—if the datatypes don't match.

Given all this information, a fairly typical reaction to an error being thrown is to use the following code:

```
} catch(SQLException se) {
  System.err.println("Error during SQL command");
  do {
    System.err.println("JDBC SQL Error: " + se.getMessage());
    System.err.println("Vendor code: " + se.getErrorCode());
    System.err.println("SQL State:   " + se.getSQLState());
  } while((se = se.getNextException()) != null);
  System.err.println("No more errors for this request");
}
```

Non-serious errors will not throw an exception. Instead, they will register a warning with the connection that you will have to look for. An example of a non-serious error is the data returned from a query being only a part of the information that was supposed to be returned. In this case, you got some data, just not all that you should have, and so a warning is issued.

You have access to warnings that have been issued through the `getWarnings()` method. The return value is an `SQLWarning` instance, which is a derived class of the `SQLException`. This means that all the data, including nested warnings, will be available.

Just like exceptions chain, warnings will too. This means that you will get a large list of them as they accumulate. If you want to clear out that list after each check, then you will need to call `clearWarnings()`. If you don't clear the list after looking at the warnings, any further warnings will be appended to the current list rather than replacing it.

Finding information about a connection

Applications typically need to know something about the underlying data source. For example, an application might want to know what character the SQL string needs in order to quote a string identifier, the version of JDBC that you have installed, or even the maximum number of open connections available. All this information and much, much more is available in the `DatabaseMetaData` instance returned by the `getMetaData()` method of the connection.

The `DatabaseMetaData` interface has approximately 150 methods in the JDBC 3.0 incarnation. We're not going to try to cover them all here! Many of the methods available in this interface are useful if you want to produce an editor or a monitoring tool for the JDBC environment. For example, you can ask for the list of SQL keywords that are supported, but not part of the SQL92 specification. These keywords are not particularly useful for a runtime-type application, but are good application server–monitoring tool.

Connecting using the core classes

Traditionally, code has used the core classes to establish the database connection. These core classes provide a set of self-registering and managing drivers that give you access to multiple databases at once. Each driver instance is represented by an instance of the `Driver` interface.

Loading the driver

The way the core code works with drivers is quite interesting. Instead of you creating driver instances and registering them with a manager, the drivers work according to a kind of self-registration mechanism.

Core drivers are stored in the DriverManager class. A requirement of the JDBC drivers is that they must self-register with the driver manager when they are first created. In this way, you can create and register a driver without ever needing to know the instance. The JDBC spec specifies that all compliant drivers must have a static constructor. Within this constructor, the driver is required to register itself with the manager as shown in the following example:

```
public class MyJdbcDriver implements Driver {
  static {
    DriverManager.registerDriver(new MyJdbcDriver());
  }
  ...
}
```

Now, this code might seem a little odd — the static initializer creating a new instance of itself after it has already been created as an instance. In fact it is not. If you remember your low-level Java handling, you'll remember that the static method is required to be called when the class is first loaded by the VM, not when the first instance is called. This allows the Class.forName() method to be used to register the driver. So in your application code you can use the following piece of code to load and register a driver without ever knowing what the class name actually is:

```
String class_name = System.getProperty("my_jdbc_driver");
Class.forName(class_name);
```

Your application code never knows what driver to use. The driver might be specified on a command line using the -D option or in a property file. The preceding piece of code makes sure that that class is loaded and registered with the driver manager, so you can now create connections to the database as needed.

If you want to have drivers self-register, you can supply a property called jdbc.drivers on the command line. This is a comma-separated list of fully qualified class names. When you query for a connection, this list is automatically checked for a conforming driver.

Requesting a connection instance

Once the drivers are loaded into the driver manager, you use them by making a connection. Apart from loading the driver, you never directly interact with them. All of your work from now on is done through the DriverManager class to obtain connections to the database.

Drivers within the core classes represent each connection as a real connection to the database. Each time you request a connection the driver must request a new internal connection to the database before returning the object to you. This process requires finding the correct driver for your request, asking the driver to establish a connection, and then dealing with any other security issues before returning the completed object to you.

You obtain a connection through one of the `getConnection()` methods of `DriverManager`. In all of these you have to supply a URL string and possibly other information. These URLs are not your standard `http://` addresses, but use a JDBC-specific form:

```
jdbc:<subprotocol>:<protocol specific name>
```

The *`subprotocol`* part is where you name the driver type or class. These vary for each driver implemented, and you need to read your driver documentation to know what to ask for. You are likely to see two common forms:

```
jdbc:mydriver://www.mydomain.com:8192/my_database
jdbc:odbc:test_db;UID=javauser;PWD=password
```

In the first form, you nominate driver `mydriver`, which then requires a name that is the host, the port, and the name of the database to use. This form is fairly common with most databases. The second form is for the ODBC bridge driver. Here you start with the `odbc` subprotocol, nominate the database name to use, and finally provide a semicolon-separated list of attribute name-value pairs — in this case, user name and password.

Name and password information usually should not be part of the connection string. As with any form of enterprise application, security considerations should be taken very seriously. The ideal method is to use an alternate connection method that passes the name and password as separate parameters or in a property list and obtains the information from a separate, trusted, secure source.

With the URL string created, you need to ask for the `Connection` instance. This is a simple one-line call:

```
String url =
  "jdbc:mydriver://www.mydomain.com:8192/my_database";
Connection conn = DriverManager.getConnection(url);
```

As with all JDBC calls, you will also need to catch the `SQLException` that may be thrown. You will get this exception if the connection cannot be established (network down), the named database doesn't exist, or some authentication information is wrong (for example, if you didn't supply a user name and password if they were needed). In the versions that supply a list of properties, you might also generate warnings about invalid property values. Although the connection is still made, check the warnings generated by calling the `getWarnings()` method on the connection.

With the connection object in hand, you are now ready to make queries on the database.

Connecting using the enterprise classes

When you are operating in an enterprise environment, JDBC encourages you to use a completely different approach. Instead of the self-registering driver and manager approach provided by the core classes, this approach uses a third-party system of registration. All of the major parts of the J2EE specification recommend using Java Naming and Directory Interface (JNDI) as the storage and lookup mechanism.

The installation process requires the use of the JNDI classes. If you want to read more about JNDI before continuing with this chapter, we recommend the LDAP primer in Chapter 8, "Working with Directory Services and LDAP" and an introduction to JNDI in Chapter 9, "Accessing Directory Services with JNDI."

Loading the driver

Enterprise drivers are represented by the interface `javax.sql.DataSource`. Unlike the core classes, enterprise drivers have no manager to load them in. There is also no need for you to go through an explicit registration step the way the core drivers did. When you are operating in the enterprise environment, it is assumed that the environment has already loaded and registered all the drivers you are going to need before your application starts. If you have downloaded a third-party driver, you will need to go to the management console or configuration files of your middleware system to register the new code.

Compared to the core `Driver`, `DataSource` offers fewer options for a database connection. Where there were four options for the core classes, you now only have two — a default and one that supplies a user name and password. You don't need to provide a URL when requesting the actual connection: This is because the assumptions are quite different within the enterprise setting. Drivers here assume that you are going to connect to a particular database, and all the information is specified in the properties that are used to register the data source in the first place. Changing the database requires the use of that middleware's management tool.

Requesting a data source still requires you to name which one you want. The name is represented as a string that always starts with `jdbc/`. Following this is the name you have assigned to the data source in the middleware-management tool. For example, if you have loaded an Oracle driver, you might use the name `jdbc/Oracle`. If your middleware is using two different databases, then you might use names such as `jdbc/oracle_payments` and `jdbc/oracle_staff`. These names can be whatever you want, so you could instead specify, say, the names `jdbc/oracle/payments` and `jdbc/oracle/staff`.

Once you have settled on a name for your driver, you might actually want to use it! To do this, you make use of the JNDI naming classes to name, locate, and then load a driver. JNDI, as you will read in later chapters, provides a directory-type view of resources. Just as your computer's file system name starts with / or `c:\` before you find the lower-level directories, you will need to provide a top-level area for the drivers. This area is represented by the `InitialContext` class that is part of the `javax.naming` package:

```
InitialContext ctx = new InitialContent();
```

With the root of your context information established, you need to provide the "path" to your driver. The path is the name that you chose earlier. When you provide the path, you ask the context to search it and find the object that it represents. In directory services–speak, this is called a *lookup* (you might be already familiar with the term from RMI's `rmiregistry`, which is a form of directory service). Fetching your `DataSource` instance is performed with the following call:

```
DataSource ds = (DataSource)ctx.lookup("jdbc/Oracle");
```

And that's all there is to it. You now have a live data source to ask for connections to the database with. Requesting a new connection through the `getConnection()` methods, as follows:

```
Connection simple_conn = ds.getConnection();
Connection passwd_conn =
  ds.getConnection("javauser", "password");
```

Of course, remember to catch the `SQLExceptions` and check for warnings as well.

Registering a Driver with the System

Registering a driver with JNDI requires knowing a lot about the implementing classes. Each time you register a driver you will need to supply a lot of extra information, such as the host name of the database, the port number, which virtual database to access, and so on. The core `DataSource` interface (and the ones you will encounter shortly) does not provide methods for setting this information, so you need to access the methods provided by the implementing class.

For example, when you want to load a Type 3 driver, you want to supply a host and port:

```
VendorDataSource vds = new VendorDataSource();
vds.setServerName("host.mybiz.com");
vds.setServerPort("1675");
```

Once all the properties have been set, you will need to register this instance with JNDI. Unlike the core-driver implementations, `DataSource` implementations do not magically register themselves with JNDI.

Registering a driver with JNDI requires creating an initial context just as you did before. With this context, you then need to bind your driver instance to a name—the same name that you use to fetch the instance from! Binding here is just like binding RMI objects to the RMIRegistry. Take a name and an instance object and tell the "system" about it:

```
IntialContext ctx = new InitialContext();
Ctx.bind("jdbc/MyDataSource", vds);
```

That is all there is to registering an enterprise driver. However, as we have mentioned before, you will rarely need to do this in your application code. Registering an enterprise driver is typically the role of your middleware provider and its administration tools.

Using resources efficiently with connection pooling

There are two major requirements for enterprise-application developers when building systems: speed, and keeping resource usage in check. Each time a connection is made, a whole heap of low-level network shuffling back and forth is done. This takes time, even when the database is located on the same machine as the middleware (a very unlikely scenario in any medium to large enterprise application!). Also, for every new connection, there is a lot of garbage. Have 10 or 12 small applications all creating and destroying connections at once, and the resource usage becomes astronomical. Your applications spend more time collecting garbage and connecting to the database than doing anything useful.

The standard solution to this problem is called *connection pooling*. It creates a set number of predefined open connections. When an application needs a new connection, the driver dips into this pool, finds an available connection, and returns it to the caller. Fetch times are instantaneous because there are no low-level connections to establish, and because you are using previously created resources, there are no garbage-collection costs either.

In all the approaches seen so far, none of the connections you've worked with have used any pooling. Each time you asked for a connection, a new live connection was established. If you wanted to use connection-pooling techniques, you had to write your own. The JDBC extension package provides a nice simple way to avoid all this hassle by providing drivers that do all this work for you.

To use connection-pooling techniques in JDBC, you change the class being loaded. Where you used the `DataSource` interface before, you now have the `ConnectionPoolDataSource` interface. However, at your code level you still use the `DataSource` interface. The JDBC driver and the management system provided by the middleware vendor hides all of these details from you. Your code to fetch a connection pooled-capable JDBC connection looks exactly the same:

```
DataSource ds =
  (DataSource)ctx.lookup("jdbc/cp/Oracle");
```

The `ConnectionPoolDataSource` interface does not extend the `DataSource` interface. It is completely separate. While a driver implementation may implement both classes, it is not required. Ideally your middleware software will define two separate paths for the pooled and non-pooled sources through the JNDI names.

Once you have the data source, you again need to obtain the connection in the same way as for the simple connection.

```
DataSource ds =
  (DataSource)ctx.lookup("jdbc/cp/Oracle");
Connection conn = ds.getConnection();
```

Using a pooled connection is just like using a normal connection. The instance of `Connection` takes care of all the underlying resources. To release a connection back into the global pool, you call the `close()` method on the `Connection` object, just as you would for any other form. When you call this method, the connection is locally closed, and all the resources are returned to the pool for other users. Shutting down the real connection to the database is the job of the `close()` method in `PooledConnection`, which you never see as it is handled by the middleware.

Using a transaction-aware driver

On the top rung of database connection types are those that are transaction-aware. Transactions enable you to place a collection of different updates into a queue and then have them all executed at once. Thus, if something fails halfway through an operation, you can roll back to the previous point where everything was OK (called save or commit points). When you are dealing with large-scale changes over a number of different data sources (not just databases), you'll need this feature.

Transaction-aware drivers are represented by the `XADataSource` interface. Just as the `PooledConnectionDataSource` has no relation to `DataSource`, neither does `XADataSource`. Still, the fetch routine is the same as for any other JDBC connection:

```
DataSource ds = (DataSource)ctx.lookup("jdbc/xa/Oracle");
```

To obtain a connection from here, you use exactly the same code as before

```
DataSource ds = (DataSource)ctx.lookup("jdbc/xa/Oracle");
Connection conn = ds.getConnection();
```

The new interface only adds one more method: `getXAResource()`. The returned interface of this method is a `XAResource` from the Java Transaction API (JTA). If you're working with raw database connections, this method is not really of use to you. However, if you're working with transaction processing, particularly in the EJB environment, this is of great importance: It is how the underlying middleware synchronizes calls across multiple data sources.

Database Data Structures

Once you have established a connection, you will want to use it to query the database, make updates, and do whatever else your application needs the database for. In Table 7-1 in the previous chapter, we introduced the set of standard datatypes provided by SQL. After making a query, you have to turn both the query results and the low-level data back into something that Java can manipulate.

Mapping SQL types to Java types

In general, the SQL datatypes for the primitives map quite easily to the Java types. Primitives in both languages map easily and have corresponding lengths. An integer that is four bytes in SQL is a four bytes `int` in Java, and so forth.

Although most types match between the two languages, there is sometimes a slight discrepancy that is too much to accommodate in the standard classes. To cope with this problem, the JDBC packages have added or extended some of the standard types, as outlined in Table 7-1. This table takes the same information that you saw in Table 7-1 and extends it to include the exact Java-type mapping. Notice that where possible, the type mapping has been to Java primitive types rather than to classes representing the type information.

Table 7-1
Mapping of SQL types to Java types

SQL Type	*Java Type*
BOOLEAN	Boolean
SMALLINT	Short
INTEGER	int
BIGINT	long
REAL	float
DOUBLE	double
DECIMAL	java.math.BigDecimal
NUMERIC	java.math.BigDecimal
CHAR	char
VARCHAR	java.lang.String
DATE	java.sql.Date
TIMESTAMP	java.sql.Timestamp
DATETIME	java.sql.Time
BLOB	java.sql.Blob

Table 7-1 contains the most frequently used SQL types. For a complete list of all SQL types and their mapping to Java, see Table B-1 of the JDBC 3.0 specification in Appendix B.

Representing the returned information of a query

Your first point of contact with the database information is the values returned from a query, which are generally represented by the output of an SQL SELECT statement. Within the Java environment, you need to encapsulate the returned values so that you can work with them. The result is the ResultSet interface that is part of the core package.

For the purposes of the discussion in this section, we will assume that you have already made a query back and received an instance of this `ResultSet`. As the data that comes from the database can have many different forms, they can contain many different things.

Understanding how ResultSet works

A result in JDBC terms is a representation of a valid query on the database. All queries will return an instance here if there is no technical problem with the query. A technical problem might be something like the database connection dying or the SQL statement string being badly formatted. So even if no items match the query, you will get a `ResultSet` back.

When a result is returned to you from the database, the database has the option of constructing it in a number of ways:

- **A read-only** `ResultSet`: This enables you to read through all of the values from the first to last, and that is it. Once you reach the end, you cannot reread the values.
- **A scrollable** `ResultSet`: This enables you to move back and forth arbitrarily through the results. With it you can jump to any known row or just move back and forth through the current list.
- **An updateable** `ResultSet`: This form is a live representation of the underlying database that enables you to insert, update, and delete rows. This form must also be scrollable.

You can hint to the database during the query process that you would like a `ResultSet` of a certain form. The database may or may not honor your request. You will see more about this later in this chapter in the section "Querying the database for information."

To check on the type of `ResultSet` that you have been returned, you need to use the `getType()` and `getConcurrency()` methods. The `getType()` method returns one of three constants defined in the interface:

- `TYPE_FORWARD_ONLY`: The result set is the read-only version that enables you to move from the first to last result and read each row once.
- `TYPE_SCROLL_SENSITIVE`: When you or anyone else makes updates, the values are reflected in the row-position number here. The end result is that successive calls to `getRow()` for each row will not return a contiguous sequence.
- `TYPE_SCROLL_INSENSITIVE`: When others make changes to the underlying data source, they will not change the order of values you see in your return results.

For the concurrency information, you have the choice of two values:

✦ CONCUR_READ_ONLY: The result set you have is readable (and may be scrollable), but you cannot change the values it gives you. It is not updateable.

✦ CONCUR_UPDATABLE: The result may be changed in any way and may have the information reflected back in the database for other users.

Result sets differ from your normal database query such as the SQL prompt. What they represent is a view into the database of the result of the query. That is, once the query string has been processed and the database connection stays up, you can be returned an instance. What happens inside that instance is then dependent on the implementation. The database may not have even finished its processing by the time you get the class back. Thus, it is a live representation of the underlying data and can change with them. It does not force the JDBC implementation to hang around until all of the data has been processed and formed into the internal values before returning to the user.

In order to deal with the live nature of a result set, JDBC describes your movement through the data in terms of a cursor. The cursor moves up and down through the results. Where you place the cursor determines the values returned from a column.

When you are first given a result, set the cursor sits before the first result. Effectively the cursor is in an undefined position. In order to read the first result, you need to move it forward using the next() method. To move up and down the result, set you can use a combination of next() and previous(). Each of these returns a boolean indicating whether the operation moved the cursor to defined data. Thus, if a query returns no data whatsoever, the next() call will return a value of false immediately. A typical piece of code used to iterate through a list of results looks like this:

```
ResultSet rs = ....

while(rs.next()) {
  .....
}
```

Columns in the returned information match the order in which they are asked for. In the previous chapter, we talked about putting columns in a specific order within the select statement using a query of the form

```
SELECT (id, name, category) FROM Products
```

Within the ResultSet that would be returned from this query, the values for the columns would match this order. One crucial difference that you will need to remember is that column numbers start from the value 1, not the value 0 like an ordinary array. If the select statement uses a wildcard for the columns, then the ordering will match that of the table declaration.

Once you have finished processing the data, the cursor will be at the end of the results (`next()` will return `false`). At this point, you should close the results in order to free resources for the next user. As with all the other JDBC interfaces, the `close()` method provides all of the cleanup. However, the specification also requires that when the object is garbage-collected, it automatically cleans up its resources.

Because a `ResultSet` is a live representation of the underlying database, each open set consumes resources. This cursor is considered to be an open reference to the database, and databases only have a limited number of cursors available (for example, Oracle 8.0*x* had only 255 available). To make sure you don't run out of resources, you should always explicitly clean up after you've finished with the data. With the huge servers in e-commerce sites today, a couple of gigabytes of RAM for the JVM to play with may mean nothing gets garbage-collected until well after you start running out of resources.

Getting information about the result

Before starting to process the results, you may need to know a bit about exactly what was returned. Metadata is available about a particular result that complements the metadata available about the connection.

`ResultSetMetaData` represents the information about a particular result. Here, you can find information such as column-header names, the numbers of columns present in the return results, and whether the values are read-only.

For example, you might want to print out information about all the columns being returned from the database for debugging:

```
ResultSet rs = ....
ResultSetMetaData meta_data = rs.getMetaData();

int num_columns = meta_data.getColumnCount();
System.out.println("There are " + num_columns + " columns");

for(int i = 1; i <= num_columns; i++) {
  System.out.print("Column ");
  System.out.print(i);
  System.out.print(" Name: ");
  System.out.print(meta_data.getColumnName(i));
  System.out.print(" Class: ")
  System.out.print(meta_data.getColumnClass(i));
}
```

Don't forget that the column numbers start from 1 rather than 0.

Reading information from the results

Now that you have the cursor positioned at a row from which you wish to read the results, the next step is to access the individual values. Doing this means using one of the many `get`*`XXX`* methods in `ResultSet`.

The getter methods of `ResultSet` work, where possible, for all column types. That is, if the column is a `REAL` datatype and you ask for it as an `int`, the type will be automatically converted for you. (The places where this is not the case should be obvious to you so we won't bother to point them out.) Each method has two forms—one that takes a column number and one that takes a column name. While both options work, using the column number is preferable: It is much, much faster to use in an enterprise setting. Internally, the database always has values represented by the column number so that any query will have to map the name (which may or may not be case-sensitive, so you have to check for that, too) to the column number. When repeated over the many thousands of accesses to database information that is common with enterprise applications, this can end up being very expensive.

If you use the same `SELECT` statement that we mentioned a little earlier, you can print out all of the returned results using the following code:

```
SELECT (id, name, category) FROM Products

ResultSet rs = ....
ResultSetMetaData meta_data = rs.getMetaData();

System.out.println("The results are:");
System.out.println("Product ID,  Name,     Category");

while(rs.next()) {
  System.out.print(rs.getInt(1));
  System.out.print("   ");
  System.out.print(rs.getString(2));
  System.out.print("   ");
  System.out.println(rs.getString(3));
}
```

SQL and databases allow a column value to be `NULL`—that is, to contain no defined value. If you know that a null value is possible in a row, you can check for it with the `wasNull()` method. Say that you want to check for the category being non-null before attempting to print it. The above snippet becomes the following:

```
while(rs.next()) {
  System.out.print(rs.getInt(1));
  System.out.print("   ");
  System.out.print(rs.getString(2));
  System.out.print("   ");
  String category = rs.getString(3);
  if(rs.wasNull())
    category = "NULL";
  System.out.println(category);
}
```

`wasNull()` only operates on the column just read—it cannot be determined before the column has been read. You always need to make a genuine read attempt before checking to see if the value was null.

Making changes to the results

One interesting capability that an updateable result set gives you is the ability to use it to make updates to the database. Even though these values are results, you may change the values of the results at any time. Changes can be any of the normal forms — insert, delete, and change.

You delete the current row with the `deleteRow()` method. If the cursor is over a valid row and the result set is updateable, this will remove the current row from the database. To delete the fifth row of the database, you can use the following snippet:

```
rs.absolute(5);
rs.deleteRow();
```

Updating the current row uses the `updateXXX` methods. These look exactly like their `get` counterparts, but require an extra parameter that is the value. You can specify the column to be changed with either a number or name. For example, you might want to fix a typo in one of the categories with the following code:

```
ResultSet rs = ....
ResultSetMetaData meta_data = rs.getMetaData();
int cat_column = rs.findColumn("category");

if(rs.getCurrency() != ResultSet.CONCUR_UPDATABLE) {
  System.err.println("Error, can't change category typo");
  return;
}

while(rs.next()) {
  String category = rs.getString(cat_column);
  if(category.equals("boks"))
    rs.updateString(cat_column, "book");
}
```

Inserting a new row is a little different in that there are no `insertXXX` methods. Instead, the `ResultSet` creates a special row just for the addition of new rows. To add a new row, you move to the place in the `ResultSet` in which you want to insert the row. Then you jump to this special row using the `moveToInsertRow()` method. You can now use the `updateXXX` methods to set the new row values (note that the column numbers here still match those of the results originally asked for). Once you have finished making the changes, use the `insertRow()` method to place the new row into the underlying database. Finally, you can move back to where you left off by calling the `moveToCurrentRow()` method.

An example of where you might use this procedure is when consistency-checking the items in the database with some other source, such as an XML file:

```
ResultSet rs = ....

if(rs.getCurrency() != ResultSet.CONCUR_UPDATABLE) {
  System.err.println("Error, can't add consistency info");
```

```
    return;
  }

  while(rs.next()) {
    int prod_id = rs.getColumn("id");
    if(external_source.contains(prod_id))
      external_source.remove(prod_id);
  }

  if(external_source.size() != 0) {
    rs.moveToInsertRow();

    while(external_source.hasMoreItems()) {
      ProductInfo info = external_source.nextItem();
      rs.updateInt("id", external_source.getId());

      ...
      rs.insertRow();
    }

    rs.moveToCurrentRow();
  }
```

You will note that we only call `moveToInsertRow()` once. Each time you call `insertRow()` the changes will be sent to the database. You may then call the update methods to put in the new values for the next row. Only when you have finished all the changes do you need to move back to the current update row. (At least in this example, it is probably not needed, because the entire `ResultSet` has finished processing.)

The results written to the database may not occur at the time that you call `insertRow()`. Depending on the commit policy you are using for transactions, the results may not be sent to the database until you call the `commit()` on the underlying connection or `close()` on the `ResultSet`. There is more information about the `commit()` method at the end of this chapter.

Taking the results home with you

A new capability in JDBC 3.0 is the ability to take a `ResultSet`, serialize it, make some changes, and return those changes to the database later. This may be useful in a PDA-type device, where you don't want the overhead of a full database but still want to have a collection of result information to play with. The idea is to place the information onto the PDA (for example), let the user use it over some period of time, and then have the user re-synchronize it later. An address book, for example, might use this capability.

Adding extra capabilities to ResultSets

Offline capabilities are not something that you want every `ResultSet` implementation to have. The large overheads dealing with serialization and the non-connected status just aren't worth it for most applications. Therefore, the JDBC designers decided to use another class to represent offline `ResultSet` information — `RowSet`.

In order to work in both environments, the `RowSet` interface extends the normal `ResultSet` and adds even more methods. The major extra new functionality is to make the `RowSet` look like a JavaBean. Set methods now exist for setting the value of the command parameters used to fill the class with data. These do not perform the same task as the update methods that change the contents of the data once the class has been filled. The getters already exist in the base interface so there was no need to add them. The new getter methods are primarily aimed at the underlying database that needs to read the values back in and re-establish any internal database connections. As all JavaBeans require listeners for changes in the bean, new methods have been added to add and remove listeners, and a listener interface — `RowSetListener` — has been added for changes in the database.

As the listeners are primarily designed for UI tool implementors, we won't cover them in this book.

One of the purposes of the `RowSet` interfaces is to provide a way to transparently pass around database results without needing a database. To accomplish this, the interface is made serializable, and two more interfaces are added: `RowSetWriter` and `RowSetReader`. These interfaces are used internally by the `RowSet` to read and write itself.

Although the interfaces and the intent of row set are good, their current implementation leaves a lot to be desired. One of their biggest drawbacks is that they are defined as a collection of disconnected interfaces that do not fit the rest of the JDBC API. So even though you have now an instance to play with, you still cannot treat it generically as an interface. You must know which explicit implementation you are playing with. Also, the purpose of the accompanying interfaces for reading and writing is very unclear. The API specification and tutorials you can find on the Internet never address these interfaces and how they fit into the general philosophy. This makes it very hard to recommend their use in current applications.

Filling a RowSet with information

Because the `RowSet` is an interface, you will need to find a concrete implementation for your use. As a specification, JDBC does not define how to access an instance of the `RowSet`. Unlike normal database connections, each `RowSet` is a separate instance, so you can't just use JNDI to locate one for you to make queries of. Each time you want a new row set you must directly instantiate the concrete instance. In terms of portability of code, that is a major problem. While it is possible to write your own implementation, it is a huge class, and we certainly don't recommend it.

You can find a sample implementation of a `RowSet` from Sun's JDC site. The `CachedRowSet` can be downloaded from `http://developer.java.sun.com/developer/earlyAccess/crs/`. You will also find a good tutorial about using row sets within a JSP at `http://developer.java.sun.com/developer/technicalArticles/javaserverpages/cachedrowset/`.

After creating an instance of the RowSet, you have to populate it with data. To do this, you use a series of commands to set up the initialization parameters and then tell it to fill itself its content based on those parameters. The rough steps you normally follow to fill a RowSet with information are:

1. Set the SQL statement that you want executed to fill the class with data.
2. Set the parameter information about where to get the information, such as user names and passwords, and the DataSource or database URL.
3. Execute the parameters, allowing the class to fill itself with data.

Providing the SQL statement to be executed is the job of the setCommand() method. In this method, you can provide any SQL statement you like, including wildcards, as a normal String. For example, if you want to fetch all the product information, you can use the following command:

```
RowSet rset = new ....
rset.setCommand("SELECT * FROM Product");
```

Naturally, you may also use all the complex SQL requests for placing columns. For obvious reasons, there is really no point in using SQL UPDATE or INSERT commands here.

Another approach you can use is to set up a standard request, but not know until runtime what some of the parameter values are. For this approach you might use a wildcard in the SELECT statement to access information. Say you don't know what category of products the user wants until he or she clicks a selection on a Web page. To make the query, you set the command and then use the setXXX methods to fill in the real values of the wildcards:

```
rset.setCommand("SELECT * FROM Product WHERE category = ?");
rset.setString(1, user_selected_category);
```

The parameter index information is the parameter position from the command string and starts at 1, not 0.

The methods you use to set connection information vary depending on what you are going to use for the data source. If you want to use the core JDBC drivers, you use the methods setUrl(), setUsername(), and setPassword().

```
rset.setUrl("jdbc:odbc:test_db");
rset.setUsername("javauser");
rset.setPassword("mypassword");
```

If you are going to use the extension data sources (including pooled connections), you use the setDataSourceName() method:

```
rset.setDataSourceName("jdbc/Oracle");
```

Internally, the implementation should determine exactly what sort of DataSource instance is returned and make use of the appropriate methods to create a Connection and use it.

You may also set other properties on the RowSet to control exactly what sort of data you want to have. For example, you may want to create a read-only set, limit the maximum data size of objects to be fetched, or use custom type maps.

Finally, tell the RowSet to go ahead and fill in the values with the execute() method call:

```
rset.execute();
```

Once this method is called, it will remove any current contents and create a new set of contents for this instance. If you've forgotten to set some values, exceptions are also thrown. However, all the setup information is retained between calls. This makes the execute() method call great if you want multiple queries for the same thing with little overhead. For example, if you want to display a single Web page that contains a listing of all printed material, books and magazines, you use the following code:

```
RowSet rset = new ....
rset.setCommand("SELECT * FROM Product WHERE category = ?");
rset.setString(1, "books");
rset.setDataSourceName("jdbc/Oracle");
rset.execute();

// do stuff with the rowset

rset.setString(1, "magazines");
rset.execute();

// now process the new information
```

Synchronizing back with the database

Because RowSets are just an extended form of ResultSet, you can make all the same changes to the underlying data source. How to get them back to the underlying database is an interesting problem, as it depends on what your RowSet represented in the first place—was it just some offline version of the ResultSet, or was it used as a live JavaBean representation of the data, or was it used in some other fashion? What you did in the first place determines how information gets back to the database.

When acting as a JavaBean, the RowSet typically represents a live view of the underlying database—just as the ResultSet does. Therefore, all the methods act in the same way. A call to updateRow() or deleteRow() will make those changes immediately.

The definition of *immediately* is also influenced by the transaction-handling of the connection. We look at this in more detail later in Chapter 23, but the actual results may not make it to the database until you call `commit()` on the `Connection` that this `RowSet` used to fill its information.

For `RowSet` instances that work as an offline representation of the database, there is no defined way of making those changes appear in the database when connections come online again (for example, re-synching your Palm Pilot's address book with the desktop PC). The JDBC specification is very unclear about how to make these changes appear, and so we can't help you much here. You will have to read the documentation for your particular implementation and find out the best method in your case.

Managing custom datatypes

With the more modern, more complex databases, you can create custom datatypes as part of the SQL99 standard. For databases that support this feature, you would like to be able to map those custom types to Java classes. JDBC enables you to do this by means of a simple lookup map. Once defined, all the connections on that database use this type map.

Creating a custom type class

Custom datatypes are represented by the `SQLData` interface. Any class that wants to present complex data must implement this interface and its methods, because the interface provides the information needed to create new instances of the actual data.

First you have to start with a data definition from the SQL schema (this is probably defined by your DBA). For illustration purposes, we'll change the `Product` table that we've been using so that now it will only take an ID integer and a custom datatype that represents all the information about an individual product:

```
CREATE TYPE ProductInfo AS (
  name        VARCHAR(64) NOT NULL,
  price       DECIMAL(6,2) DEFAULT 0.00
  in_stock    INTEGER DEFAULT 0,
  category    VARCHAR(16)
) NOT FINAL;
```

You represent this by the class of the same name — `ProductInfo`

```
public class ProductInfo implements SQLData {
  public String getSQLTypeName() {
  }
  public void readSQL(SQLInput input, String type) {
  }
  public void writeSQL(SQLOutput output) {
  }
}
```

This class represents a single instance of a piece of data from the database, but there is no restraint on how you present the data to the end user. Most of the time using public variables is an acceptable solution (ignoring the screams of the OO purists here!), and so for your class you declare the following:

```
public String name;
public float price;
public int stockCount;
public String category;
```

You also need another variable that represents the SQL type name returned by the `getSQLTypeName()`. It doesn't really matter how you store that variable for this example, because the class only ever represents one type. You can either return a constant string or keep a real variable around internally. For maximum flexibility, choose the latter option (someone may choose to create a derived type of our type later).

With the basic class setup out of the road, you now look to dealing with getting the information into and out of the database. The `readSQL()` and `writeSQL()` methods enable you to do this. Writing is just the opposite of reading, so we'll treat reading first.

You are given information about the real data in the database by the `SQLInput` class. You have no choice about the order in which that data is presented to you. When reading data from the stream, you must do it in the order in which the fields are declared in the SQL statement. If the SQL type makes references to other types, you must read those types fully before reading the next attribute for your current type. The ordering is a depth-first read of the values from the database. As your datatype is really simple, you don't need to worry about this.

```
typeName = type;
name = input.readString();

BigDecimal price_dec = input.readBigDecimal();
price = price_dec.floatValue();

stockCount = input.readInt();
category = input.readString();
```

Writing values back out is just the opposite process. You must write values to the stream in the same order in which they are declared, in the same depth-first fashion as when reading:

```
output.writeString(name);
BigDecimal dec_price = new BigDecimal(price);
output.writeBigDecimal(dec_price);

output.writeInt(stockCount);
output.writeString(category);
```

Your type-map implementation is now complete. This class can be compiled and is ready to be registered with JDBC.

Populating the type map and informing JDBC

Once you have completed the classes that represent custom datatypes, you need to register them with the system. Type mappings are registered on a per-connection basis. While it may seem annoying that you have to do this for every connection you create, this gives you more flexibility in placing different mappings for the same datatype on different connections.

Registering a new mapping involves asking for the current type map and then adding your new information to that. You start by asking for the current map from the `Connection` interface:

```
Connection conn = ....
Map type_map = conn.getTypeMap();
```

The map returned is an instance of the standard `java.util.Map`. To this you can now register your new type classes. In the map, you use the string name of the datatype as the key and the `Class` representation of your new type as the value. The string name must include the schema name that holds your type definition. If you don't have a defined schema as an SQL construct, this string is the name of the virtual database in which the type was declared. For example, if the `ProductInfo` type was declared in the `test_db` database, then the type name would be `test_db.ProductInfo`.

With the map instance in hand, all you need to do is `put()` the values into it. As it is just a general lookup map, you do not need to `set()` the map back to the connection. The map you are given is the internal one, so just call `put()` with your additional values and then continue working on other more important code.

```
Connection conn = ....
Map type_map = conn.getTypeMap();
type_map.put("test_db.ProductInfo", ProductInfo.class);
```

An alternative to this is to use `Class.forName()` to create your `Class` instance:

```
type_map.put("test_db.ProductInfo",
             Class.forName("ProductInfo"));
```

Of course, if you really want to trash all of the currently set maps (you don't want to play nice!), you can supply your own map. Just create a new `Map` instance and then use `setTypeMap()` as follows:

```
Connection conn = ....
Map type_map = new HashMap();
type_map.put("test_db.ProductInfo", ProductInfo.class);
conn.setTypeMape(type_map);
```

Working with custom type classes in code

Now, every time your code accesses a custom type in the database, your class will be returned to represent it. You can also use these same classes to set values in the database. Let's say you have your `ResultSet` from a query. You know that Column 2 contains your product-information custom type. You would like to access the custom type and use the values.

To access custom types in the table columns, use the `getObject()` method. This method will take a look at the type map that you registered before and return the class that represents the type that you have here. The return type is actually an `Object` that you must cast to the right class to use.

To use your `ProductInfo` class from Column 2, you can make the following call:

```
ResultSet rs = ...
ProductInfo info = (ProductInfo)rs.getObject(2);
System.out.println("The product name is " + info.name);
```

To set or change the value in the database, you can use the `updateObject()` method and pass it your object instance.

```
ProductInfo info = new ProductInfo();
info.name = "Java 2 Enterprise Bible";
info.category = "books";
info.price = 49.95f;
info.stockCount = 5;

rs.updateObject(2, info);
```

In this example you create a completely new set of information and update the database with it. If you just wanted to modify one item of the existing data, you can simply use the existing class instance returned and pass it back in the `updateObject()` call, as follows:

```
ResultSet rs = ...
ProductInfo info = (ProductInfo)rs.getObject(2);
if(info.category.equals("boks")) {
  info.category = "book";
  rs.updateObject(2, info);
}
```

Classes returned from the `getObject()` represent the information at the time of reading. They are not live, so once you have an instance you can do whatever you like with it. Changing the values in the instance will not change the underlying database.

That covers the introduction to the data structures that JDBC provides you. The next step is to ask the database to return these values to you.

Interacting with the Database

Having a bunch of data doesn't do you much good if you cannot access it. Between the `Connection` and the data structures you've just read about, you need a process to make queries of the database.

Two more steps exist in the process of going from a connection to having the data in your hand. The first is representing the SQL code you want to execute, and the second is making that statement happen.

Representing an SQL statement within Java

Your first step in accessing the contents of the database is to tell the connection about the SQL statement that you want to execute. As SQL is one language and Java is quite obviously another, you need to use some form of interpretative mechanism to move from Java's world to SQL's world. As a minimum, you need something to parse the SQL string and send it off to the database in whatever form the JDBC driver uses.

For a long time there have been some efforts to provide Java embedded in SQL for use in stored procedures. These are slowly merging, and an SQL/J standard is now going through the Java Community Process.

The representation of a single SQL statement

SQL works as a single command-type language. All the information needed to make one action will be entirely self-contained within that one statement. This is quite different from normal programming languages like Java or C wherein you combine groups of statements to create meaning.

A stored procedure is not an SQL statement. Stored procedures combine a programming language that embeds SQL statements with extra constructs to allow using information from multiple separate statements to be combined together. This will always involve a proprietary language, such as Oracle's PL/SQL. The exception to this rule is that a number of database vendors are moving to replace their scripting languages for stored procedures with Java code. Calling a stored procedure is a statement, however, because you only invoke the stored procedure through a single SQL statement.

All SQL statements that JDBC can execute are represented by the `Statement` interface. The core interface itself is relatively simple. You may set a number of properties about the returned data that you would like to see, and that is it.

The `Statement` interface just represents the actual SQL information. It does not represent the query as it is processed. To actually make something happen, you need to call one of the myriad `execute()` methods available to you. Which one you should call depends on the action you are about to perform. Are you asking for data or sending updates? In order to sort out the confusion about which method to call, we will introduce each of the tasks after we introduce the different statement types you can have.

For each of the types of statements you can create, there are also options to control what you get back in the `ResultSet` for queries. Each of the creation methods has a version that provides two integers — typically called `resultSetType` and `resultSetConcurrency`. The values that you pass to these parameters are the same ones that we introduced earlier in the chapter as the return values from `getType()` and `getConcurrency()`, respectively.

Standard statements for quick queries

If you know exactly what you are going to ask for, then the simplest way to grab a statement is to use the basic `Statement` interface from the connection. These forms of statements tend to represent quick one-off requests to the database in situations where you always know everything about the query.

To create an ordinary statement, use the `createStatement()` method from the `Connection` interface. This will pass you a `Statement` instance to use. This instance can now be used to make queries or updates of the database through the various `execute()` methods wherein you must pass the SQL string when you want it to be executed.

For example, to create a new statement from a `DataSource ds`, you use the following code:

```
Connection conn = ds.getConnection();
Statement stmt = conn.createStatement();
```

Creating template statements

The downside of these fast statements is the large performance cost. Each time you ask this statement to execute, it must make the full trip of parsing the SQL string and making the connection to the database and waiting for the results. For high-load server applications, the penalty can be very high. To get around this problem, you can create a form of precompiled statements that caches all the startup and return-value information — the `PreparedStatement`.

Creating a prepared statement requires the use of the `prepareStatement()` call of `Connection`. For this method, you must always pass a `String` that represents the SQL command that you want executed. If the string is properly formed, it will return an instance of the `PreparedStatement` interface. Most of the time the driver implementation will also send the SQL off to the database to compile it for later use. The idea is that you now have a preoptimized command ready to go. All you have to do is fill in any blanks and tell the database to run it.

`PreparedStatement` interfaces are really geared toward making the same query over and over — that is, the typical interaction you will see in an enterprise application server. In particular, they are best when you have a known query of which one part is dynamically set for each time it is run.

Back in the RowSet introduction, we demonstrated the use of the SQL setCommand() method and the accompanying setX methods to fill in parameter values. Well, prepared statements can work in the same way, using almost identical method calls. In your Web server, you want to always have a query waiting around to ask for the list of products in any given category. Having one complete PreparedStatement instance for each category is a waste of resources. Your code won't be flexible, either for adding or removing categories on the fly. To cope with this, you use the prepared statement with wildcards and then fill in the wildcards just before making the requests:

```
String cmd = "SELECT * FROM Product WHERE category = ?";
Connection conn = ds.getConnection();
PreparedStatement stmt = conn.prepareStatement(cmd);

...
stmt.setString(1, "book");

// now run the statement to get values back
```

The PreparedStatement interface extends the Statement interface, so all the functionality that you have there will also be available here. To this, you just add the setX methods to set all the parameter datatypes that you have seen so far.

Calling stored procedures

Stored procedures are collections of code stored inside the database that act on the tables just like regular function calls. These procedures look to some extent like ordinary Java method calls. They have parameter values and return values. Sometimes a parameter may have its value modified or be used to pass information outwards to the caller (which makes it a little different from the Java model).

To call a stored procedure, you need to have one defined. This is where your database administrator (DBA) comes in handy. Your DBA should give you the details about what is available. In keeping with previous examples, say you have a stored procedure that you can ask to list all the products from a certain category. This takes a single parameter: the category name.

```
PROCEDURE LIST_CATEGORY(IN: category)
```

Creating a stored procedure is similar to creating a prepared statement. You pass in a string with a procedure to be called using the appropriate SQL syntax (in this case the SQL CALL command). Stored procedures are represented by the CallableStatement interface, which is derived from PreparedStatement. To create an instance of CallableStatement you use the prepareCall() method from the Connection and pass it the string representing your SQL call:

```
String cmd = "CALL LIST_CATEGORY('books')";
Connection conn = ds.getConnection();
CallableStatement stmt = conn.prepareCall(cmd);
```

You can now execute the `CallableStatement` just as you would the other statement types. However, just as with prepared statements, the real idea is to use the stored procedure as a template and pass in information for each query execution. To do this, you start with the same wildcarding that you've used before in this chapter.

```
String cmd = "CALL LIST_CATEGORY(?)";
```

Stored procedures have parameters, but they can be slightly different from Java's. Java only supports parameters that are read-only. You can pass information in, but you can't use the parameters to pass information out. Stored procedures in SQL are different. Three different forms of parameters exist:

✦ `IN`: This parameter is used to pass information into the procedure. This parameter is treated as read-only and cannot be changed.

✦ `OUT`: This parameter takes no values when called, but can be read after the call returns. It is used a bit like return types in Java, but you can have many of them to returns lots of different information.

✦ `INOUT`: This parameter combines the functionalities of `IN` and `OUT`. You can set the values during the call, but they may change and hold new information on the way out.

Because each of these parameter types works differently, you need to match each parameter in the string you've passed to JDBC with the appropriate parameter type. When you pass the information to JDBC in the `prepareCall()` method call, JDBC has no knowledge of the actual script. You must tell JDBC what to expect.

Nominating parameters in callable statements are treated with a similar fashion to prepared statements. `IN` parameters use the same `set`*X* methods that you use in prepared statements to set wildcard values in SQL. `OUT` parameters need to be registered with a `registerOut`*X* method. `INOUT` parameters combine the `IN` and `OUT` functionalities, so you can use these methods to register each part.

To register information about an outgoing parameter, you must tell the statement what that parameter type is. The underlying JDBC code does not know what to expect, so you need to give it some extra information. Thus, when you call the `registerOut`*X* method, you need to supply the parameter that you are changing with an integer that tells it the type of data to expect. This integer is one of the values defined in the `Types` class that is defined in the core package. As an example, let's say your stored procedure returned the number of items in the category as an integer `OUT` parameter:

```
PROCEDURE LIST_CATEGORY(IN: category, OUT: num_items)
```

You can register the information on the `num_items` parameter and set up the call with the following code:

```
String cmd = "CALL LIST_CATEGORY(?, ?)";
Connection conn = ds.getConnection();
CallableStatement stmt = conn.prepareCall(cmd);
stmt.registerOutParameter(2, Types.INTEGER);
stmt.setString(1, "books");
```

In a departure from the other statement types, you can call the set and register methods using either a positional index or a name string. The position index works as you would expect from the previous uses. If you pass a name string, this is used to try to map the parameter to the name declared in the stored procedure in the database.

Tip

Do not try to combine parameter names and position index values within one statement. This could lead to problems or exceptions being generated by the database. Pick one and use it consistently.

Querying the database for information

You've got the driver, you've got a connection, and you've even registered interest of executing a statement. Finally you have enough information to make a query of the database!

We mentioned earlier that you need to call one of the execute methods in order to make a real query to the database. Of course, nothing you do is ever simple, and the execute method you call depends on the type of statement you created in the first place. So we'll first introduce the generic differences among execute methods before getting into more specifics.

Types of statement execution

Statements can represent either changing of information in the database or queries for information. These requests will return different types of information will be returned to the caller. In the case of updates, you want to know how many rows have been affected. In the case of queries, you want to know what the results were. Because you know you have to deal with two different return types, two different forms of the execute methods exist—`executeQuery()` and `executeUpdate()`. You can consider these a form of strong type checking. If you call `executeQuery()` when the SQL is really an update, an exception will be generated.

Sometimes when you execute the statement you may not know whether you are making an update or a query. The more general `execute()` method helps in this case. This version returns a `boolean` value. If the value is `true`, then the statement was a query; `false` indicates that the statement was an update. Of course, you want to know the results in either case, so you can use one of the convenience methods to ask for it, as follows:

```
boolean is_query = stmt.execute();
if(is_query) {
  ResultSet rs = stmt.getResultSet();
  ...
} else {
  int rows_updated = stmt.getUpdateCount();
  ...
}
```

Calling simple statements

With the simple `Statement` object, you don't have any SQL commands issued before you get to call execute. So, for these statements, you need to use one of the execute statements that takes a string. The string contains the SQL that you want to run. A simple query runs like this:

```
Statement stmt = conn.getStatement();
ResultSet rs = stmt.executeQuery("SELECT * FROM Product");
```

With the `ResultSet` in hand, you can now process the values as we discussed earlier in the chapter.

Calling prepared statements

In prepared statements, you already have the majority of the SQL data set. To execute a statement, you only need to fill in missing parameter values and call the `executeQuery()` method. This time, as you have already set the SQL data, you do not need to supply any values to `executeQuery()`.

```
String cmd = "SELECT * FROM Product WHERE category = ?";
PreparedStatement stmt = conn.prepareStatement(cmd);

...
stmt.setString(1, "book");
ResultSet rs = stmt.executeQuery();
```

Calling stored procedures

Stored procedure calls add one more interesting twist: You can have values returned as a result set, but you also have `OUT` parameters to deal with. To start with, you set up the query and execute the action just as you do with the prepared statement:

```
String cmd = "CALL LIST_CATEGORY(?, ?)";
CallableStatement stmt = conn.prepareCall(cmd);
stmt.registerOutParameter(2, Types.INTEGER);
stmt.setString(1, "books");
ResultSet rs = stmt.executeQuery();
```

After executing the statement, you will need to read the value of the OUT parameter in position index 2. In the preceding code, you have marked it as being an integer value, so you use the getInt() method from the CallableStatement interface to read the value back out.

```
int num_items = stmt.getInt(2);
```

The position index here must be the same as the one you declared when registering the OUT parameter earlier.

If you are using the generic execute() method rather than executeQuery(), the specification recommends that you always fetch the ResultSet before accessing the OUT parameter values.

Making updates to the database

Making changes to the existing database is similar to querying the database. For simple queries, you pass in the SQL statement to be executed, where the pre-built versions will not need arguments. The one crucial difference is the return value of the methods. When making a query, you get back a collection of the rows that match. When making an update, you get a number representing the number of rows that have been affected by that update.

As far as JDBC is concerned, any change to the table structure is an update. Modifying, inserting, or deleting rows all count as updates. Also considered updates are the basic database commands, such as creating, altering, or dropping tables. Because these are just SQL commands, you can create the database and all its contents from JDBC. There is no need to build external scripts for your database management should you choose not to.

The following instructions show you how to create new updates to the database. Earlier in this chapter you saw how to make changes once you have the results of a query. Those techniques are just as useful as these and the one you choose to make changes depends on what your code needs to do and on the information it already has. For example, there is no real point in making a query for all of the values and then looping through to change one column when it is far faster just to issue an SQL statement to do the same thing.

Executing simple updates

Simple updates follow the same pattern as simple queries. You must call the executeUpdate() method that takes a string argument. The string is the SQL statement to be executed.

```
Statement stmt = conn.getStatement();
int rows_updated = stmt.executeUpdate(
  "INSERT INTO ProductInfo VALUES ('Java 2 Enterprise Bible'" +
  ", 49.95, 5, 'books')"
);
```

Because this is an insert of new data, the return value of `rows_updated` will always be the value 1. If you want to update a collection of rows — say to fix a typo — you get a value that reflected the items changed.

```
int rows_updated = stmt.executeUpdate(
  "UPDATE ProductInfo SET category='books' WHERE " +
  "category = 'boks'"
);
```

Executing prepared updates

OK, by now you should be starting to get the hang of all this. The process of making updates with prepared statements follows the same pattern: Create the statement, fill in any parameters, and then execute the update. You can make the previous example completely reusable by making the following changes:

```
PreparedStatement stmt = conn.prepareStatement(
"INSERT INTO ProductInfo VALUES (?, ?, ?, ?)"
);

stmt.setString(1, "Java 2 Enterprise Bible");
stmt.setBigDecimal(2, new BigDecimal(49.95));
stmt.setInt(3, 5);
stmt.setString(4, "books");

int rows_updated = stmt.executeUpdate();
```

`CallableStatement`s are executed in exactly the same way.

Managing the database structure

One interesting, although probably less useful, use of JDBC is to write database independent way of creating a database structures. It's not often that you need to create or delete tables on the fly in your application.

Managing tables is just a matter of executing the appropriate SQL statements, such as `CREATE TABLE` or `DROP TABLE`, from your Java code. Since these commands are only used once, you use simple statements to perform the actions. Using the code in this statement is just the same as executing from a database (SQL) command prompt or setup file. For example:

```
Statement stmt = conn.getStatement();
stmt.executeUpdate(
  "CREATE TABLE Product (" +
  " product_id INTEGER NOT NULL," +
  " name       VARCHAR(64) NOT NULL," +
  " price      DECIMAL(6,2) DEFAULT 0.00" +
  " in_stock   INTEGER DEFAULT 0," +
  " category   VARCHAR(16)," +
  " UNIQUE KEY (product_id)"
);
```

You really don't need to check for the return value of this statement. If it fails, an `SQLException` will be generated.

Using Enterprise Features

At this point you should be comfortable with the run-of-the-mill features of JDBC. Over the next few pages we will introduce you to the features that are useful in an enterprise application setting, but usually not of much use in a desktop type of application.

In the enterprise environment, you have two goals: sharing resources and streamlining changes so that either everything happens or nothing happens. One failure causes all the other changes to be aborted. JDBC is part of a much larger environment, so it must not only provide these capabilities within itself, but also provide hooks to allow the same capabilities when it acts as part of the larger J2EE environment. That is, you might give up local control in order to have a larger entity synchronize control across a number of application modules and API sets.

Batching a collection of actions together

At the first level of control, you may want to batch together a number of updates to the database in one hit. This enables you to queue up a number of changes to the database and then ask that they all be performed at once. Consider a first-time user who wants to place an order—you want both to add the new user to that table and also to add the order to the the order table table. From a resource-management perspective, it is better to send both requests to the database at once than it is to send one, wait for the return, and then send another. You can achieve the same results much faster and so allow more simultaneous users on your system.

Batch requests of the database are much better suited to the update process than to the query process. In fact, the API is clearly biased toward updates; batch queries are possible, but the specification does not guarantee that they will work.

Using simple update batching

Beginning a batch of updates works just like beginning any other update. The first thing you must do is create a statement to use:

```
Statement stmt = conn.getStatement();
```

In the earlier code, the next step is to call the `executeUpdate()` method and pass it the SQL string you want evaluated. For batches, you don't want to do this, because it will immediately fire the code off to the database. Instead, you want to add the SQL command to the current batch using the `addBatch()` method. This queues the command within your `Statement` awaiting notification to send it off to the database for evaluation.

```
stmt.addBatch("INSERT INTO Customer VALUES (" +
              "'555 Mystreet Ave', 'AU', 'Justin Couch'," +
              "'+61 2 1234 5678')"
);
stmt.addBatch("INSERT INTO Order VALUES (" +
              "49.95, " +
              "(SELECT customer_id FROM Customer WHERE " +
               "name='Justin Couch' AND " +
               "phone='+61 2 1234 5678'), " +
              ""
);
```

You can submit as many queries in the batch as you want. Each request is stored internally for use. To fire the batch off to the database, you call the `executeBatch()` command. All of the currently stored commands are sent to the database for processing.

```
int[] update_counts = stmt.executeBatch();
```

Single update calls always return an integer representing the number of rows affected. When performing batch updates, there are a collection of these numbers—one for each update action—hence the return value of an array of integers this time. The array is the same length as the number of items in this batch. Each index in the array may have one of three values:

✦ Zero or any positive number, which represents the number of rows affected by the update.

✦ `SUCCESS_NO_INFO`, which means that the action succeeded but the database didn't return any information.

✦ `EXECUTE_FAILED`, which means that one of the updates failed.

Managing errors within a batch of updates

When batch updating hits an error, what happens next is to some extent undefined. The JDBC spec explicitly says that some implementations may continue to process the rest of the updates, while other implementations may exit at this point. This is not particularly useful for your code when behaviors can change on you.

Although we are jumping ahead a little here, the solution uses the capabilities of transaction handling. When dealing with transactions you want to explicitly tell JDBC that you are going to handle when to make updates with the database. This same ability is used to make sure that the behavior always returns immediately on an error. Thus, you can decide within your own code how to handle errors. This ability is known as *auto-commit* and is handled through the `setAutoCommit()` method of the connection. The default behavior is to always auto-commit, and you want to turn that off before you start setting up the batch.

```
conn.setAutoCommit(false);
Statement stmt = conn.getStatement();
```

```
stmt.addBatch( .....

...

int[] update_counts = stmt.executeBatch();
```

Now your batch will fail with a `BatchUpdateException` if there is an underlying problem. You can then retrieve the list of results to check just what failed by calling `getUpdateCounts()` from the exception instance returned.

Batching updates for prepared statements

Managing batches for prepared statements is a little different in form to using simple statements. Simple statements enable you to add a list of arbitrary SQL statements to be batched. Because a prepared statement pre-compiles the SQL command string, this is not possible. Instead, batches provide for multiple calls of the same prepared statement, but with different values for the arguments. You might use the batching action to create a batch of new products all in one hit.

Batching prepared statements starts with creating the standard `PreparedStatement` instance:

```
PreparedStatement stmt = conn.prepareStatement(
"INSERT INTO ProductInfo VALUES (?, ?, ?, ?)"
);
```

Next you need to set the values for this action using the normal `set`*`X`* methods:

```
stmt.setString(1, "Java 2 Enterprise Bible");
stmt.setBigDecimal(2, new BigDecimal(49.95));
stmt.setInt(3, 5);
stmt.setString(4, "books");
```

To indicate that you wish to batch updates, you now call the `addBatch()` method that takes no arguments. This tells the underlying implementation to store those values and get ready for another:

```
stmt.addBatch();

stmt.setString(1, "Java 2 Bible");
stmt.setBigDecimal(2, new BigDecimal(39.95));
stmt.setInt(3, 5);
stmt.setString(4,"books");
stmt.addBatch();
```

Once you have added one item to the batch, adding further items to the batch requires that you continue to notify the prepared statement of each new item. Each `setX()` method changes a value, but how does the underlying implementation know when you have finished making changes for this one item and are starting the next one? You signal your intentions by calling `addBatch()` again at the end of each lot of changes for that one item. As the preceeding example shows, if you have two requests that you would like to execute in the batch, then you must call `addBatch()` twice.

You send the updates to the database just as you have been — by calling `executeBatch()`. Again, the results are the list of successful changes.

Pooling statements for faster access

Earlier in the chapter we discussed the use of pooled connection for resource-usage control and also for faster access to the database. JDBC 3.0 has taken the concept of pooling one step further by caching the statements that you make as well!

You gain the use of statement pooling by the use of pooled connections. What this does is store the pre-compiled statements internally to the driver. Your code never has to explicitly create the statements to use this capability. Your code will notice the much faster creation times when you call `prepareStatement()` or `prepareCall()`. Pooling keeps the resources for all pooled connections. That is, registering a prepared statement on one connection will instantly make it available to other connections.

You perform checks to see if the driver supports statement pooling by using the `DatabaseMetaData` class. The `supportsStatementPooling()` method will return `true` if your driver supports this capability.

Just as pooled connections function the same as non-pooled connections, so do pooled statements. All the methods work the same; all you have to know is that someone is doing the management internally for you. In order to facilitate statement pooling, you should always make sure you explicitly close the statement after you have finished with it. This way resources may be returned to the global pool for others to use.

Managing transactions

The final piece of the JDBC API is dealing with transaction support for large-scale databases. Transactions enable you to queue up a large collection of changes and commit it to the underlying database all at once. If something goes wrong, you can remove all of the changes up to the last point you committed or marked as being useful.

Controlling when to make changes

By default, JDBC will automatically make changes available to the database when you call one of the execute methods. This process is called auto-committing, and for most applications it is a good thing. However, in the larger applications that sit in middleware systems, you may want greater control over exactly when to send items.

Commit handling is done on a per-connection basis. It sits outside the statement and affects all the statements generated from that connection. This enables you to have a number of code modules make some changes through a single connection that you supply them, wait for them to return, and then make one big commit.

The most fundamental assumption of commits and rollbacks is that you are only buffering updates heading back to the database. Removing the auto-commit does not prevent you from making multiple queries and immediately having a set of results to work with. What auto-commit holds is any changes that you might make to the returned `ResultSet` from a query going back to the database.

To allow collections of updates to be grouped together, the first thing you must do is turn off the auto-commit of updates. You do this using the `setAutoCommit()` method with a Boolean parameter value of `false`.

```
conn.setAutoCommit(false);
Statement stmt1 = conn.getStatement();
PreparedStatement stmt2 = conn.prepareStatement("INSERT....");
```

So now your code goes off and does a bunch of stuff. At the end of all this, you need to tell the database to propagate any updates. Calling `commit()` will release them.

```
conn.commit();
```

Done. It's that easy! Any changes due to be sent back to the database are now gone. If something has a problem, an `SQLException` is thrown.

What if your code has an error somewhere? What if this error is so bad that you don't want any of your changes actually being made to the database? This process is called rollback, and you use the `rollback()` method to do it. When you roll back changes, all updates that were signaled after the last time you made a `commit()` are thrown away. A common way of rolling back changes is in an exception handler, as follows:

```
conn.setAutoCommit(false);

try {
  module_1.performAction(stmt1);
  module_2.performAnotherAction(stmt2);
  conn.commit();
} catch(Exception e) {
  System.err.println("ERROR!!!! " + e.getMessage());
  conn.rollback();
}
```

Marking intermediate steps between commits with savepoints

In some cases of error handling you might not want to roll back to the complete beginning of the statements, because you may still want to preserve and commit some updates. Connections enable you to mark these positions and term them *savepoints*, duly represented by the SavePoint interface.

When you mark a save point, the assumption is that everything up to that point has worked the way you want it to. A call to rollback() will return you to the last save point. In the previous example, you just removed all the changes if there was a failure. This time you might just ignore anything if there was an error in that code module, but commit any other changes:

```
conn.setAutoCommit(false);

try {
  module_1.performAction(stmt1);
} catch(Exception e) {
  System.err.println("ERROR!!!! " + e.getMessage());
  conn.rollback();
}

conn.setSavepoint();

try {
  module_2.performAnotherAction(stmt2);
} catch(Exception e) {
  System.err.println("ERROR!!!! " + e.getMessage());
  conn.rollback();
}

conn.commit();
```

If you need more control, you can even roll back to a named savepoint. That is, you can roll back through any number of savepoints, because all they represent is a marking place. Creating a savepoint does not send the values to the database. What happens is that all of the changes so far are kept in your client-side code until either you roll back the values or you commit() them to the database. Savepoints are just a way of storing away data and changes within J2EE rather than you having to write all of your own management software. To expand on the code example, say that this time you have three modules to work with. If anything fails in the third module of a certain type, then you want to roll back to the first savepoint; otherwise you just want to ignore the local changes.

```
conn.setAutoCommit(false);

try {
  module_1.performAction(stmt1);
} catch(ModuleException me) {
  System.err.println("ERROR!!!! " + me.getMessage());
  conn.rollback();
}

Savepoint spt1 = conn.setSavepoint();
```

```
try {
  module_2.performAnotherAction(stmt2);
} catch(ModuleException me) {
  System.err.println("ERROR!!!! " + me.getMessage());
  conn.rollback();
}

conn.setSavepoint();

try {
  module_3.performThirdAction(stmt2);
} catch(ModuleException me) {
  System.err.println("ERROR!!!! " + me.getMessage());

  if(me.getErrorCode() == ModuleException.FATAL_ERROR)
    conn.rollback(spt1);
  else
    conn.rollback();
}

conn.commit();
```

That's all there is to know about basic enterprise transaction handling. There is much more to it than this—particularly when you start looking at handling commits across multiple data-source types such as LDAP, file systems, and databases. We'll address the topic in much greater detail in Chapter 23.

Summary

JDBC is a big system of APIs, and with the introduction of JDBC 3.0 it has grown enormously in capabilities. A thorough understanding of JDBC will be of great benefit not only in enterprise programming, but also in programming smaller-scale systems such as desktops and PDAs. The latest version of the specification is or will be part of the next iteration of the enterprise and standard specifications. In this chapter, we:

- ✦ Introduced the Java representation of a database JDBC.
- ✦ Examined how JDBC represents SQL information within the Java language environments.
- ✦ Explained how to make and manage connections and queries to the database and process the results.
- ✦ Looked at how JDBC provides capabilities that you need in order to work in the enterprise space.

✦ ✦ ✦

Working with Directory Services and LDAP

✦ ✦ ✦ ✦

In This Chapter

An introduction to directory services and how they differ from an RDBMS

What LDAP is and how to build LDAP systems

How to query and modify LDAP databases

How to build directory services for an enterprise application

✦ ✦ ✦ ✦

Within the enterprise application setting, directory services are just as important as the more traditional relational database like Oracle. You may have heard the term "directory service" before: Novell was the first commercial vendor to introduce a large-scale, commercial directory service with its NDS (Novell Directory Services) product in 1994 when it introduced the concept of directory services to the masses. In the context of enterprise applications, we use exactly the same technology, but (usually) in a less widely spread manager. Directory services come in a number of different flavors, but the most common is LDAP or Lightweight Directory Access Protocol.

LDAP is a very nice piece of kit to include in your programming arsenal and we find it a great shame that more programmers do not know about it or make use of its capabilities. Throughout this chapter, and the next, we hope to introduce you to LDAP and directory services in general. You'll have to get very familiar with it anyway, as it is at the core of how J2EE currently locates almost all of its information and capabilities. Future versions of J2EE are going to make this even more prevalent.

Introducing Directory Services

Like any good storyteller, we start at the beginning — by telling you what a directory service is and why you should use it in preference to a relational database. When we introduce directory services to people who have never seen them before, the most common reaction is, "Well, I can do that in XYZ database, so what's the point?" Naturally, this is the most commonly misunderstood aspect of directory services — on the outside they seem to do the same task, but internally they are very different and suit different needs.

What is a directory service?

The most common analogy used to describe directory services is the address book. Inside, information is sorted in a logical manner into various categories — even though the basic information is always the same (for example, you'll always find entries such as name, address, phone number and so on in every address book). In general you tend to read addresses from the book more often than you enter new ones.

This is a pretty good analogy for a directory service. If you filter out the salient points, you will note the following:

✦ **The information is sorted.** All the data in a directory service is sorted in a particular way as it is entered. Typically this sort is a hierarchical structure and is defined as part of the actual data structures.

✦ **Information is mostly retrieved and rarely written.** Therefore, internally the code is highly optimized toward searching at the expense of addition and deletion of data.

✦ **As in an address book, the information is stored all over the place.** It can be replicated and distributed without your knowing it.

✦ **All information is stored as a basic object** to which a collection of attributes is then associated.

In short, a directory service defines a collection of objects that contain attributes and may be ordered into groups in a hierarchical manner that makes it easy for you to find things.

Taking stock of directory services

So far we have remained really generic in our description of what a directory service is. Directory services can take many different forms. We've already mentioned one type, LDAP, and many more exist. The following list gives an indication of the types of systems that can be considered directory services:

✦ **DNS:** The domain-naming system that you use to locate your favorite Web site is a directory service. All the information is stored in a hierarchical manner (each dot in a name delimits a level in the hierarchy), the information is mostly read and rarely changed, and a basic object exists but also has a lot of attribute information associated with it. For the uninitiated, there is a lot more to DNS than just looking up the network address of a host. You can use it to locate information on mail servers, dynamically discover where to find services for a particular protocol, and much more.

- **File systems:** Yes, a file system can be considered a directory service. (We'll explain this in greater detail in Chapter 9.) Information is organized in a hierarchical manner (at least on most traditional file systems), and each object (a file) has a lot of ancillary information associated with it—the path, modification times, permissions, and so on. In most cases, a file is also read more often than it is written to.
- **LDAP:** We've already mentioned this, but it is good to go over it again. LDAP is the heart of most large-scale, well-known directory services. The two best-known examples are Novell's NDS and Microsoft's ActiveDirectory. Other examples include iPlanet's (formerly Netscape's) calendaring and roaming support for the Navigator Web browser, which uses LDAP.
- **NIS/NIS+:** If you are a UNIX user, you are probably very familiar with these systems. They are the distributed user authentication scheme used for large sites. The distributed service provides host-name resolution, user logins, access-control information, and a heap of other services. On the Microsoft side of the business, the equivalent system would be NDS or ActiveDirectory.

Comparing directory services to delational databases

So if a directory service contains collections of objects and attributes and you do searches for them, how is that any different from performing an SQL `SELECT`? The answer lies in how you want to organize your data. As we discussed earlier, directory services are designed to be search-optimized and very logically organized. The other major kicker is that because of the hierarchical nature or the directory service, there is no need for all the data to be stored in one place. You can locate each branch on a physically separate machine in a different country. Yet when you access data, you don't have to know where any of these branches are. The process asks the local server, and that server is then responsible for locating the information for you. You cannot organize data this way with a relational database.

Throughout this chapter we are going to spend a lot of time comparing relational databases and LDAP databases. For the purposes of these comparisons we are assuming that many more readers are familiar with the relational-data model and use this as a reference point to compare LDAP structures to aid in your understanding. The comparisons will not only help you understand general concepts, but will also serve as a means of highlighting the strengths and weaknesses of both systems.

Relational databases work really well in situations in which you need to access a lot of information all over the place and combine it into a single coherent answer. The examples that we've used in the database chapters involve online stores: A typical example might be a query for the list of all the orders that use a certain product and are being sent to a particular country. Due to the relational nature of the data, that is an area where your SQL database shines. Directory services are very poor in this regard. However, if you want to find the settings details for the printer in Room 523 of Building C on the northern campus, a directory service will beat the relational database hands down, because that information may be stored on one of the local servers. Relational databases, while they can replicate and distribute information, require that all copies of the information be identical, whereas directory services actually encourage the opposite — lots of small copies of only the data needed locally.

Another advantage to directory services is that LDAP is becoming the default authentication mechanism on large software systems. LDAP provides a number of security mechanisms, and because it can have customized attribute information, it is perfect for use as the database for Web servers, secure networks, printer services, calendaring systems, and even your humble company address book. It can supply all of these on a single system, and today it is rare to find enterprise or server software that does not have the ability to hook to an LDAP database for information. LDAP is one of those quiet technologies that just creeps in everywhere and that you don't notice until everyone is using it.

When should I use a directory service?

To continue with our address-book analogy, you should use a directory service (OK, let's just call it LDAP from now on!) whenever you want address book–type functionality — that is, whenever you want a heavily structured, customizable, distributed information source.

Of course, it may also be the case that LDAP is thrust upon you. If you start to use commercial software such as the iPlanet server and middleware systems, LDAP is the core of the shared information — in particular system configuration and user authentication. For example, the Web server references LDAP for login authentication, the mail server uses it to find address aliases and determine where to route incoming mail to, the middleware server uses it for authentication to prevent unauthorized access to its services, and the applications use it to hold user information.

Another really good use of LDAP services comes when you have different hardware devices that all need to share the same information. In very large-scale enterprise systems, it is quite common to have everything reference user information in the central directory service. Here you will find IVR (Interactive Voice Response) systems, firewalls, custom-built mail servers, Web services, and the call-center all using LDAP to hold a single consistent view of the world. Each of these services runs on custom hardware, and yet they can all access a common worldview.

Our last example of directory service usage is the core of J2EE itself. Directory services are accessed through the JNDI APIs. If you have worked through Chapter 7 you will have noticed that you access all the drivers through a directory-service interface. As you will see in later chapters, all the Enterprise JavaBeans (EJBs) and high-end services are accessed through JNDI as well. Put frankly — you can't avoid using directory services in a J2EE application environment.

Introducing LDAP

After the vanilla directory services that J2EE provides you, LDAP will be the directory-services capability you use most in your enterprise application. In this section, we'll introduce the major ideas about LDAP.

The J2EE environment uses the CORBA naming service COS Naming as the default service provider in JNDI. This provides a purely naming service – matching a name to an object – without all of the benefits of attributes that a directory service gives you.

A brief history of LDAP

LDAP started as an effort to simplify existing services. As you saw so often during the 1990s, that period was devoted to taking technologies that had been pioneered in the previous two decades and trimming off the overly complex pieces to leave a very simple core that was easy to understand, implement, and deploy — and that enjoyed widespread acceptance. Well-known examples are networking (OSI stack versus TCP/IP), document management (SGML versus HTML and later XML), indexing (WHOIS and WAIS versus HTTP daemon + CGI script), and portable micro-code with virtual machine (Ada pCode and Smalltalk versus Java).

The corresponding technology for LDAP was the joint ISO and ITU spec called X.500. Part of a wide-ranging set of services developed during the 1980s, X.500 was based on that other frequently used technology, the OSI Network model — commonly known as the OSI protocol stack or 7-Layer Network Model. These theoretically perfect systems that could handle any situation were bulky and cumbersome to implement. X.500, and its sibling X.400 for e-mail services, never really gained much acceptance outside of a couple of large companies and Europe. X.500 required the use of the full 7-layer model, and as a result the services were extremely difficult to manage, and the protocol used to interact with them was very slow too (given the available bandwidth of the day).

The LDAP standard is defined as part of a number of Internet RFCs. The most recent standard is RFC2251, "Lightweight Directory Access Protocol (v3)."

Like most of the other technologies that we mentioned, LDAP started its life as a way to provide a simplified, very lightweight access mechanism to the X.500 system that would run over standard TCP/IP networks. Since its inception in the early 1990s, LDAP has taken on a life of its own and does not now require any X.500 services at all — it has become its own database, rather than relying on another system. Today some LDAP implementations provide this gateway capability to X.500 systems, but the most popular do not.

Four widely used LDAP implementations exist. The open source OpenLDAP (`http://www.openldap.org`) is in use across almost every open UNIX system. Novell's NDS uses LDAP to communicate and store information. iPlanet's LDAP server is also very widely used both as a standalone system and integrated within iPlanet's other e-commerce application suites. The final major user of LDAP is Microsoft's ActiveDirectory system. However, typically for Microsoft, ActiveDirectory adds a few extra things that make it difficult to use the system in a normal LDAP-enabled environment.

How is data structured in an LDAP database?

Data within an LDAP system is defined in a hierarchical tree. How you organize that tree is up to you, but the most common arrangements follow domain names or company structure. An advantage of using this tree structure is that it enables you to break off a branch and locate it on a completely separate server from the other branches. Thus, with a logical-tree structure each branch can be physically located in its own area without needing to reference the other parts.

Organizations based on company structure are useful when you want to define or locate information based on geographical locations. For example, you can divide the information up by country, then state, and then office location, as shown in Figure 8-1. Within each office, you can keep all the local information, such as the printer and contact details of the people based there. Thus, if one of your network links goes down, the local office can still run and so can the remote ones — they just won't be able to access information for the staff there.

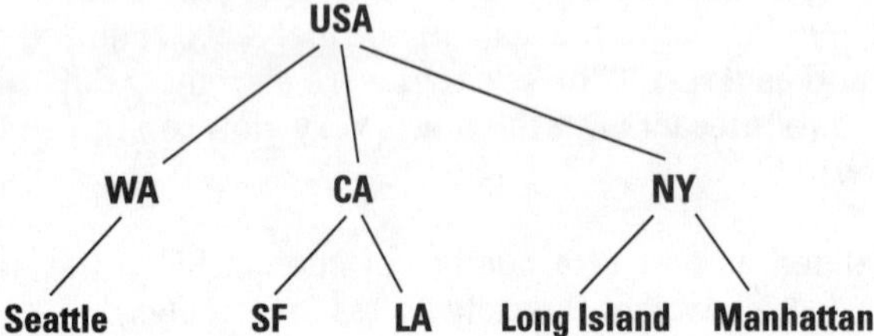

Figure 8-1: An example organization of LDAP data as a tree structure representing geographical information

Each branch in the hierarchy keeps information about its location relative to the root of the tree. So, even though your network link might have disappeared, the only difference your applications will see is that only the local information is available.

Internet address–based structures are another very common means of locating information in an LDAP database. By their very definition, domain names already include geographical information, and the name system has a very nice hierarchy already associated with it. This style of structure suits applications that deal a lot with e-mail information, such as e-commerce Web sites, because the e-mail address makes for a good lookup mechanism.

Defining one piece of data with entries

Almost all information in an LDAP database is defined as being string information. Each string consists of a name and a value. To locate an item in the LDAP, you concatenate a collection of these strings together that represent the path from the root of the tree to the entry you are interested in. A single name/value pair is called an attribute. You collect a bunch of these attributes together into a single item called an *entry*. An entry is the logical equivalent of a row in a relational database, and the name of an attribute the equivalent of the column name. When you are searching an LDAP database, or adding information to one, the smallest logical entity is an entry.

An attribute may have almost anything in it. For a given name, you may also have many different values, and this leads to multi-value attributes. For example, if you want to define an e-mail address attribute, you may actually have multiple values for that one attribute name.

Building large databases with trees

Where LDAP differs markedly from relational databases is that any entry may contain other entries. This leads to a tree structure. In a typical LDAP structure, the branches of the tree do not contain any information other than the child entries. It is not until you get to the leaf nodes that contain no children that you find sets of attributes. This is not to say that you can't provide attributes further up the tree; just that it is not a typical part of the design.

An interesting consequence of this tree structure is that for any given LDAP database, there is always only one strict "structure" within the database. Where relational databases allow a collection of tables and links among the tables, LDAP has only one tree — with many branches in it. Each branch may represent its own data just as a relational database has many different tables (that is to say, attributes found in one branch will not necessarily be found in another branch), but the LDAP database is still one logical structure.

Although there is this logical structure of a tree, it is possible to have all the data in a flat structure wherein all the parent branches are nominal only. This may seem a bit strange now, but you'll see some examples later in the chapter in which it is useful.

Linking between data structures

One of the most fundamental operations in a relational database is using a value in one table to make lookups into another table. Within LDAP, you have no way of making implicit links between two different entries. In a relational database you can define a column that contains a primary-key value to link to another table. LDAP does not contain an equivalent structure. This is where one of those optimizations directed at fast searches comes in — an entry shall have only one path to it.

While the LDAP database does not allow implicit linking among branches of the tree, you can create explicit links — and this is quite common. To create the reference between the two branches, you need only to define an extra attribute that contains the search information to the linked structure. For example, to link an employee to a department, you need only add a new attribute named `department` and store in its value the search string with which to find the department entry. The difference between relational and LDAP is that no consistency checks are enforced by LDAP — everything is just treated as a string.

Naming items in the database

The pathway from the root of the tree to an entry is referred to as the Distinguished Name or usually just DN. The DN provides the unique identifier to the path and includes the names of all the entries between the root of the tree and this entry.

You can describe an entry without all the path information using the Relative Distinguished Name (RDN). When you're searching the database this won't help much, but it is useful when you're trying to describe pieces of the data to someone else. Typically the RDN is the name of the major key used by the database to describe an entry.

A distinguished name is just a comma-delimited list of the characteristic attribute for each entry from the root to this particular entry. The interesting part is that, theoretically at least, you can use any name and any value as your structure. Practically, there is a set of conventions followed that makes the difference between the tree structure and the attributes of an entry easy to spot. We'll cover these shortly.

Standard languages

One of the more unusual aspects of LDAP systems is the lack of a standard interface language. LDAP started life as a protocol, so the definition of the protocol is the same regardless of the underlying database implementation. From the application perspective, there is no standard query language, other than a slightly modified version of the raw protocol message. In this LDAP is in complete contrast to relational databases, which have no standard interface protocol, but have a standardized query language in the form of SQL.

When querying an LDAP database, the typical query has a search term that consists of a DN or RDN, a search term that lists the name of the desired attribute, and a filter. The filter determines which information is returned to the user. We'll cover each of these items in more detail shortly.

Perhaps the best way of defining the standard language of LDAP is to say that it is a plain text string. Everything you want to do with LDAP you can do by putting the command into a string form and passing that string to the database. In the end, this means that most information is stored as and referred to as strings within the database. Other primitive types are allowed, even complex binary formats, but mostly data is kept as strings. A typical explanation for this is that if you must store a binary object in LDAP, you are probably better off using a relational database. Binary objects are too slow when it comes to searching.

Of course, a big exception to this rule is the way in which Java objects are stored in LDAP databases. With drivers and everything else being stored in the JDNI directory services, LDAP is taking on more and more of a traditional database role. Now you can access a LDAP entry for a particular printer and be given the binary driver to be installed on your operating system. So while the general rule is "text only," this rule is often violated for even simple uses.

Software using LDAP

In this chapter we've already mentioned quite a few pieces of software that use LDAP information. The following is a list of specific examples you are likely to come across in your development environment:

- **PAM (Pluggable Authentication Module):** This is a system that allows the use of modular authentication systems and provides a single common front end to them. The software has modules for standard and shadow passwords, NIS/NIS+, and LDAP. PAM is most commonly seen in the Linux and Solaris environments.
- **Apache Web server:** At least three different modules that you can use with Apache incorporate LDAP for authentication. The modules enable you to control general access to the site or more detailed access on a per-directory basis, and replace the .htaccess files.
- **Sendmail:** This is the most widely used mail agent, and it provides LDAP authentication of users and delivery information. You can define various different aliases for one person and alternate addresses through the standardized LDAP schemas.
- **IMAP/POP:** Just as Sendmail uses LDAP to hold information for the delivery and routing of e-mail, various IMAP and POP3 servers (such as the Washington University daemons) use LDAP for authentication and configuration information.
- **Netscape Navigator/Mozilla:** Since version 4.0 of the Netscape Web browser and e-mail client, LDAP has been at the center of the roaming capabilities (known as Roaming Profiles). The commercial add-on calendaring system also uses LDAP as the access point for information about users.

Defining Information in an LDAP Database

Perhaps the hardest part of trying to explain LDAP is having to deal with the problem of not having a standard language. LDAP is a protocol and a number of tools are available for the command line, and each language has its own API set, but there is no equivalent of SQL. In the relational world SQL defines both a query language and a way to define structure in a database. As you will see in Chapter 9, JNDI has its own view of the world, and that view differs widely from what the command-line tools, or other languages such as Perl and Python, offer.

LDAP does have a way of defining customized data structures through the use of *schemas*. However, schemas aren't used for the majority of business applications. The standard types provided by the various RFCs usually do the job adequately. We introduce the topic of writing custom schemas in the last section of this chapter.

Designing a new database

Combining a series of entries together, you get the tree hierarchy of an LDAP database. Because the structure of the tree defines the search criteria when you come to look things up later, it is much more important to get this representation right here than it is to get it right in a relational database. Why is this so? The distinguished name, as the unique identifier for an individual entry, also defines the structure of the tree. In combination with this, when you want to find some information in the database, the distinguished name is usually derived from outside information such as the originating e-mail address.

An example database

What does a typical DN look like? If we started by presenting a standard example, most of it would not make sense—you would need to understand the exact data structures underlying it. So before we introduce you to the fundamentals of the LDAP queries, we start with some example databases to illustrate the later concepts.

We'll start with a theoretical database for keeping customer and sales information, just like the one we used in Chapters 6 and 7. For the purpose of comparison, we will re-code SQL tables as LDAP trees, entries, and attributes.

We must point out that what follows is probably one of the worst uses of LDAP structures imaginable. It should be used as a guide only. Certainly, storing customer contact information is a prime use of LDAP, but keeping order information is not really a good or appropriate use of LDAP.

Getting started

The first major design decision you make when building an LDAP structure concerns how you are going organize information. You have this tree thing that describes all your data and yet you have to store all sorts of different items—contact information, product information, and even orders.

Working from this information, you have to decide how to organize the data structures of the tree. Just as with object-oriented programming, there is no absolute right way to do things. A number of common approaches are used for structures, but you don't need to stick with them. It is all a matter of whatever feels right for your project.

Two common arrangements for directory information trees in LDAP are illustrated in Figures 8-2 and 8-3. The first shows a company-style structure that holds information relative to the functional requirements — geographic office locations and then functional items such as printers, staff, and so on.

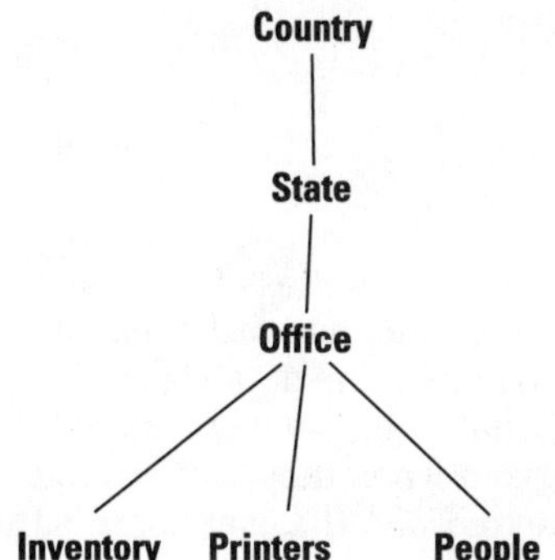

Figure 8-2: A directory-information tree organized by functional requirements

The second figure shows information organized by Internet domain name. You might be wondering why you would bother using a domain name as the tree structure. Remember that one of the key features of LDAP is the very fast searches it provides. If you have information with a domain name in it (such as customer information or running as the back-end authentication system for a mail or Web server), then you immediately have the search criteria to directly fetch entries from the database. With minimal effort you can turn that e-mail address into the distinguished name for the user: The resulting search will be very quick. Consider a database with a million customers in it — you can find something much faster in a sorted tree than you can with a linear search through a table, particularly if you want just one entry back.

For those of you who have done algorithm and data structures courses, the LDAP search is O(log *n*) while the relational search is O(*n*). Thus, for the huge datasets common in e-commerce sites, LDAP will always be faster than a relational database. Even with a primary key and indexing on that primary key rather than doing string searches, a relational database will only approach O(log *n*), whereas LDAP effectively forces this on you.

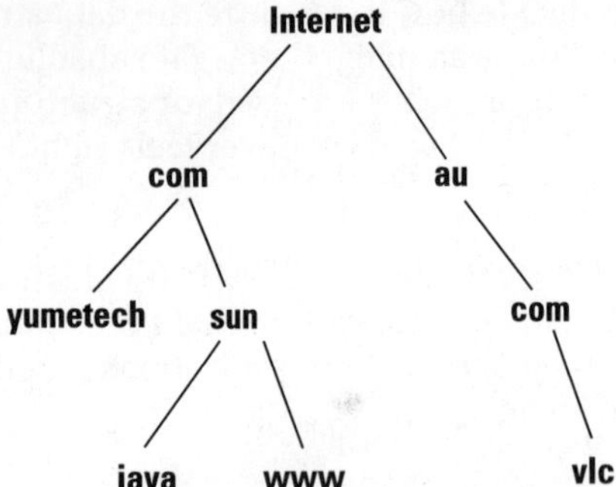

Figure 8-3: A directory-information tree organized by Internet domain name

Customer information

Because you are a business and you want to keep e-mail addresses of your customers for simple contact reasons (for example, recalls on a product and promotional deals), you are now going to insist on that e-mail address. Where in the database are you going to store this information? Well, as you already have domain-name information for their e-mail address, you can insist on requiring that when they log in to the system. The domain part becomes the hierarchy of the tree, and the user name is the unique identifier of the entry under that tree.

The rest of the information from the customer table becomes attributes for the entry. Because you already have the unique identifier for the customer, you do not need the integer identifier that the relational database uses. Apart from that, all the attributes just transfer across. (Remember that in LDAP attribute values are typically strings.) The result of this design is the structure shown in Figure 8-4.

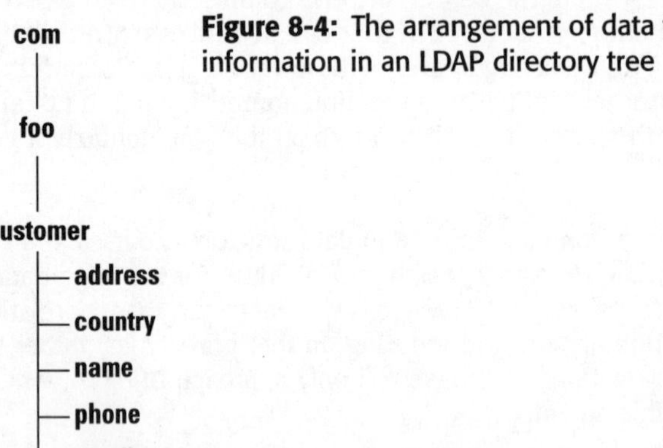

Figure 8-4: The arrangement of data for customer information in an LDAP directory tree

Product information

You have domain names for customers, but you don't have any particularly natural way of categorizing products. You have many options—you can organize everything in one flat structure, you can organize by category, or you can organize by supplier. It's a tough call, but you certainly don't want to store everything in a single flat structure, because that's not terribly efficient for lookups. In the end, let's say you punt for organizing by major category.

To individually identify a product, you are still going to need some form of unique identifier. Here, try a different tack from the one you took with the relational database: Within each category, use the natural scheme for that product as the identifier of individual items. For example, with books use the ISBN; for CDs use the catalog number. You'll end up with the structure shown in Figure 8-5.

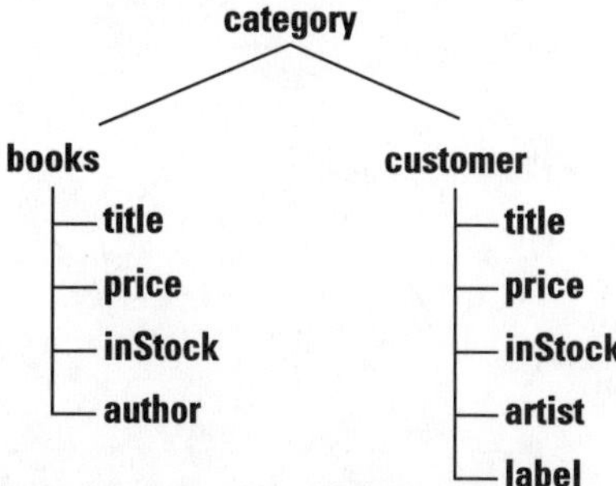

Figure 8-5: The arrangement of product data in the LDAP directory tree

Order information

As far as increasing levels of difficulty go, this is it when building LDAP data structures. Order information is a flat, sequential list with no inherent data structure. It's the worst sort of data to put into LDAP. But for the purposes of the exercise we will persevere. How do you deal with it? Well, here you are just going to have to stick with a single big, flat structure.

But with a structure like this, how do you generate the unique identifier? Unlike SQL, LDAP has no nice feature like automatically incrementing values. Indeed, no solution exists—which means that you have to fall back on the application finding the number somewhere, incrementing it itself and then placing the new incremented value back. That is hard work if you have multiple independent applications accessing the one LDAP directory tree.

Attributes are used in the body of the entity, but over in the relational database representation, most of this table is a set of primary keys of other tables. As you will recall, LDAP does not have a defined reference mechanism, and so you have to deal with this yourself. Where you have columns that are primary key references, you turn these into a string, which is the distinguished name of the entry for the appropriate data. Therefore, as Figure 8-6 shows, you will have attributes that contain ordinary information as well as attributes that contain a DN for another part of the database.

Pulling it all together

So far you have three independent data structures — customer, product, and orders — that need to be held in a database. We've avoided discussing how all of these are represented in the one database. As we've mentioned before, an LDAP directory tree always has a single root. What you need to do is organize your individual entries into one big tree in which each area is its own branch — if you don't, you'll end up with a big mess of data that looks something like Figure 8-6. So, to each tree you add another level to the distinguished name that represents the part of the tree you are in, and this allows a nice segregation of each of the individual data collections.

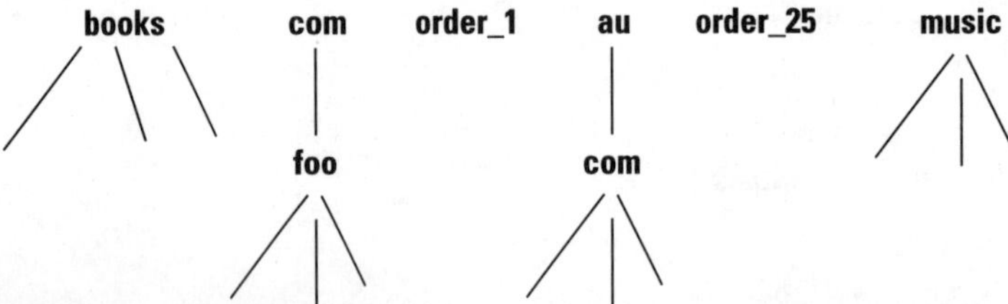

Figure 8-6: This is what happens when you try to jam all the individual structures together – chaos.

Although we've stated that the entire LDAP directory tree exists under a single root, you may have an implicit root. That is, the new tops that you've added for each area do not require a single root to be under; you could happily leave them as is. For your demonstration directory tree, that is sufficient. However, when you get to real-world situations, you will find that it is better to have a single root. The root collects all the information for a given application so that at some later stage you can add more or different information to the same database.

The final result of all of this is the structure you see in Figure 8-7. At the top you have the optional application root entry. Below the root entry you have entries for each of the data areas. Further down you'll find the data arranged as we discussed previously.

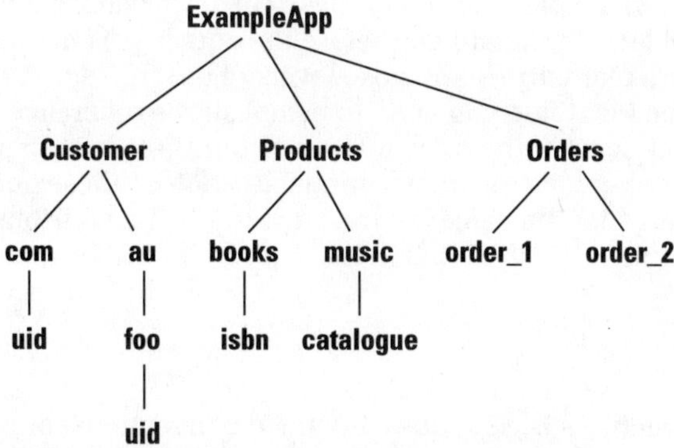

Figure 8-7: The final arrangement of your LDAP directory tree for the example application

An introduction to standard LDAP

All LDAP interactions are defined by the distinguished name and the attribute or attributes to be found or modified. So far all you have seen are a bunch of pretty pictures—how do these translate into real-world LDAP usage?

Distinguished names

Let's start your first example of a distinguished name using a product—this book. Its ISBN allocated is 0-7645-0882-2 (at least for the American edition!). Under the structure that you've just created, the DN is:

```
isbn=0-7645-0882-2, cat=books, ou=products, o=ExampleApp
```

What does all this mean? Well, let's start at the beginning—a DN is a comma-delimited list of entries that defines the path from the root of the directory tree to a particular entry. If you look at this structure and then at Figure 8-5, you should see the correspondence between each of the items declared in the list.

A distinguished name is always defined as a single string wherein the leaf entry appears first, and the last entry is the root of the tree. If you rip apart the string above, you will see how each name/value pair (as separated by the commas) represents one level in the tree that you created earlier. Whitespace is significant between sets of commas, but not right before a comma. Thus, you don't need to quote string values to include the space value. The following are all equivalent:

```
cn=Justin Couch,dc=vlc,dc=com,c=au,o=Internet
cid=justin couch,    dc=vlc    ,  dc=com,c=au, o = Internet
cid=justin Couch ,dc=vlc,  dc=com ,c=au, o =internet
```

So you've worked out what the value part of each of these entries means, but what are these funny-looking sets of letters that appear before the equals (=) character? They are the names of the particular entries for those levels of the tree. Just as your lowest level needs some unique identifier, you need to establish the difference between the entry name at each level of the tree and its attributes — remember that any and every level of the directory tree may contain attributes. These odd characters like `ou`, `o` and `cat` are just the names of the entries' defining attributes. Why such short and unintelligible names? Well, that has a lot to do with naming conventions and history.

LDAP naming conventions

Within LDAP directory-tree structures is a set of well-defined conventions for naming each level of a tree and also for naming the attributes within a tree. These are so well established that if you used them for something else, it would probably leave most experienced LDAP practitioners scratching their heads. These conventions have reached a *de facto* status. Therefore, so you will feel comfortable in this environment, Table 8-1 outlines most of the common names you will run across.

Table 8-1
The names of the conventional directory-tree hierarchy entries and attributes

Name	*Description*
`o`	The organization type or area. The value of this name is often `Internet` if data are structured by domain name; it may also be the name of the company or application if a functional structure is used.
`ou`	The organizational unit. A subsection of the company or product that enables you to define things in smaller and smaller categories. An organizational unit may contain further subunits, but they will all use the `ou` name.
`uid`	The user identifier. Usually associated with the user's login name.
`c`	The country. Typically the two-letter country code.
`cn`	The common name. Used when referring to a person's or object's ordinary name they might use in real life.
`sn`	The surname of the user.
`dc`	The domain-name component when using domain names as the tree structure.
`dn`	The distinguished name.
`mail`	The user's e-mail name or alias.
`objectclass`	The schema(s) to which this entry conforms.

When you're supplying information to LDAP, neither the attribute names nor the attribute values are case-sensitive. Keep this in mind (it would be a very poor design if structures depended on case between words anyway).

It is possible to use case-sensitive names and attributes in LDAP, but by convention, the standard schemas do not enforce case-sensitivity. If you require case-sensitive information in your LDAP data structures, then you will have to create a custom schema. By default, any non-validated data entered into an LDAP database (that is, schema checking is turned off) will not be case-sensitive.

Getting back to the example DN, you can now make more sense of it:

```
isbn=0-7645-0882-2, cat=books, ou=products, o=ExampleApp
```

At the root of the tree (the far right value) you have the organization named `ExampleApp`. Under the root you have a collection of organizational units—in this case `products`. The product unit has a number of category entries, wherein the attribute name `cat` is a custom name that you've chosen. Finally, you have the actual entry item under the category where you use the `isbn` attribute name for the unique key.

The LDIF file format

Because the protocols are different from the tools and also from the back-end database (it would be quite reasonable to implement the LDAP data structures internally as a relational database), you need some method of shuffling data back and forth, and for backing up and rebuilding databases. While no standard is defined, most LDAP databases will understand the de facto LDIF file format.

The LDIF format is very straightforward—basically one attribute exists per line. A blank line indicates the separation between entries in the database. To declare an attribute, you start with the name followed by a colon and the attribute value. If an attribute has more than one value, you just place more than one line in the file. For example:

```
dn: uid=justin,dc=vlc,dc=com,dc=au,o=Internet
cn: Justin Couch
sn: Couch
uid: justin
objectclass: top
objectclass: person
objectclass: organizationalPerson
```

LDIF is designed as a transfer mechanism, so there are no comments in it, and if you are going to have even a moderately sized database, it is really, really huge. A simple database with a thousand entries can easily take up 20MB or more.

Comments in LDIF files take the form of a line starting with the hash (#) character. You cannot use partial-line comments because all whitespace is treated as being significant to the value. Therefore, comments only work when the hash is the first character on the line.

You do not need to order attributes in any particular fashion, but by convention the first attribute mentioned for each entry is the distinguished name (the `dn` attribute). This makes it easy to sift through what each record is, because a blank line just before it always makes it easy to spot.

Strong typing with schema

Despite all the pretenses so far, LDAP does allow a relatively strong typing mechanism through the use of schema. If a particular entry says that it contains a given schema, as defined by a value(s) of the `ObjectClass` attribute, then it would be reasonable to expect attributes of that type here. That is, if you have an attribute that matches a particular name and that name is in the schema, then you know you are able to interpret the value in a particular way.

Schemas add a form of constraint checking to the database to make sure that everything that comes and goes is legal and that you don't accidentally put invalid values in and that two schemas don't clash with the use of an attribute name. While schemas are useful during the development phase of your application, they do impose quite a lot of overhead, as they are checked during every search, addition, and deletion. The result is that almost every deployed LDAP database will have schema-checking turned off for performance reasons.

A number of common schemas exist for LDAP: They are listed in Table 8-2. If you see one of these declared in the `ObjectClass`, you know what sort of functionality you can expect an application to use that particular LDAP entry for. In general, when you see these declared, they end up becoming more of a hint for the reader of the LDAP database rather than the database internals themselves. A particular application can then check these, if it so desires, to make sure that an entry contains the necessary information.

Table 8-2
Standard LDAP schema types

Schema Name	*Description*
`Top`	The root schema that all schemas are derived from. It does not contain any specific attributes.
`Person`	This is a real person so expect data such as first and last names, initials, and common names.
`OrganizationalPerson`	The person belongs to an organization so some structure information will follow.
`inetOrgPerson`	The person belongs to an organizational structure based on Internet information (for example, that is LDAP-specific rather than using the X.500 `organizationalPerson`, which may be not related to an Internet system). See RFC 2798.

Schema Name	*Description*
`inetMailUser`	The user is an Internet user with standard Internet-capable e-mail.
`inetMailRouting`	The entry can be used to perform mail routing such as aliasing to different names, changing the mail delivery protocol, or forwarding on to other servers.
`inetSubscriber`	The user has Internet mail–handling capabilities. This schema defines the types of mailboxes and mail-access protocols to use (IMAP, POP3 and so on).

Interacting with the Database

It is rare for an application to deal with an LDAP database on the protocol level. However, there is also a real lack of standard interfaces that you can use to interact at the language-independent API level, such as relational databases offer with JDBC/ODBC and SQL. Of course, this lack is the result of the fundamental difference between LDAP, which is a protocol definition, and SQL, which is a language definition. Although we introduce JNDI in the next chapter, in this one we have a difficult time formulating a generic description of how to interact with an LDAP server.

The closest thing that LDAP has to a standard interface is a set of command-line tools for addition, deletion, and viewing the database: `ldapadd`, `ldapremove`, and `ldapsearch`, respectively. All of the concepts we introduce in this section will discuss how to interact with an LDAP database in terms of these tools.

Connecting to the database

Connecting to an LDAP database should not involve any tricks that you are not already familiar with. Just as with any good enterprise service, you need to (usually) supply a user name and password to access the database as well as supplying the host and port to talk to.

Typically that user name is required to be in an LDAP style, consisting of a name-value pair. In every case that we're aware of, the attribute name is `cn` followed by the value of the user name. The host and port are the usual domain name and port number — the default port number for LDAP is 389.

Searching an LDAP database

Searching an LDAP database is the most common task you will perform. A search is just like an SQL `SELECT` — you name the table to look in (which branch of the directory tree), what you want to find (the name of the entry), and a filter to return only parts of the matching rows (attributes within the matching entry(s)).

Branch selection to narrow the search

Although it is not required, because you are always in the same tree, setting the branch of the tree to search in is a good idea. Unlike SQL, because we have a single hierarchy tree, there is no requirement to set the branch to search in—it is always the same tree. However, for efficiency reasons, it is a good idea to try to limit the scope as much as possible. Say you are looking up a customer name: You do not need to search through all the product and order areas, so you might as well confine your search to the customer area. Now, since you know that you've organized the customer area by domain name, and you have the domain name from the user's login, you can further restrict your search by setting the DN for the search criteria to be the area defined by that e-mail address. Say you wanted to look up Justin Couch. You can set the search DN to be the following:

```
dc=vlc,dc=com,c=au,ou=customers,o=ExampleApp
```

Now, when you want to look up Couch's user information, that search criteria has just limited the number of possible solutions from a million to maybe a thousand. Your search command on the command line starts with the following (note that it is supposed to be on a single line!):

```
ldapsearch -b "dc=vlc,dc=com,c=au,ou=customers,o=ExampleApp"
```

But you cannot run this command as is, because you have not told it what you are looking for yet.

Setting the search criteria

To set the search criteria for that branch, you supply the name or names of the attribute(s) you are using as the key, and then supply the value you are looking for. You can also supply a wildcard (*) character if you want all the values that match a given attribute name.

So if you want to do a search for all users whose first name is Justin, you can set the search criteria to the following:

```
ldapsearch "sn=justin"
```

Note that when dealing with the criteria on the `ldapsearch` command-line tool that you put the criteria in quotes to make sure that the shell does not accidentally interpret the equals character (=) or the whitespace as something else. Within an application, quoting is not necessary.

Filtering the returned results

When executing SQL searches, you often don't want to see everything, or to see the output in a certain order. LDAP has the same sort of abilities. You can set filters to return only certain attributes. The result filter takes the attribute names in the order in which they are to be returned, just as SQL does. Again, we're being a bit vague here because how you set the filter information depends on how you are accessing it. Say you just want to find Justin Couch's e-mail address and full name to send him a confirmation e-mail. The request is as follows:

```
ldapsearch "sn=justin" mail cn
```

The first item returns the e-mail address, and the second item is the standard attribute name for "common name"—that is, the common name that Justin Couch would like to be known by.

Modifying values in an LDAP database

To add or modify values in an LDAP database, you supply the DN for the newly added entry and then the list of attributes to be added to that. Effectively, the DN creates the entry, and then the attributes are used to fill in the details.

When you are adding or modifying entries, LDAP databases will check for the existing structure, and, if schema-checking is turned on, will determine whether you have supplied the right amount and type of data. If no schema checking is used, the LDAP database will just happily take whatever you give it. If you supply a value for an attribute that is the same as one already set, the database will not be happy with you. Remember this, because it will be very important once we come to dealing with JNDI.

Building Custom Data Structures

So far you have seen how to deal with generic data structures within LDAP. What you have learned already is a very powerful tool applicable in 90 percent of the situations in which you are likely to see LDAP. Of course, this means that another 10 percent remains, and that 10 percent is what we're going to discuss here—designing LDAP to fit custom situations.

Three areas are worth looking in terms of building your customized application. First we tell you about the most common situation—building the distinguished-name hierarchy and deciding what terms to use where. Next we look at how you can build large-scale LDAP systems, and finally we show you how to build customized data structures using schema and attributes.

Data hierarchies

We've already shown you the simple rules for building the directory information–tree hierarchies a number of times in this chapter. So far we have basically shown them fait accompli and left you to work out the details. Now we are going to spend some time discussing why you would put certain objects and names in various places in the system.

Starting at the top

Getting a good hierarchy is, believe it or not, really dependent on getting the root node and its immediate children correct. Organizing the root structures in a poor, unfocused way can make your life as a programmer extremely miserable. The database itself doesn't care much, but having to apply different sets of rules for different branches really becomes a pain for you.

Looking at the top, you want to make sure the root node is something appropriate for your application. As we've mentioned before, the root node should be something like the application or area name and will almost invariably use the `o` attribute name. There's a good reason for this — it is the organization information, who or where the data comes from. You would have to have an extremely good reason for not having the root of your directory tree use the `o` attribute.

Under the root node, you need to start looking at how to organize the data for your application. There are two schools of thought concerning the organization of data — the one we introduced earlier in the chapter, and the one we are about to introduce.

I'm upside down!

If the application does only one thing with the data, the data under the root node goes directly into the classification process. Then, once you get down towards the real data, you break it up into functional groups. One typical example of using this type of organization is dealing with user information. Here you are likely to find the following distinguished-name path:

```
uid=jones,ou=people,dc=mycompany,dc=com,o=Internet
```

Notice that you don't start dealing with the `ou` organizational structure until you get down near the leaf entries. This is in complete contrast to the structure we presented earlier in the chapter wherein the organizational units were at the top. The `ou` at the bottom approach is useful when you really only have one way of organizing the data. The example database we presented earlier had three different types of data to represent. When you're defining a product, how do domain names help you? They don't, and therefore this solution does not work in the situation presented by the example database.

Deciding how to name each level

For those concerned with the beauty of code, having the right names can mean a lot. It also helps others who come to maintain your code because you'll be using good, well-understood naming conventions.

In Table 8-1, we introduced the most common attribute names. Each of these names has a certain conventional meaning associated with it, and using it for something else will cause problems later on. So what conventions should you be concerned with?

When dealing with Internet-based addresses, always use the `dc` and `c` names for the various levels. `c` is for countries, and where it is part of the domain name, use it. If you have names that are from .com, .org, .net, or similar, then they will not contain country attributes. Below the country, for each level in the domain name, you have a `dc` value. `dc` is the domain component and makes it easy to break up information into common trees for faster searching.

For structures dealing with people and company organization, you should use the `ou` attribute. This advertises the fact that you are grouping structures based on some real-world organizational boundaries rather than on arbitrary ideas that you've come up with.

Replication

Once you get beyond a simple database with small amounts of data, coping with the demands of e-commerce and large company domains requires a little more design thought. If you are dealing with a database containing a million users, a couple of thousand products, and millions of orders, how do you build a database and hardware to deal with it? The answer is the same as with your traditional relational database — go big and get lots of 'em!

OK, what we are really talking about is distributing the processing load across a number of machines to place data where they is really needed — distributed systems.

Passing the buck

When you are building large-scale LDAP systems it is very important to consider building a distributed server. The standard approaches of replicating the entire database across all servers or splitting the database into different servers apply here just as much as they do to any other enterprise application. The great thing about LDAP is that the protocol and servers are structured so that your application will never have to care about the difference between distributed and non-distributed.

All LDAP servers implement the referral capability. What this does, when you are building your database, is signal to the local database that other parts exist that are not held locally, and tell it where to find them. The local server is therefore able to pass off requests for information it does not know how to answer. Once a result is returned from the "other" server, it is cached locally, which speeds up future accesses of that same data.

Setting up referrals

The process of setting up a server to refer to another server is software-independent. That is, you can organize name referrals in an LDIF format file.

If you want to set up your server to refer to sub-branches of the tree below your information (you are acting as a "root" server for the tree), then you can create the special attribute name `ref` in the file. To use this attribute you must first create an entry in the LDIF file that corresponds to the branch you are going to use as a referred service. Say your example server is going to have the product information located on a separate host — `products.mycompany.com`, as in the following example:

```
dn: ou=products, o=Internet
objectClass: referral
objectClass: extensibleObject
dc: cat
ref: ldap://products.mycompany.com/     \
     dc=cat,ou=products,o=Internet/
```

Here you are stating that the subtree, starting with the `dc` attribute name, can be found on the nominated server rather than locally. (Note that the last two lines are meant to be a single line with no whitespace. We've just run out of formatting room here in the book.)

To implement referrals it is recommended that you nominate both ObjectClass types of `referral` and `extensibleObject`. This will ensure that your LDIF data is portable across as many database implementations as possible.

If you want to refer to the root server from your local server, then you can skip most of the preceding explanation and just name the referral directly. Doing this takes just a single line in the LDIF file — one that states the list of URLs to try for the root servers:

```
referral: ldap://srv1.mycompany.com/ ldap://srv2.mycompany.com/
```

Note that in each case you needed only the server name; you can dispense with the DN part.

Referral is a standard part of the LDAP protocol, which means that it does not matter whether the two servers use the same software. You can have the local server use OpenLDAP while the root server for referrals is using iPlanet.

Schemas

The final customization capability we'll mention is building on the existing standard datatypes and schemas with your own. As we've hinted throughout this chapter, most production applications of LDAP turn schema-checking off, so the procedure we outline here is probably not worth the effort most of the time. If you turn schema-checking off and define all your values as strings, then you can merrily add new attributes to any entry whenever you want.

What schemas buy you is piece of mind — an assurance that your custom data handling is going to build things correctly. Most importantly, when you want to store binary data in LDAP and make sure it gets treated correctly by the underlying database.

Extensibility of schema information comes on two levels — individual attributes and whole collections of attributes (object classes).

Getting started

LDAP, being a public protocol, has some certain restrictions applied to it. If you want to play ball with everyone else, and not have to track down some weird, obscure bug, then you'll need to follow the rules. Following the rules is particularly important if you are going to be using some pre-existing LDAP server or a server that will be shared across a number of applications — any of which may require its own customizations.

Internally, LDAP support works by using numerical identifiers for each important piece of information. In this, it is just like TCP/IP, which really uses numerical addresses, but layers DNS over the top so that it is more human-friendly.

LDAP lies over the top of a global scheme used for many other applications, called the Object Identifier (OID). This number is assigned by a global body, such as IANA, for use within your application. OIDs are part of a numbering scheme used in a wide range of applications, from SNMP to LDAP.

You can find a full listing of all OID assignments at `http://www.alvestrand.no/harald/objectid/`.

It costs you nothing to get an OID allocated for your custom application. Just visit the Web page at `http://www.iana.org/cgi-bin/enterprise.pl`. Fill out the form, and you will be sent a new, unique OID for your application within a couple of days. The form mentions MIB/SNMP numbers, but you can use your number for any purpose — you only need one per company anyway.

An OID looks a bit like an IP address, and is usually of the form: 1.2.2.1.3.6. The numbers really don't matter much, but you have to know they exist. The OID that IANA gives you will have this set of numbers, which form the base of your addressing scheme. Under that base address you have to add further layers for your applications. These just add more dotted numbers. What you really want to do is create a couple of layers so that you can extend the allocated number for different application types. Remember that you can use an OID for more than LDAP, so you might as well plan ahead and add extra numbers for other applications you might build in the future.

Extending attributes

When you're building custom items for your database, the most useful will be new attribute types. These enable you to define a new name and type and give it a collection of inherent behaviors — such as marking the data as binary or making comparisons case-sensitive.

To create a new attribute type, you need to create a text file with the definition(s) in it. The syntax of the attribute definitions is described in RFC 2252. In its most simple form you declare that you are making a custom attribute type with the `attributeType` keyword, and then, in brackets, list the OID and the list of items to define the properties of the attribute. For example, you can use the following declaration to create a new case-sensitive attribute with the name `j2eeBibleString`:

```
AttributeType ( 1.2.3.4.5.6.1.1
  NAME 'j2eeBibleString'
  EQUALITY caseExactMatch
)
```

There must be whitespace between the brackets and any surrounding text. For example, `AttributeType (1.2.3.4 NAME 'foo')` is illegal because there is no whitespace between the bracket and the text.

When deciding on names for both attributes and object classes, you should avoid any possible collision problems by attaching a prefix such as your company or application name. This will help you avoid problems down the track if new standardized classes and attributes are approved by the IETF.

Within the syntax, apart from the first item, which is an OID, you have a collection of name/value pairs. The capitalized words are the defined properties that you can declare. Twelve different properties exist that you can use to define your custom attribute. Each of these attributes can then have a range of values, so we won't list all the properties available. If you really want to create custom attribute types, then we recommend you read RFC2252 to get all the gory details.

Extending ObjectClasses

With a collection of attribute types in hand, you will now probably want to use them. To use your attribute types—either custom or standard—you will want to build custom object classes. Using object classes is very much like Java's version of object-oriented programming. An object class has an inheritance model that enables you to take a previously defined object class and add more attributes.

Creating a custom `ObjectClass` is very much like creating a custom attribute type. You start with the keyword `ObjectClass` and then provide a list of the attributes that the `ObjectClass` contains. Custom object types then provide you with the option of using the `MUST` and `MAY` keywords to declare whether the attributes are always required or optional, respectively.

Say you want to build special information about a particular person that includes a photo of him or her. As you are using the personal record for identification purposes, you want to make it mandatory for every LDAP record to have a photo associated with it. You know that you already have a basic object class, `inetOrgPerson`, but you want to add the extra photo information.

```
ObjectClass ( 1.2.3.4.5.6.2.1
  NAME 'photoPerson'
  DESC 'A person that requires a photo'
  SUP  inetOrgPerson
  MUST 'myPhoto'
)
```

This definition specifies that you have a new object class called `photoPerson`. The `SUP` attribute specifies that you are extending the `inetOrgPerson` ObjectClass and that, in addition to any other required attributes of the base object class, it must include a `myPhoto` attribute.

Summary

This ends your introduction to directory services and LDAP in particular. Directory services, even though they have been around for more than 15 years, still are very much an unknown quantity to most programmers. This is unfortunate because they offer some significant benefits over traditional relational databases. For the enterprise programmer they are definitely becoming more and more important, as the inclusion of JNDI as a core API in the J2SE spec from version 1.3 indicates. In this chapter, we introduced you to the basics of directory services, including:

- A general look at what directory services are.
- Comparisons between directory services and their better-known friends the relational databases.
- The basics of what LDAP is and how to structure and define data.
- An introduction to building customized LDAP data structures.

✦ ✦ ✦

Accessing Directory Services with JNDI

✦ ✦ ✦ ✦

In This Chapter

Learning the Java Naming and Directory Interface (JNDI)

Working with LDAP databases from Java code

Adding, removing, and modifying data in any directory service

Searching a directory service for information

✦ ✦ ✦ ✦

At the heart of the J2EE system is the Java Naming and Directory Interface or JNDI. This essential piece of software provides you with all the systems for registering, storing, and retrieving the components of your enterprise application. These components may be as simple as your database connection (JDBC drivers) or as complex as a complete subsystem interface, such as an electronic-payment gateway.

In the previous chapter, we talked a lot about directory services such as LDAP. The earlier chapters introduced database connectivity with JDBC and gave you a glancing introduction to JNDI for registering and retrieving database drivers. So just what does JNDI cover?

Java Abstraction of Directory Services

As the name suggests, JNDI does more than just interface to an LDAP database or fetch drivers for an SQL database. It is in fact a collection of abstracted interfaces for any directory service or naming service. Just what is a naming service? Well, the most familiar in Java circles is RMI. This service makes available Java objects that are bound to a particular name. Make a lookup of a name and get a Java object in return.

All of these naming and directory services have a common set of requirements. You have a generic thing named by a string, and you want to find the object that it represents. Once you have that object, you can perform operations on it. JNDI is designed to provide a common means of accessing all of this information regardless of the underlying source—both directory services and naming services have the same sort of structure.

A brief history of JNDI

JNDI started its life as a way to provide an abstract interface to LDAP databases—mainly driven by the Netscape developers who were integrating LDAP in a big way into all their products. During the early development phase, it was realized that the features used to access LDAP in a programmatic way would also be useful for many other sorts of services. For example, server writers had for a long time been requesting a generic interface into the low-level details of the DNS system—`java.net.InetAddress` was just not useful for their application.

As a result of this work, it soon became clear that JNDI could be useful in many different areas. It was at about this time that the Java engineers at Sun really started hitting their stride in getting consistent with their approach to solutions and design patterns. JNDI was the second of the enterprise-aimed APIs, and the experience gained from developing JDBC clearly shows in the much more consistent and logical structure. Thus, many of the features and approaches to API design that you see in JNDI will seem familiar once we get to the more complex features, such as Enterprise JavaBeans (EJBs), in later chapters.

The homepage for JNDI is `http://java.sun.com/products/jndi/`.

JNDI is now in its third iteration (version 1.2), where it has been stable for the past couple of years. Today work is mainly focused on building implementations of drivers for many different directory services. JNDI is part of the standard J2SE distribution, and the J2EE includes the slightly tweaked version 1.2.1.

J2SE v1.4 includes the version 1.2.1 of JNDI as well as the latest implementation of most of the service providers.

Hiding the implementation

One feature of all Java enterprise APIs is the separation between the interface and the implementation of a piece of technology. JDBC instituted this standard with its driver system, and then JNDI took it to the next level with what is now called the Service Provider Interface (SPI).

The service-provider system provides a second level of interface abstraction that lies below the normal user-level interfaces you will be introduced to in this book. These interfaces enable users to code the lowest-level interaction with the underlying data source however they wish. This implementation is then plugged into the JNDI system, which deals with all the generic issues such as finding the right service implementation for the requested data, and performing data management and consistency checking.

What does a service provider represent?

Service providers perform the mapping of the naming or directory information to an underlying real system. The main requirements that a service provider must know about is that the information is represented in a hierarchical system and that at any given level you can ask for a list of attributes about that level.

In JNDI terminology, every level in that hierarchy is represented by a context. The context describes the path from the root of the hierarchy to that level. For each context you can then ask for the list of names bound to it. The name defines the next level of context information. If you are running with a directory service, then you can ask for the list of attributes of that context as well.

What service providers are available?

You can find service providers either as part of the core download or as extras around the Internet. By default you get the DNS, Filesystem, and NIS service providers. If you want to access an LDAP service, a separate download is available from Sun's download area for JNDI.

Sun Microsystems keeps a full list of known service-provider implementations at `http://java.sun.com/products/jndi/serviceproviders.html`.

JDBC usually requires individual drivers for each database implementation, but JNDI does not. The idea of JNDI is to provide a generic interface so that if you use an LDAP service provider it can be used with any LDAP database implementation.

Packages and classes

The JNDI classes exist in four separate packages of which the base package is called `javax.naming`. These packages contain only the abstract representation of the directory services — service-provider packages are contained in `javax.naming.spi`, and the actual implementation of any given service provider is in separate packages.

Within the base package you will find the definition of all the core concepts of JNDI, which we will cover shortly. In Chapter 6 you were introduced to a couple of these classes and interfaces — `InitialContext` and `Context`. Get used to seeing these as they are the core of all JNDI user code.

The classes in the base package are used to access naming services. If you want to use the directory services, you will find a set of extended classes and interfaces in the `javax.naming.directory` package. By extending the classes we provide behavior that is useful for directory services such as the ability to deal with explicit attributes.

An extra package called `javax.naming.ldap` is provided for dealing with some of the extended services provided by LDAP v3. This package provides extra interfaces for the controls and extended operations (for example, dealing with your custom data types) over the generic directory-services package. Most applications that use LDAP will not need this package; the basic, generic interfaces will be sufficient.

Finally, you have a package for dealing with updates that come from the underlying directory service. The `javax.naming.event` package provides listeners and event structures for listening to changes in the directory service, such as items being added or removed.

Connecting to a Service

As with all the other J2EE services, you need to establish a connection between your end-user code and the database. Even though JNDI provides access to both naming and directory services, the methods you use to access them differ slightly.

What is in a connection?

Before starting on making connections, we'll introduce a little bit of the JNDI lingo. If you include the directory services, JNDI provides you with three basic items: contexts, name representation, and, for directory services, attributes.

All the classes and interfaces presented in this next section can be found in the `javax.naming` package unless otherwise specified.

Understanding the context

The most basic item that you deal with in JNDI is called a context. A context, represented by the `Context` interface, describes where we are in the information hierarchy — it's a "You are here" sign if you wish. Context information enables you to move up and down the information hierarchy to explore different pieces of information.

You can query a context for further structural information. For example, you can ask a context what sub-context information it contains — in other words, what the children levels are for this level of the hierarchy.

When dealing with directory services, you will probably want to use the `DirContext` interface in the `javax.naming.directory` package. It enables you to access to the attribute information so that you can query and modify the attributes of a context.

When querying a naming or directory service, you must always start somewhere. This "somewhere" is referred to as the `InitialContext`. Initial-context information is used to establish a connection to the underlying service and any starting hierarchy. When accessing the service, you may not want to be required to traverse the entire tree from the root to the item you are interested in. To look up the domain name `www.foo.com`, you don't want to have to look up `com`, then the `foo` sub-context and finally the `www` child. Instead, the initial-context information enables you to take a short cut and go directly to the level that you need: You can provide the initial context with the name `www.foo.com` and have everything available without any extra work.

Tip If you need to deal with LDAP v3 extra capabilities, the `javax.naming.ldap` package defines an extended context type called `LdapContext` to give you access to the extended operations.

Specifying the initial context and then traversing for sub-context information is dependent on the type of information that you are looking for. When writing the application, you need to know that you are looking up a domain name rather than an LDAP distinguished name. There is no reasonable way to make this a generic task.

Putting names to objects

An important part of dealing with directory and naming services is working with the name-to-object mapping. When you provide a string name, you need to know what you are asking for. For example, does the object represent a sub-context or could it represent a link to another part of the directory service? Say you are looking up a domain name with JNDI: Do the context information or properties define an IP address, or was that domain name actually just the domain portion and not a fully qualified host name plus domain name?

A name description in the JNDI system can be either a Java `String` or an instance of a `Name` object. The `Name` is actually an interface, so you can't just create instances of it directly. Instead it is given to you when you perform some other lookup operation. You can't just create a class that extends the `Name` interface and then pass that class to JNDI. This means you must always start with a `String`. So how do you find that string to bootstrap your initial query? Well, that really depends on your application. In Chapter 8 we talked a lot about using domain names for LDAP hierarchies. Your application does some processing on the domain name (say the user entered it as part of the login process) and then passes the string through to JNDI's naming lookup system (which we'll get to shortly) to return an instance of the `Name` interface.

Tip Although the name classes are an important part of the JNDI system, in common usage I have found that they are rarely used. In general, for large-scale sites like e-commerce Web sites, the information and requests are so transient that it is simpler and faster just to run with the pure `String` representation.

Once you have a name, you have two different ways of using that name to reference an object—to name a Java object and to use a reference to another object. In the first case, you have a collection of classes in JNDI based on the `NameClassPair` class. This class maps a name for the current context onto some underlying object that can be represented within the Java application—say an image stored in the LDAP database.

References to other objects do not actually store those objects because the objects exist outside the underlying naming/directory service. In these cases, you act as a pointer to another place where that object can be found—for example, the IP address of the printer. That is, the LDAP structure that contains your office information does not contain the actual printer, but it does contain the IP address that your word processor can use to contact the printer to send in a page to be printed. For references you use the `Reference` base class. The actual contact information is then stored in a `RefAddr` class that has two derived classes, `BinaryRefAddr` and `StringRefAddr`, to store the address in binary or plain-string representations, respectively.

What Is Your Name?

Just how do you decide what a name is? If you have to pass in a `String` to get the initial-context information and then use strings to traverse the names, how do you know how to structure the names and the hierarchy? The answer is—it's all up to you.

In some systems, the naming structure is inherent. For example, LDAP and DNS have a predefined way of representing a structure. For DNS, you have a set of alphanumeric characters that are dot-delimited to a maximum length of 64 characters. In LDAP systems you have the distinguished-name syntax—a collection of comma-delimited name/value pairs. For these structures, there is no argument about how to define a name to any object or part of the context.

On the other hand, we have examples like those in Chapter 7 for dealing with JDBC drivers. You never specified what the underlying directory service was, and it appeared that you just passed some random string to the `InitialContext`, and it automagically knew what to do. In these applications you are free to use any naming system that makes sense to you. For the JDBC example you followed the style guide suggested by the specification, which told you to use slash characters (/). In reality you could use anything—commas, semicolons, asterisks, or dollar signs. So long as you understand what is going on (and maybe also write the service provider to deal with it), it doesn't matter what the scheme is. As always, good software-engineering practice dictates that you should document your system so that others understand what is going on.

Looking at Attributes

When you start looking at directory services, attributes are a very important part of the information that you are dealing with. The principal activity that attributes are involved in is looking at a series of attributes to perform some other action — such as sending out an e-mail. For this process you want to look up all the users in a certain category and then send an e-mail, but to make it look personalized you want to use their first name, last name, and title (Mr., Mrs., Dr., and so on) rather than the bland "Dear Sir/Madam." All of these are attributes.

An attribute is represented by the `Attribute` interface in the `javax.naming.directory` package, and a collection of them is represented by the `Attributes` interface. An instance of `Attribute` represents exactly one attribute of a context. Of course, this does not preclude the attribute containing multiple values, any more than the LDAP system does.

To access attribute information from a `DirContext`, you would call one of the `getAttributes()` methods that we will cover later in this chapter.

Within the `Attribute` interface you will find the standard collection of getter and setter methods to look at the value. If you are using a schema-driven underlying system, then you will also have access to the definition of your attribute so that you can determine how to process it — for example, you can check to see whether the values that the attribute contains are ordered in the underlying system or if they are case-sensitive. Again, as with context information, you have to have a prior knowledge of the underlying system to be able to deal with syntax information effectively.

Connecting to naming services

OK, now that you are familiar with the basic working interfaces for JNDI, it's time to do something useful with them. This first example will show the use of the basic naming-service interfaces, and in the next section we'll extend this example to deal with directory services.

You used JNDI as a naming service in Chapter 7 to fetch implementations of the `DataSource` interface in a J2EE environment.

In this first example you will use the RMI registry naming service. This example will enable you to perform the same functions using JNDI that you would otherwise have found in the `java.rmi.registry` package and `java.rmi.naming` class.

The RMI example in this chapter uses the classes and server defined in Chapter 15. If you are not already familiar with RMI, you may wish to read that chapter.

Using system properties

JNDI uses quite a collection of system properties to define its behavior. Although Table 9-1 only lists the most important ones, many more are in use—particularly for directory-services implementations in which you need passwords and user names for security reasons (we cover these implementations later in the chapter, in Table 9-2).

Table 9-1
The list of standard JNDI properties used to control context handling

Property Name	*Description*
`java.naming.factory.initial`	The name of the class that is the factory for providing the `InitialContext` implementation from the service provider.
`java.naming.provider.url`	The initial URL used for configuration of the initial context. Dependent on the service provider in use.
`java.naming.factory.object`	The name of the factory or factories to use for creating objects used in the name-to-object mapping. Works for both `NameClassPair` and `References`.
`java.naming.factory.state`	The name of the factory or factories to use for creating JNDI state objects.

For convenience, a number of these properties exist as constants defined in the `Context` interface. For example, to set the initial factory within the code (not on the command line) you can use the following statement to set the service provider to be the Sun's file-system implementation:

```
System.setProperty(Context.INITIAL_CONTEXT_FACTORY,
                   "com.sun.jndi.fscontext.FSContextFactory");
```

Defining the service provider

The first step in connecting to a service is to nominate the service provider you want to use. Table 9-1 lists all the system properties you can use to define the behavior of the JNDI initial lookup. If none of these properties are defined, JNDI will look up the internal property file called `jndi.properties` for the default values, where you can also place default values.

But how do you know where and when to create service providers? Well, for everyone but those rare few who may implement a service provider, the service provider comes in a neat pre-packaged form from some other company or service. This service provider should provide documentation about what class names are to be used for the various factories used to create the initial context. The normal installation process will place the JAR files in the JRE extensions directory, along with all your other extensions, such as JDBC drivers and so on.

By default, the JNDI that comes with the J2SE v1.4 release includes service providers for DNS, CORBA, RMIRegistry, and LDAP. Version 1.3 does not include the DNS service provider. For J2EE, you need to check which service providers come with your J2EE environment, because each vendor will be different.

You can define system properties in the usual way — through `System.setProperty()`, on the command line using the –D option, or in the `jndi.properties` file. Whichever way you do it, you must make sure that you at least define the initial factory (`java.naming.factory.initial`) and the service provider's URL. Say you're using Sun's RMI service provider: The class you need is `com.sun.jndi.rmi.registery.RegistryContextFactory`.

Looking up the object

Now that the system properties are set, the next step is to create the initial context. For this you just need to create an instance of `InitialContext` with the following code:

```
InitialContext ctx = new InitialContext();
```

Once you have the context you can use it to look up the object in the RMI registry (if you already know its name) using the `lookup()` method. This method returns a Java `Object`, and just as RMI's `Naming.lookup()` method requires a cast to use the object, so does this one. For example, if the `Greeter` object is registered under the name `SayHello` on the remote server, you can obtain a reference to it like this:

```
Greeter greeter = (Greeter)ctx.lookup("SayHello");
String greeting = greeter.greetByName(guestName);

System.out.println("The message is " + greeting);
```

In the RMI example, in which you just had to deal with a `RemoteException` that might be thrown, now you must also deal with the JNDI exception `NamingException`.

You can replicate other functions of the RMI `Naming` class with the JNDI methods from the context. You can use `list()` to return a `NamingEnumeration` of all the objects held in the registry, and to `bind()` and `unbind()` objects to or from the registry.

Using multiple service providers

On some occasions you may want to use JNDI with a number of different service providers. For example, in the enterprise setting you use JNDI to locate your JDBC drivers, access an LDAP database, and also perform DNS queries — all at the same time. Of course, the enterprise security environment may not be conducive to your arbitrarily setting system properties all over the place. What is useful in one part of your enterprise application may not be useful in another — for example, the root URL of the RMI object that an Enterprise JavaBean is using to communicate with different servers.

You overcome the limitations of the system-property approach with a new set of constructors for the `InitialContext`. The alternative constructors take a `Hashtable` of values. In this `Hashtable` you store the collection of system properties and their values, for this instance of the `InitialContext` to use. In this way you can store all of the relevant details for your local needs and not have to worry about what the system has set. If you provide a non-empty set of values it will override the system properties. For example, you can use the following code to change your RMI setup to use the tabled values rather than the system properties:

```
Hashtable env = new Hashtable();
env.put(Context.INITIAL_CONTEXT_FACTORY,
        "com.sun.jndi.rmi.registry.RegistryContextFactory");
env.put(Context.PROVIDER_URL, "rmi://myserver.com:1099");

InitialContext ctx = new InitialContext(env);
Greeter greeter = (Greeter)ctx.lookup("SayHello");
...
```

Context properties are copied into the `InitialContext` and any other subcontexts you create from it. This enables you to reuse the same data for many different contexts or to change them slightly each time you want to create a new initial context.

Connecting to directory services

The next example shows you how to use JNDI to access a directory service to view attribute information. For this example you will use an LDAP database (we assume you have already set it up with some data).

Creating the initial connection

Directory services are supported through the classes in the `javax.naming.directory` package, as we mentioned earlier. Here you will find implementations of the basic interfaces, such as `Context`, that you can use with a directory service rather than a naming service. For a simple example, the setup is almost identical to that of a naming service, the only difference being that you swap in the directory-services class (for example, `InitialContext` becomes `InitialDirContext`).

Directory services differ from naming services in that they typically have a higher level of security—you need at least a user name and password to access them. These can be provided using the `Hashtable`, as you did in earlier examples. For example, you can obtain a simple LDAP connection with the following code:

```
Hashtable env = new Hashtable();
env.put(Context.INITIAL_CONTEXT_FACTORY,
        "com.sun.jndi.ldap.LdapCtxFactory");
env.put(Context.PROVIDER_URL, "ldap://myserver.com/");
env.put(Context.SECURITY_AUTHENTICATION, "simple");
env.put(Context.SECURITY_PRINCIPAL, "ldapuser");
env.put(Context.SECURITY_CREDENTIALS, "mypassword");

InitialDirContext ctx = new InitialDirContext(env);
```

There are several interesting points to note in this setup. Firstly, there is how you specify what sort of security system you want to use to connect to the LDAP database. Your choice is represented by the property `java.naming.security.authentication` (or the constant `SECURITY_AUTHENTICATION` in the `Context` interface). Here you indicated that you want simple authentication, which basically means a user name and password. The other options we will cover shortly.

Next you'll find the provider URL. This URL is the location of the LDAP host, and it follows the same pattern that we introduced in the last chapter for references between parts of the database hierarchy. In this example, you said that you want to always start from the root of the distinguished-name tree for your searches. If you knew that you were dealing with only one section of the tree, say your customer information, we could add extra information to the URL to help limit the search, as in the following example:

```
ldap://myserver.com/ou=customer,o=ExampleApp
```

Once the initial context is constructed, you can query the directory service just as you would a naming service. This involves using the `lookup()` and `list()` methods, as in the preceding example. Say a customer has logged into the system and you need his or her information; you can access the relevant entry with a lookup based on the customer's calculated distinguished name:

```
String dn = "uid=me, dc=mycompany, dc=com, " +
            "ou=customer, o=ExampleApp";
Context user = (Context)ctx.lookup(dn);
```

Securing the system

With any enterprise-level application, security is a major concern. You really don't want people accessing parts of the system that they should not—or even just inappropriately sniffing data for their own gains. In the preceding example, you said that you want simple authentication—a name and password that are passed as plain text across the wire in the LDAP protocol. The JNDI system can provide much greater security should you deem it necessary.

In the Context interface is a collection of constants that define the security properties you can use with a directory service. These constants all start with the prefix SECURITY_; Table 9-2 introduces the underlying system properties.

Table 9-2
System properties used to define security settings for JNDI

Property Name	*Description*
java.naming.security.authentication	The type of authentication to be used. Has one of three values: none, simple, or strong.
java.naming.security.principal	The user name or authority used to identify who is connecting to the service. This will vary according to the underlying service provider, but it is usually a user name.
java.naming.security.credentials	Whatever credential information is needed to authenticate who the principal is. This could be a plain-text password, an encrypted password, a cryptographic key used for SSL connections, or any other object.
java.naming.security.protocol	A string describing the protocol used to actually connect to the underlying service. Typically this is set to something like ssl or kerberos.

Using these properties, you can create a very tight connection to the underlying data source. We certainly don't recommend the use of plain-text user names and passwords in a business environment and consider an SSL connection between the application and server the minimum acceptable level of security.

If you are supplying user-name credentials to an LDAP database, make sure you read the documentation about what you need to provide, as each database is different. Typically, the user information is a distinguished name, but beyond that the details differ wildly. For example, the iPlanet LDAP server requires just the dn=Directory Manager name while the OpenLDAP server requires a fully qualified DN such as dn=Directory Manager, dc=mserver,dc=com, o=Internet. Your code should be flexible enough to handle these differences.

Reading attributes

The ability to deal with attributes is the main reason for using directory services. As you saw earlier in the chapter, attributes are represented by the `Attribute` interface and can only be retrieved from the directory service–specific context `DirContext`. Say that you know your user exists and he has asked to modify his contact information. In order for the user to modify the contact information, you must first retrieve the existing information so that you can display it.

You must first specify the object name that is the child of the context object for which you want the attributes. In most cases, the name you pass is the empty string to say that you want the attributes for the current object. For example, to retrieve all of the attributes for the current object, you would use the following statement:

```
Attributes attrs = user.getAttributes("");
```

The returned `Attributes` object now contains the list of all the attributes for your current user.

Tip

You can use the named object for retrieving attributes in a high-performance application by having the context be the parent distinguished name and then performing lookups based on the child name. For example, in a customer situation, you might want to set the context to be the customer context `ou=customer,o=ExampleApp`: The `getAttributes()` method is then passed the customer name `uid=customer_id,dc=mycompany,dc=com`. This saves you having to create new context information each time you need to make a query and can result in a significant performance increase.

For efficiency reasons, you may sometimes want to fetch only a subset of the attributes. A variant of the `getAttributes()` method enables you to provide an array of strings that represent the attribute names that you wish to fetch. Say you only want their initials, last name, title, and e-mail address for an e-mail: you can create a list of the corresponding attribute IDs and pass it to the `getAttributes()` method, and the returned `Attributes` instance will contain only those items.

```
String reqd_attrs = new String[] { "surname", "initials",
    "title", "rfc822mailalias"};

Attributes attrs = user.getAttributes("", reqd_attrs);
```

If you ask for the `size()` of the `attrs` variable, you will always be returned a value of 4.

Performance optimizations

As with all the enterprise APIs, you can use various performance optimizations to get the most from your system. We have already touched on a number of them in the tips throughout the chapter. Here are a few more to add to the collection.

Each time you create a new initial context you are opening another connection to the underlying service. If you are dealing with files, this causes no real performance penalty, but if you are going across an encrypted network link to a server, it can be very costly. Avoid creating new contexts all the time by keeping the basic initial information and then querying for sub-contexts from that. Each initial context will keep the connection information. Unfortunately, this also means that JDBC does not provide with an equivalent of explicit connection pooling. You really have to rely on the underlying service-provider implementation to deal with any pooling, or write your own system over the top of the basic classes.

In most applications, pieces of code usually know when they require only a subset of the data provided by the directory service. If you use the version of `getAttributes()` that requests this subset, it provides a filtering service that you can apply at the directory-service server, thus reducing the amount of network traffic that needs to be sent. Less network traffic means faster responses and also less garbage generated on the client side.

Try to set the initial provider URL to be as specific as possible. This initial setup allows the underlying directory service to narrow the basic search terms before the search even begins, again resulting in faster searches and fewer resources used on the server side.

Interacting with Databases

Once you have the context information, you want to do stuff with it. Admittedly, most of the time you are only going to be asking for attribute information, but your application will need to be able to modify the data there — for example, by adding and removing users. This section is about dealing with data once you have that context information and you want to do something to it.

Of necessity, this section is devoted to dealing with directory services rather than naming services. However, with very little work, you can adapt the information in the section on changing the structure of the directory service to work with naming services, although modifying structures of naming services is a very uncommon thing to do.

Generalized searching

Say you have a call center in operation. A user calls in with a problem, and you want to find out that user's details — but the user can't remember his or her login name. You need to perform a search of the directory service to find all the possible matches, which obviously involves doing a search of the database. In effect, this is the equivalent of the `ldapsearch` command we mentioned in Chapter 8.

Constructing a new search

You search a directory service using the `search()` method of the `DirContext` interface. You have quite a number of options regarding how to search, but for the moment, limit yourself to a very basic search.

To search a directory service, you need to know first the context in which you are going to search, and then the name and value of any attributes that you want to match. Say our caller rings up, and we have his or her last name and initials. As the call center has caller ID, we also happen to have the country the user is calling from and probably the phone number, too.

When you pass the arguments to the search command, the context information is like the information you use to read attributes. You can either ask for everything in the current context by providing an empty string or you can ask for a sub-context specifically. What you do really depends on how you structure your application code. The search also needs a list of matching attributes, so before requesting the search you need to construct this list, as shown in the following example:

```
public DirContext[] findUser(String initials,
                             String surname,
                             String country,
                             String phone) {

  BasicAttributes search_attrs = new BasicAttributes();
  search_attrs.put("initials", initials);
  search_attrs.put("sn", surname);
  search_attrs.put("c", country);

  if(phone != null)
    search_attrs.put("phonenumber", phone);

  NamingEnumeration results =
     initial_ctx.search("ou=Customer,o=ExampleApp",
                        search_attrs);

  LinkedList found = new LinkedList();

  while(results.hasMore()) {
    SearchResults sr = (SearchResults)results.next();

    String name = sr.getName();
    Object ctx = sr.getObject();

    if((ctx == null) || !(ctx instanceof DirContext))
     found.add(initial_ctx.lookup(name));
    else
     found.add(ctx);
  }

  DirContext[] ret_val = new DirContext[found.size()];
```

```
    found.toArray(ret_val);

    return ret_val;
  }
```

In this example you have elected to use the initial context based on the root of the LDAP database. As an alternative, you could use the current context in the search, like this:

```
DirContext cust_ctx =
  (DirContext)initial_ctx.lookup("ou=Customer,o=ExampleApp");

...

public DirContext[] findUser(String initials,
                             String surname,
                             String country,
                             String phone) {
  ...

  NamingEnumeration results =
    cust_ctx.search("", search_attrs);

  ...
}
```

The return value of your `findUser()` method is the list of all the contexts that match the user details that have been provided. With this list you can place a list on-screen for your call-center operator to use to further identify the user. Once the user has been found, the exact match directory context is then used to provide any further actions for this phone call (for example, to update the user's address).

You should keep a couple of points about the search code in mind here. The `search()` method returns an enumeration of `SearchResult` instances. The `SearchResult` may not directly contain the `DirContext` it relates to, but instead contain the name of the matching sub-context. `SearchResult` is a derived class of `NameClassPair`, but the code does not guarantee that the object referred to will actually be provided (the `DirContext` instance matching the name). Therefore, to be on the safe side, your code will attempt to see if the `DirContext` is supplied as the value in the `NameClassPair` and, if it is not, will perform another lookup to find the matching instance to be returned to your method caller.

When constructing the attributes, you check to see if the phone number is provided. If your caller ID does not give you the phone number, then you can provide `null` to the argument. If you don't have it, then you should not set it as a matching value in the attributes to search against. If you do provide it with a null value, that effectively tells your underlying search algorithm to return only those users who do not have a phone number set. Another reason you may not want to provide the phone number is that it may not be the one the caller is actually registered for—if, for example, he or she is ringing from a mobile phone rather than the house phone — and using the caller ID phone number in your search would result in us not finding the right user.

Filtering the results

In addition to filtering the return values on the server side by looking for attributes, you can set the search up to provide extra filtering. Your filtering options will vary depending on the variant of `search()` you call.

First on the list of variants is the ability to request only a small list of attributes. If you know that you only need to deal with the `SearchResult` instances and not a `DirContext`, then you can use the matching attributes arguments to limit the list of attributes returned, in much the same way that `getAttributes()` enables you to use a list of required attributes. This might be useful if you want to do that initial search for caller details by simply checking the e-mail address for a match, as in the following example:

```
String reqd_attrs = new String[] { "cn", "uid",
                                   "rfc822mailalias" };
NamingEnumeration results =
   initial_ctx.search("ou=Customer,o=ExampleApp",
                      search_attrs,
                      reqd_attrs);
```

If you want to get even more picky about how much searching to do, you can also supply a filter and `SearchControls` instance. This filter acts like the filter argument to the `ldapsearch` command-line tool. `SearchControls` information is much more interesting. You can use this class to limit the scope of your search to, say, a single level of the directory-service hierarchy, or to place a maximum limit on the search results. For example, if you use your LDAP database to store all the books you have in stock, and the end user does a subject search for Java books, you might want to limit the returned results to the first 20 books found rather than listing all 2,000-odd titles that you hold, as in the following example:

```
SearchControls ctrls = new SearchControls();
ctrls.setCountLimit(20);
ctrls.setTimeLimit(5000);
ctrls.setSearchScope(SearchControls.SUBTREE_SCOPE);

NamingEnumeration results =
   initial_ctx.search("cat=books,ou=Products,o=ExampleApp",
                      "title=*Java*",
                      ctrls);
```

Tip For more details on the format of the filter string, look at RFC 2254.

Modifying existing data

Probably the most common action in a directory service is modifying the attributes. For example, users sometimes move and need to update their contact details. To update those details, you need to modify the attributes of the contexts that belong to those users.

Modifying data, in this instance, means adding, removing, or changing the attributes of a particular context. Deleting or adding a whole new context requires a different process; we address it in its own section later in the chapter on changing the structure of the directory service.

Setting up the attributes to be modified

The first step in modifying attributes is knowing which ones need to be updated and constructing the appropriate data structures. You modify attributes with the `modifyAttributes()` method of the `DirContext` interface; doing this requires an instance of `Attributes`.

The list of attributes you supply to the context must be the list of attributes to be modified and their new values. Each time you make an update to the directory service the list must be created fresh with the new values. You must remember that this list must be fresh each time—once you have made updates, you need to clear the list of existing values and then repopulate it with new values. You can't provide an attribute with a value equal to the values already in the database. This effectively prevents you from fetching a set of attributes, modifying one or two, and then passing the list back to the `modifyAttributes()` method. You need to keep two separate lists—one of the original values and one of the values that have been modified since the last time you requested an update.

For example, you could modify a user's details with a method like the following:

```
public void updateAddress(String dn,
                          String address,
                          String country,
                          String phone) {

  BasicAttributes mod_attrs = new BasicAttributes();

  if(address != null)
    mod_attrs.put("address", address);

  if(country != null)
    mod_attrs.put("c", country);

  if(phone != null)
    mod_attrs.put("phonenumber", phone);

  if(mod_attrs.size() != 0)
     // do the attribute modification....
}
```

If you are updating a multi-valued attribute, you will need to supply all the values to it. Multi-value attributes will be replaced by the new set of values, so if you want to add or change some values, the list must include all the values, including the unchanged parts; otherwise those values that are unchanged will actually be removed when you perform the update.

Requesting the modification

Once you have a list of attributes that require modification, you need to instruct the directory service to make the changes current. As we mentioned earlier, you do this through the `modifyAttributes()` method of `DirContext`.

Following the same precedents you used when fetching attributes and searching, you need to provide sub-context information. As usual, you can provide an empty string or a sub-context name to update. The next argument specifies the modification operation to be performed. You can use it to add, remove, or update the attributes.

The javadoc for each of the modification operation flags contains more detailed information on the interaction between the list of supplied changed attributes and the existing attributes.

Putting all of this together, you can complete your address-updating method with a single line of code:

```
initial_ctx.modifyAttributes(dn,
                             DirContext.REPLACE_ATTRIBUTE,
                             mod_attrs);
```

Not all directory service implementations will enable you to modify attribute information. For example, DNS does not enable you to modify attributes, for example, the domain-resolution information like the IP address. As you know what sort of service provider you are using, you should know beforehand whether it supports attribute modification. If it does not, the methods will throw an `AttributeModificationException` if you attempt to change something that cannot be changed.

Achieving greater modification control

If you want even greater control over the modifications being performed, you can supply an array of `ModificationItem` instances rather than the list of attributes and a single operation. This enables you to selectively add, replace, and remove each attribute in the list, rather than applying the same operation to the attributes. For example, you have found that the user now has two e-mail addresses, and wants to change his or her address: You can construct the following code:

```
ModificationItem[] mod_items = new ModificationItems[2];

Attribute email =
  new BasicAttribute("rfc822mailalias", new_email);
```

```
ModificationItem email_mod =
  new ModificationItem(DirContext.ADD_ATTRIBUTE, email);

Attribute addr = new BasicAttribute("address", address);
ModificationItem addr_mod =
  new ModificationItem(DirContext.REPLACE_ATTRIBUTE, addr);

mod_items[0] = email_mod;
mod_items[1] = addr_mod;

initial_ctx.modifyAttributes(dn, mod_items);
```

Changing the structure of the directory service

As part of the day-to-day maintenance of the directory service, you will probably be required to add and remove data from the system — by, for example, removing products that are no longer offered, or adding data for a new user who is registering to order something for the first time. These are structural changes to the directory service, as they involve changing the hierarchy rather than just modifying the existing items in the hierarchy.

Adding new items

Adding a new item to the directory service, naturally, requires you to know what you want to create and where you want to create it. For example, before you add a new user to your system you should already have all of the data that describe that user. When creating a new item, you are actually creating a new sub-context within the hierarchy. The existence of a sub-context implies that you know at least a name, and for directory services a collection of attributes to associate with that context. (Remember that an LDAP schema may require certain attributes in an entry, without which it will not permit the operation.)

You can create a new context for either naming or directory services using the `createSubcontext()` method. For naming services, the `Context` interface defines a method that just needs a sub-context name to return a reference to the new `Context` created. For directory services, a set of overloaded methods is provided in the `DirContext` interface that take the name as well as a list of attributes — again returning the created sub-context `DirContext` instance.

For example, you can create a new user in your system with the following code:

```
public void createUser(String dn,
                       String initials,
                       String surname,
                       String address,
                       String country,
                       String phone,
                       String email) {

    BasicAttributes attrs = new BasicAttributes();
```

```
    attrs.put("initials", initials);
    attrs.put("sn", surname);
    attrs.put("rfc822mailalias", email);

    if(address != null)
      attrs.put("address", address);

    if(country != null)
      attrs.put("c", country);

    if(phone != null)
      attrs.put("phonenumber", phone);

    initial_ctx.createSubcontext(dn, attrs);
  }
```

Note that just like the other context methods, the sub-context does not need to be the direct child of the context you are requesting to make the changes. As the previous example shows, you can create a sub-context some levels down from the root context.

Deleting an item

To delete an item from the directory service you use a process that is just the opposite of the process for adding one. Instead of creating a new sub-context, you destroy an old one. The act of destruction removes that context and all of the child contexts that it contains. A simple way to delete the entire database is to have the initial context be the root and then ask it to destroy itself—not a particularly useful thing to do!

You destroy a sub-context with the `destroySubcontext()` method of the `Context` interface. You use this same method for both naming and directory services. The destroy method needs only the name of the context to destroy. Because you are deleting the context, the details of any attributes are irrelevant to the process. A delete-user method can be as simple as this:

```
  public void deleteUser(String dn) {
    initial_ctx.destroySubcontext(dn);
  }
```

Adding and deleting contexts are not the same processes as binding and unbinding them. That is, `bind()` is not the same as `createSubcontext()`. You use the binding operations to control the name-lookup system for creating initial contexts, but after that they are irrelevant. Binding adds or removes something that already exists rather than creates something completely new on the fly.

Summary

This concludes our look at one of the most important APIs in the J2EE specification. You saw JNDI in use in earlier chapters, and in later chapters you will see just how essential it is to any J2EE-based application. JNDI is an extremely flexible API that enables you to perform tasks from looking at a file system to resolving domain-name information to interacting with LDAP directory services.

In this chapter, we introduced to you all facets of JNDI, including:

- ✦ Terminology for interacting with both naming and directory services.
- ✦ How to connect to naming services to find registered objects.
- ✦ How to connect to and query directory services such as LDAP.
- ✦ How to search and filter results in a directory service.
- ✦ How to manage the data in a directory service to modify existing entries or add or remove complete entries in the hierarchy.

✦ ✦ ✦

P A R T

IV

Communicating Between Systems with XML

✦ ✦ ✦ ✦

In This Part

✦ ✦ ✦ ✦

CHAPTER 10

Building an XML Foundation

✦ ✦ ✦ ✦

In This Chapter

Understanding the basics of XML

Representing documents with XML

Configuring applications with XML files

Communicating between applications

Understanding basic syntax rules

✦ ✦ ✦ ✦

You had a brief encounter with XML in the discussion of deployment descriptors used with servlets and JSPs. Now it's time to take a closer look at XML and related technologies. This chapter and the following three will explain why a Java developer needs to know about XML, and will introduce you to the Java APIs for parsing, transforming, and working with XML. For the most part, we will focus on XML as data and not as a language for document presentation.

For a general introduction to XML that spends more time looking at XML from the perspective of a Web developer, check out *XML Bible*, Second Edition by Elliotte Rusty Harold (Hungry Minds, 2001). Elliotte's book targets the Web-page author rather than the software developer, so his book nicely complements the material presented here.

This chapter is a brief introduction to XML and related technologies. The examples we present focus on XML's relationship to Java. After you've seen a few examples, you'll get a quick tour of the rules for well-formed XML documents. Finally, we'll run through some of the companion technologies that are often grouped under the heading of XML.

What Is XML?

XML seems to be the only technology to have been hyped more than Java was in its early days. Like Java, it has not evolved the way inventors may have anticipated. Considering the strong support for enterprise applications, it's easy to forget the early focus on applets for Java developers. Similarly, XML has its roots in Standardized General Markup Language (SGML), which was developed for handling books and other types of documents. Some powerful applications still use XML for this purpose, but the power of XML is in the promise of portable data.

An XML document consists of data placed within tags that describe the data. The tags may be your own or those of some group you belong to or standard you wish to conform to. For example, if you are creating an XML document that represents mathematical expressions, you can invent your own, or you can adopt the conventions of MathML available from the W3C at `http://www.w3c.org/Math/`. If you have created your own mathematical format, you could look to see if you can use some tool to translate your format to those of MathML and vice versa.

Ask yourself who is consuming the XML you are generating, and how. With HTML you think of an actual person viewing your content on a browser. The person is consuming the HTML document. If an HTML document is rendered in a forest and no one is there to view it, is it really rendered? An XML document, on the other hand, may be rendered for a person to view on a wide variety of devices. It also may be intended for processing by a machine, without a person being involved in the transaction at all. In one of our examples you'll see how JavaBeans are persisted through the use of XML files. Although the file is human-readable, it is not intended to be read by a person. Even in the case of a document, you may want a machine to preprocess a document in some way. Say you have a role in a play. You may want the script to highlight any lines you have to help you memorize your part.

Machines and people are good at different things. You aren't overly "puzled" when I leave out one of the *z*s in "puzzled." You can figure out what I mean. Any developer knows that applications can be halted by a typo. XML helps us create documents that humans can read and that applications can use. Just as in Java, you'll use long descriptive names to help the humans reading your document. You'll also follow the syntactical rules to help the machines reading your document.

Your opinion of what XML is will change over time. For now you can think of XML as portable data in the same way that you think of Java as portable code.

Creating XML

XML files are text files. You can create them with your favorite text editor whether it be Notepad, WordPad, SimpleText, Text Edit, vi, or emacs. Save the files as plain text with the extension `.xml`. (This extension isn't technically required, but it helps to have a reminder of the file format.) You can also easily create XML from servlets and JSPs. In Chapter 3 we generated HTML output with the following command:

```
response.setContentType("text/html");
```

There is nothing special about this. You can specify other MIME types, including XML. To generate XML, you would use the following command:

```
response.setContentType("text/xml");
```

Presenting data as XML allows you to handle the data intelligently as you can discover what is being represented by the various parts of a record. If you're on the road, you can do a database query for all seafood restaurants near your hotel. If you get the information back as XML, you can perform sorts on the data locally rather than having to go back online to retrieve the same information you already have in a different order. For example, you could take the list that's been returned and sort it by average price, by distance from your hotel, or by any other type of information contained in the XML document.

You may be surprised to discover that XML is already being used behind the scenes at Web sites you use every day. For example, Figure 10-1 shows the results of a search for "elephants" at the Google site. (`http://www.google.com`).

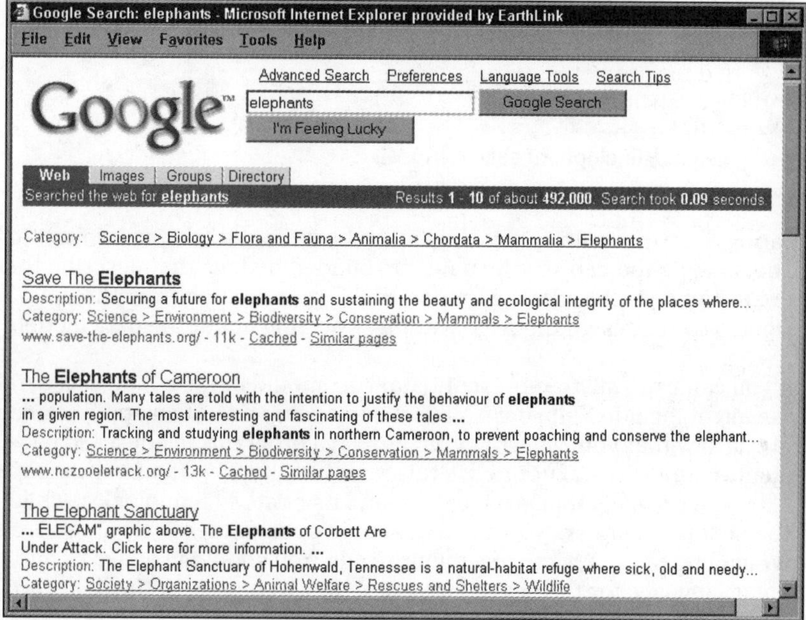

Figure 10-1: A Google search for elephants

We just entered in the keyword "elephants" and performed a basic search. The URL for the search results was given as `http://www.google.com/search?hl=en&save=off&q=elephants`. If you replace the word `search` with `xml`, you will see the XML version of the same search results, as shown in Figure 10-2.

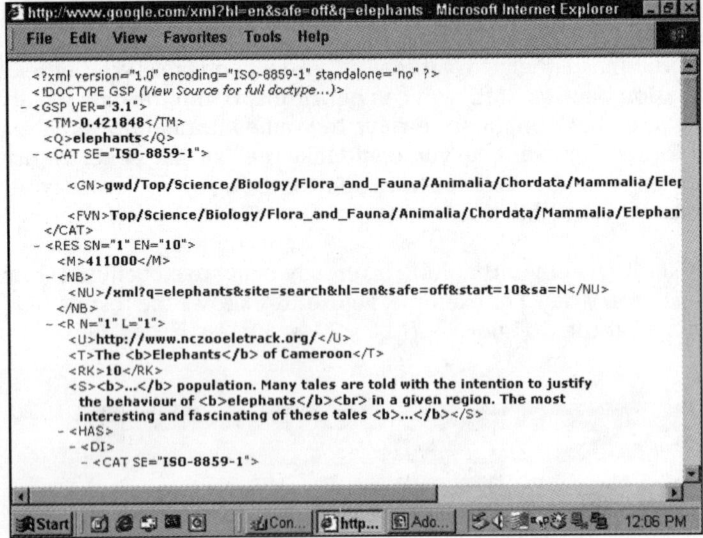

Figure 10-2: The Google elephant search in XML

By comparing the two resulting pages, you can begin to decode the information in the XML document. You can see the data surrounded by tags that describe them. The other advantage is that the tags separate the presentation from the data. The page designers can redesign the page without worrying about the data model.

Although you can use XML to represent data, you should not use XML as a database. A database might include XML, but XML is a document and not an application. In Chapter 4 you saw that you can write complex Java programs inside a JSP page, but we repeatedly cautioned you not to use this functionality. The same warning goes for XML. You can do many things using XML and its related technologies; while reading the next few chapters you may see some opportunities to do some pretty slick programming to get XML to meet your needs. You should use Java or another programming language for the heavy lifting and XML to represent the data you are lifting.

Displaying XML

XML is all about the data. None of the tags tells you anything about how the document is to be displayed. HTML, on the other hand, is all about the presentation. The good news is that it is much easier to add nice presentation to well-documented data than it is to determine the meaning of elements from the way in which they are displayed. If your document is a book, article, play, or other narrative, then you can easily apply Cascading Style Sheets as you do in HTML. If your document is more data-centric, consider whether or not it will be read by people. If nobody will ever see your document then, you don't need to worry about presentation.

If your document is intended for human consumption, and possibly also to be read by machines, then you have the added problem that you can't decide how a document will be displayed until you understand where it will be displayed. You don't want to use the same display for a browser on a personal computer that you would use for a cell phone. You probably don't want to print it out on sheets standard US letter-size paper in the same format as you display it on either device.

You can use an Extensible Stylesheet Language (XSL) document along with an XML document to specify how elements in your XML document will be mapped to HTML (or whatever your target format is). You'll see more about transforming XML in Chapter 14, when we discuss transforming XML. In this case we are using Extensible Stylesheet Language Transformation (XSLT) to format the document appropriately for a variety of clients.

Two views of the same document

We won't cover parsing an XML document until Chapter 12, but it helps to see what you're constructing if you understand how it can later be parsed. Consider the following XML document, designed to convey information about a candidate to a possible employer:

```
<?xml version="1.0"?>
<resume>
  <name> A. Employee </name>
  <address>
    <street> 1234 My Street </street>
    <city> My City</city>
    <state> OH </state>
    <zip> 44120 </zip>
    <phone>  (555) 555-5555 </phone>
  </address>
  <education>
    <school> Whatsamatta U.</school>
    <degree>  B.S. </degree>
    <yeargraduated> 1920 </yeargraduated>
  </education>
</resume>
```

One way to read through it is in an event-driven way. Just imagine yourself saying, "...and then *this* happened." In the case of this resume, you can read it as follows:

```
... and then I started the resume
... and then I started the name
... the name was A. Employee
... and then I ended the name
... and then I started the address
... and then I started the street
... the street was 1234 My Street
... and then I ended the street
```

This is not a tremendously exciting experience, but it is the way you will use the Simple API for XML (SAX) to parse an XML document. You have to keep track of the fact that the `street` is part of the `address`. You have to write down the `name` as it goes by if you want to remember it later on. We will cover SAX in Chapter 12 when we cover parsing. Its lack of memory is not just a drawback, it can also be an advantage. SAX is small, sequential, and efficient. You can sit back and wait for something to happen. If you want to know when the particular employee graduated from college, then you can listen for the event "`... and then I started year-graduated.`"

Another view of the XML document is as a tree, as shown in Figure 10-3. This is the Document Object Model (DOM). Each XML document has a single root element. In this case `<resume>` is the root element. It contains the child elements `<name>`, `<address>`, and `<education>`. You can see that `<address>` is a child of `<resume>` and also a parent to the elements `<street>`, `<city>`, `<state>`, `<zip>`, and `<phone>`. If you can see the entire structure of the document at once, then you can manipulate the data in pretty powerful ways. On the other hand, this requires a lot of resources on your part. You have to keep all this information in your head at once.

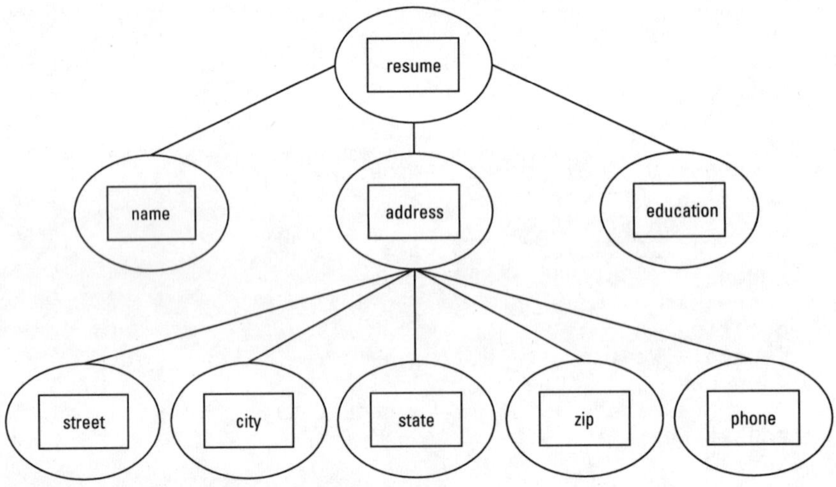

Figure 10-3: The DOM view of the resume

These are the two fundamental ways of viewing an XML document. The first is similar to the way in which you look at HTML. The second gets at the power of XML. When we get to parsers, you'll see other ways of dealing with XML documents in a more Java-centric way.

XML for Documents and Presentation

Because of XML's roots in SGML, many of the current applications of the technology have to do with the presentation of content. As an example, consider putting together a resume. Think about putting this resume together using Microsoft Word, HTML, and XML.

If you use Microsoft Word, you control exactly what the resume looks like. You can print it out for a prospective employer or attach it to an e-mail document. If the prospective employer has an application that "speaks" the same version of Microsoft Word in which you saved the document, then the employer can read what you've sent. With the electronic version, you are trusting that this format will be accessible from future versions of Word or from other software. This might be a good bet in the case of this particular example, but there are plenty of punch cards, paper tapes, and floppies full of undecipherable information.

If you decide not to go for a proprietary format, you may want to consider HTML. You can use HTML tags to change how the document will look when viewed in a browser. You can easily direct someone to the Web site containing your resume. Even for those who don't understand HTML, the source file is pretty understandable. If there comes a time when no browsers can process your document, the source code will still be human-readable.

But that brings us to a huge point. What if your document isn't intended to be read (at least right away) by another person? As computers and communication get faster, you can't always afford to have humans involved. You may want to pull out some of the information or sort the resumes I get somehow. This is where XML comes in. XML uses a markup consisting of tags that describe the document's structure and not its appearance. In Chapter 12, we'll cover parsers that enable you to pull apart the data in useful ways. You can then manipulate the XML documents. Sun's marketing department often repeats its positioning statement that XML is the noun, and Java is the verb.

A resume in Word

Here's a simple example that shows the benefits of XML as a portable document format. Start with a non-portable format. Figure 10-4 shows a resume created in Microsoft Word.

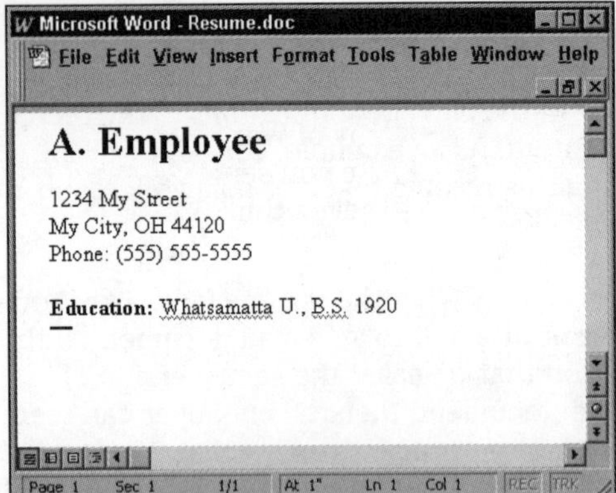

Figure 10-4: The Microsoft Word resume

Now open this file using a plain-text editor to see all the extra characters included in the file. Figure 10-5 shows a screen shot of a portion of this file.

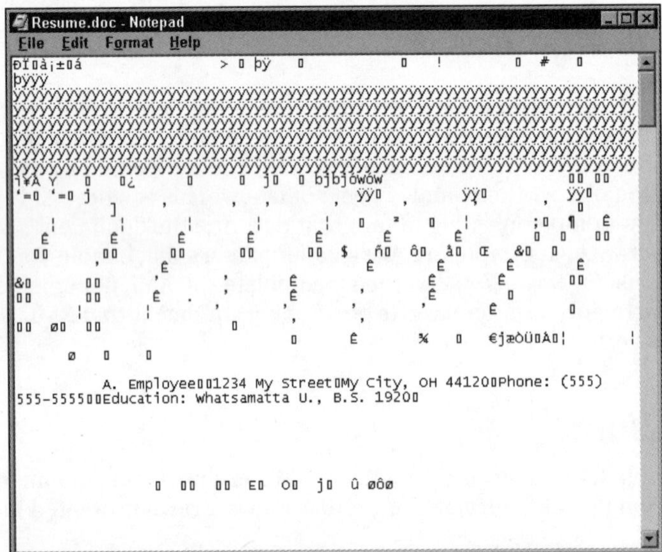

Figure 10-5: The extra information in a Microsoft Word document

Look at all that extra information. Eleven more screens full of goop follow the portion you see in Figure 10-3. If you are given this file, you've got quite a job ahead of you figuring out how to extract any useful information from it. Further down in the document is information about the author and the copy of Word, as well as information about the directory the file is stored in. Every time you send a Word document, you are sending a lot of information that you may not even think about.

If you delete even one of these special characters, you will find that you can no longer open the document with Microsoft Word. How do you go about repairing the damaged document? You can see that there are many dangers involved in dealing with these binary formats, even when the formats are generated by software that still exists on hardware running today. What do you do with older material contained on media not easily read by modern-day machines, encoded using software that no longer exists?

Using Microsoft Word has its benefits, of course. It is readily available, and you can use your Mac or Windows version of Word without any problems. You can use some of the editing features to keep track of comments. Finally, a lot of work has been put into Word by now, so a lot of features exist that you've come to enjoy. Tools for the newer technologies aren't yet at this level. For example, XML editors are not nearly as easy to use.

A resume in HTML

If you want to put your resume up on the Web, you might choose to use HTML. Your resume might begin something like this:

```
<html>
  <head>
    <title> My Resume </title>
  </head>
  <body>
    <h1> A. Employee </h1>
    1234 My Street <br>
    My City, OH 44120 <br>
    Phone: (555) 555-5555
    <p>
      <b> Education: </b> Whatsamatta U., B.S. 1920
    </p>
  </body>
</html>
```

Open this resume in a browser, and it looks like the one shown in Figure 10-6.

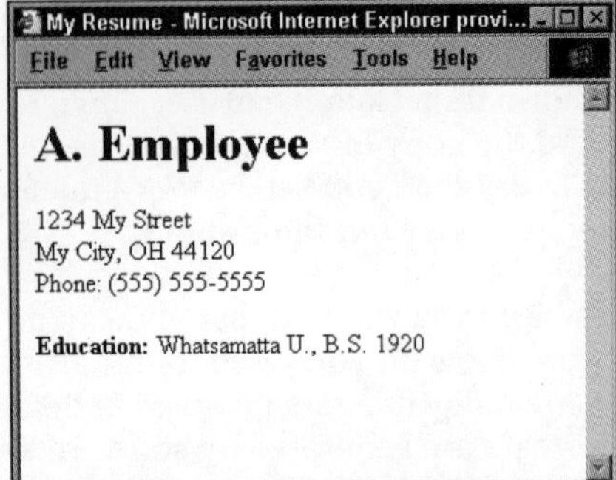

Figure 10-6: HTML resume for A. Employee

HTML is a presentation format with a well-defined set of tags. You write a page using the appropriate tags, and the browser interprets your document accordingly. The downside is that you don't get any indication of what the data on a page represents. Each line is just text. Sorting a stack of resumes written in HTML by ZIP code is not an easy task.

Another downside is that you can only display information in applications that can process HTML. You may want to scan through a set of applicant resumes on our cell phone, or you may want to download some resumes to your Palm and go through them when you're away from your desk. The data don't change, just the presentation. XML enables you to separate the content from the presentation in ways that aren't possible with HTML.

A resume in XML

Now, let's revisit the XML version of the resume. Remember, you are free to make up the tags you want. Your main goal is to make sure that the information in the preceding examples is tied to a structure that describes the data. One example could be the following:

```
<?xml version="1.0"?>
<resume>
  <name> A. Employee </name>
  <address>
    <street> 1234 My Street </street>
    <city> My City</city>
    <state> OH </state>
    <zip> 44120 </zip>
    <phone>  (555) 555-5555 </phone>
  </address>
  <education>
    <school> Whatsamatta U.</school>
    <degree>  B.S. </degree>
```

```
        <yeargraduated> 1920 </yeargraduated>
      </education>
    </resume>
```

There's not much to this code. Without knowing anything about XML, you can see that the first line specifies the version of XML being used. This is called a processing instruction (PI). It is information that the parser will need that is not part of the document structure.

Just as in HTML, in XML the tag </SOMETHING> is an end tag that matches up with the start tag <SOMETHING>. You can see that everything except the PI is between the <resume> start and end tags. This resume consists of a <name>, <address>, and <education>. The <address>, in turn, consists of a <street>, <city>, <state>, <zip>, and <phone>. (We could have further broken phone by separating the area code and even the exchange.) Keep in mind that we are creating our own format for this example. Once you understand document type definitions (DTDs) and schema (which we'll cover in Chapter 11, you may prefer to conform to an existing format or at least figure out how you might convert documents back and forth between your format and others.

Once you learn about parsers in Chapter 12, you will be able to access the data in the sample resume. You can then easily process a batch of resumes and sort them by year of graduation or ZIP code. You can even move the items around on your resume. Maybe some employers expect to see your education at the top of the resume while others expect to see it after your work experience. You'll be able to easily make these changes and have a very flexible document.

HTML had information about how the document would be presented, but not about what information the document contained. XML has information about the nature of the data contained in each part, but nothing about how they are to be displayed. In the last section of this chapter, you'll read about companion technologies for XML. Some of them are useful for rendering documents in different settings.

As a final note, this example introduced tags such as <resume>, <address>, and <education>. What exactly is a <resume>? We don't really know yet. We do know, however, that if our custom application that understands and renders this XML file should become lost to the world, others would be able to successfully interpret and render the data. Binary files, by contrast, can only be read by the applications that created them or that have the proper filters.

XML for Configuration

If you're anything like us, you probably like to customize your favorite applications a bit. You change some of the settings from the defaults that ship with the product. Maybe you assign a keyboard shortcut or change the look and feel of the application. It would be a huge pain to have to set these customizations up every time you restart the application. The configuration files are often name-value pairs stored in a text file, or sometimes special binaries that can't be easily read or altered. You saw a J2EE example of this customization in Chapters 3 and 4, when you adapted the web.xml file to configure Tomcat to run the servlets and JSPs you wrote.

For each subdirectory of the webapps directory you had to create a WEB-INF sub-directory containing the XML configuration file web.xml. For Tomcat you made modifications to this file so that the servlet container knew about various associations. One example of such a configuration file is the following:

```
<?xml version="1.0" encoding="ISO-8859-1"?>
<!DOCTYPE web-app PUBLIC
  "-//Sun Microsystems, Inc.//DTD Web Application 2.3//EN"
  "http://java.sun.com/j2ee/dtds/web-app_2_3.dtd">
<web-app>
  <servlet>
    <servlet-name>
      Hello1
    </servlet-name>
    <servlet-class>
      Greetings.Hello1
    </servlet-class>
  </servlet>
  <servlet-mapping>
    <servlet-name>
      Hello1
    </servlet-name>
    <url-pattern>
      /Hi
    </url-pattern>
  </servlet-mapping>
</web-app>
```

As in previous examples, this document begins with a PI that specifies the version of XML being used. The encoding is a formal way of specifying the character set being used as the Latin-1 character set. The following line is the document type declaration. It specifies that the document's root element is `<web-app>`, and provides information about the document type definition. You'll learn about the DTD in Chapter 11.

The actual structure of the data is pretty straightforward. The `<web-app>` consists of a `<servlet>` and a `<servlet-mapping>`. The `<servlet>` contains the name of the servlet and the class that it maps to. This is really a name-value pair that you might expect to find in a simple text-configuration file. The difference is that you know that `Hello1` is the `<servlet-name>` and `Greetings.Hello1` is the corresponding `<servlet-class>`. If you knew how the data was structured, you would have been able to retrieve this information. Similarly, the `<servlet-mapping>` contains the `<servlet-name>` and the corresponding `<url-pattern>`.

You've probably noticed by now that XML is not a space-efficient way of saving data. In fact, it is recommended that you go out of your way not to overly abbreviate tag names. Java style sheets recommend that you use descriptive names for your classes, methods, and variables. You should use the same convention for XML. The following snippet probably conveys the same information as the web.xml file you just saw:

```
    . . .
    <web-app>
  <servlet>
    <name>
      Hello1
    </name>
    <class>
      Greetings.Hello1
    </class>
  </servlet>
  <servlet-mapping>
    <name>
      Hello1
    </name>
    <url>
      /Hi
    </url>
  </servlet-mapping>
</web-app>
```

There isn't much ambiguity about what is meant by `<name>` and `<class>`. On the other hand, not much is gained by this abbreviation, which may make the document harder to read as it grows larger. We may also have other elements that are `names` but not the `name` of a `servlet`. It is best to err on the side of overly detailed names.

One of the benefits of having an XML configuration file is that we can read it and make changes using a simple text editor. (In this example we wanted to provide a URL shortcut to the servlet, so we typed in a `servlet-mapping`.) But this benefit is also a liability. If we can read the file and make changes, then so can users. Sometimes it is better to hide configuration files from them, or require them to use tools that don't allow them to break the application.

XML for Storing and Sharing Data

When you write an enterprise application, you expect to be communicating between different processes. You may be sending information back and forth, or you may be distributing code. Just as Java is a great language for portable code, XML is a great language for portable data, although you'll see in this section that it is not always the best choice. In the previous section, you saw the benefits of storing configuration files in XML; now you'll see that XML is a useful format for storing details about Java objects.

As an example, think about storing information about a Swing component. We'll create a `JFrame` and customize a few of its properties. What information would we need to send you for you to be able to recreate the `JFrame`? What is the best way to send this information to you or to another VM? We'll describe two approaches. First we'll serialize the object using Sun's proprietary format, and then we'll generate XML files using features new to JDK 1.4.

Serializing using ObjectOutputStream

The first approach we'll take is to use `java.io.ObjectOutputStream` to generate a serialized version of the `JFrame`. The following code creates a `JFrame` and sets the title, size, and default close operation of the frame. Inside the `try` block, the object is serialized and saved in the file `Test.tmp`, as shown in this example:

```
import javax.swing.JFrame;
import java.beans.XMLEncoder;
import java.io.*;

public class SerializedBeanExample {
  public static void main(String args[]){
    JFrame x = new JFrame("Look at me");
    x.setSize(200,300);
    x.setVisible(true);
    x.setDefaultCloseOperation(JFrame.EXIT_ON_CLOSE);
    FileOutputStream f;
    try {
      f = new FileOutputStream("Test.tmp");
      ObjectOutputStream e = new ObjectOutputStream(f);
      e.writeObject( x);
      e.close();
    } catch(Exception e) {}
  }
}
```

The bean is serialized into a binary format that `java.io.ObjectInputStream` can use to reconstruct the original `JFrame`. A portion of the resulting file, `Test.tmp`, is shown in Figure 10-7.

A lot of seemingly unnecessary information is included in this file. If you know what a `JFrame` is, then all you need to know is how it has been customized to make sure that your reconstructed `JFrame` is the same as the original. Although the format may seem fairly efficient, the process errs on the side of sending too much information.

Figure 10-7: The extras in a serialized JFrame object

Serialization doesn't seem any better than the situation with Microsoft Word. Why would you want to send all that information in a format that is difficult to read, parse, and figure out? One major difference is that the Microsoft Word format is designed for documents that are being stored. These documents can persist for a long time, so it is important that you be able to figure out what they say many years from now. Some people can read writings from hundreds of years ago because they were written in a medium we can read in a language we can decipher.

Although you will want to store some items that you have serialized, the main reason for serialization is to send objects from one VM to another. In Chapter 15, you will see how you can run code on one VM from another as long as you have the interface to the remote code. The key is that objects are serialized, sent over the wire, and then deserialized. In this case, you want to make sure that you aren't sending huge amounts of data over the wire. XML files can be bulkier than binary files for custom objects if you send every last piece of information. Swing components and JavaBeans can benefit from a standard XML format.

Saving state using XML

You can alternatively use the `XMLEncoder` to create a textual representation of a JavaBean. This class was added to the `java.beans` package in JDK 1.4, along with the corresponding class `XMLDecoder` and other classes that deal with the persistence of JavaBeans. The `Encoder` class is the parent of `XMLEncoder`. It works with

PersistanceDelegate and DefaultPersistanceDelegate to break an object up into some Statement objects and Expression objects that are used to recreate the instance of the JavaBean, perhaps with some help from EventHandler.

These additions to java.beans are the result of JSR (Java Specification Request) 57, and were designed to provide the mechanism for converting graphs of JavaBeans to and from XML files. (They also enable you to convert to other formats, but the current format of choice is XML.) Their purpose was to provide a format for long-term persistence of JavaBeans that is independent of the tools used to create them. (You can read more about the history of this effort at http://jcp.org/jsr/detail/57.jsp.) Although these classes are part of JDK 1.4, you can find directions in the Readme included with the download from the JSR site, telling you how to get the package to work with JDK 1.3.

You can now modify the previous example to use the XMLEncoder to create a persistent copy of the JFrame, instead of using Object OutputStream. The modifications to the previous code are shown in boldface in the following code:

```
import javax.swing.JFrame;
import java.beans.XMLEncoder;
import java.io.*;

public class XMLBeanExample {
  public static void main(String args[]){
    JFrame x = new JFrame("Look at me");
    x.setSize(200,300);
    x.setVisible(true);
    x.setDefaultCloseOperation(JFrame.EXIT_ON_CLOSE);
    FileOutputStream f;
    try {
      f = new FileOutputStream("Test.xml");
      XMLEncoder e =
        new XMLEncoder( new BufferedOutputStream(f));
      e.writeObject( x);
      e.close();
    } catch(Exception e) {}
  }
}
```

Notice that you don't have to do very much to the existing Java code. The difference in the results, however, is striking. The following is the contents of the file Test.xml:

```
<?xml version="1.0" encoding="UTF-8"?>
<java version="1.4.0-beta" class="java.beans.XMLDecoder">
  <object class="javax.swing.JFrame">
    <void property="bounds">
      <object class="java.awt.Rectangle">
        <int>0</int>
        <int>0</int>
        <int>200</int>
```

```
        <int>300</int>
      </object>
    </void>
    <void property="contentPane">
      <void property="bounds">
        <object class="java.awt.Rectangle">
          <int>0</int>
          <int>0</int>
          <int>192</int>
          <int>273</int>
        </object>
      </void>
    </void>
    <void property="defaultCloseOperation">
      <int>3</int>
    </void>
    <void property="name">
      <string>frame0</string>
    </void>
    <void property="title">
      <string>Look at me</string>
    </void>
    <void property="visible">
      <boolean>true</boolean>
    </void>
  </object>
</java>
```

This example is a bit less straightforward than the previous examples of XML, but you should still be able to figure out what is being expressed. Here the root element is <java> along with the version number and the name of the class that will be used to decode the XML file. The element <java> contains the single <object> element that identifies the object as being of type `javax.swing.JFrame`. This `object` contains six <void> elements that refer to properties being set. If you compare these elements to the original Java code, you'll be able to match most of them up.

The method `setSize(200,300)` in the Java code is represented by `<void property="bounds">`, where a `java.awt.Rectangle` is passed in as the argument with the parameters `0,0,200,300`. Even though you didn't specify it in your Java code, the dimensions of the `JFrame`'s `contentPane` are set from this same information. The `defaultCloseOperation` is set using the value of the constant `EXIT_ON_CLOSE` instead of the name of the constant. Although it is harder to read, you could have written the original line in the Java source code like this:

```
x.setDefaultCloseOperation(3);
```

In fact, during the evolution of the Swing libraries, there was a time when you had to write the line that way.

The name of the JFrame wasn't set, so it is referred to as frame0. The title was set to "Look at me" by using the single argument constructor for the JFrame. Finally, you set the visible property to true using the Java code setVisible(true).

XML Syntax

You've seen some of the benefits of having these human-readable text files instead of binary files. In the examples you've seen so far, you've been able to figure out what an XML file is telling you without knowing anything about the rules of XML. To be honest, we provided no examples that weren't very HTML-like. Now it is time to take a look at the syntax of XML.

Elements

XML applications are much more particular about syntax than HTML browsers are. You need to keep in mind that HTML was designed for presentation, and that XML is representing data in ways that can be understood both by people and by other applications. In HTML we didn't think twice about code like the following:

```
...
<P> Here is a paragraph.
<P> Here is another paragraph.
...
```

In fact, we were often sloppier than that and used the <P> tag to produce vertical space between lines. We figured that if we were beginning the second paragraph, then it should be obvious that we were no longer interested in the first paragraph.

XML is different because the tags describe the data they contain. Notice that all of our examples have a single root element that contains the rest of the elements. You need to know precisely when an element begins and ends because it is a node of a tree. You may want to manipulate the nodes and change the order. You will pick up some piece of a tree between and including a start and an end tag. As long as you follow all of the rules, an XML parser will be able to read and parse the document. Fortunately, there aren't very many rules. A document that conforms to these rules is said to be well formed.

One of the rules is that you must finish what you begin. In an XML document, you would have to fix the previous code fragment so that it read as follows:

```
...
<P> Here is a paragraph.</P>
<P> Here is another paragraph.</P>
...
```

You were supposed to do this in HTML, but browsers are taught to know what you mean, and so you were allowed to be sloppy. In XML you are forced to be explicit. What about elements that don't have any content? For example, how could you fix the following?

```
...
Here is a line. I think I'll insert a break. <br>
Here is a line separated from the previous one by a break.
...
```

One choice could be to write the following:

```
...
Here is a line. I think I'll insert a break. <br> </br>
Here is a line separated from the previous one by a break.
...
```

This seems a bit dumb (not that we all haven't had experience with badly designed syntax). If nothing could possibly go between `<br>` and `</br>`, then why create that possibility? The answer is to create an empty element. Empty elements are specially designed for elements that don't have any content. You indicate that you are combining the start and end tag by opening the tag with < and closing it with />. This way there is no confusion. Your code snippet then becomes the following:

```
...
Here is a line. I think I'll insert a break. <br/>
Here is a line separated from the previous one by a break.
...
```

An element can contain text, or one or more other elements or both. You can see this in the resume and JavaBeans examples. If you keep in mind the idea that elements are nodes on a tree and can be moved and manipulated, then it will make sense to you that elements must be properly nested. For example, the following is not allowed:

```
<outer>
<inner>
</outer>
</inner>
```

If you want to pick up the entire `<inner>` element and place it before the `<outer>` element, you would be taking the end tag for `<outer>` with you. Instead, you have to properly nest, as follows:

```
<outer>
<inner>
</inner>
</outer>
```

In these last two snippets we've omitted the indentation that we usually include for readability. There was no way to properly indent the first snippet, and we didn't want to imply in the second one that the indentation was why the second one properly parsed.

Another of the rules is that XML is case-sensitive. Again, many of us have gotten sloppy in HTML and written something like the following:

```
<html>
  <Body>
    ...
  </body>
</HTML>
```

As Java developers, this restriction shouldn't bother us. We often use different cases to indicate a class and an instance of the class. To declare an object of type `Dog` named `dog`, we might write something like the following:

```
Dog dog = new Dog();
```

The point isn't whether or not you like this naming convention, but that you aren't in need of case-sensitivity training.

As you choose an element name, you should make sure that it starts with a letter or underscore and that it doesn't contain any spaces. Following your Java naming conventions, you should choose names that are descriptive and that help you or other developers understand what you are describing.

Namespaces

You need namespaces in XML for the same reasons that you use packages in Java. You may have constructed your own version of a resume, wherein your concept of an address is different from mine. To distinguish your `address` element from mine, prefix the element name with the name of a namespace. My `<address>` consists of `<street>`, `<city>`, `<state>`, `<zip>`, and `<phone>`. Just as you would tend to package these together in Java, you should put them in the same namespace. Again, this way your `<address>` will use your `<street>`, and so on.

Let's say that our namespace will be called `J2EEBible`, and that yours will be called `reader`. Then we will refer to our `<address>` with the qualified name `<J2EEBible:address>`, and to yours as `<reader:address>`. In each case, the part before the colon is the prefix, and the part after is the local part. Really `J2EEBible` is not the namespace; it is the prefix that we will bind to a particular namespace using the following syntax:

```
xlmns:prefix="URI"
```

Here's how the use of namespaces might change the earlier resume document:

```
<?xml version="1.0"?>
<J2EEBible:resume
  xmlns:J2EEBible="http://www.hungryminds.com/j2eebible/">
  <J2EEBible:name> A. Employee </name>
  <J2EEBible:address>
    <J2EEBible:street> 1234 My Street </J2EEBible:street>
    <J2EEBible:city> My City</J2EEBible:city>
    <J2EEBible:state> OH </J2EEBible:state>
    <J2EEBible:zip> 44120 </J2EEBible:zip>
    <J2EEBible:phone>  (555) 555-5555 </J2EEBible:phone>
  </J2EEBible:address>
  <J2EEBible:education>
    <J2EEBible:school> Whatsamatta U.</J2EEBible:school>
    <J2EEBible:degree>  B.S. </J2EEBible:degree>
    <J2EEBible:yeargraduated> 1920 </J2EEBible:yeargraduated>
  </J2EEBible:education>
</J2EEBible:resume>
```

The portion in boldface shows where the namespace is declared. It is an attribute placed inside the start tag for the `<resume>` element. (We'll say more about attributes in the next subsection.) First we prefixed the tag with the name of the namespace, and then we bound the name `J2EEBible` to the URI `http://www.hungryminds.com/j2eebible/`. The URI that you choose is not necessarily a URL that can actually be typed into a browser; it is a way of uniquely identifying your namespace, just as you might use `com.hungryminds.j2eebible` to name a Java package.

You can use more than one namespace in a document. You can also use a default namespace, that any element without a prefix is associated with. You denote the default namespace using the following syntax:

```
xmlns="http://www.hungryminds.com/somedefaultnamespace/"
```

Note that there is no colon after `xmlns`, nor any prefix name. If you add the default namespace to your modified resume file, then `<J2EEBible:address>` refers to the element defined in our namespace, whereas `<address>` refers to the element defined in the default namespace.

Attributes

In addition to specifying the content between the start and end tags of an element, you can include attributes in an element start tag itself. Inside the element's start tag you include an attribute as a name-value pair using the following syntax:

```
name="value"
```

The attribute value is enclosed in quotation marks: We've used double quotes here, but you can also use single quotes. The name of an attribute follows the same rules and guidelines as the name of an element.

Consider how namespaces affect attributes. When we specified the default namespace, the name of the attribute was `xmlns`, and the value was `http://www.hungryminds.com/somedefaultnamespace/`. When we specified the namespace `J2EEBible`, the name of the attribute was `xmlns:J2EEBible`, and the value was `http://www.hungryminds.com/j2eebible/`.

The biggest question is, "when should you use an attribute?" The issue is that for the most part, any attribute could also have been created as a sub-element of the current element. The general rule of thumb for using attributes is that attributes should contain metadata or system information. Elements should contain data that you may be presenting or working with. These guidelines are not always cut and dry, however. Take a look at a snippet from the JavaBeans example earlier in this chapter:

```
<java version="1.4.0-beta" class="java.beans.XMLDecoder">
  <object class="javax.swing.JFrame">
    <void property="bounds">
      <object class="java.awt.Rectangle">
        <int>0</int>
        <int>0</int>
        <int>200</int>
        <int>300</int>
      </object>
    </void>
    ...
    <void property="defaultCloseOperation">
      <int>3</int>
    </void>
```

The attributes associated with the `java` and the first `object` elements aren't too controversial. In the `java` element, attributes are being used to specify the version and the class that can interpret this element. The first `object` element has the attribute `class`, which points to the class that you are instantiating. You could have viewed the bounds of the `JFrame` as an attribute. Similarly, you could have written the `defaultCloseOperation` in many ways, including the following:

```
<void property="defaultCloseOperation" value="3" />
<void defaultCloseOperation="3" />
<defaultCloseOperation value="3" />
```

If you were just inventing the tags you'd use in an application, none of these choices would be wrong. The actual code given in the example above was chosen over these alternatives to conform with the specification outlined in JSR-57, and this solution is best for bean persistence across IDEs. When you are designing your own XML documents, you will have to make your own decisions about what is an attribute and what is an element. Follow the rough rule of thumb about usage and rest assured that whichever choice you make for the remaining cases, lots of people will feel that you're wrong.

One limitation may influence your decision about whether something should be represented as an element or as an attribute. The following version of setting the bounds of the JFrame would not be legal:

```
<void property="bounds">
  <object class="java.awt.Rectangle"
    int="0"
    int="0"
    int="200"
    int="300" />
</void>
```

This code is illegal because you can't use the same name for two different attributes. This wasn't a problem with elements. In the original version you had four ints: Each was a different element contained between the object start and end tags. It would be legal to code this example as follows:

```
<void property="bounds">
  <object class="java.awt.Rectangle"
    xTopLeft="0"
    yTopLeft="0"
    xBottomRight="200"
    yBottomRight="300" />
</void>
```

This code may seem more descriptive than the original, but you have to remember what this XML document is being used for. You want to define the bounds of your JFrame by passing in a Rectangle. The Rectangle is constructed from four int primitives. The original code clearly conveyed this information to a Java developer. It was also generated automatically from the Java code that specified the bounds of the JFrame.

Summary

In this chapter you've been introduced to XML from the perspective of a Java developer. So far you have learned the following:

✦ Fundamentally, XML is a format that represents data along with tags that describe that data. This "self-describing" document is both human- and machine-readable. Binary files that use proprietary formats are not easily read by people or by other applications, and HTML produces content that humans can read, but that means little to machines. XML provides a robust format for both humans and machines.

- To display XML in a user-friendly form you have to use some companion technology. You can convert XML to HTML or another format using XSLT, or you can treat it as you do HTML and use it with Cascading Style Sheets. We'll further explore the first option in Chapter 14.
- When documents are represented using XML instead of HTML, the different parts become more accessible. You can more easily manipulate the document and pull out the content you are looking for.
- To standardize configuration files, a movement has sprung up in favor of using XML. You've already seen this use of XML in the web.xml configuration files for Tomcat and Enterprise JavaBeans.
- XML is used to persist data about JavaBeans and to aid development across many IDEs. The file is generated and read by the `XMLEncoder` and `XMLDecoder` classes along with helper classes that were added to the `java.beans` package in JDK 1.4.
- Elements must have properly nested start and end tags. An element may have an empty tag that is basically both a start and an end tag. When choosing names for elements, remember that XML is case-sensitive.
- Attributes are useful for including meta-information. Data that won't be rendered for the client, and that are system information, are often better represented as attributes than as elements. You can't, however, repeat an attribute name the way you can repeat an element name.

✦ ✦ ✦

Describing Documents with DTDs and Schemas

Good programming practices in Java stress separating the interface from the implementation. If you know the interface for a class, then you know how to write applications that use the methods in that class. You don't care about the implementation. Similarly, in an XML document, if you know how the data are structured, you can write Java applications that extract, create, and manipulate the document. Currently, the most popular way to specify the structure of an XML file is to use a Document Type Definition (DTD). XML Schema is an XML technology that enables you to constrain an XML document using an XML document.

In this chapter you'll begin by reading through a DTD to get a feel for the syntax. You'll then be able to use a Web resource to validate an XML document against that DTD. After that, you'll be ready to write your own DTD — one that enforces the rules you need to enforce in our running résumé example. Finally, you'll see how you can constrain the same document using XML Schema. We won't show you every aspect of constructing a DTD or a schema, but you'll learn enough that you'll be able to consult the specs for the rest of the details.

DTDs and XML Schema are not the only systems for constraining XML. The Schematron is a Structural Schema Language for constraining XML using patterns in trees. You can find out more at the Academia Sinica Computing Centre's Web site, `http://www.ascc.net/xml/resource/schematron/schematron.html`. The Regular Language description for XML (RELAX) is currently working its way through the ISO. You can find a tutorial in English or Japanese, examples, and links to software at the RELAX homepage at `http://www.xml.gr.jp/relax/`.

✦ ✦ ✦ ✦

In This Chapter

Learning the basics of Document Type Definitions (DTDs)

Validating an XML document against a DTD

Writing your own DTDs to define elements, attributes, and document structure

Using XML Schema instead of a DTD to more precisely describe datatypes

Defining your own complex types

Substituting one type for another

Producing Valid XML Documents

In Chapter 10, we began to show you what XML documents are. We considered some examples and showed you some of the basic rules of producing well-formed XML. These were basically grammatical rules. As long as the syntax was OK, we were satisfied that the XML document could be parsed by an XML parser so that you could process the information using a Java application. Consider, for example, the following sentence:

```
My ele dri brok phantenves ice 7cream.
```

It's hard to make sense of it. Perhaps the silent `7` at the beginning of `cream` doesn't help. It's also difficult because the words `elephant`, drives, and `broken` are not properly nested. The following sentence is easier to read, although it doesn't make much more sense:

```
My elephant drives broken ice cream.
```

Now the sentence is well formed. You can parse it and locate the subject, the verb and the object. Depending on where and when you went to school, you may even be able to diagram it. You can alter the sentence in many ways so that it makes sense:

```
My elephant eats delicious ice cream.
My elephant drives large trucks.
My elephant likes broken ice cream cones.
```

If your task were to make sense out of "My elephant drives broken ice cream" then, even though it is well formed, you still would be out of luck. But what if you had to follow a rule like the following:

```
If verb="drives" the object must describe one or more vehicles.
```

Now you can go to town. Maybe you need to restrict the subject to being a human being, but you can see the improvement. The sentence begins to make some sort of sense.

That is what you get when you provide a DTD or a schema for an XML document to follow. You are defining the structure of the document. If a document conforms to the specified DTD, it is said to be valid. Once you know that a document is valid according to a specific DTD, you know where to find the elements you're looking for. That's why it's a good idea to understand DTDs and schema before you start parsing and working with XML documents.

Reading a DTD

Before we show you how to create a DTD, take a look at one that corresponds to the resume document we looked at in Chapter 10. To remind you, here's the XML version of the résumé document:

```
<?xml version="1.0"?>
<resume>
  <name> A. Employee </name>
  <address>
    <street> 1234 My Street </street>
    <city> My City</city>
    <state> OH </state>
    <zip> 44120 </zip>
    <phone>  (555) 555-5555 </phone>
  </address>
  <education>
    <school> Whatsamatta U.</school>
    <degree>  B.S. </degree>
    <yeargraduated> 1920 </yeargraduated>
  </education>
</resume>
```

It was pretty easy to determine the structure of this document just by looking at it. Now the goal is to go in the other direction. Having a DTD enables you to specify the structure so that anyone who wants to create a résumé that conforms to our DTD knows which elements he or she can or must use, and the order in which those elements should go.

```
<!ELEMENT resume (name, address, education)>
<!ELEMENT address (street, city, state, zip, phone)>
<!ELEMENT education (school, degree, yeargraduated)>
<!ELEMENT name (#PCDATA)>
<!ELEMENT street (#PCDATA)>
<!ELEMENT city (#PCDATA)>
<!ELEMENT state (#PCDATA)>
<!ELEMENT zip (#PCDATA)>
<!ELEMENT phone (#PCDATA)>
<!ELEMENT school (#PCDATA)>
<!ELEMENT degree (#PCDATA)>
<!ELEMENT yeargraduated (#PCDATA)>
```

Without knowing the DTD syntax, you can figure out that the first element is called `resume` and consists of the elements `name`, `address`, and `education`. You might even assume, correctly, that there can be only one of each of those elements and that they appear in the given order. Similarly, the `address` element is also made up of one of each of the elements `street`, `city`, `state`, `zip`, and `phone`, and the `education` element consists of one each of the elements `school`, `degree`, and `yeargraduated`. The remaining elements are somehow different. Each consists of

#PCDATA. This indicates that you can think of these elements as being the fundamental building blocks of the other elements. In other words, address and education are both made up of these fundamental building blocks, which in turn consist of nothing more than parsed character data.

Connecting the document and the DTD

At this point you have an XML file and a DTD but nothing that ties them to each other. You follow the same basic rules you would follow in tying a CSS (Cascading Style Sheet) to an HTML document. For example, to indicate that this XML file references that particular DTD, you can just include the DTD in the XML file, as shown in the following example:

```
<?xml version="1.0"?>
<!DOCTYPE resume [
  <!ELEMENT resume (name, address, education)>
  <!ELEMENT address (street, city, state, zip, phone)>
  <!ELEMENT education (school, degree, yeargraduated)>
  <!ELEMENT name (#PCDATA)>
  <!ELEMENT street (#PCDATA)>
  <!ELEMENT city (#PCDATA)>
  <!ELEMENT state (#PCDATA)>
  <!ELEMENT zip (#PCDATA)>
  <!ELEMENT phone (#PCDATA)>
  <!ELEMENT school (#PCDATA)>
  <!ELEMENT degree (#PCDATA)>
  <!ELEMENT yeargraduated (#PCDATA)>
]>
<resume>
  <name> A. Employee </name>
  <address>
    <street> 1234 My Street </street>
    <city> My City</city>
    <state> OH </state>
    <zip> 44120 </zip>
    <phone>  (555) 555-5555 </phone>
  </address>
  <education>
    <school> Whassamatta U.</school>
    <degree>  B.S. </degree>
    <yeargraduated> 1920 </yeargraduated>
  </education>
</resume>
```

The portion in bold, <!DOCTYPE resume [...]>, is the document type declaration. It specifies that the root element is of type resume and then includes the DTD between square brackets. The processing instruction <?xml version=1.0?> and the DOCTYPE tag are not elements and so do not need to have matching closing tags.

It would be inefficient and overly restrictive for every XML file to include the DTD (or DTDs) it uses. Instead, suppose that you save this particular DTD in a file called resume.dtd in the same directory that contains your XML file. Then you can reference the DTD using the following document type declaration instead:

```
<!DOCTYPE resume SYSTEM "resume.dtd">
```

Here you don't include the DTD in the document type declaration but rather point to it. You can place it in another directory and use a relative URL, or you can provide an absolute URI that points to the document on your machine or another machine. Take a look at the /lib/dtds directory in your J2EE distribution. It contains various DTDs for use in enterprise applications. By storing your DTDs in this location, you can reference them from any XML document that needs to be validated against them.

The web.xml document that you used as a config file for Tomcat had the following document type declaration:

```
<!DOCTYPE web-app PUBLIC
  "-//Sun Microsystems, Inc.//DTD Web Application 2.3//EN"
  "http://java.sun.com/j2ee/dtds/web-app_2_3.dtd">
```

Here the DTD is declared to be `PUBLIC` instead of `SYSTEM`. The idea is that you aren't just using a DTD for your own idea of what a résumé should look like; this DTD will be used by tons of people customizing the web.xml file to configure their servlet containers. The validator will first try to use the first address that follows the word `PUBLIC`. In this case that address signifies that no standards body has approved this DTD, that it is owned by Sun, and that it describes Web Applications version 2.3 in English. The second address indicates the URI where the DTD can be found.

Sun has moved the address for all its J2EE DTDs to the URL `http://java.sun.com/dtd/`. The document type declaration in the current Tomcat config will most likely have been updated by the time you read this. You should install the latest version so that the changes are reflected. You will also have a local copy of these files in your J2EE SDK distribution version 1.3 or higher, in the directory /lib/dtds/.

Take a look at the web-app DTD. It includes a lot of documentation to help you understand what each element is designed to handle. Here's the specification for the `web-app` element.

```
<!ELEMENT web-app (icon?, display-name?, description?,
distributable?, context-param*, filter*, filter-mapping*,
listener*, servlet*, servlet-mapping*, session-config?,
mime-mapping*, welcome-file-list?, error-page*, taglib*,
resource-env-ref*, resource-ref*, security-constraint*, login-
config?, security-role*, env-entry*, ejb-ref*)>
```

From your experience so far you can figure out that the list in parentheses is an ordered list of elements the `web-app` contains. But now each name is followed by a ? or a *. As you'll see in the following section, the ? indicates that the element may or may not be included, and the * indicates that if it's included, there may be more than one.

Writing Document Type Definitions (DTDs)

In the previous section you saw a couple of examples of DTDs and got a feel for the basic syntax. In this section we'll run through the most common constructs used to specify elements and attributes. For more information on DTDs you should consult a book devoted to XML, such as the second edition of Elliotte Rusty Harold's *XML Bible* (Hungry Minds, 2001).

Declaring elements

From our examples, you've probably figured out that the syntax for declaring an element is the following:

```
<!ELEMENT element-name (what it contains )>
```

In Chapter 10, we covered restrictions on the name of the element. Now take a look at what an element can contain.

Nothing at all

In the resume example, let's say that the employer belongs to a secret club and wishes to give preferential treatment to others in the same club. This club membership indicator may appear in an element that contains information but doesn't appear on the page. For example, the resume may be adjusted as follows:

```
...
<resume>
  <name> A. Employee </name>
  <knowsSecretHandshake />
  <address>
...
```

You should adjust the DTD to indicate that there is now an empty element called `knowsSecretHandshake`. Of course, you have to adjust the `resume` element declaration in the DTD as well, in addition to adding the following entry:

```
<!ELEMENT knowsSecretHandshake EMPTY>
```

Nothing but text

The fundamental building blocks of the resume contain nothing but #PCDATA. This parsed character data is just text. You could have declared street as consisting of a streetNumber and a streetName. You didn't. It is declared as follows:

```
<!ELEMENT street (#PCDATA)>
```

So the contents of street can't meaningfully be further parsed by an XML parser.

Other elements

Now the fun begins. An element can contain one or more other elements. It may seem a bit silly to have it contain only one—but you can. If the parent element contains nothing but what is in the child, and only a single child element exists, then there should be a good reason for this additional layer. In any case, here's how you would declare it:

```
<!ELEMENT parent (child)>
```

You've already seen the case of a parent containing more than one child. For example, you declared the education element in the resume example as follows:

```
<!ELEMENT education (school, degree, yeargraduated)>
```

It is possible that your candidate never went to school. You can indicate that the resume element may contain one or no education elements by using a ? after the word education:

```
<!ELEMENT resume (name, address, education?)>
```

You'll notice that no symbols follow name or address. This indicates that these elements must occur exactly once each.

On second thought, your candidate may never have graduated from school, or may have graduated from one or more schools. You can indicate that an element may occur zero or more times by using a *. In this example, the resume element would be declared as follows:

```
<!ELEMENT resume (name, address, education*)>
```

Your candidate may have more than one address, and you don't want to allow the candidate to have no address or you won't be able to contact him or her. You can't, therefore, just use the * and hope that it is used correctly. You use the symbol + to indicate that an element will appear one or more times. The following example shows what this symbol looks like applied to the address element:

```
<!ELEMENT resume (name, address+, education)>
```

It is possible that your candidate has more than one degree from the same school. You can group elements to expand your options in specifying the number of degrees. Here's how you'd specify that a candidate can have one or more degrees from the same school:

```
<!ELEMENT education (school, (degree, yeargraduated)+)>
```

The element yeargraduated is grouped with the element degree so you know the year associated with each degree earned.

Finally, you may want to present options. You may want to indicate that an element can contain either a certain element (or group of elements) or another one. You can do this with the | symbol. Here's how you indicate that an address consists either of a street, city, state, and zip or of a phone:

```
<!ELEMENT address ((street, city, state, zip)| phone)>
```

Mixed content

Sometimes you want to include text without having to create a whole new element that represents this text. For example, this is an XML version of the nonsense example from the beginning of the chapter:

```
<nonsense>
  My <animal> Elephant </animal>
  drives  <vehicles> large trucks </vehicles>.
</nonsense>
```

The corresponding DTD entry is the following:

```
<!ENTITY nonsense (#PCDATA,animal,#PCDATA,vehicles,#PCDATA)>
```

Really, the format of the entry isn't different from the format of those you saw when including other elements. The difference is that #PCDATA is an allowable entry.

Anything at all

You should have a really good reason for choosing this option. You may want to use it while developing a DTD, but by the time you're finished, you should be able to convince three other people (at least one of whom doesn't like you very much) that this option is a good idea. In the event that you do choose this option, you are saying that you have some element but that it can contain whatever the person using your DTD wants. The syntax is the following:

```
<!ELEMENT looselyDefinedThing ANY>
```

Declaring entities

An entity specifies a name that will be replaced by either text or a given file. You declare an entity in a DTD as follows:

```
<!ENTITY entityName "what it is replaced by">
```

Some entities are defined for you in XML. These entities enable you to use characters that would give the parser problems. For example, if you use < or >, the parser tries to interpret these symbols as tag delimiters. Instead, you can use the entities < and > for these less-than and greater-than signs. The other three predefined entities are & for &, " for ", and &apos for '.

You can define your own constants in the same way. You can create a form letter for rejecting candidates, and personalize it by assigning the candidate's name to the entity candidate, as shown in the following example:

```
<!ENTITY candidate "A. Applicant">
```

You can now use this element in a document as follows:

```
...
Dear &candidate,
...
```

In the final document, this letter would begin, "Dear A. Applicant, ..."

Suppose that you write a lot of letters, and you want each one to have your return address at the top. You may, in addition, use some set of form letters over a long period of time. Rather than type in your return address to each letter, you can define it in the DTD for those form letters. You can hard-code it for each form letter, as shown in this example:

```
<!ENTITY returnAddress "My Name, 1234 MyStreet, My Town, OH
  44120">
```

You probably already recognize this as bad programming practice. If you move, you have to replace your address in many locations. It's a better idea to have each of these DTDs refer to a single file that contains your current address.

The reference looks similar to the syntax you used for namespaces. In this case, it looks like this:

```
<!ENTITY returnAddress SYSTEM
"http://www.hungryminds.com/J2EEBible/myAddress.xml">
```

This code refers to an XML file that you keep at the specified URI. You don't have to refer to an XML file; your target file can be a text file or even binary data. For example, you can have a picture of your house stored in an entity, pass in the link to the file and a reference to its type, and if the client application can handle the MIME type, the page will be rendered correctly.

Declaring attributes

You can think of an attribute as a modifier for an element. Here's the syntax for an attribute declaration:

```
<!ATTLIST elementName attributeName attributeType rules >
```

The element name and attribute name are self-explanatory. You have three choices for `rules`: An attribute is either `#FIXED`, `#IMPLIED`, or `#REQUIRED`.

If it is `#FIXED`, the attribute will have the value specified. For example, in the following declaration the `phone` element has an attribute, `acceptCollectCalls`, which is set to the value `false`:

```
<!ATTLIST phone acceptCollectCalls #FIXED "false">
```

The other two choices don't provide a default value. In the following case, `#IMPLIED` tells you that the attribute `acceptCollectCalls` may or may not be set in the `phone` element in an XML document:

```
<!ATTLIST phone acceptCollectCalls #IMPLIED>
```

If, as in the following declaration, you use `#REQUIRED` instead of `#IMPLIED`, then `acceptCollectCalls` must be set in each `phone` element in an XML document validated against this DTD:

```
<!ATTLIST phone acceptCollectCalls #REQUIRED>
```

Although other types of attributes exist, you will most often use `CDATA` and enumeration. The `CDATA` type means that the attribute can contain text of any sort. (You can think of `CDATA` as being opposed to the `PCDATA` we covered for elements.) Whereas `PCDATA` is parsed character data, `CDATA` is not parsed and can contain any values you like. They will not be interpreted by the parser.

The enumeration is a list of the possible values that the attribute can take on. For example, you may want to imply that `acceptCollectCalls` is a Boolean. You can do this by specifying the allowable values as being `true` or `false`, as shown in the following example:

```
<!ATTLIST phone acceptCollectCalls (true | false) #REQUIRED>
```

Validating XML

You now have all of the pieces you need to create a valid XML document. You know how to write a DTD and an XML document that conforms to it. You know how to use `DOCTYPE` to tie the two together. Your XML document has a single root element that corresponds to the element declared in the document type declaration. Now it is time to check that your document is valid. Note that you should do this *before* you go to production. You shouldn't continue to validate the document, or the output of a document-producing application, once you have entered production, as this will slow down your process.

As an exercise, try validating the resume document using Brown University's Scholarly Technology Group's XML Validation form. You'll see a welcome page, similar to the one shown in Figure 11-1, at `http://www.stg.brown.edu/service/xmlvalid/`.

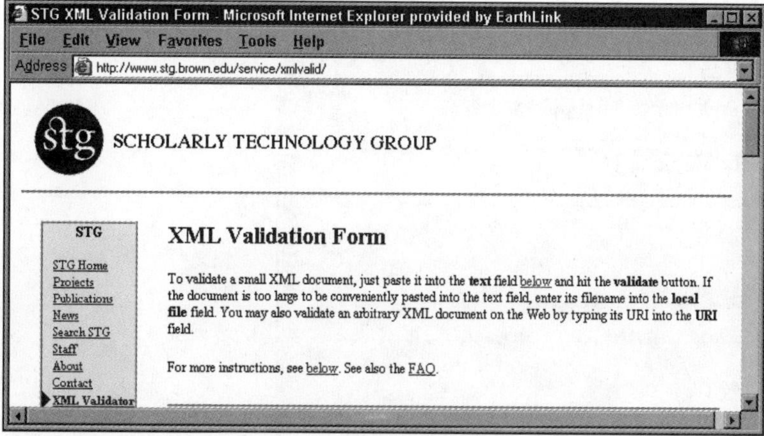

Figure 11-1: Brown University's online validator

The interface is very straightforward with helpful instructions. You can validate a local file on your machine, either by browsing to it or by typing or cutting and pasting it into the provided area. You have one version of a resume document that includes the required DTD: Type that into the text area and click the Validate button to see the result shown in Figure 11-2.

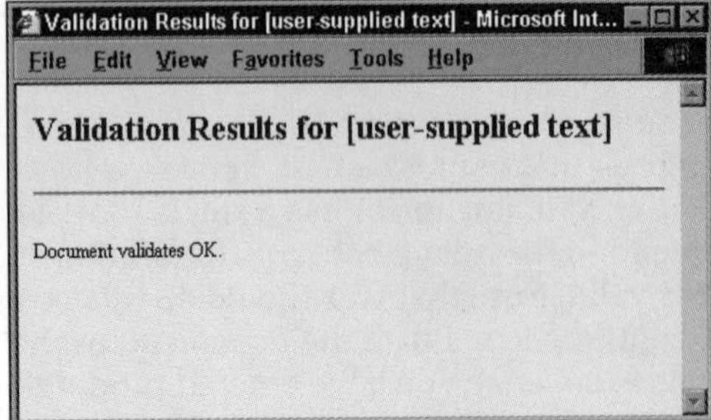

Figure 11-2: Results for a valid document

The document is valid, and that's all that the validator reports. Now delete a line, such as the `degree` element, from inside the `education` element. You will now see a report that the document is no longer valid (see Figure 11-3).

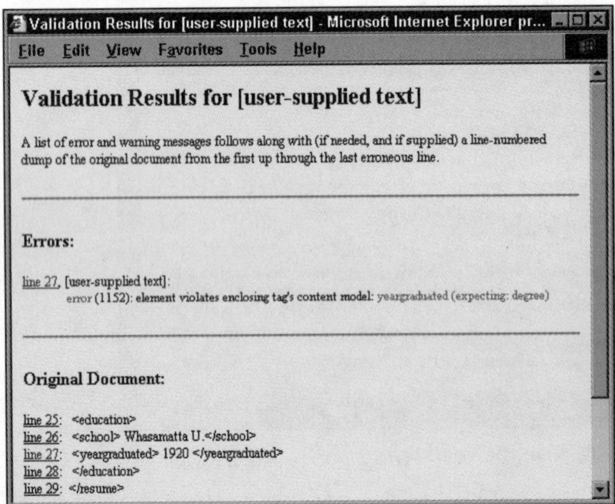

Figure 11-3: Results for a document that isn't valid

Finally, take a look at a document that isn't even well formed. Move the `</zip>` end tag inside the `phone` tag. The validator will give you a report much like the one shown in Figure 11-4.

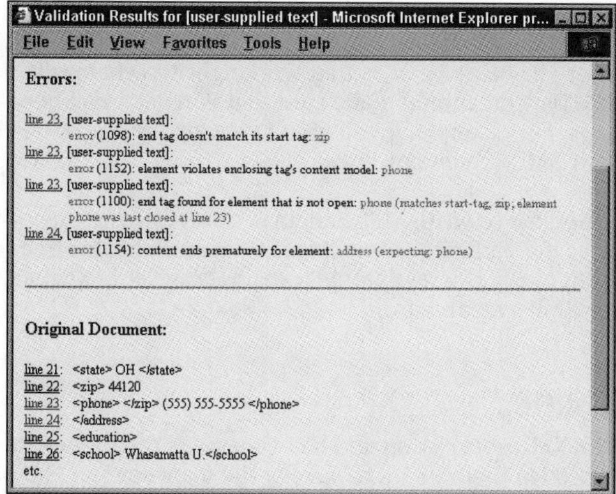

Figure 11-4: Results for a document that isn't well formed

Describing Documents with XML Schemas

A DTD may be sufficient for many of your needs. It is fairly easy to write a DTD and an XML document that validates against it. One downside is that the datatypes aren't specific enough to really constrain your document enough. For example, both the phone number (`phone`) and the candidate's name (`name`) are described as `#PCDATA`. You know that you want an integer for the phone number. More specifically, in the United States, you want a ten-digit integer. On the other hand, a name probably won't include many numbers.

A second drawback of DTDs is that you are describing XML documents with non-XML documents. An XML Schema is a well-formed XML document. In fact, it conforms to a DTD itself and so can be (but doesn't need to be) validated. It may seem as if you're cheating here, because a DTD still exists in this scenario. The point is that you will be creating or using a document that describes the structure of your XML documents. This descriptor will itself be written in XML, so you can use your favorite XML tools to parse and manipulate the schema.

The XML Schema specification is still evolving. For final syntax and details about the namespace, check out `http://www.w3.org/TR/xmlschema-1/`.

As a Java developer, you'll find it easy to get excited about XML Schema. You can use it to create complex XML types, much as you've created Java objects. The schema is to the XML document what an interface is to an instance of a class. Although the J2EE JDK currently ships with DTDs and is likely to continue to do so for a while, you can expect to see the adoption of schemas as well. (You should consider moving in that direction as well, although you might want to wait until the specification is more stable.) The other issue is that working with schemas is harder than working with DTDs. You should make sure that you get a real benefit from taking these extra steps. For example, if you aren't viewing XML as data, you may not need the extras that XML Schema provides.

You can use a standard text editor to write XML Schemas or investigate the growing selection of GUI tools. One of the earliest tools is Xeena. It is available for free from the IBM alphaWorks site at `http://www.alphaworks.ibm.com/tech/xeena`. XML Spy is a commercial IDE for XML available from `http://www.xmlspy.com`.

The shell of a schema

A schema will begin with the XML declaration and has `schema` as the root element. Follow the syntax we discussed in Chapter 10, to specify the namespace. [The particular value of the namespace has changed in the two years prior to this writing, and is likely to have changed again before you read this. Check out the W3C Web site (`http://www.w3c.org/XML/schema`).] Here's what the shell of a schema looks like:

```
<?xml version="1.0">
<xsd:schema xmlns:xsd="http://www.w3.org/2001/XMLSchema">
...
</xsd:schema>
```

You can also use the default namespace, but this format forces you to be clear about which elements are part of the schema. If you were to use the default namespace, your document would look like this:

```
<?xml version="1.0">
<schema xmlns="http://www.w3.org/2001/XMLSchema">
...
</schema>
```

For the remainder of the chapter, we'll use the first version, which gives the namespace the name `xsd`.

Recall that you used the `DOCTYPE` tag to point to a DTD. In the case of the preceding schema shell, place the `noNamespaceSchemaLocation` attribute in an XML file in the root element to point to a schema. (Assume you've saved your shell document as shell.xsd.) The process of adding the `noNamespaceSchemaLocation` looks like this fragment from the resume example:

```
<?xml version="1.0">
<resume xsi:noNameSpaceSchemaLocation="shell.xsd"
  xmlns:xsi="http://www.w3.org/2001/XMLSchema-instance">
...
```

Again, the actual URI for the namespace may change. This example is in the format you use when your XML document doesn't have a namespace. If it does, then you have to specify the namespace for the schema as well as the target namespace. In this example, assign the namespace `J2EEBible` to the `resume` elements. Now the XML document looks like this:

```
<?xml version="1.0"?>
<J2EEBible:resume
  xmlns:J2EEBible="http://www.hungryminds.com/j2eebible/">
  <J2EEBible:name>
...
```

Nothing from the XML file is pointing at the schema, so you have to alter the schema to point to the XML file. You do this in the `schema` opening tag, as follows:

```
<?xml version="1.0">
<xsd:schema xmlns:xsd="http://www.w3.org/2001/XMLSchema"
  xmlns:J2EEBible="http://www.hungryminds.com/j2eebible/"
  targetNamespace="http://www.hungryminds.com/j2eebible/">
...
</xsd:schema>
```

You've had to add the same URI twice. Once you were specifying the prefix `J2EEBible`, and the other time you were specifying the target namespace of the schema.

Elements and attributes

The syntax for specifying an element is fairly straightforward. Because you are using a namespace for the schema, you declare an element like this:

```
<xsd:element name="elementName" type="elementType" />
```

Remember that schemas are XML documents, and that as a result this tag has to be both a start and end tag for the empty element `xsd:element`. If you just use the default namespace, you can drop the prefix `xsd`. Note that other options that follow the declaration of the `name` and `type` may exist.

As before, the element name is the name you're using in the XML document, such as `address`, `phone`, or `education`. The element type will enable you to refer to many built-in types as well as to user-defined types. The way you interact with types is much more in line with your Java experience than with your experience in designing DTDs.

Now here's the syntax for declaring an attribute:

```
<xsd:element name="elementName" type="elementType" />
```

Already you can see that XML Schemas are more consistent than DTDs. However, because you can't use the specialized DTD format, you'll see as we go along that you are required to do a great deal more typing to use schemas.

One of the options that can follow the `name` and `type` in the declaration of an element or attribute is an *occurrence constraint*. Instead of the cryptic ?,*, and + from DTDs, you use the attributes `minOccurs` and `maxOccurs`. In the resume example, you can use the following syntax to specify that an applicant may include one or two phone numbers:

```
<xsd:element name="phone" type="elementType"
   minOccurs="1" maxOccurs="2" />
```

We've left out the element type because we haven't discussed it yet. What is available to you using schemas is a lot more powerful than what you used with DTDs. Sure, you can accomplish the same thing in a DTD using an enumeration, but what if the range is much wider?

Simple types

The building blocks for DTDs are fairly non-specific. XML Schema specifies more than 40 built-in types that you can use. Most of the types are pretty self-explanatory. For more details on these types, check out the online documentation at `http://www.w3.org/TR/xmlschema-1/`.

The numeric types include 13 integral types and three types to describe decimals. The types `float`, `double`, and `decimal` describe floating-point numbers. The integers include `byte`, `short`, `int`, `long`, `integer`, `nonPositiveInteger`, `nonNegativeInteger`, `positiveInteger`, `negativeInteger`, `unsignedByte`, `unsignedShort`, `unsignedInt`, and `unsignedLong`.

You can specify that `phone` is an `int` like this:

```
<xsd:element name="phone" type="xsd:int" />
```

A phone number can't be any old integer. You can assign a `nonNegativeInteger` as the type. You can even define your own simple type. Try designing a U.S. phone number as a ten-digit integer. The first digit of a U.S. phone number cannot be a 1 or a 0. You can apply many other restrictions, but for the moment just use those two. They specify that a U.S. phone number is some 10-digit integer greater than 2,000,000,000: In other words, a U.S. phone number is an integer between 2,000,000,000 and 9,999,999,999. Here's how you can define a simple type based on this observation:

```
<xsd:simpleType name="USPhoneNumber">
  <xsd:restriction base="integer">
    <xsd:minInclusive value="2000000000"/>
```

```
    <xsd:maxInclusive value="9999999999"/>
  </xsd:restriction>
</xsd:simpleType>
```

Now you can use this newly defined type in your element declaration for phone:

```
<xsd:element name="phone" type="USPhoneNumber" />
```

Allowing user-defined types is a very powerful feature that is available in schemas but not in DTDs.

You can allow the entry of more than one phone number by defining a list type, as shown in this example:

```
<xsd:simpleType name="phoneList">
  <xsd:list itemType="USPhoneNumber" />
</xsd:simpleType>
```

This means that phoneList can consist of a list of USPhoneNumbers. You probably want to make sure that at least one phone number is listed in the element phone. At this point you can restrict phoneList by specifying the minimum number of elements, as shown in this example:

```
<xsd:simpleType name="phone">
  <xsd:restriction base="phoneList">
    <xsd:minLength="1"/>
  </xsd:restriction>
</xsd:simpleType>
```

In Java, a boolean is considered an integral type that can only take the values true and false. XML Schema declares boolean to have the four possible values 0, 1, false, and true.

The three string types are string, normalizedString, and token. The normalizedString is just a string without tabs, carriage returns, or linefeeds. The token is just a normalizedString with no extraneous whitespace. The type anyURI is a string that is meant to hold the value of any relative or absolute URI.

The XML Schema provides nine time types. You can specify dates with any of the different degrees of precision allowed in the ISO standard 8601. The types allowed to specify time are time, dateTime, duration, date, gMonth, gYear, gYearMonth, gDay, and gMonthDay. These time specifications are always given so that the units go from largest to smallest as you read from left to right. An example of date is 1776-07-04. The corresponding gMonth is -07--, the corresponding gYear is 1776, and the corresponding gDay is ---04. Details of the time formats can be found in the ISO 8601 document at http://www.iso.ch/markete/8601.pdf.

In the resume example, yeargraduated should be a year. You can specify this in the schema, as follows:

```
<xsd:element name="yeargraduate" type="xsd:gYear" />
```

You can also assign the type int or a string type to the element yeargraduated. As in Java, the type of an element should help you understand what the element is and how to use it properly. If you can be more specific, you should be.

Other built-in simple types include ID, IDREF, ENTITY, and others taken from types of the same name in DTDs. These types are beyond the scope of this book, but you can find descriptions at the W3C Web site, http://www.w3c.org/TR/xmlschema-1/.

Complex types

In the previous section you saw how to create simple types based on existing simple types. The example showed you how to restrict the allowable range of an integer. You can think of that restriction as corresponding to inheritance in Java. Now you are going to look at the DTD analog to composition: building complex types out of simple types. You can then build up XML datatypes that map well to Java objects.

In the DTD version of the resume example, you declared the address element like this:

```
<!ELEMENT address (street, city, state, zip, phone)>
```

In that case you also needed individual entries for street, city, state, zip, and phone. Here's how you can declare the complex type address using XML Schema:

```
<xsd:complexType name="address">
  <xsd:sequence>
    <xsd:element name="street" type="xsd:string" />
    <xsd:element name="city" type="xsd:string" />
    <xsd:element name="state" type="xsd:string" />
    <xsd:element name="zip" type="xsd:string" />
    <xsd:element name="phone" type="xsd:string" />
  </xsd:sequence>
</xsd:complexType>
```

You have already defined a special simple type called USPhoneNumber and declared phone to be of this type. You can refer to this previous reference using the following code:

```
<xsd:complexType name="address">
  <xsd:sequence>
    <xsd:element name="street" type="xsd:string" />
    <xsd:element name="city" type="xsd:string" />
    <xsd:element name="state" type="xsd:string" />
    <xsd:element name="zip" type="xsd:string" />
```

```
      <xsd:element ref="phone" />
    </xsd:sequence>
  </xsd:complexType>
```

This highlighted portion refers to the global element phone. You can similarly group attributes together into an attribute group that you reference using ref.

To return to the element example, when you create an address element in your XML document you are forced to include street, city, state, zip, and phone in that order because of the sequence element. It makes sense to keep the street, city, state, and zip in that order because that is how that data is organized in an address. There is no standard, however, that determines whether the phone number comes before or after the rest of these items. You could collect street, city, state, and zip into a complex type called mailingAddress. If you are going to need this information by itself throughout your document, this is a good idea. Then you can collect mailingAddress and phone together into an unordered collection called address.

Since you've already seen how to create a complex type such as mailingAddress, we will just collect the elements together without naming them:

```
<xsd:complexType name="address">
  <xsd:group>
    <xsd:sequence>
      <xsd:element name="street" type="xsd:string" />
      <xsd:element name="city" type="xsd:string" />
      <xsd:element name="state" type="xsd:string" />
      <xsd:element name="zip" type="xsd:string" />
    </xsd:sequence>
    <xsd:element ref="phone" />
  </xsd:group>
</xsd:complexType>
```

Now if you enter an address, you can enter the phone either before or after the remainder of the information that must be presented in order. If instead of group you use choice, only one of the options can appear. In this case you are looking for some way to contact candidates. You don't care whether they want to be contacted by mail or by phone, but they can only give you one way to contact them. This choice is specified as follows:

```
<xsd:complexType name="address">
  <xsd:choice>
    <xsd:sequence>
      <xsd:element name="street" type="xsd:string" />
      <xsd:element name="city" type="xsd:string" />
      <xsd:element name="state" type="xsd:string" />
      <xsd:element name="zip" type="xsd:string" />
    </xsd:sequence>
    <xsd:element ref="phone" />
  </xsd:choice>
</xsd:complexType>
```

A third option is to use all instead of group or choice. In this case you are allowing the applicant to include either the mailing-address information, the phone number, both, or neither. The user can include each element surrounded by all either zero or one times.

Now suppose that you really don't want to define a separate USPhoneNumber type and then declare a phone to be of this type. If you are only using one phone number in the entire document, you may prefer to define this type locally. This type of definition is similar to an anonymous inner class in Java and is called an *anonymous type definition*. In the case of the phone example, it looks like this:

```
<xsd:complexType name="address">
  <xsd:group>
    <xsd:sequence>
      <xsd:element name="street" type="xsd:string" />
      <xsd:element name="city" type="xsd:string" />
      <xsd:element name="state" type="xsd:string" />
      <xsd:element name="zip" type="xsd:string" />
    </xsd:sequence>
    <xsd:element name="phone">
      <xsd:simpleType>
        <xsd:restriction base="integer">
          <xsd:minInclusive value="2000000000"/>
          <xsd:maxInclusive value="9999999999"/>
        </xsd:restriction>
      </xsd:simpleType>
    </xsd:element>
  </xsd:group>
</xsd:complexType>
```

There is no name following xsd:simpleType as it did in the previous example. Also, because you are defining this type in place you can't use the empty tag <xsd:element name="phone"/>. You can use a start tag and an end tag for this element. Aside from these modifications, you are basically inserting the definition of USPhoneNumber into the declaration of phone.

Finally, take a look at using one type in place of another. As an example, you can declare the education element as follows:

```
<xsd:complexType name="education">
  <xsd:sequence>
    <xsd:element name="school" type="xsd:string" />
    <xsd:element name="year" type="xsd:gYear" />
    <xsd:element name="degree" type="xsd:string" />
  </xsd:sequence>
</xsd:complexType>
```

You can extend education by including information about the major subject studied:

```
<xsd:complexType name="detailedEducation">
  <xsd:complexContent>
```

```
      <xsd:extension base="education">
        <xsd:element name="majorSubject" type=xsd:string" />
      </xsd:extension>
    </xcd:complexContent>
  </xsd:complexType>
```

You can now use the element `detailedEducation` wherever an element of the type `education` is called for. As a Java developer, you should find this very comfortable. Substituting a class that is "at least" some given type is something you do all the time.

Summary

You understand the importance of defining interfaces in your Java applications. In this chapter, we showed you the XML equivalents of this concept. Now that you are able to impose this structure and work within it, you're ready for the next chapter's look at parsing XML documents. In your quick travel through DTDs and schema, you learned the following:

- The basic syntax of a DTD enables you to very simply specify the elements and attributes in an XML document. You can pretty much create a DTD from an existing XML file and then modify it as your needs change. Start from your root element and work in by adding the biggest blocks first and then refining them.
- Once you have a DTD, you add the `DOCTYPE` document type declaration to tie the XML document to the DTD against which you are validating. You will see how to use JAXP to validate your document in Chapter 12, but here you used a validator that is available for free online.
- XML Schema provides you with another method of describing your document. A schema is an XML document itself, and so you will be able to use XML tools to parse and understand it. After the introduction to XML in the Chapter 10, you should be familiar with the syntax and able to read through a schema easily. A schema is generally more complicated than a DTD.
- In addition to using the 40-some built-in simple types, you can create your own simple types and complex types. This makes working with schemas feel more like working with Java. You learned how to extend, restrict, and group types together in creating your complex types.

✦ ✦ ✦

CHAPTER 12

Parsing Documents with JAXP

✦ ✦ ✦ ✦

In This Chapter

Creating a parser with JAXP

Configuring the parser with JAXP

Parsing a document using SAX

Responding to events with callbacks with SAX

Using DOM to view XML documents

Creating a `Document` object from an XML file or from scratch using DOM

Navigating around an XML document with DOM

Generating XML from a Java application with DOM

✦ ✦ ✦ ✦

The previous two chapters gave you an introduction to XML syntax and to the various ways of constraining XML documents. In this chapter, you'll learn the various ways in which you can use Java programs to parse, navigate an XML document using the tree structure, and to create XML. You'll learn two basic methods of working with an XML document. Either you will listen for events that the parser generates while moving through a document, or you will want to work with hierarchical view of the document.

There are various APIs for working with XML. There are the Simple APIs for XML (SAX), the APIs that support the Document Object Model (DOM), and a more Java-friendly set of APIs called JDOM. In this chapter, you'll use Sun Microsystem's Java APIs for XML Parsing, better known as JAXP. JAXP supports both SAX and DOM. JAXP allows you to use its default parser or to plug in your favorite parser. Depending on how you configure the parser and what your needs are, you can then respond to events using a SAX based parser or use the DOM to be able to manipulate and alter an XML document.

Introducing JAXP

Java technology is still evolving pretty quickly as the changes to the core have begun to slow. XML is in a rapid growth stage. Sun has slowed its Java releases to once about every 18 months; from release to release, the related XML technologies change dramatically. In order to maintain Java as an attractive platform for working with XML, Sun will release quarterly updates to the JAX Pack, Sun's collection of Java/XML offerings.

The JAX Pack

The JAX Pack is a single download from Sun that includes Java API for XML Processing (JAXP), Java Architecture for XML Binding (JAXB), Java API for XML Messaging (JAXM), Java API for XML-based RPC (JAX-RPC), and Java API for XML Registries (JAXR). You can find the JAX Pack Web page at `http://java.sun.com/xml/jaxpack.html`. It announces that the download will support SAX, DOM, XSLT, SOAP, UDDI, ebXML, and WSDL. The versions of the technology released in the JAX Pack may not be final customer ship versions of the various APIs, but Sun's goal is to get this evolving technology out faster.

You can find the latest version of JAXP at `http://java.sun.com/xml/xml_jaxp.html`. It will be included in the 1.4 release of J2SE and the 1.3 release of J2EE, and in the JAX Pack. With the JAXP 1.1 download, you'll find a number of examples and samples that will help you learn the technology.

JAXP is not a parser. What JAXP provides is an abstraction layer that enables you to use your favorite parser without worrying too much about the details of that parser. This means that you make calls using the JAXP APIs and let JAXP worry about issues such as backwards compatibility. JAXP supports both the DOM and SAX APIs. In this chapter, we'll cover each API in turn and show you their strengths and weaknesses. As you examine the needs of your particular applications, you'll find situations in which you reach for SAX and those in which you prefer to use the DOM.

Installing JAXP and the examples

Once you download and unzip the distribution, you will end up with a directory named jaxp-1.1. To complete the installation, you can either make additions to your `CLASSPATH` or you can copy three jar files to a directory that is already in the `CLASSPATH`. Because JAXP will eventually be part of the Java 2 distribution, if the jar files crimson.jar, jaxp.jar, and xalan.jar aren't in your `CLASSPATH`, you should copy them to jre/lib/ext. You can test your installation by running one of the sample applications that comes with the distribution.

Next set up your directory for the running example. Inside the jaxp1-1/examples directory create a J2EEBible subdirectory. Inside J2EEBible, create the further subdirectory cue. For this example, let's use the XML version of Shakespeare's *Richard III* that is distributed with JAXP. For simplicity's sake, copy the files rich_iii.xml and play.dtd into the J2EEBible directory. (By the way, you can find a complete distribution of Shakespeare's plays as well as other treasures at `http://sunsite.unc.edu`.)

Testing the installation

Now that you've installed JAXP, try taking it out for a quick spin. You'll learn more about SAX in the section "Reaching for SAX" later in this chapter, but you can still create a SAX-based parser and have it parse the rich_iii.xml file. You may find it helpful to direct your browser to the JavaDocs for the `javax.xml.parsers` package.

The `javax.xml.parsers` package consists of four classes, together with one exception and one error class. (The `DocumentBuilder` and `DocumentBuilderFactory` classes are used for working with the DOM objects and documents, and will be covered later in this chapter in the section "Using the DOM.") The `SAXParser` is the wrapper for implementations of `XMLReader`. If you used previous versions of JAXP, you'll notice that this is a change. In the past, JAXP only supported SAX 1.0, and so `SAXParser` wrapped the `Parser` interface; now JAXP supports SAX 2.0 using the `XMLReader` interface instead, and so `SAXParser` has been changed accordingly. The final class in the `javax.xml.parsers` package is `SAXParserFactory`. This class is a factory for creating instances of SAX 2.0 parsers and configuring them.

The `SAXParserFactory` has three get-set pairs of methods. The `setNamespaceAware()` and `isNamespaceAware()` methods enable you to specify and determine (respectively) whether or not the factory will produce a parser that supports XML namespaces. The `setValidating()` and `isValidating()` methods enable you to specify and determine (respectively) whether or not the factory will produce a parser that validates documents while parsing them. The `setFeature()` and `getFeature()` methods enable you to set and get (respectively) a specified feature in the underlying implementation of the `XMLReader`. With these six methods you can configure and view the details of the SAX-based parser you will create using the `SAXParserFactory`.

Once you have an instance of `SAXParserFactory`, you create a new instance of `SAXParser` using the `newSAXParser()` method. This will create a SAX-based parser with the setting you configured using the methods in the previous paragraph. Creating a `SAXParserFactory` is a little different from what you might expect. The constructor is declared to be `protected`. However, a `static` method named `newInstance()` creates a new instance of a `SAXParserFactory`, which means that you can create your `SAXParser` as follows:

```
SAXParserFactory spFactory = SAXParserFactory.newInstance();
SAXParser parser = spFactory.newSAXParser();
```

The fact that `newInstance()` is a static method means that, unless you need to configure it, you don't actually have to create an instance of `SAXParserFactory`. You can create a `SAXParser` more simply using the following code:

```
SAXParser parser =
      SAXParserFactory.newInstance().newSAXParser();
```

Ten of the 16 methods in the `SAXParser` class are `parse()` methods with different signatures. You also have the `getProperty()` and `setProperty()` methods, which are similar to the `getFeature()` and `setFeature()` methods you saw in the `SAXParserFactory`. You also have the getter methods `getParser()`, `getXMLReader()`, `isNamespaceAware()`, and `isValidating()`, which you can use to see the properties that have been set in the `XMLReader` and in the parser.

But, for the most part, the job of a parser is to parse, and so that's what the bulk of the methods enable you to do.

Let's put all of this together to create a SAX 2.0–based parser and instruct it to parse *Richard III*. Create the following code and save it as CueMyLine.java in the cue directory:

```
package cue;

import org.xml.sax.helpers.DefaultHandler;
import java.io.File;
import javax.xml.parsers.SAXParser;
import javax.xml.parsers.SAXParserFactory;

public class CueMyLine extends DefaultHandler{
  public static void main(String[] args) throws Exception {
    SAXParser parser =
      SAXParserFactory.newInstance().newSAXParser();
    parser.parse(new File("rich_iii.xml"), new CueMyLine());
  }
}
```

You can see that the version of `parse()` you use takes a `File` as its first argument and a `DefaultHandler` as its second argument. We'll take a closer look at `DefaultHandler` in the section "Reaching for SAX"; basically, it is just an adapter class for the `XMLReader` interface.

Compile and run this example. It should run for a little bit and then finish, and you should get the next command prompt. Big deal. Well, despite there being no evidence that anything happened, a parser was created that then parsed the file rich_iii.xml.

We're going to work with this example for a while, so let's fix up the handling of exceptions before moving on. If nothing else, this will emphasize how much is going on in the two-line body of the `main()` method. You might run into trouble configuring the parser, so you need to catch a `ParserConfigurationException`. You need an `IOException` to handle exceptions when using your parser to read from the file rich_iii.xml. You also need to catch `SAXExceptions` in case anything goes wrong during the parsing of the file. The changes are highlighted in the following snippet:

```
package cue;

import org.xml.sax.helpers.DefaultHandler;
import java.io.File;
```

```
import javax.xml.parsers.SAXParser;
import javax.xml.parsers.SAXParserFactory;
import org.xml.sax.SAXException;
import javax.xml.parsers.ParserConfigurationException;
import java.io.IOException;

public class CueMyLine extends DefaultHandler{
  public static void main(String[] args)  {
    try{
      SAXParser parser =
        SAXParserFactory.newInstance().newSAXParser();
      parser.parse(new File("rich_iii.xml"), new CueMyLine());
    } catch (SAXException e){
      System.out.println("This is a SAX Exception.");
    } catch (ParserConfigurationException e) {
      System.out.println("This is a Parser Config Exception.");
    } catch (IOException e){
      System.out.println("This is an IO Exception.");
    }
  }
}
```

You can see that more lines of code are dedicated to exceptions than to actually doing anything. Before adding more functionality, take a closer look at the file rich_iii.xml.

The play's the thing

For this example, you'll work with the copy of Shakespeare's *Richard III* that you placed in the J2EEBible directory. You can structure the information contained in a play's script in many ways; John Bosak made choices that resulted in the following DTD:

```
<!-- DTD for Shakespeare    J. Bosak    1994.03.01, 1997.01.02
-->
<!-- Revised for case sensitivity 1997.09.10 -->
<!-- Revised for XML 1.0 conformity 1998.01.27 (thanks to Eve
Maler) -->

<!-- <!ENTITY amp "&#38;#38;"> -->
<!ELEMENT PLAY     (TITLE, FM, PERSONAE, SCNDESCR, PLAYSUBT,
  INDUCT?, PROLOGUE?, ACT+, EPILOGUE?)>
<!ELEMENT TITLE    (#PCDATA)>
<!ELEMENT FM       (P+)>
<!ELEMENT P        (#PCDATA)>
<!ELEMENT PERSONAE (TITLE, (PERSONA | PGROUP)+)>
<!ELEMENT PGROUP   (PERSONA+, GRPDESCR)>
<!ELEMENT PERSONA  (#PCDATA)>
<!ELEMENT GRPDESCR (#PCDATA)>
<!ELEMENT SCNDESCR (#PCDATA)>
<!ELEMENT PLAYSUBT (#PCDATA)>
<!ELEMENT INDUCT (TITLE, SUBTITLE*,(SCENE+|
```

```
    (SPEECH|STAGEDIR|SUBHEAD)+))>
<!ELEMENT ACT (TITLE, SUBTITLE*, PROLOGUE?, SCENE+,EPILOGUE?)>
<!ELEMENT SCENE(TITLE, SUBTITLE*,
  (SPEECH | STAGEDIR | SUBHEAD)+)>
<!ELEMENT PROLOGUE (TITLE, SUBTITLE*, (STAGEDIR | SPEECH)+)>
<!ELEMENT EPILOGUE (TITLE, SUBTITLE*, (STAGEDIR | SPEECH)+)>
<!ELEMENT SPEECH   (SPEAKER+, (LINE | STAGEDIR | SUBHEAD)+)>
<!ELEMENT SPEAKER  (#PCDATA)>
<!ELEMENT LINE     (#PCDATA | STAGEDIR)*>
<!ELEMENT STAGEDIR (#PCDATA)>
<!ELEMENT SUBTITLE (#PCDATA)>
<!ELEMENT SUBHEAD  (#PCDATA)>
```

If you need a quick DTD refresher, glance back at Chapter 11. You can see, for example, that a <SPEECH> consists of one or more <SPEAKER> elements followed by one or more of the following items: a <LINE>, a <STAGEDIR>, and a <SUBHEAD>. I'm sure an argument could be made for making the SPEAKER an attribute of the <SPEECH> element, but what's important is that you understand the structure specified for you by the DTD. Here's a snippet from *Richard III* that conforms to this DTD:

```
<SPEECH>
<SPEAKER>CATESBY</SPEAKER>
<LINE>The princes both make high account of you;</LINE>
<STAGEDIR>Aside</STAGEDIR>
<LINE>For they account his head upon the bridge.</LINE>
</SPEECH>

<SPEECH>
<SPEAKER>HASTINGS</SPEAKER>
<LINE>I know they do; and I have well deserved it.</LINE>
<STAGEDIR>Enter STANLEY</STAGEDIR>
<LINE>Come on, come on; where is your boar-spear, man?</LINE>
<LINE>Fear you the boar, and go so unprovided?</LINE>
</SPEECH>
```

You have an XML file and its associated DTD. You may inadvertently make alterations so that the file is no longer well formed and/or no longer valid. Your SAX parser can provide you with some helpful feedback in either case.

Checking for well-formed documents

Now that you have a working parser, the very least it should be able to do is indicate whether or not your XML document is well formed. Try creating a problem and see what happens. Act I of the rich_iii.xml file begins with the following few lines:

```
<ACT><TITLE>ACT I</TITLE>

<SCENE><TITLE>SCENE I.  London. A street.</TITLE>
```

```
<STAGEDIR>Enter GLOUCESTER, solus</STAGEDIR>

<SPEECH>
<SPEAKER>GLOUCESTER</SPEAKER>
<LINE>Now is the winter of our discontent</LINE>
<LINE>Made glorious summer by this sun of York;</LINE>
```

Move the end tag for the <TITLE> element down a line, so that it appears here:

```
<ACT><TITLE>ACT I</TITLE>

<SCENE><TITLE>SCENE I.  London. A street.
<STAGEDIR>Enter GLOUCESTER, solus </TITLE> </STAGEDIR>

<SPEECH>
<SPEAKER>GLOUCESTER</SPEAKER>
<LINE>Now is the winter of our discontent</LINE>
<LINE>Made glorious summer by this sun of York;</LINE>
```

Run CueMyLine again, and now you see that the program actually does something. You get the following exception message, followed by a stack trace.

```
Exception in thread "main" org.xml.sax.SAXParseException:
Expected "</STAGEDIR>" to terminate element starting on line
86.
```

With the current placement of the end tag for <TITLE>, the document is no longer well formed, and the parser lets us know where there is a problem. This message is parser-dependent. Instead of using the default browser, use Xerces. (You can download Xerces from `xml.apache.com`.) Unzip the distribution and make sure that you add the file xerces.jar to your class path. Now you can specify that you are using the Xerces parser by replacing your command `java CueMyLine` with the following:

```
java -Djavax.xml.parsers.SAXParserFactory=
  org.apache.xerces.jaxp.SAXParserFactoryImpl cue/CueMyLine
```

We've included a space following the = to display the command for you. You should not include this space.

Now the message is a bit different. You get the following exception, followed by a stack trace:

```
Exception in thread "main" org.xml.sax.SAXParseException: The
element type "STAGEDIR" must be terminated by the matching end-
tag "</STAGEDIR>".
```

Put the <TITLE> end tag back where it belongs and rerun the parser to make sure you don't get any exceptions.

Before moving on, we want you to note how easy it was to plug in a different parser. Without changing any code or recompiling you were able to switch from the

Crimson parser to the Xerces parser with observable differences in the results. This is the strength of JAXP. You can, of course, write directly to the parser you use and achieve the results you want. By adding the additional level of abstraction you are creating a more flexible application that enables you to make changes as your technology evolves.

Validating

Checking that a document is valid is a more subtle process than checking that it is well formed. One of the key differences is that if a document isn't well formed, you may not be able to discern its true meaning. If a document is well formed but not valid, the meaning may be clear, but the document doesn't conform to the proscribed DTD. So, when you validate, you need to check your document against the DTD. In programming terms, when a document is not well formed, the error may not be recoverable, while a document not being valid is usually a recoverable error.

The first step is to create a validating parser. Use the `setValidating()` method from the `SAXParserFactory` class as follows:

```
package cue;

import org.xml.sax.helpers.DefaultHandler;
import java.io.File;
import javax.xml.parsers.SAXParser;
import javax.xml.parsers.SAXParserFactory;
import org.xml.sax.SAXException;
import javax.xml.parsers.ParserConfigurationException;
import java.io.IOException;

public class CueMyLine extends DefaultHandler{
  public static void main(String[] args)  {
    try{
      SAXParserFactory spFactory =
        SAXParserFactory.newInstance();
      spFactory.setValidating(true);
      SAXParser parser = spFactory.newSAXParser();
      parser.parse(new File("rich_iii.xml"), new CueMyLine());
    } catch (SAXException e){
      System.out.println("This is a SAX Exception.");
    } catch (ParserConfigurationException e) {
      System.out.println("This is a Parser Config Exception.");
    } catch (IOException e){
      System.out.println("This is an IO Exception.");
    }
  }
}
```

Notice that you have to create a `SAXParserFactory` so that you can specify that the parser to be created will be validating. Compile this program and run it, and prepare to be disappointed.

Nothing happens. The program runs and finishes, and then you get a new prompt waiting for your next command. Well, the document you're working with is valid. There's nothing to report. Now change it. Add the following `ASIDE` after Gloucester's entrance:

```
<ACT><TITLE>ACT I</TITLE>
<SCENE><TITLE>SCENE I.  London. A street. </TITLE>
<STAGEDIR>Enter GLOUCESTER, solus</STAGEDIR>
<ASIDE> Shhh. The play's ready to begin. </ASIDE>
<SPEECH>
<SPEAKER>GLOUCESTER</SPEAKER>
<LINE>Now is the winter of our discontent</LINE>
<LINE>Made glorious summer by this sun of York;</LINE>
```

Rerun the program. Nothing happens. More accurately, plenty happened, but you didn't indicate what you want to see when a problem occurs. The `DefaultHandler` implements four interfaces, one of which is `org.xml.sax.ErrorHandler`. It contains three methods that enable you to handle three different types of events — the `error()` method is used for recoverable errors; the `fatalError()` method is used for non-recoverable errors; and the `warning()` method is used for warnings.

Problems with validation are recoverable errors, so you need to override the empty implementation of `error()` provided in `DefaultHandler` and add the appropriate `import`. When you find an error, you'll just print it in the console window:

```
package cue;

import org.xml.sax.helpers.DefaultHandler;
import java.io.File;
import javax.xml.parsers.SAXParser;
import javax.xml.parsers.SAXParserFactory;
import org.xml.sax.SAXException;
import org.xml.sax.SAXParseException;
import javax.xml.parsers.ParserConfigurationException;
import java.io.IOException;

public class CueMyLine extends DefaultHandler{
  public static void main(String[] args)  {
    try{
      SAXParserFactory spFactory =
        SAXParserFactory.newInstance();
      spFactory.setValidating(true);
      SAXParser parser = spFactory.newSAXParser();
      parser.parse(new File("rich_iii.xml"), new CueMyLine());
    } catch (SAXException e){
      System.out.println("This is a SAX Exception.");
    } catch (ParserConfigurationException e) {
      System.out.println("This is a Parser Config Exception.");
    } catch (IOException e){
      System.out.println("This is an IO Exception.");
    }
  }
```

```
    public void error(SAXParseException e){
      System.out.println(e);
    }
  }
```

Now recompile and run this program, and you will get the following output:

```
org.xml.sax.SAXParseException: Element type "ASIDE" must be
declared.
org.xml.sax.SAXParseException: The content of the element type
"SCENE" must match
"TITLE,SUBTITLE*,(SPEECH|STAGEDIR|SUBHEAD)+)".
```

You are now able to validate on your local machine. Remember from the last chapter that you want to validate during development but not after. You should remember to remove the `setValidating(true)` line. Not validating during deployment is also why the default value for validating is `false`. Before moving on, you should restore rich_iii.xml to its previous valid state and rerun the program to check that it's OK.

Reaching for SAX

SAX is the Simple API for XML Parsing, and consists of a set of APIs used by various parsers to parse an XML document. A SAX parser is an event-based parser. (You can imagine yourself working through an XML document, reporting back that first this happened, then that, then this other thing . . . and then it was over.) There's good news, and there's bad news for those who use this type of device.

The good news is that it is a pretty fast means of running through a document and doesn't require much in the way of memory. The parser just keeps moving through the XML file and firing off methods based on what it is seeing. It may call a `startDocument()` method or a `startElement()` or `endElement()` method. The body of the method will specify what is done in each case. There's very little overhead with such a model. The parser doesn't have to keep track of anything but the class handling the callbacks.

The bad news is that you can't say, "Wait a minute, what was that again?" without starting all over. Also, you have no idea of the structure of the document. You need to write your own routines to keep track of where you are in the hierarchy. You also need to program what will be done for each type of event you might be interested in. Working with SAX is similar to programming `MouseAdapters`, when you specify what will be done in response to a click or some other mouse action. With SAX you specify ahead of time what your response will be to various types of events; the parser fires these callbacks when the corresponding events occur.

Many parsers use SAX. In the last section you used both Xerxes from Apache's XML site (`http://xml.apache.org`) and Sun's Crimson (which comes with the JAXP distribution and is the default parser). The example CueMyLine used JAXP to obtain a SAX-based parser. You used it to determine whether a document was well formed and valid. Now you'll respond to events generated while parsing a well-formed valid document with a SAX-based parser.

Using SAX callbacks

You've already seen the `DefaultHandler` when instantiating a validating parser. `DefaultHandler` implements four different interfaces: `org.xml.sax.ContentHandler`, `org.xml.sax.DTDHandler`, `org.xml.sax.EntityResolver`, and `org.xml.sax.ErrorHandler`. You saw that the `ErrorHandler` interface is used to handle errors and warnings that arise during the parsing of an XML document. In this section we'll focus on the `ContentHandler` interface. This is the interface that specifies the methods you'll use to respond to events generated during the processing of your XML document.

You can implement `ContentHandler` yourself, but it is easier to extend `org.xml.sax.helpers.DefaultHandler`. `DefaultHandler` is to `ContentHandler` what `MouseAdapter` is to `MouseListener`. All the methods in `DefaultHandler` are empty, so you can just override the methods you need without cluttering up your code.

We'll give you a summary of the available methods after an example. Try creating an application that counts the number of lines in *Richard III*. You can extend the previous example by adding a little bit of functionality.

Create an `int` named `totalLineCount` to track the number of lines. Every time the parser encounters a `<LINE>` element, increment `totalLineCount`. In other words, you are keeping a count of the lines of text in the script's speeches and not just every line in the file. You can do this by overriding `DefaultHandler`'s `startElement()` method. Here's the method signature:

```
public void startElement( String uri,
                          String localName,
                          String qName,
                          Attributes attributes)
  throws SAXException
```

The `uri` argument is for the namespace URI. In this case you aren't using a namespace, so you can ignore `uri`. The `localName` is the local name without the prefix; it is only available if namespace processing is turned on. The file rich_iii.xml does not use namespaces, but if you were parsing a document that did, you would have to make the method call `spFactory.setNamespaceAware(true)`. You could then use `uri` and `localName`.

Continuing with the signature of `startElement()`, the `qName` is the qualified name. This includes the prefix, if there is one. In this case there isn't, so you'll check to see if the `qName` is the string `LINE`. If it is, increase `totalLineCount` by one. The final argument is an object of type `org.xml.sax.Attributes`. This object enables you to examine the attributes of a particular element, as shown in this example:

```
package cue;

import org.xml.sax.helpers.DefaultHandler;
import java.io.File;
import javax.xml.parsers.SAXParser;
import javax.xml.parsers.SAXParserFactory;
import org.xml.sax.Attributes;
import org.xml.sax.SAXException;

public class CueMyLine1 extends DefaultHandler{
  int totalLineCount = 0;

  public void startElement(String uri, String localName,
    String qName, Attributes attributes) {
    if (qName.equals( "LINE"))  totalLineCount++;
  }
  public static void main(String[] args) throws Exception {
    SAXParser parser =
      SAXParserFactory.newInstance().newSAXParser();
    parser.parse(new File("rich_iii.xml"), new CueMyLine1());
  }
}
```

Save this snippet as CueMyLine1.java, compile it and run it. Again, nothing seems to happen. You need to report the total number of lines somewhere in your program. You can print a running count by placing `System.out.println( "Total lines =" + totalLineCount);` in the body of the `startElement()` method, but this isn't a very attractive option. All you really want is a final count. You can add a line to the end of `main()` that prints out the `totalLineCount`, but you'd have to make adjustments for calling a non-static variable from a static method. This isn't a very attractive option either. You may want to print out the total number of lines per scene or per act. You can print out the total number of lines in the play as soon as the parser has reached the end of the play.

Output the number of lines by overriding `DocumentHandler`'s `endDocument()` method to print the `totalLineCount`. When the end document event is fired, the `endDocument()` method is called, and you will see your total:

```
package cue;

import org.xml.sax.helpers.DefaultHandler;
import java.io.File;
import javax.xml.parsers.SAXParser;
import javax.xml.parsers.SAXParserFactory;
import org.xml.sax.Attributes;
import org.xml.sax.SAXException;

public class CueMyLine1 extends DefaultHandler{
  int totalLineCount = 0;

  public void startElement(String uri, String localName,
    String qName, Attributes attributes) {
```

```
    if (qName.equals( "LINE"))  totalLineCount++;
  }
  public void endDocument() throws SAXException {
    System.out.println("There are " + totalLineCount +
      " lines in Richard III.");
  }
  public static void main(String[] args) throws Exception {
    SAXParser parser =
    SAXParserFactory.newInstance().newSAXParser();
    parser.parse(new File("rich_iii.xml"), new CueMyLine1());
  }
}
```

Now, when you save, compile, and run the program, you get the following feedback:

```
There are 3696 lines in Richard III.
```

You might want to extend this application. Think about how you might track the number of lines in a particular scene. Maybe you are thinking of playing a particular role and want to know how many lines that character has. Maybe you have accepted a role and want to rehearse, and so you'd like to display your lines and the lines that come before yours so someone else can cue you. For many of these tasks, SAX isn't the best tool. If your task requires you to move up and down the hierarchy, you may be better served by the DOM. We'll look at navigating the tree in the section "Using the DOM," later in this chapter. For now, take a look at the other callbacks available to you.

Events handled by DefaultHandler

So far you've overridden the `endDocument()` and `startElement()` methods of `DefaultHandler`. Now take a look at the remaining methods declared in the `ContentHandler` interface. Each of the methods can throw a `SAXException` if something goes wrong.

Paired with the element `endDocument()` is the method `startDocument()`. These methods are invoked when the parser reaches the end or start of the document, respectively. The `startDocument()` is the first method in this interface to be called, and the `endDocument()` is the last. Each is invoked only once, so you can use them for initialization and cleanup of variables. You used `endDocument()` to get the final value of a variable: This was safe because `endDocument()` was called after all other parsing was completed. The `endDocument()` method is even called when the parser has to cease parsing because of a non-recoverable error.

Similarly, paired with `startElement()` is the `endElement()` method. It has a similar signature, taking `String`s representing the namespace URI, local name and qualified name as arguments, along with an `Attributes` object. The `startElement()` method is invoked at the beginning of every element, and the `endElement()` method is invoked at the end. For an empty element, both will still be invoked. You'll notice that no event is fired for attributes. You get at attributes by using the `startElement()` or endElement() methods and then pulling apart the attributes using the methods in the Attributes class. In between the startElement() and endElement() methods, all of the element's content is reported in order. This content may be other elements or it may be character data. The latter is handled by the characters() method.

Here's the signature of characters():

```
characters( char[] ch, int start, int length)
  throws SAXException
```

You use characters() to get information about character data. In a validating parser the ignorable whitespace information will be returned by the ignorableWhitespace() method with a similar signature. In both the characters() and ignorableWhitespace() methods, you get an array of characters, along with one int representing the start position in the array and another indicating how many characters are to be read from the array. This makes it easy to create Strings from the char arrays.

You now know how to handle elements and attributes. ContentHandler even provides the skippedEntity() method for entities skipped by the parser. What remains are processing instructions. Processing instructions don't contain other elements, so you don't need separate start and end methods for handling them. The processingInstruction() method has this signature:

```
processingInstruction(String target, String data)
  throws SAXException
```

The String target represents the target of the processing instruction (PI), and the String data contains the PI data.

The following example shows one way you might modify your running example to output the number of lines for a given character in *Richard III*. You'll need to keep track of when the given character is speaking. Whenever a new speech begins, reset the boolean mySpeech to false. Then check the character data: If it matches up with the name of the character in the play, set mySpeech to false. If the element is a LINE, increment the totalLineCount as before. If mySpeech is true, increment characterLineCount as well. This process only sounds complicated because we are using character to mean the role played in *Richard III* as well as a char being parsed by your SAX parser. Here's CueMyLine2.java with the changes highlighted:

```
package cue;

import org.xml.sax.helpers.DefaultHandler;
import java.io.File;
import javax.xml.parsers.SAXParser;
import javax.xml.parsers.SAXParserFactory;
import org.xml.sax.Attributes;
import org.xml.sax.SAXException;
```

```
public class CueMyLine2 extends DefaultHandler{
  int totalLineCount = 0;
  int characterLineCount = 0;
  boolean mySpeech = false;
  String myCharacter;

  public CueMyLine2(String myCharacter) {
    this.myCharacter = myCharacter;
  }

  public static void main(String[] args) throws Exception {
    SAXParser parser =
SAXParserFactory.newInstance().newSAXParser();
    try {
      parser.parse(new File("rich_iii.xml"),
        new CueMyLine2(args[0]));
    } catch (ArrayIndexOutOfBoundsException e){
      System.out.println("Correct usage requires an" +
      " argument specifying a character in Richard III.");
    }
  }

  public void startElement(String uri, String localName,
    String qName, Attributes attributes) {
    if (qName.equals("SPEAKER")) mySpeech = false;
    if (qName.equals( "LINE")) {
      totalLineCount++;
      if (mySpeech) characterLineCount++;
    }
  }
  public void characters(char[] ch, int start, int length)
    throws SAXException {
    String charString = new String(ch, start, length);
    if (charString.equalsIgnoreCase( myCharacter )) {
      mySpeech = true;
    }
  }
  public void endDocument() throws SAXException {
    System.out.println(myCharacter + " has " +
      characterLineCount + " of the " + totalLineCount +
      " lines in Richard III.");
  }
}
```

Save and compile this example. Now run it like this:

```
java cue/CueMyLine2 Gloucester
```

The program will respond as follows:

```
Gloucester has 698 of the 3696 lines in Richard III.
```

As an aside, when comparing the inputted character name to the name in the XML file, you should use the method `equalsIgnoreCase()`. This is because XML tags are case-insensitive, and the user will have no idea what conventions were used for character names by those who created the document.

You can see that performing even an easy task such as counting the number of lines for a specified character requires a great deal of manipulation. Now take a look at what changes when you view an XML document as a tree using the DOM.

Using the DOM

With SAX, once you parse an XML document, it is gone. You've responded to all the events, the `endDocument()` method has been called, and if you want to do anything else with the document, you have to parse it again. You should also note that the SAX APIs don't enable you to manipulate a document, navigate the hierarchy, or create a new XML document.

The Document Object Model (DOM) enables you to view an XML document as a set of objects and to use this model to work with, create, and change XML documents.

Creating a document

Parsing an XML file using a DOM-based parser is similar to using a SAX-based parser. Instead of using the `SAXParserFactory` and `SAXParser` classes, you now have to use the `DocumentBuilderFactory` and `DocumentBuilder` classes. The difference in the class names indicates the differences in how you will use them. A `SAXParser` enables you to parse an XML file with a SAX-based parser and respond to the events using callbacks. A `DocumentBuilder` enables you to parse an XML file with a DOM-based parser, but if you do this, you will have created a `Document` object. The `Document` object represents your XML document, and you'll use it to get at the document's data. Here's how you create a `Document` object from parsing the XML file with a `DocumentBuilder`:

```
package cue;

import java.io.File;
import javax.xml.parsers.DocumentBuilder;
import javax.xml.parsers.DocumentBuilderFactory;
import org.w3c.dom.Document;
import javax.xml.parsers.ParserConfigurationException;
import org.xml.sax.SAXException;
import java.io.IOException;

public class CueMyLine3 {

  Document document;

  public CueMyLine3() {
```

```
        try{
          DocumentBuilderFactory dbFactory =
            DocumentBuilderFactory.newInstance();
          DocumentBuilder documentBuilder =
            dbFactory.newDocumentBuilder();
          document =
            documentBuilder.parse(new File("rich_iii.xml"));
        } catch(ParserConfigurationException e){
          System.out.println( "There's a Parser Config problem.");
        } catch(SAXException e){
          System.out.println( "There's a SAX Exception.");
        } catch(IOException e){
          System.out.println("There's an IO exception.");
        }
      }

      public static void main(String[] args) {
        new CueMyLine3();
      }
    }
```

You can see that the main difference between the two methods, other than the differences in the relevant class names, is that the parser returns a `Document`. Compile and run CueMyLine3.java, and the `DocumentBuilder` parses rich_iii.xml and creates the `Document`. Then, not having been asked to do anything else, it stops. To get an idea of what was created, you can create a `JTree` representation of rich_iii.xml using the DomEcho02.java (located in the JAXP tutorial available from Sun at `http://java.sun.com/xml/tutorial_intro.html`).

Figure 12-1 shows a screenshot of the beginning of Act I from *Richard III*.

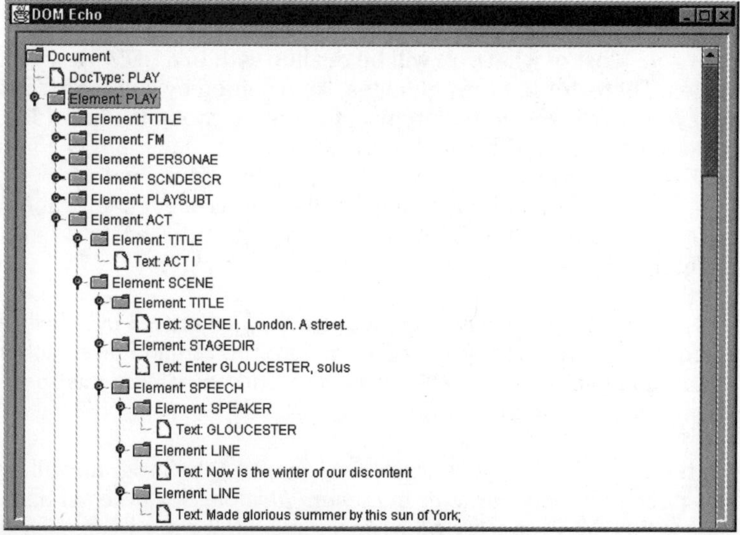

Figure 12-1: A view of *Richard III* as a JTree

Now you can clearly see the structure of the document. You can begin to imagine what it would take to navigate this document. For example, if you want to know who is speaking a line, you begin at the node, a LINE element, containing the line, travel up to its parent node, a SPEECH element, and look for its SPEAKER child element. The contents of this SPEAKER element will be the name of the character whose line you are curious about.

The contents of an element may be one level lower than you expect. Start at the node labeled Element: ACT. Its first child is the node labeled Element: TITLE. In turn, the child's first child is the node labeled Text: ACT I. This means that to get the title of the first act you have to get the data from the first child of the first child. You'll see how in code in the section "Navigating a document."

To be truthful, for the benefit of the screenshot we doctored up DomEcho02.java a little. We set validating to `true` and also called `setIgnoringElementContentWhitespace(true)` on the factory to eliminate some of the uninformative nodes in the tree. (We'll show you how we did this in the example in the section "Navigating a document.") We also eliminated the part of the application that didn't display the tree. Finally, we brushed and flossed our teeth. These are straightforward changes that you can make to the distributed code as well.

Navigating a document

The `JTree` view of Richard III shows that the top level of the `Document` object is `Document`, even though you specified that the root element is `PLAY`. This is always the case and provides you with the necessary hook into your XML documents. The package `org.w3c.dom` consists of the `DOMException` class and 17 interfaces. You will use the various interfaces specified in the package to create, navigate and manipulate the object.

The top-level interfaces are `Node`, `NodeList`, `NamedNodeMap`, and `DOMImplementation`. Most of what you will be dealing with in a DOM view of a document is `Nodes`. There are 10 types of `Nodes`, represented by sub-interfaces provided to help you handle the various types of contents contained in a `Node`. The 10 types of `Nodes` are `Attr`, `CharacterData`, `Document`, `DocumentFragment`, `DocumentType`, `Element`, `Entity`, `EntityReference`, `Notation`, and `ProcessingInstruction`. We'll provide an example that uses `Document` and `Element`. `CharacterData` has the sub-interfaces `Comment` and `Text`, and `Text` has the further sub-interface `CDATASection`.

Early books of this type were very large because they spent well over half their pages reproducing the JavaDocs available from Sun. You can find these either in the JDK 1.4 distribution or in the JAXP distribution, and we will use this space to provide examples of how to use the API.

In this example, the user will enter a character's name, and the program will output the first speech spoken by that character in *Richard III*, along with the act and scene in which the line occurs. You can use SAX to accomplish the same task: As you parse the document you can just keep the last act and scene information in memory until you need them. The advantage of the DOM approach is that you have the entire document in memory. You can provide the user with a GUI to move to the next speech by his or her character, the previous speech, or a particular speech in a particular scene. Adding this functionality would not be very difficult.

To start, make the changes to the constructor that we mentioned in the last section. To avoid extra nodes that store the ignorable whitespace as text, you need to set the parser to be validating and tell it to ignore those characters. The changes to the constructor are highlighted in the following example:

```
public CueMyLine4() {
    try{
    DocumentBuilderFactory dbFactory =
      DocumentBuilderFactory.newInstance();
      //important so you don't have extra items in the Document
      dbFactory.setValidating(true);
      dbFactory.setIgnoringElementContentWhitespace(true);
      DocumentBuilder documentBuilder =
        dbFactory.newDocumentBuilder();
      document = documentBuilder.parse(new
        File("rich_iii.xml"));
    } catch(ParserConfigurationException e){
      System.out.println( "There's a Parser Config problem.");
    } catch(SAXException e){
      System.out.println( "There's a SAX Exception.");
    } catch(IOException e){
      System.out.println("There's an IO exception.");
    }
    speechNodeList = document.getElementsByTagName("SPEECH");
  }
```

The last addition is where the fun begins. You have a `Document` object called `document`. Search through it for all elements with the tag name `SPEECH` and store them in a `NodeList` called `speechNodeList` in the order in which you would find them in a preorder traversal of your `Document` tree. A `NodeList` is a special container class that contains `Node` objects and has only two methods available. You can find the length of a `NodeList` with the method `getLength()`, and you can get the `Node` at a particular location with the method `item(int index)`. As with other collections, the indexing starts at `0`.

To start off your application you have to determine the name of the character in which you're interested, create a `CueMyLine4`, and ask it to search for the first speech by the specified character. The new `main()` looks like this:

```
public static void main(String[] args) throws Exception {
    CueMyLine4 cueMyLine = new CueMyLine4();
    try {
      cueMyLine.findCharactersFirstSpeech(args[0]);
    } catch (ArrayIndexOutOfBoundsException e){
      System.out.println(
```

```
            "Usage: java cue/CueMyLine4 <character name>");
        }
    }
```

The method `findCharactersFirstSpeech()` locates the first speech by the `String` argument whose value is a character's name. If a speech by that character is located, it will then be output to the console. Here's the idea behind `findCharactersFirstSpeech()`. In the constructor, you created a list of all of the nodes that are speeches. You can go through them one by one until you get to one whose speaker element has a value equal to the name of the character you're interested in. The speaker's name is checked using the `equalsIgnoreCase()` method, so that if the user doesn't use all caps for the character's name, the match can still be made.

Take the current `Node` returned by `speechNodeList.item(i)` and get its first child. This will be the Element: SPEAKER. If you want to get the character data contained in this element, you have to again invoke `getFirstChild()`,cast the result to be of type `CharacterData`, and invoke the `getData()` method. All together the entire line looks like this:

```
((CharacterData)speechNodeList.item(i).getFirstChild()
  .getFirstChild()).getData()
```

In your actual code, this line would appear as one line with no extra spaces. Here's the `findCharactersFirstSpeech()` method:

```
public void findCharactersFirstSpeech(String characterName){
    int i = 0;
    boolean notFoundYet = true;
    while(notFoundYet && (i< speechNodeList.getLength()-1)){
      if ( characterName.equalsIgnoreCase( ((CharacterData)
        speechNodeList.item(i).getFirstChild().getFirstChild())
          .getData())){
        notFoundYet = false;
        System.out.println("\n The first speech of " +
          characterName + " is found in Richard III ");
        outputCharactersFirstSpeech(i);
      }
      i++;
    }
}
```

What's left, now that you've located the character's first speech, is to output it. You do this with the `outputCharactersFirstSpeech()` method. Here you will navigate up the tree as well as down. You can locate the act in which the speech appears by traveling up the tree, but then you have to travel back down to get the title of the act. Similarly, you have to travel up and down to get the name of the current scene. DOM makes traveling up and down the tree pretty easy. Here's what the navigation code might look like:

```
public void outputCharactersFirstSpeech(int i){
    Element speech = (Element) speechNodeList.item(i);
    String act = ((CharacterData)
      speech.getParentNode().getParentNode().getFirstChild()
        .getFirstChild()).getData();
    String scene = ((CharacterData)
      speech.getParentNode().getFirstChild()
        .getFirstChild()).getData();
    System.out.println(act + " " + scene + ":" + "\n");
    NodeList lineNodeList =speech.getElementsByTagName("LINE");
    for (int j=0; j< lineNodeList.getLength(); j++){
      System.out.println( ((CharacterData)
        lineNodeList.item(j).getFirstChild()).getData());
    }
  }
```

Once you are inside the particular speech, you can use the `Element` version of the `getElementsByTagName()` to get all the <LINE> elements in the current `SPEECH`. You then can cycle through the lines until you reach the end. To get the name of the act, you have to get the parent of the current <SPEECH> elements parent mode and then get the first child of its first child. You then cast the resulting `Node` as a `CharacterData` object and, again, invoke the `getData()` method.

As a final step, tidy up the imports to include all the relevant classes. Listing 12-1 shows the final source file, CueMyLine4.java.

Listing 12-1: The CueMyLine4.java source file

```
package cue;

import java.io.File;
import javax.xml.parsers.DocumentBuilder;
import javax.xml.parsers.DocumentBuilderFactory;
import org.w3c.dom.Document;
import org.w3c.dom.Element;
import org.w3c.dom.NodeList;
import org.w3c.dom.CharacterData;
import javax.xml.parsers.ParserConfigurationException;
import org.xml.sax.SAXException;
import java.io.IOException;

public class CueMyLine4 {
  Document document;
  NodeList speechNodeList;

  public CueMyLine4() {
    try{
        DocumentBuilderFactory dbFactory =
         DocumentBuilderFactory.newInstance();
```

Continued

Listing 12-1 *(continued)*

```
    //important so you don't have extra items in the Document
    dbFactory.setValidating(true);
    dbFactory.setIgnoringElementContentWhitespace(true);
    DocumentBuilder documentBuilder =
      dbFactory.newDocumentBuilder();
    document = documentBuilder.parse(new
      File("rich_iii.xml"));
  } catch(ParserConfigurationException e){
    System.out.println( "There's a Parser Config problem.");
  } catch(SAXException e){
    System.out.println( "There's a SAX Exception.");
  } catch(IOException e){
    System.out.println("There's an IO exception.");
  }
  speechNodeList = document.getElementsByTagName("SPEECH");
}

public void findCharactersFirstSpeech(String characterName){
  int i = 0;
  boolean notFoundYet = true;
  while(notFoundYet && (i< speechNodeList.getLength()-1)){
    if ( characterName.equalsIgnoreCase( ((CharacterData)
      speechNodeList.item(i).getFirstChild().getFirstChild())
        .getData())){
      notFoundYet = false;
      System.out.println("\n The first speech of " +
        characterName + " is found in Richard III ");
      outputCharactersFirstSpeech(i);
    }
    i++;
  }
}

public void outputCharactersFirstSpeech(int i){
  Element speech = (Element) speechNodeList.item(i);
  String act = ((CharacterData)
    speech.getParentNode().getParentNode().getFirstChild()
      .getFirstChild()).getData();
  String scene = ((CharacterData)
    speech.getParentNode().getFirstChild()
      .getFirstChild()).getData();
  System.out.println(act + " " + scene + ":" + "\n");
  NodeList lineNodeList =speech.getElementsByTagName("LINE");
  for (int j=0; j< lineNodeList.getLength(); j++){
    System.out.println( ((CharacterData)
      lineNodeList.item(j).getFirstChild()).getData());
  }
}

public static void main(String[] args) throws Exception {
  CueMyLine4 cueMyLine = new CueMyLine4();
```

```
      try {
        cueMyLine.findCharactersFirstSpeech(args[0]);
      } catch (ArrayIndexOutOfBoundsException e){
        System.out.println(
          "Usage: java cue/CueMyLine4 <character name>");
      }
    }
  }
```

Compile it and run it with your favorite *Richard III* character as a command-line argument, and you will see where and what that character's first line is. So far you've used the DOM to parse and navigate an XML file. Finally, take a look at creating XML using the DOM.

Creating XML

So far you've parsed XML in two different ways, responded to events, and navigated a document. Now it's time for you to create XML. As an example, you'll add a prologue to *Richard III*. Looking back at play.dtd, you can see that a `PLAY` is defined as follows:

```
<!ELEMENT PLAY (TITLE, FM, PERSONAE, SCNDESCR, PLAYSUBT,
  INDUCT?, PROLOGUE?, ACT+, EPILOGUE?)>
```

So a `PLAY` may or may not contain a `PROLOGUE`, but if it does, the `PROLOGUE` should precede the first `ACT`. The DTD also specifies what a `PROLOGUE` consists of:

```
<!ELEMENT PROLOGUE (TITLE, SUBTITLE*, (STAGEDIR | SPEECH)+)>
```

In this example you'll construct a `PROLOGUE` that has a `TITLE` and a `SPEECH`, and insert it between the `PLAYSUBT` and the first `ACT`. Finally, you'll write your modified version of the play to a file that you can open with any text reader to view your changes.

You can start with CueMyLine4.java and modify it because you still need to create a `Document` object. If you were creating a new XML file from scratch, you wouldn't need to parse an existing file and create a `Document`. Instead of creating the `Document` using the `DocumentBuilder` `parse()` method, you would have had the `DocumentBuilder` build a new `Document` using the no argument constructor, like this:

```
document = documentBuilder.newDocument();
```

Start with the easy changes to the existing source file. Change all calls to `CueMyLine4` to `CueMyLine5`. Next, because you are no longer creating a `NodeList` of the speeches, you can remove the following line from the end of the constructor:

```
speechNodeList = document.getElementsByTagName("SPEECH");
```

You can also remove the outputCharactersFirstSpeech() and findCharactersFirstSpeech() methods from your code, as well as the variable speechNodeList.

The main() method is also simplified. You create a new CueMyLine5 and then invoke the methods addPrologue() and saveTheDocument(). The new main()is much simpler as shown in this example:

```
public static void main(String[] args) throws Exception {
    CueMyLine5 cueMyLine = new CueMyLine5();
    cueMyLine.addPrologue();
    cueMyLine.saveTheDocument();
  }
```

Lastly, you must write the methods addPrologue() and saveTheDocument(), and then add the appropriate import statement.

In the method addPrologue(), you begin by creating the elements prologue, title, and speech. You use the createElement() method in Document and pass in the name of the element's tag as a String. Your code should look like this:

```
Element prologue, title, speech;
prologue = document.createElement("PROLOGUE");
title = document.createElement("TITLE");
speech = document.createElement("SPEECH");
```

Now that you've created a prologue, you need to insert it in the right place in the document. This is before Act I. You can use the same method you used last time to generate a list of speeches, this time generating a list of acts, and then locate the first act. The following fragment creates a NodeList of all elements with the tag name <ACT> and then returns the first one. The result is that you get back the Node for the first <ACT>.

```
document.getElementsByTagName("ACT").item(0)
```

You now need to insert the prologue before this element. You need to be a little careful, as it is tempting to just use the following incorrect code:

```
document.insertBefore( prologue, where it goes);
```

The problem is that you are really inserting this element as a child of the <PLAY> node, which is itself a child of the <DOCUMENT> node. On the other hand, <PLAY> is the root element of this document and should be easily accessible. The method getDocumentElement() is designed to return the root element of a document. Putting this all together, you can use the following code to insert the prologue in the correct place:

```
document.getDocumentElement().insertBefore(prologue,
          document.getElementsByTagName("ACT").item(0));
```

The `title` is a child of the `prologue`. You can create the child `Node` and assign it to `title` using the `appendChild()` method in `Element`, as shown in this example:

```
prologue.appendChild(title);
```

Now you have a `<TITLE>` element with a start and end tag, but it doesn't contain any data. You can use the following code to add the text that sits between the start and end tags:

```
title.appendChild(document.createTextNode(
        "A Prologue to Shakespeare's Richard III"));
```

Use the same steps to create, add, and add content to `speech`. The following example shows the entire `addPrologue()`:

```
public void addPrologue(){
    try{
      Element prologue, title, speech;

      prologue = document.createElement("PROLOGUE");
       document.getDocumentElement().insertBefore(prologue,
        document.getElementsByTagName("ACT").item(0));

      title = document.createElement("TITLE");
      title.appendChild(document.createTextNode(
        "A Prologue to Shakespeare's Richard III"));
      prologue.appendChild(title);

      speech = document.createElement("SPEECH");
      speech.appendChild(document.createTextNode(
        "Sit back and relax here comes Act I"));
      prologue.appendChild(speech);
    } catch (DOMException e){
      System.out.println("There is a DOM Exception.");
    }
  }
```

Now that you've added a `<PROLOGUE>` section to *Richard III,* you should save your work to a file. To do this, you'll need a `Transformer` from the `javax.xml.transform` package. You create a `Transformer` using a factory, just as you created a `SAXParser` and a `DocumentBuilder`. You can do it in one step, as shown in the following example:

```
Transformer transformer =
        TransformerFactory.newInstance().newTransformer();
```

You now have the `Transformer` transform in the same way that you had the `SAXParser` parse. The `transform()` method takes two arguments: The first is the XML source and is of type `javax.xml.transform.Source`, while the second is the output target and is of type `javax.xml.transform.Result`. In this case you want the source to be generated from the `Document` object you've been modifying. You bring this about by creating a new `javax.xml.transform.dom.DOMSource` and passing the constructor your `document`. The target will be a new file named reWrite.xml. You create a new `javax.xml.transform.stream` using the constructor that takes a `File` as an argument. Add the exception handling, and your `saveTheDocument()` method looks like this:

```
public void saveTheDocument(){
    try{
      Transformer transformer =
        TransformerFactory.newInstance().newTransformer();
      transformer.transform( new DOMSource(document),
        new StreamResult( new File("reWrite.xml")));
    } catch (TransformerConfigurationException e) {
      System.out.println("There's a Transformer Config Excpt");
    } catch (TransformerException e) {
      System.out.println("There is a Transformer Exception");
    }
  }
```

You still have to add the relevant `import` statements to account for all the new classes you are using. Listing 12-2 shows the entire CueMyLine5.java file.

Listing 12-2: **The CueMyLine5.java file**

```
package cue;

import java.io.File;
import javax.xml.parsers.DocumentBuilder;
import javax.xml.parsers.DocumentBuilderFactory;
import org.w3c.dom.Document;
import org.w3c.dom.Element;
import org.w3c.dom.NodeList;
import org.w3c.dom.CharacterData;
import javax.xml.parsers.ParserConfigurationException;
import org.xml.sax.SAXException;
import java.io.IOException;
import org.w3c.dom.DOMException;
import javax.xml.transform.Transformer;
import javax.xml.transform.TransformerFactory;
import javax.xml.transform.TransformerConfigurationException;
import javax.xml.transform.TransformerException;
import javax.xml.transform.dom.DOMSource;
import javax.xml.transform.stream.StreamResult;

public class CueMyLine5 {
  Document document;

  public CueMyLine5() {
    try{
      DocumentBuilderFactory dbFactory =
        DocumentBuilderFactory.newInstance();
      dbFactory.setValidating(true);
      dbFactory.setIgnoringElementContentWhitespace(true);
```

```
      DocumentBuilder documentBuilder =
        dbFactory.newDocumentBuilder();
      document = documentBuilder.parse(new
        File("rich_iii.xml"));
    } catch(ParserConfigurationException e){
      System.out.println( "There's a Parser Config problem.");
    } catch(SAXException e){
      System.out.println( "There's a SAX Exception.");
    } catch(IOException e){
      System.out.println("There's an IO exception.");
    }
  }

  public void addPrologue(){
    try{
      Element prologue, title, speech;

      prologue = document.createElement("PROLOGUE");
         document.getDocumentElement().insertBefore(prologue,
          (Element)
document.getElementsByTagName("ACT").item(0));

      title = document.createElement("TITLE");
      title.appendChild(document.createTextNode(
        "A Prologue to Shakespeare's Richard III"));
      prologue.appendChild(title);

      speech = document.createElement("SPEECH");
      speech.appendChild(document.createTextNode(
        "Sit back and relax here comes Act I"));
      prologue.appendChild(speech);
    } catch (DOMException e){
      System.out.println("There is a DOM Exception.");
    }
  }
  public void saveTheDocument(){
    try{
      Transformer transformer =
        TransformerFactory.newInstance().newTransformer();
      transformer.transform( new DOMSource(document),
        new StreamResult( new File("reWrite.xml")));
    } catch (TransformerConfigurationException e) {
      System.out.println("There's a Transformer Config Excpt");
    } catch (TransformerException e) {
      System.out.println("There is a Transformer Exception");
    }
  }

  public static void main(String[] args) throws Exception {
    CueMyLine5 cueMyLine = new CueMyLine5();
    cueMyLine.addPrologue();
    cueMyLine.saveTheDocument();
  }
}
```

Compile and run it, and you will produce rewrite.xml. Open it up and search for `<PROLOGUE>`, and you will find the additions you made. The file, however, is quite ugly. Where are all the nice line breaks and indentations that make XML more readable? They don't appear because you told the parser to ignore the whitespace that didn't seem to matter. To output a more humanly readable file, comment out the following line:

```
dbFactory.setIgnoringElementContentWhitespace(true);
```

Summary

You can now write Java applications that make use of XML files. Although we used *Richard III* as the running example in this chapter, you can see how to apply these techniques to more data-centric files. In this chapter, you learned how to use JAXP to do the following:

- ✦ Create and configure both SAX and DOM parsers using the JAXP APIs. You can substitute other parsers, such as Xerces, for the default Crimson parser included in Sun's distribution.
- ✦ Respond to events generated by the `SAXParser` as it parses an XML file. Although nothing remains in memory, you can still think ahead and keep track of values that you will need later. SAX is a good choice when you don't need to navigate your XML file and be aware of the hierarchy.
- ✦ Instantiate a `Document` object that contains all the information and structure of your XML file in memory. Although this requires a great deal of memory, it means that you can meander around the document as you wish.
- ✦ Navigate the `Document` object. You can add and remove nodes, and determine and add to the contents of nodes. You can use these methods to transform the original XML document.

✦ ✦ ✦

CHAPTER 13

Interacting with XML Using JDOM

✦ ✦ ✦ ✦

In This Chapter

Understanding the need for a new API

Revisiting the *Richard III* examples with JDOM

Creating JDOM documents from XML, from DOM trees, or from scratch

Adding, removing, and changing nodes in a JDOM tree

Firing SAX2 events from JDOM

Outputting XML or a DOM tree from JDOM

✦ ✦ ✦ ✦

In the last chapter you used Sun's JAXP to parse and work with XML documents. It was important for you to see how Sun wants you to interact with the DOM and SAX APIs and to understand its APIs for parsing XML. In this chapter you'll learn about JDOM. In many ways, it is the solution that Sun should have come up with for parsing, creating, and transforming XML. The APIs are more intuitive than those covered in the last chapter and experienced Java programmers will find that their learning curve is fairly short. JDOM is now JSR 102 and will be incorporated into future releases from Sun. Although JDOM is very stable, the names of the packages are expected to change when it is incorporated into Sun's releases. Check out `http://www.jdom.org` to learn about the changes. The examples in this chapter use JDOM's beta 7 release.

We'll start by introducing JDOM and revisiting the examples you coded in the last chapter on JAXP. You don't need to learn JAXP before learning JDOM; in fact, you may find it easier to dive right in and use JDOM from the start. You'll notice that while some tasks are much more intuitive with the JDOM APIs than with JAXP, others aren't covered by JDOM at all. You can use the standard Java APIs to perform tasks that aren't supported by JDOM. After the introduction to JDOM, the remainder of the chapter will consist of an overview of the JDOM APIs, along with examples.

Using JDOM

One of the hardest things about learning Java is learning all the libraries you'll need to use. The language has been fairly stable for a while, but the APIs continue to grow. And yet here we are asking you to learn a new set of APIs that aren't even part of Sun's Java release. Well, JDOM is a JSR, and so it is expected to become part of Sun's J2SE release. Moreover, JDOM's way of handling XML will be easier for you to get your head around than the approach you learned for DOM, and is much more powerful than what was available to you with SAX. After exploring these issues further, and going over the JDOM download and install, we'll revisit the rich_iii.xml examples from the last chapter. You'll find a side-by-side comparison helpful when you're deciding which situations merit which technology. The creators of JDOM make it clear that JDOM doesn't solve every problem but that it makes solving many problems much easier.

Why, why, why

The big question is why. Why do you need a new set of APIs for handling XML when a full set is included in J2SE and will be updated quarterly? In the last chapter you saw that you need to use Sun's Java APIs for XML parsing in addition to the SAX and/or DOM APIs. Neither of these sets of APIs provides a familiar setting for Java programmers who want to create and transform XML documents. For example, the `NodeList` is fundamentally a list of nodes, and yet the only two methods declared in that interface are `getLength()` and `item()`. With JDOM, the lists that are returned implement the `List` interface, so you have much more flexibility in manipulating them.

JDOM is missing some of the functionality you may be used to after using the other APIs. The JDOM philosophy is not to duplicate functionality provided by the standard Java APIs. You'll frequently use the Collection APIs. In the last chapter, you were able to generate a list of all of the speeches in *Richard III* with the command `document.getElementsByTagName("SPEECH")`. JDOM doesn't enable you to do this. As you'll see during the discussion of the JDOM APIs, you can write the entire content of a document or an element or get information about the children one level down. If you know the structure of your document, only being able to see one level down isn't very restrictive.

SAX is a great tool for responding to events you encounter while parsing an XML document. The DOM is a great tool for dealing with the XML document seen as a hierarchical self-describing document. JDOM enables you to create a document from a SAX parser from a DOM tree. You can output your JDOM document to an application that is expecting SAX events, a DOM tree, or an XML document. So if you need to interact with SAX or the DOM, JDOM makes it easy. Throughout the discussion of JDOM's capabilities, we'll make comparisons to SAX and DOM.

Installing JDOM and testing the installation

Although you can anticipate JDOM becoming part of Sun's JDK, for now you can download it from the Web site `http://www.jdom.org`. On the site you'll find links to news, presentations, and to the Java Community Process page. Unzip the distribution and build it using the accompanying Ant script — after making sure that your `JAVA_HOME` environment variable is correctly set to the top level of the directory containing your JVM. (On our machine, the `JAVA_HOME` is C:\jdk1.4.) Depending on whether you're working on a UNIX box or a Windows machine, run either build.sh or build.exe to build the Java 2 implementation of JDOM. It is possible to run JDOM with Java 1.1 as long as you have installed the collections.jar available from Sun Microsystems at `http://java.sun.com/products/javabeans/infobus/#COLLECTIONS`. In this case, run build11.sh or build11.exe.

With JAXP you started by using the Crimson parser that comes with that distribution. With JDOM, start by using the Xerces parser in the lib directory of the JDOM distribution. Make sure that the xerces.jar file appears in your CLASSPATH before other XML classes. You can now compile and run one of the sample files, such as Count.java, that you'll find in the samples subdirectory of the JDOM distribution. The JavaDocs are in \build\apidocs\ in the JDOM download.

Revisiting the DOM examples

The easiest way to see the advantages of JDOM is to look at the code from the JAXP chapter — rewritten this time for JDOM. Here are the examples of navigating XML and creating XML. In the next section, "The JDOM APIs," we'll talk in more detail about what JDOM provides.

Finding a character's first speech

This example featured three basic tasks. Parse the document and create a `Document` object, find the character's first speech, and, finally, output the speech to the console. The first task is accomplished with a SAX parser using the following code.

```
SAXBuilder builder = new SAXBuilder();
document = builder.build(new File("rich_iii.xml"));
```

Using JAXP, you created a SAX parser and asked it to parse a file. Now you are asking the SAX parser to build a JDOM `Document` object. You will often use this strategy to create a JDOM `Document` from an existing XML file.

The task of locating the first speech for a given character will be handled a bit differently as well. With SAX, you can sit around and wait for a `SPEAKER` tag with a specified value and then respond by printing out all the lines until you hit the next `SPEECH` end tag. With the DOM, you have the whole document in memory so you can build a `NodeList` of all the `SPEECH`es and move through them until you find one whose SPEAKER is the character specified. You can take this approach with JDOM, but there is no need to incur the overhead of placing all the SPEECHes in memory. You'll move through a list of the ACTs. Within each ACT, you will move through a list of SCENEs. Within each SCENE, you'll move through a list of SPEECHes until you find the match you're looking for. Once you've found the desired SPEECH, you can stop looking and call the method that outputs the speech, as shown in Listing 13-1. You can see this strategy in the findCharactersFirstSpeech() method. The constraints of printing the code make the steps look a little more awkward than they are.

Listing 13-1: Locating a speech with the findCharactersFirstSpeech() method

```
package cue;

import org.jdom.input.SAXBuilder;
import org.jdom.Document;
import org.jdom.Element;
import org.jdom.JDOMException;
import java.util.List;
import java.io.File;

public class CueMyLine4 {
  Document document;

  public CueMyLine4() {
    try{
      SAXBuilder builder = new SAXBuilder();
      document = builder.build(new File("rich_iii.xml"));
    } catch(JDOMException e){
      System.out.println( "There's a JDOM problem.");
    }
  }

  public void findCharactersFirstSpeech(String characterName){
    List actList = document.getRootElement()
      .getChildren("ACT");
    allDone:
    for (int act=0; act< actList.size(); act++){
      List sceneList = ( (Element) actList.get(act))
        .getChildren("SCENE");
      for (int scene = 0; scene< sceneList.size(); scene++){
        List speechList =((Element )sceneList
          .get(scene)).getChildren("SPEECH");
        for(int speech = 0; speech < speechList.size();
          speech++){
          if ( characterName.equalsIgnoreCase(((Element)
            speechList.get(speech)).getChildText("SPEAKER"))){
            System.out.println("\n The first speech of " +
              characterName + " is found in Richard III ");
```

```
                outputCharactersFirstSpeech((Element)
                  speechList.get(speech));
                break allDone;
              }
            }
          }
        }
      }

      public void outputCharactersFirstSpeech(Element speech){
        String act = speech.getParent().getParent()
          .getChild("TITLE").getTextTrim();
        String scene = speech.getParent().getChild("TITLE")
          .getTextTrim();
        System.out.println(act + " " + scene + ":" + "\n");
        List lineList = speech.getChildren("LINE");
        for (int line = 0; line < lineList.size(); line++){
          System.out.println( ((Element) lineList.get(line))
            .getTextTrim());
        }
      }

      public static void main(String[] args) {
        CueMyLine4 cueMyLine = new CueMyLine4();
        try {
          cueMyLine.findCharactersFirstSpeech(args[0]);
        } catch (ArrayIndexOutOfBoundsException e){
          System.out.println("Usage: java cue/CueMyLine4 " +
            " <character name>");
        }
      }
    }
```

The logic for outputting the speech is the same as it was when you used the DOM. The individual calls are a bit more straightforward in JDOM than in DOM. With DOM, you have to write this to output a `LINE` from a `SPEECH`:

```
((CharacterData)  lineNodeList.item(j).getFirstChild()).getData())
```

Doing this amounted to getting a `Node` back from a `NodeList` and getting its first child. Technically this is the correct way to deal with the DOM. The text that a node contains is found in a text node that is actually a child of the node. For a Java developer, this extra level is very unintuitive. You just want to get the text from a node without worrying about this extra level. Also, because the child element is returned as a `Node`, you have to cast it to `CharacterData` before asking for its text content with the method call `getData()`.

With JDOM, you can accomplish the same action with the following easy-to-read code:

```
((Element) lineList.get(line)).getTextTrim());
```

You again have to get the appropriate item from a list. This time the result of the method call is an honest-to-goodness `List`, so it makes sense that you have to cast the result to `Element`. Finally, you ask the element for its text content without having to look for the child that actually contains this information. This code would have been even more clear if we'd used the method `getText()` instead of `getTextTrim()`. As you may be able to guess, `getTextTrim()` returns the text after trimming the unnecessary whitespace.

This discussion highlights the advantages of JDOM. It was the obscure code, such as the code needed to perform the first common task, that led Hunter and McLaughlin to first propose JDOM.

Rewriting Shakespeare

The second example again begins by generating a JDOM `Document` from a SAX parser. You then create XML and add it to the existing document. Finally, you output the altered document to an XML file. The first step is the same as in the previous example. The second step requires a little bit of creativity because you can't insert the `PROLOGUE` you are creating into a designated spot. With DOM, you can move to a specific node in the document and insert a new element in several places; with JDOM, you'll have to be a little more creative.

The code for creating a `PROLOGUE` element is simply this:

```
prologue = new Element("PROLOGUE");
```

In the DOM example, you placed the `PROLOGUE` before the first `ACT` with the following code:

```
document.getDocumentElement().insertBefore(prologue,
     (Element)
document.getElementsByTagName("ACT").item(0));
```

Now you'll perform the following slight of hand. Create a list that consists of all of the acts in the play. Now remove the acts from the document. Add the prologue to the end of the document as it now stands, and then add back the acts one by one. Here's the code to do this:

```
List actList = document.getRootElement().getChildren("ACT");
  document.getRootElement().removeChildren("ACT");
  document.getRootElement().addContent(prologue);
  for (int act =0; act< actList.size(); act ++){
    document.getRootElement().addContent((Element)
      actList.get(act));
  }
```

Now adding child elements and content to the prologue is very straightforward. When you used the DOM, you had an additional level, so adding a title to the prologue looked like this:

```
title = document.createElement("TITLE");
title.appendChild(document.createTextNode(
  "A Prologue to Shakespeare's Richard III"));
prologue.appendChild(title);
```

Now, with JDOM, it looks like this:

```
title = new Element("TITLE");
title.setText("A Prologue to Shakespeare's Rich. III");
prologue.addContent(title);
```

It may not seem very different to you, but I find `title.setText()` much more readable than asking `title` to append a child node that consists of a text node with the same text content.

Listing 13-2 shows the entire code, including the method to output the XML to a file:

Listing 13-2: Coding Shakespeare

```
package cue;

import org.jdom.input.SAXBuilder;
import org.jdom.Document;
import org.jdom.Element;
import org.jdom.JDOMException;
import java.util.List;
import java.io.File;
import java.io.FileWriter;
import org.jdom.output.XMLOutputter;

public class CueMyLine5 {
  Document document;

  public CueMyLine5() {
    try{
      SAXBuilder builder = new SAXBuilder();
      document = builder.build(new File("rich_iii.xml"));
    } catch(JDOMException e){
      System.out.println( "There's a JDOM problem.");
    }
  }
  public void addPrologue(){
   try{
     Element prologue, title, speech;

       prologue = new Element("PROLOGUE");
       List actList = document.getRootElement()
         .getChildren("ACT");
       document.getRootElement().removeChildren("ACT");
```

Continued

Listing 13-2 *(continued)*

```
        document.getRootElement().addContent(prologue);
        for (int act =0; act< actList.size(); act ++){
          document.getRootElement().addContent((Element)
            actList.get(act));
        }

        title = new Element("TITLE");
        title.setText("A Prologue to Shakespeare's Rich. III");
        prologue.addContent(title);

        speech = new Element("SPEECH");
        speech.setText("Sit back and relax here comes Act I");
        prologue.addContent(speech);

      } catch (Exception e){
        e.printStackTrace();
        System.out.println("There is an Exception.");
      }
    }
     public void saveTheDocument(){
       try{
         XMLOutputter xmlOutputter = new XMLOutputter();
         xmlOutputter.output(document, new FileWriter(
           "rewrite.xml"));
       } catch (Exception e) {
         System.out.println("There is an Exception");
       }
     }

   public static void main(String[] args) {
     CueMyLine5 cueMyLine = new CueMyLine5();
     cueMyLine.addPrologue();
     cueMyLine.saveTheDocument();
   }
 }
```

The JDOM APIs

Now that you've seen some code that uses JDOM, you're ready to look more closely at the JDOM APIs. We've divided this overview into three parts. First you look at different ways of creating a JDOM `Document`. Then you look at how to work with the `Document`. Finally, you'll want to output the `Document` in some way.

Creating a document

You begin the process by creating a JDOM `Document` object. You have several choices. You can create one from scratch using the classes in the `org.jdom` package. You can use `org.jdom.input.SAXBuilder` to create a `Document` from an existing XML document. You can also use `org.jdom.input.DOMBuilder` to create a `Document` from an existing DOM tree or from an XML document, although you would be better off using `SAXBuilder` for that.

One thing you'll come to appreciate about JDOM is the economy in the API. Very little is included that doesn't need to be there. You'll also notice that because JDOM is comprised of classes and not the interface model you saw in JAXP, creating the objects that do the work is simpler. You don't have to create a factory that creates something else that does what you want; you just create a `DOMBuilder` or a `SAXBuilder` and have it parse whatever you are using as input. For the most part, you don't need to worry about the `JDOMFactory` interface or about the `SAXHandler`, `BuilderErrorHandler`, or `DefaultJDOMFactory` classes.

Using SAXBuilder

In the examples in the previous section, "Rewriting Shakespeare," you created `Document`s using `SAXBuilder`. You can use the following code as a template for this part of the process:

```
import org.jdom.Document;
import org.jdom.input.SAXBuilder;
import org.jdom.JDOMException;

...

Document document;

...

try {
  SAXBuilder builder = new SAXBuilder();
  document = builder.build(new File("rich_iii.xml"));
  } catch(JDOMException e){
 System.out.println( "There's a JDOM problem.");
  }
```

Quite a bit is going on behind the scenes here. When you construct a `SAXBuilder` using the default constructor, you get a new `SAXBuilder` that tries to find a parser, first using JAXP and then using a default set of SAX drivers. You can specify the parser you would like to use and pass it in as a `String`, as you did from the command line using JAXP:

```
new SAXBuilder("org.apache.xerces.jaxp.SAXParserFactoryImpl")
```

You also can specify whether the parser is validating or not by passing in a `boolean` as a parameter. In short, here are the four signatures for constructors:

```
SAXBuilder()
SAXBuilder(boolean validate);
SAXBuilder(String saxDriverClass);
SAXBuilder(String saxDriverClass, boolean validate);
```

Once you have created a `SAXBuilder`, the most important thing it can do is build the JDOM tree. The `build()` method has eight different signatures. They enable you to build your document from a given `File`, `InputSource`, `InputStream`, `Reader`, `URI`, or `URL`. The template is set up to build the document from a `File`, but you can make the appropriate changes to build it from another source.

The remaining methods primarily exist to enable you to fine-tune your configuration. For example, `configureContentHandler()` and `configureParser()` enable you to configure the `SAXHandler` and `XMLReader`, respectively. You can decide how the content will be handled using methods such as `setExpandEntities()`, `setIgnoringElementContentWhitespace()`, and `setValidation()`. To customize the assignment of helpers, use methods such as `setDTDHandler()`, `setEntityResolver()`, `setErrorHandler()`, `setFactory()`, and `setXMLFilter()`.

You may have noticed that the only exception our code snippet checks for is the `JDOMException`. With so much happening behind the scenes, this may seem a bit puzzling. The magic going on here is that the `SAXExceptions` that can be thrown by the SAX parser are converted to JDOM exceptions. We haven't handled any exceptions in any of our examples, beyond printing out to the console window. You should at least add a stack trace with `e.printStackTrace()` to get an idea of what went wrong and where.

As an example, the following code produces a validating SAX parser that indicates where the problems lie:

```
package cue;

import org.jdom.input.SAXBuilder;
import org.jdom.Document;
import org.jdom.JDOMException;
import java.io.File;

public class Validator {
  Document document;

  public Validator() {
    try{
      SAXBuilder builder = new SAXBuilder(true);
      document = builder.build(new File("rich_iii.xml"));
```

```
        } catch(JDOMException e){
          e.printStackTrace();
        }
      }

      public static void main(String[] args) {
        Validator validator = new Validator();
      }
    }
```

Go ahead and make changes to the file rich_iii.xml so that it is no longer well formed or no longer valid. Compile and run Validator.java. The exception generated while the document is being parsed will be converted to a JDOMException. When the exception is thrown, the stack trace will indicate what the problem is and where it was encountered. You'll see something like "Error in line *wherever it is* of document *whatever is being parsed.* Element *such and such* doesn't allow *this element.*" Validator is a very efficient local validating parser.

Using DOMBuilder

The quickest way to understand what you can do with DOMBuilder is to look at the various build() methods. As with SAXBuilder, you can build a JDOM tree from a File, InputStream, or URL using build(File file), build(InputStream in), or build(URL url), respectively. Each method returns a JDOM Document object and throws a JDOMException. There is really no need to use a DOMBuilder to build a Document this way, as you can use a SAXBuilder for the same purpose.

What's new is that you can construct a JDOM tree from a DOM tree using DOMBuilder. If you pass build() an existing DOM Document, you will get back a JDOM Document. You can see that the signature is a bit confusing:

```
public Document build(Document domDocument)
```

In this case, the return type Document refers to the class org.jdom.Document, while the parameter type Document refers to org.w3c.dom.Document. This method does not throw a JDOMException. To avoid name collisions, provide a fully qualified name for the return type, like this:

```
org.jdom.Document document;
DOMBuilder builder = new DOMBuilder();
document = builder.build(<handle to DOM Document>);
```

So, if you start with a DOM tree, you can easily convert it to a JDOM tree. You'll see in the section "Outputting the document" that it is easy to start with a JDOM document and output it as a DOM document. This means that you can work with a DOM document using the JDOM APIs without requiring changes of the applications sending or waiting to receive a DOM document.

DOMBuilder has one build() method that does not return a Document. While you are using a DOM document to create a JDOM document, you may wish to use an element from your DOM document. DOMBuilder includes this method to help you do so, as in the following example:

```
public Element build(Element domElement)
```

As in the Document version, the return type Element and the parameter type Element refer to different classes. The return type is org.jdom.Element, while the parameter type is org.w3c.dom.Element.

You can choose from four possible constructors. The default constructor will first use JAXP to locate a parser and then try to use a set of default parsers. You can also pass in a boolean to indicate whether or not the parser should validate. With DOMBuilder, you can also pass in a String that specifies which DOMAdapter implementation to use to choose the underlying parser. Here are the DOMBuilder constructors:

```
DOMBuilder()
DOMBuilder(boolean validate)
DOMBuilder(String adapterClass)
DOMBuilder(String adapterClass, boolean validate)
```

You'll find the DOMAdapter interface in the org.jdom.adapters package. It declares two methods for getting a DOM Document object from a DOM parser. The createDocument() method is used for creating an empty JDOM Document object and enables you to decide whether or not to specify the DOCTYPE as a parameter. The getDocument() method creates a JDOM Document from an existing File or InputStream. The second parameter for getDocument() is a boolean indicating whether or not you want to validate.

In addition to the abstract class AbstractDOMAdapter, which implements the DOMAdapter interface, seven concrete implementations currently extend AbstractDOMAdapter. These wrap the behavior for getting a DOM Document object from your favorite DOM parser. The currently included implementations are CrimsonDOMAdapter, JAXPDOMAdapter, OracleV1DOMAdapter, OracleV2DOMAdapter, ProjectXDOMAdapter, XercesDOMAdapter, and XML4JDOMAdapter.

Using your bare hands

If you are creating a JDOM Document from scratch then you aren't reading from input, so your answer isn't found within the org.jdom.input package. Create a new instance of the class org.jdom.Document using one of the five constructors. At the very least you should specify the root element. You can, for example, create *Richard IV* with the following:

```
Element rootElement = new Element("PLAY");
Document document = new Document( rootElement );
```

This code creates a document with a PLAY element as its root element. Another constructor enables you to specify the DOCTYPE as well by passing in an org.jdom.DocType object. As you'll see in the next section, "Working with the document," much of your work with JDOM documents will involve Lists. You can create a new document from a List of existing content. You can also specify the DOCTYPE when creating a document from a List. Here's the signature for this constructor:

```
public Document( List content, DocType docType)
```

Finally, you'll find a default constructor, but if you use it, you would have to then create a root element and use the method setRootElement(), so you might as well use the constructor, taking a root element as a parameter.

Working with the document

You already know how to parse a document using DOM or SAX. The fact that you can do it slightly more easily with JDOM isn't enough to sell you on the technology. The strength of JDOM is in how you can work with the document. It's easy to create elements and attributes and put them together into an XML document. It's easy to locate what you want in a document and to add, remove, or alter content.

Not all of your tools will be found within the JDOM APIs. If the Java programming language has already solved a certain problem, JDOM doesn't attempt to solve the same problem again. You will have to get used to working with Lists. You will pass information in and get information out in the form of List objects. We don't cover List in this section. We will instead look at the classes you will find yourself using most: Document, Element, Attribute, ProcessingInstruction, Comment, and DocType.

The Document class

You've already seen that you can create either an empty Document or one that is generated from a List of content. In the first case, you should at least specify the root element and in either case you can specify the DOCTYPE. The two properties of a Document object are its content and its docType. The content is a List that contains the document's Comments, its ProcessingInstructions, and the root Element. From this starting point, you can find out or change any aspect of the document.

The Document class has a number of methods for accessing and changing the content. As you might expect, the method getContent() returns the content, and setContent() enables you to provide a List as the parameter that will be set to be the content of the Document. The method setContent() returns the Document. In addition, you can add and remove Comments and ProcessingInstructions using the appropriate addContent() and removeContent() methods. It may seem puzzling that you can't add an Element this way. At the top level, the Document itself only contains Comments, ProcessingInstructions and the root Element. If you want to add another Element, you will be adding it to the root Element or one of its children: Therefore, the method for doing this will be in the `Element` class and not in the `Document` class. You can work with the root `Element` using the `getRootElement()` and `setRootElement()` methods.

The Element class

The `Element` is where the action is. Most of your efforts in working with a `Document` will involve working with its elements. JDOM's `Element` class contains a ton of methods to help you out. An `Element` object also has a number of fields for keeping track of who, where, and what it is.

The name of an object is distributed among a few variables. The property `name` contains the local name of the `Element`, while the `namespace` contains the `Namespace` of the `Element`. `Namespace` is a class in the `org.jdom` package that represents an XML namespace in Java. `Element` also has a property, `additionalNamespaces`, that contains a `List` of additional `Namespace` declarations on the specific object.

Besides knowing what an `Element` is called, you need to know where it is in the hierarchy of the XML document. The `parent` property contains an `Object` that represents the parent `Element` of this `Element`, the `Document` if this `Element` is the root `Element`, or `null` if there isn't any parent. Working with this system is a bit different from working with the DOM. With the DOM, `Element`s and `Document`s are `Node`s, so you can specify this common parent type for `parent`. With JDOM, you don't have this structure. `Element` and `Document` extend `Object`. No common superclass exists. The `getParent()` and `setParent()` methods enable you to access and change an `Element`'s `parent`.

Finally, you need to know what an `Element` contains. This information is stored in the `attributes` and in the `content` properties. The `content` is a `List` of the mixed content of the `Element`. The `attributes` are a list of the attributes of the `Element`. For now, you can think of each attribute as a name-value pair. In the section "The Attribute class," you'll see more details about the class `org.jdom.Attribute`.

In the *Richard III* example `CueMyLine5`, you saw how easy it is to work with `Elements`. The following code creates an `Element`, sets its content to be the given text, and adds it as a child to the `Element prologue`:

```
title = new Element("TITLE");
title.setText("A Prologue to Shakespeare's Rich. III");
prologue.addContent(title);
```

Here you created an `Element` by specifying its name. You could also have specified the `Namespace`, the URI of the `Namespace`, or both the prefix and the URI of the `Namespace`.

You can use the `addContent()` method to add children `Elements`, `EntityRefs`, `ProcessingInstructions`, `Comments`, and text that can consist of `CDATA` or `Strings`. In the preceding code snippet, the `Element prologue` is adding the

Element title as a child. If children already exist, title will be added as the last child Element. The method getContent() returns a List containing objects of any of the types that can be added with addContent(). Each addContent() method has a partner removeContent() method that removes the specified instance of that type. For example, you can remove the title element with the command prologue.removeContent(title). This method returns a boolean indicating whether or not the operation was successful.

Instead of manipulating content, you may prefer to work with an Element's children. You can determine whether an Element has children by calling the hasChildren() method. You can find the first child Element within the current Element by name using the getChild() method. If you just want to get the first LINE of a SPEECH in *Richard III,* you can call speech.getChild("LINE"). To get a List of all the children of a particular Element you can use getChildren(). You can also call getChildren() and specify the name of the Elements you're looking for as well as the Namespace to which they belong. Note that by doing this you are only searching for Elements that are immediate children of the current Element: This is why you can't just use document.getChildren("SPEECH") using JDOM to return all the SPEECHes in the play. Many times you're more interested in getting the textual content of an element than in getting a handle to the element itself. In these cases, you can use the various getChildText() methods instead.

Just as you can remove content, you can also remove children. The method removeChildren() with no argument will remove all child elements. You can also specify the name of the element being removed. In this case, removeChild() will remove the first child element with the given name (and, if specified, the given Namespace). The method removeChildren() will remove all the child elements with the given name (and, if specified, the given Namespace). The method setChildren() is similar to setContent(): You pass in a List of Elements to be used as the children for this Element.

In an XML document, you think of elements as containing other elements as well as CDATA and other content. The content property of an Element contains information about these contents. It does not include information about an element's attributes. Although attributes can be thought of as modifiers for elements, an attribute belongs to an element and so the Element class contains getters and setters for handling Attributes.

You can get a particular Attribute object with by calling getAttribute(). In addition to specifying the name of the Attribute you're looking for, you can also specify the Namespace. The getAttribute() method returns an Attribute. You may have been expecting the value of the Attribute, but you get an Attribute object. If all you want is the value of the named attribute, use the method getAttributeValue(), which returns the value of the attribute as a String.

You can get a List of all the Attributes that this Element contains using getAttributes(). The Attributes aren't guaranteed to appear in any particular order. If an element doesn't contain any attributes, getAttributes() returns an empty list. In the rich_iii.xml example, none of the elements contains attributes, and so you will always get an empty list back. Instead, you can experiment with the web.xml file you developed in Chapters 3 and 4 when working with servlets and JSPs.

You can choose to set the value of a particular attribute or to replace the entire list of attributes with another. The `setAttribute()` method enables you to set an `Attribute` value using any of the following signatures:

```
public Element setAttribute(Attribute attribute)
public Element setAttribute(String name, String value)
public Element setAttribute(String name, String value,
                            Namespace ns)
```

So you can configure an `Attribute` object and then pass it in to the `attributes` property using the first version of the `setAttribute()` method. This works for adding a new `Attribute` to the `List` or for changing the value of an existing `Attribute`. The other two signatures are for performing the same operation by providing only the name and value of the `Attribute`. The `setAttributes()` method replaces the contents of `attributes` with the `List` being passed in.

The Attribute class

Like an `Element`, an `Attribute` needs to know what it is, where it is, and what its value is. This information is stored in the properties `name`, `namespace`, `parent`, and `value`. The `parent` is the `Element` to which this `Attribute` belongs. The `value` is a `String` containing the value of the `Attribute`.

You can create an `Attribute` from an `Element` using one of the `setAttribute()` methods described in the previous section, "The Element class." The `Attribute` class also provides constructors that enable you to create an `Attribute` by specifying the name and value of the new `Attribute` (and possibly its `Namespace`).

Once you have created an `Attribute`, you can get its value with the `getValue()` method, which returns a `String` that you can cast to its primitive type. You can also use methods such as `getBooleanValue()`, `getDoubleValue()`, `getFloatValue()`, `getIntValue()`, and `getLongValue()` to return the value of the attribute as its specific type. Each of these methods throws a `DataConversionException` if the conversion cannot be made. Only one method is required to set the value of an `Attribute`: The `setValue()` method takes a `String` as its only argument.

The ProcessingInstruction and Comment classes

In addition to the root element, a `Document`'s `contents` may also contain `Comments` and `ProcessingInstructions`. A `Comment` is fairly straightforward. It contains three fields: `document`, `parent`, and `text`. The first two locate the `Comment`, and the third contains the `Comment`'s contents. The `document` is a `Document` object if the `Comment` is outside the root element; otherwise you locate the comment using `parent`. The `parent` is an `Element` object that is the parent of this `Comment`. The `text` is just a `String` containing the text of the `Comment`.

You can create a Comment with a constructor that takes a String containing the Comment's text as its only parameter. You add the Comment to the Document or Element by using the addContent() method in the Document class or the method with the same name in the Element class.

The ProcessingInstruction class enables you to work with XML processing instructions. When handling a processing instruction, you will mainly need to know its target and its data. The mapData property holds the data in name-value pairs and returns them as a java.util.Map. The data is also stored as a String named rawData. The target of the processing instruction is a String named target. If you are creating a ProcessingInstruction, you will need to provide the name of the target and then the data as either a Map or a String.

You can set the data of a ProcessingInstruction object using one of two setData() methods. The first takes a Map and enables you to set the name-value pairs. The second takes a String that contains the rawData. The getData() method returns the rawData. You can get and set the Document and the Parent in the usual way. You can't set the target; you can only read it with a getTarget() method. You can get, set, or remove a specific value using the methods getValue(), setValue(), and removeValue(), respectively.

The DocType class

The DOCTYPE declaration from rich_iii.xml is the following:

```
<!DOCTYPE PLAY SYSTEM "play.dtd">
```

JDOM provides the DocType class for dealing with declaration. You want to know what element is being constrained: Typically it is the root element of the document. (In this case, the PLAY element is being constrained.) You also need the DocType to remember the Document that this DocType belongs to. In Chapter 11, you learned about the public and system IDs of a DOCTYPE. This information is stored as Strings in the variables publicID and systemID. Constructors exist that enable you to create a DocType object specifying the elementName and possibly the systemID and/or the publicID.

You can use accessor methods to get and set the publicID and systemID. Other methods enable you to get and set the Document to which the DocType belongs, and to access the value of the Element name being constrained. Note that getDocument() returns a Document while getElementName() returns a String containing the name of the Element.

Outputting the document

You're pretty much home free. You've created a JDOM Document and played around with it in some way. Now it's time to send it off somewhere else using the package org.jdom.output. In many cases, you will just want to save your JDOM document as an XML file. You have read in an XML document, converted it to a form in which you could easily and efficiently manipulate it, and now it is time to change it back to

XML. In other cases, you will want to generate SAX events that some other application is listening for. Or you may want to generate a DOM tree after adjusting the content of the document. Let's look at each of these cases.

Outputting a DOM tree

Although a DOM tree may be the most complex object that you can create, the process of creating it is the most straightforward. It mirrors the process for building a file with a `DOMBuilder`. The default constructor creates a `DOMOutputter`, using a DOM implementation it finds first using JAXP and then using the default parser. The other constructor enables you to specify the `DOMAdapter` implementation with which to choose the underlying parser. (Remember that you do this using one of the six concrete classes in the `org.jdom.adapters` package.)

The only method in `DOMOutputter` is `output()`, but it comes in several flavors. The most basic has the following signature:

```
public Document output( Document document) throws JDOMException
```

This time you're taking a JDOM `Document` and returning a DOM `Document`. This means that the return type `Document` refers to `org.w3c.dom.Document`, while the parameter `Document` refers to `org.jdom.Document`.

At times, however, you are going to want to output only part of a JDOM `Document` while still retaining information about its structure. In *Richard III*, for example, you may decide to rewrite the first act and then output just this first act as a DOM tree. In that case you can use the following method:

```
public Element output(Element element) throws JDOMException
```

This code takes a `org.jdom.Element` object and returns an `org.w3c.dom.Element` object. A `protected` version of this method also exists, which takes an `org.jdom.output.NamespaceStack` as its third parameter.

Similarly, you may want to save information about an attribute. In that case, you can use this method:

```
public Attr output (Attribute attribute) throws JDOMException
```

Notice that an attribute is referred to as `Attr` in the `org.w3c.dom` package and as `Attribute` in the org.jdom package. A `protected` version of this method also exists, which takes the DOM document as its second argument. Here's the signature for that method:

```
protected Attr output( Attribute attribute, Document domDoc)
  throws JDOMException
```

Outputting SAX events

You may remember from Chapter 12, that the most common way to respond to events generated bya SAX-based parser is to extend `org.xml.sax.helpers.DefaultHandler` and override the callbacks you need to implement. The `DefaultHandler` class implements the interfaces `ContentHandler`, `ErrorHandler`, `DTDHandler`, and `EntityResolver`. Your subclass of `DefaultHandler` acts as a listener for parsing events.

With JDOM you can take a JDOM tree and output SAX events using `SAXOutputter`. Another, longer route would be to save the JDOM `Document` as an XML file and then parse it and listen for callbacks as you did in the last chapter. You need to specify at least the `ContentHandler` when you create a `SAXOutputter`; you can specify the objects handling the other three interfaces as well. These are the constructor signatures:

```
public SAXOutputter(ContentHandler contentHandler)
public SAXOutputter(ContentHandler contentHandler,
                    ErrorHandler errorhandler,
                    DTDHandler dtdHandler,
                    EntityResolver entityResolver)
```

You can also use the setters `setContentHandler()`, `setErrorHandler()`, `setDTDHandler()`, and `setEntityResolver()` to set the objects implementing each of these four interfaces. You can use the final setter, `setReportNamespaceDeclarations()`,to define whether or not attribute namespace declarations are reported as "`xmlns`" attributes.

To actually send the SAX2 events, you invoke the method `output()`, which takes a JDOM `Document` object as its only parameter and then fires the registered SAX events. This method throws a `JDOMException` if it encounters problems.

Outputting XML

The `XMLOutputter` class is more complex than the other inhabitants of the `org.jdom.output` package. Eighteen different signatures exist for the `output()` method alone. Most of the methods in this class control the "prettiness" of the output. These output options even account for the difference in constructors.

```
public XMLOutputter()
public XMLOutputter(String indent)
public XMLOutputter(String indent, boolean newlines)
public XMLOutputter(String indent, boolean newlines,
                    String encoding)
public XMLOutputter(XMLOutputter referenceOutputter)
```

The constructor that takes three parameters enables you to specify the indent `String`. Usually this is just some number of spaces — in the default constructor, two spaces. The second parameter indicates whether or not new lines should be printed. In the default constructor, and the constructor taking only the indent String as a parameter, this value is false. The final parameter enables you to set the encoding using XML style names such as UTF-8 and US-ASCII. This value needs to match the encoding for a Writer if you are using one with the output() method. The method makeWriter(OutputStream out) configures the returned OutputStreamWriter to use the preferred encoding.

The remaining signature for the constructor enables you to create an XMLOutputter with the same settings as the referenceOutputter. You should experiment with CueMyLine5.java. Change the parameters when constructing your XMLOutputter. Note what happens if you set the value of the indent String to "–". See the difference between setting newlines to true and setting them to false. You'll find that you get the nicest output using the following setup:

```
XMLOutputter xmlOutputter = new XMLOutputter("  ", true);
xmlOutputter.setTextNormalize(true);
xmlOutputter.output(document, new FileWriter("rewrite.xml"));
```

I said that there are 18 different output() methods. Each of the nine pairs is designed to print out a different node type. Two output() methods each output objects of the types CDATA, Comment, DocType, Document, Element, EntityRef, ProcessingInstruction, String, and Text. One method of each pair is designed to output to a Writer; the other is designed to output to an OutputStream. You can output a whole document or, using one of these methods, part of one. When you output an Element you also output any of its Attributes, its value, and any of the child Elements it contains.

Many of the remainder of the methods in XMLOutputter enable you to tweak the settings to get different output. If your XML file is intended only to be read by other machines, you do not need to make it look pretty; you want the file to be as compact as possible. Create the XMLOutputter with the default constructor and strip away any unnecessary whitespace by calling setTextNormalize(true), as we did in the previous code snippet.

Summary

In this chapter, you didn't really learn to do anything new—you just learned how to do it better. As you played with JAXP, you may have found yourself wanting APIs that were better designed for a Java developer. Jason Hunter and Brett McLaughlin had the same feeling, and the result of their dissatisfaction is JDOM. In this chapter, you learned how to use JDOM to do many of the tasks you previously did with JAXP. You learned the following:

- You compared the JDOM code to the JAXP code for two different tasks. The first task involved searching a file for a given element and outputting the result to the console window; the second involved creating and populating a node and then outputting an XML file with the new node properly placed. Certain aspects of the second task were easier with JDOM, and others were not.
- You created a JDOM `Document` from scratch using elements of the `org.jdom` package. You also created a `Document` from a DOM tree using `DOMBuilder`, and from an XML file using `SAXBuilder`.
- You worked with the `Document` object that you created. You were able to create and work with elements and attributes using the `Document`, `Element`, and `Attribute` classes. JDOM also enables you to handle other aspects of an XML document by using `ProcessingInstruction`, `Comment`, `DocType`, and other classes.
- You output a JDOM document in different forms according to what was required. You sent it out as an XML document using `XMLOutputter`. You fired SAX 2 events from your JDOM tree using the `SAXOutputter`. You even converted your JDOM tree to a DOM tree using the `DOMOutputter`.

✦ ✦ ✦

Transforming and Binding Your XML Documents

CHAPTER 14

In This Chapter

Using XML and Cascading Style Sheets (CSS)

Creating a CSS for *Richard III*

Translating XML into HTML for browser display

Transforming your XML into XML that conforms to another DTD

Turning a DTD into Java classes using JAXB

Persisting Java objects as XML files

In this chapter you'll look at changing XML documents. The simplest change you'll make will be to transform the XML into another format, such as HTML, with the intent of presenting the contents of the document in a readable form. Before you even look at doing this, however, you'll see how you can use Cascading Style Sheets (CSS) to present XML and understand that this doesn't really transform the document. Then you'll learn how to reconcile differences between your notion of how a document should be structured and another organization's. If you want to share your document with others in a machine-readable format, you need to be able to transform an XML document that conforms to your DTD or schema to one that conforms to theirs. These techniques will be valuable to you when you're serving up your data to multiple clients.

Finally, you'll look at transforming your XML data to Java objects and Java objects back to XML. You'll use the Java APIs for XML binding (JAXB) to do a lot of the work for you. You will then write applications that work with this newly constructed Java object framework.

Presenting XML

You've seen that XML is a flexible format for storing information. Other applications can easily access and display this information. It would be nice, however, to be able to present the contents of an XML file in a Web browser or some other common existing application. You've seen nothing in the XML documents like rich_iii.xml that has indicated how the contents are to be displayed. One option is to apply Cascading Style Sheets (CSS) to XML documents just as you would apply them to an HTML file. Although this is a quick and easy solution, it will only work if the Web browser can display an XML file in the first place. A second option is to transform the XML document into an HTML document and then use the browser to display the resulting HTML file the way it normally would. In this section, you'll look at both of these options.

Using cascading style sheets

The Cascading Style Sheets (CSS) that are familiar from HTML development can be used to specify the presentation of XML documents. I'll show you a quick example of applying two different looks to a single document, and then you will see why this approach doesn't meet your needs in terms of presenting XML documents to different devices. I won't explain CSS here. You can find more information in *XML Bible, Second Edition* by Elliotte Rusty Harold (Hungry Minds, 2001) or from the W3C recommendations for Cascading Style Sheets levels 1 and 2 (available on the Web at `http://www.w3.org/TR/REC-CSS1` and `http://www.w3.org/TR/REC-CSS2/`). For this example, you'll need the files rich_iii.xml and play.dtd that you used in the previous two chapters. For instructions on finding these files you can look at Chapter 12 in the section "Installing JAXP and the examples."

Begin by opening up rich_iii.xml with your favorite browser. Figure 14-1 shows what this document looks like in IE 6.0.

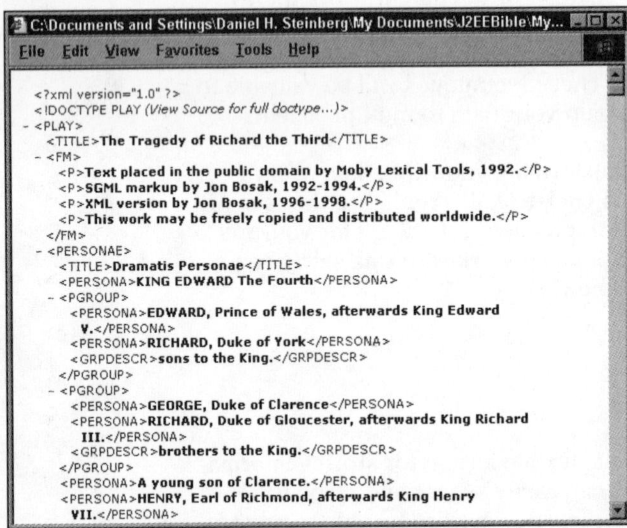

Figure 14-1: Displaying rich_iii.xml on a browser

You can see all the information contained in the play, but you wouldn't want to present it this way. Your browser may display the file differently or not at all. (If you have two different browsers, you may want to check for differences.) This inconsistency is part of the reason that you probably will not end up choosing CSS to display your documents. That's part of the challenge in using browsers to display XML. Unless you can choose the client browser, you can't control the way your page is displayed. CSS is very easy to use, but for a more robust method of displaying XML you'll more likely use XSL to actually transform XML to HTML, XHTML, WML or other useful formats.

Creating a CSS

The most basic way to alter the look of the document is to create a CSS that specifies how the various elements will be displayed. For example, you can create a program that lists the acts and scenes of *Richard III* using this style sheet:

```
PLAY {font-size:20pt;
      text-decoration: underline;}
ACT {font-size:15pt;
     text-indent: .1in;}
SCENE {font-size:10pt;
       text-indent: .3in;
       text-decoration: none;}
TITLE {display: block;}
PERSONAE, FM, SCNDESCR, PLAYSUBT,SPEECH,STAGEDIR
{display:none;}
```

Save this file as program.css in the same directory that contains rich_iii.xml. It is often helpful to look at the DTD to see the names of the elements that you want to either include or exclude. In this case, you don't want to print any of the speeches or stage directions or lists of characters. You make sure that they aren't printed by assigning the value `none` to `display` for all of them at once using `PERSONAE, FM, SCNDESCR, PLAYSUBT, SPEECH, STAGEDIR {display:none;}`. The other instructions display the `<PLAY>` element in underlined 20-point type; the `<ACT>` element is indented a tenth of an inch and is displayed in 15-point type; and the `<SCENE>` element is further indented and displayed in 10-point type. Because `<ACT>` is a child of `<PLAY>`, its contents are underlined as well. The `text-decoration:none` instruction removes the underlining in the `<SCENE>` element. You get the new lines because the `display` in `<TITLE>` is set to `block`.

Filtering the XML file with your CSS

Now that you've specified how you want to display your elements, you need to connect your XML document to this style sheet. You do this by adding the following boldface line to rich_iii.xml:

```
<?xml version="1.0"?>
<?xml-stylesheet type="text/css" href="program.css"?>
<!DOCTYPE PLAY SYSTEM "play.dtd">
<PLAY>
<TITLE>The Tragedy of Richard the Third</TITLE>
```

Save the altered file as rich_iii_css.xml and open it with your browser. Now the CSS acts as a filter that specifies whether or not an element is displayed and, if so, how it will be displayed. Figure 14-2 shows the view of the document in IE 5.5.

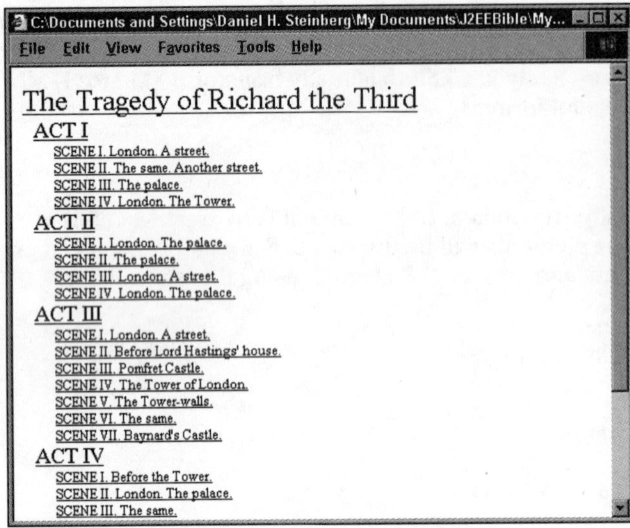

Figure 14-2: The acts and scenes from *Richard III*

Choose to view the source of this page. You may be surprised to see that even though you are only displaying a small number of lines of text on the page, the source is still the entire rich_iii_css.xml document. Sending this much information to render a small percentage of it is inefficient. When communicating with limited devices, you'll want to filter the file on the server end.

A second CSS

To get a better feel for the strengths and limitations of CSS, create another style sheet called Shakespeare.css with the following content:

```
PLAY {font-size:20pt;}
ACT {font-size:15pt;}
SCENE {font-size:10pt;}
TITLE {display: block;
       font-size: inherit;}
SPEAKER {font-weight: bold;}
LINE {font-size: 10pt;
      text-indent: .4in;
      display: block;
      }
STAGEDIR {font-style: italic;
          display: block;
          text-indent: .3in;}
PERSONAE, FM, SCNDESCR, PLAYSUBT  {display:none;}
```

This time you are creating a more script-like format. The name of the character delivering a line will appear in bold, and the lines will be indented for readability. The stage directions will be included in italics so that they are easier to spot. You give the `<LINE>` element's `display` property the value `block` so that each `<LINE>` will appear on its own physical line instead of all the lines running together in paragraph form.

In order to use this style sheet, you have to go back to rich_iii_css.xml and change the second line to this:

```
<?xml-stylesheet type="text/css" href="Shakespeare.css"?>
```

Figure 14-3 presents a view of a piece of rich_iii_css.xml as seen in IE 5.5.

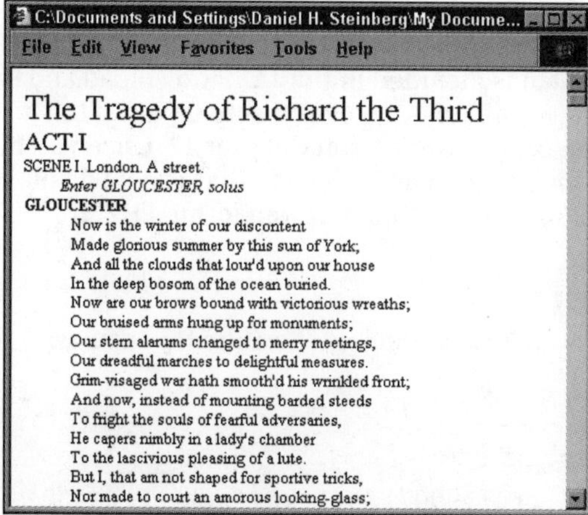

Figure 14-3: The actors' view of *Richard III*

Pros and cons of using CSS

There are positive things to be said about using CSS to deliver XML. Writing the style sheets involves very little work; you just need to find out which attributes can be set and what the possible values are. You can get your XML document to work with the CSS by adding a single line to your XML document. If your browser supports XML and CSS, then you can come up with an attractive display in minutes without any other processing.

There are, however, disadvantages. You saw that the entire XML document is still delivered to the client. This means that the client has access to all the information in the document. It also means that a client waiting for a two-line answer may have to download large files in order to get it. Performance may suffer. For clients with slow network connections or who are using constrained devices, the size of the download can be a significant issue.

There is also a drawback to having the XML document include a reference to the style sheet used to render it. In the preceding examples, you saw two different views of the same document. You had to change the XML document itself in order to change how it was rendered. With many clients using different devices to access your documents, you will want to be able to simultaneously serve up content in different device-appropriate ways. CSS does not enable you to do this.

Presenting a document with XSLT

You saw in the last section that a CSS can be used to specify how an XML document should be displayed by a Web browser. An XSLT style sheet is used to transform the XML document itself. In this section, you'll transform rich_iii.xml into an HTML document, but you can apply these same techniques to transform it into many other formats as well.

To perform the transformation, you will write a Java application that, in this case, uses the XSLT processor Xalan. (Xalan is included in the JAXP download and is also available from Apache at `http://xml.apache.org`.) You actually used this notion of transforming a document in one of the examples in Chapter 12. Once you have transformed rich_iii.xml, you will end up with an HTML file that can be displayed in any browser. The resulting file will contain nothing but well-formed HTML.

A shell for the XSLT style sheet

Unlike a CSS, an XSLT style sheet is an XML document. You should begin with the following shell:

```
<?xml version="1.0"?>
<xsl:stylesheet version="1.0"
  xmlns:xsl="http://www.w3.org/1999/XSL/Transform" >

</xsl:stylesheet>
```

In addition to the XML declaration, this file so far consists only of a single root element, `<stylesheet>`. You'll notice that the prefix mapping `xsl` has been specified and that you must specify the `version`. Save this file as program.xsl.

You can actually apply this style sheet to rich_iii.xml. It will produce a file by stripping all the existing tags and outputting the content. Of course, that isn't very useful output. In this section, your goal is to produce a well-formed HTML document. You'll have to specify how you map particular XML tags in rich_iii.xml to HTML tags. You will also have to create a Java program that processes rich_iii.xml using the style sheet.

Using JAXP to transform

You've already used the Java APIs for XML (JAXP) to transform a document. In Chapter 12, your application parsed rich_iii.xml, added a prologue, and wrote it back out. So that you don't have to go back to Chapter 12, here's a reminder of what you did with the relevant portion in bold:

```
package cue;

//many imports ...

public class CueMyLine5 {
  Document document;

  public CueMyLine5() {
    try{
      DocumentBuilderFactory dbFactory =
        DocumentBuilderFactory.newInstance();
      dbFactory.setValidating(true);
      dbFactory.setIgnoringElementContentWhitespace(true);

      DocumentBuilder documentBuilder =
        dbFactory.newDocumentBuilder();
      document = documentBuilder.parse(new
        File("rich_iii.xml"));
    } catch(ParserConfigurationException e){
      System.out.println( "There's a Parser Config problem.");
    } catch(SAXException e){
      System.out.println( "There's a SAX Exception.");
    } catch(IOException e){
      System.out.println("There's an IO exception.");
    }
  }

  public void addPrologue(){
    // refer to Ch. 12
  }
  public void saveTheDocument(){
    try{
      Transformer transformer =
        TransformerFactory.newInstance().newTransformer();
      transformer.transform( new DOMSource(document),
        new StreamResult( new File("reWrite.xml")));
    } catch (TransformerConfigurationException e) {
      System.out.println("There's a Transformer Config Excpt");
    } catch (TransformerException e) {
      System.out.println("There is a Transformer Exception");
    }
  }

  public static void main(String[] args) throws Exception {
    CueMyLine5 cueMyLine = new CueMyLine5();
    cueMyLine.addPrologue();
    cueMyLine.saveTheDocument();
  }
}
```

You need to make remarkably few changes here in order to get your application to apply the style sheet before producing output. The constructor can remain unchanged, and you no longer need to add a prologue, so you can eliminate the `addPrologue()` method and the call to it from `main()`. You need only provide the style sheet to the `Transformer` that's being created.

More concretely, create a directory called change in the same directory that contains rich_iii.xml and program.xsl. Inside this directory, place the following Transform1.java source file (the changes are in boldface):

```
package change;

import java.io.File;
import javax.xml.parsers.DocumentBuilder;
import javax.xml.parsers.DocumentBuilderFactory;
import org.w3c.dom.Document;
import javax.xml.parsers.ParserConfigurationException;
import org.xml.sax.SAXException;
import java.io.IOException;
import org.w3c.dom.DOMException;
import javax.xml.transform.Transformer;
import javax.xml.transform.TransformerFactory;
import javax.xml.transform.TransformerConfigurationException;
import javax.xml.transform.TransformerException;
import javax.xml.transform.dom.DOMSource;
import javax.xml.transform.stream.StreamResult;
import javax.xml.transform.stream.StreamSource;

public class Transform1 {
  Document document;

  public Transform1() {
    try{
      DocumentBuilderFactory dbFactory =
        DocumentBuilderFactory.newInstance();
      //important or you will have extra items in your DOM Doc
      dbFactory.setValidating(true);
      dbFactory.setIgnoringElementContentWhitespace(true);

      DocumentBuilder documentBuilder =
        dbFactory.newDocumentBuilder();
      document = documentBuilder.parse(
        new File("rich_iii.xml"));
    } catch(ParserConfigurationException e){
      System.out.println( "There's a Parser Config problem.");
    } catch(SAXException e){
      System.out.println( "There's a SAX Exception.");
    } catch(IOException e){
      System.out.println("There's an IO exception.");
    }
  }
```

```
    public void transformTheDocument(File stylesheet){
      try{
        Transformer transformer = TransformerFactory.
          newInstance().newTransformer(
            new StreamSource(stylesheet));
        transformer.transform( new DOMSource(document),
          new StreamResult( new File("alteredRichard.html")));
      } catch (TransformerConfigurationException e) {
        System.out.println("There is a Transformer Configuration
  Exception" );
         e.printStackTrace();
      } catch (TransformerException e) {
        System.out.println("There is a Transformer Exception");
      }
    }

    public static void main(String[] args) throws Exception {
      Transform1 transform1 = new Transform1();
      transform1.transformTheDocument(new File("program.xsl"));
    }
  }
```

Other than naming changes, most of the differences occur in a single line of the `transformTheDocument()` method (formerly the `saveTheDocument()` method). In the previous program, you created a `Transformer` like this:

```
Transformer transformer =
        TransformerFactory.newInstance().newTransformer();
```

Now you are creating a `Transformer` like this (the difference is in boldface):

```
Transformer transformer =
  TransformerFactory.newInstance().newTransformer(
        new StreamSource(stylesheet));
```

You have to provide a handle to program.xsl. You do this in two steps. First, `stylesheet` is a `File` that you've constructed from the `String` `program.xsl`. Then this `File` is passed as a parameter to the `StreamSource` constructor, which in turn is passed as a parameter to the `newTransformer()` method in `TransformerFactory`.

Compile and run Transform1.java. If you are getting runtime errors but were able to run `CueMyLine5` back in Chapter 12, check to make sure that no typos are present in the URI for the namespace in program.xsl. Also, you should be applying this transformation to the unchanged rich_iii.xml. If you added the CSS directive to rich_iii.xml instead of creating rich_iii_css.xml, you should go back and remove this line.

Once you have successfully run Transform1, open the generated HTML file with your browser. You will see the entire contents of the play presented as one long run-on paragraph. If you view the source, you'll see the declaration `<?xml`

version="1.0" encoding="UTF-8"?> followed by the entire contents of rich_iii.xml with all the tags removed. At this point you can transform a document; next you will learn how to produce more useful output.

Creating HTML with a template

You're going to produce an XSLT style sheet that transforms rich_iii.xml into an HTML document that lists the acts and scenes, so that the final result appears to be the same as what you produced using CSS. Because you now want to produce HTML, start by taking the root element of rich_iii.xml and mapping it to the shell of an HTML document. Add these lines to program.xsl, as follows:

```
<?xml version="1.0"?>
<xsl:stylesheet version="1.0"
  xmlns:xsl="http://www.w3.org/1999/XSL/Transform" >
  <xsl:output method="html" />
  <xsl:template match="PLAY">
    <html>
      <head> <title> Richard III Program </title> </head>
      <body>
        Transformed Richard III
      </body>
    </html>
  </xsl:template>
</xsl:stylesheet>
```

The first change is that you use the line <xsl:output method="html" /> to indicate that you are outputting HTML. One result of setting the method attribute to html is that the generated file no longer begins with the XML declaration.

The second change is contained in the <xsl:template> element. The match attribute enables you to specify that when the XSLT application encounters a <PLAY> element, it should replace it with the HTML shell provided. Save this XSLT style sheet and rerun Transform1. When you open the file alteredRichard.html in your browser, you'll see something similar to what is shown in Figure 14-4.

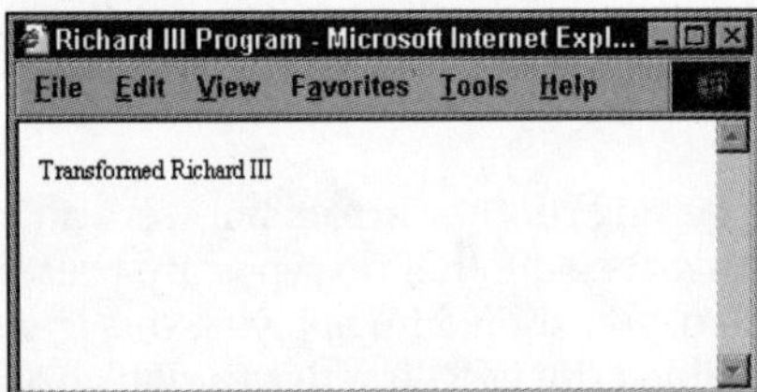

Figure 14-4: A trivial transformation of *Richard III*

Choose to view source, and you should see something like this:

```
<html>
  <head>
    <META http-equiv="Content-Type" content="text/html;
      charset=UTF-8">
    <title> Richard III Program </title>
  </head>
  <body>
    Transformed Richard III
  </body>
</html>
```

The source code demonstrates that the effects of an XSLT transform are very different from the effects of applying a CSS. In this case, the actual end product delivered to the client is different. No reference is made in the XML file to the style sheet that will be used to transform it, and no reference is made in the style sheet to which XML file it will transform. This flexibility is important because it means that you can programmatically apply different transforms to different documents.

You might ask, "Where did the rest of rich_iii.xml go?" The answer is that you didn't ask that it be included anywhere, and as a result it wasn't. As you will see in the next section, you can the `<xsl:apply-templates>` element in your XSLT style sheet to specify where the children of an element should be handled.

Generating a list of acts and scenes

Here's the plan. Instead of just printing out "Transformed *Richard III*," you'll create a style sheet that generates an HTML file that lists the acts and scenes from *Richard III*. The style sheet takes advantage of the hierarchical nature of the XML document. The `<PLAY>` element is specified like this in the DTD:

```
<!ELEMENT PLAY (TITLE, FM, PERSONAE, SCNDESCR, PLAYSUBT,
  INDUCT?,PROLOGUE?, ACT+, EPILOGUE?)>
```

In this application, you want to display the `<TITLE>` as a heading and then go on to process the `<ACT>` element. You can display the value of the `<TITLE>` element using the following XSL element:

```
<xsl:value-of select="TITLE" />
```

This empty tag will be replaced with the string value of the `<TITLE>` element. In this case, you will see "The Tragedy of Richard III." Suppose your goal is to end up with the following code for an HTML heading in the transformed document:

```
<h1> The Tragedy of Richard III </h1>
```

You can accomplish this by placing the start and end `<h1>` tags around the `<xsl:value-of>` tag, like this:

```
<h1> <xsl:value-of select="TITLE" /> </h1>
```

Now that you've displayed the value of the <TITLE>, you want to process the children of <PLAY>. You can process all the children with the following tag:

```
<xsl:apply-templates>
```

In this case, however, you don't want to process all the children. You don't want to see any of the front matter, *dramatis personae*, scene descriptions, and so on. You just want to process the acts. Again, use the `select` attribute like this:

```
<xsl:apply-templates select="ACT" />
```

Similarly, you'll display the title of the acts surrounded by <h2> tags, and the title of scenes in an unordered list. Your edited program.xsl file should look like this:

```
<?xml version="1.0"?>
<xsl:stylesheet version="1.0"
  xmlns:xsl="http://www.w3.org/1999/XSL/Transform" >
  <xsl:output method="html" />

  <xsl:template match="PLAY">
    <html>
      <head> <title> Richard III Program </title> </head>
      <body>
        <h1> <xsl:value-of select="TITLE" /> </h1>
        <xsl:apply-templates select="ACT" />
      </body>
    </html>
  </xsl:template>

  <xsl:template match="ACT">
    <h2> <xsl:value-of select="TITLE" /> </h2>
    <ul>
     <xsl:apply-templates select="SCENE"/>
    </ul>
  </xsl:template>

  <xsl:template match="SCENE">
    <li> <xsl:value-of select="TITLE"/> </li>
  </xsl:template>

</xsl:stylesheet>
```

Run Transform1 to generate the new alteredRichard.html and open it up in your browser. Figure 14-5 shows what it should look like.

Note that you have to rerun Transform1 every time you want to take a look at the effects of the changes you've made to the style sheet. As long as you are applying program.xsl to rich_iii.xml, you don't have to recompile Transform1.java, but you do need to run it to generate the new HTML file.

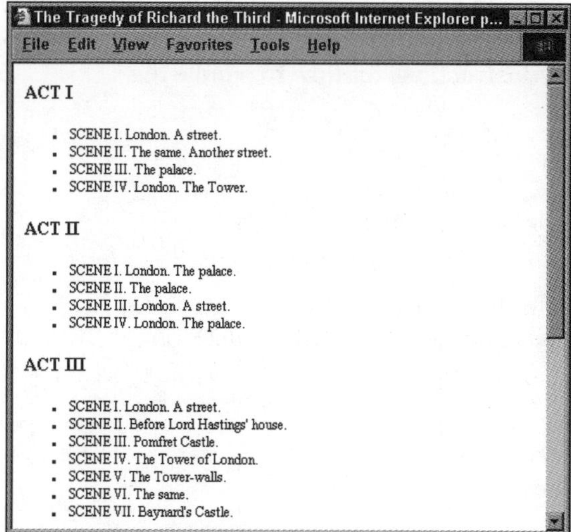

Figure 14-5: Another list of the acts and scenes in *Richard III*

A second style sheet

Now that you've been able to produce a summary of the acts and scenes of the play, you can output the play in a readable format for actors. Again you'll put the names of the speakers in boldface, put the stage directions in italics, and make sure that the line breaks have been inserted to make the play more readable. The resulting output should look like what is shown in Figure 14-6.

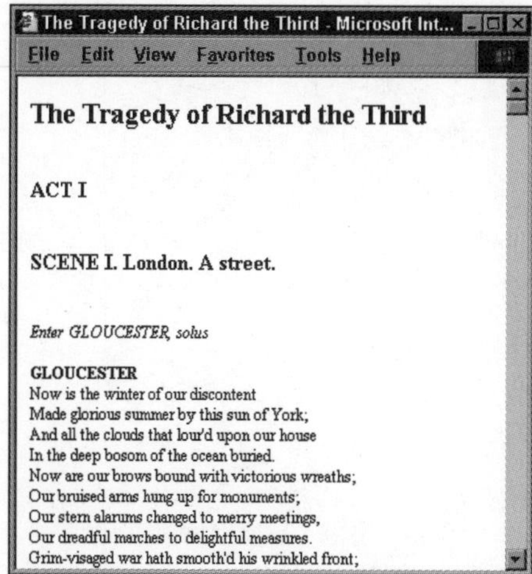

Figure 14-6: Another view of the script for *Richard III*

In the XSLT style sheet, you can just follow the following plan. To output the <TITLE> of an act or a scene correctly, the <ACT> or <SCENE> can defer the layout instructions to the <TITLE>. The instructions for how to handle the <TITLE> can be as simple as this:

```
<xsl:template match="TITLE">
  <br />
  <h2> <xsl:apply-templates /> </h2>
</xsl:template>
```

You can, similarly, set up templates for displaying the elements <LINE>, <SPEAKER>, and <STAGEDIR>. Then the template for <ACT> consists of deferring to the child elements, as follows:

```
<xsl:template match="ACT">
  <xsl:apply-templates />
</xsl:template>
```

Here's the entire revised program.xsl style sheet:

```
<?xml version="1.0"?>
<xsl:stylesheet version="1.0"
  xmlns:xsl="http://www.w3.org/1999/XSL/Transform" >
  <xsl:output method="html" />

  <xsl:template match="PLAY">
    <html>
      <head>
        <title>
          <xsl:value-of select="TITLE" />
        </title>
      </head>
      <body>
        <h1> <xsl:value-of select="TITLE" /> </h1>
        <xsl:apply-templates select="ACT" />
      </body>
    </html>
  </xsl:template>

  <xsl:template match="ACT">
    <xsl:apply-templates />
  </xsl:template>

  <xsl:template match="SCENE">
    <xsl:apply-templates />
  </xsl:template>

 <xsl:template match="SPEECH">
   <br />
   <xsl:apply-templates />
 </xsl:template>
```

```
<xsl:template match="SPEAKER">
  <br />
  <b> <xsl:apply-templates /> </b>
   </xsl:template>

<xsl:template match="TITLE">
  <br />
  <h2> <xsl:apply-templates /> </h2>
</xsl:template>

<xsl:template match="STAGEDIR">
  <br />
  <em> <xsl:apply-templates /> </em>
</xsl:template>

<xsl:template match="LINE">
  <br />
  <xsl:apply-templates />
</xsl:template>

</xsl:stylesheet>
```

XLST transformations using JDOM

So far you've used JAXP to transform rich_iii.xml using program.xsl. You could also have written your Java program using JDOM instead of JAXP. Just like the JAXP program Transform1, Transform2 is an adaptation of CueMyLine5. In Chapter 13, you created this program to make changes to rich_iii.xml by using JDOM and then saved the changes. You may need to refer back to Chapter 13 to review setting up your computer to run JDOM applications. Here's a partial listing of the JDOM version of CueMyLine5.java:

```
package cue;

// imports

public class CueMyLine5 {
  Document document;

  public CueMyLine5() {
    try{
      SAXBuilder builder = new SAXBuilder();
      document = builder.build(new File("rich_iii.xml"));
    } catch(JDOMException e){
      System.out.println( "There's a JDOM problem.");
    }
  }
  public void addPrologue(){ //...
   }
  public void saveTheDocument(){
    try{
      XMLOutputter xmlOutputter = new XMLOutputter("  ", true);
      xmlOutputter.setTextNormalize(true);
```

```
        xmlOutputter.output(document,
          new FileWriter("rewrite.xml"));
      } catch (Exception e) {
        System.out.println("Transformer Config Exception");
      }
    }

    public static void main(String[] args) {
      CueMyLine5 cueMyLine = new CueMyLine5();
      cueMyLine.addPrologue();
      cueMyLine.saveTheDocument();
    }
  }
```

As with Transform1, other than renaming the class and methods, you need to make surprisingly few alterations. You will create Transform2.java in the change directory. You will parse rich_iii.xml and then transform it using the XSLT style sheet program.xsl. Finally, you will output the transformed file as JDOMalteredRichard.html. The differences between Transform2 and CueMyLine5 are shown in boldface in the following code:

```
package change;

import org.jdom.input.SAXBuilder;
import org.jdom.Document;
import org.jdom.JDOMException;
import java.io.File;
import java.io.FileWriter;
import org.jdom.output.XMLOutputter;
import org.jdom.transform.JDOMSource;
import org.jdom.transform.JDOMResult;
import javax.xml.transform.Transformer;
import javax.xml.transform.TransformerFactory;
import javax.xml.transform.TransformerException;
import javax.xml.transform.stream.StreamSource;
import java.io.IOException;


public class Transform2 {
  Document document;

  public Transform2() {
    try{
      SAXBuilder builder = new SAXBuilder();
      document = builder.build(new File("rich_iii.xml"));
    } catch(JDOMException e){
      System.out.println( "There's a JDOM problem.");
    }
  }
  public void transformTheDocument(String stylesheet){
    try {
      Transformer transformer = TransformerFactory
```

```
          .newInstance().newTransformer(
            new StreamSource(stylesheet));

        JDOMResult out = new JDOMResult();
        transformer.transform(new JDOMSource(document), out);
        XMLOutputter xmlOutputter = new XMLOutputter("  ", true);
        xmlOutputter.setTextNormalize(true);
        xmlOutputter.output(out.getDocument(),
          new FileWriter("JDOMAlteredRichard.html"));
      }
      catch (TransformerException e) {
        System.out.println("Transformer Exception");
      }
       catch (IOException e) {
        System.out.println("IOException");
      }
    }

    public static void main(String[] args) {
      Transform2 transform2 = new Transform2();
      transform2.transformTheDocument("program.xsl");
    }
  }
```

From now on, you can decide whether you prefer to use JAXP or JDOM to transform your XML.

Transforming XML

In the last section you looked at ways of presenting your XML files to human consumers. Often the clients for your XML documents are other machines. You've seen that if you know the DTD for a given XML file then you can easily write an application that extracts the information you need. If you are processing hundreds of resumes each day, you may want to pre-screen the submissions to make certain that they meet some minimal qualification before you hand-process them. Consider the difficulties that will arise when you interact with another organization that is processing résumés that have been validated against a different DTD, one that the organization has developed in-house.

In this section, you are concerned with transforming XML documents so that they can be read and understood. This time, however, you aren't concerned with how they look but in how the data is structured. Although this type of transformation is usually applied to data-centric XML documents, you can continue with the *Richard III* example by converting a document that conforms to the existing play.dtd to a document that conforms to a new DTD that you'll define.

A second DTD for Shakespeare's plays

You've no doubt noticed by now that play.dtd defines elements but no attributes. There continue to be arguments about what belongs in an attribute and what belongs in an element. At one extreme are those who believe you should never use attributes. At the other are those who put anything they consider to be non-displayable data in attributes. The DTD play.dtd takes the "never use attributes" approach. As a reminder, here's play.dtd:

```
<!-- DTD for Shakespeare   J. Bosak  1994.03.01, 1997.01.02 -->
<!-- Revised for case sensitivity 1997.09.10 -->
<!-- Revised for XML 1.0 conformity 1998.01.27 (thanks to Eve
  Maler) -->

<!-- <!ENTITY amp "&#38;#38;"> -->
<!ELEMENT PLAY     (TITLE, FM, PERSONAE, SCNDESCR, PLAYSUBT,
  INDUCT?,PROLOGUE?, ACT+, EPILOGUE?)>
<!ELEMENT TITLE    (#PCDATA)>
<!ELEMENT FM       (P+)>
<!ELEMENT P        (#PCDATA)>
<!ELEMENT PERSONAE (TITLE, (PERSONA | PGROUP)+)>
<!ELEMENT PGROUP   (PERSONA+, GRPDESCR)>
<!ELEMENT PERSONA  (#PCDATA)>
<!ELEMENT GRPDESCR (#PCDATA)>
<!ELEMENT SCNDESCR (#PCDATA)>
<!ELEMENT PLAYSUBT (#PCDATA)>
<!ELEMENT INDUCT   (TITLE, SUBTITLE*,
  (SCENE+|(SPEECH|STAGEDIR|SUBHEAD)+))>
<!ELEMENT ACT      (TITLE, SUBTITLE*, PROLOGUE?, SCENE+,
  EPILOGUE?)>
<!ELEMENT SCENE    (TITLE, SUBTITLE*, (SPEECH | STAGEDIR |
  SUBHEAD)+)>
<!ELEMENT PROLOGUE (TITLE, SUBTITLE*, (STAGEDIR | SPEECH)+)>
<!ELEMENT EPILOGUE (TITLE, SUBTITLE*, (STAGEDIR | SPEECH)+)>
<!ELEMENT SPEECH   (SPEAKER+, (LINE | STAGEDIR | SUBHEAD)+)>
<!ELEMENT SPEAKER  (#PCDATA)>
<!ELEMENT LINE     (#PCDATA | STAGEDIR)*>
<!ELEMENT STAGEDIR (#PCDATA)>
<!ELEMENT SUBTITLE (#PCDATA)>
<!ELEMENT SUBHEAD  (#PCDATA)>
```

Now it's time to create a second DTD for specifying one of Shakespeare's plays. This exercise is not intended to suggest that this DTD needs improvements; the point of this section is to arrive at a different DTD. In the next section, you'll construct an XSLT style sheet to convert rich_iii.xml into an XML document that conforms to this new DTD.

The structure of a <SCENE>, <EPILOGUE>, and <PROLOGUE> are similar enough that you can treat them all as if they were the same thing. The description of <ACT> in play.dtd restricts each act to having one or no prologue, followed by at least one scene, followed by one or no epilogue. Although this new DTD can't enforce this existing structure, the new DTD will only be used for Shakespeare's plays, none of which violate this structure. Although it would be a bit more problematic, you can eliminate <INDUCT> and treat it as a type of <SCENE>. Doing this will require you to revise the new DTD for plays with introductions that consist of multiple scenes. For your purposes in this *Richard III* example, you can get away with the oversimplification of the new DTD. A tradeoff is that the specification of <PLAY> will be a little less clear as <scene> can refer to more than one type of element. The first optional <scene> is the introduction, the second is the prologue, and the third is the epilogue.

In the revised DTD, you can take advantage of a decision not to display the front matter or the list of characters in the play. Elements such as <TITLE>, <SUBTITLE>, and <SPEAKER> are now treated as attributes. Here's the new DTD, which you can save as newPlay.dtd (to avoid confusion later as to which DTD is being discussed, this one uses lower case for all elements and attributes):

```
<!-- DTD example derived from the revised version of J. Bosak's
  DTD for Shakespeare -->

<!ELEMENT play     (scndescr, scene?,scene?, act+, scene?)>
<!ELEMENT p        (#PCDATA)>
<!ELEMENT scndescr (#PCDATA)>
<!ELEMENT act      (scene+)>
<!ELEMENT scene    ((speech | stagedir | subhead)+)>
<!ELEMENT speech   ((line | stagedir | subhead)+)>
<!ELEMENT line     (#PCDATA | stagedir)*>
<!ELEMENT stagedir (#PCDATA)>
<!ELEMENT subhead  (#PCDATA)>
<!ATTLIST play     title    CDATA #REQUIRED
                   subtitle CDATA #IMPLIED >
<!ATTLIST act      title    CDATA #REQUIRED
                   subtitle CDATA #IMPLIED >
<!ATTLIST scene    title    CDATA #REQUIRED
                   subtitle CDATA #IMPLIED >
<!ATTLIST speech   speaker  CDATA #REQUIRED >
```

Translating with a style sheet

You can think of the two DTDs as defining different dialects. Your next job is to provide the translation. When Midwesterners refer to a carbonated beverage, they call it a *pop*. When they offer one to a New Yorker, they have to ask if the New Yorker would like a *soda* if they wish to be understood. You could use an XSLT style sheet to convert a <POP> element to a <SODA> element. Compare the two DTDs and look for ways in which you might map the elements in play.dtd to the elements and attributes in newPlay.dtd.

Creating elements

Start by considering the simplest sort of map. A <LINE> as it is defined by play.dtd is exactly mapped to a <line> as it is defined by newPlay.dtd. Whenever the translator encounters a <LINE> element, you want it to create a <line> element and put the contents of <LINE> into the newly created <line>. Here's how you arrange this:

```
<xsl:template match="LINE">
  <xsl:element name="line">
    <xsl:apply-templates />
  </xsl:element>
</xsl:template>
```

The tag `<xsl:element name="line">` creates the `<line>` element in the target file. The end tag for `<line>` will be placed where the corresponding `</xsl:element>` tag and the `<xsl:apply-templates />` tag will be replaced by the contents of `<LINE>`. Suppose for a minute that you instead used this code:

```
<xsl:template match="LINE">
  <xsl:element name="line">
  </xsl:element>
</xsl:template>
```

Because you haven't placed any content between the start and end `<xsl:element>` tags, the translator is smart enough to replace these with the empty tag `<line />`.

Creating attributes

In play.dtd the element `<SPEECH>` had `<SPEAKER>` as a child element. In newPlay.dtd the element `<speech>` has an attribute named `speaker`. In addition, `<SPEECH>` has `<LINE>`, `<STAGEDIR>`, and `<SUBHEAD>` elements that need to be mapped across to the corresponding children of `<speech>`. You can do this mapping with the following code:

```
<xsl:template match="SPEECH">
     <xsl:element name="speech">
      <xsl:attribute name="speaker">
        <xsl:value-of select="SPEAKER" />
      </xsl:attribute>
      <xsl:apply-templates />
    </xsl:element>
  </xsl:template>
```

Inside the `<xsl:element>` tags that map to the `<speech>` start and end tags, you include `<xsl:attribute>` tags that specify the name of the attribute you are declaring as an attribute of the `<xsl:attribute>` tag. The contents of the tag will be the value of the attribute: In this case the tag contains the value of the `<SPEAKER>` element.

Leaving elements out

Not all of the elements in play.dtd are being mapped over. For example, in the `<PLAY>` element, you won't be keeping the front matter or the *dramatis personae*. You could specify this in either of two ways. The first way is by explicitly listing the children of `<PLAY>` that you will keep in the target XML document, as follows:

```
<xsl:template match="PLAY">
     <xsl:element name="play">
```

```
      <xsl:attribute name="title">
        <xsl:value-of select="TITLE" />
      </xsl:attribute>
      <xsl:attribute name="subtitle">
        <xsl:value-of select="PLAYSUBT" />
      </xsl:attribute>
      <xsl:apply-templates select="SCNDESCR" />
      <xsl:apply-templates select="INDUCT" />
      <xsl:apply-templates select="PROLOGUE" />
      <xsl:apply-templates select="ACT" />
      <xsl:apply-templates select="EPILOGUE" />
    </xsl:element>
  </xsl:template>
```

An alternate approach with the same end result is to start by using the `<xsl:apply-templates>` to process all the children of the `<PLAY>` element, like this:

```
<xsl:template match="PLAY">
    <xsl:element name="play">
      <xsl:attribute name="title">
        <xsl:value-of select="TITLE" />
      </xsl:attribute>
      <xsl:attribute name="subtitle">
        <xsl:value-of select="PLAYSUBT" />
      </xsl:attribute>
      <xsl:apply-templates />
    </xsl:element>
  </xsl:template>
```

For any element that you don't want included in the resulting document, you can create an empty rule, like this:

```
<xsl:template match="FM" />
```

Setting the document type declaration

When you were transforming rich_iii.xml into an HTML document, your XSLT style sheet included the following element:

```
<xsl:output method="html" />
```

Now you are transforming one XML document into another one, so the value of `method` is now `xml`. Set the `doctype-system` attribute to `newPlay.dtd` to point to your new DTD. Here's your new `<output>` element:

```
<xsl:output method="xml" doctype-system="newPlay.dtd" />
```

The XSLT translator will turn this input into the following output in alteredRichard.xml:

```
<!DOCTYPE play SYSTEM "newPlay.dtd">
```

You can also set the `doctype-public` attribute to include a `PUBLIC` declaration in your document type declaration.

The complete style sheet

Now that you know how to construct the pieces of the style sheet, you can put them all together into a file called translate.xsl, as shown in Listing 14-1.

Listing 14-1: The translate.xsl style sheet

```
<?xml version="1.0"?>
<xsl:stylesheet version="1.0"
xmlns:xsl="http://www.w3.org/1999/XSL/Transform" >
<xsl:output method="xml" doctype-system="newPlay.dtd" />

  <xsl:template match="PLAY">
    <xsl:element name="play">
      <xsl:attribute name="title">
        <xsl:value-of select="TITLE" />
      </xsl:attribute>
      <xsl:attribute name="subtitle">
        <xsl:value-of select="PLAYSUBT" />
      </xsl:attribute>
      <xsl:apply-templates />
    </xsl:element>
  </xsl:template>

  <xsl:template match="ACT">
    <xsl:element name="act">
      <xsl:attribute name="title">
        <xsl:value-of select="TITLE" />
      </xsl:attribute>
      <xsl:attribute name="subtitle">
        <xsl:value-of select="SUBTITLE" />
      </xsl:attribute>
      <xsl:apply-templates select="PROLOGUE" />
      <xsl:apply-templates select="SCENE" />
      <xsl:apply-templates select="EPILOGUE" />
    </xsl:element>
  </xsl:template>

  <xsl:template match="SCNDESCR">
    <xsl:element name="scndescr">
      <xsl:apply-templates />
    </xsl:element>
  </xsl:template>

  <xsl:template match="INDUCT">
    <xsl:element name="scene">
    <xsl:attribute name="title">
        <xsl:value-of select="TITLE" />
```

```
      </xsl:attribute>
      <xsl:attribute name="subtitle">
        <xsl:value-of select="SUBTITLE" />
      </xsl:attribute>
      <xsl:apply-templates/>
    </xsl:element>
  </xsl:template>

  <xsl:template match="PROLOGUE">
    <xsl:element name="scene">
    <xsl:attribute name="title">
        <xsl:value-of select="TITLE" />
      </xsl:attribute>
      <xsl:attribute name="subtitle">
        <xsl:value-of select="SUBTITLE" />
      </xsl:attribute>
      <xsl:apply-templates />
    </xsl:element>
  </xsl:template>

  <xsl:template match="EPILOGUE">
    <xsl:element name="scene">
      <xsl:attribute name="title">
        <xsl:value-of select="TITLE" />
      </xsl:attribute>
      <xsl:attribute name="subtitle">
        <xsl:value-of select="SUBTITLE" />
      </xsl:attribute>
      <xsl:apply-templates />
    </xsl:element>
  </xsl:template>

  <xsl:template match="SCENE">
    <xsl:element name="scene">
      <xsl:attribute name="title">
        <xsl:value-of select="TITLE" />
      </xsl:attribute>
      <xsl:attribute name="subtitle">
        <xsl:value-of select="SUBTITLE" />
      </xsl:attribute>
      <xsl:apply-templates />
    </xsl:element>
  </xsl:template>

  <xsl:template match="SPEECH">
     <xsl:element name="speech">
      <xsl:attribute name="speaker">
        <xsl:value-of select="SPEAKER" />
      </xsl:attribute>
      <xsl:apply-templates />
    </xsl:element>
  </xsl:template>
```

Continued

Listing 14-1 *(continued)*

```
<xsl:template match="STAGEDIR">
  <xsl:element name="stagedir">
    <xsl:apply-templates />
  </xsl:element>
</xsl:template>

<xsl:template match="LINE">
  <xsl:element name="line">
    <xsl:apply-templates />
  </xsl:element>
</xsl:template>

<xsl:template match="P">
  <xsl:element name="p">
    <xsl:apply-templates />
  </xsl:element>
</xsl:template>

<xsl:template match="TITLE" />
<xsl:template match="SUBTITLE" />
<xsl:template match="SPEAKER" />
<xsl:template match="PLAYSUBT" />
<xsl:template match="PERSONAE" />
<xsl:template match="FM" />

</xsl:stylesheet>
```

Adjust Transform1.java to use translate.xsl instead of program.xsl as the style sheet. You also need to change the name of the output file from alteredRichard.html to alteredRichard.xml. Compile and run Transform1.java. Figure 14-7 shows part of alteredRichard.xml viewed in IE 5.5.

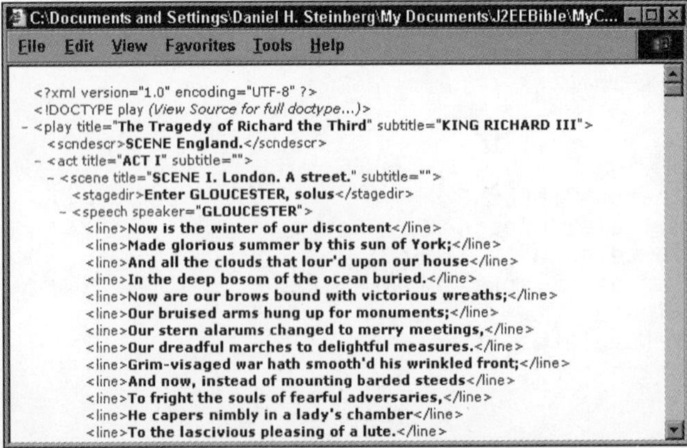

Figure 14-7: The results of applying translate.xsl

Binding with JAXB

Thus far in this chapter, you've looked at two types of transformations. You transformed elements of an XML document into HTML so that you could easily display the resulting document in a browser. You also transformed one XML document into another so an organization using a different DTD would be able to use it. Now you will look at transforming XML into Java objects so that Java developers can use them more easily. In this section, you'll create a binding schema and examine the generated files. In the next section, you'll use this binding in a sample application.

The point of binding is that you are creating a mapping. This will enable you to more quickly translate data stored in XML into Java objects, manipulate those objects, and then translate them back to persist them. As a starting point, you'll transform the play.dtd that you've been working with to get a feel for what is created by JAXB. Once you understand the default behavior of the schema compiler, you'll customize this behavior with an example that features different datatypes.

Installing and running JAXB

Currently JAXB is available as an early-access release. You can download the distribution from `http://java.sun.com/xml/jaxb/index.html`. The release notes describe the installation on a UNIX platform. There is no quick launcher for Windows, but you can easily run JAXB on a Windows box: Either copy the two jar files in the lib directory of the distribution into your \jre\lib\ext directory, or change your `CLASSPATH` to point to these two jars. Now you can run the schema compiler that generates the Java classes from the command line.

In any case, you will need a binding schema that contains instructions for the schema compiler. At the very minimum this binding schema must specify a root element. For example, the Shakespearean plays have a root element of `<PLAY>`. Create a binding schema called Shakespeare.xjs that contains the following three lines:

```
<xml-java-binding-schema version="1.0ea">
  <element name="PLAY" type="class" root="true" />
</xml-java-binding-schema>
```

Save the file in the same directory as play.dtd. Shakespeare.xjs has a root element called `<xml-java-binding-schema>` with the version specified as early-access 1.0. For now, the only other content of this file is the element `<element>` that has the `name` attribute set to the play.dtd element `<PLAY>` with instructions that this element will become a class and that it can be the root element of a document. You can specify that multiple elements can be root elements by using more than one `<element>` tag.

You can now use play.dtd to generate Java classes by using the schema compiler and passing it the name of the DTD as well as the name of the binding schema.

Open a command window and navigate to the directory containing play.dtd and Shakespeare.xjs. Enter this command:

```
java com.sun.tools.xjc.Main "play.dtd" "Shakespeare.xjs"
```

This command runs the schema-compiler application and passes in two parameters. The first is for the schema specified, in this case, by play.dtd. The second is for the binding schema Shakespeare.xjs. After a moment you'll see feedback in the console window to let you know that .java files are being generated with the names ACT.java, EPILOGUE.java, FM.java, INDUCT.java, LINE.java, PERSONAE.java, PGROUP.java, PLAY.java, PROLOGUE.java, SCENE.java, and SPEECH.java.

The generated code PLAY.java contains instance variables for each of the contained elements. Any of the elements declared to contain `#PCDATA` are variables of type `String` in the generated Java code. The elements (such as `<PERSONAE>`) that contain other elements become classes in their own right. This means that you end up with a PERSONAE.java file, and that the `PLAY` class contains a variable named `_PERSONAE` of type `PERSONAE`. You'll notice that, because play.dtd allows the element `<PLAY>` to contain one or more of the `<ACT>` elements, the schema compiler generates a class named ACT.java and the `PLAY` class contains a `List` named `_ACT` created using a utility inner class called `PredicatedLists`. Listing 14-2 shows a piece of the generated source code.

Listing 14-2: **Play class source code (excerpt)**

```
// many imports

public class PLAY extends MarshallableRootElement
  implements RootElement {

    private String _TITLE;
    private FM _FM;
    private PERSONAE _PERSONAE;
    private String _SCNDESCR;
    private String _PLAYSUBT;
    private INDUCT _INDUCT;
    private PROLOGUE _PROLOGUE;
    private List _ACT = PredicatedLists.createInvalidating(
      this, new ACTPredicate(), new ArrayList());
    private PredicatedLists.Predicate pred_ACT =
      new ACTPredicate();
    private EPILOGUE _EPILOGUE;

// accessor methods begin

    public String getTITLE() {...}

    public void setTITLE(String _TITLE) {...}
```

```
// accessors for FM, PERSONAE, SCNDESCR,PLAYSUBT, INDUCT,
// PROLOGUE, EPILOGUE are same. ACT is different it's a List.

//methods for validation

  public void validateThis()
    throws LocalValidationException {...}
  public void validate(Validator v)
    throws StructureValidationException {...}


// marshal methods turn content trees into XML documents

  public void marshal(Marshaller m) throws IOException {...}
  public void unmarshal(Unmarshaller u)
    throws UnmarshalException {...}

// unmarshal methods turn XML files into Java objects

  public static PLAY unmarshal(InputStream in)
    throws UnmarshalException {...}
  public static PLAY unmarshal(XMLScanner xs)
    throws UnmarshalException {...}
  public static PLAY unmarshal(XMLScanner xs, Dispatcher d)
    throws UnmarshalException {...}

// customized methods for equals() hashCode() and toString()

  public boolean equals(Object ob) { ... }
  public int hashCode() { ... }
  public String toString() { ... }
  public static Dispatcher newDispatcher() {...}

// inner class
  private static class ACTPredicate
    implements PredicatedLists.Predicate {...}
}
```

In the next section you'll begin an example that will give you better control over the generated code.

Introducing the user-stories example

One set of artifacts from the extreme programming (XP) methodology is user stories. These small descriptions of how a user will interact with the application are traditionally kept on index cards so that they can easily be sorted, added to, and, if necessary, torn in half. What follows is not a recommendation to store user stories electronically, but simply a manageable and easily understood example of specifying the type of the data being turned into Java objects.

In this example a user story will consist of an identifying number along with a name, a description, and an estimate of how long the story might take to complete. In XP a user story is written by the customer. Programmers can break the story down into tasks they will need to perform in order to deliver the functionality described in the story. A task will again have some sort of identifying number, name, description, and estimate. A task will also have a programmer assigned to it. If you want to track the programmer's velocity, you may want to include the actual time the programmer spends on the task.

The DTD for user stories

Here's UserStories.dtd, a possible DTD for user stories.

```
<!ELEMENT stories  (userStory)* >
<!ELEMENT userStory   (idNumber, name, description, task*,
                        estimate) >
<!ELEMENT task        (idNumber, name, description, programmer,
                        estimate, actual?) >
<!ELEMENT idNumber    (#PCDATA) >
<!ELEMENT name        (#PCDATA) >
<!ELEMENT description (#PCDATA) >
<!ELEMENT estimate    (#PCDATA) >
<!ELEMENT programmer  (#PCDATA) >
<!ELEMENT actual      (#PCDATA) >
<!ATTLIST userStory   isCompleted    CDATA "false" >
<!ATTLIST task        isCompleted    CDATA "false"
                      dateAssigned CDATA #REQUIRED >
```

A minimal binding schema for user stories

You'll need to start with a minimal binding schema that you can save as UserStories. xjs in the same directory as your XML document. You can build in some flexibility by specifying that the root of a tree can be either the `<stories>` element or the `<userStory>` element. Here's the starting point for UserStories.xjs:

```
<xml-java-binding-schema version="1.0ea">
<element name="stories" type="class" root="true" />
<element name="userStory" type="class" root="true" />
</xml-java-binding-schema>
```

Use the schema compiler to generate the Java classes with the following command:

```
java com.sun.tools.xjc.Main "UserStories.dtd" "UserStories.xjs"
```

This command causes the source files Stories.java, Task.java, and UserStory.java to be generated.

Refining the binding schema

One of the benefits of programming in Java is that it is a strongly typed language. The more accurately you can specify the types of the variables you are using, the more the compiler and runtime can help you. In Chapter 11 you saw that XML Schemas enable you to more precisely specify the datatypes. Unfortunately, JAXB can't yet work with XML Schemas, and so you have to add the information in the binding schema.

Assigning an element a primitive type

In the current example, you might prefer that an `<idNumber>` be a number and not just a `String`. Look at the relevant code generated by default for UserStory.java. The variable `idNumber` is a `String`:

```
private String _IdNumber;

public String getIdNumber() {
  return _IdNumber;
}

public void setIdNumber(String _IdNumber) {
  this._IdNumber = _IdNumber;
  if (_IdNumber == null) {
    invalidate();
  }
}
```

You can add the following line to the binding schema to specify that `<idNumber>` should be treated as an `int`:

```
<element name="idNumber" type="value" convert="int" />
```

As a result the generated variable `_IdNumber` is now of type `int` and the accessor methods are also changed. Notice in the following code that the changes include the addition of a `boolean` flag for the existence of `_IdNumber`. An exception is now thrown if `getIdNumber()` is called when `has_IdNumber` is `false`.

```
private int _IdNumber;
private boolean has_IdNumber = false;
public int getIdNumber() {
  if (has_IdNumber) {
    return _IdNumber;
  }
  throw new NoValueException("idNumber");
}

public void setIdNumber(int _IdNumber) {
```

```
    this._IdNumber = _IdNumber;
    has_IdNumber = true;
    invalidate();
  }

  public boolean hasIdNumber() {
    return has_IdNumber;
  }
  public void deleteIdNumber() {
    has_IdNumber = false;
    invalidate();
  }
```

As expected, the same changes are made to the class Task.java.

Assigning an element a non-primitive type

You must perform an extra step in order to assign a non-primitive type to an element. You have to specify a name for the type you're converting to, and then use a `<conversion>` element to specify the actual type. This sounds more confusing than it is. To treat the variable `_IdNumber` as an `Integer`, you can change UserStories.xjs to the following:

```
<xml-java-binding-schema version="1.0ea">
  <element name="stories" type="class" root="true" />
  <element name="userStory" type="class" root="true" />
  <element name="idNumber" type="value"
    convert="DummyPlaceholder" />
  <conversion name="DummyPlaceholder"
    type="java.util.Integer" />
</xml-java-binding-schema>
```

As a general coding practice, you should choose a more descriptive name (`Integer` perhaps) for your `DummyPlaceholder`. Run then preceding code through the schema compiler and your `_IdNumber` will have type `Integer`.

Working with attributes

When working with elements you can make a single change to the element `<idNumber>` and change the type of the generated variable `_IdNumber` in both Task.java and UserStory.java. Now consider the attribute `isCompleted`. It makes more sense to treat `isCompleted` as a `boolean` than as a `String`. Unlike with elements, however, you have to make this change twice: once for the `isCompleted` attribute of the element `<task>` and once for the `isCompleted` attribute of the element `<userStory>`.

The resulting binding schema now looks like this:

```
<xml-java-binding-schema version="1.0ea">
  <element name="stories" type="class" root="true" />
```

```
  <element name="userStory" type="class" root="true" >
    <attribute name="isCompleted" convert="boolean"/>
  </element>
  <element name="task" type="class" >
    <attribute name="isCompleted" convert="boolean" />
  </element>
  <element name="idNumber" type="value" convert="int" />
</xml-java-binding-schema>
```

In Task.java the following variables and methods are related to the attribute `isCompleted`:

```
private boolean _IsCompleted;
  private boolean isDefaulted_IsCompleted = true;
  private final static boolean DEFAULT_ISCOMPLETED = false;

public boolean defaultedIsCompleted() {
  return isDefaulted_IsCompleted;
}

public boolean getIsCompleted() {
  if (!isDefaulted_IsCompleted) {
    return _IsCompleted;
  }
  return DEFAULT_ISCOMPLETED;
}

public void setIsCompleted(boolean _IsCompleted) {
  this._IsCompleted = _IsCompleted;
  isDefaulted_IsCompleted = false;
  invalidate();
}

public boolean hasIsCompleted() {
  return true;
}

public void deleteIsCompleted() {
  isDefaulted_IsCompleted = true;
  invalidate();
}
```

Recall that in the DTD you set the default value of `isCompleted` to `false`. This would also be the default value for a `boolean` instance variable. The schema compiler isn't quite so sophisticated. It makes sure that the default value is stored in the constant `DEFAULT_ISCOMPLETED`. It then adds the flag `isDefaulted_IsCompleted` and sets it to `true`. You can change these entries by making changes to the DTD. For example, you can replace `false` with `#REQUIRED` or, more simply, with `true`.

Handling multiple occurrences

A user story may have more than one task associated with it. Change UserStories.dtd so that a <userStory> can contain only one <task> by removing the asterisk following task, like this:

```
<!ELEMENT userStory   (idNumber, name, description, task,
          estimate) >
```

Use the schema compiler to once again generate Stories.java, Task.java, and UserStory.java. You can see that the items in UserStory.java that correspond to the element <task> are the following:

```
private Task _Task;

public Task getTask() {
  return _Task;
}

public void setTask(Task _Task) {
  this._Task = _Task;
  if (_Task == null) {
    invalidate();
  }
}
```

This code looks like what you expect in a standard Java datatype. The variable _Task is of type Task and is accompanied by the getTask() and setTask () methods. Now you can investigate what changes when <task> can occur more than one time. Re-edit UserStory.dtd to replace the asterisk after the word task, like this:

```
<!ELEMENT userStory   (idNumber, name, description, task*,
          estimate) >
```

Use the schema compiler to again generate the Java source files. You'll see quite a few differences in the relevant code for the element <task> from UserStory.java than for the code you just examined.

The first difference is that the variable _Task is not of type Task but is instead a List created using an inner class called TaskPredicate that implements the interface PredicatedLists. Here's the relevant code snippet.

```
private List _Task = PredicatedLists.createInvalidating(this,
  new TaskPredicate(), new ArrayList());
private PredicatedLists.Predicate pred_Task = new
  TaskPredicate();

private static class TaskPredicate
  implements PredicatedLists.Predicate  {

  public void check(Object ob) {
    if (!(ob instanceof Task)) {
```

```
        throw new InvalidContentObjectException(ob,
         (Task.class));
      }
    }
  }
```

Notice that the accessors are available only to get the entire `List` named `_Task`, to delete the `List` by assigning `null` to the pointer, and to empty the list. No `setTask()` method is available.

```
public List getTask() {
  return _Task;
}

public void deleteTask() {
  _Task = null;
  invalidate();
}

public void emptyTask() {
  _Task = PredicatedLists.createInvalidating(this, pred_Task,
    new ArrayList());
}
```

A final version of the binding schema

The elements `<estimate>` and `<actual>` refer to time. If you think in terms of ideal engineering hours, this should be good enough for the purposes of this example. So convert the types generated by these two elements to `int`s. The attribute `dateAssigned` should be a date. The final binding schema could look like this:

```
<xml-java-binding-schema version="1.0ea">
  <element name="stories" type="class" root="true" />
  <element name="userStory" type="class" root="true" >
    <attribute name="isCompleted" convert="boolean"/>
  </element>
  <element name="task" type="class" >
    <attribute name="isCompleted" convert="boolean" />
    <attribute name="dateAssigned" convert="Date" />
  </element>
  <element name="idNumber" type="value" convert="int" />
  <element name="estimate" type="value" convert="int" />
  <element name="actual"   type="value" convert="int" />
  <conversion name="Date" type="java.util.Date" />
</xml-java-binding-schema>
```

The file UserStory.java

The files generated by the schema compiler tend to be quite long, and so there's no point in listing all of them. It is, however, instructive to look at one of them. UserStory.java, shown in Listing 14-3, includes all the features you've seen already in this chapter and, in addition, contains code for functionality such as validating, marshalling, and unmarshalling, which you'll use in the next section.

Listing 14-3: UserStory.java

```
import java.io.IOException;
import java.io.InputStream;
import java.util.ArrayList;
import java.util.Iterator;
import java.util.List;
import javax.xml.bind.ConversionException;
import javax.xml.bind.Dispatcher;
import javax.xml.bind.DuplicateAttributeException;
import javax.xml.bind.InvalidAttributeException;
import javax.xml.bind.InvalidContentObjectException;
import javax.xml.bind.LocalValidationException;
import javax.xml.bind.MarshallableObject;
import javax.xml.bind.MarshallableRootElement;
import javax.xml.bind.Marshaller;
import javax.xml.bind.MissingContentException;
import javax.xml.bind.NoValueException;
import javax.xml.bind.PredicatedLists;
import javax.xml.bind.PredicatedLists.Predicate;
import javax.xml.bind.RootElement;
import javax.xml.bind.StructureValidationException;
import javax.xml.bind.UnmarshalException;
import javax.xml.bind.Unmarshaller;
import javax.xml.bind.ValidatableObject;
import javax.xml.bind.Validator;
import javax.xml.marshal.XMLScanner;
import javax.xml.marshal.XMLWriter;


public class UserStory
    extends MarshallableRootElement
    implements RootElement
{

    private boolean _IsCompleted;
    private boolean isDefaulted_IsCompleted = true;
    private final static boolean DEFAULT_ISCOMPLETED = false;
    private int _IdNumber;
    private boolean has_IdNumber = false;
    private String _Name;
    private String _Description;
    private List _Task = PredicatedLists.createInvalidating(
      this, new TaskPredicate(), new ArrayList());
    private PredicatedLists.Predicate pred_Task = new
      TaskPredicate();
    private int _Estimate;
    private boolean has_Estimate = false;
```

```
public boolean defaultedIsCompleted() {
    return isDefaulted_IsCompleted;
}

public boolean getIsCompleted() {
    if (!isDefaulted_IsCompleted) {
        return _IsCompleted;
    }
    return DEFAULT_ISCOMPLETED;
}

public void setIsCompleted(boolean _IsCompleted) {
    this._IsCompleted = _IsCompleted;
    isDefaulted_IsCompleted = false;
    invalidate();
}

public boolean hasIsCompleted() {
    return true;
}

public void deleteIsCompleted() {
    isDefaulted_IsCompleted = true;
    invalidate();
}

public int getIdNumber() {
    if (has_IdNumber) {
        return _IdNumber;
    }
    throw new NoValueException("idNumber");
}

public void setIdNumber(int _IdNumber) {
    this._IdNumber = _IdNumber;
    has_IdNumber = true;
    invalidate();
}

public boolean hasIdNumber() {
    return has_IdNumber;
}

public void deleteIdNumber() {
    has_IdNumber = false;
    invalidate();
}

public String getName() {
    return _Name;
```

Continued

Listing 14-3 *(continued)*

```
}

public void setName(String _Name) {
    this._Name = _Name;
    if (_Name == null) {
        invalidate();
    }
}

public String getDescription() {
    return _Description;
}

public void setDescription(String _Description) {
    this._Description = _Description;
    if (_Description == null) {
        invalidate();
    }
}

public List getTask() {
    return _Task;
}

public void deleteTask() {
    _Task = null;
    invalidate();
}

public void emptyTask() {
    _Task = PredicatedLists.createInvalidating(this,
      pred_Task, new ArrayList());
}

public int getEstimate() {
    if (has_Estimate) {
        return _Estimate;
    }
    throw new NoValueException("estimate");
}

public void setEstimate(int _Estimate) {
    this._Estimate = _Estimate;
    has_Estimate = true;
    invalidate();
}

public boolean hasEstimate() {
    return has_Estimate;
}
```

```
    public void deleteEstimate() {
        has_Estimate = false;
        invalidate();
    }

    public void validateThis()
        throws LocalValidationException
    {
        if (!has_IdNumber) {
            throw new MissingContentException("idNumber");
        }
        if (_Name == null) {
            throw new MissingContentException("name");
        }
        if (_Description == null) {
            throw new MissingContentException("description");
        }
        if (!has_Estimate) {
            throw new MissingContentException("estimate");
        }
    }

    public void validate(Validator v)
        throws StructureValidationException
    {
        for (Iterator i = _Task.iterator(); i.hasNext(); ) {
            v.validate(((ValidatableObject) i.next()));
        }
    }

    public void marshal(Marshaller m)
        throws IOException
    {
        XMLWriter w = m.writer();
        w.start("userStory");
        if (!isDefaulted_IsCompleted) {
            w.attribute("isCompleted",
              printBoolean(_IsCompleted));
        }
        if (has_IdNumber) {
            w.leaf("idNumber", Integer.toString(_IdNumber));
        }
        w.leaf("name", _Name.toString());
        w.leaf("description", _Description.toString());
        if (_Task.size()> 0) {
            for (Iterator i = _Task.iterator(); i.hasNext(); )
{

                m.marshal(((MarshallableObject) i.next()));
            }
        }
        if (has_Estimate) {
            w.leaf("estimate", Integer.toString(_Estimate));
```

Continued

Listing 14-3 (continued)

```
        }
        w.end("userStory");
    }

    private static String printBoolean(boolean f) {
        return (f?"true":"false");
    }

    public void unmarshal(Unmarshaller u)
        throws UnmarshalException
    {
        XMLScanner xs = u.scanner();
        Validator v = u.validator();
        xs.takeStart("userStory");
        while (xs.atAttribute()) {
            String an = xs.takeAttributeName();
            if (an.equals("isCompleted")) {
                if (!isDefaulted_IsCompleted) {
                    throw new DuplicateAttributeException(an);
                }
                try {
                    _IsCompleted =
                      readBoolean(xs.takeAttributeValue());
                } catch (Exception x) {
                    throw new ConversionException(an, x);
                }
                isDefaulted_IsCompleted = false;
                continue;
            }
            throw new InvalidAttributeException(an);
        }
        {
            xs.takeStart("idNumber");
            String s;
            if (xs.atChars(XMLScanner.WS_COLLAPSE)) {
                s = xs.takeChars(XMLScanner.WS_COLLAPSE);
            } else {
                s = "";
            }
            try {
                _IdNumber = Integer.parseInt(s);
            } catch (Exception x) {
                throw new ConversionException("idNumber", x);
            }
            has_IdNumber = true;
            xs.takeEnd("idNumber");
        }
        if (xs.atStart("name")) {
            xs.takeStart("name");
            String s;
            if (xs.atChars(XMLScanner.WS_COLLAPSE)) {
```

```
            s = xs.takeChars(XMLScanner.WS_COLLAPSE);
        } else {
            s = "";
        }
        try {
            _Name = String.valueOf(s);
        } catch (Exception x) {
            throw new ConversionException("name", x);
        }
        xs.takeEnd("name");
    }
    if (xs.atStart("description")) {
        xs.takeStart("description");
        String s;
        if (xs.atChars(XMLScanner.WS_COLLAPSE)) {
            s = xs.takeChars(XMLScanner.WS_COLLAPSE);
        } else {
            s = "";
        }
        try {
            _Description = String.valueOf(s);
        } catch (Exception x) {
            throw new ConversionException(
              "description", x);
        }
        xs.takeEnd("description");
    }
    {
        List l = PredicatedLists.create(this, pred_Task,
          new ArrayList());
        while (xs.atStart("task")) {
            l.add(((Task) u.unmarshal()));
        }
        _Task = PredicatedLists.createInvalidating(this,
          pred_Task, l);
    }
    {
        xs.takeStart("estimate");
        String s;
        if (xs.atChars(XMLScanner.WS_COLLAPSE)) {
            s = xs.takeChars(XMLScanner.WS_COLLAPSE);
        } else {
            s = "";
        }
        try {
            _Estimate = Integer.parseInt(s);
        } catch (Exception x) {
            throw new ConversionException("estimate", x);
        }
        has_Estimate = true;
        xs.takeEnd("estimate");
    }
```

Continued

Listing 14-3 *(continued)*

```
    xs.takeEnd("userStory");
}

private static boolean readBoolean(String s)
    throws ConversionException
{
    if (s.equals("true")) {
        return true;
    }
    if (s.equals("false")) {
        return false;
    }
    throw new ConversionException(s);
}

public static UserStory unmarshal(InputStream in)
    throws UnmarshalException
{
    return unmarshal(XMLScanner.open(in));
}

public static UserStory unmarshal(XMLScanner xs)
    throws UnmarshalException
{
    return unmarshal(xs, newDispatcher());
}

public static UserStory unmarshal(XMLScanner xs,
  Dispatcher d)
    throws UnmarshalException
{
    return ((UserStory) d.unmarshal(xs,
     (UserStory.class)));
}

public boolean equals(Object ob) {
    if (this == ob) {
        return true;
    }
    if (!(ob instanceof UserStory)) {
        return false;
    }
    UserStory tob = ((UserStory) ob);
    if (!isDefaulted_IsCompleted) {
        if (tob.isDefaulted_IsCompleted) {
            return false;
        }
        if (_IsCompleted!= tob._IsCompleted) {
            return false;
        }
    } else {
```

```
        if (!tob.isDefaulted_IsCompleted) {
            return false;
        }
    }
    if (has_IdNumber) {
        if (!tob.has_IdNumber) {
            return false;
        }
        if (_IdNumber!= tob._IdNumber) {
            return false;
        }
    } else {
        if (tob.has_IdNumber) {
            return false;
        }
    }
    if (_Name!= null) {
        if (tob._Name == null) {
            return false;
        }
        if (!_Name.equals(tob._Name)) {
            return false;
        }
    } else {
        if (tob._Name!= null) {
            return false;
        }
    }
    if (_Description!= null) {
        if (tob._Description == null) {
            return false;
        }
        if (!_Description.equals(tob._Description)) {
            return false;
        }
    } else {
        if (tob._Description!= null) {
            return false;
        }
    }
    if (_Task!= null) {
        if (tob._Task == null) {
            return false;
        }
        if (!_Task.equals(tob._Task)) {
            return false;
        }
    } else {
        if (tob._Task!= null) {
            return false;
        }
    }
```

Continued

Listing 14-3 *(continued)*

```
        if (has_Estimate) {
            if (!tob.has_Estimate) {
                return false;
            }
            if (_Estimate!= tob._Estimate) {
                return false;
            }
        } else {
            if (tob.has_Estimate) {
                return false;
            }
        }
        return true;
    }

    public int hashCode() {
        int h = 0;
        h = ((31 *h)+(_IsCompleted? 137 : 139));
        h = ((67 *h)+(isDefaulted_IsCompleted? 59 : 61));
        h = ((31 *h)+ _IdNumber);
        h = ((127 *h)+((_Name!= null)?_Name.hashCode(): 0));
        h = ((127 *h)+((_Description!=
          null)?_Description.hashCode(): 0));
        h = ((127 *h)+((_Task!= null)?_Task.hashCode(): 0));
        h = ((31 *h)+ _Estimate);
        return h;
    }

    public String toString() {
        StringBuffer sb = new StringBuffer("<<userStory");
        sb.append(" isCompleted=");
        sb.append(printBoolean(getIsCompleted()));
        if (has_IdNumber) {
            sb.append(" idNumber=");
            sb.append(Integer.toString(_IdNumber));
        }
        if (_Name!= null) {
            sb.append(" name=");
            sb.append(_Name.toString());
        }
        if (_Description!= null) {
            sb.append(" description=");
            sb.append(_Description.toString());
        }
        if (_Task!= null) {
            sb.append(" task=");
            sb.append(_Task.toString());
        }
        if (has_Estimate) {
            sb.append(" estimate=");
            sb.append(Integer.toString(_Estimate));
```

```
        }
        sb.append(">>");
        return sb.toString();
    }

    public static Dispatcher newDispatcher() {
        return Stories.newDispatcher();
    }


    private static class TaskPredicate
        implements PredicatedLists.Predicate
    {


        public void check(Object ob) {
            if (!(ob instanceof Task)) {
                throw new InvalidContentObjectException(ob,
(Task.class));
            }
        }

    }

}
```

Using the JAXB Bindings

You can think of DTDs and Java classes as having the following correspondence. Java classes are used to produce objects; you can think of a class as a template for an object. In the same way, a valid XML document corresponds to a schema (in this case a DTD). In the preceding section, you created Java classes from a DTD so that you now have a mapping of what you can think of as templates. In this section, you'll work with the instances of the DTD and these classes. You will take an XML file and convert it to a Java object or create from scratch a Java object that could have come from a valid XML file. Conversely, you will save the Java object as a valid XML file. You'll look at both procedures in this section.

Unmarshalling: Java objects from XML documents

In this section, you'll begin to look at the process of serializing and deserializing. In this context, you will refer to this process as marshalling and unmarshalling. Start with this valid XML document called SampleStories.xml, which you can use to create Java objects:

```
<?xml version="1.0" encoding="UTF-8"?>
<!DOCTYPE userStory SYSTEM "UserStories.dtd">
<userStory isCompleted="false">
  <idNumber> 7 </idNumber>
```

```
    <name> Make Lunch </name>
    <description> Prepare something to eat. </description>
    <estimate> 1 </estimate>
  </userStory>
```

You can convert this document to a Java object by calling the `unmarshal()` method with the signature shown in this snippet:

```
public static UserStory unmarshal(InputStream in)
```

This method calls the `unmarshal()` method in `javax.xml.bind.Dispatcher`, which in turn builds the content tree and then validates it against the DTD that the schema compiler uses to generate the Java classes.

In your custom application, you will use the static `unmarshal()` method in an instance of `UserStory`. You will pass the method a `FileInputStream` constructed with the `File` constructed from your XML document. In the following small example, you can see how the content tree is built from the file SampleStories.xml and then saved as `aUserStory`:

```
import java.io.File;
import java.io.FileInputStream;

public class UserStoriesApp {
  public static UserStory aUserStory = new UserStory();

  public static void main(String[] args) throws Exception {
    File story = null;
    FileInputStream fileInputStream=null;
    try {
      story = new File("SampleStories.xml");
      fileInputStream = new FileInputStream(story);
      aUserStory = aUserStory.unmarshal(fileInputStream);
    } catch(Exception e) {
      e.printStackTrace();
    } finally {
      fileInputStream.close();
    }
     System.out.print(aUserStory.toString());
  }
}
```

For kicks, the `toString()` method prints the resulting `UserStory` to the console window. Here's what you'll see in the console window:

```
<<userStory isCompleted=false idNumber=7 name=MakeLunch
description=Prepare something to eat. task=[] estimate=1>>
```

Adding to the content tree

You just created a content tree from a valid XML file; now you'll use Java code to add a `Task` to the `UserStory`. You can use this technique to create the entire content tree from scratch. Here the `addNewTask()` method adds all the required elements and attributes. The changes are in boldface in the following code:

```
import java.io.File;
import java.io.FileInputStream;
import java.util.List;
import java.util.Date;

public class UserStoriesApp2 {
  public static UserStory aUserStory = new UserStory();

  public static void main(String[] args) throws Exception {
    UserStoriesApp2 ua2 = new UserStoriesApp2();
    File story = null;
    FileInputStream fileInputStream=null;
    try {
      story = new File("SampleStories.xml");
      fileInputStream = new FileInputStream(story);
      aUserStory = aUserStory.unmarshal(fileInputStream);
      ua2.addNewTask(aUserStory);
    } catch(Exception e) {
      e.printStackTrace();
    } finally {
      fileInputStream.close();
    }
     System.out.print(aUserStory.toString());
  }
  private void addNewTask(UserStory taskUserStory){
    List myTasks = taskUserStory.getTask();
    Task purchaseTask = new Task();
    purchaseTask.setIdNumber(1);
    purchaseTask.setName("Buy Lunch Items");
    purchaseTask.setDescription("Get a jar of peanutbutter and"
      + " a loaf of bread.");
    purchaseTask.setProgrammer("Justin");
    purchaseTask.setEstimate(2);
    purchaseTask.setDateAssigned(new Date());
    myTasks.add(purchaseTask);
  }
}
```

Now, when you compile and run this application, the output includes your newly created task. Here's the output with the changes in boldface:

```
<<userStory isCompleted=false idNumber=7 name=Make Lunch
description=Prepare something to eat. task=[<<task
isCompleted=false dateAssigned=Sat Sep 22 17:31:31 EDT 2001
```

```
idNumber=1 name=Buy Lunch Items description=Get a jar of
peanutbutter and a loaf of bread. programmer=Justin
estimate=2>>] estimate=1>>
```

Notice that although you didn't set isCompleted in the Java code it has the correct default in the generated content tree. This behavior is taken care of for you because you provided a default value in the DTD. If you were to leave out the <estimate> element for the <task> element, none would be furnished for you. To make certain that you haven't left anything out, your next step should be to validate the object.

Validating your objects

When you are moving from XML to Java code you know that a valid XML document will correctly map to the objects for the classes that JAXB has generated from the DTD. When you start with a Java object, however, you can't be sure of this. Any time you have created your own content tree or modified an existing content tree, you should validate before you save the object back to XML.

In this example you merely need to add a call to the object's validate() method to be sure that the corresponding XML document will be valid against the DTD. The new main() should look like this:

```
public static void main(String[] args) throws Exception {
  UserStoriesApp2 ua2 = new UserStoriesApp2();
  File story = null;
  FileInputStream fileInputStream=null;
  try {
    story = new File("SampleStories.xml");
    fileInputStream = new FileInputStream(story);
      aUserStory = aUserStory.unmarshal(fileInputStream);
      ua2.addNewTask(aUserStory);
      aUserStory.validate();
    } catch(Exception e) {
      e.printStackTrace();
    } finally {
      fileInputStream.close();
    }
    System.out.print(aUserStory.toString());
  }
```

Compile and run the new version of UserStoriesApp2. You shouldn't notice any differences. Now comment out the following line in the addNewTask() method, as follows:

```
purchaseTask.setEstimate(2);
```

The code will compile correctly, but when you run it you will get a javax.xml.bind.MissingContentException that informs you that the element estimate is missing. Your validation is working. Uncomment the line.

Marshalling: Java objects to XML documents

To convert the validated content tree to an XML document, you need only call the `marshal()` method. As you would expect, this process is similar to unmarshalling. You'll create a `File` that you'll write to, and then you'll create a `FileOutputStream` that you'll use to write your content tree to an XML file. Listing 14-4 shows the final version of UserStoriesApp2.java with the changes in boldface.

Listing 14-4: Final version of UserStoriesApp2.java

```
import java.io.File;
import java.io.FileInputStream;
import java.io.FileOutputStream;
import java.util.List;
import java.util.Date;

public class UserStoriesApp2 {
  public static UserStory aUserStory = new UserStory();

  public static void main(String[] args) throws Exception {
    UserStoriesApp2 ua2 = new UserStoriesApp2();
    //File story = null;
    FileInputStream fileInputStream=null;
    FileOutputStream fileOutputStream=null;
    try {
      // turn the XML file into a content tree
      File story = new File("SampleStories.xml");
      fileInputStream = new FileInputStream(story);
      aUserStory = aUserStory.unmarshal(fileInputStream);
      // add to the tree and validate it
      ua2.addNewTask(aUserStory);
      aUserStory.validate();
      // turn the content tree into an XML file
      File alteredStories = new File("alteredStories.xml");
      fileOutputStream = new FileOutputStream(alteredStories);
      aUserStory.marshal(fileOutputStream);
    } catch(Exception e) {
      e.printStackTrace();
    } finally {
      fileInputStream.close();
      fileOutputStream.close();
    }
    //System.out.print(aUserStory.toString());
  }
  private void addNewTask(UserStory taskUserStory){
    List myTasks = taskUserStory.getTask();
    Task purchaseTask = new Task();
    purchaseTask.setIdNumber(1);
    purchaseTask.setName("Buy Lunch Items");
```

Continued

Listing 14-4 *(continued)*

```
    purchaseTask.setDescription("Get a jar of peanutbutter and
a loaf of bread.");
    purchaseTask.setProgrammer("Justin");
    purchaseTask.setEstimate(2);
    purchaseTask.setDateAssigned(new Date());
    myTasks.add(purchaseTask);
  }
}
```

Compile and run UserStoriesApp2.java, and you will produce this file, named alteredStories.xml:

```
<?xml version="1.0" encoding="UTF-8"?>

<userStory isCompleted="false">
  <idNumber>7</idNumber>
  <name>Make Lunch</name>
  <description>Prepare something to eat.</description>
  <task dateAssigned="Sat Sep 22 18:06:33 EDT 2001">
    <idNumber>1</idNumber>
    <name>Buy Lunch Items</name>
    <description>Get a jar of peanutbutter and a loaf of
      bread.</description>
    <programmer>Justin</programmer>
    <estimate>2</estimate></task>
  <estimate>1</estimate></userStory>
```

It may appear that two things are missing. First, alteredStories.xml contains no document type declaration. You could argue that this information is no longer needed, or you could argue that it would still be nice to have. In any case, it's not there. Second, the `isCompleted` attribute for the `<task>` element is not there. When you printed the file to the console window, you saw that it had the value of `false` and yet, because you did not explicitly set it, the attribute is not written back to the XML file.

Extending the classes the schema compiler generates

When you use your favorite RAD tools to quickly generate a GUI for your desktop application, the next step is to customize it. The same is true when you're dealing with JAXB. The schema compiler gets you up and running quickly, but it can't provide the custom functionality that you're looking for. Your next task is to extend functionality by subclassing the Java classes generated by the schema compiler. In this example, you'll calculate the total time estimated for a user story by totaling up the individual estimates for the tasks.

The SampleStories2.xml document

To keep the Java code clean, you won't add to the XML content in your application. Here's a document called SampleStories2.xml, which includes a user story that already has several tasks defined:

```
<?xml version="1.0" encoding="UTF-8"?>
<!DOCTYPE userStory SYSTEM "UserStories.dtd">
  <userStory isCompleted="false">
    <idNumber> 7 </idNumber>
    <name> Have Lunch </name>
    <description> Enjoy a mid-day meal. </description>
    <task dateAssigned="Sat Sep 22 18:06:33 EDT 2001">
      <idNumber>1</idNumber>
      <name>Buy Lunch Items</name>
      <description>Get a jar of peanutbutter and a loaf of
        bread.</description>
      <programmer>Justin</programmer>
      <estimate>2</estimate>
      <actual>2</actual>
    </task>
    <task dateAssigned="Sat Sep 22 18:07:33 EDT 2001">
      <idNumber>2</idNumber>
      <name>Eat lunch</name>
      <description>Put peanutbutter on bread and eat
        it.</description>
      <programmer>Daniel</programmer>
      <estimate>1</estimate>
      <actual>2</actual>
    </task>
    <task dateAssigned="Sat Sep 22 18:09:33 EDT 2001">
      <idNumber>3</idNumber>
      <name>Clean up.</name>
      <description>Put away items and cleaan up
        kitchen.</description>
      <programmer>Justin</programmer>
      <estimate>1</estimate>
      <actual>1</actual>
    </task>
    <estimate> 1 </estimate>
  </userStory>
```

The final `<estimate>` element is in boldface because you'll replace the input value of `1` with the total of the estimates for the tasks. The DTD requires that you provide an estimate in order for SampleStories2.xml to be a valid document. Any `int` will do, however, as you will be ignoring this value.

Subclassing UserStory.java

The source code for UserStory.java was produced for you by the schema compiler. It provides basic functionality that you can easily extend. Create a subclass of UserStory called ChangedUserStory. In this class you will introduce a method called calculateEstimate(), which will calculate the value of the <estimate> child element of <userStory> by totaling up the values of the <estimate> elements in the <task> children elements of <userStory>. While you're at it you can change getEstimate() so that it recalculates the value of _Estimate. ChangedUserStory.java isn't very big. Here it is in its entirety:

```
import java.util.Iterator;
import java.util.List;

public class ChangedUserStory extends UserStory {

  public int getEstimate() {
    return calculateEstimate();
  }

  public int calculateEstimate(){
    int estimate=0;
    List task = getTask();
    Iterator i = task.iterator();
    while( i.hasNext()) {
      estimate += ((Task)i.next()).getEstimate();
    }
    setEstimate( estimate);
    return estimate;
  }
}
```

Using the subclass

What remains is for you to get an instance of ChangedUserStory from the XML file instead of an instance of UserStory. The key to changing your application can be found in the unmarshal() methods of UserStory. Remember that the UserStory.unmarshal() methods end up calling the unmarshal() method in the class javax.xml.bind.Dispatcher. You can override these methods in ChangedUserStory, or you can make the following changes to UserStoriesApp.java.

First, get a handle to a Dispatcher object and call its register() method to indicate that you want a call to unmarshal a UserStory to be replaced by a call to unmarshal a ChangedUserStory. Second, call the Dispatcher object's unmarshal() method and cast the returned object to type ChangedUserStory. The remainder of the changes in the file UserStoriesApp3.java are name changes, except for the call to the getEstimate() method that you overrode. This call will tell you whether the application is actually using the ChangedUserStory class.

```
import java.io.File;
import java.io.FileInputStream;
```

```
import javax.xml.bind.Dispatcher;

public class UserStoriesApp3 {

  public static ChangedUserStory anotherUserStory
    = new ChangedUserStory();

  public static void main(String[] args) throws Exception {

    UserStoriesApp2 ua2 = new UserStoriesApp2();
    FileInputStream fileInputStream=null;
    try {
      File story = new File("SampleStories2.xml");
      fileInputStream = new FileInputStream(story);

      Dispatcher d= UserStory.newDispatcher();
      d.register(UserStory.class, ChangedUserStory.class);
      anotherUserStory =
       (ChangedUserStory)d.unmarshal(fileInputStream);
      anotherUserStory.getEstimate();
    } catch(Exception e) {
      e.printStackTrace();
    } finally {
      fileInputStream.close();
    }
    System.out.print(anotherUserStory.toString());
  }
}
```

Compile and run this file, and you will see a listing of the contents of SampleStories2.xml in the console window — with one important change. The value of the final `<estimate>` element will have been changed from `1` to the calculated value of `4`.

Summary

The theme of this chapter is that XML is easily changed. Because an XML document is self-describing, it is easy to change it into another format or into another XML document that conforms to someone else's DTD. You took a closer look at how to move back and forth between XML documents and Java objects representing the same data. You learned the following:

- ✦ How to use Cascading Style Sheets (CSS) to display XML documents. The advantage of this method is that the presentation is more attractive in browsers that support this feature. The disadvantage is that the document itself isn't changed, and the way in which the document is rendered is very browser-dependent.

✦ How to use Extensible Style Sheet Language Transformations (XSLT) to actually change an XML document into other formats. In this chapter's example, you changed an XML document into an HTML document.

✦ How to use XSLT style sheets to transform an XML document conforming to one DTD into an XML document conforming to another DTD. This is a particularly useful ability when you're sharing data between organizations that have developed different ways of thinking about how the data should be organized. If you can come up with a reasonable mapping from one organization to the other, then this process can be automated.

✦ That the Java APIs for XML Binding (JAXB) enable you to take a DTD and transform it into Java classes that can be used to represent data stored in an XML document, which can then be validated against that DTD. The transformation of data stored in these XML documents to and from Java objects is called *marshalling* and *unmarshalling*, respectively. This transformation simplifies the task of working with data persisted in XML documents.

✦ ✦ ✦

Abstracting the System

P A R T

V

✦ ✦ ✦ ✦

In This Part

✦ ✦ ✦ ✦

Exploring the RMI Mechanism

✦ ✦ ✦ ✦

In This Chapter

Writing and accessing remote objects

Creating stubs and skeletons with the RMI compiler

Using the RMI registry

Sending objects across a network connection

Running remote services using the RMI daemon

✦ ✦ ✦ ✦

If you have Java on the client and the server, you can use Remote Method Invocation (RMI) to communicate between them. The client will have a piece of stub code that acts as a proxy for particular classes on the server. The client interacts with this code as if it were the remote object itself. By this we mean that you use the same methods, not that there aren't additional considerations that could affect your performance. You are passing objects back and forth across the network: You should consider carefully what it is you are passing and how frequently you are passing it.

In this chapter, we'll explore the RMI mechanism by presenting an example of having a remote Java client interact with Java classes on the server. We'll look at developing a distributed application first in a single directory, then in two directories on a single machine, then on two different machines, and finally using the RMI daemon. Each iteration of this example will introduce a new issue. Initially, nothing is really being passed back and forth, as everything is in the same CLASSPATH. This approach will enable us to discuss specific features of RMI rather than introducing them all at once.

The Components of a Basic RMI Application

We'll begin our examination of RMI with an example that enables you to create each of the components in a basic RMI application. In the next section, we will expand upon this example to create an actual distributed, albeit small, application. For now, we will concentrate on creating the interface. In this case, you will pass in a `String` called `name`, and the

`Greeter` will respond with the `String` `Hello` *`name`*. Of course, you don't need a distributed application to print a personalized greeting for a user. You can accomplish the same task using a servlet or JSP as we mentioned in Chapter 3, "Creating Dynamic Content with Servlets," and Chapter 4, "Using JavaServer Pages," even in an enterprise setting. Because you have gotten so adept at greeting others by name, this example will enable you to concentrate on the RMI implementation details.

After creating the remote interface `Greeter`, you will then create an implementation of it that will act as your remote object. The convention is to name this class `GreeterImpl`. The final class that you will hand-code for the server is `GreeterMain`. You'll use this to start up the `Greeter` service. Finally, you will need to write `WelcomeGuest` to act as the client requesting the service.

The logistics of actually running an RMI application are slightly more complicated than those shown in this section. We start with this example to clearly show the roles played by the different components. In the next section, we will explain how to specify the security, the codebase, and how to run the example over a network. We have found that many online tutorials only include examples wherein all the files are on a single machine in the same directory.

Place all the files in this example in the following directory, which we will refer to as the `Greetings` directory for short:

```
C:\J2EEBible\rmi\Greetings
```

Even with four classes running from a single directory, you will still need to start three processes to run the example. (We will explain how to run this example at the end of this section.)

The Remote interface

In order for the client and server to communicate, they have to agree on what messages may be communicated. Frequently, you want to expose the methods that can be invoked without sharing how they are implemented. This is best accomplished in Java by means of an interface. In this example, the `Greeter` interface will contain the single method `greetByName()`, which takes a `String` as an argument and returns another `String`. The following is the entire Greeter.java file:

```
import java.rmi.Remote;
import java.rmi.RemoteException;

public interface Greeter extends Remote {
  String greetByName( String name) throws RemoteException;
}
```

Of course, you could have combined the two import statements into the single statement `import java.rmi.*;` if you'd wanted. Notice that our interface extends the `Remote` interface, meaning that it is what is known as a *marker interface*. `Remote` doesn't contain any methods or constants and is just used to mark the implementing classes as being of a type that extends `Remote`. Notice also that every method must throw a `RemoteException`. (You'll see this again in Chapter 20, when we discuss Jini.) Whenever you are using remote objects or communicating across a network, Java requires you to allow for network failures and problems retrieving what you need from the remote JVM.

The `Greeter` interface serves two purposes. First, it specifies what must be contained in an implementation of the interface. This tells you or whoever will be writing the `GreeterImpl` class what must be included in it. Second, it tells the client what it can expect from an implementation. In a distributed system, you would have a copy of `Greeter.class` on the server and another copy on each client.

Implementing the Remote interface on the server

Your next task is to create the class that will live on the server and provide the implementation of the `Greeter` service. The highlighted portion in the following code completes the promise made by the `Greeter` interface. We'll call this `GreeterImpl.java` and create it with the following code, which you save in the same `Greetings` directory:

```
import java.rmi.RemoteException;
import java.rmi.server.UnicastRemoteObject;

public class GreeterImpl extends UnicastRemoteObject implements
  Greeter {

  public GreeterImpl() throws RemoteException{
    super();
    // your custom set up code goes here
  }

  public String greetByName( String name) {
    return "Hello "+ name;
  }
}
```

The class `GreeterImpl` also extends the class `java.rmi.server.UnicastRemoteObject`. This is the easiest way to create a remote object in this situation; you could also implement your own remote object or extend the class `java.rmi.server.RemoteServer`. The point is that `UnicastRemoteObject` implements the details needed for RMI, so you may as well take advantage of it.

In particular, the `exportObject()` method is defined in `UnicastRemoteObject` as a static method that makes your remote object available to incoming calls from various clients. If you are determined to roll your own, you will have to take advantage of the exportObject() method in any of its three signatures from your constructor. The constructor of a UnicastRemoteObject both creates an instance of the class and exports it. Your GreeterImpl no-argument constructor will instantiate a GreeterImpl object and then export it to make it available to receive incoming calls on an anonymous port. The result is that, because the exportObject() could throw a RemoteException, you need to declare that the constructor that contains exportObject() throws a RemoteException.

You could include a main() in GreeterImpl, but then the implementation would no longer be clean and straightforward. What remains to be written for the server side is a class GreaterMain that creates an instance of GreeterImpl and binds it to a name in the registry. Other classes will be used on the server, but they will be automatically generated by the rmic tool.

Starting up the service

Next, create the class that will start up the Greeter service. For now, we are avoiding the issue of a security manager. Security doesn't add much complexity to writing the source code, but it does complicate running the application. (We'll offer a more complete example in the next section.) If the JVM complains about access when you run the example, you will have to look ahead to the next section and include the security policy.

For now, there are only two steps: Create an instance of the GreeterImpl class, and bind it in the rmiregistry. Either of these operations could throw a RemoteException and must be called from inside a try block. The rebind() method can also throw either an AccessException or a MalformedURLException. The following code creates an instance of the GreeterImpl class:

```
import java.rmi.Naming;
import java.rmi.server.UnicastRemoteObject;

public class GreeterMain  {
   public static void main(String args[]){
    try {
      GreeterImpl greeterImpl = new GreeterImpl();
      Naming.rebind("SayHello", greeterImpl);
    }
    catch (Exception e) {
      System.out.println(e.getMessage());
    }
  }
}
```

You use the static method rebind() to associate an object with a name. It has the following signature:

```
public static void rebind(String name, Remote obj)
  throws RemoteException, MalformedURLException;
```

Other useful methods from the server's point of view are `bind()` and `unbind()`. You'll need to use `Naming` from the client to get a handle to a `Remote` object using its name. In this particular example, we have an instance of the `GreeterImpl` class that we call `greeterImpl`. That's a pretty silly name. We'd much rather refer to it as `SayHello` and so that's how we register it. Alternatively, you can add in the host and port information and specify `name` as `"//localhost:1099/SayHello"`. You can, of course, specify any other `host:port` pair as the first part of `name`. The default for `host` is the local host, and the `port` defaults to `1099`. If you decide to use a different port, you need to also specify this port when you start up the `rmiregistry`.

Turning to the client

From the client end, you would like to get hold of an object that implements the `Greeter` interface and have it greet you by the name you pass in. The code that does this is contained in the following `WelcomeGuest.java` file:

```
import java.rmi.RemoteException;
import java.rmi.Naming;

public class WelcomeGuest {

  public WelcomeGuest(String guestName){
    try{
      Greeter greeter = (Greeter) Naming.lookup("SayHello");
      String greeting = greeter.greetByName(guestName);
      System.out.println(greeting);
    }
    catch (Exception e){
      System.out.println(e.getMessage());
    }
  }
  public static void main(String args[]){
    String guestName = (args.length == 0)?" ":args[0];
    WelcomeGuest welcomeGuest = new WelcomeGuest(guestName);
  }
}
```

Quite a bit is happening inside the `try` block. First, you get a `Remote` object by invoking `Naming.lookup()`. The `lookup()` method has the following signature:

```
public static Remote lookup(String name)
  throws NotBoundException, MalformedURLException,
  RemoteException
```

Here, `name` will match that set by the first argument of `Naming.rebind()`. In this case, you can be a little lazy and refer to the `Remote` object by its name, `SayHello`, as the local host for the client and for the server is the same.

Now here's where the magic kicks in. You will hear it said that RMI means that there is no difference between making a remote and a local call. In one sense, this is completely untrue: There will be a performance difference between making a call within a single VM and making a call over a wire. This example, however, highlights the sense in which it is true. It appears that the `Naming.lookup()` method returns a `Remote` object that you cast to `Greeter`. From then on, you treat it as a `Greeter`. This means that you invoke a method such as `greetByName()` as if the object were sitting locally on your own machine. We'll look more carefully at what's actually going on later in the chapter when we discuss serialization.

Once you have assigned your `Greeter` object to `greeter`, perform the following method call:

```
greeter.greetByName(guestName);
```

The implementation of `greetByName()` is on the server. This simple method call means that you have to send a message to the server, call the method and return the result across the wire. Although the programmer doesn't need to worry about programming the transport and the transformation, you should consider the decrease in performance resulting from this remote call. We'll return to this point later in the section "Performance problems." Tool-generated helper classes are available that will help you with these remote calls. Your next step is to compile the source code and then generate these helpers.

Compiling the code

You need to compile the server source files and the client source files using javac or another standard compiler. In this case, all the files sit in the same directory, and so you can navigate to that directory and just type in `javac *.java` from the command line. This generates the four `class` files: `Greeter.class`, `GreeterImpl.class`, `GreeterMain.class`, and `WelcomeGuest.class`. Now run the RMI compiler on the `GreeterImpl` class file using the following command:

```
rmic GreeterImpl
```

If you are interested in seeing the source code for these generated files, you can use the `-keep` option. You may find it useful to see how the `greetByName()` method is transformed in this process. To see what the compiler is doing, use the `-verbose` flag.

The `rmic` application will generate a stub and a skeleton `class` file named `GreeterImpl_Stub` and `GreeterImpl_Skel`, respectively. `GreeterImpl_Stub` is a proxy for `GreeterImpl`. While `GreeterImpl` lives on the server, `GreeterImpl_Stub` will be deployed to the client's machine. Client calls to `GreeterImpl` will actually become calls to `GreeterImpl_Stub` that are in turn communicated back to `GreeterImpl`. The generated stub implements the interfaces `java.rmi.Remote` and `Greeter`. It extends the class `java.rmi.server.RemoteStub`. Currently, `RemoteStub` consists of two constructors, one of which specifies the remote reference for this `RemoteStub`.

With JRMP stubs, the method calls might also need to pass through the `GreeterImpl_Skel` class. The skeleton file lives on the server and communicates the call from the stub to the implementing class. The default behavior for `rmic` is to generate a stub and a skeleton that are compatible with both the Java 1.1 and the Java 1.2 JRMP stub-protocol versions. You can specify one version or another by using the option `-v1.1` or `-v1.2`. (The default is equivalent to the option `-vcompat`.) In version 1.2, skeletons are no longer required, and the interface `java.rmi.server.Skeleton` has been deprecated. So the call

```
rmic -v1.2 GreeterImpl
```

will create a stub and not a skeleton.

You don't need to use either version of JRMP as your protocol. You can set the `-iiop` option if you would like to generate stubs and their corresponding server-side objects, called ties (instead of skeletons), for the IIOP protocol. The examples in this chapter will use JRMP.

Running the RMI application

You will have to run three processes to get this example going. (The directions for running the example will change when we move to two different directories in the next section.) The commands are those for running Java on a Windows machine.

Begin by starting the `rmiregistry`. This is the naming registry that will enable you to bind a URL formatted name to a remote object. Open up a command window and navigate to the Greetings directory. Now start up the registry with the following command:

```
rmiregistry
```

The `rmiregistry` will listen on port 1099. If you want to have it listen on another port, you can instead enter `rmiregistry` *`xxxx`*, where *`xxxx`* is the name of the port you'd prefer. If you decide to use a different port, you must make the corresponding changes to the GreeterMain file. The registry will start up quietly and give you no indication that it is doing anything.

The second step is to start up your server. This step will soon involve specifying a security policy and the location of a codebase. For now open up another command window and navigate to the Greetings directory. Start up the `Greeter` service and register it with the `rmiregistry` with the following command:

```
java GreeterMain
```

You could include some sort of `System.out.println()` statement to print a message to the console indicating that the service is up and running. For now, we'll assume that the lack of an exception means that all is well and proceed to run the client.

The third step is to start up the client. Again, when your code is no longer in a single directory, you will need to specify a security policy. The client is allowing code from the server to arrive and execute. You need to set the permissions to allow this to happen once you are actually transporting code. For now, you can start up the client by again navigating to the Greetings directory in a new console window. Run the client with the following ordinary `java` command:

```
java WelcomeGuest
```

The client asks the `rmiregistry` for a particular object that implements the `Greeter` interface, and then the client invokes a method on the remote object. You'll get the response `Hello`. You can get a more personalized greeting by passing in a particular name. The command `java WelcomeGuest Rose` will elicit the response `Hello Rose`. Your next step will be to deploy this application to two different machines.

Running a Distributed Version

Now you are ready to run this as a distributed example. So far you have had all of the classes in the same classpath so that no real remote invocation was needed. The runtime is smart enough that if none is needed, none is invoked. If you split up the application, you will need to include the interfaces in both distributions. Because code is actually moving, you'll need to specify a security policy and a codebase. Once you're running from two directories, a minor tweak is all you need to do in order to run from two different machines. In the next section, you'll run a simple HTTP server to actually communicate over the wire.

Splitting the files into two directories

By the end of this section you will make changes to some of the files you created in the last section. For now, just split them up into a client directory and a server directory. Inside of C:\J2EEBible you have created the subdirectories GreetingServer and GreetingClient:

GreetingServer will need to contain the following files:

- ✦ GreeterMain.java, which starts up the greeter service.
- ✦ GreeterImpl.java, which provides the implementation of the service.
- ✦ Greeter.java, which provides the interface for the service.

GreetingClient will need to contain the following files:

- ✦ WelcomeGuest.java, which contains the client request for the service.
- ✦ Greeter.java, which provides the interface for the service.

So you've taken your four files and put the two that were obviously server-side files in the GreetingServer directory and the one that was obviously a client-side file in the GreetingClient directory. The interface belongs in both directories. The server needs access to it so that it knows the details of the `Remote` interface being implemented. The client needs access to it because you are casting the handle to the remote object to be of type `Greeter`.

Go ahead and compile these files in their separate directories using `javac *.java`. Then use the RMI compiler to generate the stub (and possibly skeleton). Now that you've separated the files into two directories you can more clearly see that these files sit on the server side. Generate these extra classes with the command `rmic GreeterImpl` as before.

Before going on to the next section, try to run the application as you did before. From the command line, enter `rmiregistry`. Now open a new command window and navigate to the inside of GreetingServer and type in `java GreeterMain`. You should see a message like the following:

```
access denied (java.net.SocketPermission ... connect,resolve)
```

The ellipses stand for the omitted machine address and port 1099. The point is that there is a problem getting permission to access a needed resource. The solution to this problem is to create and reference a security policy. You don't need this step when you are working from a single directory because the server and the client see the same exact CLASSPATH. No code has to be moved. Now you're going to need to move a stub between the two VMs with different classpaths. You'll need to make sure the permissions are adequate for doing so.

Creating and calling a security policy

Next you'll create an `RMISecurityManager` and set it to be the `System`'s security manager. You'll do this in both the server file GreeterMain.java and the client file WelcomeGuest.java. You change GreeterMain by importing the `RMISecurityManager` class and then using the `System.setSecurityManager()` method, as shown in the following code:

```
import java.rmi.Naming;
import java.rmi.RMISecurityManager;
import java.rmi.server.UnicastRemoteObject;

public class GreeterMain  {
   public static void main(String args[]){
   System.setSecurityManager(new RMISecurityManager());
    try {
      GreeterImpl greeterImpl = new GreeterImpl();
      Naming.rebind("SayHello", greeterImpl);
    }
    catch (Exception e) {
      System.out.println(e.getMessage());
```

```
      }
    }
  }
```

Add the same two lines to WelcomeGuest.java, as follows:

```
import java.rmi.RemoteException;
import java.rmi.RMISecurityManager;
import java.rmi.Naming;

public class WelcomeGuest {

  public WelcomeGuest(String guestName){
    try{
      Greeter greeter = (Greeter) Naming.lookup("SayHello");
      String greeting = greeter.greetByName(guestName);
      System.out.println(greeting);
    }
    catch (Exception e){
      System.out.println(e.getMessage());
    }
  }
  public static void main(String args[]){
    System.setSecurityManager(new RMISecurityManager());
    String guestName = (args.length == 0)?" ":args[0];
    WelcomeGuest welcomeGuest = new WelcomeGuest(guestName);
  }
}
```

The next step is to create a security policy file that the security manager will use. You can either create the file java.policy by hand, or you can use the policy tool application that you'll find in the bin directory of your Java distribution.

When you start up policy tool, you may be warned that your existing policy file couldn't be found in the current directory. You can dismiss this warning and use the tool to construct your new policy file. Click the Add Policy Entry button, and you will get a screen that enables you to add, edit, or remove permission. To add a permission, click Add Permission. Use the drop-down menu to choose All Permission and click OK. The Policy Entry window will then contain the following phrase:

```
permission java.security.AllPermission;
```

In this example, you are granting *carte blanche* to all classes that have access to this permission file. Of course you wouldn't want to do this when deploying an application, but it helps when you are developing. Before deploying, you should study the Java 2 security model and create an appropriate policy file. When you press Done, you return to the Policy Tool frame and see `CodeBase<All>`. Save the file as java.policy. Take a look at the policy file that you've generated:

```
/* AUTOMATICALLY GENERATED ON Fri May 11 23:02:34 EDT 2001*/
/* DO NOT EDIT */
```

```
grant {
  permission java.security.AllPermission;
};
```

The permission `java.security.AllPermission` has now been granted to all classes. Put a copy of this java.policy file in both the GreeterClient directory and in the WelcomeGuest directory. The last detail is that when you run the applications, you'll need to point to these security policies. Because you are still running on a single machine, you could have used one java.policy file and pointed to it from both applications. The main reason for using two files is that you are preparing to run this example on two different machines.

Setting the codebase

Once you are running the application from two different directories, you'll have to set the `java.rmi.server.codebase` property to the location of the code you will be loading remotely. The idea is that you register a remote object with a certain name in a certain `rmiregistry`. Then a client accesses the registry and asks for something with the name you registered.

In our example, the registry returns a reference to an instance of `GreeterImpl_Stub` to the client. The reason you didn't have to deal with security or codebase when you were running from a single directory was that the client doesn't need to do any remote code loading if it can find the stub instance in its CLASSPATH. Now that you will be working in more than one directory, you will actually be taking advantage of RMI. So the client will need to know the location of the `codebase` that contains the class definition for `GreeterImpl_Stub`.

The codebase is in the directory C:\J2EEBible\rmi\GreetingServer. Currently you are working on the same machine, so you could use the following setting for `codebase`:

```
file:///C:\J2EEBible\rmi\GreetingServer\
```

It is important to include the final backslash (\), because without it you will get an exception. Also keep in mind that you still aren't using `http` to transfer the code, although you could at this point. We'll get to that discussion after we talk about running your application on two machines.

Running the application from two directories on one machine

You are now ready to run the application. Before doing so, make one more change to the code that will count how many times the server has been accessed. Add an instance variable *n* to be incremented each time a client makes a request of the same instance of the server. The changes to GreeterImpl are shown in boldface in the following code:

```
import java.rmi.RemoteException;
import java.rmi.server.UnicastRemoteObject;

public class GreeterImpl extends UnicastRemoteObject implements
Greeter {
  public int n;
  public GreeterImpl() throws RemoteException{
    super();
    // ...
  }
  public String greetByName( String name) {
    return "Hello "+ name
      + " (this instance contacted "+ ++n +" times)";
  }
}
```

You'll need to recompile GreeterImpl and then use rmic to generate the stub (and possibly skeleton).

Start up the rmiregistry with one important change. You cannot be in the GreetingServer directory this time. You can't have the rmiregistry be in the same directory that you'll be using to access files. For kicks, you can try it and note the ClassNotFoundExceptions you get in the next step so that you recognize them later on. For convenience, you can just go to the root directory and start the rmiregistry up from there. If you're not there, enter cd \ and start up the registry by entering the usual command:

```
rmiregistry
```

The second step is to run the server. Here the only differences are that you need to point to the security policy and that you need to specify the codebase. You'll do that by assigning the java.policy you just created to the variable java.security.policy. You'll also set the property java.rmi.server.codebase to the location of GreeterImpl_Stub. In the following command, no spaces exist between the -D and java.policy. There are also no spaces between the -D and GreetingServer\:

```
java -Djava.security.policy=java.policy -Djava.rmi.server.
   codebase=file:///C:\J2EEBible\rmi\GreetingServer\
GreeterMain
```

Finally, run the client. Here the only difference is that, again, you must point to the security policy:

```
java -Djava.security.policy=java.policy WelcomeGuest Tara
```

After all that work, you will get the following response:

```
Hello Tara (this instance contacted 1 times).
```

With minimal changes, you can now run this application on two different machines.

Running an http class server

Once you are running the application on two different machines, you will need some way to communicate between them and send the data back and forth. We'll use HTTP. You may have your own HTTP server operating on your machine; if not, you can download a simple implementation from Sun at `ftp://ftp.javasoft.com/pub/jdk1.1/rmi/class-server.zip`.

You'll need to create the directory structure that matches the packaging of the class `ClassFileServer` and place it in a convenient location for running the current example. Create a directory called `examples` inside the existing J2EEBible/rmi/ directory. Create a subdirectory, classServer, inside of `examples`. Now unzip the distribution to this location.

Compile the source files and run the HTTP server from the command line by specifying the port on which you're running the server and the CLASSPATH for finding the relevant files. The idea is that you will now specify the `codebase` by pointing to this server, and that the server will in turn point to the location of the classes. So in this example, if you are running the server on port 2001, you would use the following command to start up the server:

```
java examples.classServer.ClassFileServer 2001:
C:\J2EEBible\rmi\GreetingServer
```

Running the application from two different machines

Before you can run the application, you need to make sure that your client knows the location of the `rmiregistry` it is using in the `lookup()` method. You adjust the argument of the `lookup()` method by adding `rmi://` followed by the server name and then the name you are looking up. The new WelcomeGuest file is the boldface code in the following sample:

```
import java.rmi.RemoteException;
import java.rmi.RMISecurityManager;
import java.rmi.Naming;

public class WelcomeGuest {

  public WelcomeGuest(String guestName){
    try{
```

```
        Greeter greeter = (Greeter)
          Naming.lookup("rmi://<server name here>/SayHello");
        String greeting = greeter.greetByName(guestName);
        System.out.println(greeting);
      }
      catch (Exception e){
        System.out.println(e.getMessage());
      }
    }
    public static void main(String args[]){
      System.setSecurityManager(new RMISecurityManager());
      String guestName = (args.length == 0)?" ":args[0];
      WelcomeGuest welcomeGuest = new WelcomeGuest(guestName);
    }
  }
```

You need to replace `<server name here>` with the name or address of your server. You may prefer not to hardcode the server name: That's fine. You can pass it in as a parameter at runtime if you'd prefer. Now you are ready to start up the various pieces of your distributed application.

First, on your server, open a command window, go to the root directory, and start up the `rmiregistry` with the command `rmiregistry`.

Next, start up the HTTP server. If you are using Sun's server, open up a new command window. If you have the directory structure that we've specified, navigate to just outside the examples directory. Now you can start up the server on port 2001 with the command you used earlier:

```
java examples.classServer.ClassFileServer 2001
C:\J2EEBible\rmi\GreetingServer
```

Now start up the server by opening up still another command window. Navigate to the GreetingServer directory and invoke the following command:

```
java -Djava.rmi.server.codebase=http://<server name here>:2001/
-Djava.security.policy=java.policy GreeterMain
```

Again, you need to replace `<server name here>` with the actual name or address of the server. You should not, however, use `localhost`, as this reference will not be resolved before being sent to clients and will be interpreted on the client as referring to their local machine and not back to the server.

Now you can start up the client by invoking the following command:

```
java -Djava.security.policy=java.policy WelcomeGuest Justin
```

Finally, with four VMs running on two different machines over a network, you are able to get the following response: `Hello Justin (this instance contacted 1 times)`. That was certainly worth the effort.

Using Non-Remote Objects

In the previous sections we've created an application that uses a remote object to send a `String` to a client. One of the many problems with the way we've designed this application is that there is no real intelligence on the client end, and as a result, the server is restricted to serving one specific function. Although we're not going to add much functionality to this application, we will now send an object over the wire. This will require that we talk a bit about object serialization and look a little more closely at what is going back and forth between machines. We'll finish this section with a few comments about performance.

Sending a Person object instead of a String

So far, you passed a `String` containing your name to the Greeter, which responded with a `String` of the form `Hello <name> (this instance contacted <number> times)`. You then printed this `String` to the console window. The next version will return a `Person` object that contains a `name` and a `number`. You can then do with it what you like at the client end. You can even output it to the console window as before. Here is the `Person` interface:

```
public interface Person {
  public String getName();
  public int getNumber();
}
```

Since you are returning a `Person` and not a `String`, you will need to modify the Greeter interface as follows:

```
import java.rmi.Remote;
import java.rmi.RemoteException;

public interface Greeter extends Remote {
  public Person greetByName( String name) throws
    RemoteException;
}
```

You'll need a separate directory for the client and for the server, and these two interfaces will need to be in both files. Set this application up in two directories on a single machine for development purposes. You can make the small modifications you saw in the last section to deploy this version of the application to two different machines. In the directory C:\J2EEBible\rmi\, create two subdirectories, GreetingObjectServer and GreetingObjectClient, and place both Person.java and Remote.java in each. While you're at it, place a copy of the file java.policy in each directory as well.

Next, you'll need an implementation of the `Person` interface for the server. The following `PersonImpl.java` class does all you need it to do:

```
public class PersonImpl implements Person,
  java.io.Serializable{
  String name;
  int number;

  public PersonImpl(String name, int number){
    this.name = name;
    this.number=number;
  }
  public String getName(){
    return name;
  }
  public int getNumber(){
    return number;
  }
}
```

The `PersonImpl` class has a constructor that takes the `String name` and an `int number` as arguments. It also provides getters for both variables. This file is saved in the GreetingObjectServer directory. Change GreeterImpl to accommodate the change of return type in the `Greeter` interface. You'll also set up the `Person` by passing in the `name` you receive from the client and the `number` that GreeterImpl is keeping track of. The changes to the modified GreeterImpl file are shown in bold in the following code:

```
import java.rmi.RemoteException;
import java.rmi.server.UnicastRemoteObject;

public class GreeterImpl extends UnicastRemoteObject implements
  Greeter {
  public int n;
  public GreeterImpl() throws RemoteException{
    super();
  }
  public Person greetByName( String name) {
    return new PersonImpl(name, ++n);
  }
}
```

GreeterMain does not have to be altered in any way. Compile the five files in GreetingObjectServer. Run `rmic` on GreeterImpl. Don't run `rmic` on PersonImpl, because it doesn't implement the `Remote` interface and is therefore not a remote object. The RMI compiler is smart enough to remind you of that fact if you forget. So the directory GreetingObjectServer should contain Person, PersonImpl, Greeter, GreeterImpl, GreeterMain, and the stub file GreeterImpl_Stub, and possibly the skeleton file GreeterImpl_Skel. As a reminder, we say it may *possibly* contain the skeleton file because this file is not needed for version 1.2 or higher. The server also has a copy of the file java.policy.

On the client, the file WelcomeGuest is altered as shown in bold in the following code:

```
import java.rmi.RemoteException;
import java.rmi.RMISecurityManager;
import java.rmi.Naming;

public class WelcomeGuest {

  public WelcomeGuest(String guestName){
    try{
      Greeter greeter = (Greeter) Naming.lookup("SayHello");
      Person person = greeter.greetByName(guestName);
      System.out.println("Hello "+ person.getName());
      System.out.println("You are number "
        +person.getNumber());
    }
    catch (Exception e){
      System.out.println(e.getMessage());
    }
  }
  public static void main(String args[]){
    System.setSecurityManager(new RMISecurityManager());
    String guestName = (args.length == 0)?" ":args[0];
    WelcomeGuest welcomeGuest = new WelcomeGuest(guestName);
  }
}
```

You pass in the same `String` as before, but this time `greetByName()` returns a `Person` object constructed on the server side as an instance of PersonImpl. This is a little different from what is returned by the `Naming.lookup()` call in the previous line. The `Greeter` object is a remote object. GreeterImpl implements a sub-interface of Remote. So what is passed is a stub that communicates with the GreeterImpl back on the server. Here PersonImpl is not a remote object, and so an instance is serialized and sent across the wire. What you have access to on the client side is a copy of an instance of PersonImpl. We'll say more about this process in a minute when we discuss object serialization.

The client contains the interfaces `Person` and `Greeter` as well as the files WelcomeGuest.java and java.policy. Compile WelcomeGuest, and you are ready to run this new version of the application.

Start up the `rmiregistry` from the root directory. Run the server with the following command from the directory C:\J2EEBible\rmi\GreetingObjectServer:

```
java -Djava.security.policy=java.policy
-Djava.rmi.server.codebase=file:///C:\J2EEBible\GreetingObjectS
erver\ GreeterMain
```

Run the client from the directory C:\J2EEBible\rmi\GreetingObjectClient:

```
java -Djava.security.policy=java.policy WelcomeGuest Grace
```

This time you'll get the following response:

```
Hello Grace
You are number 1
```

Object serialization

We glossed over one detail in our description of the current example. We noted that the class `PersonImpl` was an implementation of the `Person` interface. `PersonImpl` also implements the `java.io.Serializable` interface. Like `Remote`, `Serializable` is a marker interface. It indicates that an object can be serialized. You can also implement `Externalizable`. This interface extends `Serializable` and specifies the signatures for the methods `writeExternal()` and `readExternal()`.

You saw in our discussion of `GreeterImpl` that when the client requests a remote object that is created on the server, it essentially gets a handle to this object. This is often referred to as pass by reference. When we dug a little deeper you saw that actually you end up talking to a stub that in turn talks (possibly through a skeleton) to `GreeterImpl`. The class `GreeterImpl_Stub` starts off on the server and is sent to the client in much the same way that `PersonImpl` is sent. On the client, the `GreeterImpl_Stub` then acts as a proxy for `GreeterImpl`, and you communicate with the stub as if you were communicating with `GreeterImpl`. The performance isn't as good because some of the communication is happening across the wire.

In the current example, we created an instance of `PersonImpl` on the server and used it on the client. Unlike a remote object, a copy of this instance of `PersonImpl` is serialized. This means that it is transformed into byte code sent across the wire and reconstituted. There are some issues here. If you wish to save the state of an object in order to serialize it, then you have to also save the state of instance variables of it and of its superclasses. But each of these classes may also have instance variables and superclass instance variables with state that must also be saved. You may end up needing a lot of memory just to save a small class if it is part of a large connected graph of classes.

There are two ways that you can truncate what is being preserved — *truncate* meaning that the information will be lost and that you must somehow account for this loss when you are trying to recreate the object. The first way is with the keyword `transient`, which indicates that you don't want to serialize this variable. You can use this keyword when you don't need to save a particular state and you want to reduce the size of what's being sent across the wire. You can also use `transient` to modify a variable that refers to a class that is not serializable. Finally, you may wish to avoid exposing the details of a private class. The second way is to create your own `writeObject()` and `readObject()` methods that encode the data at one end of the wire and decode the data at the other end. If you skip this step, a sharp programmer may intercept and read what you thought was private data from the bytecode.

There is one other type of variable that won't be serialized. A `static` variable is not serialized, as `static` variables don't contain object-specific information. If your class has a non-serializable superclass, then your class can only be serialized if your parent class has a no argument constructor. When it is time to reconstitute your object, this constructor will be called. You'll have to fill in the lost details by hand after setting up the `transient` variables and the missing information in the objects that were built by a no-argument constructor.

Performance problems

We mentioned before that it is frequently said that RMI enables you to interact with an object on another machine as if it were running in the same process. This is true from a code standpoint. Once you have a handle to an object, you can call methods on it using the same syntax for a local object that you would use for a remote object. This is not true from a performance standpoint. When you ran the example that used two different machines, you probably noticed that it took an awful long time just to say hello. Because you also ran this code on a single machine, you know that the delay was not the result of the processing being done at each end. Even the time it took to send a simple `String` in one direction and then return the processed `String` was significant.

There are two ways that this example can scale, and you have to be aware of two issues in each case:

- ✦ There could be an increase in the size of the object being sent. Sometimes this is unavoidable, but many times it is the result of programmers not thinking about what is actually being sent.
- ✦ There could be an increase in the number of client requests for objects. Again, this is sometimes the unavoidable result of calls from various clients. On the other hand, in many cases a developer can increase the size of what's being sent in order to decrease the number of calls. In any case, you'll have to think carefully about what is right for your application and test the alternatives.

The first problem arises when you have nicely factored code. You've used your favorite design patterns to end up with a bunch of small objects that do a limited number of things. At some point, you need to send one of these non-remote objects over the wire, and so you serialize it. Suddenly your 1KB object serializes into 3MB. As we mentioned earlier, a lot of space and processing have to go into preserving the state of your simple object. Any object it references will also be preserved. In order to preserve any referenced object, you must also preserve each of the objects it references. This includes the superclasses of your original object and any of the referenced objects. You can quickly end up with a large graph of objects that all need to be preserved.

Now take a look at what you're saving. Do you really need all this stuff just to describe your little 1KB object? If your client isn't going to need certain variables, mark them as `transient` to keep the serialized object small. When you put the object back together at the client end, you can initialize these transient variables in a way that is adequate to your system.

Even if you aren't concerned about clients waiting a long time for data, for the sake of the public good you should consider reducing the size of what you send over the wire. When you send data over the wire, you are using a public resource, and sending large bits of data across can slow down what other people are trying to do. College networks noted the increase in performance when a certain music-downloading system was shut down. They hadn't noticed the gradual degradation as more and more users started transporting large files across the network.

The second problem may seem to contradict the first. Here we've told you not to send objects that are too big, and now we're telling you not to send objects that are too small. Here's a canonical example. Suppose you need to use various pieces of information contained in U.S. addresses, such as `firstName`, `lastName`, `streetAddress`, `city`, `state`, `zipCode`, `areaCode`, and `phoneNumber`. You could make multiple requests from the client for each of the pieces of information that you need. Alternatively, you can create a `PersonInfo` object that contains this information. You would then make a single request for the appropriate `PersonInfo` object and parse the information off on the client side.

The single request does require that you send a larger object across the wire, but this increase in object size is relatively minor and is offset by the additional protocol information that would need to be included with each individual request. In fact, even if you need only a couple of pieces of information, you may want to use this second approach. In other words, instead of making a remote call for the `firstName` and a second remote call for the `secondName`, you may see better performance if you make a single remote call for the `PersonInfo` object, and then, once you have it, call the `getFirstName()` and `getSecondName()` methods.

The rule of thumb is that you want fine-grained objects within a single VM, but course-grained objects between VMs because the communication is so expensive. This rule was the catalyst for many of the improvements in the EJB 2.0 spec we discussed previously.

Activating Services

Wouldn't it be nice if you could use your resources more wisely? If you have lots of services running on our server, you have to have lots of running processes. The goal of activation is to only start up a service when it is needed. In this section, you'll modify the last example to run only when it is requested by the RMI daemon. You will make slight changes to the `GreeterMain` and `GreeterImpl` classes.

Make a copy of the GreetingObjectServer directory and name it RmidGreetingServer. For simplicity, run it without a HTTP server as you did in the last example. You don't need to make any changes to any of the client code, and so you won't even need to create a new directory.

Even though it doesn't look as if there is much to change, a lot can still go wrong. Rather than spending time here discussing security, you should take the policy.rmid file from the Jini distribution and use it. It is easy to make security mistakes and have permissions prohibit you from activating your object. You will spend enough time wrestling with your daemons that you don't need to take security on as well at this point. To make it easy to run this example, put policy.rmid right in your root directory.

Changing the implementation of the Remote interface

The key change is that instead of extending `java.rmi.server.UnicastRemoteObject`, you are now extending `java.rmi.activation.Activatable`. Your first step is to get beyond the fact that this is a bad name for a class — it sounds more like the name of an interface. Once you've done that, you'll need to change the imports and the constructor. Your `greetByName()` method doesn't change at all. In the following code, you can see that in addition to `RemoteException` and `Activatable`, we are also importing `MarshalledObject` and `ActivationID`:

```
import java.rmi.RemoteException;
import java.rmi.MarshalledObject;
import java.rmi.activation.Activatable;
import java.rmi.activation.ActivationID;

public class GreeterImpl extends Activatable implements
  Greeter  {
  public int n;
  public GreeterImpl(ActivationID activationID,
    MarshalledObject marshalledObject) throws RemoteException{

    super(activationID, 0);
  }

  public Person greetByName( String name) {
    return new PersonImpl(name, ++n);
  }
}
```

Unlike before, here you don't have a no-argument constructor. Your constructor takes an `ActivationID` and a `MarshalledObject` as inputs. The `ActivationID` will allow the mechanism to identify and locate the object being activated. The `MarshalledObject` is a serialized object with information about where the class was originally loaded from. The spec requires that a remote activatable object have a constructor with this signature. In this constructor, you'll call `Activatable`'s constructor wherein you activate the object with the given `ActivationID` on a port assigned by the system.

Don't forget to create a stub using the following RMI compiler command from within the `RmidGreetingServer` directory:

```
rmic -v1.2 GreeterImpl
```

Modifying the setup class

Most of the changes take place inside the `GreeterMain` class. You can, of course, reduce the imports in the following code by using the wildcards `java.rmi.*`, `java.rmi.activation.*`, and `java.util.*`:

```
import java.rmi.Remote;
import java.rmi.Naming;
import java.rmi.activation.Activatable;
import java.rmi.activation.ActivationDesc;
import java.rmi.activation.ActivationGroup;
import java.rmi.activation.ActivationGroupDesc;
import java.rmi.activation.ActivationGroupID;
import java.util.Properties;

public class GreeterMain  {

  public static void main( String[]  args ) throws Exception
  {
    Properties properties = new Properties();
    ActivationGroupDesc agDesc = new
      ActivationGroupDesc(properties,null);
    ActivationGroupID agID =
      ActivationGroup.getSystem().registerGroup(agDesc );
    ActivationGroup.createGroup(agID, agDesc,0);

    ActivationDesc desc = new ActivationDesc("GreeterImpl",
      "file:///C:/J2EEBible/rmi/RmidGreetingServer/",null);
    Remote remote = (Remote)Activatable.register(desc);
    Naming.rebind( "SayHello", remote );
    System.exit(0);
  }
}
```

Let's step through the constructor. After creating a new `Properties` class, you create an `ActivationGroupDesc`. You are going to activate our object within an `ActivationGroup`. You begin by providing the description of this group. The `Properties` object enables you to set the `codebase`, security policy, or other properties for this group. The `ActivationGroupID` performs the same function for the ActivationGroup that the ActivationID performs for the Activatable object. Now you can go ahead and create the ActivationGroup with this ActivationGroupID and ActivationGroupDesc.

The ActivationDesc contains the information you need to activate your object. If it seems as if you are doing a lot of setup, remember that you are going to be asking processes on remote machines to start up and load a particular class and respond to your requests. Provide the name of the class you're instantiating and a fully qualified path to the codebase. Note that this path includes the trailing forward slash (/) character. You can use this constructor because you don't need to specify the ActivationGroup in this example.

There are three things left to do. First, you need to invoke register() to pass on all the information contained in the ActivationDesc so that your object can be activated. Second, as before, you need to bind a name such as "SayHello" to your object. Since you already have the name of the class in the ActivationDesc, use a handle defined by the interface Remote (or Greeter) instead of the class GreeterImpl. Finally, call System.exit(0). This, of course, is the whole point of this exercise. If you were going to leave the service up and running, you wouldn't need it to be activatable.

Running the example

We're assuming the following things. You've changed the code as outlined in the previous section and compiled it. You've used rmic to generate a new GreeterImpl_Stub. Your directories are set up as we described earlier. You've created or copied the policy.rmid file to the root directory. Begin by opening a command window and starting up the registry with the following command:

```
rmiregistry
```

Now open another window and start up the RMI daemon as follows:

```
rmid -J-Djava.security.policy=file:///C:\policy.rmid
```

Now open still another window and start up the server as before:

```
java -Djava.security.policy=java.policy -Djava.rmi.server.
codebase=file:///C:\J2EEBible\rmi\RmidGreetingServer\
GreeterMain
```

In this command, there is no space between -D and policy or between -D and RmidGreetingServer\. Unlike before, the class will run and then hit System.exit(0) and stop. You will see a command prompt. You can use this window, or open a new one to run the client with the following command:

```
java -Djava.security.policy=java.policy  WelcomeGuest Joe
```

You will get the following response:

```
Hello Joe
You are number 1
```

Networks fail, and servers crash. Go ahead and enter a few more names from this or another command window and then check out a persistence feature of `rmid` as follows. Quit the RMI daemon. Run the client another time, and you get a `ConnectException`. Go ahead and start the daemon up again and rerun the client. The number count has been reset to 1, but enough information was stored that you don't have to run `GreeterMain` again to reregister the service. For kicks, try the same cycle with `rmiregistry`, and you'll see that it isn't as resilient. You need to rerun `GreeterMain` to rebind your service in the `rmiregistry`. In Chapter 20, we'll look at a more robust registry.

Summary

RMI can be a good way to run a distributed application in Java. Despite your best efforts, however, it is often difficult to figure out what is going wrong in distributed applications. Sometimes you think you've done all that you should, and your app still isn't working. You'll find that two good resources are Sun's RMI page (accessible from `http://java.sun.com/rmi`) and its current FAQ list (`http://java.sun.com/j2se/1.3/docs/guide/rmi/faq.html`). You will often find the answer to your specific questions by checking the mailing-list archives. In our introduction to RMI, we covered the following topics:

- ✦ You learned how to create an interface for the service you would like to implement. Because you will be accessing the service from a client, it should extend the `Remote` interface. You then created a class that extended the `UnicastRemoteObject` that implements this interface.
- ✦ You generated a stub from this class using the RMI compiler. This stub travels from the server to the client to act as a proxy for the original class. You used Sun's simple HTTP server to deliver the stub code across the network. When you ran the code remotely you needed to specify where the code was located using the `java.rmi.server.codebase` property, and where a security-policy file was located using the `java.security.policy` property.
- ✦ We discussed techniques for improving performance in these distributed applications. These included limiting the number of calls you make over the network and reducing the size of the objects you send. Finally, we demonstrated that you don't need a live process for every service you want to offer on the server. By extending `java.rmi.activation.Activatable`, you are able to use `rmid` to run services on demand.

✦ ✦ ✦

CHAPTER 16

Introducing Enterprise JavaBeans

✦ ✦ ✦ ✦

In This Chapter

Learning about the concepts and terminology of Enterprise JavaBeans

Creating the two major types of beans — session and entity

Exploring the more advanced concepts and new features provided by the EJB 2.0 specification

Using EJBs within your client code — applications, servlets, or JSPs

✦ ✦ ✦ ✦

Within the Java world, the enterprise environment is the hot ticket — that is what got Java solidly placed as a real-world, useful programming language. Without a doubt, the reason for this was the release of the Enterprise JavaBeans specification. Although Sun had tried a number of times to attract serious developers with efforts like Remote Method Invocation (RMI) and JDBC, the programming and business worlds really did not take Java very seriously until Enterprise JavaBeans (EJBs) made their mark. It was as if overnight Java went from a play language to something that could build serious, industrial-quality applications — and fast.

You can read more information about RMI in Chapter 15 and about JDBC in Chapter 7.

As a platform on which to build both large and small enterprise applications — whether they be e-commerce Web sites or automated parcel-tracking systems — the J2EE environment uses the EJB as its core technology. In addition, over the last year or two XML has started to rise to equal importance in an enterprise application, the humble EJB is still at the center of most enterprise applications — usually processing or generating that XML content.

Regardless of the type of application you are developing, it is almost a given that you are going to deal with EJBs at some stage. So just what are they, how do they work, and more importantly, how do you write one?

Introducing a New Level of Abstraction

Java already has this concept of remote objects called RMI. Over in the general UNIX world, CORBA has been a major standard for well over a decade. Both of these technologies seem to offer the same or similar capabilities. Just what does the Enterprise JavaBean offer you as a programmer?

Who am I?

Trying to describe exactly what an Enterprise JavaBean is can be a tricky task. On one hand you can compare it to a collection of known technologies and tick and cross boxes of features supported. On the other hand, no matter what ticks-in-the box the marketing people give EJBs, that does not really define how they operate. We'd sound like cheesy marketing types if we said that they are a Way Of Life(TM), but that phrase encapsulates the way many programmers think of them. EJBs contain a set of rules regarding how to write them, but a corresponding set of philosophies, about when and how they are used and designed, also exists.

Just how do you look at an EJB? Well, the first step is to look at what it does and does not provide you with as a programmer.

I am not a JavaBean

The first really large-scale marketing push by Sun to develop a Java programming philosophy was the JavaBean specification. This was aimed at producing Java programs that contained a collection of very small components that could be clicked together without one component ever knowing the details of another component. Principally, this specification was aimed at the graphical user interface (GUI) components. Sun also tried to push it as a complete solution for building all software, but that failed. For various reasons, the JavaBean specification and philosophy of building applications never took root. Although Sun still pushes the JavaBeans philosophy through the Swing API, we know of no serious applications — even GUI builder tools — that have used it or currently use it.

Despite the similarity in name, an Enterprise JavaBean is not a form of JavaBean. In fact, the two have barely any commonalities at all! JavaBeans were about hiding every single detail and using reflection to find out what methods were available; EJBs are about the opposite — constructing a fixed set of known interfaces that programmers can use wherever they like by directly calling methods.

The funny thing about all of this is that in order to access an EJB from a JSP, as you will see later in the Using EJBs in JSPs section of this chapter, you need to use a JavaBean. It can get really confusing and tongue-twisting trying to make sure you get the right terms in the right spots.

An EJB implementation provides a known interface that all applications can use. The code that provides the implementation of that interface may change, but the interface is a form of contract between the provider and user. When an application uses that interface, it asks the naming service to locate and provide it with the implementation of that interface and then look after any other management details.

I don't distribute objects

If an EJB has a set of public interfaces and a set of code that distributes these implementations from one machine to another (user and service provider), then it must just be a distributed object system, the same as RMI, correct? Well, no. An EJB is an interface, and an implementation, but unlike with RMI, that is the extent of the specification. What an EJB provides is a specification that builds an infrastructure for saying how a particular component may operate, but it does not specify how that component must be shared, or communicate between the piece that the user's code talks to and the piece on the server.

The EJB 2.0 specification introduces the concept of local beans. These are EJBs that are only visible to other EJBs within the server environment. Client code, such as an application or JSP, cannot access these beans at all. Local beans are not covered in this chapter, but they will be in the next.

When implementing an EJB, you can use RMI internally. Alternatively, an EJB may directly connect to a server with JDBC or LDAP to extract information based on the user's request. Unlike RMI, the EJB does not define anything other than how a user can find and manage an object. RMI is designed to provide access to remote objects. It operates on the basic assumptions that the real service acts on a remote computer and that on the client computer the EJB system just acts as a shell for the requests. The job of the client-side stub is to collect the method arguments, package them up, and send them to the server. The server unpackages everything, processes the request, and sends the results back to the client. An EJB is the complete logic. You really don't know where the data will be processed. With some implementations it is possible that the entire bean is located on your client machine, while with others the client is held as a stub to the code running on the server. Unlike with RMI, you don't know and don't care.

Note

Although an EJB does not perform the same function as RMI, there is no reason why you can't have an EJB using RMI internally (in fact, all EJB core interfaces extend from the RMI interfaces). As far as the client code is concerned, it should not know how the EJB is implemented or where it is located. Say the bean needs to look up a collection of data: As far as the client code is concerned, that EJB may use JDBC to connect directly to a database, use RMI to pass the request off to a foreign server, or even contain a complete local copy of the database internally. That an EJB never talks to a server is entirely legal—the EJB can perform all its work in place on the client machine and never communicate with anything.

I don't know myself

We've established that an EJB is a known fixed object and that it does not do anything other than present a component to a user's computer. The question remains—how then do you fetch and load an EJB to use it? It has no `rmiregistry`; it has no associated protocol for use in a wire transaction; it doesn't even specify how to communicate! So you think we're kidding, don't you?

One of the strengths of the EJB specification is that it purposely does not specify any of these capabilities. It does one thing—define a component management infrastructure. All the rest of the business that an EJB is required to perform is left to other APIs.

What are the other things that an EJB is required to do? To locate an EJB, you use JNDI configured as a naming service. Part of your application design is to know what names you associate with each object that you want to use. You can store that EJB in a number of ways: As a BLOB in a relational database, in an LDAP database, or you even serialized onto disk somewhere. As for the functionality of the EJB, the sky's the limit. The EJB can use JDBC to talk with a database, use a raw socket to communicate in binary or text with a server, use RPC or SOAP or one of many other protocol systems, and much more. What is consistent about all these actions is that an EJB does not do any of them as part of its own specification—it relies on other specifications of the J2EE environment to provide these services.

Talking about the EJB specification as a small, limited-influence area is not quite correct. As you will see shortly, with an EJB some restrictions do exist on what the code is allowed to do. However, the application or the services that an EJB can provide are limitless. They can be used for e-commerce applications, but they can be just as easily used to build a rendering farm.

Finding a development environment

As we have just shown, the Enterprise JavaBean is a narrowly focused specification that requires a number of other specifications to work properly. For many a corporate developer, the requirement to use many different specifications to make a complete application means deciding on a development environment to support this work as nothing works as a standalone entity.

To build and run an EJB application, you need the complete J2EE environment. While you might think that the J2EE environment is just the set of APIs that we've been discussing in this book, it is much more than that. A real J2EE environment consists of the APIs, service provider implementation(s) for each of the APIs (for example, JDBC drivers, JNDI LDAP service provider, and so on), and an environment that packages EJBs, deploys them to a server, and uses the server to make the beans available to client applications.

Development environments for EJB, and hence J2EE, applications can be divided into two sets of tools—those you use to edit and compile the source code, and those you use to deploy and make available compiled code to other applications.

Editing tools for creating code

As far as editing tools are concerned, there is no real restriction on your choice—they can be as simple or complex as you like.

On the simple end of the spectrum, you can use a text editor such as vi (for the UNIX types) or Notepad. Anything that you can type text into will do. On the complex end, any of the commercial Integrated Development Environments (IDEs), such as VisualCafe, VisualAge, or JBuilder, will work. Also, many J2EE vendors include customized development tools that work well with their respective deployment environments. For example, Oracle has for years shipped J/Developer (a heavily customized version of Borland's JBuilder tool) with its application-services products.

Compiling the code really depends on the editing tool you are using. The IDEs will generally have all the required classes and build tools already built in. For those with the text editors, you will need to read the documentation for your deployment environment to find out where all the classes are stored, and make sure the `CLASSPATH` is constructed appropriately.

If you do not yet have a J2EE deployment environment and do not wish to purchase one, Sun offers a reference environment for you to use. The reference environment contains all the APIs you need for J2EE and will also double as a deployment environment. See Appendix A for a description of how to install, develop, and deploy with Sun's reference environment.

Environments to deploy beans

Now we're in a tricky area. The nature of the deployment environment is highly dependent on your project and really comes down to management and political decisions. For this reason, we are not going to recommend any, and instead, point you to Appendix C, which contains a list of the current known deployment environments. You will already be familiar with some of the big names, such as Oracle, IBM, and BEA.

If you are just starting out within the J2EE environment and your employer/institution has not yet settled on the purchase of any specific environment, yet you want to start experimenting, then Sun offers a reference environment. The reference environment is good enough to get you up and running on small projects. However, once you get to do something serious, then we strongly recommend using a commercial product. There are a couple of open-source environments that provide part or all of the J2EE specification. At the time of this writing, none of them fully support the latest EJB 2.0 specification, but a majority of the functionality is supported.

With the EJB 2.0 specification, you do not need to have the same environment for your server and client code. The earlier specification required you to use the same environment on the client and server, which badly tied the hands of developers who wanted to use the most efficient product for each part of the service. The latest specification enables you to run WebSphere as the server and Sun's reference implementation as the client, for example.

Exploring the Components of an EJB Service

Within the enterprise-application space that we presented in Chapter 1, the Enterprise JavaBean framework forms the middle tier. Internally, EJBs have their own set of tiers, too. Along with the framework comes the inevitable set of terminology and acronyms, so let's dive right in and cover those before introducing the code.

Terminology of the EJB application

An EJB looks very much like the RMI setup that you saw in Chapter 15. There are abstract interfaces that describe the capabilities that you can use and the working code with which to run the requested actions. However, where RMI only allows a single type of transaction for the remote object, EJBs introduce a set of "ratings" for the nature of the bean.

Enterprise beans consist of four major parts (discounting the actual server environment):

- ✦ An interface describing the public capabilities of the bean.
- ✦ An implementation of the public interface.
- ✦ An interface that allows you to create and manage one or more beans as a collective.
- ✦ Deployment information for when the beans are loaded onto a server.

All of these items are required in order to form a complete EJB. You cannot have one without the others.

Remote interface

For a bean to work independently of the implementation, you must specify the methods that you are making public. If you were implementing an RMI object, this interface would perform exactly the same role in the system. It presents an abstract representation of the capabilities without tying you to a given implementation class.

The methods that a remote interface presents to the world are commonly called *business logic*. Each method should provide a solution to some problem that the system wishes to address. Implied in this term is the idea that the remote interface should not contain frivolous or non-business–related methods. The whole philosophy surrounding the EJB platform is that it solves real-world business problems. The result is that all the terminology is screwed toward sounding as if it had been written by an accountant or manager rather than a programmer — it's very buzzword-friendly.

Working code – the bean

Doing something useful is the job of the bean implementation. The bean code implements all the remote-interface methods. Of course, a bean may consist of other beans. With a well-designed architecture, the beans used by the client code may not ever see the beans actually doing the work on the database — these client-visible beans may just consist of the aggregates of other beans in order to perform their logic.

A number of different types of beans exist, for the purpose of doing and representing different things. We'll describe these different classifications shortly. Each bean type has advantages, according to the type of business functionality you need to provide.

The home interface

A requirement of beans is that you cannot access them directly. The reason for this is that it allows the container determine when new instances need to be created and when they can be shared or destroyed. In order to provide a way to access any given bean, you still need some abstract representation of this container system: This is referred to as the *home interface.*

A home interface provides some of the bean life-cycle–management methods. The deal here is that it doesn't define the exact management methods, just the actions that need to be provided — create, destroy, find existing instances and a number of other tasks. You can think of this interface as a combination of a factory for producing bean instances and a static utility class providing a collection of helper methods. You know you can ask it for objects, but whether those objects are recycled or created new, you don't know and don't care.

Deployment information

Another level of abstraction applied to EJBs is the information used to control how any given bean instance is managed by the server. The beauty of this system is that it enables you to tailor the management of any given bean without needing to change a line of code. For instance, changing a bean from one with persistent information to one that is transient only takes one line in a text file — no code compilation is needed. The same bean code can act completely differently according to the deployment information that comes with it.

A number of different deployment options exist for code. Not only can you deploy a bean, but you can also deploy client code, such as JSPs and servlets. These files are known as *deployment descriptors* and are written in XML. Sometimes you will hand-write a descriptor, and other times tools will do it for you. In large, real-world applications, there will be tens or hundreds of different bean types, so hand-cutting a deployment descriptor will be a rare task for you.

If you would like to see a deployment-descriptor–generation tool at work, jump over to Appendix A, which introduces Sun's J2EE reference environment. This appendix features a complete tutorial on packaging and deploying both beans and Web components.

The bean lifecycle

On a fine day, the farmer walks into his paddock with a handful of seeds. He takes these seeds and plants them in the ground. With a little care, they sprout and grow into wonderful fruit trees. Spring arrives, and the tree blooms. Flowers become fruit. A collection of the neighboring kids jump the fence and pick some of this fruit, occasionally coming across seeds, which they spit out onto the ground. In fall, it starts to grow cold again, and the trees shed their leaves for the winter hibernation, covering the ground. Over the winter the trees lie dormant, waiting for the warm spring winds to arrive. Spring arrives, and the trees bloom, once again continuing on their cycle. Eventually, these trees become too old to produce enough fruit, so the farmer comes along with his axe and chops them down, making way for new trees. Thus is the lifecycle of the Enterprise JavaBean.

To translate this story to code, the seed is an EJB, while the paddock and atmosphere are your server. Our friendly farmer is the system administrator, and those plucky kids are your client software. EJBs have a lifecycle, too. The path through the lifecycle is dependent on the type of bean. Some beans will be continuous like the trees. They will go through periods of activity and periods of dormancy—they may also generate instances of other beans, or use other beans as part of their functionality. Other beans are like the weeds – they come and go according to the seasons and rainfall. When the bean goes dormant, this is known as *passivation*. Passivation occurs when the client no longer needs the services of a bean, but the "system" decides that it wants to keep the bean around just in case. Some beans are capable of this type of dormancy, while others are not. As you go through the chapter, we'll describe these different types of beans, how they function, and the individual lifestyle of each.

Types of beans

Kenyan, Columbian, Kona . . . .

Oh. Oops, wrong sorts of beans.

Just like their drinkable counterparts, enterprise Beans come in many different flavors. Each has a set of special capabilities, so you should understand what each type does before trying to design your application.

Properties of all EJBs

All EJBs have a set of common properties, and for good reason—the bean is a distributed object. You don't really know whether the bean is running on the client machine or on a remote server. In each of these environments, performing certain tasks can upset the existing server environment. Of course, an interesting point comes up when you're dealing with different architectures — what if the EJB server is an IBM AS/400 box, and the clients are PCs running Linux (or worse yet — Microsoft Windows)?

Only a few restrictions exist with regard to what an EJB cannot do:

✦ *Manage or synchronize threads.* All EJBs are required to be single threaded, and you cannot use `synchronized` methods.

✦ *Access files directly through the* `java.io` *package.* File access through URLs is fine, and files relative to the `CLASSPATH` using `System.getResourceAsStream()` is fine, because these actions are not dependent on a particular platform or environment. An example of the latter action is reading a properties file packaged with the bean.

✦ *Use screen functionality such as AWT or Swing.* EJBs are purely headless in operation and cannot allow the capture of keyboard or mouse operation.

✦ *Perform socket operations, such as using* `ServerSocket` *and multicast.* Also, you cannot set socket factories. However, you can create a socket connected to a foreign server for information.

✦ *Load native libraries.* For obvious reasons, a native library may or may not run in your environment, particularly when you are running different hardware architectures at different tiers of your enterprise application.

✦ The use of *static variables is heavily discouraged.* Read-only variables that act as constants are fine (for example, a variable declared as `private static final`), but using a static variable to pass information back and forth between bean instances is discouraged, as you cannot guarantee the behavior of your bean. Some servers may use multiple JVM instances to distribute the load, and static variables just won't work in that case.

Apart from these restrictions, you can do almost anything with EJB code. Threading is not permitted because the basic EJB philosophy is that you should never need to have multiple threads accessing any given bean instance. If you do find yourself in this situation, then you have used the wrong bean type, and something is also wrong with your J2EE runtime environment, as it is supposed to prevent this situation from arising.

Session beans

The first type of bean represents a single user of the system. In this situation, one servlet or application wants to have its own specific connection that maintains any information that you might need. These beans are only valid for a single client, and a new one is created each time a client needs it. Once a client has finished with the bean, that instance is discarded. A typical use of this type of beans is for a shopping-cart–type Web application wherein the session bean tracks one user as he or she adds and removes items from a "cart" before purchasing.

Session beans have two forms — those that maintain state information and those that do not. A stateless bean is one that does not keep information between calls to it, and it will typically be used to perform calculations. At its barest level, you could say that this bean does not have any internal variables (although that, strictly speaking is not true, as you will see shortly). Clients, when handed two stateless beans of the same interface, are not able to tell them apart.

A stateful bean, on the other hand, is one that keeps track of information over a number of method calls. For this bean, you can pass in information, request it back, perform operations, and so forth. Each bean becomes customized for the particular client using it. Given two stateful beans, a client is able to tell them apart. A stateful bean might be used to represent a single user's shopping cart as he or she travels from product to product on your Web site.

Entity beans

For each client, you need to have some idea of the data that that client is working on. This is the job of the entity bean. Entity beans represent some underlying data source — be it a relational database, LDAP database, or some other system. Typically an entity bean will represent one item of data. For example, consider the list of all customers of the store. For many purposes, an entity bean can be considered the Java abstraction of a particular element of the underlying data source, like a row in a table in a database.

Because entity beans represent a data source that will (probably!) last longer than the bean itself, they have the idea of *persistence*. A persistent bean is one that, when users no longer need its services, will quietly write out its state to a data store and be removed from memory until the next time it is asked for. Persistence allows beans to be managed according to memory requirements. Large systems can have hundreds of entity beans, which would mean excessive amounts of memory usage if they were all to remain in memory at once.

When dealing with persistence, the J2EE environment allows two forms — one for which the EJB server does the management, and one for which you do the management. In the former case, the server will track the number of clients using a particular bean, the current memory requirements, and any other configurable factor, and then deal with the bean. In the latter case, it is entirely up to you as the bean writer to decide when and how to write the bean's contained data to the underlying data store. While the former is easier to deal with, the latter offers more customization options.

Persistence of entity beans is not covered in this chapter. If you would like more information, please read Chapter 17.

Message-driven beans

In J2EE 1.3/EJB 2.0, a new bean type is introduced. This is the *message-driven* bean, and it represents one more part of your application. Message-driven beans represent services that exist on very large systems, such as mainframe computers. The basic idea is that these beans will communicate using non-standard services that are message-driven, rather than with method calls.

The basic purpose of message-driven beans is to integrate EJBs with legacy systems. Legacy systems are huge business and are not likely to be replaced overnight. For example, trillions of dollars worth of data are contained in airline-reservation systems, government records and financial data that cannot just be pulled to be replaced by the latest buzzword-compliant technology.

The underlying technology of message-driven beans is a messaging system. J2EE already has one of these in the form of the Java Messaging Service (JMS). However, a lot of proprietary schemes exist (for example, IBM's CICS interface) that would make use of this type of bean. The average programmer probably won't be developing message-driven beans, so we won't cover them in this introductory chapter.

To learn more about how to use JMS, please jump ahead to Chapter 22. We will describe message-driven beans in greater detail in Chapter 17. Between these two chapters, we have an example of how to integrate a JMS service with message-driven beans.

Bean containers

A bean container is the code responsible for managing beans — entity, session, message-driven and the various interfaces. You as a programmer do not have control over the bean container; the EJB specification does not give you access or any standard classes with which to work with them. The container affects both the client and the server part of the EJB code so that software running on a client machine may connect and communicate with the server software.

From the 1.3 version of the J2EE specification, you can get a level of interoperability between containers. This effectively enables you to use different vendors for the client and server J2EE environments. For example, you can use Sun's reference implementation on the client for development, and have the server running with BEA's WebLogic for serving up the beans.

A lot of confused terminology exists around this point of containers and servers. Some people refer to bean containers as EJB Containers and others as EJB Servers. When we mention the server in this book, we mean the complete running application that holds an EJB instance, management tools, load balancing, naming facilities, and so forth. The container is just the code that provides management of a given bean.

A sample application

To illustrate how to use the various beans, some sample code is needed. We are going to keep working with the examples presented in Part III of the book. The chapters in Part III described a very simple store with customers and products. We'll use all the SQL tables defined there and then add the logic over the top.

EJBs are only half the story of any enterprise application—you need a user interface, too. Our sample application will use JSPs, and we'll also show you how to do the same tasks with Servlets.

Owing to differences in the level of support for the various SQL standards by relational databases, we are going to skip a few of the fundamental details of dealing with primary keys in the tables. The example code in this chapter assumes the Cloudscape database that comes with the reference implementation, but if your RDBMS supports `AUTO_INCREMENT` on the primary key, you have to take a completely different approach, which we'll cover as well.

Deciding on beans to use

Using EJBs in an application really requires that you sit down and design the application before coding. Because different varieties of beans exist, and because each variety requires that you implement code in different forms, you need to understand the relationships between data and business logic running through your system. Only once you have worked out what needs to be represented and how should you start writing code. Unlike with some other code, you can't just slap together a bit of code and hope that it sorta works right. Proper design is absolutely essential to creating robust and efficient EJB-based code.

Designing the structure of beans is, like most code design, a matter of personal philosophy. As the old cliché goes, there's more than one way to skin a cat. For example, when you're building an entity bean to represent user data in the database, should the entity bean represent all users, or should it represent just one user?

Sample bean design

For the purposes of our sample application, we have to consider the type of data in the system. First, we have the three tables of data in the relational database—product, customer, and order information. As these are persistent information, it makes sense to treat them as entity beans—one bean for each table.

On top of the basic data, we also have to consider what the user might do with the system:

- ✦ Register as a customer.
- ✦ View and edit existing customer information.
- ✦ View and search for products.
- ✦ Purchase products.

When you look over this list, you'll see that none but the last option really justifies any representation in a bean. Registration is just a request from the customer-entity bean to make a new entry—a single method call. However, purchasing products requires a lot more information and effort. In the time-honored process of e-commerce sites everywhere, the code will send you a confirmation e-mail when you place your order.

An introduction to the EJB classes and interfaces

The list of classes and interfaces for EJBs that you as an end-user programmer need is fairly small and simple. (For a server implementer, not so, but that's another story!)

All the classes are contained in a single package — `javax.ejb`. However, as you take a look through the classes, you will notice that most of the interfaces and exceptions are dependent on the RMI classes and interfaces, typically extending them.

As part of the new capability to enable cross-vendor bean deployment, EJB 2.0 introduces a new package, `javax.ejb.spi`, for the service-provider implementation. You will never use this package in real code.

Interfaces in the package can be divided into two categories — management and implementation. Management interfaces deal with the day-to-day running of all your beans, while the implementation interfaces perform specific actions for each bean.

Bean-management interfaces

Management interfaces provide hints to the EJB server software about what sort of capabilities are to be provided to the end user. These interfaces represent the basic functions of creating, managing, and shutting down any form of bean.

Home interfaces are represented by the `EJBHome` interface. This interface provides the methods for managing the bean and its lifetime. You provide user-specific capabilities, such as creating new bean instances and finding cached copies, by extending this interface.

Providing the abstraction of the bean objects is the job of the `EJBObject` interface. It doesn't matter whether your bean is an entity or session bean: You always provide the remote interface by extending this interface.

Naming Conventions and EJBs

As you look through the example code and interfaces in this chapter, you will notice that we use a familiar naming convention. In general, classes are named after the action they perform. For example, if we have XYZ functionality, the home interface is usually called `XYZHome`. The remote interface is usually called `XYZ`, while the actual bean implementation is usually called `XYZ`<*type*>`Bean`.

Within a class, methods also follow a naming convention. Methods core to the EJB functionality all start with the prefix `ejb`. For example, the method that loads a bean from the underlying data source is called `ejbLoad()`. Other naming conventions are enforced by the particular action required, and we'll cover these as we come across them.

If you are using the new EJB 2.0 classes, you will also see two interfaces called `EJBLocalHome` and `EJBLocalObject`. These represent the new local bean capabilities. We will cover local beans in Chapter 17.

Bean-implementation interfaces

A separate set of interfaces exists for the bean-implementation code (not their remote interface). This time you use the interfaces to define specific capabilities for each type of bean.

All bean types are derived from the empty interface called `EnterpriseBean`. Session beans are represented by the `SessionBean` interface, which provides methods to control the state of the basic bean as well as session information. Entity beans, on the other hand, extend the `EntityBean` interface, which provides a much larger set of basic methods. The extra methods enable you to deal with the continuous state of an entity bean. If you are using the EJB v2.0 specification and J2EE 1.3, then you can create message-driven beans by extending the `MessageDrivenBean` interface. This is much simpler than the previous two procedures, but as we mentioned earlier, it is unlikely that you'll be called upon to implement this type of bean, and it will be covered as one of the advanced techniques in the next chapter.

Dealing with errors

Like the J2SE standard libraries, the EJB API provides a rich set of standard exceptions for describing errors in the code. The most common exception you will see is `EJBException`, but not all exceptions are derived from this class. (We will introduce the rest of the exceptions later in this chapter.) Typically, a standard exception class exists for each type of operation (for example, searches, bean creation, and bean access).

Custom exceptions are also supported by the EJB specification. In fact, as the base `Exception` class is already serializable, you don't have to do anything special at all to use them. As per normal Java programming, just make sure you declare them in the throws clause of the method signature, and the client code catches them.

EJBs add one extra requirement to the use of exceptions. When you write normal code, exceptions based on `RuntimeException` do not need to be explicitly nominated in the method signature. In addition, these exceptions do not need to be caught by your calling code. To the EJB, a runtime exception is treated as an error in the bean and will not be passed on to your calling code. Any time the container finds a runtime exception being thrown, it catches it and immediately removes the bean instance from activation. That bean instance is discarded and does not go back through the normal states of passivation, as the assumption is that something really wrong took place—for example, `NullPointerException` because a variable was not set. If you want to indicate these sorts of errors, you will need to create an explicit, non-runtime based exception and declare that in the bean's remote interface.

In older books on the EJB specification, you will see the methods of the bean implementation class throw `java.rmi.RemoteException`. This exception was required in the original EJB 1.0 specification and then was deprecated for the EJB 1.1 specification. For 2.0 you should not use `RemoteException` at all and should use `EJBException`. However, the methods of the local and home interface should still throw `RemoteException` and not `EJBException`.

Using Enterprise Beans on the Server Side

Stuck between the Web page and the database is the lowly Enterprise JavaBean. In order for the Web software to make use of the database, you need to provide this EJB thing. So what goes into creating one?

EJBs consist of two logical parts — the actual bean implementation and the client. Because the client uses the services a bean presents, you naturally have to start with the server code (really just the bean implementation). Once you have this defined and written, you can start writing the servlet, JSP, or application with which to use them.

Really, when you think about it, an EJB is only the server part of this process. The client of an EJB only deals with the interface, and those that write servlets and JSPs are not permitted to deal with the bean's implementation. Clients are just given the details and work with what has been handed to them. An EJB programmer will rarely deal with the Web interface.

Session beans

A session bean implements a single user context in the application. As we have already decided, this means that for mailing duties we will use a single stateless session bean. Session beans can be either stateful or stateless, depending on your need. Writing a stateless bean requires less work than writing a bean that must be able to keep its internal state between calls. In reality, we can implement this mailer either way, as the only state it might have to save between calls is a connection to the mail server and any message files it has read.

Creating a remote interface

All beans require two parts — the remote interface and the implementation. In order to know what you need to implement, you start with the remote interface.

Creating a remote interface for your bean starts with you creating a new interface file. After defining your interface name, you must make it extend the EJB interface `EJBObject`. You have to extend this interface so that the EJB server software knows what the method definitions are when it creates its own glue code.

Passing Objects as Method Parameters

There are many similarities between the rules of EJBs and the rules of RMI. In particular, the passing of values between the client and server observe different rules than the normal Java method call. In a traditional method call, all objects are passed in directly. This is termed *pass by reference*. Your code always has access to the real object, and any changes made by called the method will still exist once that method has exited.

For RMI, and hence EJBs, a different rule applies. For these method calls, the values are a copy. This is termed *passed by value*. Because the objects you receive inside the method (for example, the bean implementation code) are a copy of the data passed, that means that the underlying object must be serializable so it may be passed over the network. Any changes that you make to the object that has been passed to you are ignored on the client as it is a copy, and the system does not replicate those changes back to the caller.

However, just to keep you on your toes, passing in a bean reference has another set of rules. Bean references actually pass through a reference to the bean. Therefore any changes you make to the bean object, will be made to the actual bean.

Next, you must declare all the methods you want your bean to provide to the outside world. This is just like declaring an RMI interface — all the methods here declare what is publicly available to the end user. Methods that you declare in the interface also follow other RMI rules. For example, all methods must declare that they throw `java.rmi.EJBException`. If your method requires object instances rather than primitives, those objects must either be other bean interfaces, or the object must be serializable. This allows the object to be passed correctly between the bean code client and server.

As an example of what a bean remote interface may look like, the following is the representation of a mailer object in our example application:

```
public interface Mailer extends EJBObject {
    public void sendConfirmationEmail(Customer cust,
                                      Order[] orders)
        throws EJBException;

    public void sendDeliveredEmail(Customer cust,
                                   Order[] orders)
        throws EJBException;
}
```

Implementing the bean logic

The remote interface defines the basic functionality of your bean, so now you need to implement it. Here is where you stray from the RMI path. In RMI, your object implementation would `implement` the remote interface—for EJBs, you don't. Instead, you must define one of the other interfaces that define the type of bean you're creating. As this is the section on session beans, that means you should implement the `SessionBean` interface.

`SessionBean` is an interface, which means that you need to make sure you implement all the methods. For the moment, just stub them out; we'll come back to them shortly. In addition to implementing the basic methods, you should provide a public constructor explicitly, even if it is empty. This will circumvent some well-known problems with reflection to create class instances with classes that don't have an explicit public constructor.

Finally, you must provide method bodies for the business methods defined in the remote interface. Doing this is a cut-and-paste affair, but you must remove the declaration of the `RemoteException` from the throws clause required by the remote and home interfaces. If you still need to throw an exception, you may throw an `EJBException` if you wish (most people don't). Again, start by stubbing these methods out, like this:

```
public class MailerSessionBean implements SessionBean {
    public MailerSessionBean() {
    }

    public void sendConfirmationEmail(Customer cust,
                                      Order[] orders)
        throws EJBException {
    }

    public void sendDeliveredEmail(Customer cust,
                                   Order[] orders)
          throws EJBException {
    }

    public void ejbCreate() throws EJBException {
    }

    public void ejbRemove() {
    }

    public void ejbActivate() {
    }

    public void ejbPassivate() {
    }

    public void setSessionContext(SessionContext ctx) {
    }
}
```

Writing the methods

Now the fun starts — you get to write real code! Obviously you have the two business methods to fill in, but you also have all these other ones — what do they mean, and what do they do?

The way in which you implement code internally for a session bean is very dependent on whether the bean is going to remember state or not. In the case of the mailer bean, you can implement it either way. Because you know that the bean will be held for a long time and used to send many e-mails, it probably makes more sense to use a stateful bean, but you can use a stateless one instead. We'll show you how to implement both.

Creating a stateless session bean

The major characteristic of the session bean is that you cannot customize it with particular parameter information — to the outside world, every instance must look and act the same. This does not prevent you from having internal variables, though. This is good, because you have a mailer, you would probably like to be able to set up all the mail interfaces and document templates ahead of time. As the session bean is going to be held on a single client, probably for a long time, it makes sense for you to organize all these items up front.

Just because you cannot configure a stateless session bean from the outside does not mean that you can't configure it from the inside. For example, nothing prevents a session bean from connecting to a database to get information or use system properties. These are advanced topics, and we won't cover them in this chapter. You will find a good introduction in Chapter 17.

Now you have four empty methods from the bean interface, a constructor, and two business-logic methods in which you can place code. Where do you start? Well, the simplest way is to work out what each method does, and what data you need to keep lying about. Table 16-1 introduces the four methods of the `EJBObject` interface.

Table 16-1
Methods of the EJBObject interface

Method	*Description*
`ejbRemove()`	Provides notification that the bean is about to be removed from active use. The equivalent of `finalize()` for EJBs. When this method is called, you should shut down and clean up everything you are holding internally, as the bean is about to completely disappear.
`ejbActivate()`	Provides notification that the bean is about to become active after a dormant period. The chip should refresh anything internal that it might need – particularly items that cannot be serialized.

Method	*Description*
`ejbPassivate()`	Provides notification that the bean is about to go into hibernation for some reason. If the bean has any active connections (for example, mail currently being processed), it should clean up anything pending, but not remove everything completely.
`setSessionContext()`	Provides notification that the bean has just been created and become part of an active session. This provides all the contextual information so that you can perform any additional configuration. The bean has not yet been accessed by any client, it is just in the global pool.

As far as a creating a stateless bean is concerned, only one method really concerns you — `ejbRemove()`. You only need the other methods for stateful beans. In fact, if you were to implement those methods, it would be a waste of time. Figure 16-1 shows the lifecycle of a stateless session bean. Notice that there are only two states and two method calls. The other methods, such as `ejbActivate()`, are never called.

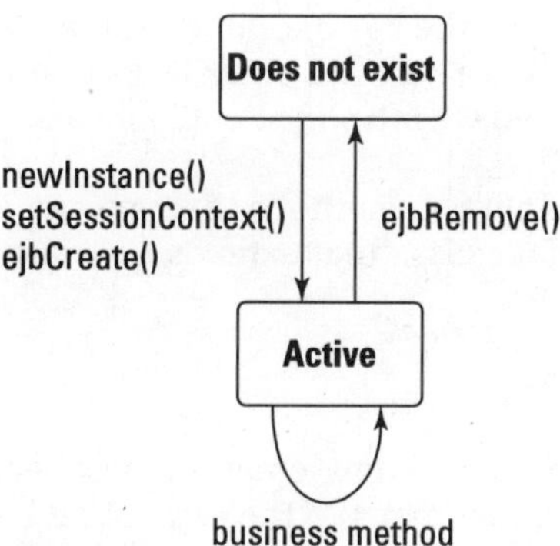

Figure 16-1: Lifecycle of a stateless session bean

One more method remains to be covered: `ejbCreate()`. Looking through the javadoc, you can see that it is not part of the `SessionBean` interface. Neither was it a part of the remote interface's business methods. Where did it come from? The `ejbCreate()` method is another part of the rules of building a bean. The EJB server calls `ejbCreate()` when it is building a new instance of a bean. This tells the bean that it has been created (although you already knew that because the constructor had been called) and that it has been accepted as a bean by the server environment. It is time to configure any internal structures that might be needed by the bean implementation (for example, that JavaMail connection).

Note The `ejbCreate()` method must always return `void` for session beans—both stateful and stateless.

From an implementation perspective, it is better to do all your setup work in the `ejbCreate()` method than do it in the constructor. You know that when this method is called that everything is fine with the system. The bean has been loaded, it is part of the server environment, and consequently you can load database drivers, e-mail interfaces, and anything else that might be useful. So in your stateless bean code, you will establish the mail connections that the bean will be required to perform.

Tip The assumptions that we make for the purpose of these examples may not be correct in every case. For entity beans, a different approach is taken when initializing items like database connections.

Writing the home interface

Now that you have completed the definition of the bean, there is one more action for you to complete: the creation of the home interface so that the client code can create instances of your session bean. Even though a stateless session bean does not contain any configuration information, a home interface must still be provided.

The job of the home interface is to provide methods that perform the management actions of beans. Think of these tasks as being like the `new` operator to create a new instance. Well, we also need to destroy beans, too. There are other tasks that home interfaces perform that you will see later on when we introduce entity beans.

For a simple stateless session bean, there are only two methods that you can provide here. Firstly, start by creating a new interface class that extends `EJBHome`:

```
public interface MailerHome extends EJBHome {
}
```

To this you are required to add just one method—one that creates a new bean instance. In this case, it is the `create()` method that maps to the `ejbCreate()` method of your bean implementation code. The `create()` method takes no arguments, because the `ejbCreate()` method also takes no argument. The return values are different, however. Where your implementation code returns `void`, the home interface requires you to return an instance of the remote interface. For example:

```
public Mailer create() throws CreateException, RemoteException;
```

Another requirement is that all create methods, not just those used by a stateless session bean, throw `CreateException`. If your client code catches this exception, it is because something has failed during the creation process. Typically this will be due to a failure in your code (maybe it threw a `RuntimeException` such as `NullPointerException`) rather than a server failure. For server or communications issues, `RemoteException` will be thrown instead.

Creating a stateful session bean

Before showing you some of the implementation of a stateful session bean's code, we'll introduce the differences between the two types of session bean. Earlier we said that for stateless beans you can't provide any configuration information that customizes the bean for a particular client. Just what did we mean by this?

Let's imagine that you have a big Web server running a large Web site. Thousands of transactions are happening at your Web site every minute. A servlet is fetching the various beans for each request and releasing them when finished. Obviously a lot of stuff is happening here. As a reasonably experienced programmer, you should know that allocating memory is an expensive operation. If you had to create a new instance in memory every time the servlet asked for a bean, the server would be very quickly overwhelmed by the performance impact of memory management. Therefore, EJB server vendors' approach to beans is similar to their approach to database connections — they create a pool of them. This pool contains a bunch of beans lying dormant. Nobody is using them. Your servlet comes along and asks for XYZ bean. The EJB server responds by dipping into this pool of unused beans. If there is one of the required type (the server will create pools of all the bean types available), the server removes it from the pool and passes it back to the servlet. If not, the server creates a new instance and passes that back to the servlet.

To learn more on database connections and pooling, please read Chapter 7.

Now consider your servlet processing away using information from that bean. The bean is calculating some value. What you really want is to make sure that, given the same input, each bean instance returned by the server will produce the same answer. The bean your servlet is using is a stateless bean. No matter which instance of the bean you use, they all look the same on the outside.

For some applications, that is not what you want. When you pass the data to the bean for calculation, you want to have it configured according to some particular set of values. If the code lets the bean go, and then fetches another one some time later, the code expects them to be different. Similarly, if the code lets go of the bean and then asks for it again, using the same configuration information, the bean should remember where it was and continue as if nothing had happened.

Writing a stateful session bean requires a little more work on your part. In order for the bean to know about its state, you will need to write code for all those other methods defined in the `EJBObject` interface.

Completing the class

Finishing off the bean implementation is a relatively simple affair for our mailer. Implementation starts with the `ejbCreate()` method, as it is here that you will need to do the setup work for the code. In this particular example, that setup work consists of initializing the mail code.

Creating Customized Bean Instances

So far we have only showed you beans with default constructors. What if you want to create a bean that has configuration information provided by the client at startup (for example, the name of the Web site or terminal operator)? That is, what if you'd like to use a constructor with one or more parameters for the bean implementation?

Internally, the bean creates a mapping between the home interface and the bean implementation code. For each different way you would like to create an instance of the bean, you must provide an implementation of the `ejbCreate()` method with matching parameters. As you can see in the preceding code, we have provided one `ejbCreate()` method that takes no arguments. Say you want to create the object with a particular `String` for a name: You will need to provide a different creation method taking a `String` parameter. For example:

```
public void ejbCreate(String name) throws EJBException {
  this.myName = name;
}
```

You do this instead of providing different constructors for the class. Because the EJB is loaded using reflection, the only constructor that will ever be called is the default, no-argument version. So in order to pass any per-instance configuration information, you need to provide these methods. You then write all your startup code in them and leave the constructor empty.

To complete the cycle, you must match the `ejbCreate()` method in your bean implementation with a corresponding method in the home interface with exactly the same arguments. For example, the home interface method declaration that matches the preceding code snippet is:

```
public Mailer create(String name)
    throws CreateException, RemoteException;
```

You implement the mail code using the JavaMail API that is part of the J2EE specification. If you are unfamiliar with JavaMail, please take a look at Chapter 5.

When initializing the code, you basically look for the really common items. Treat this method as you would a constructor. If you are writing a stateful session bean and have multiple `ejbCreate()` methods, then put all the common code in a shared method. All the rules that apply to good software engineering also apply here. Here is what the `ejbCreate()` method looks like for your mail bean:

```
public void ejbCreate() throws EJBException {
  // number formatter for price formatting
   formatter = NumberFormat.getNumberInstance();
   formatter.setMinimumFractionDigits(2);
   formatter.setMaximumFractionDigits(2);
```

```
        Properties props = new Properties();
        String mailhost = "mail.mycompany.com";

        props.put("mail.host", mailhost);
        props.put("mail.transport.protocol", "smtp");
        props.put("mail.smtp.host", mailhost);

        mailSession = Session.getDefaultInstance(props);

        try {
            smtpService = mailSession.getTransport();
        } catch(MessagingException nspe) {
            // SMTP is one of the defaults. If we get this
            // there is a serious problem!
            System.err.println("Danger, Danger! " +
                               "No SMTP mail provider!");
        }
    }
```

Next you need to fill in the business logic methods. For the example bean, these are almost identical, so we'll just show you one. Funnily enough, it is in the business-logic methods that you implement the main functionality of the code. Methods here obey all the usual rules. Remember that if your method takes parameters that are not primitives, the classes must be serializable. In this case, the parameters are other beans, which are serializable by default. For example, the business method to set the confirmation email requires the customer we are sending the message to and list of orders. These parameters are passed through to the bean implementation by using the remote interface classes like this:

```
    public void sendConfirmationEmail(Customer cust,
                                      Order[] orders)
        throws EJBException {
        String email;
        String name;

        try {
            email = cust.getEmail();
            name = cust.getName();
        } catch(RemoteException re) {
            // Argh! Can't get the details. No point continuing
            System.err.println("Error getting customer details" +
                               re);
            return;
        }

        StringBuffer buf = new StringBuffer("Dear ");
        buf.append(name);

        // put in the message contents here.....

        int id;
        int[] price;
```

```
        for(int i = 0; i < orders.length; i++) {
            try {
                // fetch the name first so that we can skip this
                // order line if something goes wrong.
                id = orders[i].getOrderID();
                price = orders[i].getCost();

                buf.append("\t");
                buf.append(id);
                buf.append(" $");
                buf.append(price[0]);
                buf.append(".");
                buf.append(formatter.format(price[1]));
                buf.append('\n');
            } catch(RemoteException re) {
                // Ignore it.
                System.err.println("Error getting order" + re);
            }
        }

        // finish of the message with a little greeting

        // send it
        sendMessage(email, "Order confirmation", buf.toString());
    }
```

Tip

For a much nicer message, you would probably like to print out the product's name, rather than just a bland ID number. The `Order` interface gives you a way to do that, by first fetching the product ID and then locating the appropriate bean using the home interface. Locating the bean is a process we have not yet covered, and so we will revisit this code later in the chapter to show you how to do it.

Although using ordinary programming strategies is useful, a few tweaks are still useful for EJB work. First, note that we attempt to get as much information up front as possible. This enables us to bug out as early as possible. Remember that EJBs are part of a distributed system, and that at any time, one piece of that system can fail. You always need to write your code to be aware of and deal reasonably with errors.

After finishing the business-logic methods, if you are implementing a stateful session bean, turn your attention to the other methods, which we will now cover. If you are implementing a stateless bean, your basic session bean is now complete.

Implementing passivation

If your bean needs to implement passivation because it is a stateful session bean, then you need to turn your attention to the `ejbPassivate()` and `ejbActivate()` methods. Inside these, you deal with the bean going into and coming out of hibernation, respectively. During the passivation period, your bean is serialized to free some memory, which implies that any bean about to be passivated must conform to the rules of serialization. For example, a serialized bean should not maintain socket connections or file references while it is in the passivated state.

Where Do My Error Messages Go?

In these examples we've been showing the code printing out to `System.err` or `System.out`. After all, your code is embedded in a Web server somewhere; it's not as though you have a nice command line on which to view all the exception traces. So where do they go?

The answer depends on the EJB server software you are running. For example, the reference implementation puts them in the $j2ee.home/logs/*machine_name*/*application_name* directory. You will need to look up the documentation for your environment for more information.

In a future release of the J2EE environment, you will be able to use the new Java logging capability included in J2SE 1.4. This will give you even more control over your logging capabilities. However, as logs are files, logging will still be controlled somewhat by the restrictions placed on EJBs, which we outlined earlier in the chapter.

Because stateful session beans can have this intermediate step, their lifecycle is a little more complex. Figure 16-2 shows the difference. Notice how, in comparison to the simple Figure 16-1, that there is an intermediate state. The intermediate state represents the time when your stateful session bean has been passivated.

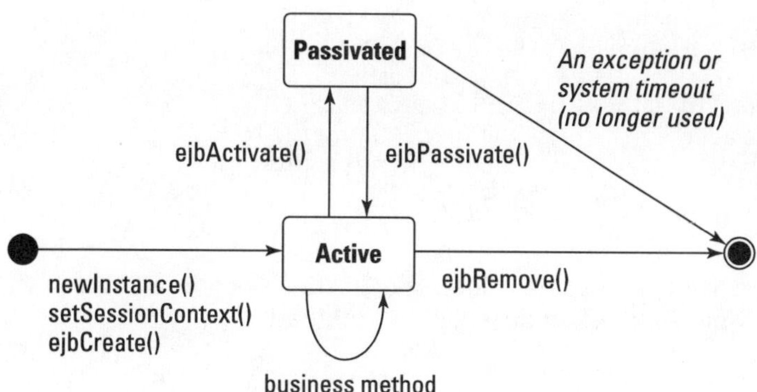

Figure 16-2: The lifecycle of a stateful session bean

While your mailer bean does not need to handle passivation (there is no state to be saved), it will be implemented anyway as an exercise. When the bean is about to be serialized, you don't want it to keep any information about the mail system in use. There really isn't any need for it, so you might as well remove the reference. The number formatter can stay, though, because it is not causing you any harm. This makes the `ejbPassivate()` method body really simple:

```
public void ejbPassivate() {
    mailSession = null;
    smtpService = null;
}
```

Recovering from passivation (activation) requires you to undo the effects that you've just created. Now you must establish those references again. You may remember that you did exactly this in the `ejbCreate()` method: So why not re-use the code here? Instead of just copying the code, you will shuffle it a little bit so that you now have a common internal method — `createMailSession()`:

```
private void createMailSession() {
    Properties props = new Properties();
    String mailhost = "mail.mycompany.com";

    props.put("mail.host", mailhost);
    props.put("mail.transport.protocol", "smtp");
    props.put("mail.smtp.host", mailhost);

    mailSession = Session.getDefaultInstance(props);

    try {
        smtpService = mailSession.getTransport();
    } catch(MessagingException nspe) {
        // SMTP is one of the defaults. If we get this
        // there is a serious problem!
        // Should throw an EJBException
        System.err.println("Danger, Danger! " +
                           "No SMTP mail provider!");
    }
}
```

With this method created, `ejbCreate()` loses a collection of code, and the `ejbActivate()` only has one task to do — call this method:

```
public void ejbCreate() {
    formatter = NumberFormat.getNumberInstance();
    formatter.setMinimumFractionDigits(2);
    formatter.setMaximumFractionDigits(2);

    createMailSession();
}

public void ejbActivate() {
    createMailSession();
}
```

That's it. A complete session bean now exists. As you have taken a completely minimalistic approach to the design and implementation of this particular bean, you can deploy it as either a stateless or stateful session bean.

Entity beans

Of all the bean types, session beans are the easiest to implement. Their behavior is relatively simple, and you have only a few methods to implement and rules to live by. Now you're ready for the next level — entity beans.

Entity beans are, by nature, long-lived objects. An entity bean is typically classified as a bean that directly represents some underlying data source, such as a database. When you ask for an entity bean, it will probably already exist, and you will just be given the handle to it. When you have finished with the bean, it doesn't just go back into the pool because there are maybe another 10 client applications that are all making use of the same entity bean. Generally an entity bean is created immediately when the server is started. When the server shuts down or crashes, that does not destroy the bean; it is more a case of suspended animation. As soon as the server restarts, that bean will exist again in exactly the same state it was in when you left it.

Types of entity beans

As with session beans, there are two types of entity beans. The types are defined by how you get data into and out of the bean: Broadly speaking, either the bean manages the data, or the EJB server manages the data.

When the bean itself manages both the data and keeping up to date with underlying data source, this is termed Bean-Managed Persistence (BMP). When you are referring to the bean itself, it is a Bean-Managed Entity Bean. In this form, the bean, whenever it becomes passivated or activated, must look after re-establishing the database connections or whatever other internal systems it might need. In some respects, this is similar to the way in which stateful session beans must work.

On the other end of the spectrum are entity beans that let the EJB server manage all their capabilities and data: This is Container-Managed Persistence (CMP). These beans are then called Container-Managed Entity Beans. Each of these terms is a mouthful, so usually the "entity" part is dropped.

Bean management is much simpler to implement than container management. A bean-managed persistence scheme is very similar to what you have already seen with stateful session beans. Container-managed beans require a lot more interaction between the bean and the EJB server and home-interface code. In addition, there is a lot of extra work to do outside the bean, including learning yet another language. For this reason, we'll stick with the simpler form for the remainder of this chapter.

Pinning down entity beans

Rules, rules. No matter where we go, we just can't escape them! Writing entity beans is no different. In addition to the basic rules about what EJBs can and cannot do, entity beans add a few more. Most of these rules are brought about because of the required behavior of representing an item in a database, so let's try to define how an entity bean works.

Entity beans represent some real data in an underlying database. If you need something to do quick calculations, write a session bean. This means that the bean is a thin veneer over the underlying data. Where you search a database for a row or rows in a table, a bean represents the result of that search, encoded in Java. Hang on! Isn't that what JDBC is about? Also, if an entity bean is just a veneer over the database, why not just use the database directly rather than going through all this extra overhead?

Take a step back. What is Java programming, and in more general, object-oriented programming all about? The most fundamental purpose is to put together little pieces of data and the code that acts on that data all in one lovely gift-wrapped box—preferably black in color. When you hand someone that item, they really don't care what's inside it, just that it works as advertised. In Java, everything starts right at the bottom—a single common class that everyone uses (`java.lang.Object`). As you move up the food chain, things get more and more complex. Classes start containing more than just data—they become composites of other classes. The ultimate class becomes the application or applet or servlet or whatever. The EJB is just one level in the process. The bean takes all the information in the database, wraps it up in some pretty clothing, and allows others to take it to the dance. When you're building huge enterprise applications, the EJB makes it much easier to follow code when you start passing around instances of the `Order` class, rather than an array of strings and integers. Having that class means that you only need to write the code once that deals with the data, rather than something for every time you want to use it. So that completes your theory lesson on object-oriented programming. What does it all mean?

An entity bean, as an abstraction of some real, underlying data, is held to some of the same rules as that data. For example, a database contains tables, and each table contains many rows of data. Somehow you have to create these abstractions and map Java code to the database. You have two options here—one is to encapsulate the entire table, and the other is to represent only a single row (or the result of a query to the database that may join multiple tables into a single result).

For the novice, it probably makes the most sense to wrap the entire table in a single bean. After all, that enables you to build a heap of methods to query directly for data and rows of people in a simple, convenient fashion. Where this approach lets you down is that in most cases, that database is going to be huge. Worst of all, that huge data size translates to enormous amounts of memory consumption on the Java server. And, to throw one more problem into the ring—what if you want data that span multiple tables? These are all design issues that you should consider when building an entity-bean instance.

No matter what you do, you have to be able to tell the system just which bean you want. Entity beans also use the home interface to locate bean instances (we'll cover implementing the home interface in the next section), but you also need some way to identify the bean you want. For example, in the database, it is easy to specify that you want a particular customer simply by using his or her unique ID (primary key) in the SQL `SELECT` statement. Entity beans have exactly the same context — a primary key that nominates a specific bean. If we say one bean "instance" is equivalent to one row of a relational database table, you can see the instant correlation between the two.

In big systems, it is quite probable that a particular piece of data will be represented by more than one instance of your entity bean. When coding applications and beans, you should never assume that your bean is going to have only one instance. For example, the data underlying the bean could be changed by another instance. Be careful, and always assume that your data are not valid when processing information from an underlying database. The entity-bean interface has a way of enforcing the integrity of the data across multiple bean instances, but you should still keep it in mind when coding.

Creating the remote interface

Implementing an entity bean requires the same basic steps as implementing a session bean. For this example, we will show the implementation of the customer entity bean from our code.

You start the process in the same way by creating a remote interface. This interface is no different from the interfaces used for session beans and so should present nothing out of the ordinary. The `Customer` remote interface is an interface that extends `EJBObject`. To this you add your normal business-method definitions. Again, you need to make sure that all the methods throw `RemoteException` as you can see from this definition of the `Customer` remote interface:

```
public interface Customer extends EJBObject {
    public int getCustomerID() throws RemoteException;
    public void setCustomerID(int id) throws RemoteException;

    public String getName() throws RemoteException;
    public void setName(String name) throws RemoteException;

    public String getAddress() throws RemoteException;
    public void setAddress(String addr) throws RemoteException;

    public String getEmail() throws RemoteException;
    public void setEmail(String addr) throws RemoteException;

    public String getCountry() throws RemoteException;
    public void setCountry(String code) throws RemoteException;

    public String getPhoneNumber() throws RemoteException;
    public void setPhoneNumber(String ph)
        throws RemoteException;
}
```

Writing the bean implementation

Next you move on to the bean-implementation code. Again, you follow the same process as for session beans—with one small twist. This time, instead of implementing the `SessionBean` interface, the code must extend the `EntityBean` interface—which is fair enough, as you are creating an entity bean, not a session bean.

In stubbing out the new methods of the entity bean, you will find that they match fairly well with session beans. All the familiar methods are there—`ejbRemove()`, `ejbPassivate()`, and `ejbActivate()`. Four new methods also make an appearance: `ejbLoad()`, `ejbStore()`, `setEntityContext()`, and `unsetEntityContext()`. Table 16-2 explains these new methods.

Table 16-2
Methods of the EntityBean interface

Method	*Description*
`ejbLoad()`	Provides notification that your bean should reload its internal data from the underlying data source, as it may have changed.
`ejbStore()`	Provides notification that any changes that the current client may have made should be stored back in the database.
`setEntityContext()`	Provides notification of the context information that this bean is in. (Identical functionality to that of the session bean's `setSessionContext()` method.)
`unsetEntityContext()`	Provides notification that any previously set context information is now becoming invalid. The bean is about to be garbage-collected, so you should clean up any remaining information or links.

Reading between the lines here, you may have noticed something interesting: The load and store events talk about reading and writing to the underlying data source. What does this mean? Well, the implication is that your bean does not need to maintain an absolutely live, completely synchronized link with the data source. The code is allowed to buffer changes locally.

An example of where buffering changes locally might be appropriate is when your bean takes a lot of client information in a series of steps and then writes it all to the database. If you know that your bean is going to need to do this, you may make use of the JDBC batch-updating calls. At the time you know your bean becomes live for a client, you can immediately start to batch any updates by calling the `addBatch()`

method of `Statement` rather than the direct `executeQuery()` method. Then, once you receive the notification through `ejbStore()`, the code can just call `executeBatch()` and update everything at once. This is a very useful tactic and a great way to optimize the performance of your application.

Revisiting bean pooling

Before moving on to discuss the implementation of a bean, think back to the issue of how the EJB server views a bean. As far as you know, the bean, when not being used by a client and sitting in the pool, is lying around in the Caribbean, sipping margaritas, waiting for the call-up to work. As far as entity beans are concerned, their lifestyle is a little more complicated than that.

In the preceding sections, you might have gotten the idea that once an entity bean has been created for a particular piece of data (say a row in a database table), that piece of data is all it represents in its life. That is not the case. Any entity-bean instance can be re-used for any similar piece of data. If you ask for a customer-entity bean, that given instance could be used to represent any customer in the database. So when you've finished with it, and it has gone back to sitting in the pool, the next time it is used it will probably represent a completely different customer. Each bean instance must be capable of being changed on demand.

How does the code acquire this capability? Through the mysterious `ejbCreate()` method. We've mentioned this strange beast in passing many times before, but never really delved into its character properly. `ejbCreate()` is the method called by our EJB server on a particular instance when a client asks for a new bean. In session beans, this method is used to create an instance of the bean configured in some given way (the parameters passed to the create method). For entity beans, the role of the create methods changes somewhat. Under the entity-bean type, create methods resemble the more traditional "creation" role. That is, when a user calls the `create()` method on the home interface, it is a sign that he or she would like to make a new instance of that bean and the data that it represents underneath (for example, a new product).

Your bean implementation is allowed to have as many different `ejbCreate()` methods as it thinks it needs. Naturally, these methods also conform to the normal method-declaration rules about parameter ordering and naming and so on, but you are not required to have only the version with no parameters. (You can even leave it out, but that really isn't a good idea.) What you are required to do for entity beans is return an instance of the primary key from the `ejbCreate()` method (remember, session beans are to return `void`). Figure 16-3 shows the basic life cycle of an entity bean and how the various method calls relate to this life cycle.

It is not really a good idea to leave out the default, no-argument constructor or `create()` method. In the enterprise environment, you really should always provide a default way to access everything.

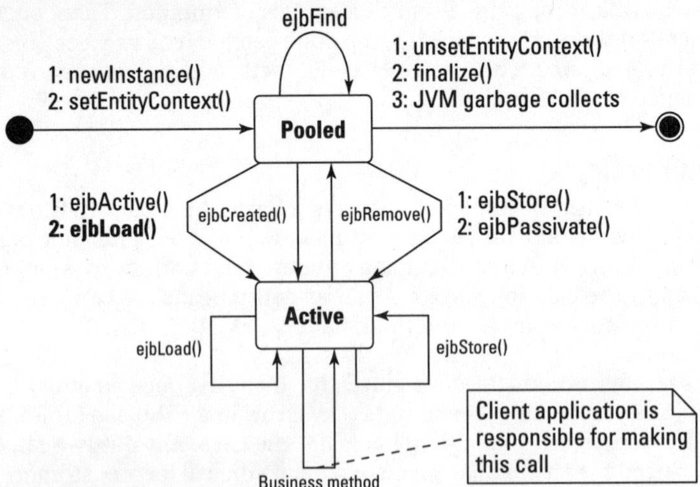

Figure 16-3: The life cycle of an entity bean and the method calls used in each transition

So, according to this life cycle, it is quite possible that a bean will be instantiated, put to work representing an existing customer, released back to the pool, then pulled out of the pool to represent a new customer, and finally garbage-collected once it is done.

Deciding on appropriate creation methods

From the preceding discussion it is quite clear that the `ejbCreate()` methods play a very fundamental role in your entity-bean implementation. These methods are what enable you to create a bean that represents a new piece of data. So just what alternatives should you supply?

When adding alternative parameter lists, you should consider how you want to let the user find and access a bean. For example, a customer bean should be able to be created based on the pre-selected customer ID (for example, a user name that the user has provided). You also want to provide a default method in case someone wants to create a new customer where an ID does not yet exist. However, there is really no point to providing a creation method based on just a telephone number; though a creation method that provides all the properties of the bean is a good idea. It allows the client code to find out all the details before attempting to create the bean, and this in turn allows a little bit of pre-processing to be performed on the client to reject an application for a new customer before you get to the point of allocating expensive system resources to it (think—processing a sign-up Web page).

Lifecycle of the Entity Bean Explained

As you have already seen in Figure 16-3, the lifecycle of the entity bean is quite complex. We will now try to make sense of it for you.

In the beginning, the bean did not exist. That's the single black circle on the left. At some point in time, the EJB container decides that it needs to load a few instances of your bean into a pool. (Typically this is done when the server first starts.) The pool contains beans that are not used by anyone. The server keeps them around just in case.

To add an instance of your bean to the pool, the server starts by creating the instance using reflection (calling `Class.forName().newInstance()`). After instantiation, the entity context information is set using `setEntityContext()`. At this time your bean is in the pool and should be ready to perform any task.

Once a bean is placed in the pool, there are three actions that it could be called on to do next: create a new instance in the underlying data source, represent an existing instance of data in the underlying source, or perform searches.

When beans are sitting in the pool, they can still be performing useful tasks. Entity beans have three types of methods that could be called while in the pool: finders, selects, and home methods (home methods are covered later in the chapter and again in the next chapter). You could consider these method calls to be the same as `static` methods of a traditional Java class. That is, utility methods that can be called without needing to create an instance of the class. When these methods are called, your bean should not need to know about any of the other state information stored in the bean. They are quick, simple queries to return a search style request for information.

In order to leave the pool, the bean has two options (well, three if you consider destroying the bean as a way of leaving). The first option is to represent a new piece of data. That is the role of the creation methods. When they are called, you should insert the appropriate row(s) into the underlying database. The second option is to represent a load of existing information. This is performed through the activation methods. When a bean is activated, it needs to check with the entity context about what piece of data it represents and then must fill its internal variables with any required information. In either option, your bean is now in the active state.

Once active, a bean will occasionally change state. For example you write values to it (for example, change the address of the customer). Because your client code maintains a reference to that bean for some length of time, somehow that data must make it back to the database. That is the job of the `ejbStore()` method. When store is called, it is a request by the container to your bean to store its internal state in the database. Occasionally, your bean gets out of sync with the database, so the container will require the bean to make itself up to date again. This is performed through the `ejbLoad()` method. Note that at this time, you are just updating the state from a known start point. You really only want to check and update information that you already know about. It is not like the `ejbActivate()` call, where you must load/replace the entire state of the bean in memory.

Continued

Continued

Once your client code has decided it no longer needs the bean reference, the container is entitled to put it back into the pool. When this happens, the `ejbPassivate()` method is called. Alternatively, the client may want to delete the data from the underlying pool. This action is performed through the `ejbRemove()` method.

Once back in the pool, that bean instance is once again able to go one of the three options. Just because the bean had to create a new data last time, does not mean that it will do the same next time it leaves the pool.

Finally, the container decides it has too many bean instances sitting in the pool, or the server is going to shut down. The first thing your bean implementation knows about this is that the `unsetEntityContext()` method is called. Once that is called, it is all over for your code, and you can expect that your code will not be called any more.

What are we going to provide for our customer entity bean then? Well, we've decided that we only want three variations:

1. No arguments, so a person can create a new default user that has no data configured.
2. A single-integer argument that is interpreted to be the customer ID. This will fetch the details of the nominated customer from the database.
3. Five parameters that correspond to the five columns of the customer database (the customer ID is automatically generated). This allows you to create a new customer with all the details set immediately.

The end result looks like this:

```
public void ejbCreate() throws CreateException, EJBException {
  ...
}

public void ejbCreate(int id)
    throws CreateException, EJBException {
  ...
}

public void ejbCreate(String name,
                      String addr,
                      String email,
                      String country,
                      String phone) {
   throws CreateException, EJBException
  ...
}
```

Accessing and finding primary keys

A couple of subsections ago we discussed the need for each bean to represent a single row in an underlying database. Part of this discussion was about the need for a unique identifier to enable you to access any given row simply and easily. So far we have not alluded to how the mapping of the unique identifier to a row in the database is performed in the bean code, and so now we need to cover this last piece of the bean puzzle.

EJBs use the same primary-key concept as the relational database. For each entity bean, you must provide a class that uniquely identifies that bean. This class is referred to as the *primary-key class* and plays a vital role in the entity-bean framework. This class is not particularly special. In fact, no EJB interface exists for you to extend. The only requirement is that this primary-key class, like all classes passed to and from beans, must be serializable. This class must present your internal code with an unambiguous way of locating a specific piece of pre-existing bean data. If you are representing a row in a database, that's simple — all your bean has to contain is the primary key for that row. For example, this is the complete primary key for the customer-entity bean:

```
public class CustomerID implements Serializable {
    public int id;

    public CustomerID() {
    }

    public CustomerID(int id) {
        this.id = id;
    }
}
```

Public variables, a default constructor, and nothing else — very simple, isn't it? It really doesn't matter what the form of this class is, so long as you can make use of it in your code. In this case, all that is used is an integer that corresponds to the `customer_id` column of the `Customer` table.

Although the example class here uses a single item of data, primary key classes may choose to use a number of values. All that you must ensure is that the class is always unique for each bean instance you create. For classes that represent multiple items of data, make sure you override the default `hashCode()` and `equals()` methods so that your EJB code performs correctly.

What good is a primary key without a way to use it? Primary keys are used in a number of new methods that are added to the bean implementation. These methods are called *finder methods* because you use them to locate bean instances and/or key information for other beans.

Finder methods are only implemented by you on bean-managed persistence-entity beans. When you use container-managed persistence, as we discuss in Chapter 17, they will not be implemented directly by you.

The name of a finder method is required to start with `ejbFind`; as with the create methods, you can take any collection of parameters. Three further restrictions exist:

✦ The return value is required to be either the primary key class or an `Enumeration` or one of the collections classes (for example, `List`) of them.

✦ You are required to have the method named `ejbFindByPrimaryKey()`, which takes the primary-key class as its argument and then returns the same primary key if it can be found in the underlying data source.

✦ All finder methods must throw `FinderException` in addition to any other exceptions that you may have.

Within the finder methods, you will need to make database connections and other processing requests. When these are called, they are logically separate from the create methods. It is entirely possible that one of your find methods will be called before the create method, as the EJB server might request that an unused pooled bean service some of the search requests from clients.

When you're deciding what finder methods to create, the best tip is to look at your list of `ejbCreate()` options. If you can create a bean based on that information, then surely someone will want to look up key information using the same items? Of course this isn't always true. Consider the call-center application again: When searching for a user who has just phoned in, you might have nothing more than a user's real name and phone number or state. This information may not be unique, but it can give you a list of primary keys with which to find the matching users. However, the create <⇨ find equivalence is a good starting point.

Bearing this in mind, the customer-entity bean is going to have two finder methods — the compulsory one, and the other that uses the customer's name.

```
public CustomerID ejbFindByPrimaryKey(CustomerID pk)
    throws EJBException, FinderException {
}

public Collection ejbFindWithName(String name)
    throws EJBException, FinderException {
}
```

One variation that you might be interested in applying here is a "find all" method that allows you to list the primary key of everyone in the database. This may or may not be convenient, depending on your application needs.

The return type of finder methods is important. Because the container uses the return type to decide how to process the primary key, there are only certain classes you can use. For single object finders, such as `findByPrimaryKey()`, only the primary key type can be used. If you are writing a finder method that returns a number of primary keys, you have two options — `java.util.Collection` or `java.util.Enumeration`. Ideally, you should only use `Collection` as the return type. `Enumeration` is only used if you need to provide backward compatibility with old JDK and J2EE specification servers. Considering that you will be using the features of EJB 2.0 and, by implication, J2SE 1.3, then this should not be an issue for you.

Writing the create methods

Enough discussion of method names! Time to move on to writing the body of the methods. First let's deal with the `ejbCreate()` methods. They define the sort of data you need to store internally as class variables.

Note The EJB specification says that the internal variables of the class should not be initialized until after the `ejbCreate()` method has been called. Your code should only set the internal variables from information provided in the parameters to the `ejbCreate()` method. Any other internal state, you should only set as the result of the various business methods. The idea is that the bean user will then fill in the rest of the data that were not provided through the `ejbCreate()` through the various business methods. For example, if you only provide a user name for the customer, you should not provide a default address, but instead wait for the `setAddress()` business method to be called.

Many parts of the entity-bean internals will be familiar to you. For a start, you have a database, so you will need to create and access the appropriate driver instance. Then you will need to obtain a connection to the database and make the requests to obtain the data. You also need to decide how to deal with the database and its data. If you have a connection and the bean is coming and going from the pool, what is the best time to fetch an instance of `Connection` or `Statement`? Remember that you also have passivation issues to deal with, as well as the finder methods.

The answer to this question is programmer-specific. Beans are long-lived, so once you've accessed a resource you can confidently keep everything around for later requests. Our personal preference is to create connections and statements as soon as possible, such as in the `setEntityContext()` method. However, if you want to use pooled database connections, you may not want to establish the connections early, as these pooled connections can be released back into the global pool.

Note Lazily creating database connections is where the new JDBC 3.0 pooled statements will become extremely handy. You can easily request a pooled connection, create a prepared statement, and release them both back into the pool. The lack of statement pooling under the older EJB 2.0 spec meant that continuously requesting new connections and statements was an expensive exercise. Now, with statement pooling, this will become a very cheap operation: It is definitely worth changing your preferred implementation style to take advantages of this new feature.

Assuming that you have some code that has already fetched your ConnectionPoolDataSource for you, you have three methods to implement, each with different behaviors. The first version takes no arguments. What this no-argument method says is that someone wants to create a new bean with no information set. Since the bean is definitely used between many different clients over time, when someone asks for a new default bean the code should clear any previously set details, like this:

```
public CustomerID ejbCreate()
    throws CreateException, EJBException {

    customerId = -1;
    userName = null;
    address = null;
    emailAddress = null;
    country = null;
    phoneNumber = null;

    CustomerID c_id = new CustomerID(-1);
    return c_id;
}
```

Note that the customerId is set to -1. The preceding is an example only because you don't know how to fetch a new customer ID. Some databases support AUTO_INCREMENT for a value in a column. In such cases, you don't need to set an ID; it will be done automatically when you insert a new row into the database. Other databases do not support AUTO_INCREMENT, so your code will need to make other arrangements to locate a unique identifier during this method. In either case, you need to make sure that an appropriate value is located and set for the returned CustomerID instance.

If your ejbCreate() method returns the same primary key twice, the EJB server is allowed to throw a DuplicateKeyException to the client code.

The second form of creation is with the user passing an identifier of the customer they wants a bean to represent. This time you will set the customerId internal variable, but leave the rest of the details unset:

```
public void ejbCreate(int id)
    throws CreateException, EJBException {

    customerId = id;
    userName = null;
    address = null;
    emailAddress = null;
    country = null;
    phoneNumber = null;

    try {
        PreparedStatement stmt =
           conn.prepareStatement(CREATE_USER_WITH_ID_SQL);
```

```
        // This is where you set the new user ID.
        // See the main text for more discussion
        stmt.setInt(1, id);
        stmt.executeUpdate();
    } catch(SQLException se) {
        throw new CreateException("Cannot create a user");
    }

    CustomerID c_id = new CustomerID(id);
    return c_id;
}
```

When the user provides all the details of a customer, simply store the details locally like this:

```
public void ejbCreate(String name,
                      String addr,
                      String email,
                      String country,
                      String phone)
    throws CreateException, EJBException {

    customerId = -1;
    userName = name;
    address = addr;
    emailAddress = email;
    this.country = country;
    phoneNumber = phone;

    try {
        PreparedStatement stmt =
           conn.prepareStatement(CREATE_USER_SQL);

        // This is where you set the new user ID.
        // See the main text for more discussion
        stmt.setInt(1, 0);
        stmt.setString(2, userName);
        stmt.setString(3, emailAddress);
        stmt.setString(4, country);
        stmt.setString(5, address);
        stmt.setString(6, phoneNumber);
        stmt.executeUpdate();
    } catch(SQLException se) {
        throw new CreateException("Cannot create a user");
    }

    CustomerID c_id = new CustomerID(-1);
    return c_id;
}
```

Remember that because no customer ID is provided, you will need to provide appropriate code to deal with this.

Writing the finder methods

At this point, you have code that allows a bean to be created and filled with appropriate data. The next step in implementing an entity bean is to write the body of the finder methods.

Finder methods have one job: to check the database to see if anything matches the passed parameters. Starting with `ejbFindByPrimaryKey()`, this code looks in the database to see if a matching key exists. If no matching key is found, an exception is generated in accordance with the rules. In the following code, you can see how all the code really cares about is that the ID exists. There is no attempt to fetch the rest of the data for that particular customer. If the ResultSet contains no matching data:

```
private static final String FIND_ID_SQL =
    "SELECT customer_id FROM Customers WHERE customer_id = ?";

public CustomerID ejbFindByPrimaryKey(CustomerID pk)
    throws EJBException, FinderException {

    try {
        PooledConnection p_conn =
            database.getPooledConnection();
        Connection conn = p_conn.getConnection();

        PreparedStatement stmt =
            conn.prepareStatement(FIND_ID_SQL);
        stmt.setInt(1, pk.id);

        ResultSet rs = stmt.executeQuery();
        if(!rs.first())
            throw new FinderException("Unknown user: " +
                                      pk.id);

    } catch(SQLException se) {
        throw new FinderException("Unknown user: " +
                                  se.getMessage());
    }

    return pk;
}
```

Looking for matching customer IDs based on a name is very simple. The code uses SQL to return a list of matching IDs. For each matching ID that is found, create a new instance of the primary key class `CustomerID` and add it to the collection that must be returned:

```
private static final String FIND_USER_SQL =
    "SELECT customer_id FROM Customers WHERE name = ?";

public Collection ejbFindWithName(String name)
    throws EJBException, FinderException {
```

```
        ArrayList ret_val = new ArrayList();

        try {
            PooledConnection p_conn =
                database.getPooledConnection();
            Connection conn = p_conn.getConnection();

            PreparedStatement stmt =
                conn.prepareStatement(FIND_USER_SQL);
            stmt.setString(1, name);

            ResultSet rs = stmt.executeQuery();

            if(!rs.first())
               throw new FinderException("No matches");

            do {
                CustomerID id = new CustomerID(rs.getInt(1));
                ret_val.add(id);
            } while(rs.next());
        } catch(SQLException se) {
            throw new FinderException("Unknown user: " +
                                      se.getMessage());
        }

        return ret_val;
    }
```

You can implement your own finder methods with a similar approach. Basically, you look for a matching ID in the underlying data source and then return an instance of a matching key. Notice here that the SQL queries only bother dealing with the `customer_id` column. You do not need to access all the other columns of the table for this task.

Implementing the load and store methods

Next on the development list are the load and store methods. These are the methods responsible for keeping the data up to date. According to the life-cycle model, the `ejbCreate()` methods are used to load data when the bean is first created; however, if the bean data change internally (say two clients have exactly the same bean and its primary key), the server uses these two methods to make sure all copies have the same world view.

`ejbLoad()` is responsible for reloading any existing data back into the database if the data have been originally loaded from there. Now, you can have this called at any time, but you will probably only have it called at the prescribed time. For example, if a default bean was created, you may not yet have used the database for data. Regardless, code should always be prepared to run in any situation.

If the bean has been recycled back into the global pool, you may already have a customer ID to play with. However, it is not a good idea to use this information, as it may be out of date. To make sure you have the latest primary key information you can make use of the `EntityContext`. In the `EntityContext` class are a number of convenient methods for accessing the current state of the bean, including the current valid primary key (`getPrimaryKey()`). Once you have the primary key, the load method fetches data from the underlying database and sets the class variables to the right data:

```
private static final String LOAD_ID_SQL =
    "SELECT * FROM Customers WHERE customer_id = ?";

public void ejbLoad() throws EJBException {

    // Fetch the primary key
    CustomerID key = (CustomerID)context.getPrimaryKey();

    try {
        PooledConnection p_conn =
            database.getPooledConnection();
        Connection conn = p_conn.getConnection();

        PreparedStatement stmt =
            conn.prepareStatement(LOAD_ID_SQL);
        stmt.setInt(0, key.id);

        ResultSet rs = stmt.executeQuery();
        if(!rs.next())
            throw new EJBException("User ID not known: " +
                                   key.id);

        customerId = key.id;
        address = rs.getString(2);
        emailAddress = rs.getString(3);
        country = rs.getString(4);
        userName = rs.getString(5);
        phoneNumber = rs.getString(6);
    } catch(SQLException se) {
        throw new EJBException("DB fetch error: ", se);
    }
}
```

Storing that data in the database is the responsibility of the `ejbStore()` method. Now you must store all the internal variable state back in the database:

```
public void ejbStore() throws EJBException {
    try {
        PooledConnection p_conn =
            database.getPooledConnection();
        Connection conn = p_conn.getConnection();

        PreparedStatement stmt =
            conn.prepareStatement(UPDATE_USER_SQL);
```

```
            stmt.setString(1, userName);
            stmt.setString(2, emailAddress);
            stmt.setString(3, country);
            stmt.setString(4, address);
            stmt.setString(5, phoneNumber);
            stmt.executeUpdate();
        } catch(SQLException se) {
            throw new EJBException("DB fetch error: ", se);
        }
    }
```

Remember that the store method is storing changes to pre-existing data, you need to use an SQL update command to place the new items in the database (you should have created a new row in the database for this ID during the `ejbCreate()` method).

In order to avoid unnecessary updates, you may want to keep an internal flag that indicates whether data have changed since the last update.

Implementing passivation

Passivation is about shutting down and rebuilding the bean when it is no longer active. Because you implement passivation by serializing the bean instance, the techniques you apply here should be the same as those you would apply for normal serialization.

When considering what to do in the passivation code, think of everything that would not normally survive a serialization process — if socket connections are not allowed to be serialized, keeping that database connection around is probably not a good idea. However, data kept locally (all those `String` references in this case) is fine, although it is practically useless. A passivated bean is one that is no longer in use by a client , so that information really isn't relevant and not worth keeping around.

Given these conditions, implementing the `ejbPassivate()` method is trivial. Just remove the reference to anything you don't like — in this case the JDBC data-source reference — like this:

```
public void ejbPassivate() throws EJBException {
    database = null;
}
```

The reverse process requires your code to replace the data-source reference you just removed. To do this, the `ejbActivate()` method calls the internal convenience method to fetch the data-source reference. This is the same method called by the `setEntityContext()` method right at the startup of the bean. Both methods are included here:

```
public void ejbActivate() throws EJBException {
    loadDatabase();
}
```

```
private void loadDatabase() throws EJBException {
    try {
        InitialContext i_ctx = new InitialContext();
        database = (ConnectionPoolDataSource)
            i_ctx.lookup(DATABASE_NAME);
    } catch(NamingException ne) {
        throw new EJBException("Could not locate " +
                               "database driver", ne);
    }
}
```

Activation in an entity bean must also perform extra tasks. Where `ejbCreate()` is used to insert new data into the database and then make the bean immediately active, the `ejbActivate()` method is called by the server when it wishes to bring a pooled bean back into use. When this method is called, you cannot assume that the bean represents exactly the same data it represented the last time it was active. During the activation process, you should make sure to load the new data.

How do you know which data to reload? You must consult the `EntityContext` to find the current primary key and reload data based on it. The code for doing this looks remarkably like the code in the `ejbLoad()` method that you wrote just a little while ago:

```
public void ejbActivate() throws EJBException {
    loadDatabase();

    // Fetch the primary key
    CustomerID key = (CustomerID)context.getPrimaryKey();

    try {
        PooledConnection p_conn =
            database.getPooledConnection();
        Connection conn = p_conn.getConnection();

        PreparedStatement stmt =
            conn.prepareStatement(LOAD_ID_SQL);
        stmt.setInt(0, key.id);

        ResultSet rs = stmt.executeQuery();
        if(!rs.next())
            throw new EJBException("User ID no known: " +
                                   key.id);

        customerId = key.id;
        address = rs.getString(2);
        emailAddress = rs.getString(3);
        country = rs.getString(4);
        userName = rs.getString(5);
        phoneNumber = rs.getString(6);
    } catch(SQLException se) {
        throw new EJBException("DB fetch error: ", se);
    }
}
```

That's all there is to dealing with passivation. If you have other database or JNDI connections in use inside your bean, you should be careful to make sure that they are managed correctly, too.

Implementing the business methods

Believe it or not, business methods are the easiest part of an entity bean to implement. So far, you have seen the code assigning values to internal variables. An entity bean has its internal state controlled by the EJB server environment it resides in. The server will tell it when to load fresh data, when to store the data, and when to change to a different mode. Any time in between the bean does not need to touch the database. This makes implementing those business methods really easy, because all the hard work has already been done!

The `Customer` entity bean has a lot of methods, so here is a sample just to show you how easy the implementation is:

```
public String getAddress() throws EJBException {
    return address;
}

public void setAddress(String addr) throws EJBException {
    address = addr;
}
```

Notice how all you do is assign the parameter to the internal variables for the setter method and return the internal variable for the getter methods. You don't need to update the database because that is done when the server calls the `ejbStore()` method.

Once you have implemented all the business-logic methods, your entity-bean implementation is complete. Compile the code to make sure it all looks correct, and then put it aside. The next step is writing the home interface so that you can access the beans you have just written.

Home interfaces and kicking off

The home interface is the last piece of the puzzle in implementing any sort of Enterprise JavaBean. The home interface represents the glue that holds together the remote interface, the bean implementation, and the EJB server in general.

How home interfaces relate to bean implementations

So far you have, in your bag of classes, a remote interface and two bean-implementation classes. Earlier in the chapter, we alluded to the need for this home-interface thing and to the fact that it is responsible for providing the life-cycle management of the bean. Just how does it fit in the middle? After all, you already have the remote interface and a bean that implements all the methods from the home interface: Just what use is another interface going to be?

Options for Storing and Loading Data in Entity Beans

The EJB specification provides you with a lot of flexibility about how and when you store your data. Although the examples we provide suggest that you just hold the values internally, that is not the only option available to you. The specification lists three options (Section 12.1.6):

- ✦ An instance loads the entire entity object's state in the `ejbLoad()` method and caches it until the container invokes the `ejbStore()` method. The business methods read and write the cached entity state. The `ejbStore()` method writes the updated parts of the entity object's state to the database.
- ✦ An instance loads the most frequently used part of the entity object's state in the `ejbLoad()` method and caches it until the container invokes the `ejbStore()` method. Additional parts of the entity object's state are loaded as needed by the business methods. The `ejbStore()` method writes the updated parts of the entity object's state to the database.
- ✦ An instance does not cache any entity object's state between business methods. The business methods access and modify the entity object's state directly in the database. The `ejbLoad()` and `ejbStore()` methods have an empty implementation.

That covers all the options. Basically you have the choice of caching all the data locally in the bean or none and just fetch it on demand as needed, or even a little bit in between.

If you think back to the discussions on the remote interface, you will remember that its purpose is to provide something that the client-side programmer can use to make requests of the bean. This enables you to define the business logic without the client ever having to know about the implementation. The question we left unanswered was "How does the client get hold of the bean?" The remote interface does not define any of the `ejbCreate()` methods, or the load and store methods needed by entity beans; just how does your client code access those methods? Enter the home interface.

EJB servers have two responsibilities related to beans: managing instances, and managing client requests to those instances. In a way, the home interface represents the client's perspective for making the requests to the EJB server. To access a bean, represented by the remote interface, a client must use the home interface. Home interfaces allow the server to hide the way in which it is dealing with bean instances. If your client code were to directly access for a bean instance, the server would have no control over the bean management, such as passivation. It is important to draw a distinct line between the client's using beans and the actual bean instances on the server. You cannot draw a direct relationship among one client, its home and remote interfaces, and the running instances on the server. It is possible that there are more clients than instances of a particular bean, or the opposite, that the server holds many more bean instances than clients on the system (remember that the server may be pooling spare beans to deal with high-load situations).

Writing a home interface

Writing a home interface starts with you creating a new interface and making it extend the `EJBHome` interface. Creating a home interface for any type of bean starts with this step. The only difference in the declarations is in the number of extra methods that must be added by your derived interface that are required by a particular bean type.

The `EJBHome` interface is really simple, as only four methods are defined: two to access information about the home interface itself, and two to remove the bean. Throughout this chapter we've been talking about creation methods, and load and store methods: Just where are they?

Because you can create an EJB in many different ways, the standard interfaces do not supply you with any specific default methods. For example, if you have a stateful session bean that requires you to pass an `int`, what point is there in having a creation method with no arguments?

To write a home interface, you start by adding create methods. You add one `create()` method for each `ejbCreate()` you have in the bean implementation. The return value of all these `create()` methods is the remote interface, and the methods must all throw two exceptions — `EJBException` and `CreateException`. (The number of create methods you have will depend on the underlying bean type. A stateless session bean will only have one method with no arguments. On the other hand, an entity bean will probably have many.)

Here is the code you would use for a home interface representing the mailer stateless session bean:

```
public Mailer create()
    throws RemoteException, CreateException;
```

Compare this to the collection of methods you would need for the customer entity bean:

```
public Customer create()
    throws RemoteException, CreateException;

public Customer create(int id)
    throws RemoteException, CreateException;

public Customer create(String name,
                       String addr,
                       String email,
                       String country,
                       String phone)
    throws RemoteException, CreateException;
```

Stateless session beans do not require any more methods. You've done everything and can now move on to packaging the beans for deployment.

Stateful beans may also end at this point. Just make sure that you have enough create methods to cover the different forms of `ejbCreate()`.

If you provided a bean implementation that used `ejbCreate()` methods (or any other methods that map from the home interface to the bean implementation) with arguments, make sure that a corresponding `create()` method with the identical argument list is a part of the home interface. If you do not declare the matching methods in the home interface, you will not be able to create that flavor of bean. Note that the return types are different, though. The bean implementation returns the primary key, and the home interface returns an instance of the bean itself.

Entity beans have a few more methods to be provided yet. These methods must cover the finder methods declared as part of the bean's implementation code. Following the same principles as the create methods, finder methods in the home interface match those in the bean implementation — minus the `ejb` prefix. Finder methods must return the primary-key class that you wrote earlier in the chapter here, too.

Here's what the finder methods look like for the customer's-home interface:

```
public Customer findByPrimaryKey(CustomerID id)
    throws RemoteException, FinderException;

public List findByName(String name)
    throws RemoteException, FinderException;
```

That completes the entity bean's home interface as well. Just compile the code to make sure there are no typos, and it is time to deploy the beans to the server.

Deploying beans to an EJB server

With the code complete, it is time to package it all up to be deployed. Depending on the version of the J2EE specification you use, the results of this section may be worthwhile or not. Under J2EE 1.2.1 and earlier, there is no predefined way to bundle a collection of files together to be deployed as a bean. As of v1.3, which uses the EJB 2.0 specification, you have a standard way to package the files on one platform and then deploy them to another. For the rest of this section, we are going to assume the 1.3 specification. If your environment is only 1.2.1-capable, treat this deployment introduction as a lot of hand-waving; we refer you to your application server's documentation.

To see how Sun's reference implementation packages and deployment tools work, refer to Appendix A.

When packaging and deploying beans, you will rarely need to use the process outlined in this section. Most tools today come with their own GUI applications to do all the hard work for you. Just start the wizard, fill in the blanks, and click Next.

There Are Methods in the Madness

The remote interface has one set of methods, the remote implementation another, and somewhere in the middle is the home interface. Each has different method names. For example, the home interface has a collection of `create()` methods, yet the remote interface has none, and the bean implementation uses `ejbCreate()`. Do all these names match up, and if they do, how do they?

EJBs and their server go through many different hoops in order to create a working environment. It is not very easy to say that method X in the remote interface corresponds to a call to method Y in the bean implementation. Regardless, the general rule is that a method defined in either the home or remote interface will correspond to a method with the prefix `ejb` in the bean implementation. For example, the `create()` method of the home interface has a matching `ejbCreate()` method in the bean implementation. Finder methods also have the same match — `findByPrimaryKey()` corresponds to `ejbFindByPrimaryKey()` in the bean implementation. Only the bean-management methods correspond to this rule. Business-logic methods do not.

The runtime correspondence of methods is a little trickier to deal with. While you might call the `create()` method on your home interface to fetch a new bean instance, on the server end this call does not directly translate to a matching call to `ejbCreate()` of the bean implementation. It very heavily depends on the current state of the server. For example, a heavily loaded bean may end up with the server creating another complete instance from scratch, causing you to need a collection of method calls.

Filling in the missing spaces

You've seen how to create a remote and home interface, as well as how to write bean implementations, but how do the interfaces talk with the bean implementation? Ah, trade secret! The J2EE specification does not specify how this communication works, only that "communication happens." After defining the interfaces, you need to run the code through a deployment tool for that server. The server will take the files, process them, and build the appropriate classes to implement them. This all happens behind the scenes.

This processing step consists of two smaller steps: automatically building the implementation classes of the interfaces, and then defining configuration information. You will no doubt have noticed that the process of writing a bean described in this chapter did not include writing implementations of the home and remote interfaces. Fulfilling this requirement is the job of the EJB container environment, because this allows each EJB server vendor to build a system optimized for their environment. In earlier versions of EJB, this meant that you could not complete your bean implementation and have different client and server software. If you used Websphere on the server, you had to use Websphere for the client, too. The EJB 2.0 specification changes this by making sure that a client and server can now be different pieces of software.

Internally, during the deployment process the deployment tool will normally take your home and remote interfaces and build the implementation classes. These implementation classes built an RMI system (with the CORBA variant RMI-IIOP) that produced a client and server set of stub classes. These classes are then compiled and placed into JAR files on the client and server machines, along with a file called a Deployment Descriptor.

Although EJB 2.0 specifies that the vendor must support RMI-IIOP communications, it also allows the use of proprietary protocols. When packaging the bean, make sure that you understand which form of communication you are generating. A bean that does not allow IIOP cannot be deployed across multiple EJB container providers.

The bean files

The process of deploying EJBs uses a number of files in addition to the Java code you have written so far. We have already mentioned the deployment descriptor — a file for describing the setup information of a bean. In addition to this are files that describe a particular bean and its classes, the client code that uses beans (say a servlet or JSP for Web use or the application code for standalone use), and the complete EJB application, all in a single file.

You will find the files just described in every EJB-server system. The following list gives a more complete description of each:

- *Deployment Descriptor* — This XML file is used to describe most of the properties of the bean. At the most simple level, you need to know the class names for each of the files, while on the other end of the scale, you can include security information about who can call what methods (we cover callers and roles in Chapter 17).
- *Bean JAR file* — Each bean must exist in a JAR file. Although this sounds draconian, it is because of the way the deployment descriptors work, and so the bean code of home, remote, and implementation classes all exist in the one file. Of course, each JAR file may contain more than one set of bean classes. If you have common library code that is accessed by many beans, these classes can still be located outside individual bean archives.
- *Application client archive* — Standalone client application code exists in its own JAR file, if needed. The client code does not need to be in a JAR file, but at the least the code that implements the client stubs for the home and remote interfaces will be.
- *Web client archive* — When you use servlets or JSPs, they will be placed into a file called a Web ARchive or WAR file. This is just a JAR file with a few extras: It keeps all the Web pieces of the application, such as HTML files, images, and so on.
- *Application archive* — Wrapping all these other files into a single deployable unit is the Enterprise Archive or EAR file. Again, this is just a JAR file with a collection of extras: It contains all the preceding archive files and more deployment information.

We haven't covered the relevant topics regarding most of these file types yet. So for the rest of this section we are going to concentrate on building a file suitable for the beans alone.

Writing a deployment descriptor

Deployment descriptors are XML files, so they are relatively easy to write in almost any tool. The job of a deployment descriptor is to describe the configuration of a bean, with the idea of letting the bean code do the real functional work, and let the configuration file provide all the details about who, what, and where to find things.

If you are unfamiliar with XML, you'll find a thorough introduction to the topic in Chapters 10 and 11.

You start writing a deployment descriptor by creating a file named `ejb-jar.xml` and adding the standard XML header and `DOCTYPE` statement:

```
<?xml version='1.0' encoding='us-ascii'?>
<!DOCTYPE ejb-jar PUBLIC
 "-//Sun Microsystems, Inc.//DTD Enterprise JavaBeans 1.1//EN"
 "http://java.sun.com/j2ee/dtds/ejb-jar_2_0.dtd">
```

Next, you place the opening tag, as defined by the preceding declaration. Inside that tag, you start by listing descriptions and the list of beans included in this JAR file. The DTD definition of the `ejb-jar` element is as follows:

```
<!ELEMENT ejb-jar (description?, display-name?,
 small-icon?,large-icon?, enterprise-beans,
 relationships?,assembly-descriptor?, ejb-client-jar?)>
```

Of all of these elements, the most useful (and the only required tag) is the `enterprise-beans` element that contains the listing of all the beans in this archive file. So take a look at a typical file that might represent the example application from this chapter:

```
<ejb-jar>
  <description>
    An example application to introduce EJBs
  </description>
  <enterprise-beans>
    <session>
      <ejb-name>Mailer</ejb-name>
      <home>MailerHome</home>
      <remote>Mailer</remote>
      <ejb-class>MailerSessionBean</ejb-class>
      <ejb-ref>ejb/MailHandler</ejb-ref>
      <session-type>Stateless</session-type>
      <transaction-type>Container</transaction-type>
    </session>
    <entity>
      <ejb-name>Customer</ejb-name>
```

```
        <home>CustomerHome</home>
        <remote>Customer</remote>
        <ejb-class>CustomerEntityBean</ejb-class>
        <persistence-type>Bean</persistence-type>
        <prim-key-class>CustomerID</prim-key-class>
        <reentrant>True</reentrant>
      </entity>
    </enterprise-beans>
  </ejb-jar>
```

All the items inside the XML file are case-sensitive, including the content between tags. For example, `<reentrant>True</reentrant>` is not the same as `<reentrant>true</reentrant>`.

All these tags are defined in the DTD for the deployment descriptor. Notice how the tags basically match the configuration information we've been showing you throughout the chapter. A session bean has a tag that says whether it is stateful or stateless, for example. Thus you can change the behavior of the bean without needing to change the source files.

The only item in the preceding file we have to explicitly point out is the `ejb-name` tag. This tag specifies the name under which this bean will be registered in JDNI. Take note of this, as you are going to need to know it shortly, when looking up the bean on the client.

The information shown in the preceding deployment descriptor is an absolutely minimal file for the two bean types. Many more configuration options exist, most of which are for topics we have not covered yet. To learn more, we recommend reading the DTD source itself, as it contains huge numbers of comments about how to use each tag.

Rolling the JAR file

With the deployment descriptor written, you now need to create the basic bean JAR file. Creating the JAR file is just like creating a standard JAR—you will need the class files and optional configuration information—such as a manifest file and, of course, the deployment descriptor.

The manifest file in an EJB JAR file performs the same task it performs for standard applications. If your bean refers to other JAR files that contain code necessary for the implementation, use the `Class-Path` entry of the manifest to refer to those extra files.

To create the JAR file, change directory to the root directory of your compiled code. Next create a directory called `META-INF` and copy it in your `ejb-jar.xml` file. If you need a manifest file, copy that in, too. Next run the standard JAR command to create your EJB archive. For example (assuming your company's code starts with the root package name `com`):

```
\classes$ jar—cf my_ejb.jar META-INF com
```

Now you have a ready-to-deploy bean JAR file on your server. From this point on, consult your server-tool documentation to learn how to proceed. But now you have finished writing the Enterprise JavaBean code. All that is left to do is create an application that will use the bean.

Using Enterprise Beans on the Client Side

Using EJBs in client code does not require the large amounts of coding that you've seen so far. In fact, using them in any application is a breeze and one of the seductive aspects of using the J2EE environment. With a well-written set of beans, it becomes easy to reuse them and create more and more applications for your company.

You can use EJBs in any environment in which you can use normal Java code. EJBs are typically used in a Web-based environment with servlets or JSPs, but applets and standalone applications are also suitable targets for beans. Non-standard systems, such as point-of-sale devices and kiosks, are perfect environments for bean technology and represent standard places that you might find a Java application making use of them.

Looking up and using beans

Regardless of what sort of environment you will be using that is accessing the beans, the basic procedure is the same and consists of the following steps:

1. Look up the bean's home interface.
2. Ask the home interface to create or find a particular bean.
3. Make calls of the bean.
4. Remove the reference, notifying the server of this so that it may reclaim the instance.

Looking up a bean

Finding a bean really starts with trying to find a bean's home interface. Remember that it is the home interface that enables you to create and manage bean instances.

Locating the home interface is as simple as using your old friend JNDI to perform a lookup of the name you specified in the `ejb-name` tag of the deployment descriptor. To look up the home interface, start with the normal JNDI `InitialContext` setup.

After obtaining the context information, you need to perform the lookup. The name that you go looking for is not just the string from the `ejb-name` tag, but must also have the prefix `ejb/`. Finally, as the `lookup()` method returns an `Object`, you will need to cast it to the necessary home interface. For example, to locate the home interface for the mailer session bean, you write the following code (ignoring exceptions):

```
InitialContext ctx = new InitialContext();
Object ref = ctx.lookup("ejb/Mailer");

MailerHome home =
    (MailerHome)PortableRemoteObject.narrow(ref,
                                        MailerHome.class);
```

The last line here is interesting. Note that you cannot just directly cast the returned reference from the lookup method. Because classes can be stubs for an interface and the RMI capabilities, we recommend that you take this extra verification step. The `narrow()` method performs a check on the returned object to make sure that it can be cast correctly to the class represented by the second argument. Although it is possible to skip this step, we highly recommend that you perform it in order to ensure that your application functions well with the rest of the world (and that the right exceptions are easily caught on the client side)—the EJB specification also states that you should perform the narrow operation

Requesting a bean from the home interface

With the home interface in hand, you must next request it to produce a bean. As you saw earlier in this chapter, the way to request this action is to use one of the `create()` methods of the bean. Naturally, the method you choose is dependent on the type of bean you have and the methods you provided in the home interface.

Creating a new bean just means calling one of the create methods and making sure you catch all the exceptions, as follows:

```
try {
    Mailer mailer = home.create();
} catch(RemoteException ee) {
    // do something
} catch(CreateException ce) {
    // do something here too
}
```

Calling business methods on the bean

Calling business methods on your newly fetched bean is just like calling any other Java method, particularly those involving RMI. Even passing in other bean references is no big deal. Again, just watch out for exceptions, including any custom exceptions you may have included.

This time, the example looks at using the Customer bean to ask for the customer's name.

```
try {
    String name = customer.getName();
    System.out.println("The customer's name is " + name);
} catch(RemoteException ee) {
    // do something
}
```

Cleaning up and removing bean references

Once your application has finished using the bean, you should notify the EJB container that it is no longer needed. This frees the server to reclaim the bean and pass it on to the next user that needs it.

You notify the server that you no longer need the bean reference using one of the `remove()` methods. You can do this in one of two places: on the home interface or directly from the bean. With most applications, it is probably simpler to use the direct method on the bean's remote interface directly, as follows:

```
mailer.remove();
```

Remember, after you have called the `remove()` method, the reference you have is dead. It cannot be used to communicate with the bean. Attempting to do so will cause an exception. If you want to use the bean again, you will need to ask the home interface to create you another one.

Calling the `remove()` method is only suitable for the session beans as it forces the container to delete the bean. When `remove()` is called, the `ejbRemove()` method is called on your bean implementation class. You've seen the code that the `ejbRemove()` method calls. For an entity bean, that means deleting the object from the underlying data store. So, while calling `remove()` on a session bean is perfectly fine, it is probably not the effect you are looking for entity beans. If you no longer need the bean reference, the simplest way of releasing its resources is to just set your client's reference to `null`.

Beans in the wild

Although the basics of using all types of EJBs in code are common to all users of EJBs, how do the individual user application types make use of the beans? Surprisingly, there isn't much difference, so take a look at each of the areas in which you are likely to find an EJB popping up its head.

Using beans in ordinary applications

Ordinary applications, such as command-line apps, don't require any extra work on the part of the programmer. Most of the work has to do with getting the updates out of the database and into a collection of text fields and tables, which really does not involve the bean code at all.

For example, if you have a text field, this example will obtain the customer's ID, find the related bean, and put the customer's address into the text field:

```
JTextField tf = new JTextField(40);

...

try {
    InitialContext ctx = new InitialContext();

    Object objref = initial.lookup("ejb/Customer");

    CustomerHome home =
     (CustomerHome)PortableRemoteObject.narrow(objref,
                                     CustomerHome.class);

    String cust_id_str = idTextField.getText();
    int id = Integer.parseInt(cust_id_str);

    Customer customer = home.create(id);
    tf.setText(customer.getName());
} catch(Exception e) {
  System.err.println("Something died...:" + e.getMessage());
}
```

How you run a command-line application depends on the environment you are in. To learn how to run a command-line app using the J2EE reference implementation, please read Appendix A.

Using beans in servlets

As far as EJBs are concerned, operating in a servlet environment is no different from operating as a command line. At its most simple, just grab the initial context, ask for the home interface, and start working with the bean(s) you need.

Usage patterns of beans in a servlet environment is quite different from usage patterns of beans in an application. Applications tend to have (relatively) long lives working on a single piece of data. Servlets, on the other hand, have very short and sharp usages of beans. This contrast means that the ways in which you handle the respective interfaces will be quite different. An application may grab the home interface and grab a bean instance almost immediately afterward, while a servlet will grab the home interface at startup and then sit around waiting for a request to be processed before asking for a bean.

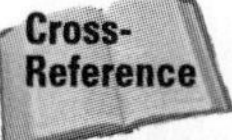

You'll find an introduction to writing servlets in Chapter 3.

Given these different usage patterns, we recommend the following rules of thumb for dealing with beans in a servlet environment:

- Establish references to all the home interfaces you are going to need during the `init()` method.
- Create and remove bean instances on the fly during the processing of the `service()` or `doXXX` methods. Make sure you free the reference and call `remove()` on the bean before exiting from these methods if using session beans, to avoid overburdening the EJB server.
- Try to minimize the servlet design to use as few beans as possible. Don't create one big super-servlet to process all request types. Smaller servlets mean fewer home interfaces to keep around, and a much easier time load balancing both servlets and beans.
- Remember the roles of stateful session beans and how servlets work. Stateful session beans don't work as well in a servlet environment as the other types do. This is mainly because a different servlet instance from the one that created the bean in the first place may be called to process a given set of state information.

Using beans in JavaServer Pages with JavaBeans

JavaServer Pages (JSP) represent an interesting challenge when you are attempting to integrate with EJBs. This is because of the way a JSP accesses Java-based information through either custom tags or scriptlets. Unlike applications and servlets, a JSP does not contain long-term code that can be used to buffer home interfaces or even direct references to EJB objects. Instead, you must go through an intermediary in the form of a normal JavaBean that can perform these tasks for us.

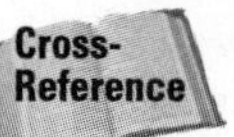

Chapter 4 provides an introduction to JSPs and how to use them with JavaBeans.

Using EJBs with servlets may take one of two paths. The simplest path is to use a JavaBean to reference the EJB. Alternatively, you can use custom tags to directly represent bean information. The examples will start with the JavaBean option.

The first step in the integration of EJBs and JSPs is writing a JavaBean wrapper class. This wrapper class is responsible for acquiring the home interface, creating the target bean, processing the information, and then making the results available to the JSP. Because the wrapper is a normal JavaBean, the code is required to follow all the normal rules for beans — including naming conventions for methods. As for the EJB part, because the JavaBean is just a wrapper, the methods will simply mirror the methods in the EJB.

Let's start the example by creating a page that will edit a customer's details. After entering the user ID, this page will present the page with all the editable items on it. The user can then edit fields and submit the details back. Ignoring the start page, a single JavaBean for both dynamic pages will represent the customer in the database. This JavaBean will be named `CustomerBean`.

The process of writing the class follows the normal procedure: You declare the class and a public constructor. Because a JavaBean has no equivalent of the servlet `init()` method, you will need to fetch the home interface in the constructor, as follows:

```
public class CustomerBean {
    private CustomerHome home;

    public CustomerBean() {
        try {
            Context initial = new InitialContext();
            Object objref = initial.lookup("ejb/Customer");

            home =
              (CustomerHome)PortableRemoteObject.narrow(objref,
                                                 CustomerHome.class);

        } catch(Exception e) {
            // Just print the error out
            System.out.println("Error finding home interface" +
                               e.getMessage());
        }
    }
}
```

Next, you need some methods to process information coming from the JSP. First you will need a method to take the action performed by the JSP. Remember that two JSPs will be accessing this bean instance—one to fetch the original data and one to update it—and so the bean needs to know which action has been requested. Action information, as it always comes from a HTTP request, will be a string, as shown in the following code:

```
public void setAction(String act) {
    action = act;
}

public String getAction() {
    return action;
}
```

You have to store data internally for these methods, because at the time that these values are set, the code is not be doing the processing. Processing is the responsibility of the next step—the implementation of the `processRequest()` method. Why have we included an extra method? Well, because the process requires setting or reading quite a few properties (name, phone number, e-mail, and so on), your bean code cannot assume that any one setter is the last call to happen. The only way that it can be guaranteed is to make use of an extra trigger scriptlet that is part of the JSP source, which we haven't covered yet.

The code for our JavaBean will work for both showing the initial data and allowing the user to modify data. The `processRequest()` method looks at the value of the action parameter and acts accordingly, as this example shows:

```
public void processRequest() {
    if(action.equals("show")) {
        CustomerID id = new CustomerID(customerId);
        Customer cust = home.findByPrimaryKey(id);

        userName = cust.getName();
        address = cust.getAddress();
        country = cust.getCountry();
        phoneNumber = cust.getPhoneNumber();
        email = cust.getEmail();
    } else if(action.equals("update")) {
        CustomerID id = new CustomerID(customerId);
        Customer cust = home.findByPrimaryKey(id);

        cust.setName(userName);
        cust.setAddress(address);
        cust.setCountry(country);
        cust.setPhoneNumber(phoneNumber);
        cust.setEmail(email);
    }
}
```

Note that the customer is fetched from the database each time, which allows the bean to be explicitly updated each time the user fetches the page. Most Web users check updates by checking their details after having edited them. This ensures that they will always have the right values.

On to the JSP source. This follows the same patterns that you learned in Chapter 4. First include the bean in your JSP and add a scriptlet to force the execution, as follows:

```
<html>
<jsp:useBean id="customerBean" scope="session"
  class="CustomerBean" />
<jsp:setProperty name="accountBean" property="*" />
```

The wildcard is used on the `setProperty` tag to tell the JSP to update all properties all the time. Next is the command to execute for this when the page is requested:

```
<% customerBean.processRequest() %>
```

The way in which you process bean actions depends on the page you want. For a simple page to edit the customer details, use the following example code. (Note that this is just standard JSP code for accessing any JavaBean. You won't have to do anything special to the JSP source in order for it to use EJBs.)

```
<html>
<head>
<title>Show customer details</title>
</head>
<body>
<h1>Show customer details<h1>
<form method=POST action="edit_customer.jsp">
<br>
<input type=hidden name="customerID" value="<jsp:getProperty
name="customerBean" property="customerID" />" >
<input type=hidden name="action" value="update">

Customer ID: "<jsp:getProperty name="customerBean"
property="customerID" />"
<br>
Name: <input type=text name="name"
  value="<jsp:getProperty name="customerBean" property="name"
 />" >
<br>
Address: <input type=text name="name"
  value="<jsp:getProperty name="customerBean" property="name"
 />" >
<br>
Country: <input type=text name="name"
  value="<jsp:getProperty name="customerBean" property="name"
 />" >
<br>
Email: <input type=text name="name"
  value="<jsp:getProperty name="customerBean" property="name"
 />" >
<br>
Phone: <input type=text name="name"
  value="<jsp:getProperty name="customerBean" property="name"
 />" >
<br>
<input type=submit name=submit value="Update Now">
</form>
</body>
</html>
```

That completes the code you need in order to integrate a JSP and EJB into the one action. Simply deploy the code according to your J2EE environment tools, and you're up and running.

Using beans in JavaServer Pages with custom tags

An alternate way of using EJBs within a JSP is through the use of custom tags. You have already been introduced to writing custom tags for JSPs in the "Using Custom Tags" section of Chapter 4. Because of this, we'll skip the basics here and concentrate on the work you need to do to integrate the tag library code with EJBs.

Tag libraries are an extremely flexible way of creating content. There are many options for creating a custom tag, so we'll just stick with a simple one. From this example, you can expand to include the more complex tag types. For this example, you will write a simple tag that displays the customer information. Input to this tag will be the customer ID, and the output will be a list of the information known about that customer.

Let's start the example with the JSP tag declaration:

```
<%@ taglib uri="J2EEBible-ejblib.tld" prefix="ejb" %>
<ejb:customer customerID="123456" />
```

The tag declaration follows the same form as you saw back in Chapter 4. This should not be surprising for you as a custom tag is a custom tag, no matter what that tag contains or where it sources its data. Our custom tag requires a single parameter that is the customer ID. Here we've just hardcoded the value, but in your real bean, that may be provided by a text field in a lead-up page prior to this one.

Working with custom tags and EJBs has all of the interesting code in the tag class. Because the tag is a single element, with no body, you only need to extend the `TagSupport` class. Without a closing tag, you then only need to provide the `doStartTag()` method. In addition, the usual `get` and `set` methods are required to process the attribute `customerID`. This is the outline of what your custom tag class will need to look like:

```
public class CustomerTag extends TagSupport {
  private CustomerHome home;
  private int customerId;

  public CustomerTag() {
    ????
  }

  public int doStartTag() {
    ????

    return SKIP_BODY;
  }

  public String getCustomerID() {
        return Integer.toString(customerId);
  }
```

```
  public void setCustomerID(String id) {
    customerId = Integer.parseInt(id);
  }

  public void release() {
  }
}
```

From this outline, you can see most of the standard features relating to custom tags. There's the constructor, the `doStartTag()` method (both of which require some code) and the methods for processing the `customerID` attribute. Of interest here is how you process the attribute information. Notice that the code has elected to take the value from the JSP as a `String` and then process it internally. You may provide alternative classes, such as `Integer` in the TLD rather than the default `String`.

You are still missing the important part: interacting with the EJB. You should remember from the other examples the basic process that is needed—fetch the home interface and then access the bean information. As usual, Java gives you plenty of options, but this is the one we recommend. Use the constructor to load the home interface of the `Customer` EJB. You would use the constructor rather than fetching the home interface in the `doStartTag()` method. The reason for this is for efficiency. The home interface is a common item, and you don't need to be fetching it every single time. So place that code in the constructor:

```
public CustomerTag() {
  try {
    Context initial = new InitialContext();
    Object objref = initial.lookup("ejb/Customer");

    home = (CustomerHome)PortableRemoteObject.narrow(
     objref, CustomerHome.class);
  } catch(Exception e) {
    // Just print the error out
    System.err.println("Error finding home interface" + e);
  }
}
```

If you allocate items in the constructor, you should naturally follow it up with an implementation of the `release()` method so that you can free them.

```
public void release() {
  home = null;
}
```

That leaves the `doStartTag()` method for you to fill in. You should probably be able to guess exactly what needs to be done now. In this method, you fetch the EJB corresponding to the provided customer ID and then write out some formatted text to the output like this:

```
public int doStartTag() {
  JspWriter out = pageContext.getOut();

  try {
    CustomerID id = new CustomerID(customerId);
    Customer cust = home.findByPrimaryKey(id);

    out.write("Customer ID: ");
    out.write(customerId);
    out.write("<br>");

    out.write("Name: ");
    out.write(cust.getName());
    out.write("<br>");

    out.write("Address: ");
    out.write(cust.getAddress());
    out.write("<br>");

    out.write("Country: ");
    out.write(cust.getCountry());
    out.write("<br>");

    out.write("Email: ");
    out.write(cust.getEmail());
    out.write("<br>");

    out.write("Phone: ");
    out.write(cust.getPhoneNumber());
    out.write("<br>");
  } catch(Exception e) {
    out.write("There was an error processing the customer");
    out.write(e.getMessage());
  }

  return SKIP_BODY;
}
```

That's all you need to do to integrate EJBs with custom tags in JSPs. As you can see from the two different examples, there is really not that much difference in difficulty between the approaches. Which you choose is more a matter of personal and/or company preferences.

Summary

During this chapter, you received an extensive introduction to the core of the J2EE specification—Enterprise JavaBeans. You could reasonably argue that the rest of the specifications in J2EE are there to support the requirements for EJBs. As you can see, EJBs are a huge topic, and so far we have barely scratched the surface of what you can do with them (stay tuned for more in the next chapter!). However, what we have covered so far is enough to get you up and running on most simple and medium-complexity projects. We gave you:

- An introduction to the concepts and terminology of EJBs.
- Instructions for writing basic session and entity beans.
- Instructions for integrating EJBs within other J2EE systems, such as servlets and JSPs.

✦ ✦ ✦

CHAPTER 17

Using Advanced EJB Techniques

In This Chapter

Examining the capabilities introduced in the EJB 2.0 specification

Looking at the new Message-Driven Beans

An introduction to writing container-managed entity-bean persistence

Dynamically configuring beans for deployment

Adding security to your beans

EJBs provide a huge range of capabilities to the end user. In the previous chapter, we introduced you to the basics of writing the most common forms of EJBs. Those techniques are useful in many situations and form the core of any EJB-based application. However, there are many more useful techniques yet to be introduced, and as we alluded to in the previous chapter, there are more types of EJBs to cover.

The techniques covered in this chapter are aimed at the true enterprise-level system — a system wherein you have a central system providing hundreds of services with many different client-application types. As the first step in moving on to larger systems, we show you how to extend for better performance the basic classes that you already have from the previous chapter. Basic entity and session beans can only provide you with so much, and the EJB specification team realized this. The J2EE v1.3 specification includes the new EJB 2.0 standard, which provides for a huge increase in the number of and, more importantly, the interaction between, beans and databases. Along with this new specification come a lot of new languages and concepts, so hold on, we have a lot to cover!

Extending Enterprise Beans

Within the basic bean structures that we introduced in the previous chapter, you have a lot of room to explore different strategies in the enterprise application. Most of the new techniques we introduce in this section revolve around getting more out of your existing application.

While you can take these approaches and bolt them into the basic design, it will be more beneficial for you to revisit the complete architecture as a result of having learned to use these new tools.

Local beans for better performance

At the top of the list of EJB users' wish lists has been the ability to allow beans to be more efficient in communication. Prior to the EJB 2.0 specification, a bean was a bean. They all acted the same. It did not matter whether the bean client was used on the same machine as the bean server or on another one halfway around the world: All the underlying connections took the same approach of using the network to access the bean and its methods, even if they did exist on the same server and even in the same JVM. Many large-scale system designs took the EJB philosophy and applied it to everything—not only was the outside world presented with an EJB interface, but internally the design used beans that were never seen in the outside world. The effect was a severe performance penalty for beans that referenced other beans residing on the same machine.

In order to fix this problem, the new specification introduces the concept of local beans. These are beans that are never seen outside of the server context, which allows the server to make a number of performance optimizations (for example, making direct method calls rather than using RMI-IIOP).

Local beans still maintain the concept of client and server usage. For local beans, the only permitted client is another bean residing on the same machine. Beans on other machines cannot be clients of the local bean.

Requirements of local beans

Programming local beans requires applying a few restrictions over and above those required by ordinary EJBs. These extra requirements are the result of the fact that local beans are a purely server-side construct—that is, an EJB client such as a JSP or servlet will never see these beans.

- Local beans must exist in the same JVM as the beans that use them. This restricts their usage and deployment capabilities to whatever the user bean needs.
- All data is live between the local bean and the bean using it (pass-by-reference). That is, the user ends up with a live copy of the local bean, and both should assume that any data passed back and forth will be live rather than a copy. For example, an array of values from the local bean to the user bean will be a single piece of data, so the user should not write new values into the array for fear of corrupting the state of the local bean.
- Any bean may be a local bean. Session and entity beans are valid local clients.
- It is possible for a bean implementation class to have both local and remote definitions, but it is not encouraged.

As any sort of bean can be a local bean, you can add a lot of flexibility to your application. That is, local beans are not a new type of bean, just an extended (or restricted, depending on your viewpoint) set of capabilities layered over the existing bean types.

The choice between local beans and remote beans is highly dependent on your application. If you look at the example beans in the previous chapter, you will see that nothing really lends itself to the use of a remote bean. For example, the mailer bean must be available to every client so that the clients can send e-mail. The same goes for customer and order information, because these beans are accessed by the Web component of the application. With more analysis and a bigger set of data, our example application could make use of local beans — for example, in keeping more detailed product information, like various models of the same product.

Sometimes it is worth having both local and remote beans for the same information. For example, if the example application had a new super-bean that performed order processing, it would be worth having a local bean that represented customer and product information in addition to the remote versions that the Web components are using. So don't think that if you have a remote bean you can't use a local bean for the same information and vice versa.

Interfaces for local beans

With each new capability comes a new set of interfaces to implement. For local beans, two new interfaces exist: the home interface (`EJBLocalHome`) and the bean object (`EJBLocalObject`). Even though you must implement these interfaces as you do the remote beans, you have a lot less work to do.

Local interfaces still perform and require the same tasks as remote interfaces. You can't take shortcuts just because your bean is now local. Accessing beans still means going through a home interface as well as taking the usual steps, such as calling create methods. If you are still confused about the various relationships, have a look at Figure 17-1, which illustrates the details using UML.

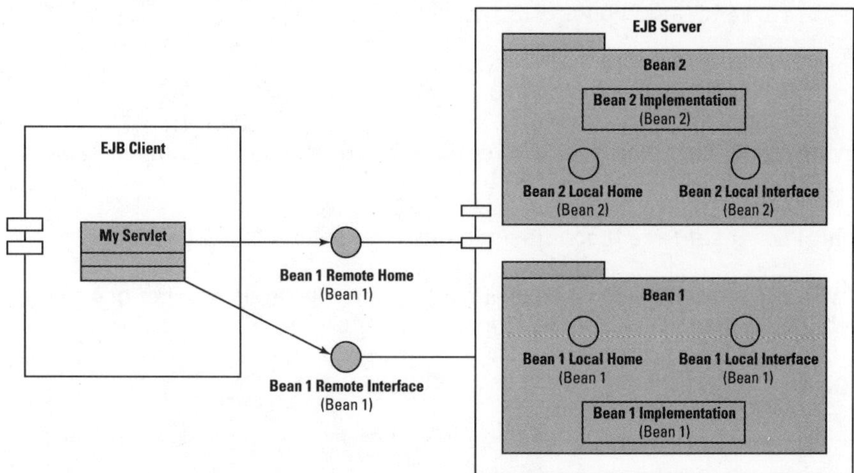

Figure 17-1: A UML depiction of the relationships among local interfaces, remote interfaces, and the bean implementation

From the client perspective, there are no new interfaces to deal with. Now that the bean is local to the client, no method calls that you make will need to catch a `RemoteException`. Maintaining the status quo is the new `AccessLocalException`, which indicates that the client is not allowed to use this method because the method is not a local call (for example, because a remote client such as a JSP tried to access the bean). All the other exceptions remain the same, meaning that you will still need to deal with them from their respective method calls.

Writing local beans

You implement local beans using the same process you use for remote beans. First create the bean interface, then write the home interface, and finally the bean implementation itself. For illustrative purposes, we shall convert the product beans of the previous chapter.

Starting with the bean interface, you need to write an interface that extends the `EJBLocalObject` interface.

```
public interface LocalProduct extends EJBLocalObject
```

To date, no naming conventions for local interfaces have been suggested, so in this book we will start all local objects with the prefix `Local` to distinguish them from the remote versions.

As with all bean interfaces you will need to provide a number of methods that allow access to the data. Unlike with the remote equivalent, because the bean is local, these methods are not required to throw any exceptions. So, taking the lead from the remote `Product` EJB, you add methods to the interface as follows:

```
public int getProductID();
public void setProductID(int id);

public String getName();
public void setName(String name);
```

Moving along, the home interface requires you to extend the `EJBLocalHome` interface as follows:

```
public interface LocalProductHome extends EJBLocalHome
```

As with the remote home interfaces, you need to declare a number of `create()` methods, each of which throws a `CreateException`:

```
public LocalProduct create() throws CreateException;

public LocalProduct create(int id) throws CreateException;
```

Note the lack of RemoteException that the remote version of the bean had to throw in the previous chapter. The remote product EJB is an entity bean that requires declarations of a number of finder methods. You will still need to write the finder methods for the local version, too:

```
public LocalProduct findByPrimaryKey(ProductID id)
    throws FinderException;

public List findByCategory(String cat, String name)
    throws FinderException;

public List findAllInCategory(String cat)
    throws FinderException;
```

Primary-key information is required for all entity beans. As you might have noticed in the preceding snippet, the code reuses as the primary-key class the ProductID class from the remote version. As the primary-key class is not dependent on any form of the EJB interfaces, you are free to use it wherever you like (even using the same class for different bean types). In this case, reusing the class gives you an advantage, because the local and remote beans represent the same data.

Once you have completed the local interfaces, the rest of the writing process is the same as for remote beans. Local bean-implementation classes are still required to implement EntityBean or SessionBean interfaces as appropriate. This requirement does not change between local and remote versions.

Using local beans

The process of gaining access to a local bean is no different from the process of gaining a reference to a remote bean. The use of home and remote interfaces remains the same, and you still use JNDI to find the initial reference to the home interface. Of course, the most important difference between using local beans and using remote beans is that you can't use a local bean in an environment such as a servlet or JSP. You can only use local beans in the same context (EJB container) as another bean.

Apart from that consideration, all the code looks the same. To complete the picture of using local beans, this is what the code looks like in an environment such as another bean:

```
InitialContext ctx = new InitialContext();
Object ref = ctx.lookup("ejb/LocalProduct");

LocalProductHome home =
    (LocalProductHome)PortableRemoteObject.narrow(ref,
                                      LocalProductHome.class);

ProductID id = new ProductID(some_id);
LocalProduct product = home.findByPrimaryKey(id);
```

Deploying local beans

Deploying a local bean is the same as deploying any other bean. The various classes and the deployment descriptor must be wrapped into a JAR file and deployed to an appropriate server.

Normally the vendor's tools will take care of the complete process for you. Fill in the appropriate fields of the deployment wizard, and everything is taken care of. If you wish to roll your own, the only difference between remote beans and their local brethren is the element names used in the deployment descriptor.

A deployment descriptor for a local bean starts with the same headers as a normal bean:

```
<?xml version="1.0"?>
<!DOCTYPE ejb-jar PUBLIC
  "-//Sun Microsystems, Inc.//DTD Enterprise JavaBeans 1.1//EN"
  "http://java.sun.com/j2ee/dtds/ejb-jar_2_0.dtd">

<ejb-jar>
  <description>
    An example application to introduce local interfaces
  </description>
  <enterprise-beans>
    <entity>
      <ejb-name>LocalProduct</ejb-name>
```

The next step is to provide the names of the classes that have the home and remote interfaces. Of course, you don't have a remote interface this time, but a local interface. To describe these new capabilities, you replace the `home` and `remote` elements with `local-home` and `local` elements, respectively:

```
      <local-home>LocalProductHome</local-home>
      <local>Customer</local>
```

After this point in the descriptor, the file looks the same. To complete the description, you will need to provide the following elements:

```
      <ejb-class>LocalProductEntityBean</ejb-class>
      <persistence-type>Bean</persistence-type>
      <prim-key-class>ProductID</prim-key-class>
      <reentrant>True</reentrant>
    </entity>
  </enterprise-beans>
</ejb-jar>
```

Now the descriptor is complete, and you can roll the EAR file as before.

Method-data granularity

As with any non-trivial application, performance considerations are always important in the design process. When it comes to enterprise beans, you use a set of design considerations similar to that of any other remote-object technology, such as RMI or CORBA. For the purpose of these considerations, we make the very fundamental assumption that the client will be on a separate machine from the server. Each time you ask for data, the system has to ensure that you get the latest copy and must therefore require extra network traffic. The result is that a good designer will alter the way he or she makes data available to the client.

Designing for remote beans

When you are designing the code surrounding remote beans, the network is your primary concern. By placing a network between the user of the data and the source of the data, you create a lot of extra overhead: Requests must be sent and received, data must be written to and from the underlying stream, error detection/correction handling and many other tasks. As a result, the response time between asking for and receiving a piece of data is very long (potentially in the order of seconds for a heavily loaded system).

As a programmer you will be very aware of performance issues in any application. It's typically the number-one complaint we programmers have to deal with. If it takes a second or so every time a request is made to a bean, then reducing the number of time-consuming requests as much as possible certainly becomes a goal. What does this mean from a design perspective?

If the goal is to reduce network traffic as much as possible, you want to get your money's worth each time you do make a request. If you are returning only one piece of information, you might as well return as much as possible. The design implications are quite clear: Don't use a lot of methods that only return one value, and do use a few methods that return a lot of information in one hit. In EJB terminology, the class that returns all the data as a single item is called a *Value Object.*

Remember that for any method that returns a class rather than a primitive type, the returned class must be serializable. If the class is not serializable, a `RemoteException` will be thrown.

Implementing value objects in remote beans

Let's take our customer bean example as the basis for illustrating how to change an EJB to use value objects. In the previous chapter, you saw a bean declaration that looks like this:

```
public interface Customer extends EJBObject {
  public int getCustomerID() throws RemoteException;
  public void setCustomerID(int id) throws RemoteException;
```

```
    public String getName() throws RemoteException;
    public void setName(String name) throws RemoteException;

    public String getAddress() throws RemoteException;
    public void setAddress(String addr) throws RemoteException;

    public String getEmail() throws RemoteException;
    public void setEmail(String addr) throws RemoteException;

    public String getCountry() throws RemoteException;
    public void setCountry(String code) throws RemoteException;

    public String getPhoneNumber() throws RemoteException;
    public void setPhoneNumber(String ph) throws RemoteException;
  }
```

Notice how there are a lot of methods that all return one value. In the "Beans in the wild" section of the previous chapter, you saw how to integrate an EJB with a JSP or servlet. With what you now know about performance penalties, think about how slow that JSP will be to process and then display the contents of the Web page. Each one of those lines where you wrote data out to the page, either through a bean or custom tag, required a request across a network. That means your JSP using that model is going to be a real dog.

The now obvious solution to this problem is to change the bean so that it now uses a single value object to fetch the values that your JSP needs. The role of the value object is to provide a very simple container for all those values that you would have previously fetched individually. Looking through the method calls above, that looks like you will need to deal with strings and ints.

Creating a value object class starts with the normal class declaration. Because value objects are returned as parameters in a remote call, they need to satisfy the same rules as any other class that you may use — they must be serializable. That makes the outline of your value object class look something like this:

```
public class CustomerValues implements Serializable {
  public CustomerValues() {
  }
}
```

Remember that serializable objects require an explicit public, no-argument constructor.

Now you need to provide variables that represent each of the fields. The simplest implementation is to just use a public variable per method that you had in your previous bean instance (this will horrify the OO-purist who would insist on having setter and getter methods!). This is how the class would now look with the addition of the public variables:

```
public class CustomerValues implements Serializable {
  public int customerID;
  public String name;
  public String address;
  public String email;
  public String country;
  public String phoneNumber;

  public CustomerValues() {
  }
}
```

For your next step, you need to modify the bean's remote interface to take advantage of this new class. Two options exist — replace all the methods with a set/get method pair that just takes the `CustomerValues` class, or add it as an additional methods. Which choice you make is personal preference. For the purposes of this exercise, all the methods will be replaced by a single pair of set/get methods using the value object.

Having made this decision, you can rewrite the remote interface to look like this:

```
public interface Customer extends EJBObject {
  public CustomerValues getCustomerInfo()
    throws RemoteException;
  public void setCustomerInfo(CustomerValues)
    throws RemoteException;
}
```

Next you need to update the bean implementation class (you don't need top do anything with the home interface) to reflect the changes in the remote interface. Due to the way you constructed the example in the previous chapter, the change in the implementation is quite simple. Start by deleting all of the methods that correspond to the old business methods and replace them with the stubs of the two new methods.

```
public class CustomerEntityBean implements EntityBean {
  ...

  public CustomerValues getCustomerInfo()
    throws EJBException {
  }

  public void setCustomerInfo(CustomerValues info)
    throws EJBException {
  }
}
```

Two methods to fill in, what do you do? Well, so long as you can copy the values from the values class to the internal cached variables, it really doesn't matter what you do. So, let's look at the `setCustomerInfo` method first:

```
public void setCustomerInfo(CustomerValues info)
  throws EJBException {
    customerId = info.customerId;
    userName = info.name;
    address = info.address;
    emailAddress = info.email;
    country = info.country;
    phoneNumber = info.phoneNumber;
}
```

And that leaves us with the `getCustomerInfo()` method. This method is required to return an instance of CustomerValues so you need an instance to return! Either create it locally in the method, or use a global instance for the class. The global instance is the preferred option. Why? Won't different callers end up overwriting the data that a previous caller requested? No. Remember that remote EJBs always pass data by value. That means that each time a method returns data, the caller ends up with a copy of the data you returned. Thus you can change information as much as you want, and each client will have his or her own individual copy. The final method implementation of your bean is:

```
private CustomerValues customerInfo = new CustomerValues();

public CustomerValues getCustomerInfo()
  throws EJBException {

  customerInfo.customerId = customerId;
  customerInfo.name = userName;
  customerInfo.address = address;
  customerInfo.email = emailAddress;
  customerInfo.country = country;
  customerInfo.phoneNumber = phoneNumber;

  return customerInfo;
}
```

As you can see, there is not that much work required to convert a standard bean design to a high-performance version using value objects. So, if you know that you are going to have beans that are heavily used by your application and performance is a major consideration, value objects are a worthwhile change.

Designing for local beans

Looking at the opposite situation—wherein the client and bean are held in the same VM—the other approach applies. This time, instead of trying to corral all the data into a single reply, each piece of data is requested through a separate method.

The disadvantages for the remote beans are the advantages in this situation: You need only to access data that you need rather than having to access all of it. In addition, you have the greatest chance of accessing the most up to date information (the bean may have changed its data between method calls if another client is also working with the same bean).

For local beans, you want the methods that you provide to return primitive data whenever possible. This ensures the fastest possible communications and removes the overhead of copying data or allocating new class instances to return data. Earlier in the chapter, we mentioned that one of the restrictions on local beans is that they must pass a reference to the data to the client. Traditional code works the same way. For example, passing an array enables the receiver to change the contents of the array directly. In the context of remote beans, that array would be made as a copy of the original and passed to the client code. Any changes made in that array would be kept on the client and not reflected back at the server. With local beans, the opposite applies — unless the local bean implementation takes explicit steps to make a copy of the data before returning it.

Inter-bean communication

Rarely do beans work in isolation from each other. Even in the simple example application that we've been walking you through you can see evidence of a number of beans colluding to make a complete application. For example, the Mailer bean uses the Customer and Order beans to do its work. In each of these examples, the receiver bean (typically a session bean) has been given the bean instances to work with directly. What happens when your code is inside one bean and would like to make a call to another bean?

Passing a reference to this

In traditional desktop applications, the use of callback style methods (such as event listeners) is very common not only for GUI work, but also for internal structures. If desktop applications use them, why wouldn't bean-based middleware components wish to do the same thing? Things become a little more interesting when you're dealing with callback methods. If a normal EJB is represented by a remote or local interface that is separated from the implementation, how do you call a method on another bean type that requires an instance of your bean type?

The answer can be found in context classes, which we looked at briefly in the previous chapter. Bean-context information can be found in the bean type — specific interfaces that extend from `EJBContext`. For example, if you are writing an entity bean, you would use the `EntityContext` interface that is passed through to you with the `setEntityContext()` method.

Having the entity context is the first step. Now, how do you move to passing your bean instance to the target bean? In each of the derived-context classes are two methods: `getEJBObject()` and `getEJBLocalObject()`. These return a reference to the remote or local interface respectively that describes your bean to the outside world that can be passed as an argument to a method call. Because your remote interface extends `EJBObject` (or `EJBLocalObject`), you can then cast the return value to the right interface and pass the result to the target bean. For example:

```
private EntityContext entityCtx;

public void doSomething() {
    MyEntityEJB me = (MyEntityEJB)entity.getEJBObject();
    targetBean.addData(me);
}

public void setEntityContext(EntityContext ctx) {
    entityCtx = ctx;
}
```

Even if you attempt to pass `this` as a reference to the target bean, the Java compiler will complain about it as well. Because your bean-implementation class does not extend the remote/local interface, it is not a valid argument to pass to the method anyway—hence the compiler error.

Accessing one bean from another

One very common operation that is performed in beans is accessing of other beans for information. An example that we've made mention of previously, is the use of a session bean to provide most of the business logic while entity beans provide the data. We also expect that another common use for accessing one bean from another is within entity beans where the client-facing remote interface presents the large-scale structure, but internally, the data use a number of local beans.

In order to illustrate how beans interact, let's create a new bean that does the order processing for us. This bean will be a session bean that represents an order-processing pipeline.

Combining beans in transactions

As enterprise applications become larger and work with more data, the requirements to keep the worldview of that data consistent also rise. In the enterprise world, regardless of the programming language used, this is known as transaction management. Throughout this book we have introduced you to the individual transaction-management capabilities within a specific API. Enterprise JavaBeans, as a collection technology, bring a number of these important APIs together into a single environment. Now we focus on combining these APIs with the transaction-management system so you will be able to control transactions at a higher level.

Keeping Valid Contexts

We have not used the context classes very much so far, but this is about to change. Many of the advanced techniques require you to use the context information available in the `EntityContext` and `SessionContext` interfaces.

These context classes provide you with references to information about the environment in which a given bean instance finds itself. In the previous chapter, in the section "Implementing the load and store methods," we introduced the usage of these interfaces. We also mentioned in passing throughout that chapter the `setXContext()` methods for each of the bean types. The one important point that we didn't cover was the exact time at which the context information becomes valid. Even though you have a reference to the context object, not all the information is available for you to use. When you are building new bean instances, availability of context information is very important for correct functionality.

In bean instances that need to use context information, your code must wait until after the `setXContext()` method for valid context information to be available, even though you already have a reference to the context class (see the figures of the previous chapter that describe lifecycles of the various bean types). If your bean has been created through an `ejbCreate()` method, and you need context information, the context information will not yet be available. In order to use valid context information, you may provide another method, `ejbPostCreate()`, which has exactly the same argument signature as the `ejbCreate()` method that was called. When the bean container calls the post-create method, you know that all the context information is available for your use.

The EJB specification says that you must have an `ejbPostCreate()` method for every `ejbCreate()` method, even if the `ejbPostCreate` method is empty. In our experience, and even in the examples provided by Sun, this is not necessary. The tool that builds and deploys EJBs appears to provide default definitions and implementations of the post-create methods if you don't write them yourself.

Transactions and transaction management can occur at many different levels of an application. J2EE has a whole API set devoted specifically to the transaction-management capabilities with the Java Transaction API (JTA). We cover JTA in depth in Chapter 23. That chapter covers the large-scale issues involved in using transactions over a large application. Although the following examples will use interfaces from the JTA packages, in this chapter we will concentrate on transaction management purely within a bean, rather than across the many bean instances that a full JTA session would involve.

EJBs offer two forms of transaction management: You can do all the transaction handling, or you can let the container do it. The right choice for you depends on your needs and the complexity of the interactions with the underlying database and surrounding beans.

Managing transactions within a bean

Throughout the EJB introductions so far, the basic assumption has been that a single entity-bean instance represents one piece of data in a database — one row of one table. This is not a hard and fast requirement; an entity bean may represent a complex arrangement of data. Maintaining your own transactions on this complex data is termed bean-managed transactions.

Because all of the actions going on below the surface of an EJB container, simply grabbing transaction handlers directly from the database handlers will result in all sorts of problems and is a tight and twisty maze. If you wish to manage your own steps in the transaction process, EJBs provide you with a convenient handle, which is available through the bean's context.

Transaction management within a bean starts with the `UserTransaction` class (part of the JTA API — `javax.transaction.UserTransaction`). You need to obtain a copy of it from your bean's context class. The access method is `getUserTransaction()`, which you will find in the base interface `EJBContext`. Once you have an instance of the transaction interface, it becomes the focus of all your transaction handling. Instead of using the JDBC transaction methods (or those of any other API), you now use the methods provided by `UserTransaction`. Why? Well, if you are interacting with a database through a bean, and your bean was called by another bean that was also interacting with the database, the container wants to make sure that everything is properly committed — an all-or-nothing policy. By circumventing that policy using your own transaction handling, you can break the integrity of the data.

Tip EJB transactions do not support all of the JTA transaction capabilities. The two biggest missing features are named rollback points and nested transactions.

Using a `UserTransaction` is just like using the JDBC transaction methods. As your code performs data processing, you call `begin()`, `commit()`, and `rollback()` as necessary. Here is a typical piece of code for which you would use transactions in the bean:

```
public void updatePricing() {

    UserTransaction trans = ejbContext.getUserTransaction();

    InitialContext ctx = new InitialContext();

    DataSource p_conn = (DataSource)ctx.lookup("jdbc/Oracle");
    Connection conn = p_conn.getConnection();

    trans.begin();
```

```
        try {
            // do some stuff here with the JDBC connection

            trans.commit();
        } catch(SQLException se) {
            trans.rollback();
        }
    }
```

Externally managing a transaction

When the transaction is externally managed, you need do nothing in your code. The EJB container makes sure that each time one of your business-logic methods is called, it will begin a new transaction part and then commit the changes after your method has completed. If your method throws an exception, no changes will be sent through, and a rollback will be issued.

Declaring the transaction type

Whatever choice you make at the code level, you need to tell the server about it when the bean is deployed. You impart this information in the deployment descriptor using the element `transaction-type`. Each bean type has this element, although its place in the order varies somewhat.

Declaring the transaction type to be used is a simple affair — you only have two choices: `Bean` or `Container`. If you want to do the transaction management yourself, then you use the following declaration:

```
<transaction-type>Bean</transaction-type>
```

Otherwise, to let the container do all the hard work, you use this declaration:

```
<transaction-type>Container</transaction-type>
```

Using Message-Driven Beans

A new form of bean is introduced in EJB 2.0. This bean is not available to user code, such as servlets or JSPs. The function of this new form of bean is to provide interaction with other existing enterprise systems (such as mainframes) and to place the information from that interaction into the underlying database(s). Tasks that use previously existing code take many more lines of code to implement and the performance they provide is not as good.

The role of message-driven beans in an application

As the enterprise application starts to encompass more parts of the traditional corporate-computing workload, the number of roles that Java and J2EE are required to fill likewise increases. The introduction of message-driven beans (MDB) with the latest EJB and J2EE specifications is designed to merge Java-based systems with their pre-existing counterparts. Airlines and car manufacturers have spent too many millions of dollars building their computing infrastructure to just throw it away for the latest fad technology. In order for Java and J2EE to be accepted in these environments, they must play nicely with existing systems.

The missing link

Prior to the EJB 2.0 specification, the focus of the EJB specification was mainly on establishing an infrastructure and a set of rules that would work. Once the various enterprise vendors established that the basic processes involved in an EJB system worked, they moved on to filling in the holes that have been left. Two holes are particularly important — integration with existing large-scale systems and a much more tightly defined and flexible container-managed persistence scheme. Message-driven beans fill in the first hole; later in the chapter, we will discuss the second hole.

The problem that MDBs were provided to solve was the problem of interaction between the larger existing systems and the smaller systems that the J2EE and EJBs were typically aimed at. For example, as government departments and large industries like airlines rushed to get online, they really didn't want to upset their core technologies. Those technologies were typically based around big-iron boxes running a collection of custom, proprietary software. Providing a "Web presence" by tearing down the entire system and replacing it with a completely new Java-based application is just not on.

In the mainframe arena, it is rare to find a public standard. Almost every interaction relies on some proprietary protocol. This causes a problem for Java because Java tries to stick with tried-and-true protocols wherever possible. So along comes the Java Messaging Service (JMS). JMS is designed to interact with systems using the native communication method — messages — rather than realtime-based network protocols. Examples of these forms of applications are Lotus Notes, SAP R/3, and IBM's CICS protocol. The main feature of these systems is that changes are notified in a message form that does not require interactive feedback. Effectively, all change notifications can be queued and then processed at some later time. This is in complete contrast to standard networking processes, such as RMI or CORBA, which require immediate feedback.

With earlier versions of the J2EE specification, you could not interact with these forms of systems. JMS existed as a specification, but it was not part of J2EE. If you wanted to include a CICS system into the application, you had to go it alone to write your own interface outside the "standard" J2EE system. This would involve writing a standalone Java client application that would listen using a proprietary API or JMS and then use EJBs or JDBC to update the J2EE database with the new knowledge. Quite an inefficient way of doing things.

To learn more about JMS, please turn to Chapter 22.

Now things have changed, and interacting with big-iron systems is a routine affair thanks to the inclusion of JMS and MDBs in the J2EE specification. These two specifications represent the two halves you need in order to interact with these existing systems in a standardized manner while reducing the amount of code the developer needs to write and maintain.

Properties of message-driven beans

Message-driven beans are a new form of EJB. How do they fit into the overall scheme of things with regard to your application? What code is the client for this form of bean, and who manages the state of any given bean?

Trying to describe a message-driven bean is difficult without a simple up-front statement: MDBs are for processing messages from the outside world and passing those messages to the underlying data source. The basic assumption is that an MDB's sole purpose in life is to process messages from some message queue that some other external application fills with message details. Typically, that processing results in data being modified in the assumed-to-exist database (or directory service).

Further examination of this set of assumptions reveals some more interesting properties:

- As the bean only processes messages from the outside world, it does not have any clients. It only listens to a queue of messages. How that queue is filled, we don't really care.
- Because clients don't have direct access to the bean (they just post messages to the queue), you do not have a remote, local, or home interface.
- The lifecycle of message-driven beans is controlled entirely by the EJB server, because no client can request the creation and destruction of instances of the bean.
- No requirement exists for the processing of any particular type of message, although processing JMS message queues are expected to be the typical use. Proprietary messaging APIs can be used.
- Message-driven beans conform to all the other requirements of EJB implementations — they can connect to databases, directory services, and other servers, but they cannot create separate threads, be a network server, or use static methods and variables.

The EJB 2.0 specification does not require support for any message service other than JMS. Support for other message queue types may be available, but is dependent on the J2EE environment provider.

A message-driven bean also acts like a cross between a session bean and an entity bean. Like session beans, MDBs do not maintain any form of state or customization. Like entity beans, MDBs have a persistence that exists over multiple lifespans of the bean. This persistence is in the form of the message queue. When the bean/server is not operating, messages are maintained in the queue until the server returns, and the bean can process the pending messages. Of course, this only works if the underlying queue type supports buffering messages. If it doesn't, you can't do anything about lost messages.

Requirements of message-driven beans

Session and entity beans have requirements for methods that are to be implemented, and MBDs also have requirements. These requirements are much less stringent for MDBs than for the other types:

- There can be only one `ejbCreate()` method that takes no arguments.
- The bean must implement the JMS interface `MessageListener`.
- A public default constructor, even if it is empty.

Even though the specification says that MDBs are not dependent on JMS directly, it is clear that they still need to implement a JMS interface. The reason for this apparently contradictory situation is that it will be easy to relax the requirements in a future version of the specification without effecting existing implemented beans. The `MessageDrivenBean` interface does not directly extend the `MessageListener` interface and the requirement enforced is by wording in the specification only. If you want, you can make your code non-portable and stick with one particular EJB server in order to use another messaging system.

After implementing the JMS `MessageListener` interface and any processing it requires, you do not need to implement any other JMS code. The beauty of this is that it saves you a lot of lines of code mucking about with JMS setup. All those details are handled by the EJB server environment and any configuration information you provide in the deployment descriptor.

Coding a message-driven bean

Coding a MDB is quite simple, compared to coding any other bean type. Gone are the requirements for home and remote/local-interface declarations. You have only one class to implement and only one interface to extend. Most of the real work involves setting up the deployment information in the deployment descriptor.

Implementing the bean code

Implementing a message-driven bean starts with you creating a class that extends the `MessageDrivenBean` interface. Two required methods exist: `ejbRemove()` and `setMessageDrivenContext()`. You should be familiar with these methods from the other bean types. The only minor change from the other beans types is that, because there are no home interfaces, you only need one `ejbCreate()` and no passivation methods.

For illustrative purposes, this example code will process a generic queue that you can manually feed messages to. Alternatively, you can make the queue that processes a mail queue. In either case, we assume a simple text message will be provided.

The start of the class declares the class name and the two required interfaces:

```
public class QueueProcessingBean
    implements MessageDrivenBean, MessageListener
{
}
```

Most of the interesting activity belongs in the `onMessage()` method required by the JMS `MessageListener` interface. This method takes a single argument — the `Message` object to be processed. `Message` is a base class for many different forms of message types; in this case, we are going to assume a text message has been sent, such as an e-mail message or XML document:

```
public void onMessage(Message msg) {
    String txt = ((TextMessage)msg).getText();
}
```

What you choose to do with the message from here on depends on your application requirements. For example, you might want to process the string (or, if you used a `BytesMessage`, a raw stream) as an XML document. You could then build a JAXP parser:

```
StringReader sr = new StringReader(txt);
InputSource source = new InputSource(sr);

SAXParserFactory factory = SAXParserFactory.newInstance();

SAXParser parser = factory.newSAXParser();

// Do lots of configuration work here

parser.parse(source);
```

The EJB server environment is free to create as many instances of any given message-driven bean as it feels are necessary. Because of this, any given bean instance may only process a fraction of the total messages on the nominated queue. You should always write your `onMessage()` method so that it does not rely on sequential messages being received.

That's all there is to writing a JMS bean implementation. Writing message-driven beans is easy to deal with because the container does all the hard work for you. All that remains is for you to tell the container what message queue you want the code to process, and that takes place through a deployment descriptor.

Chapter 22 contains a much longer example of the integration of a JMS service with a message-driven bean to process that service. If you would like to know more about these bean types, please skip over to that chapter for more information.

Deploying a message-driven bean

As we stated earlier, most of the work that goes into setting up a message-driven bean is performed through the configuration options provided in the deployment descriptor. It is here that you tell the EJB server environment which message queue to assign to a certain bean, how many messages to buffer, and many more details to be covered shortly.

Writing the information in the deployment descriptor starts with making the usual declaration of the bean type — in this case a message-driven bean:

```
<enterprise-beans>
  <message-driven>
    <ejb-name>Mailer</ejb-name>
    <home>MessagerHome</home>
    <remote>Messager</remote>
    <ejb-class>MessageBean</ejb-class>
    <ejb-ref>ejb/MessageHandler</ejb-ref>

    ???
  </message-driven>
</enterprise-beans>
```

So far, so good. All the starting information is the same as for the other beans. Next you need to declare the transaction type. The specification for MDBs recommends that you always let the container manage the transaction system.

After setting the transaction type, you move into the JMS specific fields. You have three to work with here: They are, in order of declaration, `message-selector`, `acknowledge-mode`, and `message-driven-destination`. Each of these items is optional, but you should declare at least one of them. Because using them requires a more detailed knowledge of JMS, we'll only skim the details here and refer you to Chapter 22 for more information.

The `message-selector` element describes optional conditions that you can use to filter which messages arrive at your bean. For example, your bean only wants to receive messages dealing with orders that cannot be processed. The `acknowledge-mode` field deals with how the container should respond to messages that have been processed by your bean. Because the container does the majority of the message processing before it even gets to your bean code, you should never explicitly acknowledge a message. The two options provided are: automatic, immediate acknowledgement or lazy acknowledgement that may result in duplicate copies being sent. (See the `javax.jms.Session` class for more details.)

Even though it is described as optional, the `message-driven-destination` element is required. This element describes where your messages are coming from so your bean can process them! It consists of two parts: the type of source (`Topic` or `Queue`) and, if the source type is a topic, whether the messages should be kept when no beans or server exist to deal with them.

```
<message-selector>category = 'Books'</message-selector>
<acknowledge-mode>Auto-acknowledge</acknowledge-mode>
<message-driven-destination>
  <destination-type>javax.jms.Queue</destination-type>
  <subscription-durability>Durable</subscription-durability>
</message-driven-destination>
```

Understanding Container-Managed Persistence

When we last looked at entity beans, you had to write a lot of trivial code for every bean. The trivial (and repetitive) tasks included making connections to databases, and making a query and then updating the details in the local variables. Wouldn't it be nice if you could just avoid doing all that work and tell the system what data you want and let it deal with all the information? Welcome to the world of container-managed persistence.

Container-managed persistence (mostly referred to as CMP) enables you to specify a basic set of interfaces and the data to be filled in, and from there the "system" takes care of the rest of the details of mapping your requirements to the underlying data source. The ability to very quickly knock out beans or modify existing beans using this structure has led to their rapid adoption in the enterprise developer's toolkit. Need to add a new data field? Simply add four lines of code and an extra element declaration to the deployment descriptor and re-deploy your bean (a five-minute job for an experienced practitioner).

Introducing CMP concepts

Although CMP beans are entity beans, they have a philosophy that is very different from that of the entity beans you saw in the previous chapter. In the previous chapter, you learnt about beans that managed their own data, an arrangement that is termed bean-managed persistence (BMP). CMP beans offload the task of managing data to the EJB server, and so involve a whole new set of rules and terminology.

In the change from EJB 1.1 to 2.0, a number of major changes were made to the requirements for CMP beans. The result is that the two specifications are incompatible. A 1.1 bean will not work in a 2.0 environment or vice versa. In this book, we will concentrate on the latest version of the specification; if you need to write code for an older system, please have a look at the various tutorials available on the Internet that have been linked from Sun's EJB homepage: `http://java.sun.com/products/ejb/`.

A bean without code

The most important aspect of CMP beans is that you actually write very little code. CMP beans, by definition, have their data managed by the container. All you need to do is provide the Java fields and abstract access methods to get to that data. Keeping a bean up to date with the underlying data source is the job of the container.

When the container manages the bean's data, the lifecycle model is mainly handled by the container. Whereas before you had to write methods for load/store and activate/passivate handling, the container now does this. The lifecycle model still looks exactly the same, but you as a programmer don't have to worry about the details that you had to worry about before.

Relationships with underlying data sources

If you don't have to write code to establish the connection with a data source, how do you make the connection between your code and that data source? Doing this is the job of the EJB container when you deploy a bean.

Deploying a CMP bean requires the deployment tool to take your class, analyze it, and provide all the missing implementation code. How does the deployment tool provide the missing code? It takes your class and extends it with the vendor-specific code. You never see this code, and it only appears after the deployment process takes place. That is, your code always stays the same regardless of the server vendor used, and each deployment tool will generate its own code.

Because the deployment tool and EJB container are responsible for creating the working runtime code, the deployment tool is also responsible for mapping your fields to some underlying storage system. You don't really know how this mapping is done, and you don't have any choice in the matter. All you can do is tell the server which fields to store and relationships to other beans. The vendor may use a relational database or a file: That is up to the server vendor to decide. That means that the database that was being used to store data for bean-managed persistence is now irrelevant. The container stores and retrieves all the values, and your application no longer needs to maintain its own separate database.

CMP bean requirements

At its heart, a CMP bean is just a normal entity bean. That means that you must follow the normal requirements for a home and remote and/or local interface declarations. Your bean implementation must still extend the `EntityBean` interface, too. However, as we have hinted, the other requirements when the container manages persistence are quite different from the requirements when the bean is managing it.

So what are the new rules for CMP beans?

- ✦ The class that extends `EntityBean` must be declared `abstract`.
- ✦ A field that is CMP managed must start with a lower case letter. However, the field cannot be defined in your code.

- `get` and `set` methods to access the field information must be declared `abstract` and `public`. The method must match the field name, with the exception that the first letter is capitalized. For example, to set the CMP integer field `foo`, the method would be `public abstract void setFoo(int value)`.
- Parameters to the `get` and `set` methods must follow the serialization rules— primitive types or classes must be serializable.
- If a field references other bean types, the field type must be the local interface for a single reference. If you wish to maintain a reference to a number of items of that other bean type, the field type must be either `java.util.Collection` or `java.util.Set`. These references can't be made available through business methods of the remote interface, but can be made available through the local interface
- All fields and relationships to be managed by the container must be specified in the deployment descriptor. If the field/relationship is not nominated in the deployment descriptor, then the container will not magically look after it for you.
- Normal business methods are allowed, and you must provide the bodies of these in your bean implementation.

You must be aware of several other restrictions that that we have not covered here. These restrictions involve runtime arrangements of bean references, and we'll cover them in due course as we introduce you to coding a CMP bean.

Writing a CMP entity bean

Writing CMP entity beans follows the same well-worn path as writing the other bean types. You start by defining home and remote interfaces, move on to the implementation code, and finish up with the deployment process. Like the others, CMP beans have their own quirks with regard to how the various methods must be defined, and we'll cover them as we introduce you to the code.

Implementing a CMP entity bean is a process in two parts—dealing with straight property value information, and dealing with relationships (references) to other bean instances. The container-managed relationships to other beans can be quite hairy to deal with, so we will cover them in a separate section following this one. In order to introduce container-managed fields, we are going to re-visit an old favorite—the product information from the virtual store example we have been using throughout the book. Products don't have any relationships to other beans, so they are a natural fit for this introduction to CMP fields. In the following section, where you will be introduced to relationship management, the code will use the order bean.

Writing home and remote interfaces

The home, local, and remote interfaces are little different from those used for BMP entity beans. The restrictions that were listed for CMP beans don't really apply at this level. For example, if you have a remote interface, it is not allowed to return instances of local beans.

Starting with the home interface, you must provide the `create()` method declaration(s). These perform the same task that they normally perform — creating a new instance of the bean type. CMP beans are still entity beans, so don't forget that you are still required to provide finder methods — at a minimum `findByPrimaryKey()`. Finder methods that return more than one key still return a `java.util.Collection` or `java.util.Set` instance. For example, the product remote home interface would look like this:

```
public interface ProductHome extends EJBHome {
    public Product create()
        throws CreateException;

    public Product create(int id)
        throws CreateException;

    public Product findByPrimaryKey(ProductID id)
        throws FinderException;

    public Collection findByCategory(String cat, String name)
        throws FinderException;

    public Collection findAllInCategory(String cat)
        throws FinderException;
}
```

Now, if you think that looks familiar, you're correct! This is exactly the same as the home-interface declaration that was used for BMP entity beans. You should not expect any different! The whole idea behind home and remote interfaces is that you can change the bean implementation without client code ever knowing the difference — even to the point of making a major functional change to the way data are stored.

Surprise number one is out of the way, so what do you expect should happen for local and remote interfaces? You think that we should just copy the BMP version, too? Actually, in this case — no. Why? Here's a hint:

```
public int[] getPrice() throws RemoteException;
public void setPrice(int dollars, int cents)
   throws RemoteException;
```

Can you see the problem here?

In the preceding code, the `get` method returns a different datatype from the `set` method. CMP beans do not recognize that a number of individual `int` values can be the same thing as an array of them. When you attempt to deploy a bean with this declaration, the tool will issue an error. How do you fix this problem?

The answer lies in the restriction list we presented earlier—the return type of the getter method should match the parameter type of the setter. Because you clearly can't return a number of individual `int` values, the solution is to change the setter parameters to be an array of `int` values:

```
public abstract int[] getPrice() throws RemoteException;
public abstract void setPrice(int[] cost)
    throws RemoteException;
```

Alternatively, you can make use of a simple value object class with two public variables for dollar and cent values. Just remember that you need to make the class serializable, and there should be no complaints from the EJB deployment tools. For example:

```
public class CostDetails implements Serializable {
    public int dollars;
    public int cents;

    public CostDetails () {
    }
}

....

public CostDetails getPrice() throws RemoteException;
public void setPrice(CostDetails cost) throws RemoteException;
```

By nature, the EJB deployment tool is required to implement the right functionality to map this custom datatype to its internal storage system.

Starting the bean implementation

The bean implementation class starts in the same way as other entity beans. So that you can tell the difference between the various different entity beans, this example will be named `ProductCMPBean`. It starts with the following line of code:

```
public abstract class ProductCMPBean implements EntityBean
```

One difference here from BMP beans is that the class is made abstract. This is a requirement because the class will contain a number of abstract methods and because a normal Java compiler would complain anyway if the class was not declared abstract.

As this class is an implementation of a bean, you need to follow the same conventions and requirements as you do with other beans. For example, naming conventions still apply for methods like `ejbCreate()` and `ejbRemove()`. Also, don't forget that you must supply an explicit public no-argument constructor.

Declaring the CMP field methods

With BMP bean implementations, when the remote or local interface defines business methods, these are directly reflected in the implementation class. CMP beans are no different. What you do with those methods is different.

In the BMP bean example, the methods that you provided in the remote-interface declaration provided access to the individual field information. In order to implement the business logic methods from the remote interface in the BMP bean implementation, you needed to keep local variables, talk to a database, and provide methods to perform these actions. For CMP beans, those fields in the remote interface just happen to match data that you would like the bean container to manage for you. Revisiting the restrictions for CMP entity beans, this means that any method that wants to represent CMP data should be declared abstract. Wonderful! That's a whole pile less code to write. Now, instead of you having to deal with all of the database-access code, the bean implementation code just copies the method declarations from the remote interface into the `ProductCMPBean` class, sticks the word `abstract` into the declaration, and everything is done!

```
public abstract int getProductID();
public abstract void setProductID(int id);

public abstract String getName();
public abstract void setName(String name);

public abstract int[] getPrice();
public abstract void setPrice(int[] cost);

public abstract int getStockCount();
public abstract void setStockCount(int count);

public abstract String getCategory();
public abstract String setCategory(String cat);
```

Although the ability to palm off the implementation details to the container makes for quicker coding, the downside is the lack of control over values coming in. For example, if you want to check for the category string that belongs to a specific set, you can't. A workaround for this problem is to have the bean provide the raw method, but expose a different method name through the remote interface and have that method call the now-private container-managed method.

In a change from all the other bean implementation types, notice that the method declarations do not declare exceptions.

Writing create methods

Your next task is to write the create methods that are used to insert new information into the underlying data source (for CMP beans, that translates to creating a new bean instance). Implementing create methods for CMP beans requires a different approach from those you have used previously. Sure you still need to look the same on the outside (you must still return the primary-key class from all `ejbCreate()` methods), but internally you have a different set of rules to play with.

You need to be aware of two differences, both of which are the result of the implementation changes enforced by the container management of field data.

Under this new system, when setting values of the data represented by the bean, you don't have direct access to the actual variable. Remember that you had to declare all the methods as `abstract` and that the container provided the implementation of the beans. This means that each time you want to access the value of one of these pieces of data, you need to call the appropriate getter method. When you want to set the value, such as in an `ejbCreate()` method, you must therefore call the appropriate setter method. For example, you have a create method that provides all the data for a new product:

```
public ProductID ejbCreate(String name,
                           int[] price,
                           int  stockCount,
                           String category) {
    setName(name);
    setPrice(price);
    setStockCount(stockCount);
    setCategory(category);

    ....
}
```

Now that the container is managing the bean and all its accompanying data, one important requirement has suddenly become an issue—the primary key. This is an important issue, because the primary key is the means the bean uses to determine the data it should represent. With BMP entity beans, you just called on the underlying database to generate a new unique identifier for you to the use as the primary key. As the container now manages the storage of that data, the unique key-generation capability has been lost. Problem is, you still need to create a primary key!

In a departure from the requirements for BMP entity beans, finder methods for the container-managed variant must return either `java.util.Collection` or `java.util.Set`, `Enumerations` are not permitted. Sets are used when you wish to ensure that each bean contained is unique.

Options for generating primary keys

You can generate a unique primary key in a number of ways, and the best choice depends on your needs for the overall system design. In some cases, you might want the bean client to provide the primary key. Alternatively, you can generate the ID internally (by asking another bean to do it for you), or even allow the container to manage primary-key generation.

The ability to force the bean client to provide you with a unique ID is available when the user would like to provide something that will be easy to remember—for example, a bean that has a unique user name for a login. When providing these keys, the client code should check with another bean that can provide third-party confirmation that the bean is unique. This is the ideal use for a stateless session bean. The session bean can be in contact with the underlying authorization system, such as LDAP or a database, and check that the supplied name is unique. If the session bean gives the OK, request the creation of a new entity bean.

An alternative to letting a third-party action control uniqueness is to let the container do it. One rule of the container is that if the primary key returned from the `ejbCreate()` method already exists, the container will throw a `CreateException` to the client. So if the create method takes the user name and returns it, and the user name already exists, the container will force the uniqueness rule anyway.

To make the client supply you with a primary key, just make sure that the `create()`-method definition in the home interface provides you with the required data—a string for the user name, for example:

```
public String ejbCreate(String productCode,
                        String name,
                        int[] price,
                        int  stockCount,
                        String category) {
    setName(name);
    setPrice(price);
    setStockCount(stockCount);
    setCategory(category);

    setProductId(productCode);

    return productCode;
}
```

It is now the bean user's responsibility to generate the ID and pass it to your bean.

If you prefer that the bean generate a unique ID internally, then your bean implementation will have to go looking for that ID. But where is it going to find a unique key? Well, you can make contact with another database and ask it to generate one for you, just as you would have done with the BMP bean implementation. Naturally, this requires that you have two databases — your database and the database in which the entity beans are stored by the container. This may not be a problem for you if you are representing a really large enterprise system, but if you only have a small system with just a few beans, as in the example application, the extra hassle is probably not worth it. So why not apply some of the principles you've already learned, and encapsulate the "generate me a unique ID" functionality into another bean?

Providing a unique-number generator should be the job of an entity bean rather than a session bean. You still need some form of persistence so that the numbers always remain unique if the server crashes. Given the choice of a local or remote interface, it is better to use a remote bean because the functionality may well be located on another server or system (alternatively, provide both local and remote interfaces for the one bean). For the purpose of this exercise, assume that you have the following home- and remote-interface declarations:

```
public interface UniqueNumberGenerator extends EJBObject {
    public int nextIdentifier() throws RemoteException;
}

public interface UniqueNumberHome extends EJBHome {
    public UniqueNumberGenerator findByPrimaryKey(String type)
        throws FinderException, RemoteException;
}
```

In order to use this unique-number generator, you are going to need an instance of it. Of course, that instance is going to be needed inside the `ejbCreate()` method of the `ProductCMPBean` so that you can create the primary-key class that is needed for the return value. Because you are generating a unique primary key internally for the product bean implementation, there is no need to ask for a value in the create-method declarations in either the home interface or bean implementation.

To complete the `ejbCreate()` method implementation you must add the code to fetch the key-generator bean, ask it for a value, create a new primary-key class, and then clean up the bean reference:

```
public ProductID ejbCreate(String name,
                           int[] price,
                           int  stockCount,
                           String category)
    throws CreateException {

    ProductID product_id = null;

    try {
        InitialContext ctx = new InitialContext();
        Object home_ref = ctx.lookup("ejb/KeyGen");

        UniqueKeyHome home =
```

```
            (UniqueKeyHome)PortableRemoteObject.narrow(home_ref,
                                            UniqueKeyHome.class);

        UniqueKeyGenerator key_gen =
            home.findByPrimaryKey("products");

        int id = key_gen.nextIdentifier();
        setCustomerID(id);

        product_id = new ProductID(id);
    } catch(Exception e) {
        // any error is bad, so barf for all of them
        throw new CreateException("Cannot create unique ID");
    }

    setName(name);
    setPrice(price);
    setStockCount(stockCount);
    setCategory(category);

}
```

Tip

The preceding example code assumes that the bean used to generate the unique key is a remote object and therefore that it requires the use of `narrow()` before using the home interface.

Note that if there is any error in attempting to obtain a unique identifier that the code does not proceed any further.

Implementing automatically generated primary keys

Finally, you have the option of letting the container manage the primary keys. This is quite easy to do and is the suggested method for most beans for which you don't need to know or care about uniqueness (such as an address field of a customer bean). This style is known as automatic primary-key generation.

To implement automatic primary-key generation, you must make quite a few extra changes to a standard CMP bean. The idea is that the container will create classes when you deploy the bean and will manage all the details. The two most obvious changes affect the return types of `ejbCreate()` and `findByPrimaryKey()`. Because you don't know the class that the container will select for the primary key, both of these methods must return `java.lang.Object`.

You must take other precautions when using this form of primary key. First, no code that you have written in the bean implementation can rely on the return value of `EJBContext.getPrimaryKey()`. Because you don't know what the class is, you should not make assumptions about the value of the primary key. Doing so will only lead to non-portable code.

A Hidden Message

If you take a look through the EJB specification, you will find that it talks about many more methods than we have introduced here. The most interesting of these is the method `ejbSelect()`. (Most of the others you will have seen in earlier examples.)

When you need to define code that makes a query of the underlying data structure, it helps if you have some local knowledge of the data. Sometimes you will want to find out about other beans, or properties of a collection of beans. Instead of writing all the code yourself, you can be lazy and let the bean do it for you. This is the job of the `ejbSelect()` methods. These select methods are only available to your bean implementation class, as you are not allowed to expose them through the home, remote or local interfaces.

As you will see later in the chapter, you can describe relationships between beans and finder methods using EJB QL. This SQL-like language is used in the deployment descriptor to perform these tasks. The `ejbSelect()` method(s) is part of the infrastructure that EJB QL can be applied to in order to perform lookup tasks. The EJB container supplies the method implementation at deployment time, so all you need to do is declare the abstract method name and parameters that you want to use, and fill in the appropriate blanks in the deployment descriptor.

Sometimes you might want to provide the equivalent of static methods for your beans—methods for which you don't want or need to create an instance of the bean. Because beans do not enable you to declare static methods, you need an alternative arrangement. To handle this situation, EJBs have what are termed *home methods*. These are extra methods, declared in the home interface, that are not create, find, or remove methods. To map these through to your bean, just create a method name that starts with `ejbHome` and that matches the rest of the method name and argument list supplied by the home interface (in basically the same pattern as that of finder methods in BMP entity beans). Calling a home method creates a situation similar to that of finder methods—they are called on pooled, inactive instances of the bean and work in much the same way that a static method would. Under earlier versions of the EJB specification, you would previously have used session beans to perform these tasks. The intention now is that you can replace all those session beans with home methods.

Completing the bean implementation

At this point, the only remaining coding task is finishing off any other methods that you might need. For the simple product bean presented here, no more code remains to be written. All the public methods in the remote interface are handled by the CMP code, while the create methods have been dealt with. What about the finder methods? An entity bean requires finder methods, which haven't been implemented.

Finder methods are one of the bonuses of CMP beans. You don't need to implement them. A finder method is effectively a search of the underlying database for a matching set of details. If you don't know how the data is stored, you can't effectively search for the data either, you need to leave those details to the container. Although you leave the actual implementation to the container, you still need to tell it how to use the arguments to find the right bean instance. The mapping of the arguments to a request and implementation code is the job of the newly introduced EJB Query Language. EJB QL is a huge topic that we will cover later in the chapter.

Other methods are also swept along in this scheme. For example, you do not need to implement `remove()` or entity-context methods if you don't need them.

Business methods that use the bean's state, but that do not represent container-managed fields, should take care in their use of bean information. Because the bean can change details without your knowing it, your code should never store the values in local variables between method calls. Each time one of your business methods is called you should fetch the values again.

You can call `ejbLoad()` within your own business methods to make sure that everything is up to date before fetching the values.

Writing the deployment descriptor

Unlike the other bean types, the deployment descriptor is more important than the actual bean code. While the bean code just defines a set of abstract methods, it is the deployment descriptor that matches up these methods to real data, defines relationships between beans, and provides the definition of the finder methods.

Of course, the easy way out of writing the deployment descriptor is to let your vendor's tool do all the work for you!

Starting with the now familiar `enterprise-bean` tag, the deployment descriptor describes an entity bean:

```
<entity>
  <ejb-name>Product</ejb-name>
  <home>ProductHome</home>
  <remote>Product</remote>
  <ejb-class>ProductCMPBean</ejb-class>

  ???

</entity>
```

After the `ejb-class` element, you need to describe the type of persistence to use. For container-managed beans, the word `Container` is used. Next, you define the primary key class and re-entrant properties as you would for BMP entity beans:

```
  <persistence-type>Container</persistence-type>
  <prim-key-class>ProductID</prim-key-class>
  <reentrant>True</reentrant>
```

So far, so good. Everything looks the same as for bean-managed persistence. At this point you would close the `entity` element if it were bean-managed. However, this is not the case, and now the fun starts.

The next tag tells the container what version of container-managed persistence is being used. Remember that this is really important because the earlier schemes are not compatible with the latest specification. For EJB 2.0 spec beans, the value you use for the `cmp-version` element is `2.x`.

```
<cmp-version>2.x</cmp-version>
```

Jumping ahead of ourselves a little here, the next tag describes a name that the EJB QL will use to access this particular bean. For the moment, the value will be set to `Product`; we will explain it in more detail a little later in the chapter.

```
<abstract-schema-name>Product</abstract-schema-name>
```

You now need to list all the fields that the container is required to manage. Each field name must have a name — the same name that you used for the `get` and `set` methods. With each field, you can have an optional description string too, as follows:

```
<cmp-field>
  <description>Product category</description>
  <field-name>category</field-name>
</cmp-field>
<cmp-field>
  <field-name>name</field-name>
</cmp-field>
<cmp-field>
  <field-name>stockCount</field-name>
</cmp-field>
<cmp-field>
  <field-name>price</field-name>
</cmp-field>
<cmp-field>
  <description>The primary key</description>
  <field-name>productID</field-name>
</cmp-field>
```

As you can see, you list each field individually. If the field is not mentioned here, the container will not know about it, and errors will be generated at deployment time.

The primary key is what anchors entity beans together. The next tag specifies the primary-key class so that it can be used in the finder-method implementations. You must make sure that the primary-key field is also one of the fields nominated with a `cmp-field` element:

```
<primkey-field>productID</primkey-field>
```

If your bean does not refer to any other beans and only has the single finder method of `findByPrimaryKey()`, this is the end of the deployment descriptor. You can add more, but we won't discuss these parts right now because we need to introduce to you EJB QL to cover the extras.

If you are letting the container specify the primary-key class, you should not declare the `primkey-field` element. Instead, use the `prim-key-class` element with the following declaration:

```
<prim-key-class>java.lang.Object</prim-key-class>
```

Container-managed relationships

Rarely will an entity bean stand alone. Entity beans represent data, and most applications have some relationship between pieces of data, and therefore you expect that there will be relationships between beans. Already we have shown one set of relationships—orders contain customers, products, and an employee. You need to maintain these relationships externally.

Fields that represent links to other beans are termed container-managed relationships (CMR). On the outside, they look almost identical to container-managed fields. Many of the rules are the same, but naturally there are a few minor differences.

Working with bean relationships

For many applications, a nice object-oriented design can go much further than simple large-container classes. Internally, you may wish to break out data representation even further. For example, an address is a common item for both customers and suppliers, so why not treat it as a separate class (that is, a bean) that can be used in both the customer and supplier beans?

Providing simple representations of internal data is just what local beans were designed for. Container-managed persistence relieves you of the burden of having to write code, so why not combine the two and let the container manage the links between bean instances as well? What a wonderful idea! The less code you have to write, the faster and more reliable you can make software. As an added bonus, the boss and marketing are happy, too.

A limitation of the current CMR system is that you can only define local beans for management. If you want to present that combined information to a remote client, then your bean has to do some data shuffling and present data in a different form to remote users, such as by finding remote versions of the same bean or using a value object class.

Because CMR fields look a lot like database-table relationships (they even use many of the same terms), you can also arrange the relationships in a variety of ways. Taking a leaf from the database book of terminology, the basic relationship classifications are as follows:

✦ *One-to-one* — The parent bean has one child bean, and the child has only one parent.

✦ *One-to-many* — The parent bean has many children, but the children only have a single unique parent.

✦ *Many-to-many* — The parent bean has many children, while a child bean can have many parents.

Defining methods for CMR fields

CMR fields still require accessor methods so that the container can set and retrieve values. As with fields, you have methods for single-valued fields, but now you have extra options for methods to take multi-valued fields to accommodate one-to-many and many-to-many relationships. As usual, the methods must be declared public and abstract.

When referring to CMR fields, the container provides your bean with references to the local interface; there is no need to go through a home interface. When you provide a method that looks after a one-to-one relationship (either `set` or `get`), the parameter type must be the local interface, not the bean implementation class. For example, the order bean would declare methods for the customer as follows:

```
public abstract void setCustomer(LocalCustomer   cust);
public abstract LocalCustomer getCustomer();
```

In order to provide access to multi-valued fields, whether one-to-many or many-to-many, the CMR methods may take an instance of `java.util.Collection`. The collection contains local interfaces for all related child beans. For example, if you modify the order to reference all the products (until this point the order only referred to a single product purchased), then you declare the CMR field methods as follows:

```
public abstract void setProducts(Collection products);
public abstract Collection getProducts();
```

Remember that you cannot make these relationships available to bean clients through a remote interface. Local interfaces are fine, but because the references are to local beans, it is not valid to make these interfaces available to remote users.

Making use of related beans within your bean implementation is the same as with fields. Because there is no class variable to access, you need to use the get and set methods. For relationships that are multi-valued, you have a Collection to work with. While you can determine the real class and cast up, it is usually easier just to ask for an Iterator and use that to traverse the values, as follows:

```
Collection products = getProducts();
Iterator itr = products.iterator();

while(itr.hasNext()) {
    LocalProduct product = (LocalProduct)itr.next();

    ....
}
```

Tip

If the field does not contain any relationships, the return value will be a valid container instance that is empty.

Note here that there is no need to narrow() the local interface down to the right class, as you have to when working with a home interface. You can be assured that all class references handed to the Collection will be valid before you start.

Moving references about

Once you have the collection to play with, it is useful to do something with the contained beans. For example, the remote interface of the order bean might want to present a total price of all items that have been ordered, or to copy one order to another.

When working with referenced beans, particularly when copying data that have a single parent relationship, you need to be careful about how you pass the references around. If you are not careful, relationships can change without your being aware of it. Take a look at a couple of examples of how these relationships can change automatically.

In both one-to-one and one-to-many beans, as you can see in Figure 17-2, both parent and child have one relationship in both directions (parent to child and child to parent). If you assign the parent a new child that is already the child of another parent, then the child shifts its allegiance to the new parent.

In psuedo-code, the internal actions taken by the EJB container would look like this:

```
child = p2.getChild();
p2.setChild(null);
p1.setChild(child);
```

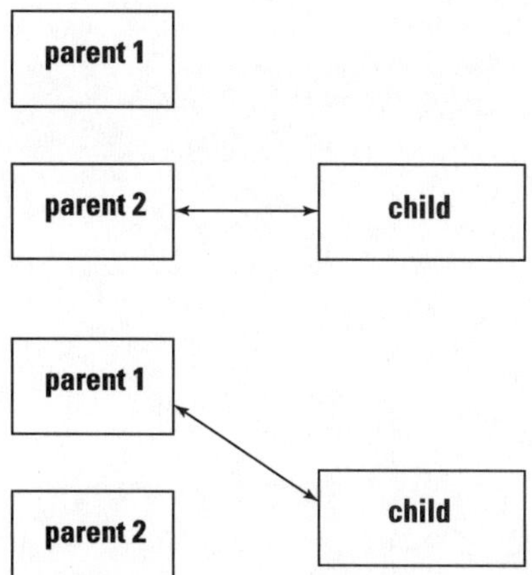

Figure 17-2: A one-to-one relationship shifts the parent relation to the new parent.

In many-to-many relationships, the child beans are assigned a new `Collection` for the parents. As you can see in Figure 17-3, the new collection contains the old list of parents, plus the new parents. The psuedo-code for the EJB container takes a little more work now. For each child bean, the container must grab the list of current parents, add a child, and then reset the collection. (Remember that each child bean can potentially have a different set of parents, meaning that you must treat each one individually.)

```
Collection new_children = ....
Iterator itr = new_children.iterator();

while(itr.hasNext()) {
  ChildType child = (ChildType)itr.next();
  Collection parents = child.getParents();
  parents.add(new_parent);
  child.setParents(parents);
}

new_parent.setChildren(new_children);
```

Note that the container does not need to clear the old parent of the child nodes. Instead, it fetches the current set of parents, adds the new parent, and then replaces the values.

One final word of caution when dealing with CMR fields. If you are working with a collection and iterating over the values, then you need to be careful about how you work with the contents of the `Collection`. Iterating over the contents does not cause any problems, but if you wish to add or remove values (such as to assign the child to a new parent), then you must exercise care.

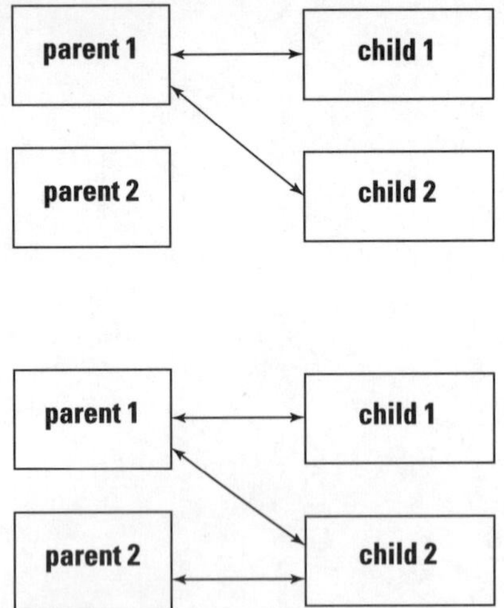

Figure 17-3: The relationships for child beans that now have new parents added

When moving a bean between two fields, where the bean is sourced from an `Iterator`, you should make sure that you take explicit steps for each part of the process. That is, if you attempt to use the collection to implicitly remove the bean from one parent bean and place it in another, then an exception will be generated. The correct way to move a bean reference when using iterators is to use the `remove()` method before adding that bean to the new parent.

```
Collection new_children = ....
Iterator itr = current_parent.iterator();

while(itr.hasNext()) {
  ChildType child = (ChildType)itr.next();
  itr.remove();
  new_children.add(child);
}

this.setChildren(new_children);
```

Deployment-descriptor additions for CMR fields

With relationships being added to the mix of items for the container to manage, you now need to tell the container what to manage and how to manage it. Once again, this is the job of the deployment descriptor.

Adding information for CMR fields comes right after the `primkey-field` element from the last time we looked at the deployment descriptor. Actually, the new information comes a long way after the XML you have already seen — right at the end of the file, after the closing `enterprise-beans` tag.

Defining relationships between beans is the role of the relationships tag. In the general scheme of things, this element is found just after the enterprise-beans element.

```
<ejb-jar>
  <enterprise-beans>
   ....
  </enterprise-beans>
  <relationships>
   ...
  <relationships>
</ejb-jar>
```

Contained in the relationships is a set of elements that defines one single relationship, either unidirectional or bi-directional.

Each relationship declaration is defined by the element ejb-relation. The relationship defines a marker name used in EJB QL declarations, and information about how the relationship is structured — for example, what the related class is, whether it is single- or multi-valued, and so on.

The relationship declaration starts by defining a name with the ejb-relation-name element. This name is important because it not only defines to the reader what is being managed, but also serves as an identifier when, later on, you come to write the EJB QL that says exactly which beans are to be related. When defining a name, you should make sure that it is a single word. Although whitespace is acceptable here, errors will be generated if you come to use it later in the EJB QL statements. Also, the name must be unique within a given deployment descriptor. You may, however, use the same name in different deployment descriptors, although for clarity's sake we always advise against doing that. If you want to define the order-to-customer relationship, for example, you use the following declaration:

```
<ejb-relation-name>Order-Customer</ejb-relation-name>
```

The convention we are using here is to capitalize the first letter of each word. For example, if your order consists of a number of items, you would use Order-Item as the naming convention.

Next you define the details of one relationship — in EJB terminology, a role. The role is a unidirectional definition, such as the order to the customer, or the customer to the order. A role is defined by the ejb-relationship-role element and contains another name, multiplicity information, the name of the EJB being used as the source, and the CMR field that all this information belongs to.

Before explaining all the terms, we'll present a short snippet of the complete declaration:

```
<ejb-relationship-role>
  <ejb-relationship-role-name>order-has-customer
  </ejb-relationship-role-name>
  <multiplicity>One</multiplicity>
  <relationship-role-source>
    <ejb-name>Order</ejb-name>
  </relationship-role-source>
  <cmr-field>
    <cmr-field-name>customer</cmr-field-name>
  </cmr-field>
</ejb-relationship-role>
```

Working through this example, you see that it starts with a declaration of yet another name with the `ejb-relationship-role-name element`. Again, as with the relationship name, you should not use any whitespace. Multiplicity indicates how many references this bean has to the destination bean. Only two legal values exist here: `One` and `Many`. Because this relationship is one-to-one between the order and the customer (we're assuming that a customer can only have one order active at a time), the value to use is `One`. Following the multiplicity is the source information—the "from" part of the relationship. In the relationship-role-source tag, you define the name of the bean acting as the source. This name must be one of the matching names from an `ejb-name` element that you declared way back in the `entity` declaration. Finally, you declare the name of the field that will receive the references to the destination bean. This field is just like the other non-relationship fields in that the first letter should be lower case.

The preceding example defines a unidirectional relationship. In this case, the order knows about the customer, but the customer does not know about the order. When a customer logs on to your Web site, he or she may want to see the current pending orders. This means that you would like to provide the reverse relationship, hence making the relationship bi-directional. That is, orders know about their customers, and customers know about their orders. Apart from including the extra methods in the Customer bean, you now need to add the extra declarations to the deployment descriptor.

In order to define the reverse relationship details, you start with the example `relationship-role` shown earlier in this section. Following that, you declare a second `relationship-role` that provides the reverse details. To define the reverse relationship, you use the same set of declarations with a few small changes, as follows:

```
<ejb-relation-name>Order-Customer</ejb-relation-name>
<ejb-relationship-role>
  ....
</ejb-relationship-role>
```

```
<ejb-relationship-role>
  <ejb-relationship-role-name>customer-has-orders
  </ejb-relationship-role-name>
  <multiplicity>Many</multiplicity>
  <relationship-role-source>
    <ejb-name>Customer</ejb-name>
  </relationship-role-source>
  <cmr-field>
    <cmr-field-name>orders</cmr-field-name>
    <cmr-field-type>java.util.Collection</cmr-field-type>
  </cmr-field>
</ejb-relationship-role>
```

For the reverse relationship details, just change all the references to make the source and destination point in the opposite direction. Because the customer may have many orders, you make an addition to the `cmr-field` element. The `cmr-field-type` element indicates which class should be used to hold the values. As you have already seen, only two valid classes exist for the EJB 2.0 specification: `Collection` and `Set` from `java.util`. Whatever you place here should match the parameter type of the accessor methods defined in the bean interface. If your multiplicity type is defined as `Many`, you are required to have this element.

The processes of providing details for the other relationship types are just variations on the process we just outlined. For unidirectional relationships you only need one `ejb-relationship-role` element, and for bi-directional relationships you need two. By playing with the combinations of multiplicity and roles, you can define any set of organization between two beans.

Cleaning up after yourself

One element remains for the deployment descriptor, and this affects a very important behavior — cleaning up when a bean is removed. If you delete a bean and that bean references a collection of other beans, what should happen? Should all the referenced beans also be deleted, or should they remain?

Specifying the deletion behavior is the job of the `cascade-delete` element. In the above examples, the element, which is optional, is not declared. When it is not declared, the relationship does nothing when the source bean is deleted for that role. That is, the source bean is deleted, but any referenced beans are not deleted.

If you do provide the `cascade-delete` element, then the source, when deleted, will automatically attempt to delete the destination beans too, where possible. Asking for cascade deletion is pointless if the destination bean has a multiplicity of `Many`: The destination beans refer to many source beans, and so they cannot be deleted until all their source beans have been deleted, too.

If you are familiar with the UML, using the `cascade-delete` functionality is exactly the same as specifying a containment relationship (the filled diamond arrowhead).

EBJ QL

One more piece of the container-managed persistence system remains. So far we have introduced you to describing the bean's Java code and deployment information, but the missing link is specifying exactly which bean instances should be part of the association. For one order instance there are thousands of potential customer instances, but our code only allows one. How do you tell a particular bean instance to use a particular order instance?

Specifying relationships using existing technologies such as Java and XML won't work because the languages are not designed for the terseness required. The solution is to use a new "language" to allow this definition to take place. What was chosen? Nothing. The EJB Query Language, which looks suspiciously like SQL, was designed specifically for the task of linking objects and relationships.

By convention, we indicate all EJB QL keywords using uppercase letters. These keywords are case-insensitive, so `SELECT` is the same as `select`. However, all of the other words used, such as the names of variable declarations and schema types, are case-sensitive.

The language definition

EJB QL is based on the SQL syntax, with a number of additions to allow specification of a Java-based entity. At the same time, the list of commands is reduced to exactly one: the `SELECT` statement.

EJB QL is provided so that you can define a search mechanism for entity beans that are managed by the container. It cannot be used to locate non-CMP beans. Within the context of an entity bean, you can use EJB QL in two places: nominating the beans that should be placed into a CMR field, and the finder/select methods.

The EJB QL statement for finding a bean or beans has the following form:

```
SELECT a value FROM a bean type or field WHERE some condition
```

Only the `WHERE` section is optional.

CMP entity beans define a term called an *abstract schema type*, which you use when talking about the values you can place into the `FROM` or `SELECT` portions of the EJB QL. The schema type is a longhand way of talking about the datatype. For example, if you have an Order bean to represent one order, the abstract-schema type is `Order`. Now, what if the bean has a field called `customer` that refers to the Customer entity bean through the `LocalCustomer` local interface? The abstract-schema type of that field is `Customer`. You can refer to this field using the declaration `Order.customer`. If you think this looks suspiciously like an SQL statement to a table and column declaration, you are almost right.

Abstract schema–typing names are actually defined by the names you place into the deployment descriptor. Do you remember the `abstract-schema-name` tag we used earlier? The name that you place in that tag is the real name you must use in an EJB QL statement when referring to a particular customer. So even though your entity-bean Java class might be called `CoffeeShop`, if the deployment descriptor calls it `DepartmentStore`, then the EJB QL must refer to it as `DepartmentStore`.

The SELECT clause

The first section of the EJB QL statement describes the type of data that is "returned." According to the abstract-schema type, the value you specify here can be either a single value or multiple values. Another factor that will be taken into account is what you are using the method for — finders or selects.

Two forms of the `SELECT` statement exist:

```
SELECT schema-type-variable.cmr-field
```

and

```
SELECT OBJECT(variable_name)
```

In the terminology of the EJB specification, the first form is called a *single valued path expression*. The expression is like nominating a class and field type. The schema-type variable is defined later in the statement, but the field name must be one of the CMR fields, such as `products` from the Order bean. You typically use this when you want to nominate a particular field type of a bean as the return value.

You use the second form when you don't need to use a field of a bean, but instead need to say, "find me any matching object" from the underlying storage. Again, the variable name is declared later in the statement.

In both forms, you have the option of declaring the keyword `DISTINCT`, which will remove duplicate matching entries. For example, if the query is used to define a finder method that returns a `Collection` or `Set`, it will guarantee that only one of each matching bean instance exists.

If the return type is `Set`, then even if you don't declare the `DISTINCT` keyword the container will assume that you have used it. The mathematical property of a set is that no duplicate entries exist.

The FROM clause

The second, compulsory part of an EJB QL is the `FROM` clause. With this clause you specify the bean type that you are searching for the required data, and also declare the variable that is used by the `SELECT` clause.

Declaring the FROM clause starts with specifying the keyword and then includes the abstract schema name and then the variable name. In other words, this declaration looks just like a normal Java variable declaration. For example, if you want to fetch information from the Order bean, the declaration is as follows:

```
FROM Order o
```

Compiling a complete query, you can ask for the customer of an order with the following statement:

```
SELECT o.customer FROM Order o
```

Here you see the combination of the variable declaration using the abstract-schema type Order, which you have named o; you then said that you would like to access the customer field from the order. At this point, the query is not particularly useful, as the query does not say which order you want. However, if you want a method that says, "find all customers of all orders," then the preceding query is perfect. Notice how analyzing the query can immediately show you what the return type is: This query will make the return value a Collection or Set, depending on which method it is assigned to.

The FROM clause can sometimes have an optional keyword, AS, between the abstract-schema name and the variable name. The following two statements are equivalent:

```
SELECT o.customer FROM Order o
SELECT o.customer FROM Order AS o
```

Of course, you don't need to feel restricted to having just a single variable declaration. The FROM clause allows multiple declarations, provided you separate them with commas. Each item can be a different schema type, too. For example:

```
FROM Order o, Product p
FROM Order o1, Order o2
```

To use the field value of another bean, you can use the IN keyword. Say you want access to all the products nominated in an order in another part of the query statement: This is a case in which you need to use IN:

```
FROM Order o, IN(o.products) p
```

In the statement in this form, you see that the first declaration is of the order bean, that the second declaration uses the order to nominate the products field, and that one of these values, to be known as the value p, is in the field. By implication, the variable p is of the abstract-schema type Product, because this can be derived from the deployment-descriptor information.

Another implied trait here is that you can use IN only when you are talking about a collection of items. Using an IN declaration does not make sense if you are referring to a single-value field. How can you find something that is "in" a single value?

The WHERE clause

So now you're getting picky and want the customer of only one particular order. You have to narrow down the very general query into a specific bean instance using the `WHERE` clause. In this clause, you provide conditional information that is evaluated to narrow down the return values.

After the `WHERE` keyword, you can use a variety of expressions. Each of these expressions will start with some field value of the bean, followed by an operator and finishing with a value for the operator to work with. Expressions can be combined, just like your normal Java expressions, if you use combinations of Boolean and arithmetic math.

Tip If you are familiar with SQL, you can use all the SQL operators for arithmetic and Boolean math, and string search.

In the most typical case, you will be comparing one field of a bean against a value, such as a name string or numerical value. Getting back to the customer request you saw earlier, say you already know the order ID: In that case, a complete query to access the customer that the order belongs to would be as follows:

```
SELECT o.customer FROM Order o
WHERE o.orderID = 56789
```

When using string values as the comparison, you need to quote the string you are comparing against using the single quote character ('). For example, to find all orders for books, you would do the following:

```
SELECT OBJECT(o) FROM Order o
WHERE o.product.category = 'book'
```

This example brings up an interesting point—in this case, the assumption is that the order bean has only a single product. If you go with the small change that we have been assuming in this chapter, that the order contains multiple products, then this example is an illegal statement. The reason for the illegality is that `o.products` can evaluate to multiple bean instances.

In order to create a legal statement in this situation, you need to make use of the `IN` keyword to set up individual references to each product instance in that list. Effectively, you are using the `FROM/IN` combination to iterate through all the products contained in an order instance, and then using `WHERE` to refine the search to a specific comparison. Your EJB QL statement will look like this:

```
SELECT OBJECT(o) FROM Order o, IN(o.products) p
WHERE p.category = 'book'
```

You can add more complexity to the query by adding Boolean logic elements. For example, if you want to find all books with the word "Java" in the title, you combine the two comparisons using the AND keyword, like this:

```
SELECT OBJECT(o) FROM Order o, IN(o.products) p
WHERE p.category = 'book' AND p.name LIKE '%Java%'
```

EJB QL statements are supposed to represent method calls, right? So where in the above examples are any relations to the parameters of the methods? Ah, one more thing to cover!

In EJB QL terminology, the parameter of a method is known as an *input parameter* for the statement. An input parameter is represented by a question mark (?) followed by a number that indicates the parameter position. The position comes from the method declaration the statement is associated with. Parameter positions always start at 1. Say you have the following method declaration:

```
public Collection ejbFindByName(String category,
                                String name)
```

Given this declaration, the category parameter would be defined as ?1, and the name parameter as ?2.

```
SELECT OBJECT(o) FROM Order o, IN(o.products) p
WHERE p.category = ?1 AND p.name LIKE ?2
```

Using EJB QL statements

Once you are happy with the various statements that you want to use, you need to associate each of these statements with the method that will use it. Yet again, this job falls to the deployment descriptor.

Associating an EJB QL statement with a method begins with specifying the query element. You specify the query element as the very last child of the entity element—after the CMP fields, primary key, and any environment information:

```
<entity>
  ...
  <cmp-field> .... </cmp-field>
  <primkey-field>orderID</primkey-field>
  ...
  <query> ??? </query>
</entity>
```

The query element contains a fair bit of information—aimed primarily at correctly identifying the method with which you are associating the statement. The element can be broken down into two main parts and one optional part.

Apart from the EJB QL text of the query, you need to define the method that should use the query statement. Because the descriptor is XML, describing a method can be quite tedious and verbose. Each method is described by a name and set of arguments in the deployment descriptor. As you are aware, methods can be overloaded, so a name alone is not sufficient — some of the time. If you don't have an overloaded method name that you are lining up with a query, then you can take some shortcuts.

Method declarations are handled by the `query-method` element. The first child element is the name of the method, enclosed in the `method-name` element. After the method name come the parameters (if any) collected together in the `method-params` element.

```
<query>
  <query-method>ejbFindByCategory</query-method>
  <method-params> ??? </method-params>
</query>
```

The method name provided must be the name in the bean-implementation class, not the home interface. In other words, every name you use here should start with `ejbFind` or `ejbSelect`.

In this example, only one method in the product home interface has the name `findByCategory`. That means you can leave the `method-params` element empty. You can't remove it entirely, because it is required, but an empty declaration is allowed.

A single method parameter is declared using the single `method-param` element (note the lack of an *s*). The parameter declares the datatype (class or primitive) rather than the name. So if your method takes a string, then you would use the following declaration:

```
<method-param>java.lang.String</method-param>
```

The full declaration is as follows:

```
<method-params>
  <method-param>java.lang.String</method-param>
</method-params>
```

For more than one parameter, you must declare the types in the order in which they are declared in the Java class. Examining the `LocalProductHome` local home interface, you can see that the `findByCategory` method takes two strings as the parameters. The deployment descriptor representation of the method is as follows:

```
<query>
  <query-method>ejbFindByCategory</query-method>
  <method-params>
    <method-param>java.lang.String</method-param>
    <method-param>java.lang.String</method-param>
  </method-params>
</query>
```

Now you need to tidy up by adding the EJB QL statement using the `ejb-ql` element. This final element is declared after the `method-params` element. To include the EJB QL statement, just wrap it in the opening and closing tag like this:

```
<ejb-ql>SELECT ENTITY(p) FROM Product p
        WHERE p.category = ?1 AND p.name LIKE %?2% </ejb-ql>
```

If you have a statement that uses the greater-than or less-than characters (< or >), you cannot use these characters directly. Remember that the text here is XML, which means these are reserved characters that must be encoded using `>` and `<` in accordance with the rules of XML.

You have now completed all the work that is needed to describe queries for a container-managed entity bean. There are many small, detailed areas that are left to be explored — various command types, use of the home methods and combining beans together into an application. We'll leave these up to you to become acquainted with as you grow in your confidence when using EJBs.

Managing Bean-Security Issues

In the enterprise setting, security is an absolutely essential requirement of the application. Security extends far beyond just sticking a firewall in front of your Web server and hoping for the best. Security *must be considered* in every part of the system. Think of all the great credit-card cracks on the Web — the server was set up right, but a failure to check the input validity, or open database access to all comers, allowed people to walk right through the back door without even looking at the front door.

Dealing with security issues comes down to first, knowing who is using your system, and second, making sure that the user can only access what his or her status allows. If you don't know who the user is, then the second part is very difficult to do.

If you don't provide any security information in the deployment descriptor, the EJB vendor will assume that there is none and give everyone complete access to your code.

Identifying the user

The first step in providing security on any site is knowing exactly who is using your system. While the anything-goes approach may be appropriate for your prototype application, allowing the warehouse staff access to the customers' credit-card numbers is really not a good idea (not to mention an extremely embarrassing situation for your CEO to deal with).

Even when you are building a public system, such as a Web site, for which you don't want to make every user provide a login, an implied user still exists. That "user" still needs to access files (static Web pages) and maybe parts of the database (for example, to search for products), but some level of access is granted or denied even here. Obviously, you don't want to provide the anonymous user with access to all your customers and all their details, so even "no user" is considered a user in these systems.

Whose job is it anyway?

Another way of looking at security issues is to break down the system into the collection of pieces that require a certain level of access to other pieces. The Web server needs access to the servlet engine, and the servlet needs access to the EJB server. However, the Web server does not need direct access to the EJB server. It is in this way that you start to break down the system in order to provide good security.

The task of analyzing security requirements does not fall solely on you, the programmer. Providing a secure system requires involving people responsible for the network, the servers, and the administrator of the EJB servers. Under the EJB model, the majority of the security implementation is not up to you. Apart from the ever-present deployment descriptor (which is still essential in the overall security system), the job falls to the people running the servers.

Look ma, no code

Although some programmatic capabilities exist to help you handle security, these should not be your primary means of making the system secure. The only way to ensure full security is to cooperate to build a self-supporting mesh between the EJB system (as well as the greater J2EE environment) and the underlying server operating system(s).

Since security is not part of the coding process, it is the responsibility of the deployment descriptor. The idea here is that you, as the programmer, do not need to worry about exactly who is allowed access to various capabilities. Over time, you can expect access requirements to change, and you really don't want to recompile and re-deploy beans every time a slight variation occurs.

Another reason for separating the two parts involves third-party code. Say you purchase a collection of off-the-shelf beans: The provider has no understanding of your specific security requirements. Most likely you don't even have the source code, so the only way you can control access is through the use of configuration items — the deployment descriptor.

Terms and conditions

Once again, a collection of new terminologies is associated with EJBs. Many of these terms are imported from the generalized Java security model, although a few are new.

You can't control bean-security issues through the policy files used by J2SE. These policy files only control functions of a particular API, such as file I/O or threading, and they won't work because they must be available across all clients and servers. In addition, the environment (for example Java code embedded in an Oracle database as a trigger) may not support them.

The assignment of a set of access restrictions is known as a *role* in EJB terminology. A role acts as a grouping mechanism. You don't use it to predefine access capabilities or users who wish to attempt certain tasks; rather it acts as a means of collecting like-minded methods together after you have written them.

A particular user of the system is known as a *security principal*. When your servlet code needs to access an EJB, it has an identity, which is the principal's name. The name represents the user attempting to perform the task. The role information forms the other half of the request. At some point during the deployment, the person responsible for deploying beans will pull up the administration tool and provide a mapping of principal names to roles. Consider it a many-to-many mapping where a single principal may be allocated a number of roles, but a role may be assigned to many principal names. How the roles and principles are arranged depends on your application requirements.

Determining who is calling

As we alluded to earlier, some programmatic ways of accessing security information exist. The two methods provided enable you to determine the identity of the principal calling you and to check the role of the caller.

The J2EE specification explicitly warns against using these methods as means of controlling secure access to your code. They should be treated as purely informational, because if your method has been called, the assumption is that the EJB container has already performed all the necessary checks.

Finding out the identity of the principal calling your code is the job of the `getSecurityPrincipal()` method of the `EJBContext`. The return value of the method is `java.security.Principal`, which represents the underlying authorization mechanism (for example, Keberos or NIS). You can then obtain the name of the user as a `String` with the `getName()` method.

So why would you want to know the name of the user calling you? Let's say you are running an application that is a data-entry terminal, such as a terminal in the dispatch warehouse. The user logs on and then starts processing orders. The terminal brings up the next order pending. Off goes the storeman to acquire the items, parcel them up, and call the courier. Before the storeman can move on to the next item, the order is marked as being processed, and the next order comes up. As far as he or she is concerned, "Order completed" is the only button on the screen. Down the back, on the EJB server, the database requires a record of who actually processed the order. Instead of having to ask the storeman to enter his or her name each time, you can use the `getSecurityPrincipal()` method to access the login name and assign it to your database record. For example, you might find the following business method in the Order bean (ignoring exception handling):

```
public void orderCompleted() {
  Principal operator = ejbContext.getSecurityPrincipal();
  String op_name = operator.getName();

  InitialContext ctx = new InitialContext();

  Object home_ref = ctx.lookup("ejb/EmployeeLocalHome");
  EmployeeLocalHome home = (EmployeeLocalHome)home_ref;

  Employee emp = home.findByPrimaryKey(op_name);

  // now assign the reference to the employee bean here as we
  // are assuming a CMR field
  setEmployee(emp);
}
```

Notice that the code uses the operator's login name as the primary key for the employee bean. The assumption here is that the login name is always unique and therefore valid for a unique identifier for a bean. To access the real details of the employee, you can then look up the bean or one of the other server-administration tools. Using the operator details, the code then looks up the representative bean and assigns it to this order-bean instance so that the relationship is established and then maintained by the EJB container using container-managed relationship capabilities.

On the odd occasion when the deployment-descriptor handling of role-based information is not sufficient, you can enforce tighter rules using the `isCallerInRole()` method from `EJBContext`. For example, the bean might impose a maximum number of simultaneous requests for a particular role, backed by information in a database.

The `isCallerInRole()` method takes a single argument of a `String`, representing the name of the desired role to check against. In return you are given a Boolean value indicating whether the caller is using the nominated role. For example, if you want to check that the user about to process an order as complete is actually the storeman, then the following code becomes useful:

```
public void orderCompleted() {
  if(!ejbContext.isCallerInRole("stores"))
    throw new SecurityException("The caller is not " +
                     "authorized to complete an order");
  ...
}
```

It is important to understand that the role information that is checked is what the caller is acting as, not what your bean code is currently acting as. These may well be two separate things — you could allow four roles to access your code, but be described by a completely different role.

Profiling the user for access capabilities

Now we get into the specifics of applying role and security information to individual bean instances. All the information in this section is described in the deployment descriptor. As you will see, it is quite verbose as a process and will usually be easier to set up in the tool provided by your EJB server vendor. However, read on, as you will need to understand the terminology used in all those wizard dialog boxes.

Security information is defined in so many places in a deployment descriptor that deciding where to start can be a daunting exercise. In order to make the following sections more understandable, we're going to introduce the ideas in the order in which you might consider security issues from the deployment perspective. Unfortunately, that means that we'll be jumping all over the deployment descriptor to insert the new information provided in each step. We hope not to confuse you too much!

The Role Chain of Execution

In all but the simplest systems, your particular bean may be at the end of a long series of method calls. In order to reach your code, a request may have passed through a servlet or two, a JMS message queue, and then a few layers of beans. By the time you receive a request, how do you know whether the original caller was actually allowed to access the information?

Roles have the interesting ability to form a chain. The original caller sets the role, and then all subsequent method calls maintain that role. So even if you are buried under 10 levels of method calls and beans, you will still maintain the original caller's role. In this way, you can determine whether the original caller was a servlet, message queue, or any other type of bean.

For example, if you have a servlet and you set its role to be `customer_servlet`, then your order bean's `ejbCreate()` method will return `isCallerInRole("customer_servlet")` as `true`. However, if the order was placed as a telephone operator using a kiosk application, the method will return `false`. Even if you are called by other beans between the servlet and your code, the role is not changed by any of the intermediaries.

The only time you have a chance of influencing the role used is when your bean is directly accessed by application code. For example, a kiosk application accesses your bean directly. The application does not have a role associated with it, so the EJB container will take the role assigned to your bean as the originating role.

Declaring role information

The first task in building security information is deciding on the various roles that will be assumed by the beans and the bean clients. Ideally you will decide in a very early stage of the project's analysis and design, not right at the end when you have finished testing.

You start the process by declaring all the roles to be used by the beans. Role declarations take place in the `security-role` element, which is in turn held in the hitherto-unseen `assembly-descriptor` element.

You declare `assembly-descriptor` as the last child of the `ejb-jar` element—after the `enterprise-beans` element in which you have so far been placing all your information:

```
<ejb-jar>
  <enterprise-beans>
    ...
  </enterprise-beans>
  <assembly-descriptor>
    ...
  </assembly-descriptor>
</ejb-jar>
```

The `assembly-descriptor` element starts by listing all the security-role elements. Each declaration of the `security-role` covers exactly one role in the bean. So, if you need 20 roles, 20 declarations of `security-role` will exist.

The security roles defined by the `security-role` elements are scoped to the ejb-jar file level, and apply to all the enterprise beans in the ejb-jar file. If you have two JAR files that nominate the same roles, they are treated as independent entities as far as the container is concerned.

Inside the `security-role` element is only one required tag—the name of the role being declared:

```
<assembly-descriptor>
  <security-role>
    <role-name>customer_servlet</role-name>
  </security-role>
</assembly-descriptor>
```

You can add a description string with each role's name, just as you can with most other items in the deployment descriptor.

Declaring role names is just the first step. It is a declaration of who might want to use the system for the deployment tool to look at in order to start putting things in order. The next step is to assign a role to an individual bean to be used when no other information is known about the caller (that is, when no role information is present yet).

Forcing a bean to run as a particular user

To define information about the default security information for a bean, we now jump back to the deployment-descriptor declarations dealing with a specific bean instance (such as `entity` or `session` elements).

When declaring user information for a bean, you have two options: provide a specific role name to run under every time, or always use whatever the caller provides. The choice here is binary—you can't provide both paths. In either case, you start by specifying the `security-identity` element. The new element is placed between the `primkey-field` and `query` elements if you are using an entity bean, and after the `transaction-type` element if you are using a session bean, as shown in the following example:

```
<enterprise-beans>
  <entity>
    ...
    <primkey-field>OrderID</primkey-field>
    <security-identity>
      ???
    </security-identity>
    <query>
      ...
    </query>
  </entity>
  <session>
    ...
    <transaction-type>Container</transaction-type>
    <security-identity>
      ???
    </security-identity>
  </session>
</enterprise-beans>
```

`security-identity` has one of two children elements: `run-as` or `use-caller-identity`. As the names suggest, these control either a role name to be used by the bean, or a direction in which to use the caller's identity information.

For the former case, you provide a `role-name` element as the child that declares the role that should be used. The name here must be one of the names that you have just declared in the `security-role` section:

```
<security-identity>
  <run-as>
    <role-name>servlet_customer</role-name>
  </run-as>
</security-identity>
```

In order to use caller identity, you need only the empty element declaration. The rest is assumed from the runtime context.

```
<security-identity>
  <use-caller-identity/>
</security-identity>
```

Message-driven beans do not permit the use of use-caller-identity semantics. The deployment tool should flag an error if you declare them.

Nominating security information

Earlier you saw the use of the programmatic methods for checking the caller-role information. When you do this, you need to let the container know that you are going to be performing these checks, and exactly what you will be checking for. The effect of these checks is to imply the roles the bean code wants to check for as part of the deployment process.

References to roles declared in code are contained in the `security-role-ref` element. This element is placed just before the `security-identity` element if you declared it earlier. In the role declaration, you place the name of one role that you have declared in code and an optional element that provides a link between the code declaration and one of your defined declarations in the `security-role` section. If more than one role is being checked in the bean's code, you just declare more `security-role-ref` elements.

```
<entity>
  ...
  <primkey-field>OrderID</primkey-field>
  <security-role-ref>
    <role-name>stores</rolename>
  </security-role-ref>
  <security-identity>
    ...
  </security-identity>

  ...

  </entity>
```

Security-role nomination is not available to message-driven beans.

You use link information when you wish to map the code's role declarations to your own preferred declarations. For example, a third-party bean declares a name that conflicts with one of your names, so you want to map it to something else or to a broader category:

```
<security-role-ref>
  <role-name>stores</role-name>
  <role-link>warehouse_staff</role-link>
</security-role-ref>
```

Whatever you declare in the role-link element must have been previously declared in the `security-role` section.

Getting picky with per-method security

Once you have defined the larger perspective of security, you can become much more detailed in your requirements. Should you require it, you can become as detailed as individual method calls when singling out who can access what functionality.

In each of the following pieces of functionality, the method is always described by a single structure: the `method` element. Different behaviors are then wrapped around this structure. The purpose of the `method` element is to describe, in as much detail as necessary, the method signature. So you start with the bean affected:

```
<method>
  <ejb-name>Product</ejb-name>
</method>
```

Next you need to declare which methods in the bean are affected. If you want to use all methods (the most typical case), you can use the special wildcard character, the asterisk (*), in the `method-name` element, as follows:

```
<method>
  <ejb-name>Product</ejb-name>
  <method-name>*</method-name>
</method>
```

If you wish to have different permissions on each method, then you provide the name of the method in the `method-name` element. Because we are dealing with security information, this method name is always the name used in the home or remote/local interface, not the bean implementation: That is you should never see a method starting with `ejb`. For example, here we declare a finder method:

```
<method>
  <ejb-name>Product</ejb-name>
  <method-name>findByCategory</method-name>
</method>
```

Mapping the Bean's View to the Real World

From your perspective, the security net starts with the deployment descriptor. In the deployment descriptor, you describe the access requirements of the various pieces of code in terms of roles. In order for these definitions to take effect, they must mean something in the greater scope of the entire system.

Roles don't have any meaning in the real world of the server's operating system. They are not required to, either. Roles are only a construct of the EJB server software. If the roles do have any relationship to user details on the underlying system, it is purely due to the server administrator's creating matching information.

However, roles are much smaller in scope than a standard user login, so it would be unusual to see a direct mapping of EJB roles to system users. A role may only encompass a single method call out of thousands of beans. If your system consisted of hundreds or thousands of beans, the management issues would become a nightmare as you tried to keep the EJB parts synchronized with the servers.

When you have only one of this method in the class, you can stop here. However, when you have overloaded methods, such as `create()`, you might want to single a specific method out for separate treatment by providing the method arguments. To specify a particular method based on the argument list, use the `method-params` element, which looks and works identically to the examples you saw earlier with EJB QL:

```
<method>
  <ejb-name>Product</ejb-name>
  <method-name>findByCategory</method-name>
  <method-params>
    <method-param>java.lang.String</method-param>
    <method-param>java.lang.String</method-param>
  </method-params>
</method>
```

Finally, you have one more way to provide restrictions — some classes have both remote and local interfaces declared for accessing a particular bean. The most common restriction here is to prevent the caller from accessing some methods that are available in both the remote and local interfaces. For example, a setter method may be available to all local users, but only to remote users of a specific role. Declaring whether a method belongs to a remote or local interface declaration is the job of the `method-intf` element. This element is inserted between the `ejb-name` and `method-name` elements. There are four valid values: `Local`, `Remote`, `Home`, and `LocalHome`.

```
<method>
  <ejb-name>Product</ejb-name>
  <method-intf>Remote</method-intf>
  <method-name>findByCategory</method-name>
```

Now that you know how to declare methods, it's time to use them in something. You can declare methods to be completely off-limits, or you can create a free-for-all.

At the tightest end of the spectrum is the list of methods that cannot be called at all. These methods are listed in the `exclude-list` element. `exclude-list` is placed as the last element of the `assembly-descriptor` (before the `exclude-list` are a couple of elements that we'll be covering shortly). Inside `exclude-list` you list all the methods that should not be accessed:

```
<assembly-descriptor>
  ...
  <exclude-list>
    <method>
      <ejb-name>Product</ejb-name>
      <method-name>setProductID</method-name>
    </method>
    <method>
      <ejb-name>UnusedBean</ejb-name>
      <method-name>*</method-name>
    </method>
  </exclude-list>
</assembly-descriptor>
```

Lightening up the heavy-handed restrictions is the job of the `method-permission` element, which can be found just ahead of the `exclude-list`. In this element, you place the list of methods and the roles that are allowed access.

Inside the `method-permission` element, you find a collection of individual methods and the role(s) that are allowed to access them. Each permission declaration starts with the list of acceptable role names, followed by the `method` declarations of all the methods affected by these permissions:

```
<assembly-descriptor>
  <method-permission>
    <role-name>stores</role-name>
      <role-name>call-center</role-name>
    <method>
      <ejb-name>Product</ejb-name>
      <method-name>getProductID</method-name>
    </method>
    <method>
      <ejb-name>Order</ejb-name>
      <method-name>*</method-name>
    </method>
  </method-permission>
  <method-permission>
    <role-name>customer-servlet</role-name>
    <method>
      <ejb-name>Customer</ejb-name>
```

```
      <method-name>*</method-name>
    </method>
  </method-permission>
  <exclude-list>
    ...
  </exclude-list>
</assembly-descriptor>
```

The EJB 2.0 specification does not mention the order of priorities when declarations conflict with each other. It is best to double-check everything you provide to make sure no conflicts exist.

If you would like to go all the way and let any user call a method, you can substitute the empty element unchecked for the list of `role-name` in the `method-permission`. The result is that the server always lets requests to these methods go through:

```
<method-permission>
  <unchecked/>
  <method>
    <ejb-name>Customer</ejb-name>
    <method-name>*</method-name>
  </method>
</method-permission>
```

If you don't declare a method in any of the permissions, then the bean container must assume that you want unchecked semantics.

This completes the introduction to setting up security for EJB systems. As we mentioned before, security is more than just a few lines in a configuration file. In order for it to be effective, you need to involve everyone in the requirements and implementation.

Dealing with Bean-Configuration Issues

The last topic that we wish to cover with regard to beans is dealing with configuration issues. You've been inundated with one aspect of configuration already: specifying deployment information with the deployment descriptor. What we have not covered so far are all the small details, like environmental properties — items that you have traditionally used Java properties files and the `java.util.Properties` class to deal with.

The J2SE 1.4 API introduces a standardized preferences API for the first time in the `java.util.prefs` package. J2EE 1.3 requires only J2SE 1.3, and so you may or may not have access to these capabilities.

Under the EJB specification, providing property information to configure your beans is just as important as before. Although beans like stateless session beans are not supposed to be individually configured, plenty of areas still exist in which you can provide configuration information for business logic. These include areas in which you might need a constant defined, such as maximum and minimum values of a range check.

Summary of existing configuration techniques

Before venturing into the approved method of providing configuration information to beans, let's quickly go back over the previously existing options and where they fail in the EJB worldview.

Properties files

Until the release of J2SE 1.4, no standard system for storing and loading user preferences existed. If a programmer wanted to create a portable application that was configurable, the only option, apart from creating a custom system, was to use text-properties files and use the `Properties` class to load and save the information.

J2EE requires a heavy restriction on the use of file I/O. The use of the `java.io.File` class is not permitted within a bean implementation. This leaves you rather handicapped because you have no real way of reading, and more importantly no way of saving again, a properties file. There is a potential alternative method to locate and open the file using `ClassLoader`'s `getSystemResourceAsStream()` method and storing the property file in the EJB-JAR file. This tactic is thwarted by the rule that bean implementations are not permitted to access the current class loader that the method call relies on.

JNDI driver registration

Throughout this book you have been seeing examples of how configuration and storage information is maintained. For example, JDBC drivers are registered by the system, and you access the current driver through JNDI. Each of these drivers is externally configured as part of the J2EE middleware-vendor's software.

Because no standard configuration mechanism exists for low-level drivers, this lack of a standard system does not make the idea of portable environment variables particularly appealing. Each time you move to a new system, you need to build a new set of configuration files. If you are providing a bean library for others to use, the requirement that each customer build his or her own set of configuration files can be a major headache.

Providing system-agnostic configuration properties

Providing property information falls to the pairing of JNDI and the deployment descriptor. Once again, the deployment descriptor holds the values to be used during runtime, while your bean-implementation code accesses values through JNDI.

Accessing properties in code

In your bean-implementation code, accessing environment properties starts with creating a JNDI `InitialContext` instance. Accessing property values starts with you performing a `lookup()` operation on the name of the variable (just like you've done before with JDBC data sources and bean home interfaces). This obviously requires you to know what those property names are beforehand. The root name to use in the JNDI context is the same as that of all other J2EE items: `java:comp/env`. Below this, you provide the name of the property that you are after. For example:

```
InitialContext i_ctx = new InitialContext();
Context env = i_ctx.createSubcontext("java:comp/env");

Object prop = env.lookup("MyProperty");
```

The J2EE specification makes no recommendations for naming conventions for properties, unlike for JDBC drivers or EJBs. Properties are only visible to their particular beans, so there is no need to come up with really long, convoluted names.

Property values are restricted to using only the primitive types available in Java. Effectively, that means strings, integers, and floating-point values. When you access a value through the `lookup()` method you will then need to cast the return value to the appropriate class type, as follows:

```
Integer max_int = (Integer)env.lookup("MaxRange");
Integer min_int = (Integer)env.lookup("MinRange");

int max_value = max_int.intValue();
int min_value = min_int.intValue();
```

That's all there is to using properties in your bean code. The next step is to declare the property values.

Declaring property values

Completing the task of using property values requires us to wander back to our old friend, the deployment descriptor. Properties are defined with the bean in which they are used, rather than as a global setting. Therefore you can have properties with the same name in different beans that use different datatypes and values! We really don't recommend it, though, and always suggest using clear, meaningful names for each property.

Property values are contained in the env-entry element, which you can find just after the primkey-field of entity beans, and in the transaction-type element of session and message-driven beans. You must declare one env-entry per property. Within env-entry, you then provide a name, the Java class type that it must use, and the value, in that order. For example, to declare the MaxRange value we used in the preceding code snippet, you need to declare the following in the deployment descriptor:

```
<env-entry>
  <env-entry-name>MaxRange</env-entry-name>
  <env-entry-type>java.lang.Integer</env-entry-type>
  <env-entry-value>20</env-entry-value>
</env-entry>
```

The name declaration will have the java:comp/env prefix added to it by the container at deployment time.

This is fairly straightforward as far as the deployment descriptor is concerned. The only mildly interesting part is that the entry type must be the fully qualified Java class type rather than just the class name.

If you need more than one property defined, then just use more env-entry elements. For example:

```
<entity>
  <ejb-name>MyBean</ejb-name>
  ...
  <env-entry>
    <env-entry-name>MaxRange</env-entry-name>
    <env-entry-type>java.lang.Integer</env-entry-type>
    <env-entry-value>20</env-entry-value>
  </env-entry>
  <env-entry>
    <env-entry-name>MinRange</env-entry-name>
    <env-entry-type>java.lang.Integer</env-entry-type>
    <env-entry-value>-5</env-entry-value>
  </env-entry>
  ...
<entity>
```

Who Is Looking After the Code?

Code, code, code. When you look back over the past two chapters, all we ever talk about is how you can write this bit of wonderful code that does all these terrific things. Barely do we stop to consider that there are people also involved in the system. If you read between the lines, you will have noticed passing references to other people – system administrators, architects, users and more. EJBs fulfill one very small part of a very big system – it is a little, tiny, bit of code in amongst a billion dollar company that employs thousands of people. Surely at least one or two of these might be a bit interested in what you are doing with the company's money and very expensive hardware.

Before you even start looking at code, and well after you have finished, there are many other people involved in the process of giving your fellow workers a useful piece of software. The EJB specification defines a number of roles that make up the process of getting the code from the drawing board to the user. As you could imagine, not all these roles involve code cutting.

The roles outlined in this section only consider the EJB worldview. Where you have middleware, you will need a client application, and a datastore. The roles described here do not consider these other roles of the full application development.

EJB development roles

The EJB specification defines six roles involved in the development of an EJB. All of these roles have some relationship to the process of developing code. Depending on the size of your organization and the project, a person may fulfill more than one of these roles. However, as you can see, these roles are distinct phases in the development process.

The bean provider

That's you — the code cutter. You are required to code the complete bean: home and remote interfaces, local interfaces if needed, and the implementation class. If you must use other code libraries inside your implementation, then you may need to code those as well. After coding, *and testing*, your bean you are also responsible for creating the EJB-JAR file. That is, you must put together the deployment descriptor and create the JAR file.

At this stage, the assumption is that you are coding one bean at a time. That bean represents a specific piece of information, and you are the expert in that area. Your role does not need to consider higher-level issues such as transaction management or how the beans may be deployed on the server. If you have container-managed beans, then you must also provide the EJB QL statements.

The application assembler

After a collection of beans have been written, they need to be assembled into the EAR file so that it may be deployed to the server. This function is performed by the application assembler. They take your collection of EJB-JAR files and add more information to the deployment descriptor. The main function of this role is to consider architectural issues such as how transactions are to be managed.

An application will consist of more than just the beans. A further task for this role is to collect the work of the client-side developers, such as servlets, JSPs and any standalone applications, and include those in the EAR files.

The deployer

With all the code packaged, ready to go, the next role is to deploy that EAR file onto the middleware server. The deployer role must resolve any external dependencies during this process. That means if your bean requires JDBC data sources or environment entries to be set, the deployer must provide all of that information. Put simply, this person customizes the beans to the particular environment that they will exist in.

The person fulfilling the role of the deployer is not likely to be a code-cutter. Typically he or she is an expert in that particular environment — for example he or she will have an Oracle or Websphere certification.

The server provider

Unless you are working on an Open Source project like JBoss, you are unlikely to be fulfilling this role within your company. The role of the server provider is taken by the various product vendors, such as Oracle, IBM or BEA. They are required to provide you with server software, which may involve many different products. For example, you might have DB2 database from IBM, BEA's Weblogic for the middleware and Apache/Tomcat for the web tier. Each of these is a server provider role.

The container provider

In most cases, the container provider role is the same thing as the server provider role. While the server provider role can be quite general, this role focuses purely on the job of taking bean code and providing tools to make those beans available to all takers.

The container provider is required to provide deployment tools as well as the software that manages the runtime instances of the beans. If there are clusters of servers, then the container provider must also provide the management facilities for the cluster.

The system administrator

Finally the management of the whole system — servers, networking, communications and software falls to the system administrator role. This role is just your standard sysadmin that has to deal with installing software, fixing broken printers and keeping the users happy.

Non-development roles

In addition to the development roles, there are also roles that do not involve the development. These roles are not defined in the EJB specification, but you are going to come across these people once you start developing real-world code.

The Business Analyst

Before you even start coding, someone has to decide what needs to be coded. Deciding what needs to be coded must start with a person talking to other people, such as the users. In this role, the business analyst is responsible for doing that thing that all techies detest — talking to the end user. Believe it or not, that's a really useful thing to do, because with happy users, you have happy managers. With happy managers, you have a much better life. The key to happy users is to provide them with software that they want, not what you feel like hacking up in your spare time between games of Q3 or Everquest.

Business analysts are the people that do a lot of the basic footwork of getting around to all of the people that have a vested interest in the project and trying to make sense out of all their wishes. They filter the various wishes and build a list of requirements and the tasks the users will be performing. Sometimes they may get involved in specifying the user interface layout. It will be your job to take the information they present and turn it into a usable application.

The end-user

The most important role of all. Without the end user, you would not have an application. Your job is to make them happy (well, most of the time anyway).

In terms of your application development process, the end user should be involved all along. Obviously, they are involved right at the start and finish of the project. In between, you should also be seeking to bring them into the process. Sometimes you will find that a particular process cannot be implemented, so you'll have to work out an alternate approach. Even if things are going well, the user should be seeing your progress and helping you to do some of the testing. For example, they might (will!) decide that a particular process might be better done in a different manner. Better to do that change early in the development rather than right at the end or even end up with unhappy users after you have finished.

The management

Everybody loves to hate them. Of course, the management role is just as important as any other in the software development. Not only do they make sure you get paid, but they are the ones that have to sponsor your project work. Management roles extend all the way from your team leader up to the CEO. At each stage, there are a different set of responsibilities, but each makes sure that development proceeds, or stops. They will also feed requirements into your development — deadlines, testing requirements, hardware and more.

Summary

Writing and deploying Enterprise JavaBeans is a huge part of any enterprise-level application. As they have gained more acceptance, the specification has grown to include new uses for them. This chapter has covered most of the new functionality included in the EJB 2.0 specification. As you can see, it is a big chapter already, without covering the now-obsolete EJB 1.1 spec!

We covered many detailed topics in this chapter. The most important of these were:

- Advanced EJB topics such as method granularity
- The new EJB local interfaces
- Writing the new message-driven beans
- Container-managed persistence of entity beans, as well as the new EJB QL
- Providing a secure EJB environment
- Providing configurable properties to all bean types

✦ ✦ ✦

CHAPTER 18

Introducing CORBA

✦ ✦ ✦ ✦

In This Chapter

Understanding CORBA

Overview of Object Management Architecture (OMA)

Learning the structure and function of Object Request Broker (ORB)

Understanding Interface Definition Language (IDL)

Writing a simple CORBA application

✦ ✦ ✦ ✦

The success of a software product depends on the following factors: code reusability, code efficiency, and code maintainability. Of these criteria, reusability is probably the most important, as it drives the other two — that is, code that is written with reusability in mind tends to be both efficient and easily maintainable. So, the object-oriented techniques plays an important role in mainstream software design.

The Need for CORBA

The need for design of "objects" that could be used across networks by multiple users resulted in the development of CORBA specifications. These specifications, developed by the Object Management Group (OMG), were designed exclusively for a distributed-applications framework. Developers using these specifications can create applications that can be used across multiple configurations and that are both fault-tolerant and sophisticated in their core functionality.

Business units today, even within the same organization, have the flexibility to use diverse IT software, hardware, and networking systems. Business units therefore look for applications that are supported by these diverse systems. CORBA enables developers to develop applications that work seamlessly across these systems.

Consider the following example: A needs to send a package to B. A and B are in different locations. Assume that A sends his package through the postal service to B. Earlier, the only information A could receive about the status of the package was an acknowledgement of receipt at the other end by B. Now, however, thanks to the improvements brought about by the Internet, A can not only know whether the package has reached its destination, but can also track it throughout its transit, enabling A (the sender), B (the recipient), and the postal service to know exactly where the package is at any given time. The postal service enables this by providing access to a tracking application that both sender and receiver can use to get the status of the package.

This is a simple example that illustrates how diverse systems across multiple organizations are required to execute the same code object. CORBA is a set of tools that can be used to develop objects whose central feature is global usability.

What Is CORBA?

CORBA is the acronym for *Common Object Request Broker Architecture*. It is an open, vendor-independent specification developed by the Object Management Group (OMG) to support applications designed to work across networks (both within the same organization and across multiple organizations). This model, because it enables the interoperability of distributed objects across diverse architectures and platforms, allows clients to access and execute various objects across networks with ease. Basic architectural features provided by the CORBA architecture are as follows:

- *Location transparency*—This allows client applications to access objects across the network without knowing where they reside. As far as the client is concerned (at least in theory), the object being called could be in the same server as the client, in another server on the same LAN, or ten thousand miles away, accessed through a WAN.
- *Support for distributed networks*—CORBA-compliant products are all platform-independent, which allows applications to work on a wide range of systems. A CORBA object can be invoked, by any client that uses the proper interface definition, regardless of the hardware and software platforms running on the client system.
- *Seclusion of interface and implementation*—Because clients "talk to" (that is, invoke) objects only through appropriately defined interfaces, implementation changes in the server do not directly affect the client. In fact, clients are unaware of implementation changes in the object, as they interact only through interface definitions, which are constant for an object invoked from a client. This feature of CORBA enables you to modify and upgrade objects without having to also change how clients invoke the object—or, indeed, anything else about the clients.

The Object Management Architecture

Understanding the Object Management Architecture (OMA) is critical to developing a proper understanding of how CORBA works. The OMA acts as the base for the CORBA architecture. It is a mature model, enabling location-transparency of objects across heterogeneous networks. The OMG originally designed the OMA specifications, like CORBA, in order to standardize applications developed for CORBA.

Figure 18-1 illustrates the structure of the OMA. Its relevance to CORBA is that it uses an ORB to mediate communication between services provided through objects and the client applications that invoke them.

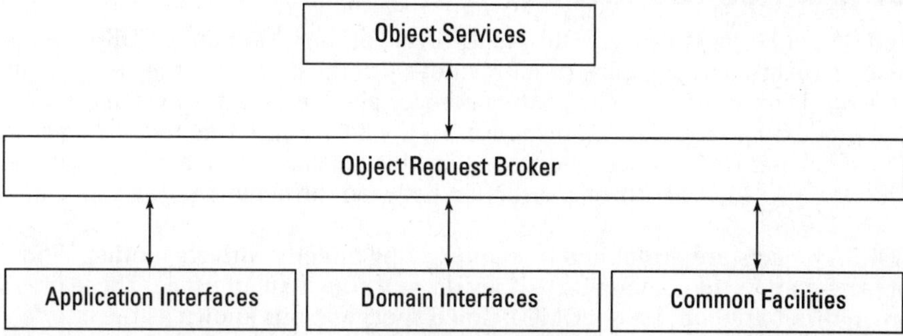

Figure 18-1: Object Management Architecture (OMA)

Object services

Several object services are made available to applications that invoke them, and are standardized under the Common Object Service Specification (COSS). Utilities that provide functionality for managing and maintaining objects is one example of the types of services in this category. This service is an object service that performs lifecycle management of objects — one that starts from the creation of the object and tracks it throughout its lifecycle, tracking changes made to it and to referring applications as well. You can find a list of CORBA services in the later sections (CORBA Services).

Common facilities

These are generic application interfaces that assist user applications. This category includes function such as standardization of time functions. As they are generic, these interfaces are typically applicable to and usable by most application domains.

Domain interfaces

These are also generic application interfaces; they differ in their functionalities, which tend to be specific to a particular function or industry, such as accounting, payroll, finance, telecommunications, transportation, and so on.

Application interfaces

These are interfaces to non-standardized (or custom) applications, created to solve a specific problem. These interfaces are used by clients to access applications.

Object Request Broker

The Object Request Broker (ORB) is the heart of the OMA and of CORBA. It allows objects to interact with each other regardless of the platforms they reside and execute on. The ORB is the coordinating core for all objects in the system, receiving and processing requests and responses from objects and from requesting clients across the network. A client requesting an object gains access to it through the ORB. The ORB provides a layer of abstraction between the client and the application.

CORBA objects are prohibited from interacting directly with each other. When two objects do have to communicate, they do so through an interface. These interfaces are in turn based on a set of OMG-defined specifications known as the Interface Definition Language (IDL). Applications use IDL to create common interfaces with which clients and objects can interact with other objects independent of the underlying programming languages and platforms they have been designed to run on. IDLs in turn are mapped to any programming language using an appropriate IDL compiler. As interfaces are designed to be language-independent, accessing the CORBA object is relatively simple. Multiple ORBs communicate by means of a messaging protocol known as Internet InterOperable Protocol (IIOP).

Structure and Action of ORB

Figure 18-2 shows the structure of the ORB. The various elements are as follows:

- *Client*—The application that requests the remote object.
- *IDL compiler*—The IDL compiler creates the language maps of IDL code, based on the programming language(s) used.
- *IDL stub*—The IDL interface created on the client by the IDL compiler. It ensures the *marshalling* of the appropriate parameters involved in the invocation of the remote object. Marshalling is the process by which the necessary

parameters for calling the remote object's method are inserted into the remote object and sent to the server for processing.

✦ *IDL skeleton*—The IDL interface created on the server by the IDL compiler. It ensures the *unmarshalling* of parameters involved in the invocation of the remote object. Unmarshalling is the process by which the skeleton extracts the parameters from the remote object for processing. It has the same functionality as the IDL stub, except that it resides on the server instead of the client.

✦ *Dynamic Invocation Interface (DII)*—The DII allows applications to call remote objects without the help of the client stub. In effect, this allows clients to call remote object methods whose types are unknown. DII also improves performance, as it allows client applications to execute other tasks until the request is served.

✦ *ORB interface*—The ORB interface has some local functions that object implementations and clients can use to talk to other CORBA services, such as the naming service and the lifecycle service.

✦ *Dynamic Skeleton Interface (DSI)*—The same as the DII, with the difference that it resides on the server.

✦ *ORB*—The architecture of the ORB is discussed in detail later on in this section.

✦ *Object implementation*—The layer in which the remote objects are implemented. Typically, the IDL skeleton or DSI layer communicates with this object implementation to access the real remote object.

✦ *Object adapter*—The object adapter helps the ORB locate the target object implementation in the server.

✦ *Interface repository*—This repository stores all the interface definitions defined by the IDL. The ORB uses it as a lookup directory for all interface definitions when the DII is used. It acts as a substitute for the client stub when there is a need to type-check objects.

✦ *Implementation repository*—This repository stores information about object implementations.

Every client that can invoke an object, and every server on which an object resides, has at least one ORB component. The chief purpose of ORB is to facilitate and manage requests between clients and the (remote) objects they invoke. Actual communication between clients and objects takes place through the IDL stub and the IDL skeleton; the ORB monitors and manages the process. These communications (mainly requests and responses) between clients and objects, and between objects that the ORB mediates, typically take the form of IIOP messages.

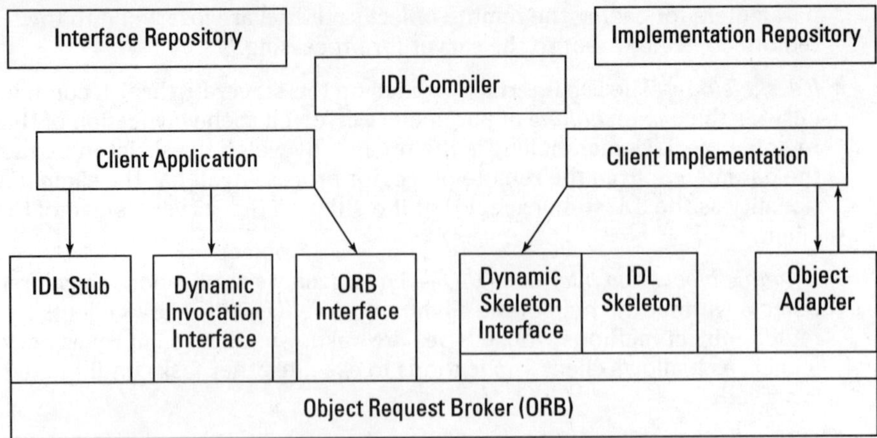

Figure 18-2: Structure of the Object Request Broker (ORB)

Upon initialization, the ORB performs the following series of steps for each object:

1. Initialize the ORB component.
2. Get the initial object reference for the Naming Services.
3. Convert the object reference to a string.
4. Connect the object reference to the server object and then disconnect.

Figure 18-3 illustrates how ORB achieves its purpose.

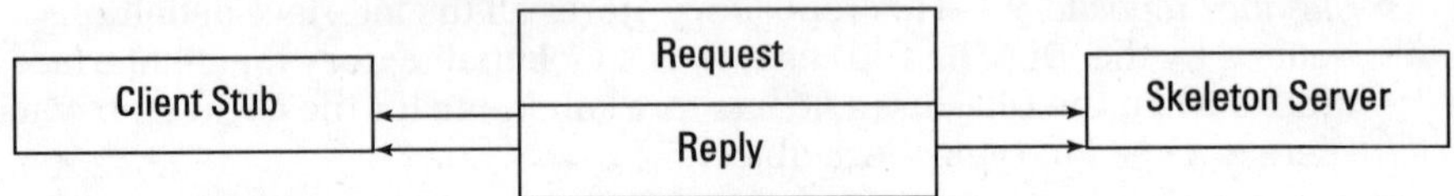

Figure 18-3: Interaction between server and client

The following are the steps a client typically goes through when it calls a (remote) CORBA object through ORB:

1. To call the remote object, the client first needs an object reference. Because the remote object can be accessed from within any ORB framework, it is also referred to as an Interoperable Object Reference. Once the client obtains the Object Reference, the IDL stub containing the necessary interface definitions creates and sends a CORBA defined request object containing the necessary parameters to the ORB. The process of inserting the parameters into the request object is called marshalling. As explained in the bulleted list at the beginning of this section, this process can also be done through the DII.

2. The ORB then sends an IIOP message through the network to locate the remote object needed.
3. The server application, upon "seeing" the request, creates an instance of the actual object and informs the ORB that it exists. It then waits for the request from the clients.
4. After getting the request from the client, the ORB finds the target object from the request object and passes control to the generated IDL skeleton or the Dynamic Skeleton Interface (DSI) of the CORBA object.
5. This IDL skeleton/DSI layer extracts the appropriate input, as well as the processing and output parameters, and then invokes the methods that pass the parameters. This process is known as unmarshalling. The object implementation does not need to know whether the object was called by the IDL skeleton layer or the DSI layer.
6. The skeleton receives the return values and any exceptions, creates the response message and sends it to the ORB.
7. The ORB sends this response back to the client by way of an IIOP message.
8. The ORB on the client side extracts the data from the response message and sends it to the stub.
9. The stub extracts the returned data and returns it to the client application.

Dynamic Invocation Interface (DII)

Remote calls to CORBA objects are made when the client calls a method that is resident in the remote object. The client calls the method by means of the client stub created by the IDL compiler, which "knows" the method—that is, the number and type of the parameters, the exceptions that will occur, and the return type. This is how objects are invoked through static invocation, in which the client has all the details about the object at compile time.

The Dynamic Invocation Interface (DII), as the name suggests, allows client applications to dynamically call remote objects. This process does not require a client stub; instead, the ORB uses the Interface Repository to check and resolve calls to the remote objects. This in effect enables client applications to invoke and use objects that were not available at compile time. In addition, it allows client applications to use newly created objects that are available at runtime. Dynamic invocation is also useful in synchronous applications. Usually, the client makes a request for the object and waits until the server sends the response back to it. With the help of dynamic invocation, the client can send the request to the server and monitor the response, simultaneously executing other tasks until it receives the response. This improves the performance and efficiency of the application. Additionally, client applications are not restricted to use any particular remote objects and need not be recompiled when they use new objects. The only drawback is the programming effort required to replace the stub in the client application.

The following are the steps involved in making calls using the DII:

1. The remote object's reference must be obtained.
2. The request object is composed with details such as parameters, return type, and exceptions it might cause.
3. Finally, the requested object is invoked and the results awaited.

This process is similar to the one used for static invocation, in which the client stub performs the entire process. In case of DII, the operations performed by the client stub are handled by the application itself.

Dynamic Skeleton Interface (DSI)

The Dynamic Skeleton Interface (DSI) resolves client requests dynamically to transfer control to the target CORBA object. The DSI helps clients locate target CORBA objects that the clients do not have compile-time knowledge of. When a client submits a request, the ORB interface attempts to locate the target object with the help of this interface, thus performing the role of the static skeleton. The DSI makes use of the Interface Repository to resolve object calls.

Interface Repository

The Interface Repository acts as a dictionary, containing definitions of the remote objects. It plays an important role in the dynamic invocation of remote objects, and does some of the work of the client stub in dynamic invocations. Because the Interface Repository holds the definitions of all object interfaces, client applications that use it do not need to restrict themselves to the use of objects that were available when their applications were compiled. Client applications can use it to invoke objects created after application compile time through dynamic invocation. The Interface Repository is also used to check the accuracy of the inheritance graphs.

Implementation Repository

The Implementation Repository contains all the relevant information about object implementations. The ORB uses it as a dictionary to monitor the process of locating and activating remote objects. It also stores additional information associated with the object implementation that could potentially be useful to the ORB.

Object adapters

Adapters are units in the ORB that serve as intermediaries between the ORB and the object implementation. The ORB uses the object adapter to obtain information about CORBA objects. In order to execute the operations on the CORBA object as requested by the client, the ORB in the server must determine the details of the implementation of that particular object. The function of the object adapter is to find the correct object implementation. The object that implements the CORBA interface is called the *servant* object; it may also be called the *object implementation*.

When a client invokes a method on the CORBA object, the client ORB bundles the request and sends it to the server ORB. The server ORB then passes the client request to the object adapter. The object adapter, which maintains details about all the servant objects (object implementations) that implement the CORBA object, locates the appropriate servant object and passes control to the static skeleton layer or the DSI. The skeleton layer extracts the input parameters and passes them to the servant object (object implementation) to perform the necessary operations, as illustrated in Figure 18-4.

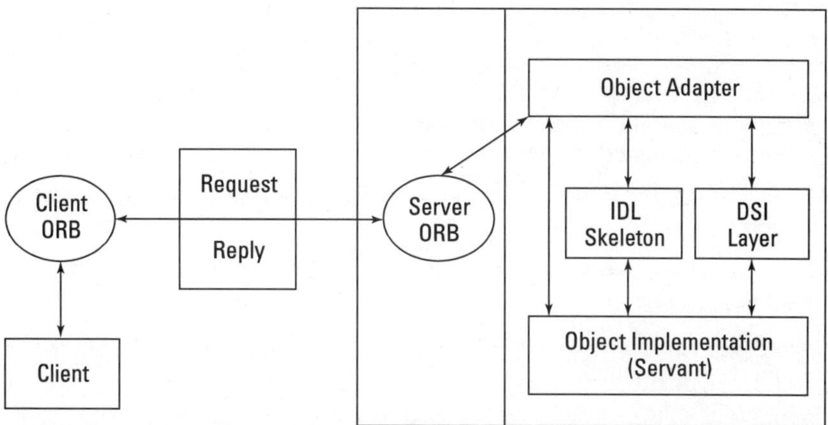

Figure 18-4: Structure of the object adapter

Before you can understand object adapters, you must understand the servant object. The term "servant object" indicates that this is the object that is created in and residing in the server, and that it actually implements the CORBA interface. Since servant objects implement the CORBA interface, the object adapter must have access to the relevant information about CORBA entities and their associated servant objects. Object adapters perform the following functions:

- *Registering servant objects*—Servant objects, once created, must be registered with the object adapter so that the adapter is aware that that particular servant exists in the server. The object adapter identifies the servant objects with the help of an *object ID* (defined later in this section) that acts as a unique (within the adapter only) key for identification.
- *Activating and deactivating CORBA objects*—*Activation* is the process by which the CORBA object is made eligible to service client requests. It typically involves creating and associating a servant object with a CORBA entity. *Deactivation* is the process by which the association between the CORBA entity and the servant object is removed, during which the servant object may be destroyed.
- *Maintaining the object map*—It is the responsibility of the object adapter to maintain an associative map of the CORBA object and its servant so that the servant can be located when a client makes a request.

Two types of object adapters are in use, Basic Object Adapters (BOAs) and Portable Object Adapters (POAs).

Basic Object Adapters

Basic Object Adapters are the simplest type of object adapter in use. These are the adapter whose interfaces were initially introduced by the OMG. The object adapter's function is to help the ORB in the server locate the right target object when the ORB receives the client request. The BOA provides interfaces for creating, activating, deactivating, and destroying objects, and also monitors them in the server. The BOA uses certain activation models to maintain server processes. These are as follows:

- *Shared server model*—As the name indicates, this model allows the server to share the existence of the various CORBA objects, thus enabling support of CORBA objects of different types.
- *Unshared server model*—This model allows only one CORBA object of a particular type to reside in the server.
- *Persistent object model*—This model allows the server to be launched by the user code, a shared server that supports CORBA objects of different types.
- *Server-per-operation model*—This model creates a separate server process for all incoming requests.

The BOA was the first adapter type introduced by the OMG, and largely because of the lack of standardization associated with several of its key features, it has some deficiencies that reduce its portability. For example:

- No standard interface defines the association between the object adapter and the skeleton layer.
- No common specification is available for registering servant objects.
- No standard interface exists for the multi-threading environment.

Portable Object Adapter

Portable Object Adapter (POA) is the recent, flexible object adapter in use. It maintains the objects by assigning them a unique ID called the *object ID*. This adapter maintains an active object map that is used to map the CORBA servant objects with the object IDs. This object ID will be unique well within the POA. When the client passes an object reference, the client ORB sends an object key that is used to locate the target object. The object ID is a part of that object key. The object key may also contain information about the POA.

Unlike BOA, the Portable Object Adapter uses the concept of nesting, starting with a root POA. This allows the server to have multiple POAs that can cover different CORBA objects, and it also provides functions to establish the association between the object adapter and the skeleton layer. The Portable Object Adapter supports multi-threading, which does not exist in the Basic Object Adapter. Portable Object Adapters are the most common adapters in use now.

The Portable Object Adapter incorporates policies to maintain and organize the objects in use. Some of the important policies are:

- Object ID assignment policy
- ObjectID uniqueness policy
- Lifespan policy
- Request processing policy
- Implicit activation policy
- Servant retention policy

Object references

Client applications can get references to a CORBA object in many different ways. The two important means of obtaining object references are Naming Services and stringified object references.

Naming Services

As the name suggests, Naming Services refer to the locators of object references. Naming Services provided by CORBA enable storage of object references in the depository by assigning unique names to them. This name-reference binding helps the service locate object references at client requests. Naming contexts store this name-reference binding, known as the *name component*, in the naming service. The naming context can be a single object-reference binding, or a group of object-reference bindings stored hierarchically. Since the naming context acts as a lookup directory that clients can use to obtain object references, it is the server's responsibility to insert the object reference with a name—that is, to create the naming context in the Naming Services.

Following are the details of how Naming Services work to connect servers and clients to objects, when Naming Services are first invoked:

1. The resolve_initial_references function of the ORB is called as the first step to obtain the CORBA object reference from the root (the initial object reference).
2. The initial object reference thus obtained from the ORB is a generic CORBA object reference. The client and server need to handle it as a NamingContext object; so, the generic CORBA object reference is converted into a Naming Context object.
3. The `Helper` class of the `NamingContext` interface then converts this generic CORBA object reference to a NamingContext objects.

4. On the server side, now that the server has access to the naming context, it has to create a component to be stored in the naming context.
5. The server then creates a `NameComponent` with a unique identifier to identify that particular object reference.
6. The NameComponent and the object reference are then bound in the naming context.
7. On the client side, the client gets a NamingContext reference from the ORB, which is then converted into a naming-context object.
8. The client also creates a name component to query the naming context about that particular object reference.
9. The naming context then resolves the name component and returns the object. As the type of the returned object is generic, the object is converted to a specific object reference with the help of its `Helper` class.
10. Now the client can invoke the methods on that particular object and perform all the operations.

Note that in Java, the naming service used is known as the COS Naming Service. All necessary interfaces required to be able to use this naming service are available in a package called `org.omg.CosNaming`. CORBA applications in Java need to import this package in order to use the naming service.

The following example, which creates an object reference-name binding using Naming Services, may help you understand Naming Services better. First, assume the existence of a CORBA application called Welcome, which welcomes a new user with the message "Welcome to CORBA." Consider the steps the server performs to add the object-reference binding in the naming service:

1. Implement the interface. Assume that the implementation already exists:

```
class WelcomeServant extends _WelcomeImplBase {
// Implementation code goes here
}
```

2. Create an instance of the object in the main server application. Also create the ORB object. Then, add the object to the ORB with the help of connect() method of the ORB:

```
public class WelcomeServer {
    public static void main(String args[])
    {
        ORB orb = ORB.init(args,null);
        WelcomeServant wsRef =  WelcomeServant();
        orb.connect(wsRef);
    }
}
```

3. Get the initial object reference from the ORB by calling the resolve_initial_references method in the ORB interface, as follows (Where `"NameService"` is the initial name of the service):

```
org.omg.CORBA.Object objtRef =
ORB.resolve_initial_references("NameService");
```

4. This method returns a CORBA object. In order to use it as a naming context object, you must narrow it down to a naming-context object by invoking the `narrow()` method present in the `NamingContext Helper` class:

```
NamingContext nmctRef  = NamingContextHelper.narrow(objtRef);
```

5. Subsequently, a name component is created, and is used to uniquely identify the CORBA object (`"Welcome"`). The first parameter is the ID, and the second parameter is its kind (which, in principle, can be null):

```
NameComponent nct = new NameComponent("Welcome","");
```

6. Since only object-reference binding exists, and no hierarchical structure is involved, a single-dimensioned array of `NameComponents` is created to store the object-name binding:

```
NameComponent  nctStore [] = {nct};
```

7. This name is then bound to the object by the following method:

```
nmctRef.rebind(wsRef,nctStore);
```

   You can perform the name-object binding by calling either the `bind()` or the `rebind()` methods of the `NamingContext` interface.

On the client side, steps 2–6 are repeated to create the NamingContext object. As the client has to query on the NamingContext object, it invokes the `resolve` method of the `NamingContext` interface to return the object. This object must be narrowed down to the specific object the client requested.

Stringified object references

As the name suggests, the object reference is stored as a string so that the client can make use of it. As you saw with the Naming Services, you obtain the initial object reference by calling the `resolve_initial_references()` method of the ORB. This generic object reference is narrowed down to the naming context object type by calling the `narrow()` method of the naming-context object's `Helper` class. The name component is created for the CORBA object and is bound with a unique name. The ORB interface has a function called `object_to_string()` that converts this object reference to a string, which can be stored in a Java file. When a request comes in for an object reference from the client, the client can access the file containing the object reference and use it. This is useful in an environment where no Naming Services are available.

Internet Inter-ORB Protocol

The Internet Inter-ORB Protocol (IIOP) is the protocol with which the ORB achieves its objectives. When a client requests a CORBA object, it uses an inter-operable reference to identify the CORBA object in the server. The ORB on the client side then passes this reference to the ORB in the server, which identifies the CORBA object and processes the request. The client ORB and the server ORB communicate through the Internet Inter-ORB Protocol. As the name indicates, this protocol carries inter-operable references across wide-area networks (such as the Internet) to facilitate communication between CORBA objects, as shown in Figure 18-5.

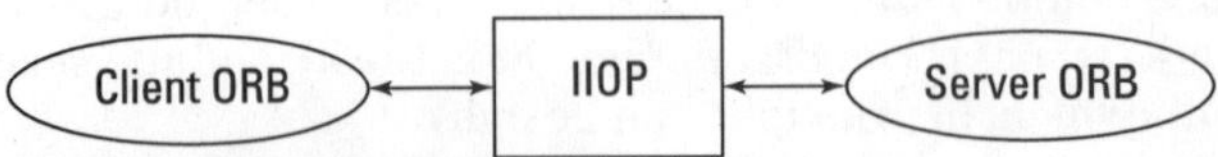

Figure 18-5: IIOP protocol

The IIOP specification uses a data format called Common Data Representation (CDR), which supports several of the datatypes in the OMG IDL. The IIOP protocol uses this format along with some specific message formats to send messages across the ORBs. The message format supported by IIOP can be transmitted across a variety of protocols that are currently in vogue, including TCP/IP and SNA, and this helps CORBA achieve location transparency. The main advantage of using the IIOP protocol is platform independence, which helps CORBA objects interact with each other even when they are not physically located on the same server.

Interface Definition Language

Remote objects can be accessed from client applications only when the client invokes a method on that particular object. Clients, to be able to identify these objects, must have the definition of the remote object's interface at compile time. This interface definition is provided by the Interface Definition Language (IDL). The IDL file stores the interface definitions of the remote objects needed by client applications. IDL files are typically not written in any programming language, but instead can be mapped to any programming language with the appropriate IDL-Language compilers. For IDL-to-Java mapping, for example, you would use the idltojava compiler (in version 1.2) or the idlj compiler (version 1.3 and above) to create the equivalent interface definitions.

The following is a simple IDL file with an interface called Sample.idl:

```
module SampleApp {
    interface  Sample {
        string sayName();
    };
};
```

This is only a simple definition of an IDL file. The following is a list of some of the features of the syntax that IDL file definitions use:

- ✦ The first module statement in the IDL file corresponds to the package statement in Java. If this IDL file is actually compiled for Java mapping, it would have generated a package with the name SampleApp.
- ✦ The second statement, namely the interface statement, is similar to the interface definition in Java.
- ✦ The third statement specifies an operation in IDL. This is an operation that must be performed by the interface. In Java, this operation would correspond to object's methods.

The equivalent Java mapping for the file Sample.idl is as follows:

```
package SampleApp;
public interface Sample
extends org.omg.CORBA.Object, org.omg.CORBA.portable.IDLEntity
{
    String sayName();
}
```

In addition to the equivalent Java file for the interface, the IDL compiler also creates other files. For this particular example, if you look in the folder SampleApp, you will see that the compiler creates a total of five files for this particular IDL file:

- ✦ Sample.java
- ✦ SampleHelper.java
- ✦ SampleHolder.java
- ✦ _SampleImplBase.java
- ✦ _SampleStub.java

Sample.java is the file that contains the mapping of the IDL interface in Java. As the name indicates, SampleStub.java is the client stub, and SampleImplBase.java the IDL skeleton created by the IDL compiler. This leaves SampleHelper.java and SampleHolder.java.

The `Helper` classes allow the applications to write objects to and read them from the stream. They also help to convert generic object references to specific objects in use with the help of the `narrow()` method defined in the `Helper` class, and list the repository ID of the object. The Helper classes also allow the applications to extract data from or add them to a special datatype (called Any) that the IDL uses.

The `Holder` classes provide functionality for manipulating the in/out parameters used in the interfaces. Since Java does not provide any mechanism for resolving the in/out parameters, `Holder` classes help pass the parameters properly to achieve the correct results. For example, the `omg.org.CORBA` package offers `Holder` classes for all the basic datatypes, while user-defined datatypes have their `Holder` classes defined as `<user type>Holder.java`, and `Holder` classes for basic datatypes in turn are defined as `<datatype>Holder`. `Holder` classes for basic datatypes are typically initialized with default values.

The following general rules apply to the IDL definitions: Identifiers are usually case-sensitive, comments can be written as C++ or Java comments, and all statements end in a semicolon.

An IDL file supports the use of basic datatypes, complex datatypes (such as structures, unions, enums, arrays, and so forth), and user-defined exceptions. Much like Java interfaces, it also supports the inheritance of interfaces.

Constants

Constants can be defined in IDL just as in any other programming language. Constants play an important role in many applications. For example, if a generic application calculates the area of all available geometric shapes, it becomes necessary to define pi as a constant in the IDL file. Pi will in turn be mapped as a Java constant, as in the following example.

IDL Definition

```
module SampleApp {
    interface Sample {
        const float PI = 3.14;
    };
};
```

Java Definition

```
package SampleApp;
public interface Sample  extends org.omg.CORBA.Object,
org.omg.CORBA.portable.IDLEntity {
    final float PI = (float) (3.14D);
}
```

Basic Datatypes

Basic datatypes are mapped in the same way as constant datatypes. Table 18-1 indicates how basic datatypes are mapped. All datatypes in IDL are shown with their equivalents in Java. Note that the int and Long datatypes are not interchangeable; take care when defining datatypes as one or the other.

Table 18-1
IDL Datatypes

IDL Datatype	*Java Datatype*
Boolean	boolean
Char	char
string	java.lang.String
short	short
Long	int
long long	long
Float	float
double	double

The following is the code for the basic datatypes as an IDL definition.

IDL Definition

```
module SampleApp {
    interface Sample {
        attribute boolean b;
        attribute char c;
        attribute string s;
        attribute short sh;
        attribute long i;
        attribute long long l;
        attribute float f;
        attribute double d;

    };
};
```

The following code is the Java file generated for the previous idl file with the same basic datatype definitions. The Java file not only maps the data types but also creates the set-get methods for the attributes.

Java Definition

```
package SampleApp;
public interface Sample extends org.omg.CORBA.Object,
org.omg.CORBA.portable.IDLEntity {
```

```
        boolean b();
        void b(boolean arg);
        char c();
        void c(char arg);
        String s();
        void s(String arg);
        short sh();
        void sh(short arg);
        int i();
        void i(int arg);
        long l();
        void l(long arg);
        float f();
        void f(float arg);
        double d();
        void d(double arg);
    }
```

The Boolean data type in IDL can take either a `TRUE` or a `FALSE` value, which maps to true or false, respectively, in Java.

Complex Datatypes

In this section I describe how complex datatype translations are handled in IDL.

Structures

Structures written in the IDL file are mapped as separate class-file definitions in Java, in a sub-package defined under the main package. The file also creates `Holder` and `Helper` classes for the structure definition. The following code definition illustrates how the structures are mapped in Java:

IDL Definition

```
module SampleApp {
    interface Sample {
        struct usr_time {
            short hour;
            short min;
            short sec;
        };
    };
};
```

Java Definition

The Sample.Java file corresponding to the definition for the structure does not contain any code. In this situation, the `struct` definition in the IDL file will eventually be mapped as a separate final class, and, accordingly, the Sample.java file will not contain any definitions. The mapped class files can be available as a sub-package under the main Samplepackage. The mapped `usr_time` class looks like this:

```
package SampleApp.SamplePackage;
public final class usr_time implements
org.omg.CORBA.portable.IDLEntity {

    //    instance variables
    public short hour;
    public short min;
    public short sec;

    //    constructors
    public usr_time() { }
    public usr_time(short __hour, short __min, short
    __sec) {
        hour = __hour;
        min = __min;
        sec = __sec;
    }
}
```

`SamplePackage` is the sub-package created under the `SampleApp` package, and it holds the `struct` variables as its member variables. It also has a default constructor and a constructor that initializes its member variables, and creates `Holder` and `Helper` classes for these exceptions, which are available as separate Java files.

Typedefs

The typedef defines the user-defined type that will be used in the application. For example, in a college admission application, in order to store the course in which the student is enrolled, a user-defined datatype called COURSE is created. This will be a string datatype, but defining and using an intuitive name for the datatype makes the name clearer.

IDL Definition

```
module SampleApp {
    interface Sample {
        typedef string COURSE;
    };
};
```

As the typedef also creates a separate class file, no code will be available in Sample.java. This definition will be available under COURSEHelper.java in the sub-package called `SamplePackage`, which falls under the main `SampleApp` package.

Java Definition

```
package SampleApp.SamplePackage;
public class COURSEHelper {

// It is useless to have instances of this class
private COURSEHelper() { }
public static void write(org.omg.CORBA.portable.OutputStream
out, String that)  {

    out.write_string(that);
}

public static String read(org.omg.CORBA.portable.InputStream
in) {

    String that;
    that = in.read_string();
    return that;
}

public static String extract(org.omg.CORBA.Any a) {
org.omg.CORBA.portable.InputStream in =

    a.create_input_stream();
    return read(in);
}

public static void insert(org.omg.CORBA.Any a, String that) {

    org.omg.CORBA.portable.OutputStream out =
    a.create_output_stream();
    a.type(type());
    write(out, that);
    a.read_value(out.create_input_stream(), type());
}

private static org.omg.CORBA.TypeCode _tc;
synchronized public static org.omg.CORBA.TypeCode type() {

if (_tc == null)
_tc= org.omg.CORBA.ORB.init().create_alias_tc(id(),
"COURSE",
org.omg.CORBA.ORB.init().get_primitive_tc(org.omg.CORBA.TCKind.
tk_string));

return _tc;
}
public static String id() {
   return "IDL:SampleApp/Sample/COURSE:1.0";
}
}
```

Enums

An enumerated datatype holds a set of predefined values. For example, assume an admission application that must store different test results. Possible test results might be pass, fail, and hold. If the application stores these as numeric values, the person reviewing the results might not know what each value signifies. If they are stored as PASS, FAIL, and HOLD, anybody who views the results will know exactly what each label signifies. You can arrange this setup with an enumerated data type, for which the definition looks like this:

IDL Definition

```
module SampleApp {
    interface Sample {
        enum TestResult {PASS,FAIL,HOLD};
    };
};
```

The equivalent Java definition for the enum data type is mapped as a final static class in Java—that is, the .java file will not contain any definition. This class will instead be generated in a sub-package called `SamplePackage` under the `SampleApp` package. `Holder` and `Helper` classes are also created for the enum data types. The definition for the Java equivalent to the preceding IDL definition is as follows:

Java Definition

```
package SampleApp.SamplePackage;
public final class TestResult implements
org.omg.CORBA.portable.IDLEntity {

     public static final int _PASS = 0,
                  _FAIL = 1,
                  _HOLD = 2;
     public static final TestResult PASS =
     new TestResult(_PASS);

     public static final TestResult FAIL =
     new TestResult(_FAIL);

     public static final TestResult HOLD =
     new TestResult(_HOLD);

     public int value() {
         return _value;
     }
     public static final TestResult from_int(int i)
     throws  org.omg.CORBA.BAD_PARAM {
           switch (i) {
             case _PASS:
                 return PASS;
             case _FAIL:
```

```
                return FAIL;
            case _HOLD:
                return HOLD;
            default:
                throw new org.omg.CORBA.BAD_PARAM();
        }
    }
    private TestResult(int _value){
        this._value = _value;
    }
    private int _value;
}
```

Arrays

Arrays play an important role in most applications, as they have proven to be a simple structure in which to store values. Arrays are a common feature of several applications, which in effect makes them a necessity in virtually every language. Going back to our college admission–application example, assume that the admission application has to store test scores for 50 students. In order to do this, the application can use an array. In the following example, two arrays are defined — one to store the names of the students and another to store their test scores.

IDL Definition

```
module SampleApp {
    interface Sample {
        string name[50];
        float testMarks[50];
    };
};
```

The array definitions in IDL trigger an equivalent `Holder` class under the package called `SamplePackage`. The `Holder` classes are created for both array variables. The equivalent Java mapping of the IDL definition is as follows:

Java Definition

```
package SampleApp.SamplePackage;
public final class nameHolder
    implements org.omg.CORBA.portable.Streamable
{
    //    instance variable
    public String[] value;
    //    constructors
    public nameHolder() {
    this(null);
    }
    public nameHolder(String[] __arg) {
    value = __arg;
    }
    public void
    _write(org.omg.CORBA.portable.OutputStream out) {
```

```
            SampleApp.SamplePackage.nameHelper.write(out,
            value);
        }

        public void
        _read(org.omg.CORBA.portable.InputStream in) {
            value =
            SampleApp.SamplePackage.nameHelper.read(in);
        }

        public org.omg.CORBA.TypeCode _type() {
            return
            SampleApp.SamplePackage.nameHelper.type();
        }
    }
```

The preceding code is created for the array variable name; a similar mapping is done for the array variable `testMarks` also.

Exceptions

Exceptions play a major role in error-handling. Earlier, when execution errors occurred in programs, the program would typically terminate and the user wouldn't know why. This has now changed, thanks to exception handling. Now, if a method has an error, it throws or raises an exception. If the method has an error-handler, execution control passes to the error-handler routine. If it does not, it goes to the calling program and looks for an error-handler. And so on up the program hierarchy until it finds an appropriate error-handler. If it does not find one, the program then terminates.

Exceptions are of two types — *system exceptions* and *user exceptions*. System exceptions can be raised by the system in situations such as when invalid parameters are passed to remote objects, or if problems are encountered during memory allocation. User exceptions are created mainly by users or clients who take on error-handler roles. Exceptions raised by methods are passed back to their calling objects through the ORB.

User exceptions are defined much like the struct datatype in IDL. They can have members but not methods. In fact, even user exceptions defined without any members are allowed and treated as valid. The following code shows how to write the exceptions in IDL.

IDL Definition

```
module SampleApp {
    interface Sample {
        exception NoNameFoundException {};
        exception MarksNotFoundException {
            string name;
        };
    };
};
```

Like the struct definition, this definition does not create any code in the .java file. It creates a separate class file under the sub-package `SamplePackage`, whose definition has the following structure:

Java Definition

```
package SampleApp.SamplePackage;
public final class NoNameFoundException
extends org.omg.CORBA.UserException implements
org.omg.CORBA.portable.IDLEntity {

    //    constructor
    public NoNameFoundException() {
    super();
    }
}
package SampleApp.SamplePackage;

public final class MarksNotFoundException
    extends org.omg.CORBA.UserException implements
org.omg.CORBA.portable.IDLEntity {

    //    instance variables
    public String name;
    //    constructors
    public MarksNotFoundException() {
    super();
    }
    public MarksNotFoundException(String __name) {
    super();
    name = __name;
    }
}
```

`Holder` and `Helper` classes for these exceptions are also created and are available as separate Java files.

Interfaces

CORBA interfaces, like Java interfaces, have attributes and operations. Attributes are little more than the public member variables, while operations are the methods associated with those interfaces. Parameters passed to methods may be in, out, or inout parameters. The action associated with each parameter is self-evident. If the type of parameter is designated as in, it is an input parameter, meaning that it sends values from the client to the server for processing. The client stub must marshal this parameter properly before passing it on to the server. Parameters designated as out are values processed and set by the server, which means that parameters designated as out will be manipulated only by the server. Parameters marked inout will be accessed and manipulated by both clients and servers. The client stub marshals the parameters, while the server processes requests and sends the output.

Going back to the college application example: Assume that an application has to determine an applicant's grade by finding the average of the scores of two test papers. This requires that test scores be passed as input parameters and the grade as the output parameter. The requirement definition is as follows:

```
module SampleApp {
    interface Sample {
        attribute string name;
        attribute float score1;
        attribute float score2;
        string  calculateResult(in float score1,in float
score2,out char grade);
    };
};
```

The equivalent code in Java looks is as follows:

```
package SampleApp;
public interface Sample extends org.omg.CORBA.Object,
org.omg.CORBA.portable.IDLEntity {
    String name();
    void name(String arg);
    float score1();
    void score1(float arg);
    float score2();
    void score2(float arg);
    boolean calculateResult(float score1, float score2,
org.omg.CORBA.CharHolder grade);
}
```

In the Java file, the attributes are mapped as member variables of the interface, which therefore contains both `set` and `get` methods for member variables. The in parameters are maintained as in the IDL definition, while the out parameter is resolved as a `CharHolder` object. Since the server will manipulate it directly, the `CharHolder` object is passed as a parameter. This `CharHolder` object will be initialized to `0` (the default value for a variable of the char datatype).

Interfaces can be inherited just like Java interfaces. Any derived interface can have its own attributes and methods, in addition to inherited interface definitions. Inheritance from multiple interfaces is also possible.

The idltojava compiler

The idltojava compiler is the tool used to create the Java mapping for the OMG IDL. You can download it from the `http://www.java.sun.com`.

The idltojava compiler is not included in JDK 1.2, and so you must download it separately. In recent versions of JDK 1.3 and 1.4, the compiler is available bundled with the JDK development kit itself, and is called idlj compiler in the recent versions.

The syntax of the idltojava command is as follows:

```
idltojava -<flags> -<options> <IDL file name>
```

These are two of the important flags used in the idltojava compiler:

✦ `flist-flags`—Lists the status of all the flags. The value can be `on` or `off`.

✦ `fcpp`—Specifies that the IDL source should run through the C/C++ preprocessor before being compiled. The value can be `on` or `off`; the default value is `on`.

To set the status of the flag to `off`, you use the keyword `no`. To change the status of the flag `fcpp` from `on` to `off`, you use the following command:

```
idltojava -fno-cpp <IDL file name>.
```

This command tells the idltojava compiler not to run the IDL source code through the C/C++ preprocessor before it is compiled.

Example: Calculating Simple Interest

Now try a simple CORBA application to call a method to calculate simple interest for bank deposits. Recall that simple interest is calculated by the following formula:

Simple Interest = Principal* Period (in years)* Annualized Interest Rate (%)

The following are the steps in developing the interest calculation application:

1. Writing the IDL interface
2. Compiling the IDL interface by an IDL compiler to create the equivalent Java files
3. Coding the interest server
4. Coding the interest client
5. Running the server and the client

Step 1: Writing the IDL interface

Take as an example an interest calculator, for the calculation of simple interest. Essential input parameters for the interest calculator are the principal amount, the term of the deposit in years, and the annualized rate of interest. The application stores these three parameters as the interface's members. In order to uniquely identify deposits, a customer name and Social Security number are also associated with each set of details.

The steps involved in creating the IDL interface are as follows:

1. Create a file called Interest.idl by opening a text editor.
2. Enter the following code:

```
module InterestApp {
    interface Interest {
            attribute string Name;
            attribute string Ssn;
            attribute double Principal;
            attribute unsigned long Years;
            attribute float Rate ;
            double calculateInterest();
    };
};
```

3. Set the PATH and CLASSPATH variables for the downloaded idltojava compiler.
4. Next, compile the file with an idltojava compiler, using the following command at the command prompt. Go to the folder where the IDL file is present. If the file is present in the root directory then, give the following command at the command prompt:

```
C:\> idltojava Interest.idl
```

This code will create an equivalent Java file in which:

- ✦ The module statement in the IDL file will correspond to the package name in the Java file, and the interface will correspond to the interface statement in Java (the server will implement this interface).
- ✦ The IDL statement attribute will correspond to the public members defined in Java.
- ✦ The IDL operation (in this case, double `calculateInterest()`); will correspond to the method statement in Java.

Step 2: Compiling the IDL file

The steps involved in compiling the IDL file are as follows:

1. Go to the command prompt.
2. Open the folder that holds the Interest.idl file.
3. At the command prompt, run the following command:

```
idltojava Interest.idl.
```

This will create Java-equivalent files under the directory named InterestApp, which will have five files under it:

- ✦ Interest.java: This is the Java-equivalent file for the IDL file that you created. It contains the Java code.
- ✦ InterestHelper.java: The `Helper` class converts the generic CORBA object reference to the "Interest" object reference with the help of the `narrow()` method present in the `Helper` class.
- ✦ InterestHolder.java: The `Holder` class resolves the inout parameters.
- ✦ _InterestImplBase.java: This is the IDL skeleton, which will be used on the server.
- ✦ _InterestStub.java: This is the client stub.

The Java mapping for the IDL file Interest.idl in the file Interest.java will look like this:

```
package InterestApp;
public interface Interest
extends org.omg.CORBA.Object, org.omg.CORBA.portable.IDLEntity
{
    String Name();
    void Name(String arg);
    String Ssn();
    void Ssn(String arg);
    double Principal();
    void Principal(double arg);
    int Years();
    void Years(int arg);
    float Rate();
    void Rate(float arg);
    double calculateInterest();
}
```

Step 3: Coding the InterestServer

In order to create and run the server, you must first implement the CORBA object. In the server, the CORBA object is implemented through an object known as the servant. The servant object resides in the server and performs all the operations requested by the clients, as outlined in the following steps:

1. Create a file called InterestServer.java by opening the text editor. The first statement in the server file is to import the `InterestApp` package and other relevant CORBA packages, as follows:

```
import InterestApp.*;
import omg.org.CORBA.*;
import omg.org.CosNaming.*;
import java.io.*;
```

2. **Next, implement the servant object in the server. The skeleton created by the IDL compiler acts as the base class for the servant object.**

```
class InterestServant extends _InterestImplBase {
// Implement the defined interface
// Declare the variables
    string name;
    string ssn;
  double principal;
    int years;
    float rate;

// Implement the get and set methods for all members in a
// similar fashion

public string name(string arg)
{
     name = arg;
}
string name()
{
   return name;
}
}
```

3. **Implement the method** `calculateInterest`**, which calculates the simple interest:**

```
double calculateInterest()
{
                    return(principal*years*rate/100);
}
```

4. **Define the public class and the** `main()` **function. (Because CORBA functions may cause system exceptions at runtime, it is good practice to introduce a** `try-catch` **block.)**

```
public class InterestServer {
    public static void main(String args[]){
    try {
    // Code goes here
     }catch(Exception e) {
        System.out.println("Message:" + e);
            e.printStackTrace();
     }
     }
  }
}
```

5. **Use the** `init()` **method to create and initialize the ORB (each server is required to have one). The** `init()` **method has two parameters: The first is the command-line argument for the main method (this could be** `null`**), and the second contains application-specific properties. For this example, assume**

that you do not have application-specific properties—that is, pass `null` for that parameter.

```
        // Create ORB
    ORB orb = ORB.init(args,null);
```

6. Create the servant object and attach it to the ORB instance with the following statements:

```
    InterestServant IntRef = new InterestServant();
orb.connect(IntRef);
```

7. Get an initial object reference. The most common way to do this is through the COS Naming Service provided with the Java IDL. To use the COS Naming Service you must import the `org.omg.CosNaming` package, as follows:

```
// Get the root naming context
org.omg.CORBA.Object objtRef =
orb.resolve_initial_references("NameService");
```

   The preceding code invokes the `resolve_initial_references` method to obtain an initial object reference to the server. The string `"NameService"` is passed on as the initial name service.

8. Use the `narrow()` method of the `NamingContextHelper` interface to narrow down the initial object reference obtained (a generic CORBA object) to its naming context object:

```
NamingContext nctRef = NamingContextHelper.narrow(objtRef);
```

9. Specify the complete path of an object as an array of `NameComponents`. Note that the name component contains a string to identify the interest server, which you will use as follows:

```
NameComponent nct = new NameComponent("Interest","");
```

   The first parameter of the `NameComponent` constructor is an ID that identifies the server; the second parameter is its kind. For this example, pass `null` for the kind parameter, and `"Interest"` for the interest server.

10. As the path to the `Interest` object is a single-entry, create a single-dimensional `NameComponent` array called path, and assign to it the `NameComponent` variable `nct` (which you created in the previous step):

```
NamingContext path[] = {nct};
```

11. use the `rebind` statement to bind the object with its name in the naming context:

```
nctRef.rebind(path,IntRef);
```

12. Wait for clients to invoke the objects. This is done by the following code:

```
java.lang.Object sync = new java.lang.Object();
synchronized(sync)    {
    sync.wait();
}
```

The code for InterestServer.java is as follows:

```
import InterestApp.*;
import org.omg.CORBA.*;
import org.omg.CosNaming.*;
import org.omg.CosNaming.NamingContextPackage.*;

class InterestServant extends _InterestImplBase {
// Implement the Get - Set Procedures for the Member
// variables

   string name;
   string ssn;
     double principal;
     int years;
     float rate;

   public String Name()
    {
        return name;
    }
  public void Name(String arg)
  {
       name =arg;
  }

    public String Ssn()
    {
        return ssn;
    }
    public void Ssn(String arg)
    {
      ssn = arg;
    }

    public double Principal()
    {
        return principal;
    }

    public void Principal(double arg)
    {
       principal = arg;
    }

    public float Rate()
    {
        return rate;
    }
```

```
    public void Rate(float arg)
    {
      rate = arg;
    }
    public int Years()
    {
        return years;
    }

    public void Years(int arg)
    {
      years = arg;
    }


  // Implement the method to calculate simple interest

    public double calculateInterest()
    {
        return (principal * years * rate / 100);
    }

}

public class InterestServer {

    public static void main(String args[]) {

    try {

    // Create the ORB
    ORB orb = ORB.init(args,null);

   // Create an instance of the servant object (object
   // implementation)
    InterestServant IntRef = new InterestServant();
    orb.connect(IntRef);

    // Get the initial root context and narrow it to the
  // Naming Context object
org.omg.CORBA.Object objtRef =
orb.resolve_initial_references("NameService");

NamingContext nctRef = NamingContextHelper.narrow(objtRef);

// Create a new Name component for the Interest object
NameComponent nct = new NameComponent("Interest","");
NameComponent path[] = {nct};

// Attach the Interest object's namecomponent into the //
Naming Service

nctRef.rebind(path,IntRef);
```

```
// Wait for client's requests
java.lang.Object sync = new java.lang.Object();
synchronized(sync){
    sync.wait();
}
}catch(Exception e) {
    System.out.println("Error" + e);
    e.printStackTrace(System.out);
} // end of try-catch
} // end of main

} // end of class InterestServer
```

Step 4: Coding the Client

1. Create a file named InterestClient.java by opening the text editor.
2. Import the `InterestApp` and other relevant CORBA packages:

```
import InterestApp.*;
import omg.org.CORBA.*;
import omg.org.CosNaming.*;
import java.io.*;
```

3. The next statement is the class definition, which defines the `Client` class and calls the main function. (Because CORBA functions may cause system exceptions at runtime, it is good practice to include a `try-catch` block.)

```
     public class InterestClient {

    public static void main(String args[]){
    try {
        // Code goes here
    }catch(Exception e) {
        System.out.println("Message:" + e);
        e.printStackTrace();
    }
    }
  }
```

4. Declare a variable called `interestAmount` to hold the value of the calculated interest and initialize it to `0.0`.
5. Use the `init()` method to create and initialize the ORB (each server is required to have one). The `init()` method has two parameters, the first of which is the command line argument for the main method, and the second of which contains application-specific properties (which is a `Property` object). For this example, assume that you do not have application-specific properties — that is, pass `null` for that parameter. In some situations, the first parameter of the method may also be `null`.

```
     // Create ORB
    ORB orb = ORB.init(args,null);
```

The preceding code returns an instance of the ORB.

6. The next step is to get an initial object reference, using the COS Naming Service provided with the Java IDL. In order to use the Cos Naming Service, import the `org.omg.CosNaming` package:

```
// get the root naming context
org.omg.CORBA.Object contextobj =
orb.resolve_initial_references("NameService");
```

   The method `resolve_initial_references` is used to get an initial object reference from the Naming Services. The string `"NameService"` is passed as a parameter for the resolve_initial_references method.

7. Narrow the initial object reference obtained from a generic CORBA object, to a specific naming-context object holding the name bindings. The names available in this object are unique. You use the `narrow()` method of the `NamingContextHelper` interface to perform the function of narrowing down:

```
NamingContext rootContext =
NamingContextHelper.narrow(contextobj);
```

8. Specify the complete path of an object as an array of `NameComponents`. Note that the name component contains a string that identifies the interest server, and which you use as follows:

```
NameComponent nct = new NameComponent("Interest","");
```

   The first parameter of the `NameComponent` constructor is an ID that identifies the server; the second parameter is its kind. For this example, pass `null` for the kind parameter and `"Interest"` for the interest server.

9. As the path to the `Interest` object is a single-entry, create a single-dimensional `NameComponent` array of called path, and assign the `NameComponent` variable `nct` (which you created in the previous step):

```
NamingContext path[] = {nct};
```

10. Next, pass the path value to the naming service, which, in turn, calls the `resolve()` method to get a reference to the interest server object. Use the `narrow()` function of InterestHelper.java to convert the generic CORBA object that the `resolve()` function returns to the `Interest` object:

```
Interest interestRef =
InterestHelper.narrow(rootContext.resolve(path));
```

11. Now, using the CORBA object reference, set the member variables and call the method to calculate the simple interest:

```
    interestRef.Name("John");
    interestRef.Ssn("123-45-6789");
    interestRef.Principal(10000);
    interestRef.Years(1);
    interestRef.Rate(10);

double interestAmount = interestRef.calculateInterest();
```

   As the `calculateInterest()` method returns a double value, you declare a local variable of type `double` and store the value in that variable.

12. Output the set and calculated values by calling a `System.println` **statement:**

```
System.out.println("Name          :"    + interestRef.Name());
System.out.println("SSn           :"    + interestRef.Ssn());
System.out.println("Principal  :$"+ interestRef.Principal());
System.out.println("Years         :"   + interestRef.Years());
System.out.println("Rate           :"   + interestRef.Rate() +
"%");
System.out.println("Interest      :$"  +  interestAmount);
```

The full source code of InterestClient.java is now as follows:

```
import InterestApp.*;
import org.omg.CORBA.*;
import org.omg.CosNaming.*;
import org.omg.CosNaming.NamingContextPackage.*;


public class InterestClient {

public static void main(String args[]) {
try {

// Initialise the interestAmount variable to 0.0 to
// hold the interest value

double interestAmount = 0.0;

// Create ORB

ORB orb = ORB.init(args,null);


// Get the initial root context and narrow it to Naming
// Contextobject
org.omg.CORBA.Object contextobj =
orb.resolve_initial_references("NameService");

NamingContext rootContext =
NamingContextHelper.narrow(contextobj);

// Initialise the Name component for the Interest
// object

NameComponent nct = new NameComponent("Interest","");
NameComponent path[] = {nct};

// Get  the Interest object reference
Interest interestRef =
InterestHelper.narrow(rootContext.resolve(path));
```

```
// Assign values to the member variables
interestRef.Name("John");
interestRef.Ssn("123-45-6789");
interestRef.Principal(10000);
interestRef.Years(1);
interestRef.Rate(10);

// Call the method to calculate the interest and store
// it in the variable
interestAmount = interestRef.calculateInterest();

// Display the results
System.out.println("Name       :"   + interestRef.Name());

System.out.println("SSn         :"   + interestRef.Ssn());

System.out.println("Principal  :$"  + interestRef.Principal());

System.out.println("Years       :"   + interestRef.Years() +
"year(s)");

System.out.println("Rate         :"   + interestRef.Rate() +
"%");

System.out.println("Interest    :$"  +  interestAmount);

}catch(Exception e) {
   System.out.println("Error" + e);
   e.printStackTrace(System.out);

} // end of try-catch
} // end of main
}  // end of class WeatherClient
```

Step 5: Compiling and Running the Application

1. Compile InterestServer.java and InterestClient.java using the `javac` command.
2. Before running the application, start the COS Naming Service provider in both client and server applications to get the initial reference of the object. tnameserv is the naming service I use in this example (this server is available when the Java IDL is installed).

   To start the tnameserv naming service, use the following command at the command prompt:

   ```
   tnameserv -ORBInitialPort <portnumber>
   ```

   The user may specify any port number (the default is 900). It is advisable to use port numbers greater than 1024 when the user has to specify the port number. Note that you must use the same port numbers when starting the naming service and when running the server and client applications.

3. Start the interest server application with the following command in the command prompt:

```
java InterestServer -ORBInitialPort <portnumber>
```

where *<portnumber>* is either the port number specified by the user or the default port (900).

4. Run the InterestClient application with the following command:

```
java InterestClient -ORBInitialPort  <portnumber>
```

where *<portnumber>* is either the port number specified by the user or the default port (900). This command will set the input parameters as specified in the client program, calculate the simple interest, and display the results. The results will be as follows:

```
Name    :John
SSN    :123-45-6789
Principal   :$10000
Years        :1 year(s)
Rate          :10 %
Interest     :$1000
```

CORBA Services

OMG has provided several CORBA services, which are available for use. These are the common object services, which interact with the ORB. OMG provides a specification called Common Object Services Specifications for these services (COSS). Few important services include:

- Naming services
- Event services
- Transaction services
- Security services
- Lifecycle services
- Trader services
- Time services
- Externalization services
- Concurrency services
- Licensing services
- Notification services
- Property services

Differences between CORBA and RMI

On the surface, CORBA's architecture is quite similar to that of RMI. However, some major differences distinguish the CORBA architecture and make it a preferred alternative to RMI:

- The RMI architecture is based on the Java programming language, involving as RMI does the serialization of objects at the lower level. The RMI architecture does allow applications to use C and C++ through the Java Native Interface; nonetheless, RMIs foundation in Java is still a constraint on applications that use other programming languages. In contrast, CORBA applications provide generic interfaces that can be mapped to any programming language.
- The use of Java in real-time applications is greatly limited, in spite of its several advantages. This feature of Java enables objects written using the CORBA architecture to participate in real-time applications.
- CORBA provides a solid base for future technologies with the definition of standard specifications that can be applied to multiple applications. This enables a programmer to build a basic infrastructure in any distributed network system.

Automatic garbage collection, which is available in the Java architecture, is not available in CORBA.

Summary

The main aim of this chapter is to give an idea about what CORBA is, and to know about the other important components of the CORBA architecture. It also tries to help the readers to build a simple CORBA application. To summarize, I covered the following topics in this chapter:

- An overview of CORBA.
- Descriptions of the Object Request Broker (ORB), the Dynamic Invocation Interface (DII), and the Dynamic Skeleton Interface (DSI).
- An overview of object adapters.
- The use of the Interface Definition Language (IDL).
- Writing a simple CORBA application.

✦ ✦ ✦

CHAPTER 19

CORBA Applications in the Enterprise

✦ ✦ ✦ ✦

In This Chapter

Developing a complete CORBA application

Accessing the CORBA object, with standalone client applications and with servlets

✦ ✦ ✦ ✦

In this chapter, you'll see a CORBA application that deals with a CORBA weather object. The weather object stores weather details for a city on different dates. This object consists of the following characteristics:

- City name
- Current date
- High temperature
- Low temperature
- Humidity
- Forecasts

The CORBA application provides procedures for the following operations:

- Storing weather details for various cities into a database
- Converting the temperature from Fahrenheit to Celsius
- Retrieving the weather details
  - for all the cities
  - for a particular city
  - for a particular city and a particular date

Build the CORBA Object

Start with the CORBA object by writing the IDL file:

```
module WeatherApp {
    interface WeatherObject {
       struct Weather {
            string city;
            string currDate;
            float highTemp;
            float lowTemp;
            long humidity;
            string remarks;
        };

    typedef sequence<Weather> WeatherReport;
    boolean commitData(in Weather wthrobj);
    WeatherReport retrieveData();
    WeatherReport findDataCity(in string cityname);
    Weather findData(in string cityname,in string dt);
    float convertTemp(in float tempinFahr);

    };
};
```

The characteristics of the weather object are defined as a structure. The IDL file also contains the associated methods for the weather object. The methods are as follows:

- `retrieveData()`—Retrieves weather details for all the cities stored in the database. The return value of this method is defined as a sequence of weather objects. A sequence is like the arrays, but its size is not fixed when it is defined in the IDL file. A sequence will be mapped as a Java array.
- `findDataCity()`—Returns weather details for a particular city on different dates. This method also returns a sequence of weather objects.
- `commitData()`—Saves weather details into a database.
- `findData()`—Retrieves weather details for a particular city on a particular date.

The IDL file is compiled with the idltojava compiler with the following command at the command prompt:

```
C:>idltojava Weather.idl
```

This idltojava compiler creates the equivalent Java files under the directory WeatherApp. The generated files are as follows:

✦ WeatherObject.java — The generated Java file

✦ _WeatherObjectImplBase.java — The generated static skeleton file

✦ _WeatherObjectStub.java — The generated client stub

✦ WeatherObjectHelper.java — The `Helper` class, which contains the `narrow()` method to convert the general CORBA object references into specific object references

✦ WeatherObjectHolder.java — The `Holder` class, which helps to resolve the inout parameters

In addition to these files, a subfolder called `WeatherObjectPackage` is created under the `WeatherApp` package. This WeatherObjectPackage contains the Java files for the structures and sequences defined in the IDL file. These files are as follows:

✦ Weather.java — Contains the definition of the Weatherobject structure in Java

✦ WeatherHelper.java — The `Helper` class for the weather object

✦ WeatherHolder.java — The `Holder` class for the weather object

✦ WeatherReportHolder.java — The `Holder` class for the sequence `WeatherReport`

✦ WeatherReportHelper.java — The `Helper` class for the sequence `WeatherReport`

Develop the CORBA Server

Now you'll develop the CORBA server and implement the methods defined in the IDL file. The first step in developing the CORBA server is to implement the weather object using the methods defined in the IDL. Take a look at how the methods are implemented. In the example in this section, the weather details are stored in a table called weather. For example, let me create this weather table in Microsoft Access. To access this table, you need to create a data-source name in the machine for this weather table. Let me create a data source called "Weather" in the machine that you will use. You will use this data-source name to get the connection for the database. With this connection, all the methods will interact with the database to store and retrieve the details from the table. The combination of the city and the date acts as the primary key for this table. The details of creating the data-source name are available in Chapter 7.

Start by defining a method called `getConn()` that gets a connection to the database:

```
Connection getConn()
{
try {

// Load the class driver
Class.forName("sun.jdbc.odbc.JdbcOdbcDriver");

// Get the connection to the weather table
con = DriverManager.getConnection("jdbc:odbc:Weather");

}catch(ClassNotFoundException cnfe){
System.out.println("Class Not Found Exception" +
cnfe.getMessage());

}catch(SQLException sqle) {
System.out.println("SQL Exception" + sqle.getMessage());
}
return con;
}
```

The `getConn` method loads the JDBC-ODBC driver and creates a connection to the database.

Let me explain the methods that are present in the IDL file in detail. The first method is `commitData()`, which saves the weather details into the weather table.

```
void commitData(WeatherApp.WeatherObjectPackage.Weather w )
```

It is defined as follows:

```
public boolean
commitData(WeatherApp.WeatherObjectPackage.Weather w)
{
  try {

    // Get the connection to the weather table
    con = getConn();

  // Create the Statement object
  st= con.createStatement();

  // Create the INSERT string
  String sql = "insert into Weather values ('" +
  w.currDate + "','" + w.city + "'," +
  w.highTemp +  "," + w.lowTemp + "," +
  w.humidity + "," + "'" + w.remarks + "')";

  // Execute the INSERT String
    st.executeUpdate(sql);
```

```
    }catch(SQLException e){
    System.out.println("SQL Exception");
    return false;
    }// end of try-catch

    return true;
  } // end of function commitData
```

The `commitData()` method gets the connection from the database by calling the `getConn()` method. Once it gets a connection, it creates a `Statement` object to execute the query. The weather details are stored in the weather object, which is passed as an input parameter. With this input parameter, the `INSERT` query is built, and the query is executed. The return value indicates whether the weather details were stored into the table or not.

The second method that I am going to explain is the `retrieveData()` method, which retrieves all the records from the weather table.

```
Method : WeatherApp.WeatherObjectPackage.Weather[]
retrieveData()
```

The method is defined as follows:

```
public WeatherApp.WeatherObjectPackage.Weather[] retrieveData()
    {
WeatherApp.WeatherObjectPackage.Weather[] wtrList = null;

try {

    // Get the connection
    con = getConn();
    st= con.createStatement();

    // Execute the SELECT query
    rst = st.executeQuery("select * from Weather");

    // Create a Vector component
    Vector v = new Vector();

    while (rst.next())
    {

     WeatherApp.WeatherObjectPackage.Weather wtr =
     new WeatherApp.WeatherObjectPackage.Weather();

     wtr.city = rst.getString("City Name");
     wtr.currDate = rst.getString("Current Date");
     wtr.highTemp = rst.getFloat("High Temperature");
     wtr.lowTemp = rst.getFloat("Low Temperature");
     wtr.humidity =rst.getInt("Humidity");
     wtr.remarks =rst.getString("Forecasts");
```

```
        // Add the weather object into a Vector component
        v.add(wtr);
        }// end of while

    // Create an array of weather objects
    wtrList = new
    WeatherApp.WeatherObjectPackage.Weather[v.size()];

    // Copy the vector component into the array of weather
    // objects
    v.copyInto(wtrList);

    }catch(SQLException sqle) {
    System.out.println("SQL Exception" + sqle.getMessage());
    } // end of try-catch
    return wtrList;
    } // end of function retrieveData
```

The retrieveData() method retrieves all the records present in the table. It gets a connection to the table by calling the getConn() method and creates a Statement object. As this method has to create a list of all the records present in the weather table, the SELECT query is built accordingly and given to the Statement object. The results returned by this query are stored in a ResultSet object. The weather object is created to hold a single record of the weather table. The ResultSet object is traversed to read the records one by one so that the values can be stored in a weather object. This weather object is added into a vector component. Because the number of records is known only at runtime, you use a vector component to store the weather objects. Once all the weather objects are stored in the vector component, an array of weather objects is created by giving the vector component's size as the size of the array. Then the contents of the vector component are copied into this array, and it is sent as a return value.

Let me explain the next method, findDataCityMethod : public WeatherApp.WeatherObjectPackage.Weather[] findDataCity(String city).

The method findDataCity() retrieves all the weather details about a city, which is passed as an input parameter. The method is defined as follows:

```
public WeatherApp.WeatherObjectPackage.Weather[]
findDataCity(String city)
{
WeatherApp.WeatherObjectPackage.Weather[] wtrList = null;

try {

    // Get the connection to the weather table
    con = getConn();
    st= con.createStatement();

    // Create the SELECT string
```

```
    String sql = "select * from Weather where
    [City Name] ='" + city + "'";

    // Execute the SELECT string
    rst = st.executeQuery(sql);

   // Create a Vector component
    Vector v = new Vector();
    while (rst.next())
    {

    // Create a Weather object
    WeatherApp.WeatherObjectPackage.Weather wtr = new
    WeatherApp.WeatherObjectPackage.Weather();

    // Store the table values into the Weather object
    wtr.city = rst.getString("City Name");
    wtr.currDate = rst.getString("Current Date");
    wtr.highTemp = rst.getFloat("High Temperature");
    wtr.lowTemp = rst.getFloat("Low Temperature");
    wtr.humidity =rst.getInt("Humidity");
    wtr.remarks =rst.getString("Forecasts");

    // Add the Weather object into the Vector component
    v.add(wtr);

    }// end of while

    // Create an array of Weather objects
    wtrList = new
    WeatherApp.WeatherObjectPackage.Weather[v.size()];

    // Copy the vector component into the array of
    // weather objects
    v.copyInto(wtrList);

    }catch(SQLException sqle) {
    System.out.println("SQL Exception" +
    sqle.getMessage());

    }// end of try-catch
    return wtrList;

}// end of function findDatacity
```

The `findDataCity()` method is similar to the `retrieveData` method, but the `SELECT` query is different. The `SELECT` query is built specifically for Microsoft Access Database. The `SELECT` query fetches all the records that match the city name passed as the input parameter. The array of weather objects is passed as the return value.

The next method I will talk about is the `findData()` method.

```
Method : public WeatherApp.WeatherObjectPackage.Weather
findData(String city,String dt)
```

The `findData()` method retrieves a particular record for the particular city and date specified as the input parameter. The method is defined as follows:

```
public WeatherApp.WeatherObjectPackage.Weather findData(String
city,String dt)
{
WeatherApp.WeatherObjectPackage.Weather wtr = new
WeatherApp.WeatherObjectPackage.Weather();

try {

    // Get the connection to the weather table
    con = getConn();
    st= con.createStatement();

    // Create the SELECT string
    String sql = "select * from Weather where
    [City Name] ='" + city + "'" +
    "and [Current Date] = #" + dt + "#";

    // Execute the SELECT string
    rst = st.executeQuery(sql);
    rst.next();

    // Store the table values into the Weather object

    wtr.city = rst.getString("City Name");
    wtr.currDate = rst.getString("Current Date");
    wtr.highTemp = rst.getFloat("High Temperature");
    wtr.lowTemp = rst.getFloat("Low Temperature");
    wtr.humidity =rst.getInt("Humidity");
    wtr.remarks =rst.getString("Forecasts");

    }catch(SQLException sqle) {
    System.out.println("SQL Exception" +
    sqle.getMessage());

    } // end of try-catch
    return wtr;

}// end of function findData()
```

The `findData()` method gets the connection to the weather table by calling the `getConn()` method and creates a `Statement` object to execute the query. It builds the `SELECT` query with the input parameters, and the `SELECT` query is executed. This query returns only one record, and so you can store it in the weather object, which is the return value for this method.

The next method that I will explain is the `convertTemp()`.

```
Method : float convertTemp(float tempinFahr)
```

The `convertTemp()` method converts the temperature from Fahrenheit scale to Celsius scale. The temperature is stored in the Fahrenheit scale in the database. In order to provide the temperature in the Celsius scale, the `convertTemp()` method is used. The method is defined as follows:

```
public float convertTemp(float tempinFahr)
{
    float celsius;
    celsius = (float)((tempinFahr -32) / 1.8 );
    return celsius;
}
```

The `convertTemp()` method accepts the temperature in the Fahrenheit scale as the input parameter and sends the calculated temperature in the Celsius scale as the return value.

The preceding methods are implemented by the weather object. The main() function of the CORBA server looks like this:

```
public class WeatherServer {
    public static void main(String args[]) {
 try {

    // Initialize ORB
    ORB orb = ORB.init(args,null);

    //Create an instance of Weather object
    WeatherObjectServant weatherRef = new
    WeatherObjectServant();

    orb.connect(weatherRef);

    // Get the initial root context and narrow it to
    // Naming Contextobject

    org.omg.CORBA.Object objRef =
    orb.resolve_initial_references("NameService");

    NamingContext ncRef =
    NamingContextHelper.narrow(objRef);

    // Initialize the Name component for the weather
    //object

    NameComponent nc = new
    NameComponent("Weather","");
```

```
        NameComponent path[] = {nc};

        // Attach the Weather object's
        // NameComponent into the naming service
        ncRef.rebind(path,weatherRef);

        // Wait for client's requests
        java.lang.Object sync = new
        java.lang.Object();

        synchronized(sync){
            sync.wait();

        } // end of synchronized
        }catch(Exception e) {
        System.out.println("Error" + e);
        e.printStackTrace(System.out);

        } // end of try-catch
    } // end of main
} // end of class
```

In the main() function defined as above, the ORB is created for the server and initialized. An instance of the servant object is created and attached to the ORB component. The next step is to get the initial object reference, using the COS Naming Service provided with the Java IDL. In order to use the COS Naming Service, you must import the org.omg.CosNaming package. The initial object reference obtained by calling the resolve_initial_references method is narrowed down to a namingContext object from a generic CORBA object that holds the name bindings. The name component contains a string to identify the Weather server. As the path to the weather object is a single entry, a single-dimensional NameComponent array of called path is created, and assigned the NameComponent variable nc, which was created in the previous step. The object is bound with its name in the naming context by means of the rebind statement. The server waits for clients to invoke the objects.

The source code of WeatherServer.java is as follows:

```
import java.sql.*;
import java.io.*;
import java.util.*;

import WeatherApp.*;
import WeatherApp.WeatherObjectPackage.*;

import org.omg.CORBA.*;
import org.omg.CosNaming.*;
import org.omg.CosNaming.NamingContextPackage.*;


class WeatherObjectServant extends _WeatherObjectImplBase {
```

```
// Initialize the variables required to interact // with
database

        Connection con = null;
        Statement st = null;
        ResultSet rst = null;


public boolean
commitData(WeatherApp.WeatherObjectPackage.Weather w)
{
    try {
        //Get a connection to the database
        con = getConn();
        st= con.createStatement();

        // Build the INSERT query
        String sql = "insert into Weather values ('" +
        w.city + "','" + w.currDate + "'," +
        w.highTemp + "," + w.lowTemp + "," +
        w.humidity + "," + "'" + w.remarks + "')";

        //Execute the Query
        st.executeUpdate(sql);

       }catch(SQLException e){
      System.out.println("SQLException"+e.getMessage());

    } // end of try-catch

      return true;
} // end of function commitData

public WeatherApp.WeatherObjectPackage.Weather[] retrieveData()
{
WeatherApp.WeatherObjectPackage.Weather[] wtrList = null;

    try {

    //Get a connection to the database
    con = getConn();
    st= con.createStatement();

    //Build & execute the SELECT query
    rst = st.executeQuery("select * from Weather");

    // Create a new vector component
    Vector v = new Vector();

    // Traverse through the ResultSet object
    // to store the weather details in the
    // vector component
```

```
        while (rst.next())
        {

        WeatherApp.WeatherObjectPackage.Weather wtr =
        new WeatherApp.WeatherObjectPackage.Weather();

        wtr.city = rst.getString("City Name");
        wtr.currDate = rst.getString("Current Date");
        wtr.highTemp = rst.getFloat("High Temperature");
        wtr.lowTemp = rst.getFloat("Low Temperature");
        wtr.humidity =rst.getInt("Humidity");
        wtr.remarks =rst.getString("Forecasts");

        v.add(wtr);
        } // end of while

        wtrList = new
        WeatherApp.WeatherObjectPackage.Weather[v.size()];

        v.copyInto(wtrList);

        }catch(SQLException sqle) {
       System.out.println("SQL Exception" +
       sqle.getMessage());
       } // end of try-catch

       return wtrList;

    } // end of function retrieveData

    public WeatherApp.WeatherObjectPackage.Weather[]
    findDataCity(String city)
    {
    WeatherApp.WeatherObjectPackage.Weather[] wtrList = null;

    try {

        //Get a connection to the database
        con = getConn();
        st= con.createStatement();

        //Build the SELECT query
        String sql = "select * from Weather where
        [City  Name] ='" + city + "'";

        //Execute the SQL Query
        rst = st.executeQuery(sql);

        //Create a Vector component
        Vector v = new Vector();

        // Traverse through the Resultset object to
        // the weather details in the vector component
```

```
    while (rst.next())
    {

    WeatherApp.WeatherObjectPackage.Weather wtr =
    new WeatherApp.WeatherObjectPackage.Weather();

    wtr.city = rst.getString("City Name");
    wtr.currDate = rst.getString("Current Date");
    wtr.highTemp = rst.getFloat("High Temperature");
    wtr.lowTemp = rst.getFloat("Low Temperature");
    wtr.humidity =rst.getInt("Humidity");
    wtr.remarks =rst.getString("Forecasts");

    v.add(wtr);

    } // end of while

    wtrList = new
    WeatherApp.WeatherObjectPackage.Weather[v.size()];

    v.copyInto(wtrList);

    }catch(SQLException sqle) {
    System.out.println("SQL Exception" +
    sqle.getMessage());

    } // end of try-catch
    return wtrList;
} // end of function findDataCity

public float convertTemp(float tempinFahr)
{

 // Convert temperature from Fahrenheit to Celsius
 float celsius;
 celsius = (float)((tempinFahr -32) / 1.8 );
 return celsius;
}

public WeatherApp.WeatherObjectPackage.Weather findData(String
city,String dt)
{
WeatherApp.WeatherObjectPackage.Weather wtr = new
WeatherApp.WeatherObjectPackage.Weather();
try {

    //Get the conncetion
    con = getConn();
    st= con.createStatement();

    //Build and execute the SELECT query
    String sql = "select * from Weather where" +
    "[City Name] ='" + city + "'" +
    "and [Current Date] = #" + dt + "#";
```

```
        rst = st.executeQuery(sql);
        rst.next();

        wtr.city = rst.getString("City Name");
        wtr.currDate = rst.getString("Current Date");
        wtr.highTemp = rst.getFloat("High Temperature");
        wtr.lowTemp = rst.getFloat("Low Temperature");
        wtr.humidity =rst.getInt("Humidity");
        wtr.remarks =rst.getString("Forecasts");

        }catch(SQLException sqle) {
        System.out.println("SQL Exception" +
        sqle.getMessage());

        }// end of try-catch
        return wtr;

    } // end of function findDataCity

    Connection getConn()
    {
    try {

    //Load the class driver and get the connection
    Class.forName("sun.jdbc.odbc.JdbcOdbcDriver");
    con = DriverManager.getConnection("jdbc:odbc:Weather");

    }catch(ClassNotFoundException cnfe){
    System.out.println("Class Not Found Exception" +
    cnfe.getMessage());

    }catch(SQLException sqle) {
    System.out.println("SQL Exception" +
    sqle.getMessage());
    } // end of try-catch
    return con;

    } // end of function getConn

    } // end of class WeatherObject

    public class WeatherServer {
        public static void main(String args[]) {
        try {

        //Create ORB
        ORB orb = ORB.init(args,null);

        //Create the Servant object
        WeatherObjectServant weatherRef = new
        WeatherObjectServant();
        orb.connect(weatherRef);
```

```
        //Get the initial object reference
        org.omg.CORBA.Object objRef =
        orb.resolve_initial_references("NameService");

        NamingContext ncRef =
        NamingContextHelper.narrow(objRef);

        //Create a new name component for the Weather object
        NameComponent nc = new NameComponent("Weather","");
        NameComponent path[] = {nc};

        // Attach the Weather object's reference to the
        // naming service

        ncRef.rebind(path,weatherRef);

        // Wait for clients to invoke requests
        java.lang.Object sync = new java.lang.Object();
        synchronized(sync){
            sync.wait();
        } // end of synchronized

        }catch(Exception e) {
        System.out.println("Error" + e);
        e.printStackTrace(System.out);
        } // end of try-catch
    } // end of main
} // end of class WeatherServer
```

Develop the CORBA Client

Now that you have implemented the CORBA object in the server, take a look at how some clients can access this object. In this section, you are going to see how the CORBA object is accessed from standalone client applications and from servlets.

Accessing the CORBA object from a client application

The standalone client application can take the weather details for a city and store them in the database; it can also list the weather forecasts for all the cities, and get a city name from the user and populate the weather details for that city. Take a look at how the client does these things.

```
import WeatherApp.*;
import WeatherApp.WeatherObjectPackage.*;
import java.io.*;
import org.omg.CORBA.*;
import org.omg.CosNaming.*;
import org.omg.CosNaming.NamingContextPackage.*;
```

```
public class WeatherClient {
public static void main(String args[]) {
try {

//Create ORB
ORB orb = ORB.init(args,null);

// Get the initial root context and narrow it to
// Naming Contextobject

org.omg.CORBA.Object contextobj =
orb.resolve_initial_references("NameService");

NamingContext rootContext =
NamingContextHelper.narrow(contextobj);

// Initialise the Name component for the Weather
//object
NameComponent nc = new NameComponent("Weather","");
NameComponent path[] = {nc};

// Get  the Weather object reference
WeatherObject woRef =
WeatherObjectHelper.narrow(rootContext.resolve(path));

WeatherApp.WeatherObjectPackage.Weather wtr = new
WeatherApp.WeatherObjectPackage.Weather();

// Add an entry to the table
wtr.city = "Denver";
wtr.currDate = "11/26/2001";
wtr.highTemp =20;
wtr.lowTemp = 10;
wtr.humidity =10;
wtr.remarks ="Fairly clear";
woRef.commitData(wtr);

// Retrieve all the records from the table
WeatherApp.WeatherObjectPackage.Weather[] wtrList = null;

wtrList = woRef.retrieveData();

//Print the weather details

int i = 0;
while (wtrList[i].city != null)
{
System.out.println("Date of Forecast " +
wtrList[i].currDate);

System.out.println("Forecasts for the city :" +
wtrList[i].city);

System.out.println("=======================================
=================");
```

```
System.out.println("High Temperature :" +
wtrList[i].highTemp + "F" + "          " +
woRef.convertTemp(wtrList[i].highTemp) + "C" );

System.out.println("Low Temperature :" +      wtrList[i].lowTemp
+ "F" + "          " +      woRef.convertTemp(wtrList[i].lowTemp)
+ "C");

System.out.println("Humidity Factor " +      wtrList[i].humidity
+ "%");

System.out.println("Forecasts for the day : " +
wtrList[i].remarks);

i++ ;
if (i > wtrList.length-1)
    break;

}// end of while

}catch(Exception e) {
System.out.println("Error" + e);
e.printStackTrace(System.out);

} // end of try-catch
} // end of main
} // end of class WeatherClient
```

In the client application, the ORB component is created and initialized. The initial object reference is obtained, and the `narrow()` method of the `NamingContext` interface is used to convert it into a naming context object. The name component for the weather object is created, and it is used to get a reference to the weather object. Now you have the weatherobject reference. Take a look at how the methods are called from the client application.

1. Call the `commitData()` method. Add the weather details for a city — say Denver — and pass them on, as follows:

   ```
   City Name : Denver
   Current Date :11/26/2001
   High Temperature : 30
   Low Temperature : 10
   Humidity: 12
   Forecasts : Scattered Thunderstorms
   ```

   These are the weather details for the city of Denver. Now create an instance of the weather object, called wtr, to assign these weather details. Call the `commitData` method and pass wtr as the input parameter. The call to this method will store these details in the weather table.

2. Call the `retrieveData()` method. This method retrieves all the records from the weather table. Because it is going to return one or more records from the

table, an array of weather objects is used to store the return value. The call to the retrieveData() method looks like this .

```
WeatherApp.WeatherObjectPackage.Weather[] wtrList = null;
wtrList = woRef.retrieveData();
```

This method returns a list of all the records present in the Weather table. The while loop prints the weather forecast for the city by traversing through the list of weather objects.

3. Call the findDataCity() method. The findDataCity method takes the city name as an input parameter. The city name is passed as an input parameter to the findDataCity method, as follows:

```
//Retrieve the weather details for a city
DataInputStream din = new DataInputStream(System.in);
System.out.println("Enter the city name");
String city = din.readLine();
wtrList = woRef.findDataCity(city);
```

This method can return one or more records; therefore it is stored in an array of weather objects. while . A while loop can be used to read the array of weather objects to print the forecast details. The sample code for this loop looks like this :

```
    int i = 0;
    while (wtrList[i].city != null)
    {
    System.out.println("Date of Forecast " +
    wtrList[i].currDate);

    System.out.println("Forecasts for the city :" +
    wtrList[i].city);

    System.out.println("High Temperature :" +
    wtrList[i].highTemp + "F" + "          " +
    woRef.convertTemp(wtrList[i].highTemp) + "C" );

    System.out.println("Low Temperature :" +
    wtrList[i].lowTemp + "F" + "          " +
    woRef.convertTemp(wtrList[i].lowTemp) + "C");

    System.out.println("Humidity Factor " +
    wtrList[i].humidity + "%");

    System.out.println("Forecasts for the day : " +
    wtrList[i].remarks);

    i++ ;
    if (i > wtrList.length-1)
        break;
}
```

4. Call the findData() method. This is a method that finds the weather details for a city on a particular date. This method takes the city and date as the

input parameters and returns the matched record. The readers can look at the sample code described above to print the forecast details.

5. Call the `convertTemp()` method. In the sample code to display the output details, this method is called to convert the temperature from Fahrenheit scale to Celsius scale. The high and low temperatures are displayed, both in Fahrenheit and in Celsius.

Compiling and running the application

1. Compile the WeatherClient.java and WeatherServer.java files.
2. Start the naming service with the command tnameserv:

```
c:> tnameserv  -ORBInitialPort <port number>
```

<*port number*> can be any number. (The default is 900.) If the users give the port number, then it is advisable to give port numbers greater than 1024.

3. Start the WeatherServer with the following command:

```
java WeatherServer -ORBInitialPort <port number>
```

<*port number*> can be any number. (The default is 900.) If the users give the port number, then it is advisable to give port numbers greater than 1024.

4. Run the client with the following command:

```
java WeatherClient -ORBInitialPort <portnumber>
```

<*port number*> can be any number. (The default is 900.) If the users give the port number, then it is advisable to give port numbers greater than 1024.

Figure 19-1 shows the output screen, which displays the output details after the client calls the `retrieveData()` method of the `CORBA` object.

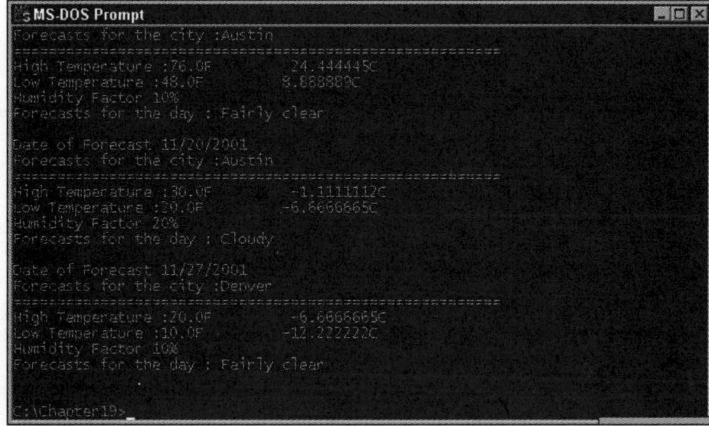

Figure 19-1: Output resulting from a call to the retrieveData() method

Figures 19-2 and 19-3 show the output that will be generated if the client calls the methods `findData()` and `findDataCity()`.

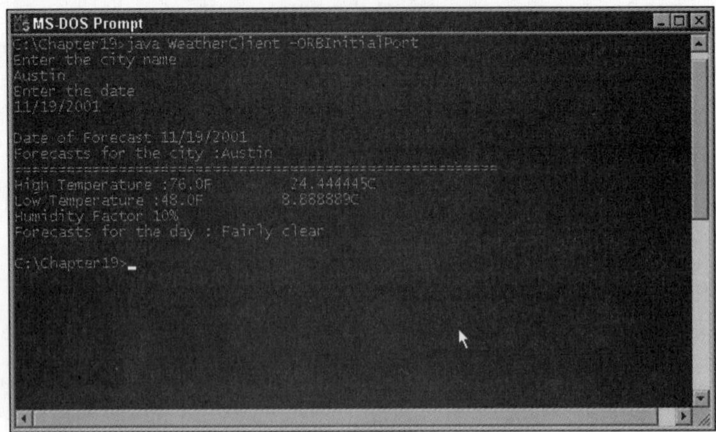

Figure 19-2: Output screen resulting from a call to the findData() method

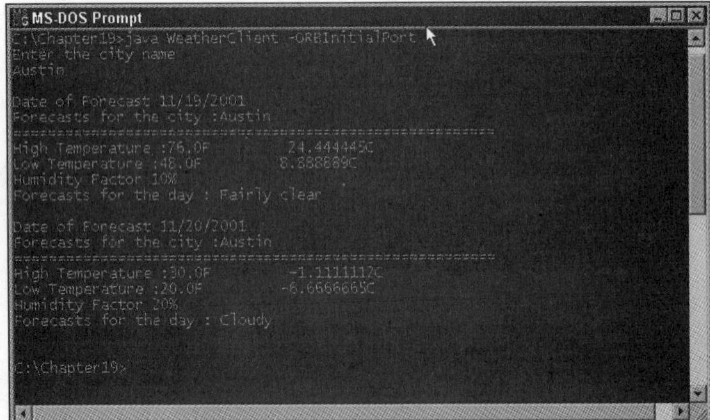

Figure 19-3: Output screen resulting from a call to the findDataCity() method

Accessing the CORBA object from servlets

You can access the CORBA object through various client applications. In this section, you'll learn how to access the CORBA object from Java servlets. Consider a Web application that wants to know the weather forecasts for a particular city. Through an HTML page, this application gets the city name as the input from the user. The HTML page calls a servlet, which in turn calls the findDataCity() method of the CORBA weather object. The findDataCity() method returns the weather forecasts for this particular city for different dates. These details are then displayed to the user in the form of a table.

First, take a look at what the input page (called findWeather.html) contains. This page contains a text field called txtCity and a command button called cmdSubmit. The user enters the city name and clicks the Submit button to retrieve the weather details for a given city. When the user clicks the Submit button, a call is made to the servlet (called WeatherServlet), which retrieves the weather details for this city.

The source code snippet findWeather.html looks like this:

```
<html>
<script language=javascript>
function Submit() {
    document.frmWeather.submit();
}
</script>
<form name=frmWeather method = post action =
"/servlet/WeatherServlet">
<h1> Weather Forecasts</h1>
<body>
<h4> Please enter the city name to get the weather forecasts
</h4>
City name :<input type =text name=txtCity id= txtCity >
<input type=button name=cmdSubmit value=Submit
onclick=Submit()>
</form>
</body>
</html>
```

The entry page for this application is defined in findWeather.jsp. A form called frmWeather is defined, and the control is transferred to the servlet from this page by giving the servlet in the action property of the form. This form defines two fields, the text field, called txtCity, which accepts the city name from the users, and a command button, called cmdSubmit, which submits the query. When the user clicks the Submit button, a Javascript function, called Submit(), is called and submits the form. Now control is transferred to the servlet that processes the request. Take a look at how this servlet is implemented.

To invoke the methods on the CORBA object, the client first needs an object reference. As in the standalone client application you saw earlier in the chapter in the section "Accessing the CORBA object from a client application," the servlet should do the following:

✦ Create and initialize the ORB

✦ Get the initial object reference

✦ Initialize the name component with the weather object

✦ Get the weatherobject reference

✦ Call the methods on the CORBA object

The initialization of the ORB takes place in the init() method of the servlet. The init() method for this servlet looks like this:

```
public void init(ServletConfig config) throws ServletException
{

// Call super as  I am rewriting the init() method
super.init(config);

try {
    String []args = null;

    // Create and Initialize ORB
    ORB orb = ORB.init(args,null);

    //Get the initial object reference
    org.omg.CORBA.Object contextobj =
    orb.resolve_initial_references("NameService");
    rootContext= NamingContextHelper.narrow(contextobj);

    nc = new NameComponent("Weather","");

    }catch(Exception e){
    System.out.println("Exception");
    } // end of try-catch
}// end of init
```

The first call in the init() method calls the super.init(config) in order to call the init() method of the HttpServlet, because you are overwriting this method. Then, the ORB is created and initialized. You can define the ORBInitialPort and the ORBInitialHost in a Properties object in this method, which you can pass as the second parameter to the ORB. The initial object reference is obtained, and the naming context object is created. A new name component for the weather object is also created with the unique ID Weather.

The HTML page that receives the user input will use the POST method to submit the request to the servlet.

Now, code the doPost() method of the HttpServlet so that the request will be processed:

```
public void doPost(HttpServletRequest req,HttpServletResponse
res) throws ServletException,IOException {

WeatherApp.WeatherObjectPackage.Weather[] wtrList = null;
try {

// Get the object reference
NameComponent path[] = {nc};
WeatherObject woRef =
WeatherObjectHelper.narrow(rootContext.resolve(path));

res.setContentType("text/html");
PrintWriter out = res.getWriter();

//Get the input that is the city name
String city = req.getParameter("txtCity");

// Invoke the method on the CORBA weather object        wtrList
= woRef.findDataCity(city);

//Display the details in a table
out.println("<html>");
out.println("<body>");
out.println("<h1>");
out.println("Welcome to FindWeather.com");
out.println("</h1>");
out.println("<table border = 1>");
out.println("<h4>City Name:");
out.println(wtrList[0].city + "</h4>");
out.println("<tr>");
out.println("<th width =100>Date</th>");
out.println("<th width =100>High Temperature");
out.println("(in F)</th>");
out.println("<th width =100>Low Temperature");
out.println("(in F)</th>");
out.println("<th width =100>Humidity </th>");
out.println("<th width =100>Forecasts</th>");
out.println("</tr>");
int i = 0;
while (wtrList[i] != null)
{
    out.println("<tr>");
    out.println("<td>" + wtrList[i].currDate + "</td>");
    out.println("<td>" + wtrList[i].highTemp + "</td>");
    out.println("<td>" + wtrList[i].lowTemp + "</td>");
    out.println("<td>" + wtrList[i].humidity +"</td>");
    out.println("<td>" + wtrList[i].remarks + "</td>");
    out.println("</tr>");
```

```
        i++;
        if (i > wtrList.length-1)
            break;
    }// end of while

    out.println("</table>");
    out.println("</body>");
    out.println("</html>");

    }catch(Exception e) {
     System.out.println("Exception" + e);
    } // end of try-catch
    } // end of doPost
```

In the doPost method, you obtain the request from the HTML page by calling the req.getParameter() method. This retrieves the city name entered by the user. Now the CORBA object reference is created and used to call the findDataCity() method. The city name is passed as the input parameter to this method. The return value from this method is stored in an array of weather objects. This array is traversed to display the weather details in a table.

The full source code for the WeatherServlet.java file looks like this:

```
import javax.servlet.*;
import javax.servlet.http.*;
import java.io.*;
import org.omg.CORBA.*;
import org.omg.CosNaming.*;
import org.omg.CosNaming.NamingContextPackage.*;
import WeatherApp.*;
import WeatherApp.WeatherObjectPackage.*;

public class WeatherServlet extends HttpServlet {

NameComponent nc = null;
NamingContext rootContext = null;
WeatherObject woRef = null ;

public void init(ServletConfig config) throws
ServletException {

// Call super as I am rewriting the init() method
super.init(config);

try {

String []args = null;

// Create and Initialise ORB
ORB orb = ORB.init(args,null);
```

```
//Get the initial object reference
org.omg.CORBA.Object contextobj =
orb.resolve_initial_references("NameService");

rootContext=NamingContextHelper.narrow(contextobj);
nc = new NameComponent("Weather","");
}catch(Exception e){
System.out.println("Exception");
}// end of try-catch
}// end of function init

public void doPost(HttpServletRequest req,HttpServletResponse
res) throws ServletException,IOException {

WeatherApp.WeatherObjectPackage.Weather[] wtrList = null;
try {

// Get the object reference
NameComponent path[] = {nc};
WeatherObject woRef =
WeatherObjectHelper.narrow(rootContext.resolve(path));

res.setContentType("text/html");
PrintWriter out = res.getWriter();

//Get the input that is the city name
String city = req.getParameter("txtCity");

// Invoke the method on the CORBA weather object
wtrList = woRef.findDataCity(city);

//Display the details in a table
out.println("<html>");
out.println("<body>");
out.println("<h1>");
out.println("Welcome to FindWeather.com");
out.println("</h1>");
out.println("<table border = 1>");
out.println("<h4>City Name:");
out.println(wtrList[0].city + "</h4>");
out.println("<tr>");
out.println("<th width =100>Date</th>");
out.println("<th width =100>High Temperature");
out.println("(in F)</th>");
out.println("<th width =100>Low Temperature");
out.println("(in F)</th>");
out.println("<th width =100>Humidity </th>");
out.println("<th width =100>Forecasts</th>");
out.println("</tr>");

int i = 0;
while (wtrList[i] != null)
{
```

```
        out.println("<tr>");
        out.println("<td>" + wtrList[i].currDate + "</td>");
        out.println("<td>" + wtrList[i].highTemp + "</td>");
        out.println("<td>" + wtrList[i].lowTemp + "</td>");
        out.println("<td>" + wtrList[i].humidity +"</td>");
        out.println("<td>" + wtrList[i].remarks + "</td>");
        out.println("</tr>");

        i++ ;
        if (i > wtrList.length-1)
           break;
    }// end of while

    out.println("</table>");
    out.println("</body>");
    out.println("</html>");
    }catch(Exception e) {
    System.out.println("Exception" + e);
    } // end of try-catch

    }// end of function doPost
    }// end of class WeatherServlet
```

Compiling and running the servlet

Now you'll use the JRun Web server to determine whether the WeatherServlet is working properly. The class file of the WeatherServlet and the WeatherApp folder created by the idltojava compiler should be placed in the \JRun\servers\default\default-app\web-inf\class folder. The HTML page is placed in a folder called project under \JRun\servers\default\default-app.

1. Start the naming service by typing the following command at the command prompt:

   ```
   c:\>tnameserv  -ORBInitialPort  <port number>
   ```

   <port number> can by any number (the default is 900). If you give a port number here, then you must send the same port number as a property to the ORB object in the init() method. If the user gives a port number, then it is advisable to use a port number greater than 1024.

2. Start the CORBA Weather Server by typing the following command at the command prompt:

   ```
   C:\> java WeatherServer -ORBInitialPort <portnumber>
   ```

   <port number> can by any number (the default is 900). If the user gives a port number, then it is advisable to use a port number greater than 1024.

3. Start the JRun Default Web server. Open the browser window and type the following command in the link column to test the servlet:

   ```
   http://localhost:8100/project/findWeather.html
   ```

Figure 19-4 shows the input page.

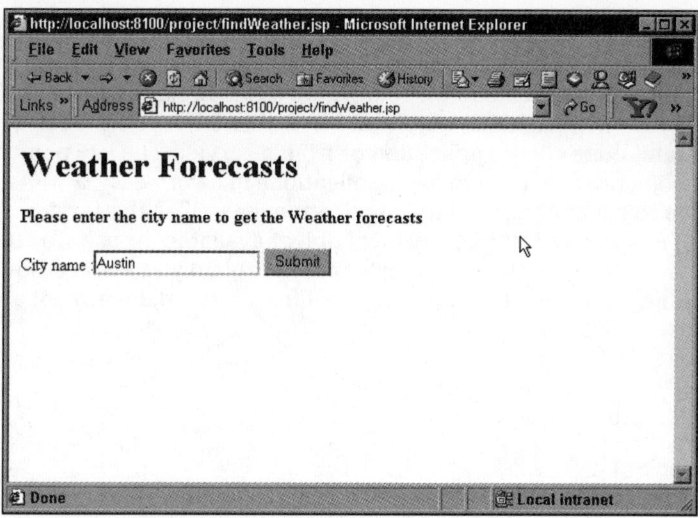

Figure 19-4: Input page for entering the city name

The user enters the city name as `Austin`; when the user clicks the Submit button, control is transferred to the servlet that processes the request. The servlet calls the `findDataCity` method of the CORBA weather object and displays the weather forecast details for Austin in a table. Figure 19-5 shows the response of the servlet.

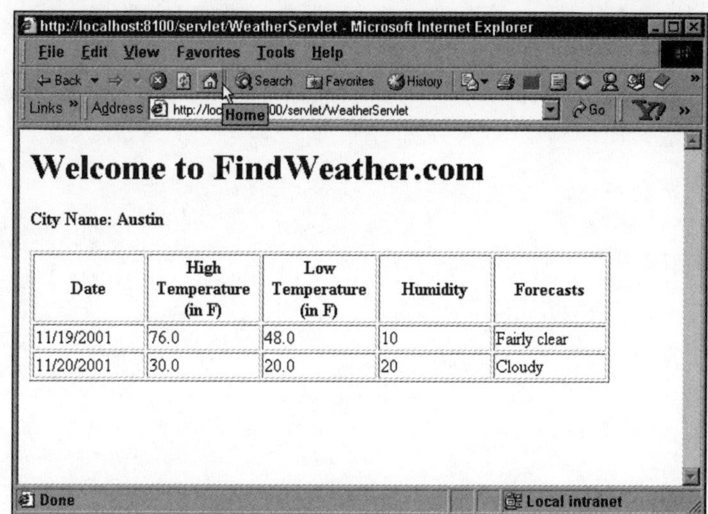

Date	High Temperature (in F)	Low Temperature (in F)	Humidity	Forecasts
11/19/2001	76.0	48.0	10	Fairly clear
11/20/2001	30.0	20.0	20	Cloudy

Figure 19-5: Weather forecast for Austin

The servlet application acts as a client to access the CORBA weather object. The servlet can also call all the other methods defined in the CORBA weather object.

Summary

This chapter mainly concentrates on how to develop a CORBA application. In this chapter, we saw how to write a `CORBA` object and how that `CORBA` object can be accessed from a standalone client application or from a servlet. The key point here is that the `CORBA` object can be used in any applications in a very easy way. As you have seen earlier in this chapter, the client application, as well as the servlet, manipulates the `CORBA` object just like any local object available for use. To summarize, in this chapter we have worked on an example to explain you learned how to develop a `CORBA` object and how it can be accessed from a standalone client application and from a servlet.

✦ ✦ ✦

CHAPTER 20

Why Dream of Jini?

✦ ✦ ✦ ✦

In This Chapter

Running and accessing Jini services in the Jini distribution

Creating your own services and joining a lookup service

Requesting and using services you discover on a lookup service

Adding attributes to services and selecting services based on those attributes

Caching discovered services to reduce network traffic

Using RMI to split a service between a proxy and a piece that doesn't travel to the client

✦ ✦ ✦ ✦

You've seen several architectures for distributed computing. For each of them, you've had to know where to look for the services, how to look for them, and how to communicate with them. With Jini, a service announces its availability. A client looking for a service can discover it and use it by asking around for a service that implements an interface. Referring to these processes as "announcing" or "asking around" may seem casual, and in many ways the process itself is fairly casual.

In this chapter, you'll take a simple non-distributed calculator example and turn it into a Jini service. You'll then add more and more of the features of Jini, making the service more robust. You can't cover all Jini's features in a single chapter, but this chapter will take you well on the way to understanding discovery, joining and leaving, leasing, caching, and using RMI in distributing a Jini service.

A Quick Look at Jini

Jini is a collection of simple ideas that combine to provide a powerful environment for network services. You can forget whether the service is provided by hardware, software, or both. You just concentrate on what you want done and contract with a service to provide it. When you create a service and want to make it available, you announce your product, and others on the network are able to discover it.

Jini is not, however, a naming/directory service. Deciding how to catalog your services is hard. What if a service provides more than one function and forgets to advertise itself in multiple places? What if, as you'll see in Chapter 21, using a slightly different word for the same category results in no matches? Additionally, once you have matched with a service, you have to know how to interact with it.

As you know from using Java, you know how to use a class if you know its interface. So Jini services need to implement one or more interfaces that may be known to the client. The client can then search for services that implement the interfaces with the functionality they need. This process may not be fine-grained enough. In the examples in this chapter, a client can search for a calculator and then later look more closely for a calculator that adds or subtracts. You can specify the lookup group you're in, so you don't end up ordering pizza from a pizza service that isn't close enough to deliver.

Unlike Web Services and CORBA, Jini depends on there being Java at both the client and service ends. The client is downloading Java code to his or her machine and using it to perform a service or to act as a proxy for a service being provided remotely. This code helps the client understand how the service can be used. If the service comes with additional functionality that the client didn't anticipate, it can announce these capabilities to the client. Jini not only notifies you when a service is available, but it also is designed so that you can discover when a service is no longer there for you to use. Services negotiate and renew leases, so a mechanism is in place to ensure that they check in once in a while to announce their continued presence.

Why do we need Jini?

Jim Waldo, chief architect for Jini, makes the point that computers are now involved in our everyday lives in ways that we don't even notice. If you drive to work, you've already interacted with a dozen computers before sitting down at your desk. We can't afford to have a human involved in every computer interaction. They need to be able to interact without us being involved. Waldo often cites Peter Deutsch's Eight Fallacies of Distributed Computing. You can find them listed on James Gosling's Web site at `http://java.sun.com/people/jag/Fallacies.html`. They are preceded by the warning that "[e]ssentially everyone, when they first build a distributed application, makes the following eight assumptions. All prove to be false in the long run and all cause big trouble and painful learning experiences." The Eight Fallacies are as follows:

- The network is reliable.
- Latency is zero.
- Bandwidth is infinite.
- The network is secure.
- Topology doesn't change.
- There is one administrator.
- Transport cost is zero.
- The network is homogeneous.

One of the goals for Jini is to make the developer aware of the risks involved in distributed computing. Start by asking the simplest questions. Instead of hoping that the network never fails, ask what happens when the network eventually does fail. Even more simply, ask what happens when the machine that hosts a service crashes. Imagine a system on which your running application can get a good idea of "what else is out there," and take advantage of this new knowledge.

Jini resources

The installation, setup, and startup phase is the most frustrating part of working with Jini. If something isn't working right, it is likely that others have encountered a similar problem. In addition, while you are creating your Jini services and clients, you will most likely recreate problems that others have seen. You may want to check out Bill Venners' Jini resources on his Artima site at `http://artima.com/jini/`. In addition to providing great Jini advice and reprints of his *JavaWorld* articles, Bill provides links to other sites and commentary on useful resources on the Web. Jan Newmarch has an online Jini tutorial at `http://pandonia.canberra.edu.au/java/jini/tutorial/Jini.xml`, and Noel Enete's nuggets, available at `http://www.enete.com/`, are quite helpful. Keith Edwards' Jini Planet is online at `http://www.kedwards.com/jini/`. Keith's troubleshooting section is invaluable. Wish we'd found it long ago.

Although the Jini community is a subset of the Java community, Jini folks tend to be a bit different. You'll find links to the Jini community, as well as ongoing projects that you are encouraged to join, upcoming events, resources, and discussions at `http://www.jini.org`. For the really good bits, you'll have to join (it's free). The official Jini releases have code names corresponding to stops along the MBTA Red Line in Boston heading into Harvard Square (and hopefully out again). The Alewife release is the 1.2 release currently in beta. It is designed to get Jini up and running faster and more efficiently than in past releases. The Davis release will address security issues in Jini technology.

Introducing Our Example

In this chapter, our running example will be a simple calculator. It will be able to add and subtract two numbers. You'll start with the non-distributed version running on a single machine. Although you could easily have a single class that adds and subtracts based on what method is called, you'll use `Adder` and `Subtractor` classes that implement the `Calculator` interface. A separate client will then create an `Adder` object and a `Subtractor` object and ask each to perform its calculations.

Although this seems unnecessarily complex, when you later create Jini services you will be better able to separate what is required by Jini. You'll continue to modify the example to add more and more Jini functionality as the chapter progresses. So that you can modify the various commands for your settings, create the files for this example in the C:\J2EEBible\NonDistributedCalculator directory.

The Calculator interface

The `Calculator` interface specifies two methods, shown in the following code. The `getOperationName()` method returns a `String` that describes the operation being performed. The `getValueOfResult()` method returns the result of the operation on the two arguments being passed in. For simplicity, this application will only add and subtract numbers that are of type `int`.

```
package NonDistributedCalculator;

public interface Calculator {
  public String getOperationName();
  public int getValueOfResult(int firstOperand,
                              int secondOperand);
}
```

The Adder and Subtractor classes

There isn't much to do to implement the `Calculator` interface. The `Adder` needs only to return the `String` `"sum"` from the `getOperationName()` method and the sum of the two operands from the `getValueOfResult()` method.

```
package NonDistributedCalculator;

public class Adder implements Calculator {
  public String getOperationName(){
    return "sum";
  }
  public int getValueOfResult(int firstOperand,
    int secondOperand){
    return firstOperand + secondOperand;
  }
}
```

The `Subtractor` method is analogous to `"sum"` replaced by `"difference"` and to the difference of the two operands being returned from the `getValueOfResult()` method.

```
package NonDistributedCalculator;

public class Subtractor implements Calculator{
  public String getOperationName(){
    return "difference";
  }
  public int getValueOfResult(int firstOperand,
    int secondOperand){
    return firstOperand - secondOperand;
  }
}
```

The Client

The `Client` is just a class for exercising these Calculator services. Its only real method is `getAndDisplayResult()`, which takes a `Calculator` along with the two operands. It then asks the `Calculator` for the operation name and will get `"sum"` if the `Calculator` is an `Adder` and `"difference"` if the `Calculator` is a `Subtractor`. It then gets the results of the calculation and displays them. You can already view `Adder` and `Subtractor` as services and see how you could easily extend the application to include other operations.

```
package NonDistributedCalculator;

public class Client {

  public void getAndDisplayResult(Calculator calculator,
    int firstOperand, int secondOperand){

    String operationName = calculator.getOperationName();
    int operationResult =
      calculator.getValueOfResult(firstOperand, secondOperand);

    System.out.println("The "+operationName + " of " +
      firstOperand + " and " +
      secondOperand + " is " + operationResult);
  }

  public static void main(String[] args){
    Client client = new Client();
    client.getAndDisplayResult(new Adder(), 5, 6);
    client.getAndDisplayResult(new Subtractor(), 24,7);
  }

}
```

In the next section, you'll download and install Jini and get it configured and running. You'll then return to this example and convert it to a set of Jini services and a client.

Getting Jini Up and Running

You may remember from Chapter 15 that getting all the RMI services running properly is difficult. For the most part, the Jini community has addressed that issue by creating a version that is easy to install and to run.

Note

As with RMI, it is a good idea to run these examples on at least two different machines, each of which is connected to a network (an internal network is fine). You may recall that when you ran RMI examples in which the client and server code were in the same file or even on the same machine, shortcuts were taken. If you aren't able to develop on two different machines, at least test in such a setup before deploying.

Installing Jini

Download the latest version of the Jini Technology Starter kit by following the links from http://java.sun.com/jini. (In this chapter, I use version 1.2 beta in all the examples.) Unzip the distribution. The code in this chapter was tested on a Windows box and on a UNIX box (actually a Mac running OS X). In each case, I unzipped the distribution into a directory named files. On the Windows machine, this directory is C:\files, and on the Mac, it is <*home directory*>/files. This isn't a huge point, but it will help you see how to adjust the configuration file to your own settings.

The instructions for the rest of the chapter are given in terms of the Windows installation on a single machine. Jini actually runs more easily on a Mac. In particular, if you want to develop Jini applications on a Windows machine that isn't connected to the network, you'll have to look around the Jini FAQs for the latest information on how to configure your computer.

Other books give the exact same directions twice, once for Windows users and once for UNIX users. The differences are mainly that Windows bat files are replaced by UNIX shell scripts and that the paths have to be altered in the usual ways. That is, the base of the path depends on where you install Jini and your other files, and the direction of the separators changes from \ on Windows to /on UNIX.

Create two subfolders inside the C:\J2EEBible directory. Name one of them CalculatorClient and the other CalculatorService. Again, you may want to have CalculatorClient on one machine and CalculatorService on another. As a final step, you'll follow the directions in the next paragraph to place two files in your CalculatorClient directory that you'll need later on. (These instructions are included here and not later so that when you install Jini on another machine and something isn't quite working right, you'll find them and say, "Oh yeah, that's right.")

Open up a command window and navigate into CalculatorService. You are going to pull a single file from each of two jar files in the Jini distribution. You'll use the jar utility and specify the path to the jar files and the actual class files you're looking for. Type in the following:

```
jar xvf C:\files\jini1_2\lib\jini-ext.jar
net\jini\lookup\ServiceDiscoveryManager$LookupCacheImpl$LookupL
istener_Stub.class
```

There is a space between jar and net and not the line break that you see in the preceding code. You should type your command in all on a single line. You have specified that you are extracting a particular file and that you want verbose output. Of course, UNIX users should reverse the direction of the slashes and adjust the file location of jini-ext.jar to agree with their installation. You should see the following response:

```
extracted
net\jini\lookup\ServiceDiscoveryManager$LookupCacheImpl$LookupL
istener_Stub.class
```

Extract the other class with this command:

```
jar xvf C:\files\jini1_2\lib\jini-core.jar
net\jini\core\event\RemoteEventListener.class.
```

You will get feedback telling you that the class had been extracted. You're now ready to run the GUI tool.

The GUI tool

You can set up the various Jini components from the command line using multiple windows or you can just use the GUI tool that ships as a part of Jini. In this book, you'll use the GUI tool, but if you prefer the command line you can see the commands that result from pressing the start buttons on the tool and enter those by hand. The reason you may not want to use the command-line method is that you are constantly specifying the additions to the `CLASSPATH`. It is tedious to repeatedly type in these long unenlightening strings, and it is easy to make a mistake. Instead, you will probably want to open up the GUI tool and locate the appropriate properties file. You will modify the settings so that the various services run on your machine for your configuration. You will then save these settings into a modified properties file and open it up each time to avoid having to remember your customized settings.

You should be warned (again) that getting Jini up and running is the most frustrating part of working with Jini. The situation has greatly improved since the early days. If you continue to have problems, check the installation docs to see if anything has changed since the 1.2 beta release. Make sure you have a network connection and that you have configured it as described in the following section. Yell loudly. Check out the Jini resources section for links to helpful hints. Many of them include troubleshooting techniques.

Start up the GUI launcher

To start up the GUI launcher, type in the following code, after making adjustments to the various paths:

```
java -cp files/jini1_2/lib/jini-ext.jar;files/jini1_2/lib/
jini-examples.jar com.sun.jini.example.launcher.StartService
```

Here you are, of course, running the StartService application and adding both the jar file that contains it and a jar file with other Jini utilities to the `CLASSPATH`. You will be running this launcher enough that you should save this command into a bat file or a shell script that you can easily run. The GUI launcher application starts up, and the window in Figure 20-1 appears.

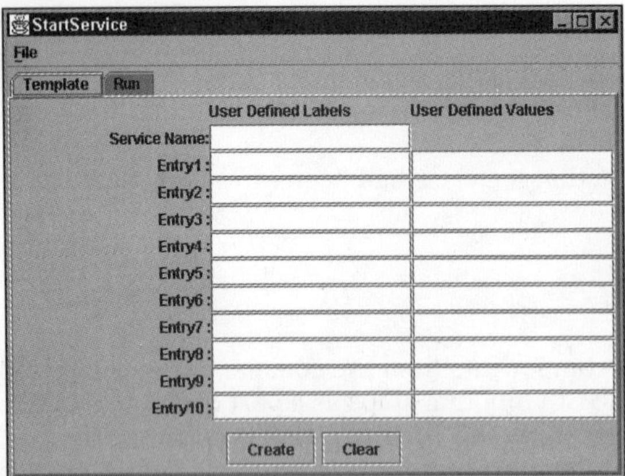

Figure 20-1: The Jini StartService launcher

The cool thing about this application is that it is flexible enough that you can use it to start up any Java application. The template that you see in Figure 20-1 enables you to add the command-line parameters you need to pass in. Click the Run tab, and you will see a start button and a stop button for the application you just added. You can use them to run any of your own Java applications.

In this chapter, you'll just use StartService to launch your Jini-related applications. Load the configuration file by selecting File ➪ Open Property File, and then navigate to the example\launcher subdirectory in your Jini 1.2 distribution. There you'll see two property files, one for Windows and one for UNIX. Choose the one that is appropriate for your needs. Mac OS X users should choose UNIX.

You should see many tabs added to your StartService launcher. Click the Run tab, and you should see something like what is shown in Figure 20-2.

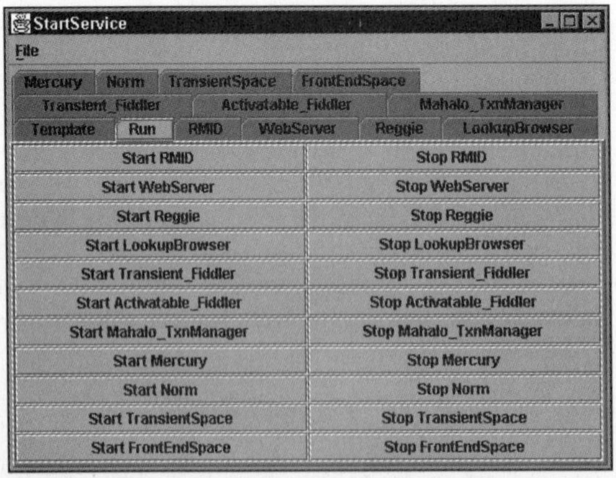

Figure 20-2: Applications you can run from the launcher

In the following sections, you will customize the default settings and then save your new settings to your own properties file that you can use the next time you start up the launcher.

Startup rmid

You may remember from your experience with RMI that working with the RMI activation daemon introduced some complexity. In Jini this complexity is, for the most part, hidden from you. You start up rmid and a Jini lookup service (in our case Reggie). Usually, this is where the difficulties come in starting Jini. After you start up Reggie, you may get one or more errors or exceptions until you get your configuration right. To configure rmid, use the default settings shown in Figure 20-3.

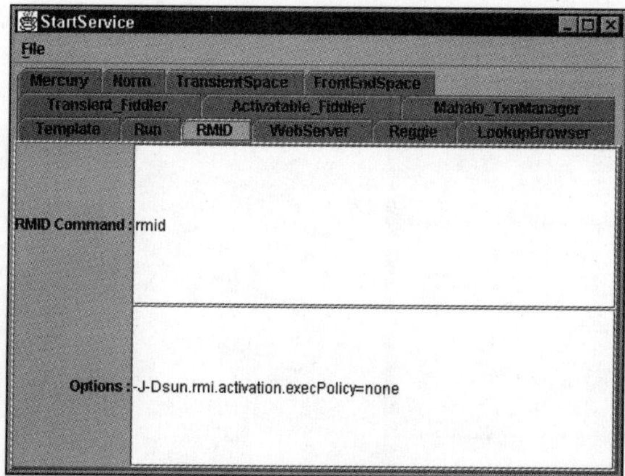

Figure 20-3: The rmid settings

Go ahead and return to the Run tab and click Start RMID. The console window should display the following:

```
the command line is: rmid -J-Dsun.rmi.activation.execPolicy=none
```

You could also have started rmid by typing that command yourself. The GUI tool is just a convenience to keep you from having to do that.

As discussed in Chapter 15, you will want to change the security policy once you are ready to deploy your application. For general security improvements to the Jini architecture, you should watch for news of the Davis release at `http://www.jini.org/`.

If you have to cycle rmid (in other words, shut it down and restart it), you should discard the log file before starting it up again. In other words, use the stop button labeled "Stop RMID" or the command `rmid -stop` to kill rmid. Then delete the log file generated by rmid. Then use the Start RMID button on the GUI launcher to start rmid again. If you start up rmid and get a screen filled with problems, look for the log file and delete it.

Start up a Web server

Really there is no reason why the Web server has to be started up next. You could have started it before rmid or after Reggie. The instructions are given in this order to match the order of the buttons on your GUI tool.

In the course of this chapter, you will start up several Web servers. You will need to serve up files from the CalculatorService and CalculatorClient directories. For now you are setting up a Web server to serve up the jar files in the \lib subdirectory of the jini1_2 distribution. The \lib subdirectory includes, among others, the reggie.jar file. The port is set to 8081, and the Web server itself is in the tools.jar file in the lib directory. Your Web server configurations should look like what you see in Figure 20-4.

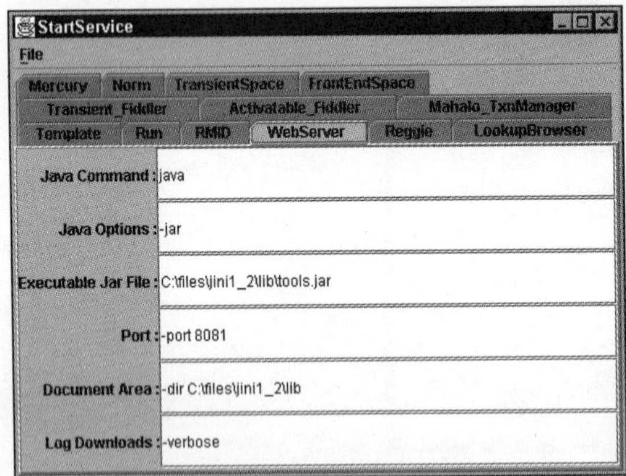

Figure 20-4: The Web server configuration

Start up your Web server from the Run tab. Here's the resulting command:

```
java -jar C:\files\jini1_2\lib\tools.jar -port 8081 -dir C:\files\jini1_2\lib
-verbose
```

You will use other ports for the Web servers being used for CalculatorService and CalculatorClient in our example application. As long as it's unused, it doesn't much matter which port you choose. You will need to make sure your other Jini applications know about and use whichever port you choose. The default is now 8081. In earlier Jini days, the default was 8080, and so some people change to that. In Chapters 3 and 4, however, you would have used 8080 to run Tomcat. If you are running Tomcat and Jini, then you need to make sure you are not using the same port for each. The long and the short of it is that it doesn't matter which port you choose, and so for this example we will stay with the default of 8081 in the default properties files shipped in the Jini distribution.

Start up Reggie

As I mentioned earlier, you'll find most of your initial problems in getting a Jini service up and running in this step. You should check the resources for troubleshooting, but the basic setup is this. Make sure you are connected to a network and that the RMI activation daemon is running. If you have tried to start up reggie before, make sure you have deleted the log that was created. If you are on a UNIX system, you will have to create the directory into which reggie will write its log. For example, if your log is to be written into the file /Users/yourName/files/reggie_log then reggie_log should not exist but the directory /Users/yourName/files must exist.

You will need to specify where reggie.jar is. If you have expanded the jini1_2 somewhere other than in the default location, you will need to make the usual adjustments. You will also need to specify the codebase, as you did with RMI. As with RMI, you shouldn't use `localhost` because that means different machines to different users. You would be indicating `localhost` because the code is on your machine. Then a client from another machine contacts you and asks where the files are that it needs to download. It is told `localhost`. The client says, "Oh, I know where `localhost` is. It's on my machine." You want to use the URL for the machine running reggie. In this case, we are connected to a router, and the machine's address is 192.168.1.101.

You will also need to specify the port. All that matters here is that the port matches the setting you chose for the Web server. The Web server will be used to access reggie, so these values must match. As before, you need to specify a policy file. (You will most likely want a more restrictive policy file than the policy.all that you're using in this example when it's time to deploy your application.) You can choose to keep the log file wherever you'd like. You'll be saving this property file so you'll be storing whatever settings you now enter. If reggie doesn't start up correctly and you want to cycle reggie without cycling rmid, you can just input another value for the log directory as a temporary measure.

Figure 20-5 shows the reggie settings.

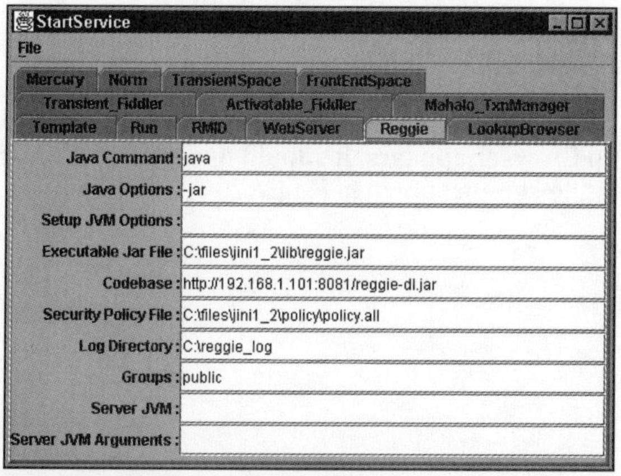

Figure 20-5: The reggie settings

Hold your breath and start up reggie using the start button in the Run tab. If all goes well, reggie should start pretty quietly. You'll have to wait a little while for things to settle down to see if it really started up correctly. You can wait 30 seconds or to see if any error messages appear. You usually find out in less than a minute. Now it's time to see what you've done.

Start up a Lookup Browser

You now have a running Jini service. It's hard to tell. There's no visual evidence that anything is happening. The Lookup Browser will find lookup services and enable you to find information about the various services that their providers have made available. In your first application, you'll write a fairly ordinary service, and later on you'll provide information so that clients can locate the services they want.

The settings for the Lookup Browser are similar to the ones for reggie. You will again need to specify a security policy and codebase as well as the location of the jar file containing the `Browser` class file and the full name of the class being run. Make the adjustments to the values shown in Figure 20-6 to fit the location of the Jini distribution and your IP address and port number.

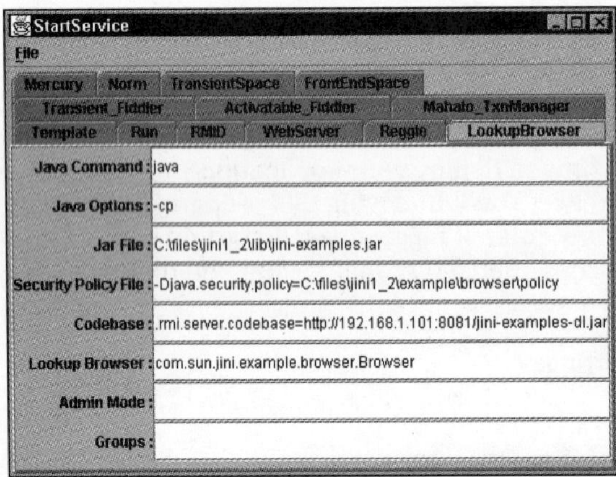

Figure 20-6: The Lookup Browser settings

After a few seconds, the Lookup Browser appears. It should find your running reggie service, and you should see the screen shown in Figure 20-7.

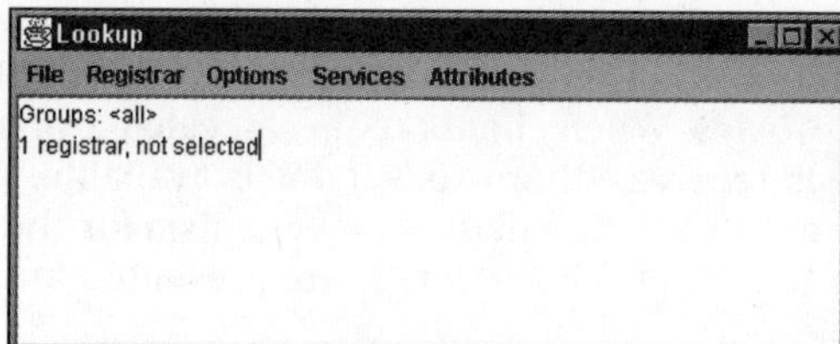

Figure 20-7: The Lookup Browser

Select the only host being displayed and you can find out more information about the reggie services by using the checkboxes for the items in the other menus. You'll see more on this later in this chapter, but have fun poking around for now. At this point, if you have another machine on the same network, go ahead and follow the steps for starting up rmid, a Web server, reggie, and a Lookup Browser. You should see each machine discover and register with the other. This is *automatic discovery*, and joining is just part of the magic of Jini. While you're at it, kill off reggie and the Web server in one of the machines. After a while the other machine realizes that the reggie service on the remote machine is no longer there. You will again see only a single host listed. Again, magic. Leasing means that you won't continue to believe you have access to resources that are no longer there. You'll learn more about these features as you move through the examples in this chapter.

Save your properties file

OK, this probably doesn't deserve a separate heading, but nothing is more frustrating than finally getting Jini working and quitting the tool, only to have to configure it again later. Before you quit, choose File ⇨ Save As and save your property file under some useful name, such as customJini.properties. For convenience, place the file in the directory that is first opened when the JFileChooser appears. That way you can quickly load your config files without searching around.

A Simple Proxy Jini Calculator Service

You'll modify the non-distributed calculator example to run as a Jini service. Imagine that an adding service could just make itself available, and you could use it whenever you needed to add two numbers together. Perhaps this example seems trivial, but you can imagine a spell-checking service, a printing service, or a service for ordering dinner. For simplicity, begin by creating a subdirectory called ProxyCalculator in both the CalculatorClient and the CalculatorService directories.

In this version of the example, you will begin by modifying the `Calculator` interface. The classes that perform the actual addition and subtraction will be sent from the server to the lookup service as proxies. When clients request a calculator service from the lookup service, they will receive either proxy if one is available. What really changes in this version of the example is the delivery mechanism for the service and the request mechanism for the client. Those details are presented in this section.

Remember that you can run this application with the CalculatorClient directory on one machine, the CalculatorService on another, and the actual lookup service on a third. For the purpose of this example, I will assume that you are running on a single machine with the directories set up as specified . Inside of the ProxyCalculator subdirectory of CalculatorService, you will create the `Calculator` interface as well as the `AdderProxy`, `SubtractorProxy`, `AddingService`, and `SubtractingService` classes described in the following sections. The ProxyCalculator subdirectory of CalculatorClient will contain the same `Calculator` interface as is found in CalculatorService. It will also contain the `CalculatorClient` class described in the following section.

The Calculator interface

As in all Java programming, the interface is like a contract between two classes. One class wants to use another class that, to it, looks like a calculator. Another class promises to behave like a calculator when it implements the `Calculator` interface. This means that the client class knows what messages it is allowed to send to the service that implements the interface, and the implementing class knows how it is expected to respond. You can see that both the client side and the service side must know what the interface is, so the following `Calculator` interface must be in both the CalculatorClient and the CalculatorService directories.

```
package ProxyCalculator;

import java.rmi.Remote;
import java.rmi.RemoteException;

public interface Calculator extends Remote{
  public String getOperationName() throws RemoteException;
  public int getValueOfResult(int firstOperand,
    int secondOperand) throws RemoteException;
}
```

The chief additions here are that `Calculator` now extends `java.rmi.Remote` and that each of the two methods now throws a `java.rmi.RemoteException`. It is important to know when you could be making a remote method call and to be able to handle the problems that could arise.

The proxies for the adding and subtracting services

In the original application, the Adder and Subtractor classes performed the actual calculation. As you convert them to Jini services, you will need to divide up the responsibilities between the piece that actually travels to the client machine and the piece that remains on your server. Later in the chapter you'll create a thin client that calls back to the server for all the results. For now, the calculating abilities will be contained in the proxy objects, and the server will contain the logic for delivering the service.

Inside the directory CalculatorService you will create the two files AdderProxy.java and SubtractorProxy.java. Because the AdderProxy will be delivered over the wire, it needs to be serializable. Other than that very few changes to Adder are necessary. Because the proxy does not need to communicate with the service to return results to the client, the proxy does not need to accomplish anything extra. Here's the code:

```
package ProxyCalculator;

import java.io.Serializable;

public class AdderProxy implements Calculator, Serializable {
  public AdderProxy(){}

  public String getOperationName(){
    return "sum";
  }
  public int getValueOfResult(int firstOperand,
    int secondOperand){
    return firstOperand + secondOperand;
  }
}
```

Similarly, Subtractor needs to be changed to the following:

```
package ProxyCalculator;

import java.io.Serializable;

public class SubtractorProxy implements Calculator,
Serializable{
  public SubtractorProxy(){}
  public String getOperationName(){
    return "difference";
  }
  public int getValueOfResult(int firstOperand, int
secondOperand){
    return firstOperand - secondOperand;
  }
}
```

Create the services

Once you have separated out the actual functionality that you are presenting to the client, you can take a clear look at the delivery mechanism. In this first example, you will use a very simple model. You will set up a security manager as follows:

```
private void setUpSecurityManager(){
    if (System.getSecurityManager() == null) {
      System.setSecurityManager(new RMISecurityManager());
    }
  }
```

When you run the application, you will pass in a security policy as a command-line argument. If, however, a user forgets to do this, your application will create a `java.rmi.RMISecurityManager` for him or her.

The next step is to set up the `net.jini.lookup.JoinManager`, as follows:

```
private void setUpJoinManager(){
    try{
      JoinManager joinManager =
        new JoinManager(new AdderProxy(), null,
         (ServiceIDListener)null, null, null);
    } catch (IOException e) {}
  }
```

Two signatures are possible for the `JoinManager` constructor. In the one you've used, the first parameter is a handle to the proxy service. In other words, an instance of `AdderProxy` will be communicating back to this instance of `AddingService`, so when setting up the `JoinManager` for `AddingService` you have to tie it to the object that is referring back to `AddingService`. The other parameters have been set to `null` and will be explained in later examples as you add their functionality.

It may look odd to see a `null` cast to the type `ServiceIDListener`. This is because the signatures of the two constructors differ only in their type. You use the constructor that takes a `ServiceIDListener` if you are registering your service for the first time and haven't yet been assigned a `ServiceID`. Each service should have a unique `ServiceID` so that if you register your service with more than one lookup service, a client can tell that the two or more apparently different services it is finding are really the same. The first time you register a service you can find out the `ServiceID` it's been assigned and then subsequently use this `ServiceID` by using the other constructor for `JoinManager` when registering with other lookup services. In this chapter, you won't actually be coding in this storage of the `ServiceID`.

Here's the entire code for AddingService:

```
package ProxyCalculator;

import net.jini.core.lookup.ServiceItem;
import java.io.IOException;
import java.rmi.RemoteException;
import java.rmi.RMISecurityManager;
import net.jini.lookup.JoinManager;
import net.jini.lookup.ServiceIDListener;

public class AddingService {

  public AddingService() throws IOException {
    setUpSecurityManager();
    setUpJoinManager();
  }

  private void setUpSecurityManager(){
    if (System.getSecurityManager() == null) {
      System.setSecurityManager(new RMISecurityManager());
    }
  }

  private void setUpJoinManager(){
    try{
      JoinManager joinManager =
        new JoinManager(new AdderProxy(), null,
          (ServiceIDListener)null, null, null);
    } catch (IOException e) {}
  }

  public static void main(String args[]) {
    try {
      new AddingService();
      Thread.sleep(5000);
    } catch (IOException e) {
      e.printStackTrace();
    } catch (InterruptedException e){
      e.printStackTrace();
    }
  }
}
```

Similarly, here's SubtractingService:

```
package ProxyCalculator;

import net.jini.core.lookup.ServiceItem;
import java.io.IOException;
import java.rmi.RemoteException;
import java.rmi.RMISecurityManager;
import net.jini.lookup.JoinManager;
import net.jini.lookup.ServiceIDListener;
```

```
public class SubtractingService {

  public SubtractingService() throws IOException {
    setUpSecurityManager();
    setUpJoinManager();
  }

  private void setUpSecurityManager(){
    if (System.getSecurityManager() == null) {
      System.setSecurityManager(new RMISecurityManager());
    }
  }

  private void setUpJoinManager(){
    try{
      JoinManager joinManager =
        new JoinManager(new SubtractorProxy(), null,
          (ServiceIDListener)null, null, null);
    } catch (IOException e) {}
  }

  public static void main(String args[]) {
    try {
      new SubtractingService();
      Thread.sleep(5000);
    } catch (IOException e) {
      e.printStackTrace();
    } catch (InterruptedException e){
      e.printStackTrace();
    }
  }
}
```

At this point you can skip down to the sections on compiling and running the application before getting the client up and running. You can run your adding and subtracting services and see that you can view them in the lookup browser. You won't be able to see much, but you can verify that they are there, and then you can see them go away.

The Jini Calculator client

You can separate the functionality that uses the `Calculator` from the parts of the client that register with the lookup service to find the `Calculator`, as you did on the service side. This separation made practical sense on the service side because you were delivering the proxy object to the client via the lookup service. On the client side more needs to be done, but it can all be done by a single object.

As in the case of the service, you've got to start by ensuring that a `java.rmi.SecurityManager` has been set up. Before you perform the calculation, you have quite a bit of setup work to do. This shouldn't be surprising if you consider what you're trying to accomplish. You want to perform a calculation using an object that you don't have. Not only don't you have it, you don't really know where it is. Not only that, but you don't really know where anyone is who knows where the service might be.

As a first step, you set up a `net.jini.lookup.ServiceDiscoveryManager` as follows:

```
private void setUpServiceDiscoveryManager() throws
  RemoteException, IOException{
  serviceDiscoveryManager =
    new ServiceDiscoveryManager(null,null);
}
```

Later in the chapter, you'll expand on this basic setup to include caching. For now, as a next step, you're going to ask the `ServiceDiscoveryManager` that you've just constructed to find you the service you're looking for. Before you do that, you must somehow describe the service you are looking for. You do this using a `net.jini.core.lookup.ServiceTemplate`, which you'll set up as follows:

```
private void setUpServiceTemplate(){
  Class[] types = new Class[] { Calculator.class };
  serviceTemplate = new ServiceTemplate(null, types, null);
}
```

If you know the particular `ServiceID` of the service you are searching for, you can specify it as the first argument of the `ServiceTemplate` constructor. If not, you can pass in an array containing `Class` elements that, in this case, specify the interface you are trying to match. You will get back services that at least satisfy this specification. The final argument is not currently being used. It will hold an array of attributes. In this example you are searching for a `Calculator`. This means that you aren't specifying whether the item you get back is capable of adding, subtracting, or some other service. You can specify the type of `Calculator` by passing in an attribute that describes more carefully the operation desired. You can either process that restriction here as you look for services or apply a filter to the list of services that you get back from the lookup service.

Now that you have set up the `ServiceTemplate` you can use it to have your `ServiceDiscoveryManager` return a `net.jini.core.lookup.ServiceItem`, as follows:

```
private void setUpServiceItem(){
  try {
    serviceItem = serviceDiscoveryManager.lookup(
      serviceTemplate,null,200000);
  } catch (InterruptedException e){
    e.printStackTrace();
  } catch (RemoteException e){
    e.printStackTrace();
  }
}
```

The important feature to note is that in this example you are using the `lookup()` method from the `ServiceDiscoveryManager`. Later you will use the `lookup()` method from a different object to perform the same task. The `null` you are passing in indicates that you are not specifying a `ServiceFilter`. The `200000` is a `long` that specifies how long in milliseconds you are willing to wait for a result. After that amount of time the `ServiceDiscoveryManager` will return a matching `ServiceItem` or a `null`. Here's the entire client code:

```
package ProxyCalculator;

import net.jini.core.lookup.ServiceTemplate;
import java.io.IOException;
import java.rmi.RemoteException;
import java.rmi.RMISecurityManager;
import net.jini.lookup.ServiceDiscoveryManager;
import net.jini.core.lookup.ServiceItem;
import net.jini.lookup.ServiceDiscoveryListener;

public class CalculatorClient  {
  private ServiceTemplate serviceTemplate;
  private ServiceDiscoveryManager serviceDiscoveryManager;
  private ServiceItem serviceItem;

  public CalculatorClient() throws IOException {
    setUpSecurityManager();
    setUpServiceDiscoveryManager();
    setUpServiceTemplate();
    setUpServiceItem();
    performCalculation();
  }

  private void setUpSecurityManager(){
    if (System.getSecurityManager() == null) {
      System.setSecurityManager(new RMISecurityManager());
    }
  }

  private void setUpServiceTemplate(){
    Class[] types = new Class[] { Calculator.class };
    serviceTemplate = new ServiceTemplate(null, types, null);
  }

  private void setUpServiceDiscoveryManager() throws
    RemoteException, IOException{
    serviceDiscoveryManager = new
      ServiceDiscoveryManager(null,null);
  }
```

```
  private void setUpServiceItem(){
    try {
      serviceItem = serviceDiscoveryManager.lookup(
        serviceTemplate,null,200000);
    } catch (InterruptedException e){
      e.printStackTrace();
    } catch (RemoteException e){
      e.printStackTrace();
    }
  }

  public void performCalculation(){
    try{
      int operand1 = 7;
      int operand2 = 4;
      Calculator calculator = (Calculator) serviceItem.service;
      System.out.println("The " + calculator.getOperationName()
        + " of " + operand1+
        " and " + operand2 +" is " +
        calculator.getValueOfResult(operand1,operand2));
    } catch (RemoteException e){
      e.printStackTrace();
    }
  }

  public static void main(String args[]) {
    try {
      new CalculatorClient();
      Thread.sleep(1000000);
    } catch (IOException e) {
      e.printStackTrace();
    } catch (InterruptedException e){
      e.printStackTrace();
    }
  }
}
```

At this point you have no knowledge of which service will be returned, so you just print out the result along with a `String` describing which service was used. In a later example you'll build some intelligence into this part of the process.

Compile the application

Navigate into your CalculatorClient directory and enter the following command to compile `Calculator.java` and `CalculatorClient.java` at the same time:

```
javac -classpath C:\files\jini1_2\lib\jini-
core.jar;C:\files\jini1_2\lib\jini-ext.jar
ProxyCalculator/*.java
```

You should know a couple of things about this command. First, if you have not added a pointer to . in your CLASSPATH settings you may have to change the preceding command to the following:

```
javac -classpath C:\files\jini1_2\lib\jini-
core.jar;C:\files\jini1_2\lib\jini-ext.jar;.;
ProxyCalculator/*.java
```

Next, if you are working on a UNIX machine, you will have to make adjustments to the command. These are the usual changes, but I'll be explicit once, and then you can make the adjustments as needed throughout the rest of the chapter. If you have expanded the Jini distribution in the files directory, then your command is as follows:

```
javac -classpath /files/jini1_2/lib/jini-
core.jar:/files/jini1_2/lib/jini-ext.jar:.:
ProxyCalculator/*.java
```

Navigate to the CalculatorService directory and compile all the source files inside the ProxyCalculator directory with the same command.

Run the distributed application

This process consists of several steps, so let's take them one at a time. Although you could choose to perform them in a different order, this order enables you to verify that things are proceeding correctly. These steps assume that you have the RMI activation daemon, a Web server, reggie, and a lookup browser running on a single machine.

Start up a Web server for the service items

You've already started up a Web server that will serve up reggie and the other Jini services in the lib directory. Now you are going to start up a Web server that will serve up your adding and subtracting services. The easiest way to do this is to use the Jini GUI launcher and change the port and the codebase settings. You can't use port 8081 because that port is already being used by the running Web server. In this chapter you'll use port 8085, unless you have already assigned it for another purpose. Whichever port you choose, make sure you remember it, because you will need it in the next step.

Configure the Web server as shown in Figure 20-8, and then start it from the Run tab.

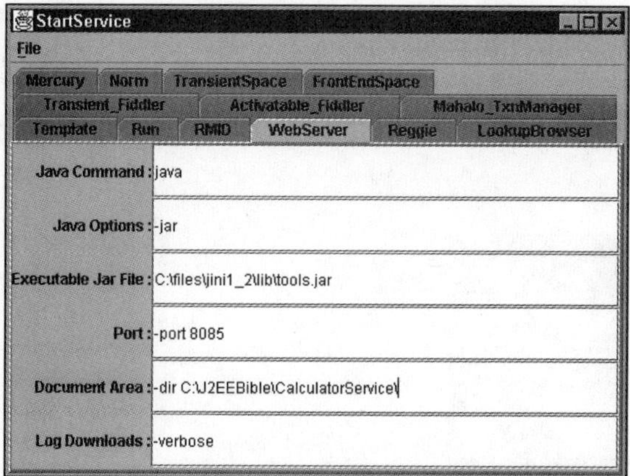

Figure 20-8: Web-server settings for the service side

Start up the services

Now you're ready to start up the services. Basically this just means that you're ready to announce to nearby lookup services that you have services available that implement `Calculator`. You aren't even really letting anyone know that these particular services add or subtract. Now that you have a Web server configured, open up a command window and navigate into CalculatorService.

In addition to specifying the same `CLASSPATH` settings that you provided when you compiled the source files, you also need to specify a security policy and the codebase. For the security policy, you can use one of those provided in the Jini distribution. Inside of the jini1_2\policy directory you will find an assortment of security-policy files. For now, use policy.all as it is the most permissive. Make sure that the codebase setting matches what you set when configuring the Web server. One final piece of advice is that you need to include the slash (/) that follows the port number. If you leave it out, you will get an error message that won't point you in the right direction.

Type in the following command to run the `AddingService` leaving a space between the codebase and the classname:

```
java -classpath C:\files\jini1_2\lib\jini-
core.jar;C:\files\jini1_2\lib\jini-ext.jar;.;
-Djava.security.policy=C:\files\jini1_2\policy\policy.all
-Djava.rmi.server.codebase=http://192.168.1.101:8085/
ProxyCalculator/AddingService
```

Take a look at your Lookup browser. You should see that you can select from at least one registrar. Go ahead and select the one running on your local machine. At this point you should see a message telling you that two services are registered. Now select Options ➪ Service classes. You should see the services shown in Figure 20-9.

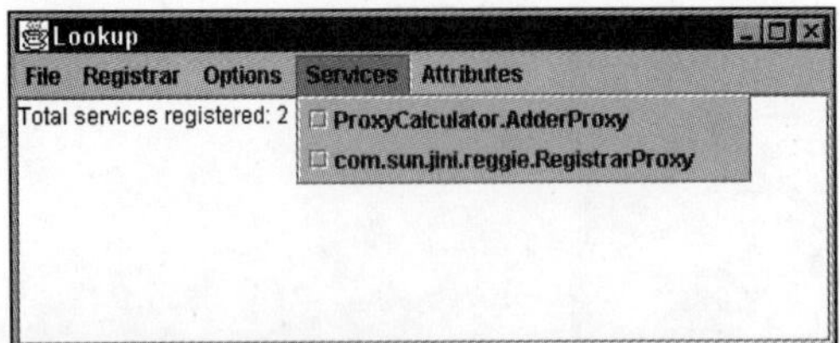

Figure 20-9: Viewing your services in the lookup browser

Start up the `SubtractingService` as follows:

```
java -classpath C:\files\jini1_2\lib\jini-
core.jar;C:\files\jini1_2\lib\jini-ext.jar;.;
-DJava.security.policy=C:\files\jini1_2\policy\policy.all
-Djava.rmi.server.codebase=http://192.168.1.101:8085/
ProxyCalculator/SubtractingService
```

Almost magically, the lookup browser announces the availability of the new service.

Start up a Web server for the client

Before running the client, look back to the section on installing Jini to make sure you have extracted two files. You should have extracted net\jini\lookup\ServiceDiscoveryManager$LookupCacheImpl$LookupListener_Stub.class from jini-ext.jar and net\jini\core\event\RemoteEventListener.class from jini-core.jar. For convenience, you should have placed these inside of your CalculatorClient directory. In fact, serving up these files is the reason that at this point you need to run a Web server pointing at this directory.

Set up the CalculatorClient Web server the same way you set up the CalculatorService Web server. Use the Jini GUI tool to launch the Web server. This time use port 8086 and set up the codebase to point at C:\J2EEBible\CalculatorClient. Your configuration should look like the one shown in Figure 20-10.

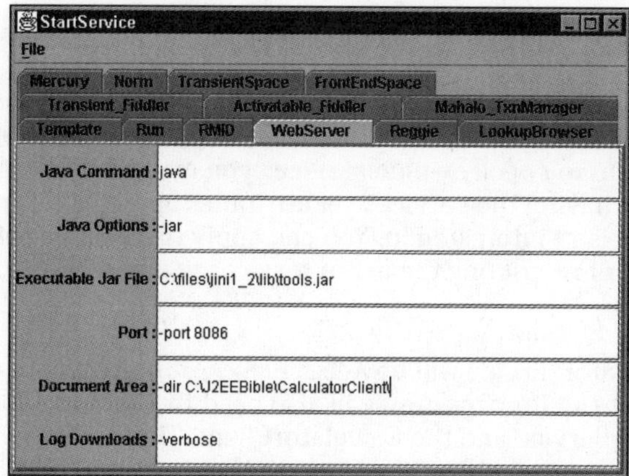

Figure 20-10: Configuring the CalculatorClient Web server

Now start the Web server from the Run tab.

Run the client

The instructions for running the client are the same as those for running the service. (As a reminder, the client, the service, and the lookup service could all be on different machines, and the instructions would be the same.) Open up a command window and navigate to the CalculatorClient directory. Enter the following command to run the client:

```
java -classpath C:\files\jini1_2\lib\jini-
core.jar;C:\files\jini1_2\lib\jini-ext.jar;.;
-DJava.security.policy=C:\files\jini1_2\policy\policy.all
-Djava.rmi.server.codebase=http://192.168.1.101:8086/
ProxyCalculator/CalculatorClient
```

There will be a pause, and you will see one of the following two lines in your console window:

```
The sum of 7 and 4 is 11.
The difference of 7 and 4 is 3.
```

You will need to Ctrl+C to stop the `CalculatorClient`.

Use Attributes in the Jini Calculator

In the last example, you saw that you got whatever Calculator object happened to be available. If more than one was available, you didn't have any choice in the matter. There are many ways for you to specify which services you may be interested in. In this section you'll look at having the services set attributes and at having the client filter out those he or she isn't interested in. You can apply these same principles to Groups or other means of restricting the list of services you're willing to interact with.

As before, the classes in CalculatorService will be AdderProxy, SubtractorProxy, AddingService, and SubtractingService. You will also need the Calculator interface in both the CalculatorService and the CalculatorClient. The CalculatorClient will now consist of the classes MultiCalculatorClient, FilterForAdder, and FilterForSubtractor.

Set a service's attributes

In the last section you were able to use the lookup browser to view the available services. If you chose the Service Info option from the Attributes menu, you are only able to see entries for reggie. You didn't set any attributes for the AdderProxy or for the SubtractorProxy. This is your next task. Make the following changes to AddingService (shown in boldface):

```
package ProxyCalculator;

import net.jini.core.lookup.ServiceItem;
import java.io.IOException;
import java.rmi.RMISecurityManager;
import net.jini.lookup.JoinManager;
import net.jini.lookup.ServiceIDListener;
import net.jini.core.entry.Entry;
import net.jini.lookup.entry.ServiceInfo;

public class AddingService {
  Entry[] attributes;

  public AddingService() throws IOException {
    setUpSecurityManager();
    setUpServiceInfo();
    setUpJoinManager();
  }

  private void setUpSecurityManager(){
    if (System.getSecurityManager() == null) {
      System.setSecurityManager(new RMISecurityManager());
    }
```

```
}
private void setUpServiceInfo(){
  attributes = new Entry[1];
  attributes[0] = new ServiceInfo("Add", "J2EEBible team",
    "HungryMinds", "Version 1", "community", "AOK");
}

private void setUpJoinManager(){
  try{
    JoinManager joinManager = new JoinManager(new
      AdderProxy(), attributes, (ServiceIDListener)null,
      null, null);
  } catch (IOException e) {}
}

public static void main(String args[]) {
  try {
    new AddingService();
    Thread.sleep(5000);
  } catch (IOException e) {
    e.printStackTrace();
  } catch (InterruptedException e){
    e.printStackTrace();
  }
}
```

The main change is that when you create your instance of `JoinManager` you want to specify the attributes you are assigning to the `AdderProxy`. The second parameter for the `JoinManager` constructor takes an array of type `Entry`, which can accommodate as many attributes as you'd like to create and pass in. You'll be passing in a `ServiceInfo` object as the first and only element of the `Entry` array. These standard `ServiceInfo` attributes are set up in the `setUpServiceInfo()` method. In this example you'll use the `ServiceInfo` constructor, which passes in the `String "Add"` as the name of the service, `"J2EEBibleTeam"` as the manufacturer, `"HungryMinds"` as the vendor, `"Version 1"` as the version, `"Community"` as the model, and `"AOK"` as the serial number.

You can also change the `SubtractingService` to include attributes, as follows:

```
package ProxyCalculator;

import net.jini.core.lookup.ServiceItem;
import java.io.IOException;
import java.rmi.RMISecurityManager;
import net.jini.lookup.JoinManager;
import net.jini.lookup.ServiceIDListener;
import net.jini.core.entry.Entry;
import net.jini.lookup.entry.ServiceInfo;

public class SubtractingService {
```

```
Entry[] attributes;

public SubtractingService() throws IOException {
  setUpSecurityManager();
  setUpServiceInfo();
  setUpJoinManager();
}

private void setUpSecurityManager(){
  if (System.getSecurityManager() == null) {
    System.setSecurityManager(new RMISecurityManager());
  }
}

private void setUpServiceInfo(){
  attributes = new Entry[1];
  attributes[0] = new ServiceInfo("Subtract",
    "J2EEBible team", "HungryMinds", "Version 1",
    "community", "AOK");
}

private void setUpJoinManager(){
  try{
    JoinManager joinManager =
      new JoinManager(new SubtractorProxy(), attributes,
        (ServiceIDListener)null, null, null);
  } catch (IOException e) {}
}

public static void main(String args[]) {
  try {
    new SubtractingService();
    Thread.sleep(5000);
  } catch (IOException e) {
    e.printStackTrace();
  } catch (InterruptedException e){
    e.printStackTrace();
  }
}
```

Compile these source files as before, and you are prepared to run the service without any changes to `Calculator`, `AdderProxy`, or `SubtractorProxy`.

Create filters on the client side

The proxies are now delivered, along with some information about them. You'll want to use this information. In this case you will find all the services that implement `Calculator` and then apply filters to this list. You can imagine that you have a long list of `Calculator` objects and that you ask each one in turn, "Can you add?" More formally, you are going to look at the attributes sent with each `ServiceItem` by looking at the first member of the `attributeSets` array. The value of the `name` will be checked against the String "Add" and later "Subtract". You might also be interested in checking against other attributes.

The FilterForAdder class implements the ServiceItemFilter interface. The interface specifies a single method called check() that takes a ServiceItem as its only parameter and returns a boolean. Generally this means that you get the ServiceItem and use it to access some defining feature and return true if the ServiceItem is to be labeled that it matches the criteria and false if it isn't to be so labeled. Here's how to filter to check if the ServiceItem has the name attribute with the value Add.

```
package ProxyCalculator;

import net.jini.lookup.ServiceItemFilter;
import net.jini.core.lookup.ServiceItem;
import net.jini.lookup.entry.ServiceInfo;


public class FilterForAdder implements ServiceItemFilter{
 public boolean check(ServiceItem serviceItem){
   String name =
((ServiceInfo)serviceItem.attributeSets[0]).name;
   if (name.equalsIgnoreCase("Add")){
     return true;
   } else {
     return false;
   }
 }
}
```

The FilterForSubtractor class is another ServiceItemFilter. This one checks for name to have the value "Subtract":

```
package ProxyCalculator;

import net.jini.lookup.ServiceItemFilter;
import net.jini.core.lookup.ServiceItem;
import net.jini.lookup.entry.ServiceInfo;


public class FilterForSubtractor implements ServiceItemFilter{
 public boolean check(ServiceItem serviceItem){
   String name =
((ServiceInfo)serviceItem.attributeSets[0]).name;
   if (name.equalsIgnoreCase("Subtract")){
     return true;
   } else {
     return false;
   }
 }
}
```

Use ServiceItemFilter objects

When you ask the ServiceDiscoveryManager to return a ServiceItem, you will be placing additional restrictions regarding which objects may be returned to you. You do this by passing in a net.jini.lookup.ServiceItemFilter as a parameter in the setUpServiceItem() method call, as follows:

```
serviceDiscoveryManager.lookup(
        serviceTemplate,serviceItemFilter,20000);
```

You'll get an AdderProxy when you use the FilterForAdder and a SubtractorProxy when you use a FilterForSubtractor. The entire code looks like this with the changes to the previous client in boldface:

```
package ProxyCalculator;

import net.jini.core.lookup.ServiceTemplate;
import java.io.IOException;
import java.rmi.RemoteException;
import java.rmi.RMISecurityManager;
import net.jini.lookup.ServiceDiscoveryManager;
import net.jini.core.lookup.ServiceItem;
import net.jini.lookup.ServiceDiscoveryListener;
import net.jini.lookup.entry.ServiceInfo;
import net.jini.lookup.ServiceItemFilter;

public class MultiCalculatorClient  {
  private ServiceTemplate serviceTemplate;
  private ServiceDiscoveryManager serviceDiscoveryManager;
  private ServiceItem addingServiceItem,
    subtractingServiceItem;

  public MultiCalculatorClient() throws IOException {
    setUpSecurityManager();
    setUpServiceDiscoveryManager();
    setUpServiceTemplate();
    System.out.println(
      "First locate an adding service and use it");
    addingServiceItem = setUpServiceItem(new FilterForAdder());
    performCalculation(addingServiceItem);
    System.out.println(
      "Next locate a subtracting service and use it");
    subtractingServiceItem = setUpServiceItem(new
      FilterForSubtractor());
    performCalculation(subtractingServiceItem);
  }

  private void setUpSecurityManager(){
    if (System.getSecurityManager() == null) {
      System.setSecurityManager(new RMISecurityManager());
    }
  }
```

```
  private void setUpServiceTemplate(){
    Class[] types = new Class[] { Calculator.class };
    serviceTemplate = new ServiceTemplate(null, types, null);
  }

  private void setUpServiceDiscoveryManager() throws
RemoteException, IOException{
    serviceDiscoveryManager = new
ServiceDiscoveryManager(null,null);
  }

  private ServiceItem setUpServiceItem(ServiceItemFilter
serviceItemFilter){
    try {
      return serviceDiscoveryManager.lookup(
        serviceTemplate,serviceItemFilter,20000);
    } catch (InterruptedException e){
      e.printStackTrace();
      System.out.println("No matching Service");
      return null;
    } catch (RemoteException e){
      e.printStackTrace();
      return null;
    }
  }

  public void performCalculation(ServiceItem serviceItem){
    try{
      int operand1 = 7;
      int operand2 = 4;
      Calculator calculator = (Calculator) serviceItem.service;
      System.out.println( (
        (ServiceInfo)serviceItem.attributeSets[0]).name);
      System.out.println("The " +
        calculator.getOperationName()+ " of " + operand1+
        " and " + operand2 +" is " +
        calculator.getValueOfResult(operand1,operand2));
    } catch (RemoteException e){
      e.printStackTrace();
    }
  }

  public static void main(String args[]) {
    try {
      new MultiCalculatorClient();
      Thread.sleep(1000000);
    } catch (IOException e) {
      e.printStackTrace();
    } catch (InterruptedException e){
      e.printStackTrace();
    }
  }
}
```

Run the example

You'll run this example exactly as before. First compile the source files in the CalculatorClient and CalculatorService directories. Start up a Web server for each of these locations. Run the `AddingService` and `SubtractingService` and verify that they appear in the lookup browser. Because you have created attributes for the services, you can also view the attributes in the lookup browser for these two services, as shown in Figure 20-11.

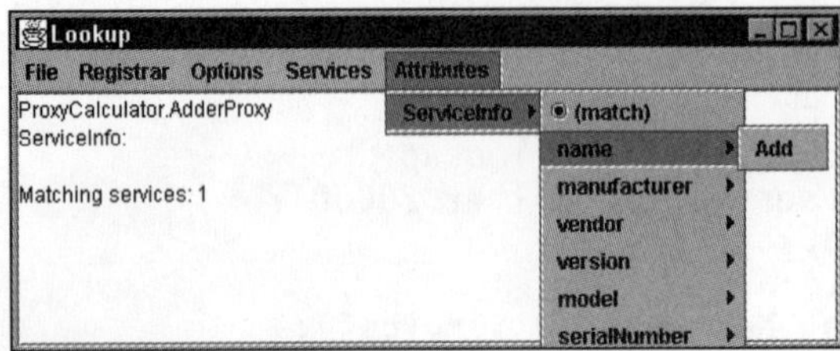

Figure 20-11: Attributes for the AdderProxy

Now that you know the attributes are there, go ahead and run your client application `MultiCalculatorClient`. You should see the following in your console window:

```
First locate an adding service and use it
Add
The sum of 7 and 4 is 11
Next locate a subtracting service and use it
Subtract
The difference of 7 and 4 is 3
```

You may also find it interesting to open up the other console windows and view the activity of the various Web servers. You can see which files are being requested and which are being served up.

Cache the Services

By this point in the book you know that you should minimize unnecessary network calls. In the current example, once you've gone to the trouble of checking with lookup services to determine which services are available, you can cache the results on the client. In this section you'll look at two caching examples. In the first example, the cache returns a `ServiceItem` instead of requesting that the `ServiceDiscoveryManager` check with the lookup services. In the second example, you'll build a smarter mousetrap. You will ask to be notified when the cache discovers a service you are waiting for.

A simple LookupCache example

In previous examples, you created an instance of a ServiceDiscoveryManager and used its lookup() method to return a ServiceItem. Now you will create a net.jini.lookup.LookupCache and allow it to fill with all the objects that implement the Calculator interface, as follows:

```
private void setUpLookupCache(){
    try{
      lookupCache=serviceDiscoveryManager.createLookupCache(
        serviceTemplate, null, null);
      Thread.sleep(10000); //need to allow Cache to fill
    } catch (RemoteException e){
      e.printStackTrace();
    } catch (InterruptedException e){
      e.printStackTrace();
    }
  }
```

The createLookupCache() method takes a ServiceTemplate as its first parameter. You could have also passed in a ServiceItemFilter so that the createLookupCache() method would return only Calculator objects that add. You'll use the final parameter in the next example when you add a ServiceDiscoveryListener.

The other major change to this version of the client is that you use the lookup() method from LookupCache, and not from ServiceDiscoveryManager, to return the ServiceItem. The changes are shown in boldface in the following code:

```
package ProxyCalculator;

import net.jini.core.lookup.ServiceTemplate;
import java.io.IOException;
import java.rmi.RemoteException;
import java.rmi.RMISecurityManager;
import net.jini.lookup.ServiceDiscoveryManager;
import net.jini.core.lookup.ServiceItem;
import net.jini.lookup.ServiceDiscoveryListener;
import net.jini.lookup.entry.ServiceInfo;
import net.jini.lookup.ServiceItemFilter;
import net.jini.lookup.LookupCache;

public class CacheCalculatorClient  {
  private ServiceTemplate serviceTemplate;
  private ServiceDiscoveryManager serviceDiscoveryManager;
  private ServiceItem addingServiceItem,
    subtractingServiceItem;
  private LookupCache lookupCache;
```

```
public CacheCalculatorClient() throws IOException {
  setUpSecurityManager();
  setUpServiceDiscoveryManager();
  setUpServiceTemplate();
  setUpLookupCache();
  System.out.println(
    "First locate an adding service and use it");
  addingServiceItem = setUpServiceItem(new FilterForAdder());
  performCalculation(addingServiceItem);
  System.out.println(
    "Next locate a subtracting service and use it");
  subtractingServiceItem = setUpServiceItem(new
    FilterForSubtractor());
  performCalculation(subtractingServiceItem);
}

private void setUpSecurityManager(){
  if (System.getSecurityManager() == null) {
    System.setSecurityManager(new RMISecurityManager());
  }
}

private void setUpServiceTemplate(){
  Class[] types = new Class[] { Calculator.class };
  serviceTemplate = new ServiceTemplate(null, types, null);
}

private void setUpLookupCache(){
  try{
    lookupCache=serviceDiscoveryManager.createLookupCache(
      serviceTemplate, null, null);
    Thread.sleep(10000); //need to allow Cache to fill
  } catch (RemoteException e){
    e.printStackTrace();
  } catch (InterruptedException e){
    e.printStackTrace();
  }
}

private void setUpServiceDiscoveryManager() throws
  RemoteException, IOException{
  serviceDiscoveryManager = new
    ServiceDiscoveryManager(null,null);
}

private ServiceItem setUpServiceItem(ServiceItemFilter
  serviceItemFilter){
  return lookupCache.lookup(serviceItemFilter);
}
```

```
    public void performCalculation(ServiceItem serviceItem){
      try{
        int operand1 = 7;
        int operand2 = 4;
        Calculator calculator = (Calculator) serviceItem.service;
        System.out.println("The " +
          calculator.getOperationName()+ " of " + operand1+
          " and " + operand2 +" is " +
          calculator.getValueOfResult(operand1,operand2));
      } catch (RemoteException e){
        e.printStackTrace();
      }
    }

    public static void main(String args[]) {
      try {
        new CacheCalculatorClient();
        Thread.sleep(1000000);
      } catch (IOException e) {
        e.printStackTrace();
      } catch (InterruptedException e){
        e.printStackTrace();
      }
    }
  }
```

You can see that the suspect feature in this code is that you have to wait for the cache to fill up. How long should you wait? You may be creating an application with constraints on the upper or lower limits of how long you can wait. In any case, you may want to experiment by changing this value by using a command-line argument to enter different values at runtime. In the next example you will create a more robust version of the client.

Use a ServiceDiscoveryListener

In the last example, you improved some of the client performance by reducing the calls over the wire. You will be able to actually observe the benefits of the code you're adding when you run the example in this section. This time when you set up the `LookupCache` you will create a `net.jini.lookup.ServiceDiscoveryListener`. In this case the class `CalculatorDiscoveryListener` implements `ServiceDiscoveryListener`, as follows:

```
  private void setUpLookupCache(){
      try{
        lookupCache=serviceDiscoveryManager.createLookupCache(
          serviceTemplate, null,
          new CalculatorDiscoveryListener());
      } catch (RemoteException e){
        e.printStackTrace();
      }
    }
```

The other big change is that no call to the performCalculation() method exists in the constructor. Remember that you're changing your event model. In the past you'd take care of a few tasks, get a handle to the ServiceItem, and then perform your calculation. Now you are waiting around to be notified that an appropriate ServiceItem has been found. The inner class responsible for listening for the service discovery will fire the performCalculation() when it gets the signal that the service is in place. Here's the code for the inner class.

```
class CalculatorDiscoveryListener implements
    ServiceDiscoveryListener{
    public void serviceAdded(ServiceDiscoveryEvent event){
      performCalculation(event.getPostEventServiceItem());
    }
    public void serviceChanged(ServiceDiscoveryEvent event){}
    public void serviceRemoved(ServiceDiscoveryEvent event){}
  }
```

A ServiceDiscoveryListener has to implement the methods serviceAdded(), serviceChanged(), and serviceRemoved(). In this case it is enough to call performCalculation() when the serviceAdded() method is fired through the event callback.

Put this all together, and here's your SmartCacheCalculatorClient:

```
package ProxyCalculator;

import net.jini.core.lookup.ServiceTemplate;
import java.io.IOException;
import java.rmi.RemoteException;
import java.rmi.RMISecurityManager;
import net.jini.lookup.ServiceDiscoveryManager;
import net.jini.core.lookup.ServiceItem;
import net.jini.lookup.ServiceDiscoveryListener;
import net.jini.lookup.entry.ServiceInfo;
import net.jini.lookup.ServiceItemFilter;
import net.jini.lookup.LookupCache;
import net.jini.lookup.ServiceDiscoveryListener;
import net.jini.lookup.ServiceDiscoveryEvent;

public class SmartCacheCalculatorClient  {
  private ServiceTemplate serviceTemplate;
  private ServiceDiscoveryManager serviceDiscoveryManager;
  private LookupCache lookupCache;

  public SmartCacheCalculatorClient() throws IOException {
    setUpSecurityManager();
    setUpServiceDiscoveryManager();
    setUpServiceTemplate();
    setUpLookupCache();
  }
```

```
  private void setUpSecurityManager(){
    if (System.getSecurityManager() == null) {
      System.setSecurityManager(new RMISecurityManager());
    }
  }

  private void setUpServiceTemplate(){
    Class[] types = new Class[] { Calculator.class };
    serviceTemplate = new ServiceTemplate(null, types, null);
  }

  private void setUpLookupCache(){
    try{
      lookupCache=serviceDiscoveryManager.createLookupCache(
        serviceTemplate, null,
        new CalculatorDiscoveryListener());
    } catch (RemoteException e){
      e.printStackTrace();
    }
  }

  private void setUpServiceDiscoveryManager() throws
RemoteException, IOException{
    serviceDiscoveryManager = new
ServiceDiscoveryManager(null,null);
  }

  private ServiceItem setUpServiceItem(ServiceItemFilter
serviceItemFilter){
    return lookupCache.lookup(serviceItemFilter);
  }

  public void performCalculation(ServiceItem serviceItem){
    try{
      int operand1 = 7;
      int operand2 = 4;
      Calculator calculator = (Calculator) serviceItem.service;
      System.out.println("The " + calculator.getOperationName()
        + " of " + operand1+ " and " + operand2 +" is " +
        calculator.getValueOfResult(operand1,operand2));
    } catch (RemoteException e){
      e.printStackTrace();
    }
  }

  class CalculatorDiscoveryListener implements
    ServiceDiscoveryListener{
    public void serviceAdded(ServiceDiscoveryEvent event){
      performCalculation(event.getPostEventServiceItem());
    }
    public void serviceChanged(ServiceDiscoveryEvent event){}
    public void serviceRemoved(ServiceDiscoveryEvent event){}
  }
```

```
    public static void main(String args[]) {
      try {
        new SmartCacheCalculatorClient();
        Thread.sleep(1000000);
      } catch (IOException e) {
        e.printStackTrace();
      } catch (InterruptedException e){
        e.printStackTrace();
      }
    }
  }
```

Once you've compiled the files you can see the effect of using the `CalculatorDiscoveryListener`. Start up the `SmartCacheCalculatorClient`. Now go to the CalculatorService directory and start up either the `AddingService` or the `SubtractingService`. You choose. You'll see the results in the console window from which you are running the client. Now go ahead and run the other service, and you'll see the corresponding results.

Ready for the bad news? Go ahead and run the `AddingService` again. You'll see that the client reports that again you've added seven and four to get eleven. This isn't really bad news; you just need to rethink how you want to use the `serviceAdded()`, `serviceChanged()`, and `serviceRemoved()` methods. In this elementary example, we just used a straightforward approach. Imagine that you had produced a GUI for the calculator. You may want the add button to be enabled when the service is added and disabled when it is removed.

Use RMI Stubs as Thin Proxies

In the preceding section you made changes to the client to improve the performance by limiting the number of network calls that you might make. In this section you will reduce the size of the proxy object that you are sending to the client. Actually, in this simple example you aren't getting much in the way of savings. So far in this chapter you've been able to send the entire service functionality to the client. What if the service is too complex and large for you to be able to send more than the instructions for invoking the methods? In other words, you'll be sending an RMI stub to the client and keeping the functionality on the service side. This brings back the cost of sending many calls across the wire, but later you can use what you learned in the RMI chapter to tune this by using coarser grained objects.

Just as the changes in the preceding section had no effect on the service code, these changes to the service and proxy have no effect on the client.

The RMI version of the proxy

It doesn't appear that you are making many changes to the proxy object. The chief difference in the RMI version is that you aren't going to deploy this proxy object anymore but instead are going to deploy a stub generated from it. You are preparing the stub to communicate back over the wire to the object that will stay with the service object and actually perform the calculation. Here's the new proxy code.

```
package ProxyCalculator;

import java.io.Serializable;
import java.rmi.server.UnicastRemoteObject;
import java.rmi.RemoteException;

public class RMIAdderProxy extends UnicastRemoteObject
implements Calculator, Serializable {

  public RMIAdderProxy() throws RemoteException{}

  public String getOperationName(){
    return "sum";
  }

  public int getValueOfResult(int firstOperand,
    int secondOperand){
    return firstOperand + secondOperand;
  }
}
```

Not only must you compile this class, but you also need to use the RMI compiler to generate the stub:

```
rmic ProxyCalculator.RMIAdderProxy
```

You will see that the class `RMIAdderProxy_Stub` has been generated.

The RMIAddingService

Surprisingly, little needs to change in the service. The changes are highlighted in this code listing.

```
package ProxyCalculator;

import net.jini.core.lookup.ServiceItem;
import java.io.IOException;
import java.rmi.RMISecurityManager;
import net.jini.lookup.JoinManager;
import net.jini.lookup.ServiceIDListener;
import net.jini.core.entry.Entry;
import net.jini.lookup.entry.ServiceInfo;
import java.rmi.RemoteException;
```

```
public class RMIAddingService {
  Entry[] attributes;
  RMIAdderProxy rmiAdderProxy;

  public RMIAddingService() throws IOException {
    try{
      rmiAdderProxy = new RMIAdderProxy();
    } catch (RemoteException e){
      e.printStackTrace();
    }

    setUpSecurityManager();
    setUpServiceInfo();
    setUpJoinManager();
  }

  private void setUpSecurityManager(){
    if (System.getSecurityManager() == null) {
      System.setSecurityManager(new RMISecurityManager());
    }
  }
  private void setUpServiceInfo(){
    attributes = new Entry[1];
    attributes[0] = new ServiceInfo("Add", "J2EEBible team",
      "HungryMinds", "Version 1", "community", "AOK");
  }

  private void setUpJoinManager(){
    try{
      JoinManager joinManager = new JoinManager(rmiAdderProxy,
        attributes, (ServiceIDListener)null, null, null);
    } catch (IOException e) {}
  }

  public static void main(String args[]) {
    try {
      new RMIAddingService();
      Thread.sleep(5000);
    } catch (IOException e) {
      e.printStackTrace();
    } catch (InterruptedException e){
      e.printStackTrace();
    }
  }
}
```

Compile and run the `RMIAddingService`. For contrast you can run the `SubtractingService` again. Open up the Lookup browser, and you can check under the Services item to see that the `SubtractorProxy` and the `RMIAdderProxy_Stub` are the proxies that were sent to the lookup service and on to the clients.

Summary

This quick look at Jini may have left you thinking that it is very complicated. Actually, its power comes from the simplicity of the ideas involved. In this chapter, you learned the following:

- ✦ You created a `JoinManager` that allows a service to join one or more lookup services and announce the capabilities of the service it provides.
- ✦ On the client side, you created a `ServiceDiscoveryManager` that enabled you to query nearby lookup services to find out if any of them had a service that matched the type you were looking for. If you found a match, you were able to use the functionality provided by the service by invoking methods on the discovered `ServiceItem`.
- ✦ You then added attributes to your services. This means that you enabled clients to do a more fine-grained search for services that were, for example, made by a certain company, of a certain version or later, or capable of a certain action.
- ✦ You added caching capabilities to your client so that you didn't have to make so many requests across the network. You even provided for smart caching, with which you respond to services being added to, changed, or removed from the cache.
- ✦ For services that were too large to send in their entirety, you used your knowledge of RMI to create a stub that you sent as a proxy for your service.

✦ ✦ ✦

PART

VI

Building Big Systems

✦ ✦ ✦ ✦

In This Part

✦ ✦ ✦ ✦

CHAPTER 21

Implementing Web Services

✦ ✦ ✦ ✦

In This Chapter

Exposing a standard Java class as a Web service

Using SOAP to send messages

Deploying Web services using deployment descriptors

Discovering Web services written by other developers

Describing Web services using WSDL

Sending the state of a JavaBean wrapped up in a SOAP envelope

✦ ✦ ✦ ✦

When you first learned the basics of object-oriented programming, you were probably told to think of objects making requests of each other. When you invoke a method on an object to which you have a handle, you are basically asking the other object, "Hey, could you do something for me?" As you've seen so far in this book, making such requests is not so simple when you are designing a distributed application. You have to worry about how you find the remote object, how you communicate with it, and how it will get the response back to you. At this point, you've seen lots of alternatives for running an enterprise application. You can build applications that use servlets, JSPs, or EJBs. You can instead choose to create a distributed application written in Java on both the server and the client that uses RMI (or Jini on top of RMI). At the other end of the spectrum, you can create a language-independent approach using CORBA.

The idea of Web services is one that goes back to your first experiences with object-oriented programming. If you want to invoke a method in a remote Web service, or just send it information that might elicit a response, you send it a request. Often, you send this request in the form of a Simple Object Access Protocol (SOAP) message. Although you'll learn the details of this type of message in this chapter, the most important characteristic is that it is an XML message and so is easily read by both people and machines. If a response is required, it too can be sent in the form of a SOAP message. By agreeing on the protocol, you free yourself from wondering what language the service you are using is written in. Likewise, the service doesn't care about the language in which the client contacting it is written.

In this chapter, you'll begin by writing a simple Web service that just returns the `String` you send it. This elementary application will enable you to explore several different ways of deploying your Web service. You can also take a look at the actual message being sent from client to server and also the message being sent from server to client. The examples in this chapter use the Apache open-source application Axis to serve your Web services from inside Tomcat. These are open-source offerings that are available for free from the Apache Software Foundation.

When you create a Web service that you would like others to use, you need to get the word out somehow. You can use a registry that uses a protocol called Universal Discover, Description, and Integration (UDDI). This process is generally known as *publishing* your Web service. As a developer, you can also use the registry to find other Web services. Once you've found these other services, you can look around for information that will enable you to connect to the service and use it. In this chapter you'll see what's involved in these last two steps, commonly known as *find* and *bind*. In the final section you'll look at serializing a JavaBean and sending it as part of the SOAP message.

A HelloWorld Service

As a first example, you'll use RPC to echo `String` input that you will then display. As usual in a beginning enterprise HelloWorld example, it's a long way to go for such a modest result. The point of the example is, of course, the process and not the end result. In this section you'll set up Axis and create a HelloClient that will communicate with an existing Web service. You will then construct the service and run it from within Axis. In the last portion of this section, you will use a utility called tcpmon to monitor the request and response being sent across the wire. You may be surprised to see that even these simple strings are wrapped in XML files to be parsed and used at the other end.

You will use this very easy "toy" example throughout this chapter. It will enable you to see the entire code that a variety of settings requires. Although a more complex example might be more interesting, it wouldn't explain any more about Web services, and you would find yourself able to view only pieces of the files as you adapted and extended the example.

Setting up Axis

You can download the latest release of the Axis software (formally known as xml-axis) from `http://xml.apache.org`. Follow the instructions to install it for your particular Web server. In this chapter, the instructions are given for Axis 1.0 alpha2 running on Tomcat 4.0. Tomcat is available from `http://jakarta.apache.org`. You may want to take a look back at Chapter 3 for information on installing and using Tomcat.

With Tomcat it is very easy to set up and run Axis. Unzip Axis and save it somewhere convenient. The following instructions assume that Axis is on a Windows machine in the directory C:\axis-1_0 and that Tomcat is in the directory C:\jakarta-tomcat-4.0; adapt these instructions to fit your setup. Copy the directory C:\axis-1_0\webapps\axis into the directory C:\jakarta-tomcat-4.0\webapps. Copy the axis.jar from C:\axis-1_0\lib to C:\jakarta-tomcat-4.0\webapps\axis\WEB-INF\lib. You will also want to copy either xerces.jar or both jaxp.jar and crimson.jar to the same location. (You can get xerces.jar in the xerces download from `http://xml.apache.org`; the files jaxp.jar and crimson.jar are included in the JAXP download available at `http://java.sun.com/xml`.) We happen to have xerces.jar installed.

Update your `CLASSPATH` information to include these jar files and then start up Tomcat using either the startup.sh or startup.bat files. You can skip the steps for testing your installation for now: In the alpha2 release of Axis, they don't work as written. You'll test the installation in the HelloWorld example in the next two sections.

A HelloWorld Web service client

You are going to adapt an example shipped as part of the Axis distribution in the subdirectory \samples\userguide\example1. Save the following as HelloClient.java inside the directory J2EEBible\Greeting.

```
// ...Apache copyright and notices in distributed file.

package Greeting;

import org.apache.axis.client.ServiceClient;

public class HelloClient {

  public static void main(String [] args) {
    try {
      String inputName = (args.length<1)? "World": args[0];
        String endpoint =
      "http://nagoya.apache.org:5049/axis/servlet/AxisServlet";

      ServiceClient client = new ServiceClient(endpoint);
      String name = (String)client.invoke(
        "http://soapinterop.org/", "echoString",
          new Object [] { inputName});

      System.out.println("Hello " + name + ".");
    } catch (Exception e) {
      System.err.println(e.toString());
    }
  }
}
```

This is as simple as a service can get. If you pass in a command-line argument, then it is saved as the `String inputName`. If not, then `inputName` is set to the value `"World"`. In either case, a new `org.apache.axis.client.ServiceClient` is created. A `ServiceClient` is used to invoke an Axis service from the client side. Here you are constructing a `ServiceClient` by passing in the URL of the endpoint.

The action happens when you call the `invoke()` method. `invoke()` has four signatures. Here you are using this one:

```
public Object invoke(String namespace, String method,
  Object[] args) throws AxisFault
```

So the name of the method you are invoking is `echoString()`, and you are passing `inputName` as a parameter for this method. `invoke()` returns an `Object` that you are casting as a `String` called `name` and outputting in the next line. It is notable that you aren't assuming very much about the remote application you are communicating with. You don't have a handle to an object the way you would with RMI. All you know is that some method named `echoString()` is going to take the `String` you pass it and return a `String` to you.

Compile HelloClient.java. If you have a network connection, go ahead and run it by typing **java Greeting/HelloClient Smedley**. You will probably have to wait quite a while for your call to go over the network, execute, and return. When it does, you will see `"Hello Smedley."` in the console window. Execute HelloClient without an argument, and you will wait just as long to see `"Hello World."` in your console.

A local greeting service

Now that you've written a simple client, you can write and deploy a simple service for HelloClient that tests your Axis installation. Your HelloService only needs to contain a method that takes a `String` as an argument and returns that `String` to the caller. Here's HelloService.java:

```
public class HelloService{

  public String echoName( String name ){
    return name;
  }
}
```

Really, that's it. You don't even need to compile it. Just rename it and put it inside the Axis directory that you moved into the Tomcat distribution. Rename it HelloService.jws and place it inside the C:\jakarta-tomcat-4.0\webapps\axis directory.

Now you have to modify the client to look in the right place and request that the correct method be called. The changes are shown in boldface in the following code:

```
package LocalGreeting;

import org.apache.axis.client.ServiceClient;

public class HelloClient {
  public static void main(String [] args) {
    try {
     String inputName = (args.length<1)? "World": args[0];
     String endpoint =
       "http://localhost:8080/axis/HelloService.jws";
     ServiceClient client = new ServiceClient(endpoint);
     String name = (String)client.invoke("echoName",
       new Object [] { inputName});
     System.out.println("Hello " + name + ".");
     } catch (Exception e) {
       System.err.println(e.toString());
     }
  }
}
```

The first change is that this HelloClient.java is in the directory J2EEBible\LocalGreeting, and so the package is changed accordingly. The second change is that the `endpoint` is now on your local machine. (You may need to replace this text with the actual name of your machine and a different port if you use one.) The rest of the URL corresponds to the file HelloService.jws sitting inside of the axis subdirectory of webapps. The third change is that you are now using a different signature for `invoke()`—one that doesn't take a `String` argument for the namespace. Using this call is equivalent to using the following code:

```
invoke("","echoName", new Object [] { inputName})
```

The final change is that the name of the method being invoked has changed from `echoString()` to `echoName()`.

Start up Tomcat. Compile HelloClient.java but not HelloService.jws. Run HelloClient.java. There will be a long pause while HelloService.jws is located and compiled into HelloService.class. You will be able to see that the class file is located in the same directory as HelloService.jws. The class file will then be used to perform the service. Run HelloClient again, and you will see that it executes a bit more quickly.

Behind the scenes with tcpmon

When you are running a client-server application on a single machine, it is nice to be able to verify what is actually happening behind the scenes. You might remember from Chapter 15 that optimizing shortcuts are taken when your client and server files were located in the same directory. You can quickly verify that you are contacting the HelloService through the Web server by shutting Tomcat down and running HelloClient again. This shows that your service requires Tomcat, but what is actually being sent over the wire?

The Axis distribution includes a utility called tcpmon (for TCP Monitor) that enables you to monitor what is being sent back and forth. Open up a console window and start up tcpmon with the following command:

```
java org.apache.axis.utils.tcpmon
```

This brings up the TCPMonitor GUI, as shown in Figure 21-1.

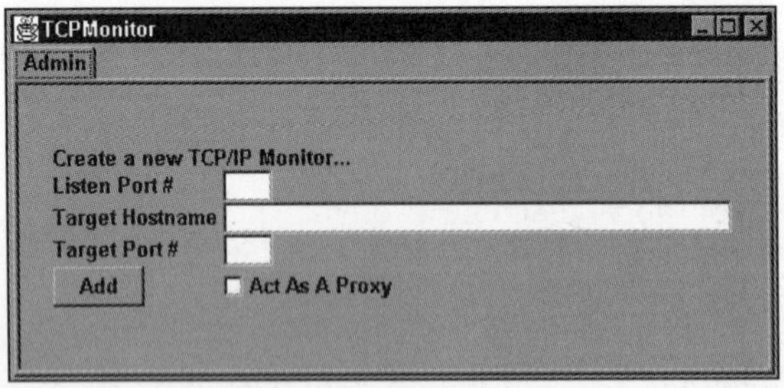

Figure 21-1: The TCPMonitor

You want to intercept calls between your client and your server. Pick a port to listen on — port 8088, for example. The target host name in this case is localhost, and the target port is 8080 because that's the host and port on which Tomcat is listening. (You may need to adjust these values to accommodate your local setup.) Click Add.

You'll have to go back and change HelloClient.java so that the target is port 8088; otherwise you won't be able to view the conversation between HelloClient and HelloService. You need only to change `endpoint` to this:

```
String endpoint =
  "http://localhost:8088/axis/HelloService.jws";
```

Now recompile and rerun HelloClient with the command-line argument `Sam`, as follows:

```
java LocalGreeting/HelloClient Sam
```

The TCPMonitor will show something like this as the request:

```
POST /axis/HelloService.jws HTTP/1.0

Content-Length: 341

Host: localhost

Content-Type: text/xml; charset=utf-8

SOAPAction: "/echoName"


<?xml version="1.0" encoding="UTF-8"?>
<SOAP-ENV:Envelope xmlns:SOAP-
ENV="http://schemas.xmlsoap.org/soap/envelope/"
xmlns:xsd="http://www.w3.org/2001/XMLSchema"
xmlns:xsi="http://www.w3.org/2001/XMLSchema-instance">
 <SOAP-ENV:Body>
  <echoName>
   <arg0 xsi:type="xsd:string">Sam</arg0>
  </echoName>
 </SOAP-ENV:Body>
</SOAP-ENV:Envelope>
```

You'll look at SOAP in greater depth in the next section. For now, take a look at the `<SOAP-ENV:Body>` element. The method name is sent as the element `<echoName>` and contains the value of the command-line element as its first and only element. This value is included as the child element `<arg0>` with the type of string included as an attribute. Without writing any XML or even being aware that XML was involved, you have sent a well-formed and valid XML document.

By placing tcpmon between your client code and your service code, you enable yourself to see the SOAP messages being sent as requests and responses. This is a great way to run down a bug when you're not sure where it is occurring. You can check to make sure the expected message is being sent. If it isn't, you need to take a look at your client code. If the request looks correct, you can start looking at your service code. The response may also include error messages in the form of *"faults"* that help you locate a problem.

Not that it makes a difference, but you did go to the trouble of assigning the variable you were passing the name `inputName`, and if you would like to preserve that name in the XML SOAP request, you can modify the HelloClient like this:

```
package LocalGreeting;

import org.apache.axis.client.ServiceClient;
import org.apache.axis.message.RPCParam;
```

```
public class HelloClient {
  public static void main(String [] args) {
    try {
      String inputName = (args.length<1)? "World": args[0];
      String endpoint =
        "http://localhost:8088/axis/HelloService.jws";
      ServiceClient client = new ServiceClient(endpoint);
      String name = (String)client.invoke("echoName",
        new Object [] { new RPCParam("inputName", inputName)});
      System.out.println("Hello " + name + ".");
      } catch (Exception e) {
        System.err.println(e.toString());
      }
    }
}
```

The subtle change to your SOAP request is just that the name of `<arg0>` has been changed to `<inputName>`. The change is boldfaced in the following snippet:

```
POST /axis/HelloService.jws HTTP/1.0

Content-Length: 351

Host: localhost

Content-Type: text/xml; charset=utf-8

SOAPAction: "/echoName"

<?xml version="1.0" encoding="UTF-8"?>
<SOAP-ENV:Envelope xmlns:SOAP-
ENV="http://schemas.xmlsoap.org/soap/envelope/"
xmlns:xsd="http://www.w3.org/2001/XMLSchema"
xmlns:xsi="http://www.w3.org/2001/XMLSchema-instance">
 <SOAP-ENV:Body>
  <echoName>
   <inputName xsi:type="xsd:string">Sam</inputName>
  </echoName>
 </SOAP-ENV:Body>
</SOAP-ENV:Envelope>
```

You'll see the following code as the response in the TCPMonitor:

```
HTTP/1.1 200 OK

Content-Type: text/xml; charset=utf-8

Content-Length: 444

Date: Tue, 02 Oct 2001 18:16:58 GMT

Server: Apache Tomcat/4.0 (HTTP/1.1 Connector)
```

```
Set-Cookie:
JSESSIONID=C250D5F3F188E8B48161585158E781A8;Path=/axis


<?xml version="1.0" encoding="UTF-8"?>
<SOAP-ENV:Envelope SOAP-
ENV:encodingStyle="http://schemas.xmlsoap.org/soap/encoding/"
xmlns:SOAP-ENV="http://schemas.xmlsoap.org/soap/envelope/"
xmlns:xsd="http://www.w3.org/2001/XMLSchema"
xmlns:xsi="http://www.w3.org/2001/XMLSchema-instance">
 <SOAP-ENV:Body>
  <echoNameResponse>
   <echoNameResult xsi:type="xsd:string">Sam</echoNameResult>
  </echoNameResponse>
 </SOAP-ENV:Body>
</SOAP-ENV:Envelope>
```

Again, concentrate on the contents of the `<SOAP-ENV:Body>` element. It contains the element `<echoNameResponse>`, which contains the child element `<echoNameResult>`, which is, again, of `type` string. This string "Sam" will be converted back into a Java `Object` and cast to a `String`.

Understanding Simple Object Access Protocol (SOAP)

You saw in the last section that even when you were only intending to send the `String Sam` back and forth across the wire, HelloClient packaged it up inside an XML document and used HTTP to send this much bulkier file to the HelloService as a SOAP message. In turn, the HelloService opened up the envelope, consumed the SOAP message, and generated a response. Again, the response amounted to sending the `String Sam` back to HelloClient. In reality, a SOAP message with the appropriate HTTP headers was constructed and sent back across the wire. In this section, you'll get a feel for the structure of the messages being passed back and forth.

The structure of a SOAP message

Take another look at the SOAP message that HelloClient sent to the HelloService:

```
<?xml version="1.0" encoding="UTF-8"?>

<SOAP-ENV:Envelope
  xmlns:SOAP-ENV="http://schemas.xmlsoap.org/soap/envelope/"
  xmlns:xsd="http://www.w3.org/2001/XMLSchema"
  xmlns:xsi="http://www.w3.org/2001/XMLSchema-instance">

  <SOAP-ENV:Body>
```

```
    <echoName>
      <inputName xsi:type="xsd:string">Sam</inputName>
    </echoName>
  </SOAP-ENV:Body>

</SOAP-ENV:Envelope>
```

You can see that a SOAP message is basically just an XML message, though it cannot contain processing instructions or a document type declaration. Its structure is deliberately uncomplicated. (You can read through the formal specification at the W3C site online at `http://www.w3.org/TR/SOAP`.) The SOAP message generated by Axis is consistent with the W3C naming convention of using `SOAP-ENV` as the namespace prefix associated with the SOAP namespace `http://schemas.xmlsoap.org/soap/envelope`. The other namespace prefix, which is not used in this particular document, is `SOAP-ENC`: This prefix maps to the SOAP namespace `http://schemas.xmlsoap.org/soap/encoding`. `SOAP-ENV` is used for the SOAP envelope and `SOAP-ENC` for SOAP serialization.

The metaphor for a SOAP message is that it consists of a note inside an envelope, perhaps with other important information included as well. In particular, a SOAP message consists of a SOAP envelope that is an element named `<Envelope>`. The `<Envelope>` element may contain a `<Header>` as its first child element. The only other element that `<Envelope>` may contain is the `<Body>` element.

The SOAP envelope

The root element of a SOAP message is `<Envelope>`. In addition to containing the `<Body>`, and possibly the `<Header>`, the envelope may also contain attributes set to help with the processing of the message. In the sample message sent by HelloClient, the attributes set were all namespace declarations. For example, the prefix `SOAP-ENV` was given the value `http://schemas.xmlsoap.org/soap/envelope/`. In addition to these basics, the envelope can contain additional child elements so long as they come after the `<Body>` element and are namespace qualified. Additional namespace-qualified attributes are allowed as well.

The SOAP header

The `<Header>` element is optional. If you use one, it must be the first child element of `<Envelope>`. The SOAP specification requires that a SOAP application first identify all parts of the SOAP message intended for that application. It is possible to send a SOAP message to several SOAP applications, each of which will process some or all of it. It is also possible that a SOAP message be sent from one SOAP application to another being modified along the way. You can do this by using the `actor` attribute in the child elements of `<Header>`, as in the following code:

```
<SOAP-ENV:Header>
  <ns:Example xmlns:ns="some namespace URI"
    actor="target URI for application handling this"
    ...
  </ns:Example>
</SOAP-ENV:Header>
```

If the SOAP application is not the final destination of the SOAP message, then the parts identified as requiring processing by the current SOAP application will be removed from the SOAP message after the message is processed and before it is sent on to the next destination.

The SOAP specification then requires that a SOAP application ensure that all the parts of the message that must be processed can be processed. If they can be processed, the application should process them. You use the attribute mustUnderstand and give it a value of 1 to indicate that this particular child element of <Header> must be processed. Here's a code snippet using mustUnderstand:

```
<SOAP-ENV:Header>
  <ns:Example xmlns:ns="some namespace URI"
    mustUnderstand="1"
    ...
  </ns:Example>
</SOAP-ENV:Header>
```

Setting the attribute mustUnderstand to a value of 0 is the same as not including it in the first place.

The SOAP body

HelloClient used the <Body> element to specify the RPC. This element contained the name of the method being invoked, as well as the value of the parameters. Notice that the child elements of <Body> did not have to be namespace qualified. HelloService used the <Body> element to return the result of invoking the method. Notice also the naming conventions. The client sent an <echoName> element to call the echoName() method in HelloService. In return, HelloService sent an <echoNameResponse> element that contained the child element <echoNameResult>.

The child element <inputName> is intended to be a parameter for the echoName() method. You can see that the code xsi:type="xsd:string" specifies the data type of the element <inputName>. The namespace prefixes xsi and xsd point to http://www.w3.org/2001/XMLSchema and http://www.w3.org/2001/XMLSchema-instance, respectively. You'll recognize the allowable simple data types as being the same as those you saw in Chapter 11. (For more information about compound types, consult section 5.4 of the SOAP specification at http://www.w3.org/TR/SOAP.)

Another use of the <Body> element is to return information in the form of error messages when the SOAP application can't process the message. These error messages are included in the <Fault> child element of the <Body> element. The errors are explained by the contents of the subelements <faultcode>, <faultstring>, <faultactor>, and <detail>. You can think of these subelements as being analogous to the familiar HTTP status codes: Instead of a number for the <faultcode>, you see names that begin with one of the following four roots: VersionMismatch,

MustUnderstand, Client, or Server. You can think of these as the 100-level status codes, 200-level status codes, and so on, respectively. The advantage of these codes over their HTTP counterparts is that you can build on them. The specification suggests, as an example, that you can use a <faultcode> element with the contents Client.Authentication. The intention of the <faultcode> element is to provide information about the error to machines. These <faultcode> elements are supplemented by information in the <faultstring> and <detail> elements. The <faultactor> element contains information about which SOAP application caused the fault to happen. This information corresponds to the URI of the actor in which the fault happens, as with the information contained in the actor attribute for children of the <Header> element.

In Axis, the class org.apache.axis.AxisFault is used to interact with <Fault> elements. AxisFault contains the fields faultActor, faultCode, faultDetails, and faultString, along with accessor methods for getting and setting them.

SOAP and HTTP

Take a look at the first lines of the message sent by HelloClient and at the first lines of the response generated by HelloService. Before the XML begins in the request, you see the familiar beginnings of an HTTP header. You can see that the method is POST and you see a summary of information about the message itself. You can think of this as the HTTP envelope for the SOAP envelope:

```
POST /axis/HelloService.jws HTTP/1.0
Content-Length: 351
Host: localhost
Content-Type: text/xml; charset=utf-8
SOAPAction: "/echoName"
```

Similarly, the response generated by the HelloService begins with the following information:

```
HTTP/1.1 200 OK
Content-Type: text/xml; charset=utf-8
Content-Length: 444
Date: Tue, 02 Oct 2001 18:16:58 GMT
Server: Apache Tomcat/4.0 (HTTP/1.1 Connector)
Set-Cookie:
JSESSIONID=C250D5F3F188E8B48161585158E781A8;Path=/axis
```

Just as you aren't required to use SOAP in order to create Web Services, you aren't required to use HTTP to send SOAP messages. SOAP does, however, specify a binding of SOAP with HTTP. These two examples show the results of placing SOAP messages inside HTTP requests and responses. You can see the security concerns that would arise from this unauthorized tunneling.

Because a SOAP message is an XML document, you'll notice that the content type in each of the sample messages above is set to text/xml. You can see in the request that a SOAP HTTP Request uses HTTP POST. You can also see that the response is returned with a status code of 200. The specification requires that if a failure occurs during the processing of a request that the server issue a status code of 500 (indicating an internal server error) and that the `<Body>` element of the accompanying SOAP message include a `<Fault>` element with more information about the error.

Deploying Web Services

In the last two sections you got a simple Web service up and running and took a look at what was being sent between the client and the service. The deployment was pretty basic. You took your source code and changed the suffix from .java to .jws and then placed the source file with the new suffix in the appropriate place and accessed it. In this section, you'll look at other methods of deploying your Web services.

As you run these examples, don't forget to cycle Tomcat (shut it down and start it back up) so that the Web server refreshes its configuration.

Setting up for the example

Create the directory J2EEBible/DeployedGreeting. Copy your HelloClient.java file from J2EEBible/LocalGreeting and your HelloService.java file that you created and later renamed HelloService.jws. Open up HelloService.java and add this package declaration before any other non-comment code:

```
package DeployedGreeting;
```

Open up a terminal window and navigate to J2EEBible and compile HelloService.java:

```
javac DeployedGreeting/HelloService.java
```

Now you're going to place this newly created HelloService.class file where Axis will be able to find it. Go to your Tomcat distribution. Inside the axis directory, navigate down to the classes folder and create a new folder called DeployedGreeting. You should be working in the *<tomcat-installation>*\webapps\axis\WEB-INF\classes\DeployedGreeting directory. Copy HelloService.class into DeployedGreeting. If you would like to reassure yourself that no monkey business is going on, you can remove HelloService.jws and the automatically compiled HelloService.class from the *<tomcat-installation>*\webapps\axis directory.

Using deployment descriptors

The deployment-descriptor syntax is the part of Axis that is going to change. You can get the basic idea of using the deployment-descriptor from this section, but the actual syntax will be different in the final release, so you should check out the release's user guide to see the commands for the Web Service Deployment Descriptor (WSDD). For now, you can at least get a feel for how this mechanism will work. It should feel similar to using the entries you wrote in web.xml when you studied servlets and JSPs in Chapters 3 and 4.

Creating the file deploy.xml

Inside of J2EEBible\DeployedGreeting, create the following file, deploy.xml:

```
<admin:deploy xmlns:admin="AdminService">
  <service name="HelloService" pivot="RPCDispatcher">
    <option name="className"
      value="DeployedGreeting.HelloService"/>
    <option name="methodName" value="*"/>
  </service>
</admin:deploy>
```

You can see that the root element is `<deploy>`. You are passing in the information that the service to be deployed will be known as HelloService, and that the actual class being used is the `HelloService` class in the `DeployedGreeting` package.

Processing the file deploy.xml

The next step is to actually deploy your Web service. You do this using an Axis application. Open up a terminal window and navigate to J2EEBible\DeployedGreeting. Now process deploy.xml with the following command:

```
java org.apache.axis.client.AdminClient deploy.xml
```

You should see the following feedback:

```
Processing file: deploy.xml
<Admin>Done processing</Admin>
```

You've now deployed your Web service. If you would like to take a look at the components that have been deployed, you can use AdminClient but pass it the command-line argument `list`, as follows:

```
java org.apache.axis.client.AdminClient list
```

You will get the feedback `Doing a list` followed by a long listing with the root element `<engineConfig>`. You should see a list of `<handler>` and `<chain>` elements as child elements of the `<handlers>` element. This list will be followed by the `<services>` element. One of the children of `<services>` will be a `<service>` child element containing exactly what deploy.xml contained. In other words, you should see the following <service> element somewhere on your screen:

```
<service name="HelloService" pivot="RPCDispatcher">
  <option name="className"
    value="DeployedGreeting.HelloService"/>
  <option name="methodName" value="*"/>
</service>
```

The remaining elements are <transports> elements and <typeMappings> elements.

If this information went by too quickly on the screen, you can also find it in the server-config.xml file in <tomcat-install>/webapps/axis/WEB-INF.

Creating and running undeploy.xml

You will also want a mechanism for removing a Web service. For this you will create the file undeploy.xml inside J2EEBible\DeployedGreeting:

```
<admin:undeploy xmlns:admin="AdminService">
 <service name="HelloService"/>
</admin:undeploy>
```

Again, you can use AdminClient to process this file:

```
java org.apache.axis.client.AdminClient undeploy.xml
```

If you generate a list of deployed services, you'll see that HelloService is no longer one of them.

To continue with this example, deploy your service once again by processing the deploy.xml file.

Running your deployed service

At this point you've saved your service in the classes directory on the server and you've deployed it by processing the deploy.xml file. Now you just need to access it. In this section, you'll make a couple of changes to your client, and you'll also look at deploying your service as a jar file.

Changing HelloClient.java

You need to make a couple of changes to your client. Open up HelloClient.java and make the following boldfaced changes:

```
// Apache copyright and distribution notes ...
package DeployedGreeting;

import org.apache.axis.client.ServiceClient;
```

```
public class HelloClient {
  public static void main(String [] args) {
    try {
      String inputName = (args.length<1)? "World": args[0];
      String endpoint =
"http://localhost:8080/axis/servlet/AxisServlet/HelloService";
      ServiceClient client = new ServiceClient(endpoint);
      String name = (String)client.invoke( "echoName",
        new Object [] { inputName});

      System.out.println("Hello " + name + ".");
    } catch (Exception e) {
      System.err.println(e.toString());
    }
  }
}
```

You've changed the package to DeployedGreeting and you've changed the URL being accessed as highlighted in the preceding code. If you changed the port when you were using the tcpmon, you should change it back to 8080. You are also using the AxisServlet to serve up your Web service, so you have to include servlet/AxisServlet in the path. Finally, you deployed the service under the name HelloService so that is how you should refer to it.

Compile and run HelloClient.java, and your Web service will run as before.

Deploying HelloService as a jar

In your first local deployment, you put the single source file HelloService.jws in the axis directory inside Tomcat's webapp directory. If your Web service requires more than one file, placing them all inside this directory could get a bit messy. In your second deployment, you moved the class files inside the classes directory inside webapps/WEB-INF, being careful to preserve the directory structure under which those class files were compiled. A deployment descriptor then redirected the user input to the actual location of the class files. As an alternative, you can jar your files up and save the resulting jar file in the lib directory.

In this case, open up a terminal and navigate inside of the J2EEBible directory. Now jar up your class file with the following command:

```
jar cvf DeployedGreeting.jar
  DeployedGreeting/HelloService.class
```

To deploy your service, take the created jar file, DeployedGreeting.jar, and copy it into the directory <tomcat-install>\webapps\axis\WEB-INF\lib. Your earlier deploy.xml file configured the axis server correctly to deliver the current version of the service. If you'd like to be sure that you aren't still seeing the results of the HelloService.class file, remove the DeployedGreeting directory from the <tomcat-install>\webapps\axis\WEB-INF\classes directory.

Cycle Tomcat and then rerun HelloClient: It should behave as before. Dropping a jar file into the lib directory is an easy way to deploy your Web service.

Finding Web Services with UDDI

Universal Discover, Description, and Integration (UDDI) will enable you to discover services, explore their interfaces, and decide how to integrate them with your applications. The idea is that a service provider will publish a description of a Web service in a UDDI registry, which other developers can then search for this description. Once a developer understands the interface, he or she can write a SOAP client that can work directly with the SOAP service. This process is known as *publish, find, and bind.*

In this chapter you are concentrating on the find and bind part of this process. If you are interested in publishing your Web services, you should consider registering with one of the registries described in this section. If you simply want to explore the process, you can download a free Web Services Toolkit (WSTK) from IBM's alphaWorks at `http://www.alphaworks.ibm.com/tech/webservicestoolkit`. This is quite a large download, and it provides many of the same facilities as Axis. It will enable you to set up a local UDDI registry that you can experiment with.

UDDI resources

Most of the resources for UDDI are on the Web. A good place to start is `http://www.uddi.org`, which provides information about creating a UDDI implementation. The focus of this section, however, is just on using the registry. If you click the Find icon on the screen, you are given the option of using the UDDI Business Registry from IBM or from Microsoft. These are two of the big players behind SOAP and UDDI. At this point it doesn't much matter which registry you use. There is currently no fee for registering with or using either service. Figure 21-2 shows a portion of the advanced Business Search page on IBM's UDDI Business Registry.

The available categories match up with the UDDI specification. Under the locator field is a drop-down menu that enables you to search by North American Industry Classification System, Universal Standard Products and Services Code, or the ISO 3166 Geographic Taxonomy. Microsoft's UDDI browser is a bit easier to use if you don't know what you are looking for. You can drill down in any of these classifications to see the categories and subcategories. You can easily choose to search for a string in a business name as well as in a business location, business identifier, discovery URL, RealNames keyword, or other category. Figure 21-3 shows the Microsoft UDDI Registry.

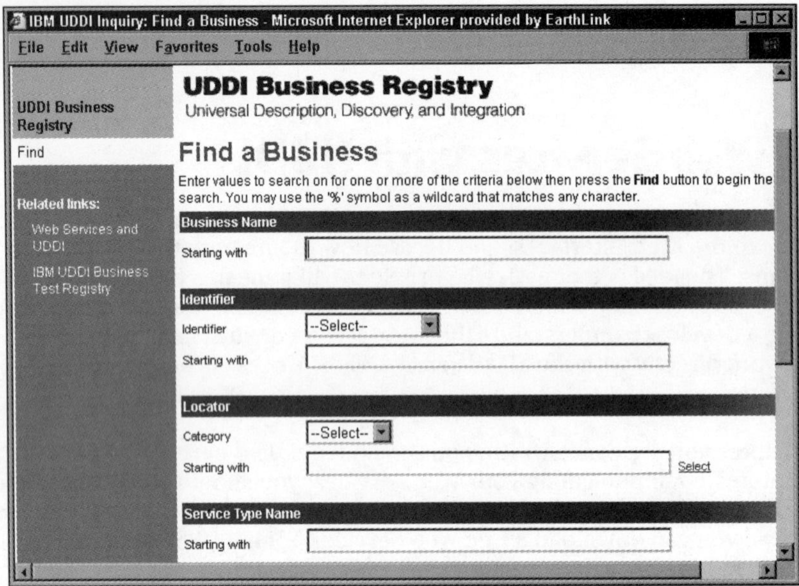

Figure 21-2: IBM's UDDI Business Registry search

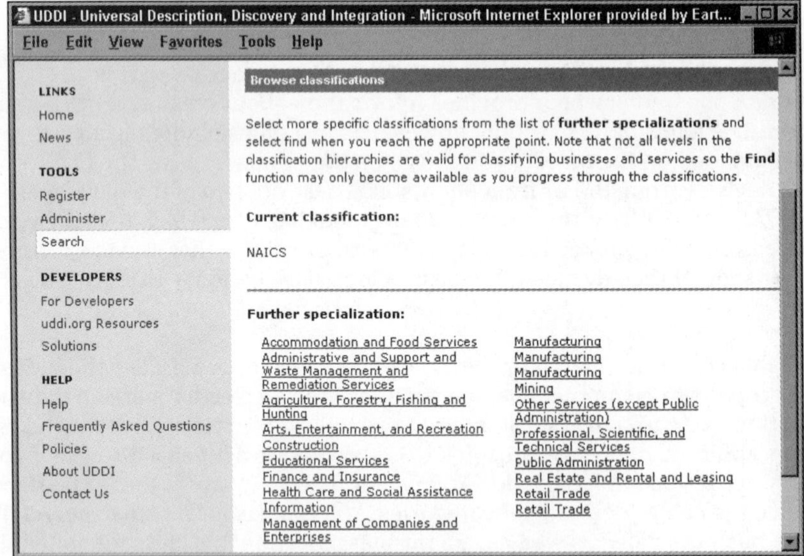

Figure 21-3: Microsoft's UDDI Business Registry search

You should be warned that at this point the search capabilities of either registry are fairly limited. You can search for a business, service, or service type, but if you and the service provider use different words, you are unlikely to be successful. Of course, with the good search engines out there, the limitations of this system are a bit frustrating. The good news is that this is likely to improve pretty soon. You may be able to search for *weather* and find links to Web services provided by the National Oceanic and Atmospheric Administration.

IBM and Microsoft have made major commitments to UDDI and have provided free resources online. IBM provides links to many UDDI resources at `http://www-3.ibm.com/services/uddi/testregistry/index.html`. Microsoft provides links from its UDDI Registry browser. Both Microsoft and IBM provide software-development kits that are available for free from their respective sites. Another resource is the Web Services Test Area from IBM's alphaWorks, at `http://demo.alphaworks.ibm.com/browser/`.

Exploring Web services using UDDI

Point your browser to the IBM Web Services Test Area. If you don't see something similar to what is shown in Figure 21-4, you may have to fill in the text field, click the Find button, and then expand the IBM Web Services TestArea folder.

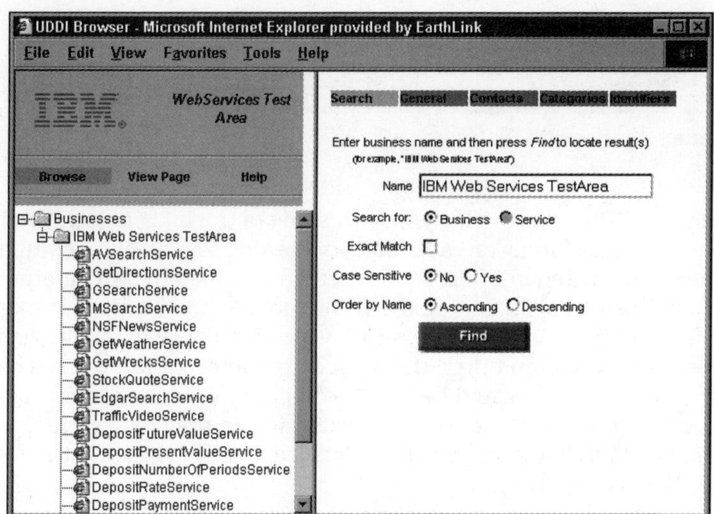

Figure 21-4: IBM's Web Services Test Area

Click GetWeatherService in the list in the left-hand window, and you will see a table in the right-hand window that gives details about the service, including access points for various protocol types and the location of the Web Services Description Language (WSDL) implementation files. You'll look a little more carefully at a WSDL file in the next section, but right now you may want to follow the link contained in the first WSDL file to the weather-interface WSDL file at `http://demo.alphaworks.ibm.com/browser/services/weather-interface.wsdl`. Figure 21-5 shows an excerpt from this file.

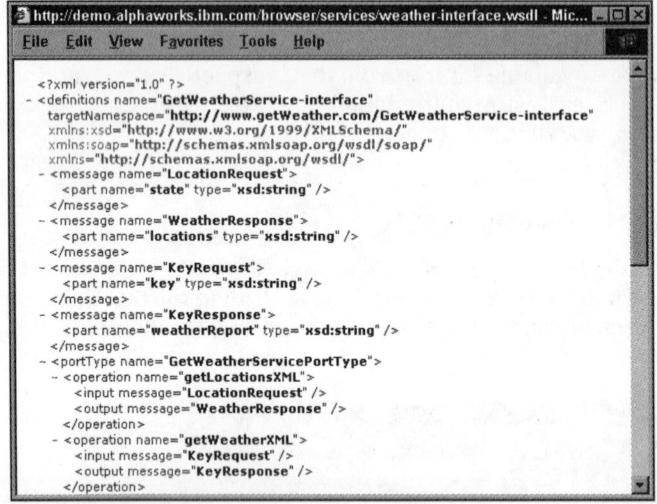


```
<?xml version="1.0" ?>
- <definitions name="GetWeatherService-interface"
   targetNamespace="http://www.getWeather.com/GetWeatherService-interface"
   xmlns:xsd="http://www.w3.org/1999/XMLSchema/"
   xmlns:soap="http://schemas.xmlsoap.org/wsdl/soap/"
   xmlns="http://schemas.xmlsoap.org/wsdl/">
 - <message name="LocationRequest">
     <part name="state" type="xsd:string" />
   </message>
 - <message name="WeatherResponse">
     <part name="locations" type="xsd:string" />
   </message>
 - <message name="KeyRequest">
     <part name="key" type="xsd:string" />
   </message>
 - <message name="KeyResponse">
     <part name="weatherReport" type="xsd:string" />
   </message>
 - <portType name="GetWeatherServicePortType">
   - <operation name="getLocationsXML">
       <input message="LocationRequest" />
       <output message="WeatherResponse" />
     </operation>
   - <operation name="getWeatherXML">
       <input message="KeyRequest" />
       <output message="KeyResponse" />
     </operation>
```

Figure 21-5: Weather-interface WSDL file

You can see that the WSDL file provides you with some of the information you need to interact with this service. Tools are available for turning this file into a stub file similar to the ones you created in Chapter 15 when you studied Remote Method Invocation (RMI). In the next section, you'll use the tool included with Axis to generate Java code from a WSDL file. You'll generate your own because the published WSDL file is incomplete: You aren't provided with all the information you need to actually use this Web service. It would be nice if you could view the appropriate WSDL file, as it serves as an interface to the Web service. In the next section, you'll start by generating a WSDL file from your HelloService Web service, and then you'll use it to generate the client-side stub file.

For now, explore the other feature of the IBM Web Services Test Area. You can play with the Web services published there. Select the View option instead of the Browse option in the left-hand window. You will now see a working version of the GetWeatherService in the right-hand window. You can select a U.S. state from the drop-down list and then be presented with a list of locations for which weather reports exist. Select one of them, and you will see its short-term weather forecast, as shown in Figure 21-6.

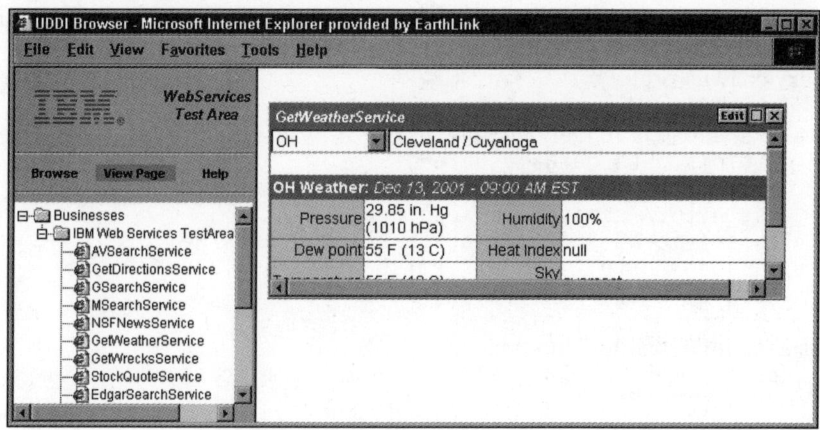

Figure 21-6: GetWeatherService GUI

This Test Area enables you to register your Web services and explore them as a user might. As you look around at various registered Web services, you'll notice that many of the URIs don't really enable you to play with them. Many of the URIs are local links and are really just being used by developers such as you for the purpose of playing around with the new technology. These are early and exciting times for Web services.

Creating and Working with WSDL files

In this section you'll see how easy it is to write a client if you have access to the service — even without seeing the source code. All you really need to know is where the service is and how you are able to communicate with it. The WSDL file includes information about the interface of the service as well as about the format of the SOAP messages that will be sent back and forth. Tools exist that can take all the information contained in the WSDL file and produce a proxy for the service on the client. You can then interact with the proxy as you would interact with the service. You should remember at all times that you aren't really making local method calls. You will still incur the penalty involved in communicating with a remote object.

Generating a WSDL file from HelloService

Axis enables you to generate a WSDL file from a .jws file or from a deployed service itself.

Begin by generating a WSDL file from HelloService.jws. You can view the HelloService by pointing your browser at `http://localhost:8080/axis/HelloService.jws?wsdl`. By appending the query `?wsdl` to the end of the URI, you enable yourself to see the WDSL for that particular Web service. (Of course, your Web server must be running.) You don't need to save the WSDL file locally, because you will be able to use it to generate Java files in the next section regardless of whether it is local or on the server. The following code shows the WSDL for HelloService.jws:

```
<?xml version="1.0" encoding="UTF-8"?>
<definitions  targetNamespace=
    "http://localhost:8080/axis/HelloService.jws"
  xmlns="http://schemas.xmlsoap.org/wsdl/"
  xmlns:serviceNS="http://localhost:8080/axis/HelloService.jws"
  xmlns:soap="http://schemas.xmlsoap.org/wsdl/soap/"
  xmlns:xsd="http://www.w3.org/2001/XMLSchema">

  <message name="echoNameResponse">
    <part name="echoNameResult" type="xsd:string"/>
  </message>

  <message name="echoNameRequest">
    <part name="arg0" type="xsd:string"/>
  </message>

  <portType name="HelloServicePortType">
    <operation name="echoName">
      <input message="serviceNS:echoNameRequest"/>
      <output message="serviceNS:echoNameResponse"/>
    </operation>
  </portType>

  <binding name="HelloServiceSoapBinding"
    type="serviceNS:HelloServicePortType">
    <soap:binding xmlns:soap=
      "http://schemas.xmlsoap.org/wsdl/soap/" style="rpc"
      transport="http://schemas.xmlsoap.org/soap/http"/>

    <operation name="echoName">
      <soap:operation
        xmlns:soap="http://schemas.xmlsoap.org/wsdl/soap/"
        soapAction="" style="rpc"/>
      <input>
        <soap:body
          xmlns:soap="http://schemas.xmlsoap.org/wsdl/soap/"
          encodingStyle=
            "http://schemas.xmlsoap.org/soap/encoding/"
          namespace="" use="encoded"/>
      </input>
      <output>
        <soap:body xmlns:soap=
          "http://schemas.xmlsoap.org/wsdl/soap/"
          encodingStyle=
            "http://schemas.xmlsoap.org/soap/encoding/"
          namespace="" use="encoded"/>
      </output>
    </operation>
  </binding>
```

```
    <service name="HelloService">
      <port binding="serviceNS:HelloServiceSoapBinding"
        name="HelloServicePort">
        <soap:address xmlns:soap=
          "http://schemas.xmlsoap.org/wsdl/soap/"
          location=
            "http://localhost:8080/axis/HelloService.jws"/>
      </port>
    </service>
  </definitions>
```

This seems like quite a lot of XML to describe a very simple service. Remember that the entire HelloService.jws was only this:

```
public class HelloService{

  public String echoName( String name ){
    return name;
  }
}
```

However, a lot of information in the WSDL file seemed to have been taken care of by your application. The root element is `<definitions>` and begins with the declarations of the various namespaces. Next the request and response messages are described. The request coming in from the client will be called `echoNameRequest` and will contain a single string. The response will be called `echoNameResponse` and will contain a string named `echoNameResult`. You can see how this response corresponds to the SOAP messages you intercepted using tcpmon. The `<portType>` element contains a child element that names the operation `echoName` and formally declares which message is the input and which is the output. The `<binding>` element includes the description of the operation as a remote procedure call and specifies the encoding of the incoming and outgoing messages. Although longer than you might expect, the WSDL file is easy to understand.

Generating the client from the WSDL

In the last section you saw how to produce a WSDL file from the Web service. You or someone else could also have written the WSDL file from scratch. In any case, if you have a WSDL file, you can use it to generate files on the client side to interact with the Web service. As the example file, use the WSDL file associated with HelloService.jws. You can either save the file you accessed with your browser in the last section and process it, or process the file remotely. You'll use the application Wsdl2java to transform the WSDL file into the Java files that you need.

Create a new directory, J2EEBible/GeneratedGreeting. Make sure that Tomcat is still running. From the command line, navigate into this directory and then type the following:

```
java org.apache.axis.wsdl.Wsdl2java
  http://localhost:8080/axis/HelloService.jws?wsdl
```

Three files are generated inside J2EEBible/GeneratedGreeting. The file HelloServiceSoapBindingStub.java is a stub like the stubs you saw when you learned about RMI. The stub is a local proxy for the remote Web service. You communicate with the stub and let it take care of the details of conveying this information to and from the remote object. The interface `HelloServicePortType` extends the `java.rmi.Remote` interface and includes the signature of the method `echoName()`. The generated class `HelloService` provides a handle to a local object that can communicate with your remote object. It returns an instance of the stub that is configured correctly. In the remainder of this section, you'll look at `HelloServicePortType` and `HelloService`; then you'll create a client application to connect to the `HelloService`.

The generated interface HelloServicePortType

In the WSDL specification, a port type is a set of operations and the messages involved in these operations. In the WSDL generated by `HelloService`, the `<portType>` element was the following:

```
<portType name="HelloServicePortType">
  <operation name="echoName">
    <input message="serviceNS:echoNameRequest"/>
    <output message="serviceNS:echoNameResponse"/>
  </operation>
</portType>
```

Like all port types, this one has a name. It specifies a single operation, which also has a name, and it consists of an input followed by an output. The Wsdl2java application transforms this information into the following interface, `HelloServicePortType`:

```
/**
 * HelloServicePortType.java
 *
 * This file was auto-generated from WSDL
 * by the Apache Axis Wsdl2java emitter.
 */

public interface HelloServicePortType extends java.rmi.Remote {

  public String echoName(String arg0) throws
    java.rmi.RemoteException;
}
```

The interface contains a single method signature for the method `echoName()`. The signature of the method comes from the further details of the input and output `<message>` elements. The output `<message>` element contains this single child element:

```
<part name="echoNameResult" type="xsd:string"/>
```

From this, you know that the return type of echoName() must be String. The input <message> element contains this single child element:

```
<part name="arg0" type="xsd:string"/>
```

You can see how this element is converted to the parameter type String and the name of arg0 for echoName(). The remote exception is required because the interface extends java.rmi.Remote.

The generated class HelloServiceSoapBindingStub

One of the things that makes the generated stub class hard to read is the lack of import statements: All the classes are referred to by their fully qualified names. The stub file needs to implement the interface HelloServicePortType. In this case that amounts to the requirement that it implement echoName(). The generated code looks like the code you wrote in the second version of HelloClient. After setting the values of certain variables, it makes the remote request by calling the invoke() method, like this:

```
Object resp = call.invoke("", "echoName", new Object[]
      {new org.apache.axis.message.RPCParam("arg0", arg0)});
```

Notice that the generated code only assumes that it will get some Object in return. The variable resp is declared to be of type Object. This Object is cast to a String before it is returned by the echoName() method. In your version of HelloClient, you treated the returned value as a String by casting it immediately.

In the boldfaced portions of the following code, if you squint and tilt your head just so, you should make out the image of the client you created by hand:

```
/**
 * HelloServiceSoapBindingStub.java
 *
 * This file was auto-generated from WSDL
 * by the Apache Axis Wsdl2java emitter.
 */

public class HelloServiceSoapBindingStub extends
  org.apache.axis.wsdl.Stub implements HelloServicePortType {

  private org.apache.axis.client.ServiceClient call
    = new org.apache.axis.client.ServiceClient(
        new org.apache.axis.transport.http.HTTPTransport());

  private java.util.Hashtable properties
    = new java.util.Hashtable();
```

```
public HelloServiceSoapBindingStub(java.net.URL endpointURL)
  throws org.apache.axis.SerializationException {

  this();
  call.set(org.apache.axis.transport.http.HTTPTransport.URL,
    endpointURL.toString());
}

public HelloServiceSoapBindingStub() throws
  org.apache.axis.SerializationException {}

public void _setProperty(String name, Object value) {
      properties.put(name, value);
}

// From org.apache.axis.wsdl.Stub
public Object _getProperty(String name) {
  return properties.get(name);
}

// From org.apache.axis.wsdl.Stub
public void _setTargetEndpoint(java.net.URL address) {
  call.set(org.apache.axis.transport.http.HTTPTransport.URL,
    address.toString());
}

// From org.apache.axis.wsdl.Stub
public java.net.URL _getTargetEndpoint() {
  try {
    return new java.net.URL((String)call.
      get(org.apache.axis.transport.http.HTTPTransport.URL));
  }
  catch (java.net.MalformedURLException mue) {
    return null; // ???
  }
}

// From org.apache.axis.wsdl.Stub
public synchronized void setMaintainSession(boolean session){
  call.setMaintainSession(session);
}

// From javax.naming.Referenceable
public javax.naming.Reference getReference() {
  return null; // ???
}

public String echoName(String arg0) throws
  java.rmi.RemoteException{
  if (call.get(org.apache.axis.transport.
    http.HTTPTransport.URL) == null) {
    throw new org.apache.axis.NoEndPointException();
  }
  call.set(org.apache.axis.transport.
```

```
        http.HTTPTransport.ACTION, "");
      Object resp = call.invoke("", "echoName", new Object[]
        {new org.apache.axis.message.RPCParam("arg0", arg0)});

      if (resp instanceof java.rmi.RemoteException) {
        throw (java.rmi.RemoteException)resp;
      }
      else {
        return (String) resp;
      }
    }
  }
```

In addition to the echoName() method, you should also pay attention to the first constructor. Note that the second constructor is a no-argument constructor that doesn't actually do anything, but to allow for cases in which it does contain functionality, it is called by the first constructor. The first constructor takes a URL as an argument and uses the ServiceClient set() method to set the value of org.apache.axis.transport.http.HTTPTransport.URL in the message to the value that was passed in. As you'll see next, this is what allows the generated class HelloService to act as a Factory.

The generated class HelloService.java

When the time comes to write the client, you will actually create a HelloService object and not a HelloServiceSoapBindingStub. The HelloService class will enable you to construct the HelloServiceSoapBindingStub that you need and expose it as an object of type HelloServicePortType. When all is said and done, all you want to do is invoke the right method in the Web service; the HelloServicePortType is the interface that enforces the signature of this method.

The generated class HelloService sets the endpoint URL as a constant called HelloServicePort_address to the value http://localhost:8080/axis/HelloService.jws, which it read from the WSDL file. It also provides two getHelloServicePort() methods. One takes a java.net.URL as an argument and returns a HelloServicePortType that is communicating with that address. The other doesn't take any arguments and uses the first version of getHelloServicePort() to return a HelloServicePortType that is communicating with the final value storied in the HelloServicePort_address variable.

```
/**
 * HelloService.java
 *
 * This file was auto-generated from WSDL
 * by the Apache Axis Wsdl2java emitter.
 */

public class HelloService {

  // Use to get a proxy class for HelloServicePort
```

```
  private final java.lang.String HelloServicePort_address
    = "http://localhost:8080/axis/HelloService.jws";

  public HelloServicePortType getHelloServicePort() {
    java.net.URL endpoint;
    try {
      endpoint = new java.net.URL(HelloServicePort_address);
    } catch (java.net.MalformedURLException e) {
      return null; //unlikely as URL was validated in wsdl2java
    }
    return getHelloServicePort(endpoint);
  }

  public HelloServicePortType getHelloServicePort(
    java.net.URL portAddress) {
    try {
      return new HelloServiceSoapBindingStub(portAddress);
    } catch (org.apache.axis.SerializationException e) {
      return null; // ???
    }
  }
}
```

Writing the class Main.java

To use the generated files, you do the following:

1. Create an instance of the class `HelloService`.
2. Use the `getHelloServicePort()` method to create a stub that acts as a proxy for the Web service and only presents its interface.
3. Use the proxy to call the `echoName()` method as you would a local method.

Note that as with other remote calls, you should be aware of the costs of making such a call. Even though the code is the same as it is when you make a local call, you can see when you execute the application that the response takes a while.

Here's the class `Main.java`:

```
public class Main {
  public static void main(String[] args) throws Exception{
    try {
      String inputName = (args.length<1)? "World": args[0];
      HelloService helloService = new HelloService();
      HelloServicePortType port
        = helloService.getHelloServicePort();
      String response = port.echoName(inputName);
      System.out.println("Hello " + response + ".");
    } catch (Exception e) {
      System.err.println(e.toString());
    }
  }
}
```

The generated classes wrote the Axis code for you and enabled you to concentrate on what you actually want the client to do and what you want its interface to be.

Using WSDL files to create a service

For completeness, you should know that the Wsdl2java application can also take a WSDL file and create the appropriate files for the server side. You may have a WSDL file that describes a Web service, but you may not have access to the actual Java class files (or application files in whatever language they may be written in). Just as you generated a stub file and an interface and a class to implement the client side, you can generate a skeleton file and a class to implement the server side.

You won't actually deploy the server-side files this time, but start by creating the directory J2EEBible/GeneratedGreeting2. Open up a terminal window and navigate to that directory and, with Tomcat running, type in the following command:

```
java org.apache.axis.wsdl.Wsdl2java --skeleton
  http://localhost:8080/axis/HelloService?wsdl
```

The only difference between this and the early command is the addition of the flag indicating that you want to create a skeleton. This time two files are created. One is the skeleton file: This is the file that you will use as your Web service. It uses the other file, which is the implementation file. The implementation file is the one that you customize so that the service does what you want it to. Remember that these files are generated from the WSDL file that specifies the interface for the messages and the Web service. The WSDL file can't specify the actual action of the Web service.

Note that the interface `HelloServicePortType` is not regenerated. You will need this interface, as it is referenced in the generated classes. This is consistent with your experience with RMI, in which the interface has to be present on both the client and the server.

The generated class HelloServiceSoapBindingSkeleton

The skeleton consists of two constructors, an implementation of the `echoName()` method and a variable of type `HelloServicePortType`. The constructors enable you to assign the `HelloServicePortType` variable `impl` either to an instance of the generated class `HelloServiceSoapBindingImpl` or to an instance of another class that implements the `HelloServicePortType` interface. Here's the automatically generated code.

```
/**
 * HelloServiceSoapBindingSkeleton.java
 *
 * This file was auto-generated from WSDL
 * by the Apache Axis Wsdl2java emitter.
 */
```

```
public class HelloServiceSoapBindingSkeleton {
  private HelloServicePortType impl;

  public HelloServiceSoapBindingSkeleton() {
    this.impl = new HelloServiceSoapBindingImpl();
  }

  public HelloServiceSoapBindingSkeleton(
    HelloServicePortType impl) {
    this.impl = impl;
  }

  public Object echoName(String arg0)
    throws java.rmi.RemoteException {
    Object ret = impl.echoName(arg0);
    return ret;
  }
}
```

The `echoName()` method uses the `echoName()` method in the object named `impl`. You don't have to edit this skeleton file, as it defers the actual implementation of `echoName()` to the implementation file. Notice that the return type for `echoName()` is `Object`. This saves a step. You have to send the return value over the wire as an `Object` that will get cast to a `String` on the client side, so you do not need to change the type here.

The class HelloServiceSoapBindingImpl

The implementation class contains an outline that you have to fill in. Here the method `echoName()` returns a `String` because `HelloServiceSoapBindingImpl` implements the interface `HelloServicePortType`. When `HelloServiceSoap BindingImpl` sends this string on to the skeleton class, the skeleton ignores the fact that it has an object of type `String` and sends an ordinary `Object` over the wire.

```
/**
 * HelloServiceSoapBindingImpl.java
 *
 * This file was auto-generated from WSDL
 * by the Apache Axis Wsdl2java emitter.
 */

public class HelloServiceSoapBindingImpl
  implements HelloServicePortType {

  public String echoName(String arg0)
    throws java.rmi.RemoteException {
    throw new java.rmi.RemoteException ("Not Yet Implemented");
  }
}
```

All you have to do is fill out this method to `return arg0` in a `try` block, and you have implemented the service. The preceding example was a very easy service, but these generated files on the server side perform the same function that the generated files performed on the client side. The generated files act as a framework that enables you to concentrate on coding up the service you are creating and accessing. The code for communicating this information can be generated by an application. As with all automatically generated code, you may want to tweak it here and there, but this code should get you up and running quickly.

Sending a Java Object to your Web Service

In this section, you'll extend the running example to pass a Java object inside a SOAP message. Up until now, you've only passed a `String`, and this has kept the details uncomplicated. You'll be relieved to see that, for the most part, most of the work in this extended example is done for you by Axis.

In Chapter 14 you learned about data binding. You saw that it makes sense to persist Java objects in XML. With JAXB you began with a DTD and transformed it into a collection of Java classes. From using JAXB, you got a correspondence between Java objects and the elements defined in the DTD. This correspondence made it easy to handle the XML files that described objects for which you already had mappings.

When dealing with Web services, you need to look at this setup from the opposite vantage point. You already have Java objects and, for the most part, don't want to be bothered with setting up a DTD or schema that conforms to their structure. You just want to be able to send the objects between your client and Web service. Remember that when you are dealing with a Web service, you don't know the language being used at the other end of the wire and you don't really care. What you really need to do is convert the state of the Java object to some reasonable format and send the object over the wire. You're already sending XML when you send your SOAP message, so it is natural to use XML to send the state of your Java object.

In this section, you'll use JavaBeans and take advantage of the built-in functionality of Axis. If you need more control over the serialization, you can adapt these ideas to suit your own needs.

The classes for the JavaBean version of HelloService

You'll need three classes to make the Java Bean version of HelloService work. First you will need to code up the bean itself. You'll keep a copy of this class on both the client and the server. You'll also need to slightly rewrite the HelloService.java code so that your method is accepting an object of type `HumanBeanCounter` and not just a `String`. Most of your work will be in changing the HelloClient.java code so that you are creating an instance of a `HumanBeanCounter` and bundling it up and sending it off to the server. In the next section, you'll make the corresponding changes to the deployment descriptor.

The bean class HumanBeanCounter

To see how to pass a JavaBean, you'll create a simple object that contains a `String` and an `int`. Here's the source for the file HumanBeanCounter.java:

```
package BeanGreeting;

public class HumanBeanCounter {
  private String name;
  private int age;

  public String getName(){
    return name;
  }

  public void setName(String name){
    this.name = name;
  }

  public int getAge(){
    return age;
  }

  public void setAge(int age){
    this.age = age;
  }
}
```

There's nothing tricky going on here. The class `HumanBeanCounter` contains two private variables, `age` and `name`, along with public-accessor methods to get and set each of them.

The service class HelloService

The service class isn't much more complicated than it was when it received a `String` and immediately returned it in the `LocalGreeting` or the `DeployedGreeting` versions. It still consists of a single method, `echoName()`. This time `echoName()` takes an object of type `HumanBeanCounter` and returns a `String` based on the value of private variables belonging to this object. The values of the variables are accessed using the standard JavaBean `get`*`XXX`*`()` methods.

```
package BeanGreeting;

public class HelloService{

  public String echoName( HumanBeanCounter human ){
    return human.getName() + ", I would never have guessed" +
      " that you're " + human.getAge() + " years old.";
  }
}
```

Just to belabor this point — there's some magic going on. Remember that the HumanBeanCounter is created on the client machine and is sent to the server after being encoded in XML. This XML message is now once again accessible as a Java object.

The client class HelloClient

The file that needs to change the most is HelloClient.java. In the following code, the first changes to main() are additions that create and initialize an instance of HumanBeanCounter:

```
package BeanGreeting;

import org.apache.axis.client.ServiceClient;
import org.apache.axis.utils.QName;


public class HelloClient {

  public static void main(String [] args) {
    try {
      String inputName = (args.length<1)? "World": args[0];
      int inputAge = (args.length<2)? 1000000 :
        Integer.parseInt(args[1]);

      HumanBeanCounter person = new HumanBeanCounter();
      person.setName(inputName);
      person.setAge(inputAge);
//change the port back to 8080 in the line below

      String endpoint =  "http://localhost:8088/axis/servlet"
        + "/AxisServlet/HelloService";
      ServiceClient client = new ServiceClient(endpoint);
      client.addSerializer(HumanBeanCounter.class,
        new QName("urn:HelloService", "HumanBeanCounter"),
        new org.apache.axis.encoding.BeanSerializer(
          HumanBeanCounter.class));

      String name = (String)client.invoke("HelloService",
        "echoName", new Object [] { person});
      System.out.println("Hello " + name + ".");
    } catch (Exception e) {
      System.out.println("Parameters <String name> <int age>");
      System.err.println(e.toString());
    }
  }
}
```

The change that is central to transforming the JavaBean is the addition of the call to the addSerializer() method. The addSerializer() method takes as its first parameter the Java class that you will be serializing. In this case, that class is HumanBeanCounter.class. The second parameter is an org.apache.axis.utils.QName that is the xsi:type of the XML type that will be associated with HumanBeanCounter.class. With the third parameter, you are passing in a newly created BeanSerializer object with the class it is serializing set to HumanBeanCounter. Note that you'll need to be careful when deploying this service to make sure that the contents of the deployment descriptor are consistent with what you've specified in the addSerializer() method call.

Deploying and running the application

As you would for the DeployedGreeting version of this service, create a BeanGreeting directory inside the <tomcat-install>\webapps\axis\WEB-INF\classes directory. Move a copy of HelloService.class and HumanBeanCounter.class inside. Cycle Tomcat. You are now ready to write and run the deployment descriptor. Once that's done, you can compile and run HelloClient. In this section, you'll compare the SOAP request sent under these circumstances with the SOAP request sent when only a String is being passed as the parameter for the service's echoName() method.

The deployment descriptor

Your deployment descriptor requires an additional child element for the <service> element. Add the <beanMappings> element boldfaced in the following code. You are defining the bean mappings to be consistent with those you set up in HelloClient.java:

```
<admin:deploy xmlns:admin="AdminService">
  <service name="HelloService" pivot="RPCDispatcher">

    <option name="className"
      value="BeanGreeting.HelloService"/>
    <option name="methodName" value="echoName"/>

    <beanMappings>
      <myNS:HelloService xmlns:myNS="urn:HelloService"
        classname="BeanGreeting.HumanBeanCounter"/>
    </beanMappings>

  </service>
</admin:deploy>
```

Save this file as deploy.xml inside J2EEBible/BeanGreeting. Use AdminClient to deploy BeanGreeting.HelloService. Create a list of deployed services with the AdminClient, and you'll see the following element. Notice the additional <typeMappings> element. In addition to the settings you passed in using deploy.xml, the `<typeMappings>` also includes the values of the classes it will use to serialize and deserialize.

```
<service name="HelloService" pivot="RPCDispatcher">
  <option name="methodName" value="echoName"/>
  <option name="className" value="BeanGreeting.HelloService"/>

  <typeMappings>
    <typeMapping classname="BeanGreeting.HumanBeanCounter"
      deserializerFactory=
        "org.apache.axis.encoding.BeanSerializer$BeanSerFactory"
      serializer="org.apache.axis.encoding.BeanSerializer"
      type="ns:HelloService" xmlns:ns="urn:HelloService"/>
  </typeMappings>
</service>
```

The changes to the SOAP message

Open a terminal, navigate to J2EEBible, and compile and run HelloClient.java. By running it with the command-line arguments `Abe` and `45`, you are sending the following SOAP message, which you can intercept using tcpmon:

```
POST /axis/servlet/AxisServlet/HelloService HTTP/1.0

Content-Length: 530

Host: localhost

Content-Type: text/xml; charset=utf-8

SOAPAction: "HelloService/echoName"


<?xml version="1.0" encoding="UTF-8"?>
<SOAP-ENV:Envelope xmlns:SOAP-ENV=
  "http://schemas.xmlsoap.org/soap/envelope/"
  xmlns:xsd="http://www.w3.org/2001/XMLSchema"
  xmlns:xsi="http://www.w3.org/2001/XMLSchema-instance">

  <SOAP-ENV:Body>
    <ns3:echoName xmlns:ns3="HelloService">
      <arg0 href="#id0"/>
    </ns3:echoName>

  <multiRef id="id0" xsi:type="ns5:HumanBeanCounter"
    xmlns:ns5="urn:HelloService">
    <age xsi:type="xsd:int">45</age>
    <name xsi:type="xsd:string">Abe</name>
  </multiRef>

 </SOAP-ENV:Body>
</SOAP-ENV:Envelope>
```

As a reminder, when you were just sending a String from HelloClient, the <Body> element in its entirety was as follows:

```
<SOAP-ENV:Body>
    <echoName>
      <inputName xsi:type="xsd:string">Sam</inputName>
    </echoName>
  </SOAP-ENV:Body>
```

You can see that in the new code echoName belongs to the HelloService namespace. It takes an argument whose type is defined below, and so you see the pointer to the <multiRef> element that follows. The <multiRef> element contains the elements that correspond to the two attributes of the HumanBeanCounter class. Each of these elements, <age> and <name>, has simple types, but you can see how this model could be extended.

As you should expect, the returned SOAP message is similar to the reply in the version of the service you constructed earlier. The only difference in the <Body> element is the specification of a namespace as in the request:

```
<SOAP-ENV:Body>
  <ns3:echoNameResponse xmlns:ns3="HelloService">
    <echoNameResult xsi:type="xsd:string">Abe, I would never
have guessed that you&apos;re 45 years old.</echoNameResult>
  </ns3:echoNameResponse>
 </SOAP-ENV:Body>
```

Sending a JavaBean

You've sent quite a few SOAP messages in this chapter. For the most part, the idea has been to avoid working with the actual XML. In this section you have already used a utility to serialize the JavaBean before sending it over the wire. This subsection shows you how you might create a simple SOAP message from an XML file. Using the information from the XML chapters, you could, of course, create the XML document from scratch. This section details an alternate approach.

The XML file person.xml

Create a new directory, J2EEBible/MessageGreeting. Inside it, save the following person.xml file:

```
<?xml version="1.0" encoding="UTF-8"?>

<humanBean>
  <name> Bee </name>
  <age> 50 </age>
</humanBean>
```

Really, you'd just like to be able to pick this file up, trim off the first line, and tuck it inside a SOAP envelope. This is what you will do in HelloClient.java.

The client file HelloClient.java

The first job of the client is to create a `Document` object by parsing the file person.xml. The first bit of boldfaced code in the following example creates a `Document` object, exactly as was done in Chapter 12 on the Java APIs for XML parsing:

```
package MessageGreeting;

import org.apache.axis.client.ServiceClient;
import org.apache.axis.message.SOAPEnvelope;
import org.apache.axis.Message;
import org.apache.axis.message.SOAPBodyElement;

import java.io.File;
import javax.xml.parsers.DocumentBuilder;
import javax.xml.parsers.DocumentBuilderFactory;
import org.w3c.dom.Document;
import org.w3c.dom.Element;

public class HelloClient {

   public static void main(String [] args) {
     try {
       DocumentBuilderFactory dbFactory =
         DocumentBuilderFactory.newInstance();
       DocumentBuilder documentBuilder =
         dbFactory.newDocumentBuilder();
       Document document = documentBuilder.parse(new
         File("MessageGreeting/person.xml"));

       SOAPEnvelope envelope = new SOAPEnvelope();
       envelope.addBodyElement(new
         SOAPBodyElement(document.getDocumentElement()));

       //change the port back to 8080 in the line below
       String endpoint =
"http://localhost:8088/axis/servlet/AxisServlet/HelloService";
       ServiceClient client = new ServiceClient(endpoint);

       client.setRequestMessage(new Message(envelope));
       client.invoke();

     } catch (Exception e) {
       System.out.println("Params <String name> <int age>");
       System.err.println(e.toString());
     }
   }
}
```

The second boldfaced task is to create a SOAPEnvelope and add the Document created from person.xml as the SOAPBodyElement for this SOAPEnvelope. The final task is to create a Message object from the SOAPEnvelope and pass it to the ServiceClient as the request message. The last boldfaced line is required, which may seem a bit odd. You aren't making a remote procedure call, so you aren't directly invoking a named method. On the other hand, your code so far has just set up a ServiceClient with the appropriate SOAP message and a destination. You need to somehow say, "send the message." The method invoke() sends the SOAP message.

The message sent by the client

Use the application tcpmon to intercept the following message sent by the client:

```
POST /axis/servlet/AxisServlet/HelloService HTTP/1.0

Content-Length: 344

Host: localhost

Content-Type: text/xml; charset=utf-8

SOAPAction: "/humanBean"

<?xml version="1.0" encoding="UTF-8"?>

<SOAP-ENV:Envelope
  xmlns:SOAP -ENV="http://schemas.xmlsoap.org/soap/envelope/"
  xmlns:xsd="http://www.w3.org/2001/XMLSchema"
  xmlns:xsi="http://www.w3.org/2001/XMLSchema-instance">

  <SOAP-ENV:Body>
    <humanBean>
      <name> Bee </name>
      <age> 50 </age>
    </humanBean>
  </SOAP-ENV:Body>
</SOAP-ENV:Envelope>
```

This technique enables you to include a particular XML message as the <Body> element of a SOAP message. You can likewise modify part or all of a SOAP message, as it is just an XML message.

Summary

In this chapter, you looked at the process of creating, exposing, and using Web services. In its most basic form, a Web service doesn't differ much (if at all) from existing Java classes that you may have just sitting around at home. On the other hand, you may need to create a Web service that interacts directly with the request and response SOAP messages. Whether or not Web services end up being the industry standard, Microsoft and IBM are strongly behind this technology, and it is worth investigating it and deciding if it is right for your needs.

✦ You took a simple Java class and converted it to a Web service. This didn't involve changing the code of the service; you just needed to place the source where Tomcat and Axis could serve it up. You then wrote a client that could contact your service. The client sent a `String` and expected a `String` in return.

✦ You looked at the syntax of the request and response messages being sent back and forth. The single `String` that you were sending and receiving was wrapped inside an XML document inside an element called the SOAP `<Body>`, which was in turn inside the SOAP `<Envelope>` element that contained information on how this `<Body>` element was to be processed. In addition to this information, the messages contained the usual HTTP information before the SOAP message began.

✦ Just placing your Web service's source file in a directory is an easy way to deploy your service, but you learned about a much more flexible way when you had to deploy many classes inside some directory structure. You can place these class files in their existing directories inside the classes folder, or you can jar them up and place the jar file inside the lib folder. You then learned to write and run a deployment descriptor to tell Axis where to find the class files.

✦ You explored the UDDI registries at Microsoft and IBM to find Web services written by others. You searched the registries and found information about Web services you may want to use.

✦ You learned to generate WSDL files from Web services. These files describe the Web services and enable you to use various tools to generate stub files for the client and skeleton files for the server. Using WSDL files, you can automatically generate much of the code that you need for the remote infrastructure. You can also provide other developers with WSDL files so that they can write to your Web services.

✦ You saw that it is easy to serialize a JavaBean and send it from the client to the service as XML inside the SOAP message. Once the JavaBean has arrived, the service can access it as if it had been created locally. If you don't want to use a JavaBean, you also saw how to send XML from an existing file inside your SOAP message.

✦ ✦ ✦

CHAPTER 22

JMS

✦ ✦ ✦ ✦

In This Chapter

Understanding Java Message Service (JMS)

Setting up a JMS system

Developing applications with JMS

✦ ✦ ✦ ✦

Building enterprise-level applications requires more than just EJBs. You will need to interact with both new applications and legacy applications in order to create comprehensive and robust applications. Message-oriented middleware is a proven technique you can use to access and integrate these other systems into your application.

This chapter shows you how you can interact with message-oriented systems the Java way. It introduces you to the Java Message Service (JMS) and gives you the information you need to start communicating with messages from a Java application and brings you up to speed on another tool in the J2EE developer's toolbox.

Messages in the Middle

Message-oriented middleware (MOM) has proven to be a great facilitator in application integration. It allows applications to interact with each other without requiring each application to know intimate details about the others. This is especially useful in enterprise environments, in which integrating multiple applications with Web servers has become commonplace.

Applications cooperate with each other by defining a set of messages that they accept and produce. They don't care where the messages come from as long as they follow the expected format. Likewise, the applications don't care where messages they produce go; they just assume that the proper applications are listening. This is loose coupling at the application level.

So how do these messages get from the output of one program to the input of another? Say hello to MOM. The applications use the services of a message-oriented middleware program whose job it is to hand messages back and forth between the different applications. Using this middleware frees programmers from worrying about (or coding for) issues such as message handshaking, message-delivery guarantees, programming-language dependencies, timing, transactions, and many others. All of these issues are handled by the middleware.

Life before JMS

The idea of well-defined applications interacting with others to produce a greater whole has been central to UNIX since its inception. In the mid-80s, message-oriented middleware came along to support that idea by supplying a robust communication layer that freed programmers from having to deal with the intricacies of system communications.

MOM vendors have been refining and extending their products for almost 20 years. MOM products have evolved from a simple asynchronous queue to elaborate systems with publishers, subscribers, brokers, message reformatting, differing quality of service (QOS) capabilities, and more. During that time, programmers have been able to choose the most appropriate middleware products for their needs.

MOM Meets JMS

Java arrived on the scene in the mid-90s and brought with it the idea that code should be portable. While many of the existing MOM vendors provided a Java interface, the resulting code was not portable. It tied the user to using that specific software vendor and only ran on platforms supported by the vendor. Sun, along with many of the MOM vendors, recognized this problem and created a generic API designed to provide access to the majority of features supported by most MOM products. This API is known as Java Message Service (JMS). The role JMS plays in messaging is similar to the role that Java Database Connectivity (JDBC) API plays in database access.

No matter what the underlying native API is for a messaging product, Java programs can use it as long as it supports the JMS API. In fact, many of the existing MOM providers have just added another JMS interface onto their existing APIs. For instance, IBM's MQSeries is available on a wide variety of platforms with a wide variety of programming interfaces. Once JMS was published, IBM built a JMS interface on top of its own native interface. This allows Java programs to exchange messages with programs written in other languages (C, COBOL, Smalltalk, and others).

JMS for application independence

A major benefit of using the JMS API is application independence. If you write your application following the JMS API, your application can run on any of the JMS-compliant middleware products on the market. This gives you an enormous amount of freedom when it comes to selecting specific vendors. If you are not getting the support you require, or if your application can take advantage of another vendor's implementation, you can migrate to a new vendor with few or no code changes.

Pure JMS providers

Since the JMS specification was released, a number of software companies have created messaging systems in Java whose only interface is the JMS API identified by Sun. These vendors have been able to optimize their products for use with Java and the JMS API. Some of these products are iBus from Softwired, SonicMQ from Progress, FioranoMQ by Fiorano, and JMQ from Sun. One advantage these products have over their non-Java cousins is the ability to deploy wherever there is a Java Virtual Machine (JVM) available.

JMS support in version 1.2 of the J2EE specification was optional. However, version 1.3 of the J2EE specification requires a J2EE-compliant platform to provide a JMS implementation. This integration should make deploying and configuring messaging applications on the J2EE platform easier and more consistent. It also helps ensure that the messaging integration with the J2EE is more stable and complete.

Since JMS is becoming a standard part of the J2EE platform, you need to understand how you can use JMS and messaging systems in your enterprise applications. Specifically, what messaging models are supported by JMS and how do you use them?

Types of Messaging Systems

According to the JMS API, messaging systems can be separated into two main categories. In this section, you will learn about the *point-to-point* and *publish/subscribe* models of messaging.

Point-to-point

Point-to-point messaging is a messaging style in which one application sends a message directly to a specific message queue. Only one application retrieves the message from the queue. In this case only two messaging clients are involved: one to send, and one to retrieve.

An example of a point-to-point system might be a queue for incoming orders. Anyone can send an order to the queue, and one order processor will remove the order from the queue and process it. In any order transaction, there is one sender and one receiver.

Publish/subscribe

The publish/subscribe model of messaging is very different from the point-to-point model. In this model the sender of the message sends (publishes) the message to a topic. Anyone who is interested in receiving messages on a given topic subscribes to that topic. As a result, when the sender sends the message to the topic, each subscriber receives a copy of the message. In this case, the message has one sender and potentially many (or zero) recipients.

One of the most important aspects of this type of messaging is that the sender doesn't know anything about the subscribers. It doesn't know how many subscribers there are, where they are located, or what they do with the messages.

One publish/subscribe example might be someone publishing a set of stock quotes on a regular basis. Another example from the order-entry system of the previous section might involve publishing the order information to a topic as the order is processed. Several subscribers might receive that message. The order-fulfillment department will begin filling the order once it receives the message. The customer-service department might send out confirmation and support information once it receives notice of the order. The billing department might receive the message and generate a bill. The business-planning department might receive the message and update its information for reporting purposes.

While these definitions seem fairly cut and dried, you may encounter some messaging systems that blur the two models into systems with varying capabilities. However, they should behave as expected with standard JMS code. To take advantage of unique features, you may have to write some non-standard JMS code. At that point, your code may not be portable.

JMS Overview

Before diving into the details of JMS programming, there are several things that you should be familiar with. These include some basic messaging terminology, an overview of the interfaces involved, and a high-level operational view of JMS systems.

Messaging terminology

Here are some simple definitions of the terminology you will be encountering as you read more about JMS. These definitions are simple and to the point, but they should give enough information to understand the explanations.

- *Message*—Encapsulates the information sent between the sender and the receiver. It consists not only of the body of the message (the data), but also of a header and optionally a set of properties.
- *Header*—Contains information used by both the clients and the JMS provider to identify and route the messages. All message types have the same header structure.

- *Body*—Contains application-specific data. It can take one of several forms, depending on the message type. It can be simple text strings, serialized objects, XML, a binary stream, and so on.
- *Administered object*—Objects created and maintained outside the JMS application. They provide a generic means of accessing a message provider and connecting with predefined queues and topics. Programmers use a naming service like the Java Naming and Directory Interface (JNDI) to locate administered objects.
- *Connection*—The link between the application and the JMS provider. A connection must be established with the provider before anything else can be done.
- *Session*—Designed to manage the sending and receiving of messages. A session is created on top of a connection. It is responsible for creating producers and consumers, creating message objects, handling transactions, controlling acknowledgements, and so on.
- *Destination*—The target of a JMS message. It can be either a queue or a topic, depending on the model of operation.
- *Queue*—The destination for the point-to-point model of operation. Messages are sent to a queue and then retrieved from the queue by a single receiver.
- *Topic*—The destination for the publish/subscribe model of operation. Messages are sent to a topic where the JMS provider sends a copy of the message to each subscriber of the topic.
- *Producer*—The source of a message. Two types of producers exist: senders and publishers. Senders send messages to a queue in the point-to-point model. Publishers send messages to a topic in the publish/subscribe model.
- *Consumer*—A consumer is the recipient of a message. Two types of consumers exist: receivers and subscribers. Receivers receive messages from a queue in the point-to-point model. Subscribers receive messages from a topic in the publish/subscribe model.

Interface overview

The JMS API is the key to writing generic messaging code. Therefore, you need to become familiar with the interfaces involved. The following sections give an overview of these interfaces. The following tables describe each interface, while the diagrams give you a sense of how they are related to each other.

Note

JMS defines a set of interfaces and abstract classes. You don't create instances of JMS classes; instead you work with objects from a JMS provider that implement the JMS interfaces. You get the initial provider objects by looking them up in a namespace. From that point on, all objects created from these initial objects are provider-specific, but they implement the JMS interfaces.

Table 22-1 describes the interfaces you will use to create and process messages. These interfaces are used for both point-to-point and publish/subscribe messaging models.

Table 22-1
Message interfaces

Interface Name	*Description*
`Message`	Basic interface for all message types. Defines the header, properties, and body of the message. Specific message types will implement this interface.
`BytesMessage`	Defines a message body containing a sequence of bytes. Useful for carrying existing message formats and interfacing with non-Java systems.
`MapMessage`	Defines a message body containing a map with strings as the keys and Java objects as the values. Objects can be retrieved by name or sequentially.
`ObjectMessage`	Defines a message body with a single serializable Java object. If more than one object must be sent, you should send a collection of objects.
`StreamMessage`	Defines a message body that can be accessed as a stream of Java objects. The methods used to read and write StreamMessage objects are very similar to those in `java.io.DataInputStream` and `java.io.DataOutputStream`. Useful for writing primitives and objects in a sequence.
`TextMessage`	Defines a body that holds a `String` object. Used for basic text messages as well as messages containing XML.

Table 22-2 describes the interfaces you will use when programming with the point-to-point messaging model.

Table 22-2
Point-to-point interfaces

Interface Name	*Description*
`Queue`	The destination for point-to-point messages. You send messages to a queue, and specify the queue when creating a sender or a receiver.
`QueueSender`	Sends messages to the given queue. Defines the `send` method used to kick off a message.

Interface Name	*Description*
`QueueReceiver`	Retrieves messages from a given queue.
`QueueSession`	Creates senders, receivers, and various types of messages for a given connection.
`QueueConnection`	Establishes a connection with the JMS provider. Used to create sessions for an application to use.
`QueueConnectionFactory`	A provider-specific class that creates connections to the JMS provider. Usually looked up in a JNDI namespace.

Table 22-3 describes the interfaces you will use when programming with the publish/subscribe messaging model.

Table 22-3
Publish/subscribe interfaces

Interface Name	*Description*
`Topic`	The destination for publish/subscribe messages. You send messages to a topic, and topic subscribers receive copies of the message. Multiple publishers and subscribers are allowed on any given topic.
`TopicPublisher`	Publishes messages to the given topic. Defines the `publish` method used to kick off a message.
`TopicSubscriber`	Subscribes to a given topic. Provides both blocking and non-blocking `receive` calls as well as asynchronous calls to a registered message listener.
`TopicSession`	Creates publishers, subscribers, and various types of messages for a given connection.
`TopicConnection`	Establishes a connection with the JMS provider. Used to create sessions for an application to use.
`TopicConnectionFactory`	A provider-specific class that creates connections to the JMS provider. Usually looked up in a JNDI namespace.

The following figures show a static view of the classes and their relationships with each other. Figure 22-1 shows the classes involved in creating messages, as well as the various types of messages.

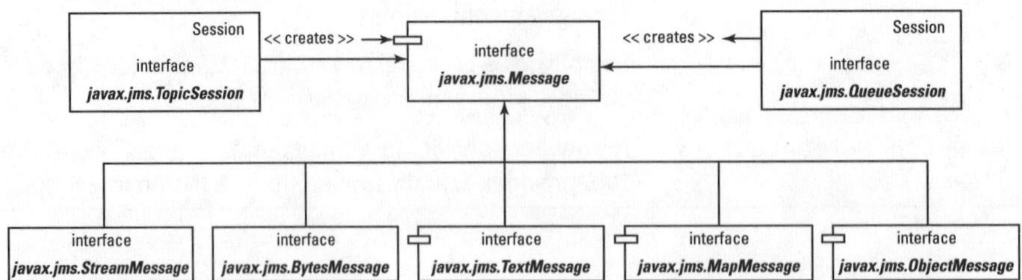

Figure 22-1: The relationships among the message classes and their producers

Figure 22-2 shows the classes involved in point-to-point messaging, as well as the relationships among them.

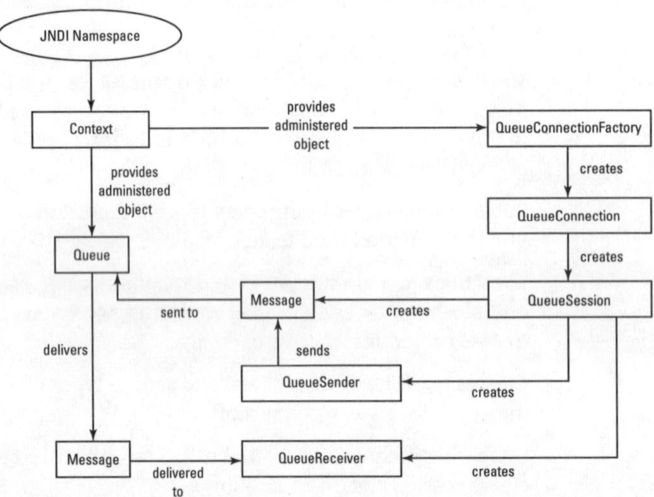

Figure 22-2: The relationships among the interfaces used with point-to-point messaging

Figure 22-3 shows the classes involved in publish/subscribe messaging and the relationships among them.

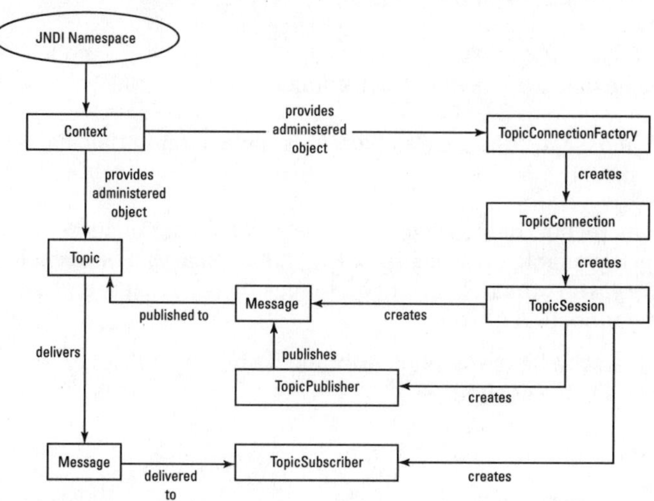

Figure 22-3: The relationships of interfaces used in publish-subscribe messaging

Operational overview

Using JMS is a fairly simple and straightforward process and can be divided into two parts — *initialization* and *message processing*. Initialization establishes a connection to the underlying messaging provider and creates the destinations, senders, and receivers. Message processing involves sending and receiving messages.

The following steps are involved in the initialization of the JMS:

1. Look up a connection factory (`QueueConnectionFactory` or `TopicConnectionFactory`).
2. Create the connection using the factory (`QueueConnection` or `TopicConnection`).
3. Create a session from the connection (`QueueSession` or `TopicSession`).
4. Look up a destination (`Queue` or `Topic`).
5. Create a sender or receiver from the session using the destination (`QueueSender/Receiver` or `TopicPublisher/Subscriber`).
6. For asynchronous receivers/consumers, register a message listener to be notified when messages are available.

You can send messages once the JMS objects have been initialized—just follow these steps:

1. Create a message object from the session.
2. Set the contents of the message.
3. Send the message using the sender or producer.

You can also receive messages once the JMS objects have been initialized—to do this, follow these steps:

1. For synchronous receipt of messages, use the receiver or consumer to retrieve the next available message (blocking if necessary). For asynchronous message delivery, start the delivery of messages by invoking the `start` method of the connection object.
2. With the handle to the `Message` object obtained above, you can extract the message data and process them.

JMS System Setup

A complete JMS application includes several pieces—the client application, the messaging provider software, and some sort of a directory containing administered objects. The messaging-provider software and the directory must be set up before the JMS client application can run.

Your first step is to set up the JMS provider software. This process is provider-specific, and the amount of effort required will vary greatly. It can be as simple as obtaining the software and running a simple installation program, or as complicated as running several installation programs, creating dedicated servers, setting up environment variables, creating specific user accounts to run the messaging software, and so on. Pure Java implementations tend to be fairly simple to set up.

JMS presents a standard interface that makes integrating with various messaging systems much easier. One of the reasons that JMS programs can be independent of the underlying messaging system is that key objects that are specific to each messaging system are not hard-coded into the application. You create and maintain these objects separately from the application and then look them up when necessary. These objects are called *administered objects.*

Administered Objects

Administered objects are objects that you set up in a directory service before your application runs. By using administered objects, you can defer binding these objects with your application until runtime. This enables you to exchange any of these objects for new or different ones without having to change and recompile your code.

In JMS you store instances or references to factory and destination objects (queues or topics) as administered objects. Factory objects establish connections to the underlying JMS provider while destination object represent targets for outgoing messages or the sources for incoming messages. Storing factory objects as administered objects makes code portable among JMS providers. Storing a destination object as an administered object allows you to vary the final destination without modifying your code, providing a great deal of runtime flexibility.

Administered objects can be serialized versions of the classes provided by the provider or they can be references to factory classes that will create the objects on demand. Either way, the process of getting a handle to a factory object or a destination object is the same—look it up and retrieve it using the Java Naming and Directory Interface (JNDI). The JNDI API provides programmers with a standard way to look up and use objects.

In order to obtain a handle to a factory object, you get the JNDI context and then perform a lookup of a specific name. This process is illustrated in the following code (assuming a `TopicConnectionFactory` object has been bound to the string `"TopicConnectionFactory"` in the JNDI namespace):

```
// create the initial context
Context ctx = new InitialContext(env);

// Get the topic connection factory
String tcf = "TopicConnectionFactory";
TopicConnectionFactory tcf =
  (TopicConnectionFactory)ctx.lookup(tcf);
```

The process of obtaining a handle to a destination object is similar (assuming you have bound the `Topic` object to the name `"TestTopic"`):

```
// assuming we have the initial context from above
// Get a topic object
Topic topic = (Topic) ctx.lookup("TestTopic");
```

To learn more about JNDI, including options for setting up the initial context and storing and retrieving objects in the JNDI namespace, please turn to Chapter 9.

Before you can look up an object in the directory, it must be placed there. This process can be very simple or fairly complicated. Most JMS providers include some sort of utility for getting the appropriate objects into the JNDI namespace. Some of them are simple command-line tools providing the bare-minimum methods. Others are full-blown directory explorers that provide a graphical user interface enabling insertions, modifications, deletions, and attribute manipulation.

One current trend is to use the Java Management extensions (JMX) to manage the administered objects. If you do this, any JMX-compliant management software will be able to control the administered objects over a wide variety of protocols.

Many JMS providers include a set of convenience classes that hide the details of JNDI from you. You can typically call static methods on these classes to return connections, topics, and the like. While they can make life a little bit simpler, these classes will also make your code dependent on that particular JMS provider.

Sending and Receiving Messages

One of the easiest ways to understand the JMS API is to follow a JMS message from creation to consumption. Take a look at the following code excerpts. Each one illustrates the steps you must follow to send or receive a simple text message using the different JMS models. This is not how you would normally program a robust JMS application, but it serves as an example of the steps that you will have to follow. Also note that these examples contain no exception handling or error recovery.

Following each code excerpt you will find a description of each step. Reading through the code and descriptions will give you a good understanding of the various JMS components and how they relate to each other.

The following code and description would be sufficient for sending a single message to a destination, and then receiving it from that destination.

I will present the same scenario for both point-to-point and publish/subscribe scenarios.

Point-to-point – sending messages

The following code excerpt shows how to send a simple JMS message using the point-to-point model of JMS:

```
// Step 1
// Look up an administered QueueConnectionFactory object
Context ctx = new InitialContext();
Object obj = ctx.lookup("ConnectionFactory");
QueueConnectionFactory qcf =
   (QueueConnectionFactory) obj;

// Step 2
// Create a connection with the factory
QueueConnectionFactory qcon =
   qcf.createQueueConnection();
```

```
// Step 3
// With the connection we can create a QueueSession
QueueSession qsession =
               qcon.createQueueSession(false,

Session.AUTO_ACKNOWLEDGE);

// Step 4
// Before creating the sender, look up the queue
Queue queue = (Queue) ctx.lookup("testQueue");

// Step 5
// Create the QueueSender object
QueueSender qsender = qsession.createSender(queue);

// Step 6
// Create a simple text message and send it out
Message msg =
   qsession.createTextMessage("Simple text message");

// Step 7
// Send the message out
qsender.send(msg);
```

Step 1. Before you can do anything else, you need to establish a connection with the JMS provider. You do this with administered objects, as described in the section "Administered Objects." In this preliminary step, you retrieve the connection factory that has been placed into the JNDI namespace. First create an initial context (using default JNDI parameters from a jndi.properties file). Once you have created the initial context, you can look up an object that is bound to the name `"ConnectionFactory"`. Finally, cast the object to the appropriate type—in this case `QueueConnectionFactory`.

Step 2. Once you have retrieved the `QueueConnectionFactory` object from the JNDI namespace, you can use it to create a connection to the JMS provider. Note that this connection factory is specific to the JMS provider. It knows how to establish a connection—what protocols to use, what steps are required, and so on. But since it implements the `ConnectionFactory` interface, all you have to do is call the appropriate routine—in this case `createQueueConnection`.

Step 3. The next step is to create a session from the connection. You do this with the `createQueueSession` method, which takes two arguments. The first is a Boolean flag that indicates whether the session is to be transacted or not. (See the later section "Use transactions with JMS" for more details.) The second argument is the acknowledgement mode to be used for this session. Notice that there are predefined constants that you should use in specifying the mode.

Step 4. In this step, you retrieve another administered object – the queue. This example assumes you have previously placed a queue object into the JNDI namespace as described in the administered objects section. You can use the same context you created in Step 1. Look up the queue object that has been bound to the name `"testQueue"`, cast it to a `Queue` object, and assign it to the handle `queue`. You can perform this step at any time before the next step. It is not dependent on any of the first three steps (apart from the setting up of the initial context).

Step 5. Once you have the `Queue` object, you are ready to create a `QueueSender` object that you will use to send messages to the queue. The session has a method called `createQueueSender` that takes a `Queue` object as a parameter. It creates the sender and connects it to the specified queue.

Step 6. This is where you create the message to be sent. In this case you are creating an instance of `TextMessage`. Use the session to create an object that will hold a text message by calling the `createTextMessage` method. If you want to send other types of messages, you can call one of the other methods on the `QueueSession` object (`createObjectMessage`, `createStreamMessage`, and so on).

Step 7. Finally, you can send the message to the destination queue. You do this by invoking the `send` method of the `QueueSender`, passing as an argument the message object to be sent.

Point-to-point – receiving messages

The following code excerpt shows how to receive a simple JMS message using the point-to-point model of JMS:

```
// Step 1
// Look up an administered QueueConnectionFactory object
Context ctx = new InitialContext();
Object obj = ctx.lookup("ConnectionFactory");
QueueConnectionFactory qcf =
    (QueueConnectionFactory) obj;

// Step 2
// Create a connection with the factory
QueueConnectionFactory qcon =
    qcf.createQueueConnection();

// Step 3
// With the connection we can create a QueueSession
QueueSession qsession =
    qcon.createQueueSession(false,
                            Session.AUTO_ACKNOWLEDGE);

// Step 4
// Before creating the receiver we need a queue
Queue queue = (Queue) ctx.lookup("testQueue");
```

```
// Step 5
// Create the QueueReceiver object
QueueReceiver qreceiver =
    qsession.createReceiver(queue);

// Step 6
// Start the delivery of messages
qcon.start();

// Step 7
// Receive the message from the queue - blocking call
TextMessage tm = (TextMessage) qreceiver.receive();
// receive() may return null on closed connection
if (tm != null)
   System.out.println("Message received: "
                      + tm.getText());
```

Steps 1–4. These steps are identical to the steps for sending a message. You are just establishing a connection with the JMS provider.

Step 5. Once you have the `Queue` object you are ready to create a `QueueReceiver` object that you will use to receive messages from the queue. The session has a method called `createReceiver` that takes a `Queue` object as a parameter. It creates the receiver and connects it to the specified queue.

Step 6. Enable the connection to deliver messages. By default, the connection's message delivery is disabled in order to allow you to set everything up before dealing with incoming messages. Once you are ready to handle incoming messages, call the method on the `Connection` object.

Step 7. Call the `receive` method on the `QueueReceiver`. This method will block while waiting for a message to be delivered into the queue. Once you receive the message, cast it directly to a `TextMessage`. (In a real application you would have to be much more cautious before casting objects). Once you have the `TextMessage`, retrieve the text of the message with the `getText` method. Finally, print out the text from the message.

Publish/subscribe – sending messages

The following code excerpt shows how to send a simple JMS message using the publish/subscribe model of JMS:

```
// Step 1
// Look up an administered TopicConnectionFactory object
Context ctx = new InitialContext();
Object obj = ctx.lookup("ConnectionFactory");
TopicConnectionFactory tcf =
   (TopicConnectionFactory) obj;
```

```
// Step 2
// Create a connection with the factory
TopicConnectionFactory tcon = tcf.createTopicConnection();

// Step 3
// With the connection we can create a TopicSession
TopicSession tsession =        tcon.createTopicSession(false,
   Session.AUTO_ACKNOWLEDGE);

// Step 4
// Before creating the sender, look up the topic
Topic topic = (Topic) ctx.lookup("testTopic");

// Step 5
// Create the TopicPublisher object
TopicPublisher tpub = tsession.createPublisher(topic);

// Step 6
// Create a simple text message and send it out
Message msg =
   tsession.createTextMessage("Simple text message");

// Step 7
// Send the message out
tpub.send(msg);
```

Step 1. Before you can do anything else, you need to establish a connection with the JMS provider. You do this with administered objects, as described in the administered objects section. In this preliminary step, you retrieve the connection factory that has been placed into the JNDI namespace. First, create an initial context (using default JNDI parameters from a jndi.properties file). Once you have created the initial context you can look up an object that is bound to the name `"ConnectionFactory"`. Finally, cast the object to the appropriate type—in this case `TopicConnectionFactory`.

Step 2. Once you have retrieved the `TopicConnectionFactory` object from the JNDI namespace you can use it to create a connection to the JMS provider. Note that this connection factory is specific to the JMS provider. It knows how to establish a connection—what protocols to use, what steps are required, and so on. But since it implements the `ConnectionFactory` interface, all you have to do is call the appropriate routine—in this case `createTopicConnection`.

Step 3. The next step is to create a session from the connection. You do this with the `createTopicSession` method, which takes two arguments. The first is a Boolean flag that indicates whether the session is to be transacted or not. (See the later section on JMS transactions for more details.) The second argument is the acknowledgement mode to be used for this session. Notice that there are predefined constants that you should use in specifying the mode.

Step 4. In this step you retrieve another administered object — the topic. This example assumes you have previously placed a topic object into the JNDI namespace as described in the section "Administered Objects." You can use the same context you created in Step 1. Look up the topic that has been bound to the name "testTopic", cast it to a Topic object, and assign it to the handle topic. You can perform this step at any time before the next step. It is not dependent on any of the first three steps (apart from the setting up of the initial context).

Step 5. Once you have the Topic object, you are ready to create a TopicPublisher object that you will use to send messages to the topic. The session has a method called createTopicPublisher that takes a Topic object as a parameter. It creates the sender and connects it to the specified topic.

Step 6. This is where you create the message to be sent. In this case you are creating an instance of TextMessage. Use the session to create the message object by calling the createTextMessage method. If you want to send other types of messages, you can call one of the other methods on the session object (createObjectMessage, createStreamMessage, and so on).

Step 7. Finally, you can send the message to the destination topic. You do this by invoking the send method of the TopicPublisher, passing as an argument the message object to be sent.

Publish/subscribe – receiving messages

The following code excerpt shows how to receive a simple JMS message using the publish/subscribe model of JMS:

```
// Step 1
// Look up an administered TopicConnectionFactory object
Context ctx = new InitialContext();
Object obj = ctx.lookup("ConnectionFactory");
TopicConnectionFactory tcf =
   (TopicConnectionFactory) obj;

// Step 2
// Create a connection with the factory
TopicConnectionFactory tcon =
   tcf.createTopicConnection();

// Step 3
// With the connection we can create a TopicSession
TopicSession tsession =
   tcon.createTopicSession(false,
                           Session.AUTO_ACKNOWLEDGE);

// Step 4
// Before creating the sender, look up the topic
Topic topic = (Topic) ctx.lookup("testTopic");
```

```
// Step 5
// Create the TopicSubscriber object
TopicSubscriber tsub = tsession.createSubscriber(topic);

// Step 6
// Start the delivery of messages
tcon.start();

// Step 7
// Receive the message from the queue - blocking call
TextMessage tm = (TextMessage) tsub.receive();
// receive() may return null on closed connection
if (tm != null)
   System.out.println("Message received: "

                           + tm.getText());
```

Steps 1–4. These steps are identical to the steps for sending a message. You are just establishing a connection with the JMS provider.

Step 5. Once you have the `Topic` object, you are ready to create a `TopicSubscriber` object that you will use to receive messages from the topic. The session has a method called `createSubscriber` that takes a `Topic` object as a parameter. It creates the subscriber and connects it to the specified topic.

Step 6. Enable the connection to deliver messages. By default, the connection's message delivery is disabled in order to allow you to set everything up before dealing with incoming messages. Once you are ready to handle incoming messages, call the `start` method on the `Connection` object.

Step 7. Call the `receive` method on the `TopicSubscriber`. This method will block while waiting for a message to be delivered to the topic. Once you receive the message, cast it directly to a `TextMessage`. (In a real application, you would have to be much more cautious before casting objects.) Once you have the `TextMessage`, retrieve the text of the message with the `getText` method. Finally, print out the text of the message.

MessageListeners

Both the point-to-point and publish/subscribe models can deliver messages to your application asynchronously. All that you need to do is create a `MessageListener` and register it with the `QueueReceiver` or the `TopicSubscriber`.

The `MessageListener` interface is very simple. It contains a single method to be implemented:

```
void onMessage(Message message);
```

You can create a standalone class shown below that contains the `onMessage` method, or you can add the method to an existing class:

```
public class Receiver implements MessageListener {
   public void onMessage(Message message) {
      TextMessage tm = (TextMessage) message;
      if (tm != null)
        System.out.println(
                  "Msg rcvd: " + tm.getText());
   }
}
```

Once you have defined this class, register it with the `QueueReceiver` or the `TopicSubscriber`. In the point-to-point example, you would insert this code between steps 5 and 6:

```
// Step 5.5
// Create a message listener and register it
MessageListener ml = new Receiver();
qreceiver.setMessageListener(ml);
```

In the publish/subscribe example, you would insert this code between steps 5 and 6:

```
// Step 5.5
// Create a message listener and register it
MessageListener ml = new Receiver();
tsub.setMessageListener(ml);
```

Step 7 is not necessary in either case, because the `MessageListener` processes the incoming messages as required.

Connections and sessions

Connections allow you to interact with a JMS provider in the same way that database connections allow you to interact with a database. Before you can send or receive any messages, you must establish a connection with the JMS provider and create one or more sessions.

In the process of establishing a connection, the JMS provider typically allocates some system resources outside the JVM. As a result, connections are fairly heavy objects and should be reused whenever possible. The most common approach is to create a single connection within the JVM or application and then use it for multiple purposes.

Since the process of creating a connection with a JMS provider varies from provider to provider, it is abstracted into a standard `ConnectionFactory` interface. Depending on the messaging model you use, publish/subscribe or point-to-point, you will use either the `TopicConnectionFactory` or a `QueueConnectionFactory`. You place the appropriate connection factory into the namespace and retrieve it at runtime by looking it up. This removes any provider-dependency from your application.

The following code samples show how to look up a connection factory. They assume that a connection factory (whether it is a `QueueConnectionFactory` or a `TopicConnectionFactory`) has been placed into the JNDI namespace under the name `"ConnectionFactory"`.

You can retrieve a queue connection factory in the point-to-point messaging model as follows:

```
// Establish an initial jndi context
Context ctx = new InitialContext();

// Look up a queue connection factory
qcf = (QueueConnectionFactory)
      ctx.lookup("ConnectionFactory");
```

Likewise, you can retrieve a topic connection factory in the publish/subscribe model as follows:

```
// Look up a topic connection factory
tcf = (TopicConnectionFactory)
      ctx.lookup("ConnectionFactory");
```

Create a connection

Once you have the connection factory, you can use it to create the actual connection to the JMS provider. Depending on the type of connection factory you have, you will use either the `createQueueConnection` or the `createTopicConnection` method.

Assuming you have the `QueueConnectionFactory` described earlier, you can create a `QueueConnection` as follows:

```
// Use the factory to create a queue connection
QueueConnection qcon = null;
qcon = qcf.createQueueConnection();
```

Similarly, if you have the `TopicConnectionFactory` described earlier, you can create a `TopicConnection` as follows:

```
// Use the factory to create a topic connection.
TopicConnection tcon = null;
tcon = tcf.createTopicConnection();
```

As I mentioned at the beginning of this section, connections are fairly heavy objects that should be created once and then reused whenever necessary. As a result, you may want to keep a reference to your connection as a member of your class, or somewhere else where it can be retrieved on demand.

Create sessions

Sessions serve as the middleman between a connection and the client application. You typically use your connections only during setup and cleanup. All other access to the provider is by means of a `Session` object. Using the `Session` object, you can create producers or consumers, create a temporary destination, create message objects, and control transactions. Sessions also manage other things for you behind the scenes. They hold messages until they have been acknowledged, distribute messages to registered listeners, and more.

Once you have a connection, creating a session is easy—just invoke the `createQueueSession` or `createTopicSession` method (depending on the type of session you have). `Session` objects are lightweight objects, and you can create multiple sessions from a single connection. You can create a queue session as follows:

```
// With the connection, create a QueueSession
QueueSession qsession = null;
qsession = qcon.createQueueSession(
    false, Session.AUTO_ACKNOWLEDGE);
```

Creating a topic session is similar to creating a queue session:

```
// With the connection, create a TopicSession
TopicSession tsession = null;
tsession = tcon.createTopicSession(
    false, Session.AUTO_ACKNOWLEDGE);
```

Notice that constants are defined in the `Session` interface for the various acknowledgement modes. Use these constants as parameters, and you will cut down on runtime errors and maintenance problems.

Sessions are intended to be single-threaded. It doesn't matter how many threads use a session, but only one thread should use it at a time. Since no code is provided to guarantee single-thread access, you must provide it yourself. The session guarantees that all registered `MessageListener` objects will be invoked serially, so you aren't required to provide code to handle that.

Create producers and consumers

In order to send or receive messages, you use producer or consumer objects, respectively. Again, according to the model you are using, you will obtain the appropriate producer or consumer from the session.

For point-to-point messaging, you will create a `QueueSender` for sending messages to a queue, and a `QueueReceiver` for receiving messages from a queue. The following code shows how you do this:

```
// Create the QueueSender object from the session
QueueSender qsender = null;
qsender = qsession.createSender(queue);

// Create the QueueReceiver object from the session
QueueReceiver qreceiver = null;
qreceiver = qsession.createReceiver(queue);
```

The situation is similar for the publish/subscribe model. You will create a `TopicPublisher` for publishing messages to a topic, and a `TopicSubscriber` for receiving messages from a topic. The following code shows how you do this:

```
// Create the TopicPublisher object from the session
TopicPublisher tpublisher = null;
tpublisher = tsession.createPublisher(topic);

// Create the TopicSubscriber object from the session
TopicSubscriber tsubscriber = null;
tsubscriber = tsession.createSubscriber(topic);
```

Messages in Detail

So now that you know how to send and receive messages, how do you go about creating messages with your data? This section focuses on the message objects themselves, including the message header and the various types of message bodies.

If you look at the `Message` interface, you will see that messages have three main components: a header, a body, and a set of properties. Let's take a look at each of these.

Message header

The message header is the envelope of the message. It provides all the information required for the message to reach its destination. You directly control the value of some of the header fields, while the JMS provider fills in others.

Note that in the simplest of JMS applications, none of these fields must be explicitly set or read by the application. They exist to help in the routing of messages and provide the capability for writing certain types of applications. Take a look at each field and think about the conditions under which you might use that information.

Table 22-4 describes each field — what it is used for and how it is set.

Table 22-4
Message header fields

Field Name	***Set By***	***Description***
`JMSDestination`	`Send` method	Specifies where this message should be sent. Filled in by the JMS provider.
`JMSDeliveryMode`	`Send` method	Identifies the mode used to deliver this message – either persistent or non-persistent. The JMS provider fills this field in after sending the message.
`JMSMessageID`	`Send` method	Contains a unique identifier for the message. Filled in by the JMS provider as part of the send process.
`JMSTimestamp`	`Send` method	Contains the time that this message was passed to the `Send` method. Set by the JMS provider as part of the send process.
`JMSCorrelationID`	Client	Contains an ID for linking messages together. The client will typically set this to the message ID of the referenced message.
`JMSReplyTo`	Client	May contain a destination to which replies should be sent. The client will specify the value for this field if it is expecting a response.
`JMSRedelivered`	Provider	Contains an indication that this message may have been delivered previously.
`JMSType`	Client	Contains a message-type identifier supplied by the client. The requirements for this field may vary from provider to provider.
`JMSExpiration`	`Send` method	A calculated value from the client-supplied time-to-live value. If GMT is later than this expiration time, the message is destroyed.
`JMSPriority`	`Send` method	Contains the value the client specified when sending the message.

Message properties

In addition to the preceding properties, you can define your own properties to a message. The primary reason for assigning your own properties is to facilitate message selection.

Once you have a message object, you define a property for the message simply by calling one of the `setXXXProperty` methods, where *XXX* is one of the following: `Boolean`, `Byte`, `Double`, `Float`, `Int`, `Long`, `Object`, `Short`, and `String`. As you can see, the JMS API supports a variety of datatypes for use as message properties. Each property consists of a string name and an associated value.

As an example, the following code sets a customer name property as a string, and an order ID as an integer:

```
TextMessage msg = tsession.createTextMessage();
msg.setStringProperty("CUSTOMER_NAME", "MyCustomer");
msg.setIntProperty("ORDER_ID", 12345);
```

You can read a property value from an incoming message in a similar manner by using the `getXXXProperty` methods. Following the same example, once you have received the preceding message, you can read the properties with the following code:

```
String customer =
    msg.getStringProperty("CUSTOMER_NAME");
int ordered = msg.getIntProperty("ORDER_ID");
```

The message selection section later in the chapter demonstrates the use of properties for filtering incoming messages.

Properties should mainly be used for holding message-selection criteria. While you can create simple messages with the data entirely in properties, it is not a good idea. JMS providers may not handle data in properties as efficiently as data in the body of a message. However, having appropriate properties defined for message selection can be a very efficient use of resources since it might prevent a JMS provider from sending messages across the wire unnecessarily.

Message body

The message body holds the core data of the message. You can place any type of data into the body of a message by selecting the appropriate message type. JMS identifies five different message types: `TextMessage`, `MapMessage`, `BytesMessage`, `StreamMessage`, and `ObjectMessage`. By selecting the most appropriate type of message, you allow the JMS provider to handle the message in the most efficient way.

Text messages

Text messages store data in the body as a simple string. You will typically use this format whenever your information can be represented most efficiently as a string. You can also use it to send XML messages as strings.

This example shows how to use a `TextMessage` object:

```
// Creating a text message
String text = "Sample text for TextMessage";
TextMessage msg = session.createTextMessage();
Message.setText(text);

// Reading a text message
String txt = message.getText();
```

Some providers include an XML-specific message type. It's a bit more convenient and provides some additional benefit. However, it is not an official JMS message type, and by using it you make your code less portable.

Map messages

A `MapMessage` stores the body of its message using a map, which is made up of a set of name/value pairs. The datatypes allowed in properties are allowed here as well. Here the name is a `String`, and the value is one of the defined datatypes. You add name/value pairs to the message using the `setXXX` methods and retrieve them using the `getXXX` methods.

This example shows how to use a `MapMessage` object:

```
// Creating a MapMessage object
MapMessage msg = session.createMapMessage();
String custName = "John Doe";
int custAge = 40;
long orderDate = new Date().getTime();
msg.setString("CUSTOMER_NAME", custName);
msg.setInt("CUSTOMER_AGE", custAge);
msg.setLong("ORDER_DATE", orderDate);

// Reading the MapMessage
String s = msg.getString("CUSTOMER_NAME");
int age = msg.getInt("CUSTOMER_AGE");
long date = msg.getLong("ORDER_DATE");
```

Bytes messages

To store a sequence of bytes as the body of a message you use a `BytesMessage`. This message format is useful if you want to minimize the amount of data being sent, if you need to conform to existing message formats, or in any other situation in which it makes the most sense to write out data as a sequence of bytes.

This example shows how to use a BytesMessage object:

```
// Creating a BytesMessage object
byte[] data;  // data from a network data packet
BytesMessage msg = session.createBytesMessage();
msg.writeBytes(data);

// Reading the BytesMessage
byte[] msgData = new byte[256];
int bytesRead = msg.readBytes(msgData);
```

Stream messages

You use a StreamMessage to write out a sequence of primitive types. The same types allowed for properties and MapMessages are allowed here. With this message format, the sender and the receiver must agree on the order of the fields so that both can read and write fields in the same order.

This example shows how to use a StreamMesssage to accomplish the same result as the MapMessage:

```
// Creating a StreamMessage object
String custName = "John Doe";
int custAge = 40;
long orderDate = new Date().getTime();
StreamMessage msg = session.createStreamMessage();
msg.writeString(custName);
msg.writeInt(custAge);
msg.writeLong(orderDate);

// Reading StreamMessage - must be in the same order
String s = msg.readString();
int age = msg.readInt();
long date = msg.readLong();
```

Object messages

An ObjectMessage enables you to write any serializable object to the message body. You can only store one object in the message. To store multiple objects, you will need to create a collection of the objects and write out the collection object to the message.

This example shows how to use an ObjectMessage object to accomplish the same result as the previous examples (assuming the Customer object encapsulates the desired data):

```
// Creating the ObjectMessage object
String custName = "John Doe";
int custAge = 40;
long orderDate = new Date().getTime();
Customer cust = new Customer();
cust.setCustomerName(custName);
```

```
cust.setCustomerAge(custAge);
cust.setOrderDate(orderDate);
ObjectMessage msg = session.createObjectMessage();
msg.setObject(cust);

// Reading the ObjectMessage
Customer cust = (Customer) msg.getObject();
```

Application Development with JMS

This section is where the rubber meets the road. You have seen a summary of the JMS specification and which classes do what. This section provides summary ideas and simple programming notes dealing with the JMS classes.

Connections and sessions

The following notes summarize the use of connections and sessions and provide some simple programming tips regarding their use.

- ✦ Connections are heavy objects.
- ✦ Create a connection once and then save the handle for future use. Create all sessions from this one connection.
- ✦ Sessions are lightweight, single-threaded objects.
- ✦ Because they are lightweight, you can create numerous sessions.
- ✦ Sessions are not reentrant — they can't be accessed simultaneously from multiple threads. If you are sharing a session between threads, you must ensure that only one thread accesses a session's resource at a time.

Resource management

While Java provides automatic garbage collection of objects, there are some guidelines you should follow with JMS to ensure that system resources are freed up as soon as possible.

- ✦ In general, free all JMS resources as soon as possible.
- ✦ Connections allocate resources outside the JVM, and you should free them as soon as you know they are not needed any more. Explicitly freeing objects releases resources immediately while relying on the garbage collector to free them results in resources that are tied up longer than necessary.
- ✦ When releasing JMS objects, you do not have to perform a `close()` on each one. By invoking `close()` on the `Session` or `Connection` object, you ensure that all child objects (those created from the session or the connection) will be closed correctly.

Persistence and durable subscriptions

Persistent or durable messages are messages that are preserved even when destination computers are powered down or not responding. When the destination is available, the message is delivered.

- Applications that require persistent messages must send messages with the delivery mode set to `PERSISTENT`.
- You can set the mode for all messages using the `setDeliveryMode()` method of the `QueueSender` or `TopicPublisher`. If you want to specify the mode on a message-by-message basis, you can use the long form of the `send()` method, which accepts the delivery mode as one of the parameters. The default mode is `PERSISTENT`.
- Applications that must receive messages from topics that were sent while the application was not running must use durable subscriptions.
- You can create durable subscriptions by using the `createDurableSubscription()` method for the `TopicSubscriber`.

JMS and threads

Any complex Java application will require the use of multiple threads. Using JMS with threads is straightforward as long as you understand the relationship of `Connection` and `Session` objects with regards to threads.

- Connections can be shared across threads
- Sessions are intended to be single-threaded objects. In order to share a session among threads, you must provide your own code to ensure single-threaded access to the session.
- Applications that use multiple threads to process messages should provide each thread with its own `Session` object.

JMS transactions

Transactions are one of the main features of a J2EE system. Using transactions correctly is imperative for creating robust systems. JMS is designed to work with transactions, but you must understand the ramifications of placing JMS calls within a transaction.

- Sessions are the transaction-management objects for JMS messages.
- Each session is a single-threaded grouping of send and receive operations controlled by a transaction.
- Transactions are specified when you create the session.

✦ The `createXXXSession` method takes as its first parameter a Boolean that specifies whether the session will be transacted or not. If this Boolean is set to `true`, all sends and receives are part of a transaction. As soon as one transaction completes (commits or is rolled back) the session starts another transaction.

✦ Rolled-back sent messages are never transmitted to their final destination; they are destroyed. One of the ramifications of this fact is that you can never send a message and receive a response from within a single transaction.

✦ Consumed messages are recovered and redelivered after a rollback.

✦ Only operations on producers or consumers created from the same session can be combined in a transaction.

✦ Messages may be sent to multiple queues, or received from multiple queues, as long as the same `QueueSession` was used to create all the receivers and senders involved. Likewise, messages may be received from or published to multiple topics as long as all the subscribers and publishers were created from the same `TopicSession`. You can include both send and receive operations in a transaction as long as you are not trying to send a message and get a response back as a result.

Putting it All Together – an Example

This section contains a simple example of sending and receiving messages. Here you will see an application that starts out very simply—it sends and receives messages. Next I will add some properties to the messages and implement message selection.

Simple sending and receiving of text messages

The example is made up of two classes, `JMSPublish` and `JMSSubscribe`. The code for the first example follows in its entirety. In subsequent examples, while adding features to these classes, changes to these classes are shown in bold (only the changes are shown).

JMSPublish

Here is the complete listing for `JMSPublish`. It sends the specified message to the given topic a number of times.

```
import javax.jms.*;
import javax.naming.InitialContext;
import javax.naming.Context;
import javax.naming.NamingException;
```

```
/**
 * JMSPublish is a simple example of an application that
 * publishes a number of messages to a given topic. It
 * uses the publish/subscribe model of JMS operation.
 *
 * This application assumes that the topic has already
 * been set up and can be looked up in the JNDI space.
 * Likewise, it assumes that a TopicConnectionFactory
 * has been placed into the JNDI space.
 *
 * @version 1.0
 * @author Bruce Beyeler
 * @param args[0] topic connection factory name
 *               (bind name in JNDI context)
 * @param args[1] topic name (bind name in JNDI context)
 * @param args[2] message to be sent to the queue
 * @param args[3] optional number of messages to be sent
 */
public class JMSPublish {
   /**
    * Contains a reference to the TopicConnectionFactory
    * that has been looked up from the JNDI namespace
    * under the specified name.
    */
   TopicConnectionFactory tcf;

   /**
    * Holds the connection to the JMS provider.
    */
   TopicConnection tcon;

   /**
    * Holds the TopicSession created from the
    * connection - used to publish messages
    */
   TopicSession tsession;
   /**
    * The TopicPublisher created from the TopicSession
    */
   TopicPublisher tpub;

   /**
    * The topic where messages will be published
    */
   Topic topic;

   /**
    * The message to be published
    */
   String message;
```

```
/**
 * The number of times the message is to be sent
 */
int count;

/**
 * This method validates the command-line arguments,
 * creates an instance of the JMSPublish class, and
 * calls the publishMessages() method.
 */
public static void main(String[] args) {
   // make sure enough parameters were specified
   if (args.length < 3) {
      System.out.println(
         "Usage: SimpleJMSSend tcf_name topic_name"
         + " message [count]");
      System.exit(1);
   }

   // let someone know we are here
   System.out.println("JMSPublish - beginning.");

   // parse the arguments and set up local variables
   String tcfName = args[0];
   String topicName = args[1];
   String message = args[2];
   int count = 1;

   /*
    * Read the count value if it exists. If it
    * doesn't or isn't valid, use a default of 1.
    */
   if (args.length >= 4) {
      try {
         count = Integer.parseInt(args[3]);
      } catch (NumberFormatException ne) { }
   }

   // Create an instance of this class
   System.out.println(
      " - creating an instance of JMSPublish...");
   JMSPublish publisher =
      new JMSPublish(tcfName, topicName);

   // now invoke the publishMessages() method
   // which does the real work
   publisher.publishMessages(message, count);

   // clean up the object
   System.out.println(
      " - cleaning up JMSPublish...");
   publisher.cleanup();
```

```
      System.out.println("JMSPublish - exiting.");
   }

   /**
    * Constructor for the JMSPublish object. This
    * constructor attempts to set up all the required
    * JMS pieces and ready the object to begin
    * publishing.
    * @param tcfName   the name of the topic connection
    *                  factory to use
    * @param topicName the name of the publishing topic
    */
   public JMSPublish(String tcfName, String topicName) {
      try {
         /*
          * Look up the TopicConnectionFactory object
          *
          * We are using the default jndi initial
          * context. If you wanted to specify an initial
          * context, you cold create your own properties
          * object and put in the properties for:
          *    java.naming.factory.initial
          *    java.naming.provider.url
          *    java.naming.factory.url.pkgs
          */
         Context ctx = new InitialContext();
         tcf =
           (TopicConnectionFactory) ctx.lookup(tcfName);

         // Create a connection with the factory
         tcon = tcf.createTopicConnection();

         // Create a TopicSession with the connection
         tsession = tcon.createTopicSession(
            false, Session.AUTO_ACKNOWLEDGE);


         // Look up the topic before creating sender
         topic = (Topic) ctx.lookup(topicName);

         // Create the TopicPublisher object
         tpub = tsession.createPublisher(topic);
      } catch (JMSException e) {
         System.out.println(
            "--JMSPublish: JMSException caught\n" + e);
      } catch (NamingException e) {
         System.out.println(
            "--JMSPublish: NamingException caught\n"
            + e.toString());
      }
   }
```

```
    /**
     * This method prepares for this object to be
     * discarded. It is responsible for deallocating any
     * system resources that may have been allocated. In
     * this case all that is required is to close the
     * connection. The connection object will in turn
     * ensure that all objects created from the
     * connection are closed properly.
     */
    private void cleanup() {
       try {
          // close the connection -
          // it will close all other generated resouces
          tcon.close();
       } catch (JMSException e) {
          System.out.println(
             "--cleanup: JMSException caught\n" + e);
       }
    }

    /**
     * This method takes a message to be sent and
     * publishes it to the topic the given number of
     * times. It uses TextMessage for the message it
     * creates.
     */
    public void publishMessages(String msg, int count) {
       try {
          // First, create a TextMessage from the
          // string we have received.
          Message txtMsg =
             tsession.createTextMessage(msg);

          // now publish it the specified number of times
          for (int i = 0; i < count; i++) {
             System.out.println("    - sending message: "
                                 + msg);
             tpub.publish(txtMsg);
          }
       } catch (JMSException e) {
          System.out.println(
             "--publishMessages: JMSException caught\n"
             + e);
       }
    }
}
```

JMSSubscribe

Here is the complete listing for `JMSSubscribe`. It registers as a message listener to the given topic and then prints out each message it receives.

```
import javax.jms.*;
import javax.naming.Context;
import javax.naming.InitialContext;
import javax.naming.NamingException;
import java.io.IOException;

/**
 * JMSSubscribe is an example application that will
 * subscribe to the given topic and will print out any
 * messages that it receives. It will continue this
 * until the user presses the enter key.
 *
 * This app uses the publish/subscribe model of JMS. It
 * assumes that the TopicConnectionFactory and a topic
 * have been initialized in the JNDI namespace and are
 * available under the given names.
 *
 * @version 1.0
 * @author Bruce Beyeler
 * @param args[0] TopicConnectionFactory name
 *                (bind name in JNDI context)
 * @param args[1] topic name (bind name in JNDI context)
 */

public class JMSSubscribe {
    /**
     * Contains a reference to the TopicConectionFactory
     * looked up from the JNDI namespace under the
     * specified name.
     */
    TopicConnectionFactory tcf;

    /**
     * Holds the connection to the JMS provider
     */
    TopicConnection tcon;

    /**
     * Holds the TopicSession created from the connection
     * - used to publish messages to the given topic
     */
    TopicSession tsession;

    /**
     * The TopicSubscriber created from the TopicSession
     */
    TopicSubscriber tsub;
```

```
/**
 * The topic where messages will be published
 */
Topic topic;

/**
 * This method validates the command-line arguments,
 * creates an instance of the JMSSubscribe class, and
 * registers a message listener.
 */
public static void main(String[] args) {

   // make sure enough parameters were specified
   if (args.length < 2) {
      System.out.println(
         "Usage: JMSSubscribe tcf_name topic_name");
      System.exit(1);
   }

   // let someone know we are here
   System.out.println(
      "JMSSubscribe - beginning ..."
      + " press enter to exit.");

   // parse the arguments and set up local variables
   String tcfName = args[0];
   String topicName = args[1];

   // Create an instance of this class
   System.out.println(
      " - creating an instance of JMSSubscribe...");
   JMSSubscribe subscriber =
      new JMSSubscribe(tcfName, topicName);

   // now wait until the user presses the enter key
   try {
      System.in.read();
   } catch (IOException e) { }

   // clean up the object
   System.out.println(
      " - cleaning up JMSSubscribe...");
   subscriber.cleanup();
   subscriber = null;

   System.out.println("JMSSubscriber - exiting.");
}
```

```
/**
 * Constructor for the JMSSubscribe object. This
 * constructor attempts to set up all the required
 * JMS pieces and ready the object to begin
 * receiving.
 * @param tcfName   the name of the
 *                  TopicConnectionFactory to use
 * @param topicName the name of the topic
 */
public JMSSubscribe(
        String tcfName, String topicName) {
    try {
        /*
         * Look up a TopicConnectionFactory object.
         *
         * We are using the default jndi initial
         * context. If you wanted to specify a
         * specific initial context, you could create
         * your own properties object and put in
         * properties for:
         *    java.naming.provider.url
         *    java.naming.factory.initial
         *    java.naming.factory.url.pkgs
         */
        Context ctx = new InitialContext();
        tcf =
          (TopicConnectionFactory) ctx.lookup(tcfName);

        // Create a connection with the factory
        tcon = tcf.createTopicConnection();

        // Create a TopicSession with the connection
        tsession = tcon.createTopicSession(
            false, Session.AUTO_ACKNOWLEDGE);

        // Before creating the sender we need to
        // look up the topic
        topic = (Topic) ctx.lookup(topicName);

        // Create the TopicPublisher object
        tsub = tsession.createSubscriber(topic);

        // Create a message listener and register it
        MessageListener ml = new Receiver();
        tsub.setMessageListener(ml);

        // Now start the connection to enable the
        // receiving of messages
        tcon.start();
    } catch (JMSException e) {
```

```
            System.out.println(
               "--JMSSubscribe: JMSException caught\n"
               + e);
         } catch (NamingException e) {
            System.out.println(
               "--JMSSubscribe: NamingException caught\n"
               + e);
         }
      }

      /**
       * This method prepares for this object to be
       * discarded. It is responsible for deallocating any
       * system resources that may have been allocated. In
       * this case all that is required is to close the
       * connection. The connection object will in turn
       * ensure that all objects created from the
       * connection are closed properly.
       */
      private void cleanup() {
         try {
            // close the connection - it will close all
            // generated resouces
            tcon.close();
         } catch (JMSException e) {
            System.out.println(
               "--cleanup: JMSException caught\n" + e);
         }
      }

      /**
       * Receiver is a message listener that just prints
       * out the message received.
       */
      class Receiver implements MessageListener {
         public void onMessage(Message message) {
            try {
               TextMessage tm = (TextMessage) message;
               if (tm != null)
                  System.out.println(
                     "Msg rcvd: " + tm.getText());
            } catch (JMSException e) {
               System.out.println(
                  "--Receiver.onMessage: JMSException"
                  + " caught\n" + e);
            }
         }
      }

   }
```

Running JMSPublish as shown previously produces the following output, which is based on the JBoss 2.4.1 implementation of JBossMQ, using the default setup and default connection factories and topic:

```
>java JMSPublish TopicConnectionFactory topic/testTopic "Test
message from JMSPublish" 5
JMSPublish - beginning.
 - creating an instance of JMSPublish...
    - sending message: Test message from JMSPublish
    - sending message: Test message from JMSPublish
    - sending message: Test message from JMSPublish
    - sending message: Test message from JMSPublish
    - sending message: Test message from JMSPublish
 - cleaning up JMSPublish...
JMSPublish - exiting.
>
```

Running JMSSubscribe as shown previously yields the following output:

```
>java JMSSubscribe TopicConnectionFactory topic/testTopic
JMSSubscribe - beginning ... press enter to exit.
 - creating an instance of JMSSubscribe...
Msg rcvd: Test message from JMSPublish
Msg rcvd: Test message from JMSPublish
Msg rcvd: Test message from JMSPublish
Msg rcvd: Test message from JMSPublish
Msg rcvd: Test message from JMSPublish

 - cleaning up JMSSubscribe...
JMSSubscriber - exiting.
>
```

Add properties

To illustrate message properties, you can add a message count property to the simple example above. You define a property called message_count that increments by one every time you send out a message. The receiving end can query this message count.

To add the message count property to the message, you can call the setIntProperty method, passing it the name message_count and the integer value to set it to. To retrieve the message count from the message, you call getIntProperty and pass it the name message_count.

JMSPublish modifications

You must make two changes to JMSPublish: You must add a class member to hold the count, and you must call the setIntProperty on the TextMessage object before sending it out. The messageCount declaration looks like the following:

```
/**
 * Counter for the number of messages that have been
 * sent by this object.
 */
int messageCount = 0;
```

You can set the message count property in the publishMessage method. To set the property, you invoke the setIntProperty method on the message object as shown here:

```
// now publish it the specified number of times
for (int i = 0; i < count; i++) {
   System.out.println("    - sending message: "
                   + msg);
   txtMsg.setIntProperty(
      "message_count", ++messageCount);
   tpub.publish(txtMsg);
}
```

JMSSubscribe modifications

Similarly, the only necessary changes to JMSSubscribe occur in the message listener. Instead of just printing out the received message, retrieve the property and print that out. The code looks like this:

```
public void onMessage(Message message) {
   try {
      TextMessage tm = (TextMessage) message;
      if (tm != null) {
         System.out.println(
            "Msg rcvd: " + tm.getText());
         int c = tm.getIntProperty("message_count");
         System.out.println("message_count: " + c);
      }
   } catch (JMSException e) {
      System.out.println(
        "--Receiver.onMessage: JMSException caught");
      System.out.println(e.toString());
   }
}
```

Applying these changes and renaming the files to JMSPublish2 and JMSSubscribe2 yield a slightly different output. The JMSPublish2 output is as follows:

```
>java JMSPublish2 TopicConnectionFactory topic/testTopic "Test
message from JMSPublish2" 5
JMSPublish - beginning.
 - creating an instance of JMSPublish...
    - sending message: Test message from JMSPublish2
    - sending message: Test message from JMSPublish2
    - sending message: Test message from JMSPublish2
    - sending message: Test message from JMSPublish2
    - sending message: Test message from JMSPublish2
 - cleaning up JMSPublish...
JMSPublish - exiting.
>
```

The JMSSubscribe2 output is as follows:

```
>java -cp JMSSubscribe2 TopicConnectionFactory topic/testTopic
JMSSubscribe - beginning ... press enter to exit.
 - creating an instance of JMSSubscribe...
Msg rcvd: Test message from JMSPublish2
message_count: 1
Msg rcvd: Test message from JMSPublish2
message_count: 2
Msg rcvd: Test message from JMSPublish2
message_count: 3
Msg rcvd: Test message from JMSPublish2
message_count: 4
Msg rcvd: Test message from JMSPublish2
message_count: 5

 - cleaning up JMSSubscribe...
JMSSubscriber - exiting.
>
```

Add message selection

To filter incoming messages, you will use the message-selection feature of the incoming messages. By specifying a selector string (a string that looks fairly similar to query strings in SQL), you can inform the JMS provider that you are interested only in certain messages. This method becomes more efficient as the number of clients the provider is serving increases. Message selectors are based on a subset of the SQL92 syntax and use header properties as their variables. Any property defined in the header can be used in the selector expressions (JMS, JMSX, or user-defined).

This example uses the message count property to filter incoming messages. Suppose you want to receive only messages 3 and 8. You can specify this in a selector by using an arithmetic expression. Your selector will look like this:

```
(message_count = '3') OR (message_count = '8')
```

You use this selector syntax to work with JBoss 2.4.1. According to the JMS specifications, you do not need to place single quotes around the 3 or the 8; in fact, doing this might cause problems with other JMS providers.

In order to provide the most flexibility, JMSSubscribe3 takes the selector as the last command argument rather than hardcoding the selector into the constructor. This enables you to play around with various selectors and see which ones give you the results you desire.

Modify the main method of JMSSubscribe to accept an additional argument and pass it to the constructor:

```
public static void main(String[] args) {
   // make sure enough parameters were specified
   if (args.length < 3) {
      System.out.println(
 "Usage: JMSSubscribe tcf_name topic_name selector");
      System.exit(1);
   }

   // let someone know we are here
   System.out.println(
      "JMSSubscribe - beginning ... "
      + "press enter to exit.");

   // parse the arguments and set up local variables
   String tcfName = args[0];
   String topicName = args[1];
   String selector = args[2];

   // Create an instance of this class
   System.out.println(
      " - creating an instance of JMSSubscribe...");
   JMSSubscribe3 subscriber =
     new JMSSubscribe3(tcfName, topicName, selector);

// remainder of method not shown
```

Additionally, you need a new constructor to take the additional parameter and call the second form of `createSubscriber` that takes a selector as an argument. The constructor signature change is as follows:

```
public JMSSubscribe3(
   String tcfName, String topicName, String selector)
```

This is the call to `createSubscriber`:

```
// Create the TopicSubscriber object - pass in// the selector
to use
tsub=tsession.createSubscriber(topic, selector, false);
```

Running the code again with the changes made to JMSSubscribe3 and passing in the selector produces the following results. After modifying the parameters to `JMSPublish2` to output 10 messages, the resulting output is as follows:

```
>java JMSPublish2 TopicConnectionFactory topic/testTopic "Test
message from JMSPublish2" 10
JMSPublish - beginning.
 - creating an instance of JMSPublish...
    - sending message: Test message from JMSPublish2
    - sending message: Test message from JMSPublish2
    - sending message: Test message from JMSPublish2
    - sending message: Test message from JMSPublish2
    - sending message: Test message from JMSPublish2
    - sending message: Test message from JMSPublish2
    - sending message: Test message from JMSPublish2
    - sending message: Test message from JMSPublish2
    - sending message: Test message from JMSPublish2
    - sending message: Test message from JMSPublish2
 - cleaning up JMSPublish...
JMSPublish - exiting.
>
```

The JMSSubscribe3 output is shown here:

```
>java JMSSubscribe3 TopicConnectionFactory topic/testTopic
"(message_count = '3') OR (message_count = '8')"
JMSSubscribe - beginning ... press enter to exit.
- creating an instance of JMSSubscribe...
Msg rcvd: Test message from JMSPublish2
message_count: 3
Msg rcvd: Test message from JMSPublish2
message_count: 8

 - cleaning up JMSSubscribe...
JMSSubscriber - exiting.
>
```

JMS and J2EE

JMS is a very useful tool in enterprise applications. Up until the recent changes to the EJB specification, its use in J2EE applications has been somewhat limited. You could send and receive messages, but there was no asynchronous way of calling EJBs upon receipt of a message. The EJB 2.0 specification and the J2EE 1.3 specification have made JMS a key component in fully compliant J2EE platforms.

Connect to corporate and legacy systems

JMS is one of the means you can use to connect with existing systems. Many systems already use some form of message-oriented middleware software. Most MOM vendors have created JMS interfaces to their systems: This means that new applications or Web front ends can directly tap into an existing system without modifying any of its code.

For those systems that don't use MOM, JMS may still be a viable option. Many system vendors are creating JMS adapters that communicate natively with their existing application and support a JMS interface for new application integration.

Message-driven beans

Message-driven beans (MDBs) were added in the EJB 2.0 specification. MDBs finally allow an EJB to be called asynchronously. Previously you couldn't set up a bean to respond to a message (say an incoming order) and process it; instead you had to set up some external entity to listen for messages and then invoke the EJBs through their remote interfaces.

With the addition of MDBs, an EJB container now sets itself up as the listener for a message. When the container receives the message, it invokes the MDBs `onMessage` method.

Message-driven beans differ from other JMS applications in that the EJB container has done the majority of the initialization work. The container creates the consumer (either a receiver or subscriber), registers a message listener, and sets the acknowledgement mode. All of the information required to perform these tasks is defined in the MDB deployment descriptor.

For a complete description of the steps involved in creating and deploying Message Driven Beans, please turn to Chapter 17.

As an example of a Message Driven Bean, consider the following scenario. Customers have placed their orders with you, and you have outsourced the fulfillment of those orders. In order to be able to notify the customer that his or her order has been shipped, you receive a notification from the fulfillment house that it has shipped the order. You have set up a queue in your server that will receive the following information in the form of an XML message: order ID, shipment method, tracking number, and due date.

Your Message Driven Bean will receive the message, look up the customer based on the order ID, and e-mail him or her a notification of the shipment.

The code for the `onMessage()` method is as follows:

```
public void onMessage(Message message) {
    try {
        // process the message and get the data.
        // NotificationMessage will take an XML message,
        // parse out the values and make them avaialable
        // as properties.
        String msg = ((TextMessage) message).getMessage();
        NotificationMessage nm =
            new NotificationMessage(msg);
        String orderId = nm.getOrderId();
        String shipperName = nm.getShipperName();
        Date shipDate = nm.getShipDate();
        Date dueDate = nm.getDueDate();

        // now look up the customer by the order id
        Context initial = new InitialContext();
        Object objref = initial.lookup("ejb/Order");

        OrderHome home =
            (OrderHome) PortableRemoteObject.narrow(
                objref, OrderHome.class);
        Order order =
            home.findByPrimaryKey(new OrderID(orderId));
        int customerID = order.getCustomerID();

        // now that we have the customer id, get
        // the email address
        objref = initial.lookup("ejb/Customer");
        CustomerHome custHome =
            (CustomerHome) PortableRemoteObject.narrow(
                objref, CustomerHome.class);
        Customer customer = custHome.findByPrimaryKey(
            new CustomerID(customerID));
        String email = customer.getEmail();
```

```
            // now that we have the email, create
            // the message to send out
            StringBuffer sb = new StringBuffer();
            sb.append("Dear ");
            sb.append(customer.getName());
            sb.append("\nThis email is to notify you that ");
            sb.append("your order number ");
            sb.append(orderId);
            sb.append(" has been shipped. The shipping");
            sb.append(" information is as follows:\n");
            sb.append("Shipper: ")
            sb.append(shipperName);
            sb.append("\nTracking number: ");
            sb.append(trackingNumber);
            sb.append("\nShip Date: ");
            sb.append(shipDate);
            sb.append("\nDue Date: ");
            sb.append(dueDate);
            sb.append("\nThank you for your order.");

            // use the mail session bean to send out the msg
            objref = initial.lookup("ejb/Mailer");
            MailerHome mailHome =
               (MailerHome) PortableRemoteObject.narrow(
                  objref, MailerHome.class);
            Mailer mailer = mailHome.create();
            mailer.sendMessage(
              email, "Your order has shipped", sb.toString());
        } catch (Exception e) {
          // log error to your logging facility
          e.printStacktrace();
        }
    }
```

Distributed applications

JMS also plays a large role in distributed enterprise applications. JMS provides an asynchronous means of hooking various pieces of an enterprise application together. If one of the pieces is down or unavailable, the rest of the application does not have to sit around waiting for it to respond.

Many components of enterprise applications may not be J2EE-aware but yet may have JMS capabilities. Small handheld devices and legacy systems are typical examples. But as long as they can send and receive JMS messages, these components can be an integral part of the entire application.

Some of the features of JMS lend themselves readily to distributed computing. For example, sending requests that need processing to a specific queue and then having multiple processes read from this queue solves the problem of load balancing and scalability very effectively.

Summary

In this chapter, you took a whirlwind tour of the JMS specification. While I didn't cover everything in the spec (entire books are devoted to JMS), I covered enough to get you up and running with the JMS API.

What did I cover in this chapter? The key concepts, terminology, and procedures for sending and receiving JMS messages, including:

- ✦ An overview of message-oriented-middleware
- ✦ The types of JMS messaging (point-to-point and publish/subscribe)
- ✦ An overview of the JMS API
- ✦ Administered objects and their role in JMS applications
- ✦ Tips for application development using JMS
- ✦ Examples illustrating the JMS API
- ✦ The role of JMS in J2EE applications

✦ ✦ ✦

CHAPTER 23

Managing Transactions with JTA/JTS

✦ ✦ ✦ ✦

In This Chapter

Looking at transactions in J2EE applications

Understanding basic transaction processing

Looking at the Object Management Groups (OMG) OTS, the Java Transaction API (JTA), and Java Transaction Service (JTS)

Using JTA/JTS with Enterprise JavaBeans

Understanding container-managed and bean-managed persistence

✦ ✦ ✦ ✦

Enterprise applications can vary in complexity and size. Most large-scale applications persist data in a relational or object-oriented database while they run. Critical data such as a checking account or a home mortgage must be treated with care.

Unchecked failures during application processing can result in corrupted or incorrect data. For instance, an application processing a payment against your home mortgage may experience an exception during the operation in which the amount you paid is subtracted from the principal you owe. When the exception occurs, the entire operation that was being performed should be undone. Otherwise, you might end up with an incorrect balance on your mortgage.

Applications that work with critical data use transactions to give themselves a way to undo changes they have made. In this chapter, we will look at transaction-processing basics and, more formally, at transaction processing in J2EE. We will also look at how to use the Java Transaction API (JTA) and Java Transaction Service (JTS) with Enterprise JavaBeans in your applications. To help you understand the history behind JTS and JTA, we will also briefly touch on a couple of distributed transaction–processing standards: Extended Architecture (XA) and Object Management Group (OMG) Object Transaction Service (OTS).

What Are Transactions?

A transaction can loosely be described as a unit of work. Transactions do not imply a single action or a large number of actions that an application can perform. A transaction is a unit of work whereby an application or application server indicates that some work is being performed and that certain agreed-upon behavior is expected.

Over the years, the definition of the behavior of a transaction has evolved along with different transaction-processing standards. The set of requirements that transactions adhere to does not change and is not tied to a specific implementation of a transaction-processing system, because they transcend implementation-specific details. Transactions, therefore, are commonly defined by a set of requirements, also called *characteristics* or *properties*.

Transaction requirements

A transaction must be an all-or-nothing operation. Its operations, no matter how many or how few, must either all complete or all fail. This is especially important when transactions involve multiple tables or databases, or are distributed transactions. The term *atomic* (or *atomicity*) is used to describe this characteristic of a transaction.

Transactions must be consistent: They must take the system from one consistent state to the next consistent state. For instance, when you begin a transaction that updates a checking account, the account is in a well-known state; when the transaction ends, the checking account must still be in a well-known state. No ambiguities must exist about what state the checking account is in.

Transactions must also hide the intermittent, inconsistent states from other applications while they are processing. As you will read later on, some DBMSes permit limited reading of data at the user's discretion. The term *transaction isolation* is commonly used to describe the way in which transactions hide their states from other processes and threads during execution.

Results, if the transaction was successful, should be persisted at the end of the transaction. When a transaction ends, all the data it intended to modify should have been modified and the results safely stored by the DBMS. The term *transaction durability* is commonly used to describe this characteristic of a transaction. This characteristic must be enforced even if a failure occurs after the commit of a transaction. For instance, if an EJB component performs an update to a table and then receives an exception of some type, the transaction results should be persisted regardless. This behavior ensures that application-scoped exceptions that have nothing to do with the data do not affect the transaction processing.

Collectively, these requirements are referred to as the *ACID* properties of a transaction. ACID is an acronym for *Atomic*, *Consistent*, *Isolated*, and *Durable*, each of which refers to one of the requirements or characteristics just mentioned.

Understanding these basic requirements will give you a better idea of what transactions are up to and what transaction managers do with transactions. You will deal with several terms when working with transactions.

Transaction-processing terms

✦ *Commit*—Refers to the point at which the operations performed during a transaction are written to the database. After a commit, changes cannot be automatically undone or rolled back without manual intervention—or some pretty fancy database-recovery tools. Before the commit occurs though, you do have an opportunity to undo any changes that have been performed.

```
PerformUpdate()
If (updates were not successful)
    rollback
Else
    commit
```

✦ *Rollback*—Refers to the operation of undoing, before the transaction has been committed, the modifications that have taken place during a transaction. This operation is possible even if only part of the intended updates were started before an exception occurred. The database management system then reverts the state of the updates to before the modifications occurred. The following pseudo-code illustrates the concept of rollback:

```
If (conditionA is true)
    PerformUpdate()
   If (result is not true)
      rollback
   Else
      commit
Else
   Don't do anything
```

In some database management systems, the rollback process may only roll back to a specific point in time. This is common in large-scale enterprise systems in which applications have only a small window in which to execute. Any delays are costly, so when an exception occurs, rather than rolling back the entire set of updates, the application rolls back only those that have occurred since the last checkpoint. When the application is restarted after the exception, the updates begin occurring after the last checkpoint.

✦ *Demarcate*—To indicate where a transaction begins and where it ends. This means that, depending on how your application handles transaction management, you may have a line of code that explicitly indicates that a transaction should be started, and another line that explicitly indicates that the transaction should end and be committed. The following pseudo-code illustrates how demarcating transaction boundaries might look:

```
If (conditionA is true)
    Start a  new transaction
    Update some data
    If no exceptions occurred
       commit
    Else
       Rollback the update
Else
    Do something else
```

Transaction demarcation can be done programmatically or declaratively. The former involves the use of programming-code statements that mark the boundaries of a transaction, and the latter involves some runtime configuration that can change easily, which tells the transaction manager how transaction boundaries are done. Later in this chapter, in the section "Container-managed transactions," you will see how EJB deployment descriptors are used to declare transaction boundaries.

✦ *Locking*—Setting an object against which a transaction will be performing operations, so that its state does not change unpredictably while the transaction is in progress. Transactions can be running stored procedures against a row in the database; if another transaction is allowed to update that row and the stored procedure later rereads or continues, the results of the transaction will be unpredictable and quite possibly incorrect. Later in this chapter, in the section "Transaction isolation," you will see how to programmatically alter the isolation of a transaction to permit limited access to an object that a transaction may be updating.

The database administrator and the application developer should work together to decide which type of locking to use in their application, in order to ensure the best performance from the database and the transaction-processing monitors.

✦ *Optimistic locking*—Refers to a specific type of locking that you perform by establishing some marker or timestamp when an object is initially accessed. The marker is established on the object; the actual implementation of how this occurs is usually irrelevant to the user, as long as it works as advertised. When changes are attempted against the object, the timestamp or marker is checked to see if it has changed. If it has, an error or some exception is raised; otherwise the updates are committed. This type of locking allows the best performance of the two types of locking, because the target object is only locked while commits or rollbacks are taking place.

✦ *Pessimistic locking*—Refers to a type of locking in which a lock is obtained against the object being operated on for the entire duration of the transaction. From the time the transaction begins to the time it is either committed or rolled back, the object is locked. The object is eventually unlocked at the end of the transaction. While this locking approach simplifies the equation somewhat, in the long run it can cause serious performance degradation because of the locks it obtains against the entire object.

✦ *Propagation*—Refers to the process by which transaction context is passed around in a distributed-processing environment. Transaction context is the internal state of the transaction. The context can consist of information about what threads are associated with it or the resources being affected by the transaction. The Transaction Manager is generally responsible for establishing and maintaining the transaction context.

Transaction-processing components

Transaction processing is a complex business that involves several components. Each component is responsible for a different piece of the overall process. As you will read later in this chapter, standards such as X/Open and OMG OTS help to ensure that these components can interoperate while coordinating transaction and resource management. Now take a look at some of the major components involved in transaction processing.

Application client

The application client is the component that the rest of the components in the picture are there for. An application client can be as simple as a single object or as complex as an entire application. Application clients make use of data through the use of transactions in order to ensure that their interaction with the data is controlled and can easily be corrected if something goes wrong.

Application clients can start a transaction that spans multiple resources. Another component, which you will see shortly, the transaction manager, is responsible for coordinating the transaction across these resources.

Transaction manager

The transaction manager is the interface between the application client and the rest of the transaction-processing components. The method of interaction with the transaction manager really depends on the implementation of the transaction manager. However, as you will see later in this chapter, standards such as JTA are intended to standardize access to transaction managers through the use of a common API built on top of other industry standards.

The transaction manager is responsible for coordinating the actual demarcation of transaction boundaries, either at the request of an application server or container or at the request of an application client. The transaction manager is also responsible for obtaining access to the resources that the application client wants to work with. If anything goes wrong, it is up to the transaction manager to initiate the rollback and release of resources that the transaction may have been using.

The transaction manager is also sometimes referred to as the *transaction coordinator*.

Resource manager

The resource manager is the component responsible for coordinating access to the resources affected by a transaction, usually a DBMS. A resource manager can be as simple as a JDBC driver that manages access to a database and its tables, or JMS queue connection that allows an application to access a JMS queue. Resource managers are generally capable of participating in distributed transactions by adhering to distributed transaction–processing standards like XA from the OpenGroup.

Transaction-processing monitors

Transaction-processing monitors are used to complement DBMS functionality. They balance the load to resources used by transactions, such as threads and database connections. Transactions themselves can incur significant overhead, depending on the implementation.

Transaction-processing monitors can lower this overhead through different types of actions. In some older implementations, transactions may actually incur the cost of creating an operating-system process; newer implementations lower this cost by using a lighter-weight thread. Threads, while not completely without overhead, can be created and destroyed and potentially reused much more easily than can an operating-system process. Threads can potentially access shared data more easily because they may all be running in the same process, and thus may not need to cross address-space boundaries.

TP monitors can also distribute requests among several different DBMSes using standard or implementation-specific load-balancing techniques. This reduces the time it takes to start a transaction, as well as potentially reducing the time it takes to run a transaction. Even with TP monitors, transactions battle for CPU time and access to resources, and the more transactions you try to run on the same machine, the slower the result will come back. When requests are distributed among several DBMSes, the resource contention is lessened and in some cases becomes unnoticeable.

The following are some of the more popular transaction-processing monitors available for both UNIX and Windows. Some TP monitors are add-ons to DBMS products, and some are integrated into the DBMS software.

- ✦ BEA Tuxedo
- ✦ WebSphere Application Server Advanced Edition
- ✦ Microsoft COM+
- ✦ BEA TopEnd

While TPM's are commonly used with DBMes, they are also used in other types of applications and architectures. For instance, a TPM could be used in an application that uses messaging. In this type of application, the TPM could be used to distribute messages among several queues, possibly changing the priority of messages so that others process more quickly than others.

It's no secret that transaction-processing monitors are big business. If you've been involved with writing applications that use transactions, you are probably familiar with the reports routinely published by DBMS and TPM vendors, giving benchmarking numbers for their respective products. Vendors like Microsoft and Oracle are big competitors in this business.

To get an idea of the work that goes into benchmarking TPMs, visit `http://www.tpc.org`. This is the Web site for the Transaction Processing Monitoring Council.

Transaction benchmarking

The Transaction Processing Performance Council (TPC) is a consortium of hardware and software vendors that work to provide accurate and timely benchmarking data about transaction-processing monitors and database performance. With the advent of the Web and e-commerce, the TPMC is also extending the types of applications it benchmarks to include HTTP servers.

Benchmarking data is accumulated for DBMSes and TPMs using commercially available products with different hardware configurations. Single-node and multi-node (clustered) configurations are tested for performance in terms of number of transactions per hour, how long a certain type of transaction may take, and how much a transaction costs in terms of resources to execute a particular type of transaction, just to name a few parameters.

The benchmarks are run in environments that simulate real-world scenarios involving order processing, order taking, and retail stores both on and off the Web. The environments are set up so that they involve a number of variables that occur in real-world environments, such as number of users, contention against resources, database design, size, and complexity.

To get a better idea of the types of benchmarking they do, take a brief look at each of the benchmarking categories the TPMC provides:

✦ *TPC*— This benchmark is probably one of the more comprehensive and complex of the four, because of the way it is executed. The TPC benchmark is an online transaction processing (OLTP) benchmark that measures the number of new-order transactions per minute. This benchmark can be further refined to indicate how much a particular transaction costs in terms of resources, and how fast it may be carried out.

This benchmark simulates a small order-entry environment that supports activities such as entering orders, delivering orders, recording payments, checking the status of orders, and monitoring inventory levels. A mixture of five different transaction types of varying complexity are either executed immediately, as they would be online, or queued for deferred execution. Since the goal of these benchmarks is to simulate real-world transaction-processing performance as accurately as possible, the benchmark environment is further enhanced by the following attributes:

- Simultaneous execution of multiple transaction types of varying complexity
- Online and deferred transaction execution
- Multiple users
- Moderate system and application execution time
- Non-uniform distribution of data access through primary and secondary keys
- Databases consisting of many tables with different sizes, attributes and relationships
- Contention against data resources during read and write

✦ *TPC-H*—This benchmark differs from the first in that is designed to measure transaction performance in a decision-support environment. Service industries that provide high-volume call support, such as call centers or business offices of public utilities, are two examples of such environments. This benchmark is designed to measure the number of queries per hour that a system can perform. Typically this benchmark is run in an environment that simulates large volumes of data, executing queries of varying complexity that provide, in some cases, mission-critical information.

✦ *TPC-R*—This benchmark, like TPC-H, is also a decision-support–based benchmark. However, it differs in that it enables optimizations based on advanced knowledge of the queries being performed. This benchmark also measures the number of transactions per hour.

✦ *TPC-W*—This benchmark is designed to measure the number of Web transactions per second. A Web transaction can be anything from requesting a Web page (which could be static or dynamically generated) to updating a database. The benchmark is designed to simulate an online retail store, and each transaction is subject to a response-time constraint. To maximize the accuracy of the results, this benchmark uses real-world attributes similar to those used by the TPC benchmark.

Distributed transactions

In simple applications, transactions may perform actions against a single database, a single table, or some combination of the two. Simple applications may fall at the low end of the spectrum of the types of applications that are written today; at the other end of the spectrum are complex applications.

Transactions in complex applications can touch multiple databases that can be on the same network or scattered across a WAN. This means that transaction managers and DBMSes must be highly coordinated in order to ensure that transactions that span multiple databases adhere to the transaction requirements described earlier.

Two-phase commit

Two-phase commit is a protocol that transaction managers follow to ensure that a sequence of operations in a distributed transaction occur properly. Two-phase commit is the standard protocol used in distributed-transaction processing. It enlists the use of transaction managers and resource managers to ensure that every resource manager is willing to commit the transactions.

Two-phase commit occurs in a couple of steps: First the resources are queried to determine whether they are available, and second they are queried to determine whether they are willing to make the updates requested. If any one of the resource managers is unwilling to commit the changes, the entire transaction must be rolled back to maintain the integrity of the data. The first step is referred to as the *prepared* phase, and the second step is referred to as the *commit* phase. Figure 23-1 illustrates the concept of two-phase commit.

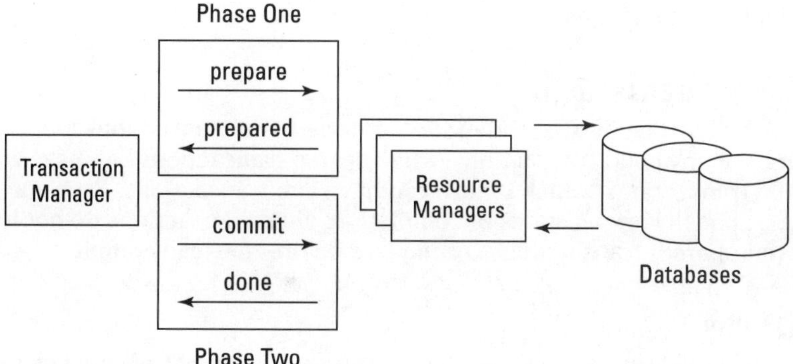

Figure 23-1: Two-phase commit

Transaction-processing standards

As with any software that deals with a major area such as data management and data access, different vendors initially tend to have different ideas about how things should be done. But over time, as vendors realize, customers want standardization. These customers could be those responsible for implementing transaction managers, or customers writing applications that use transactions.

Transaction management in J2EE has a rich history of standards on which to draw. Some standards apply to vendors looking to implement transaction managers, and some apply more to application developers writing applications that make use of transaction-management capabilities.

Database administrators or system administrators who are responsible for configuring access to machines in a network may also have to understand the function of transaction-management facilities. Having standards makes these people's jobs easier, and the more entrenched a standard becomes, the less likely it is to change frequently.

Users versus implementers

Transaction-processing standards often contain specifications that present their information from the point of view of a user, as well as from the point of view of an implementer. Generally speaking, the user of a transaction could be a person sitting at a computer using an order-entry application, or the components of the application itself.

Users are concerned with how they can use the facilities of a transaction manager, what APIs they will need to use, and how and when should they use those APIs.

An implementer is concerned with how the transaction manager will manage a transaction's lifecycle, and how it will establish connections to resources and coordinate transactions across multiple resources if needed. An implementer must also be concerned with things like marking transaction boundaries, enlisting resources, and coordinating transactions.

Flat and nested transactions

A transaction will be one of two models: *flat* or *nested*. Flat transactions are those that cannot have any child transactions, while nested transactions can have zero or more child transactions, which in turn can have sub-transactions. Each sub-transaction can be in various states of completion; child transactions do not have to wait for their parent transactions to complete before they can complete.

Interoperability

Another reason standards make life easier for transaction-manager implementers as well as for software developers is that they enable products to interoperate. For instance, imagine that you have more than one DBMS (such as Microsoft SQL Server and Oracle), and that you need to write applications that access or modify data in both. From a developer's point of view, it would be easiest if you could use a common framework that would coordinate the update across different implementations. If the implementations use proprietary protocols or interfaces, this becomes impossible. If products cannot interoperate, organizations are forced to either choose a specific vendor or use more resources to ensure that their applications will work across the disparate DBMSes.

Interoperability can take different forms, such as using a common network-communications protocol, or messaging protocol. Imagine for a moment that the Hypertext Transfer Protocol (HTTP) had never come to be: Web-browser users might have been forced to use different Web browsers depending on the Web server they were accessing. While this particular scenario seems completely far-fetched, the reality is that interoperability is a big issue in software development and always will be. And if transaction-management vendors and DBMS vendors had not worked together at least a little, writing applications that use transactions would be quite difficult. In that case, you might have had to write code specific to a particular DBMS vendor in order to work with a particular database or to use transactions in your application.

As you will see later in this chapter, JTS/JTA attempts to provide a common interface for working with transaction managers, regardless of underlying implementation. Along with already well-established standards for resource management and distributed-transaction processing, this makes the outlook seems less bleak.

Now that we've beaten the interoperability horse to death, take a look a brief look at two well-established standards in the software industry: the X/Open Distributed Transaction Processing Model specification and the Object Management Groups (OMG) Object Transaction Server (OTS) specification.

X/Open Distributed Transaction Processing Model

Decades ago, the X/Open group defined a model for distributed-transaction processing. Its model primarily defines two sets of interfaces: these represent, respectively, the interface between client and transaction manager and the interface between transaction manager and resources. The former is referred to as the `TX` interface, and the latter as the `XA` interface. The `TX` interface enables application programs to mark transaction boundaries using the methods listed in Table 23-1.

Table 23-1
TX interface methods

Method Name	*Description*
`tx_open`	Opens the transaction manager and associated set of resource managers.
`tx_close`	Closes the transaction manager and associated set of resource managers.
`tx_begin`	Begins a new transaction.
`tx_rollback`	Rolls back a transaction.
`tx_commit`	Commits a transaction.
`tx_set_commit_return`	Commits a transaction.
`tx_set_transaction_control`	Commits a transaction.
`tx_set_transaction_timeout`	Sets a transaction timeout interval.
`tx_info`	Returns information about a transaction, such as its status.

Table 23-2 shows the methods of the `XA` interface.

Table 23-2
XA interface methods

Method Name	*Description*
`xa_start`	Directs a resource manager to associate an applications request to a transaction identified by the supplied identifier.
`xa_end`	Ends the association of a resource manager with a transaction.
`xa_prepare`	Prepares the resource manager for the commit operation. This method is called by the transaction manager in phase one of the two-phase commit process.
`xa_commit`	Commits the transaction. This method is called by the transaction manager in phase two of the two-phase commit process.
`xa_recover`	Retrieves a list of prepared, heuristically committed or heuristically rolled back transactions.
`xa_forget`	Forgets the heuristic transaction associated with the given transaction identifier.

The `XA` and `TX` interfaces, collectively known as the X/Open Distributed Transaction Processing Model, are supported by a number of transaction-management software vendors, such as BEA, Encina, and IBM.

OMG Object Transaction Service

The Object Transaction Service (OTS) is designed to standardize the transaction-processing monitor functionality through the use of an ORB. The OTS, originally intended for use in managing transactions of CORBA objects, has become the foundation of the Java Transaction Service (JTS). Table 23-3 shows some primary OTS interfaces and a brief description of each.

Table 23-3
OTS interfaces

Interface Name	*Description*
`Current`	Enables you to set the transaction boundaries using methods like `begin()`, `commit()`, and `rollback()`.
`TransactionFactory`	Responsible for explicit transaction creation.
`Control`	Responsible for explicit transaction-context management.
`Terminator`	Responsible for committing or rolling back a transaction.

Interface Name	Description
Coordinator	Responsible for coordinating transactions.
RecoveryCoordinator	Responsible for coordinating recovery.
Synchronization	Implemented to receive notification of transaction status.
TransactionalObject	Implemented by transactional objects.

The OMG OTS specification also describes the components involved in an OMG OTS transaction model. These components are responsible for collectively providing the transactional capabilities an application is using. Take a look at each of these components:

- The *transaction client* is the component or program invoking operations on a transactional object. This is the application or component that a developer writes.
- A *transactional object* is a CORBA object that represents persistent data. Its behavior is affected by whether or not its operations are invoked inside a transaction.
- A *recoverable object* is an object that directly maintains persistent data and participates in transaction protocols.
- A *transactional server* is a collection of one or more transactional objects.
- A *recoverable server* is a collection of objects, one of which is recoverable.
- A *resource object* is an object that is registered in the transaction service for participation in the two-phase commit protocol.

Java Transaction Service

The Java Transaction Service is an implementation of a Java Transaction Server that implements the OMG OTS 1.1 specification and supports the XA/Open Distributed Transaction Processing Model. The Java Transaction Server sits as a layer below the JTA, which sits as a layer over the OMG OTS implementation. As an EJB developer, you do not need to understand the intricacies of JTS and OMG JTS, because JTA is designed to be the primary interface with which to enable transaction management in applications.

On the other hand, if you are interested in implementing a transaction manager for an application server or perhaps in a transaction-processing monitor, the relevance of JTS and OMG JTS becomes more apparent. While understanding the underlying architecture results in a greater understanding of transaction management, this chapter does not attempt to provide all the details a transaction-manager implementer needs.

As you saw earlier, transaction processing involves many components, one of which is the transaction manager. The transaction manager provides a range of functionality. To further understand what functionality you can access from the JTA in the JTS, the JTS is able to do the following:

- Provide applications and application servers to control the scope and duration of a transaction. As you have seen, you can affect scope and duration by programmatically or declaratively marking the boundaries of a transaction.
- Allow multiple components to perform work as a single atomic transaction.
- Enable you to associate a global transaction with the resources being used by a transaction.
- Coordinate the completion of transactions that span multiple resources.
- Provide synchronization for transactions.
- Enable interoperation with other transaction managers by means of the CORBA ORB/OTS interfaces. Coordination among transaction managers is transparent to clients of the transaction manager.

The transaction manager is also required to support a distributed flat-transaction model. Earlier in the chapter, we mentioned that a flat transaction is one that cannot have child transactions. The transaction manager is not required to support nested transactions.

The transaction manager also maintains the association between the transaction context of the executing thread and the transaction being executed. The transaction context is either null or refers to a specific global transaction. The transaction manager also enables you to associate multiple threads with the same transaction concurrently, either in the same JVM or in multiple JVMs.

With distributed transactions, the transaction manager propagates the context of a transaction automatically between transaction managers.

And lastly, the transaction manager is required to use the interfaces defined in the X/Open distributed transaction processing model to make sure that the integrity of all affected resources is maintained.

Java Transaction API

While it is possible to use JTA/JTS with Web components, this chapter deals with the use of JTA/JTS with Enterprise JavaBeans. As you saw in Chapters 16 and 17, Enterprise JavaBeans come in two varieties: entity and session. The former represents a piece of data your application is working with, and the latter represents application logic.

EJBs can manage their own transactions, or they can enlist the EJB container to manage their transactions. Most EJB containers today support the use of JTA and JTS to perform transaction management.

You often see the two acronyms, JTA and JTS, together. This does not mean that you as a developer will necessarily be using both directly. The Java Transaction API is the developer's means of accessing transaction management. JTA makes use of JTS to provide the necessary functionality. JTA is designed to provide transaction capability to applications, regardless of the underlying transaction models implemented by the vendors.

JTA interfaces and classes

As a developer of EJBs and user of transaction-management facilities, you actually have a relatively small number of interfaces to worry about. This, of course, makes using transactions in your application much easier. Table 23-4 lists the primary interfaces of the Java Transaction API located in the `javax.transaction` package as part of the J2EE SDK.

Table 23-4
JTA interfaces

Interface Name	*Description*
`Status`	Defines a series of static fields with values representing the various states that a transaction could be in at any given moment.
`Synchronization`	Enables an interested party to be notified before and after a transaction completes.
`Transaction`	Represents the transaction itself and exposes methods that enable you to query the state and affect the transaction outcome—for example, by rolling it back. Applications that are only intended to use transactions should never try to manipulate a transaction directly using this class. Instead, use the `javax.transaction.UserTransaction` interface.
`TransactionManager`	Allows an application server to manage transaction boundaries on behalf of application components that may be running in it.
`UserTransaction`	Allows an application to explicitly manage transaction boundaries.

Now look a little more closely at a couple of the interfaces mentioned in the preceding table, interfaces that warrant further discussion given their relevance to your application code.

The UserTransaction interface

The `javax.transaction.UserTransaction` interface is the means by which applications can programmatically mark their transaction boundaries. As you will read later on in "JTA transactions," your use of this interface depends on the type of transaction management you desire in your application. You should not use the `javax.transaction.UserTransaction` interface during container-managed persistence to mark transaction boundaries.

The `javax.transaction.UserTransaction` interface defines a set of methods (Table 23-5) that enable you to mark transaction boundaries and retrieve limited information about the transaction in progress.

Table 23-5
UserTransaction interface methods

Method Name	*Description*
`begin`	Causes a new transaction to be created and associated with the current thread of execution.
`commit`	Causes the current transaction to complete and the associated thread to become unassociated with the transaction.
`rollback`	Causes the current transaction to be rolled back and the associated thread to become unassociated with the transaction.
`getStatus`	Returns the status of the current transaction. (See Table 23-6 in "The Status interface" section for a list of possible status codes.)
`setRollbackOnly`	Modifies the current transaction so that its only outcome is to be rolled back.
`setTransactionTimeout`	Modifies the timeout value that was established after the call to the `begin()` method.

The Status interface

The `javax.transaction.Status` interface, as mentioned in Table 23-6, defines a series of static integer fields with values that represent the various states that a transaction may be in during its execution. As an application user of JTA, you may find these status fields of limited value, depending on the type of transaction management you're using. For instance, if you are using container-managed transactions, the status of the transaction really matters only to the container managing the transaction.

Table 23-6
Status interface fields

Field Name	*Description*
`STATUS_ACTIVE`	The transaction is associated with a target object and is in an active state.
`STATUS_COMMITTED`	The transaction is associated with a target object and has been committed.
`STATUS_COMMITTING`	The transaction is associated with a target object and is in the process of committing.
`STATUS_MARKED_ROLLBACK`	The transaction is associated with the target object and has been marked for rollback.
`STATUS_NO_TRANSACTION`	No transaction is associated with the target object.
`STATUS_PREPARED`	The transaction is associated with a target object and has been prepared.
`STATUS_PREPARING`	The transaction is associated with a target object and is in the process of preparing.
`STATUS_ROLLEDBACK`	The transaction is associated with a target object, and the outcome of the transaction has been determined to be rolled-back.
`STATUS_ROLLING_BACK`	The transaction is associated with a target object and is in the process of rolling back.
`STATUS_UNKNOWN`	The transaction is associated with a target object, but its status cannot be determined. This may be an intermittent state that the transaction passes through. Subsequent queries against the status of a transaction may yield one of the other values listed in this table.

As you can see from Table 23-6, various levels of states exist. This enables an interested caller to find out the status of a transaction at various stages and act accordingly.

The Synchronization interface

The `javax.transaction.Synchronization` interface enables an interested application server to become notified before and after a transaction has completed. It defines two methods, summarized in Table 23-7, which the server can use to receive notification of these two transactional events.

Table 23-7
Synchronization interface methods

Method Name	*Description*
`beforeCompletion`	Called by the transaction manager prior to the start of the transaction completion process.
`afterCompletion`	Called by the transaction manager after a transaction is committed or rolled back. Takes a single-integer argument representing the status of the transaction.

Application clients generally do not use the `Synchronization` interface. A similar interface exists for application components and clients who want to be notified of transaction states. The `javax.ejb.SessionSynchronization` interface is listed in Table 23-8. This interface is of course optional and can be implemented by session beans.

Table 23-8
SessionSynchronization interface methods

Method Name	*Description*
`afterBegin`	Called when a new transaction has started. Subsequent operations will operate in the scope of a transaction.
`beforeCompletion`	Called when the transaction is about to be committed.
`afterCompletion`	Called after the transaction commit has occurred. A Boolean is passed to this method to indicate the success or failure of the transaction.

As you will also see later in this chapter, session beans can use the `javax.transaction.Synchronization` interface to reinitialize the values of fields.

How Do I Use JTA/JTS?

The answer to this question depends on the type of control you want over transactions in your application. Your bean may fall into one of two categories: *container-managed* or *bean-managed* transactions. The answer also depends on whether you're using a session bean, an entity bean, or a message-driven bean. Each type of bean has individual rules, which are discussed in the following sections.

It should also be noted that while JTA is traditionally used with EJBs, it can also be used with servlets or standalone Java applications that require transaction services.

Container-managed transactions

Container-managed transactions are those that an EJB container carries out on the part of the EJB. They are among the easiest means of enabling transaction support in your application. They are also among the more restrictive, in that you cannot control when the rollback of an operation can occur. The EJB container is also responsible for reinitializing the instance variables of an EJB, should a rollback occur while you're working with an entity bean. The EJB container invokes the `ejbLoad()` method of the bean, which reloads the instance-variable data from the database.

You can use container-managed transactions for both entity and session beans. They start right before the method is invoked and commit right before the method exists.

Transaction attributes for EJB

The JTA specifies a series of attributes that EJB developers can use to indicate when and how transactions should be handled for their EJB. Transaction attributes also define the scope of a transaction. Transaction attributes can be applied toward individual methods of an enterprise bean or toward the entire bean.

One thing that can affect how you assign transaction attributes is the behavior of the client that will be calling the EJB. A client that calls a method of the EJB may or may not have a transaction in progress when it calls the method. As an EJB developer, you may or may not decide to require that a caller of a method of your EJB must have a transaction already in progress. You may decide to make things easier for the users and have the EJB container start the transaction automatically.

Before continuing, let's briefly touch on how transaction attributes relate to the client. A client is usually defined as a single process or thread of execution that makes a request of a resource, presumably within a single transaction. However, in the case of EJBs, the client can be another EJB that may or may not already have a transaction in progress. The transaction attribute of the code being called may be different from that of the caller, but this does not mean the code being called cannot have its transaction requirements met.

Table 23-9 shows the allowed attribute names and a description of each.

Table 23-9
Transaction attributes

Attribute Name	*Description*
`Required`	If the client is running within a transaction, the method executes within the client's transaction. If the client has not already started a transaction, the container starts a new transaction before starting the method.
`RequiresNew`	If the client is running within a transaction, the method is executed after all of the following occurs: 1) The client's transaction is suspended. 2) A new transaction is started. 3) The method is started. 4) The client's transaction is resumed. If the client has not started a transaction, a new transaction is started before executing the method.
`Mandatory`	If the client has not started a transaction, and the method is invoked, the container will throw a `javax.transaction.TransactionRequiredException`. You should use this value if you want to hold callers responsible for marking the transaction boundaries.
`NotSupported`	If the client has started a transaction, and the method is invoked, the client's transaction is suspended during the execution of the method. If the client has not started a transaction, no transaction is started. A value of `NotSupported` can provide some measure of performance increase, and starting and ending transactions involve overhead.
`Supports`	
`Never`	If the client has started a transaction, and the method is executed, the container will throw a `RemoteException`.

Specify transaction attributes

You specify transaction attributes in the EJB deployment descriptor. This enables you to change the transactional requirements of your EJB with little or no code changes, and you can change the attributes many times over the course of development. In Chapter 16, you were introduced to EJB deployment descriptors.

Whether you are brave enough to code the EJB deployment descriptor by hand or whether you opt to use a GUI tool such as the J2EE deployment tool, you can easily specify transaction attributes. Here is a fragment of an EJB deployment descriptor of which the elements use the values described in Table 23-9:

```
<container-transaction>
      <method>
        <ejb-name>OrderEJB</ejb-name>
        <method-intf>Remote</method-intf>
        <method-name>placeOrder</method-name>
        <method-params>
          <method-param>int</method-param>
          <method-param>int</method-param>
          <method-param>int</method-param>
        </method-params>
      </method>
      <trans-attribute>Required</trans-attribute>
    </container-transaction>
```

Here an EJB named `OrderEJB`, with a method named `placeOrder`, has a transaction attribute of `Required`.

Even though transaction attributes can be set at many stages during application development, the responsibilities of determining the correct values and determining which methods need which attribute values should fall on the EJB developer. The EJB developer knows the application and its requirements better than anyone else and understands how the different components will call each other.

Performance implications of transaction attributes

Deciding on the correct transaction attribute requires more than just the correct people. It also requires a good understanding of concepts such as the two-phase commit, locking, and TP monitors, and an understanding of the overall design of the application. When you assign a transaction attribute to a bean or method of a bean, you must realize the implications for the performance of the application. For instance, in some cases it may be tempting to simply assign a default transaction-attribute value of `RequiresNew` or `Required` to every method of a bean during the use of the J2EE deployment tool. You might make this decision because of uncertainty on a developer's part or a misunderstanding about how another component of the application works. But assigning transaction attributes improperly or when the method or component doesn't need a transaction at all can degrade the overall performance of the component and possibly the entire application.

You may recall from earlier in the chapter that many components are involved in carrying out a transaction. First, transactions are expensive to start in some cases, and they may also create locks on resources they don't need, tying up valuable resources that could be used elsewhere. The resources that might be tied up are the resources used by the transaction-processing monitor, which will then have to decide what to do with a transaction. The transaction manager will also now have to waste resources managing the lifecycle of a transaction it doesn't need to manage. In the case of a distributed transaction, the transaction must be coordinated across the affected databases, tying up resources on those machines as well.

In short, assign transaction attributes with care. If during development it's easier to take the defaults, make sure that when deploying the EJB you review your transaction-attribute settings. You should take into account the caller of a particular EJB and whether or not that caller may have a transaction already in progress. You take these steps, as described in Table 23-9, to ensure that transactions don't step on each other; this involves suspending the caller's transaction until the bean's transaction is finished. If you assign a transaction attribute to a method that doesn't need it, the calling transaction will be suspended unnecessarily.

What not to do when using container-managed transactions

Container-managed transactions are there to make your life as an EJB developer easier. So, despite your best intentions, do not try to help out by executing any code that interferes with the transaction management, such as by trying to initiate a rollback or commit a transaction or change the behavior of auto-committing transactions. Also, do not try to obtain a new transaction while in container-managed transactions.

Operations such as these can affect the transactional boundaries that have been established by the container and, in short, can really mess things up.

When things go awry

Things can go wrong during the execution of a method. A database may be unavailable for some reason, or a runtime exception may occur. As you are no doubt aware, when things go wrong during a transaction, operations and updates that were occurring must be undone or rolled back. Container-managed transactions can be rolled back in two ways.

The first way is to let the container do the rollback. The container will only do a rollback if the EJB throws a system exception. A system exception is one defined in the J2EE API. The two most common system exceptions are `javax.ejb.EJBException` and `javax.transaction.SystemException`. A system exception usually indicates that either a failure in the underlying network transport or something less severe, such as a SQL exception, has occurred.

When system exceptions occur, they are wrapped in a `java.rmi.RemoteException` and propagated back to the caller of the method.

Application-specific exceptions are those that you define in your own application and that represent failures unique to your application. In the well-known example, a transfer from savings to checking, you might define an exception named `InsufficientFundsException`, to be thrown in the event that there isn't enough money in the savings account to satisfy the request.

If an application-specific exception is thrown, the transaction rollback is not automatic but may be initiated by a call to the `setRollBackOnly()` method of the `EJBContext` interface. Listing 23-1 illustrates the use of system exceptions in an EJB method.

Listing 23-1: Rolling back container-managed transactions

```
public void changeBalance(float newBalance){

        try {

            updateBalance(newBalance);

        } catch(Exception ex) {

            try {

                context.setRollBackOnly()

            } catch (SystemException ex) {
                throw new EJBException("Rollback failed");
            }

            throw new EJBException("Transaction failed");
        }
}
```

In Listing 23-1, the `updateBalance()` method is called: If an exception occurs during the execution of this method, the `setRollBackOnly()` method of the `javax.ejb.EJBContext()` method is called to indicate that when the method exits, the transaction should be rolled back.

If a failure occurs during the processing of the request, a `javax.ejb.EJBException` is thrown. This exception will cause the EJB container to roll back the transaction.

Unlike system exceptions, application exceptions do not cause the exception to be wrapped in a `java.rmi.RemoteException`. The application exception is returned to the caller of the method as is.

Reinitialize session beans

Session beans have some different behavior when a transaction fails and is rolled back. Unlike an entity bean, of which the instance variables are automatically reset via a call to the bean's `ejbLoad()` method, a session bean's instance variables are not reinitialized automatically. It should be noted that the use of the `javax.ejb.SessionSynchronization` interface is entirely optional.

The `javax.ejb.SessionSynchronization` interface allows a session bean to be notified of various states that a transaction is in, giving the session bean the opportunity to reinitialize the state of its fields. The EJB container is responsible for invoking the methods of the `javax.ejb.SessionSynchronization` interface.

You can to use the `afterBegin()` method to be notified after the transaction has begun but before the method of the EJB is invoked. You can also use it as a place to load the instance variables of a session bean if you desire.

You can use the `beforeCompletion()` method to be notified after the EJB method has finished but before the transaction commits. When the `beforeCompletion()` method is invoked, you have one last opportunity to roll back the transaction using the `setRollBackOnly()` method of the `javax.transaction.UserTransaction()` interface.

The last method, `afterCompletion()`,is invoked when the transaction has completed. It takes a single Boolean argument indicating whether or not the transaction was committed: either a value of `true`, committed, or a value of `false`, meaning rolled back. If the transaction was rolled back, it is in this method that you can reinitialize the instance variables — either by setting them to a default or by reading some values from the database. Listing 23-2 shows the source of a session bean, illustrating the use of the `javax.ejb.SessionSynchronization` methods.

Listing 23-2: A shopping-cart session bean using javax.ejb.SessionSynchronization

```
/*
 *
*    ShoppingCartBean to illustrate the use of
*    SessionSynchronization interface.
 *
 */

import java.util.*;
import javax.ejb.*;
import java.sql.*;
import javax.sql.*;
import javax.naming.*;

public class ShoppingCartBean implements SessionBean,
                                         SessionSynchronization
{

   private List cartItems = null;
   private int customerId = 0;
   private SessionContext context;
   private Connection con;
   private String dbName = "java:comp/env/jdbc/CatalogDB";
```

```
public void addItem(int productId {

   cartItems.add(new Integer(productId));

}

public double getCartItems() {

   return cartItems;
}

public double getNumberOfItems() {

   return cartItems.size();
}

public boolean submitOrder() {
}

public void ejbCreate() throws CreateException {

   try {
      makeConnection();
      cartItems = new List();
   } catch (Exception ex) {
       throw new CreateException(ex.getMessage());
   }

}


public void ejbRemove() {

   try {
       con.close();
       cartItems.clear();
   } catch (Exception ex) {
       throw new EJBException("ejbRemove SQLException: " +
                              ex.getMessage());
   }
}

public void ejbActivate() {

   try {
      makeConnection();
   } catch (Exception ex) {
       throw new EJBException("ejbActivate Exception: " +
                              ex.getMessage());
   }
}
```

Continued

Listing 23-2 *(continued)*

```
public void ejbPassivate() {

     try {
       con.close();
     } catch (Exception ex) {
         throw new EJBException("ejbPassivate Exception: " +
                                ex.getMessage());
     }
  }


  public void setSessionContext(SessionContext context) {
     this.context = context;
  }

  public void afterBegin() {

     System.out.println("afterBegin()");
     try {
        cartItems = new List();
     } catch (Exception ex) {
         throw new EJBException("afterBegin Exception: " +
                                ex.getMessage());
     }

  }

  public void beforeCompletion() {

     System.out.println("beforeCompletion()");
  }

  public void afterCompletion(boolean committed) {

     System.out.println("afterCompletion: " + committed);
     if (committed == false) {
        try {
           cartItems.clear();
        } catch (Exception ex) {
            throw new EJBException("afterCompletion
                                   SQLException: " +
                                   ex.getMessage());
        }
     }
  }

  public ShoppingCartBean() {}
```

```
    private void makeConnection()
        throws NamingException, SQLException {

        InitialContext ic = new InitialContext();
        DataSource ds = (DataSource) ic.lookup(dbName);
        con =  ds.getConnection();
    }

}
```

In Listing 23-2, the `ShoppingCartBean` class implements the required methods of the `javax.session.Synchronization` interface and prints a message when the container calls into the methods `afterBegin()`, `beforeCompletion()`, and `afterCompletion()`.

Bean-managed transactions

Bean-managed transactions are those that the EJB controls itself. The EJB is responsible for marking the boundaries of the transaction as well as for initiating a rollback of the transactions and any operations that may have been in progress. In bean-managed transactions, the EJB is also responsible for reinitializing any instance variables.

JDBC transactions

JDBC transactions are those managed by the transaction manager of the DBMS. You mark the boundaries of JDBC transactions using the `connect()`, `commit()`, or `rollback()` methods of the `java.sql.Connection` interface. You might have noticed that, unlike JTA transactions, JDBC transactions have no method to explicitly start a transaction. JDBC transaction starts are implicit and begin with the most recent call to one of the aforementioned methods. You may already have been exposed to JDBC transactions if you've written a Java servlet that directly accesses a database. Listing 23-3 shows an example of an Enterprise JavaBean that uses JDBC transactions to mark its boundaries.

Listing 23-3: Using JDBC transactions

```
public void changeBalance(float newBalance){

        try {

            con.setAutoCommit(false);

            updateBalance(newBalance);

            con.commit();
```

Continued

Listing 23-3 *(continued)*

```
} catch(Exception ex) {

        try {

            con.rollback();

        } catch (SystemException ex) {
            throw new EJBException("Rollback failed");
        }

        throw new EJBException("Transaction failed");
    }

}
```

The changeBalance() method begins by setting the auto-commit behavior of the java.sql.Connection interface to false. The beginning of the transaction has already been marked at this point. You may recall from earlier in the chapter that JDBC transactions boundaries are implicit. When the java.sql.Connection instance was created, the beginning of the transaction boundary was marked.

Next, the changeBalance() method calls a method to update the database. (For the purpose of this example, the code that comprises the updateBalance() method has been omitted.) What will most likely occur is that the bean will perform updates to the database.

Next, you call the commit() method of the java.sql.Connection, and if all goes well, the method executes. If an exception occurs while the begin(), updateBalance(), or commit() methods occurs, you can make an attempt to roll back the transaction using the rollback() method of the java.sql.Connection interface.

JTA transactions

JTA transactions are those managed by the J2EE transaction manager. The J2EE transaction manager supports managing a single transaction across multiple databases if you desire.

You mark the boundaries of JTA transactions by using the begin(), commit(), and rollback() methods of the javax.transaction.UserTransaction interface. Listing 23-4 shows an example of an EJB method that uses a JTA transaction to mark its boundaries.

Listing 23-4: Using JTA transactions with bean-managed transactions

```
public void changeBalance(float newBalance){

       UserTransaction ut = context.getUserTransaction();

        try {

           ut.begin();

           updateBalance(newBalance);

           ut.commit();

       } catch(Exception ex) {

           try {

               ut.rollback();

           } catch (SystemException ex) {
               throw new EJBException("Rollback failed");
           }

           throw new EJBException("Transaction failed");
       }
}
```

In Listing 23-4, the `changeBalance()` method begins by creating an instance of the `javax.transaction.UserTransaction` interface using the `getUserTransaction()` method of the `EJBContext` interface. Next, it marks the beginning of the transaction using the `begin()` method. You then call the `updateBalance()` method, which is presumed to be a method elsewhere in the bean. (For the purpose of this example, the code that comprises the `updateBalance()` method has been omitted.) What will most likely occur is that the bean will perform updates to the database.

Next, the `commit()` method of the `javax.transaction.UserTransaction` interface is called, and if all goes well, the method executes. If an exception occurs while the `begin()`, `updateBalance()`, or `commit()` methods occurs, you can attempt to roll back the transaction using the `rollback()` method of the `UserTransaction` interface.

What not to do when using bean-managed transactions

As with container-managed transactions, you should not use certain methods while using bean-managed transactions. You should not use the `getRollbackOnly()` or `setRollbackOnly()` methods of the `javax.ejb.EJBContext` interfaces. These methods should only be used with container-managed transactions.

Transaction timeout

When a transaction begins, a number of factors may affect the time it takes to execute. No solid rule exists for how long a transaction should take. The type of application in which the transaction is running could affect how long you are willing to wait for a transaction to complete before giving up.

Transaction timeout is the amount of time you are willing to wait for a transaction to begin and commit. The length of time a transaction takes can be affected by things such as network traffic, availability of resources such as databases, or length of an operation being performed during a transaction. In distributed applications, a transaction that affects multiple databases has to coordinate itself across multiple network nodes: Some nodes may be down, and the request may be routed along a different path until it reaches the intended node. The length of time may also be affected by the amount of work being done by a particular application component at the same time. Even though EJB containers support the pooling of objects, this does not guarantee that one will be available when you try to make a request; in addition, a transaction-processing monitor may decide that your request needs to go to a different server, which may increase the amount of time it takes to execute a request.

All of these factors can affect your decision of how long a timeout value to assign. Web-based applications should generally have a low timeout value: Users are usually not willing to wait a very long time before they become bored or frustrated at how long a particular operation is taking.

The timeout value

Default timeout values vary according to the DBMS or application server you are using. The J2EE SDK has a default timeout value of zero. You can change the transaction timeout value by looking in the default.properties file in the config subdirectory of the J2EE installation directory and looking for the following property:

```
transaction.timeout
```

The value you assign is in seconds. If the value is zero, the transaction will not time out. If the number of seconds elapses before the transaction is complete, the transaction is rolled back.

Who is affected by transaction timeout?

The transaction timeout property only affects beans using container-managed transactions. You can also programmatically change the timeout value for beans that are using bean-managed transactions and JTA by using the `setTransactionTimeout()` method of the `javax.transaction.UserTransaction` interface. The `setTransactionTimeout()` takes a single primitive integer argument that specifies the timeout in number of seconds. If you pass a value of zero to this method, the default timeout value is restored.

Transaction isolation

Transaction isolation involves making a decision about whether or not you want to isolate the data being modified during a transaction. For instance, you may want applications to be able to read data from a particular table regardless of whether a transaction is in progress. Under normal circumstances, when a transaction starts, access to the table being updated is locked while the update is in place. Transaction isolation enables you to make a conscious decision about whether or not you want other application code to be able to read that table while it is being updated.

The implications of this type of behavior are quite evident: Other application code may read the wrong data. An application may read the data before the transaction commits, and if the transaction is rolled back, the data that application is reading will be corrupted.

The J2EE does not define any standards for transaction isolation, but it does provide means of configuring the way transaction isolation is handled: the `setTransactionIsolation()` method of the `java.sql.Connection` interface. You cannot alter transaction isolation for entity beans using container-managed transactions. Table 23-10 shows the allowed values for the `setTransactionIsolation()` method.

Table 23-10
Transaction isolation levels

Level Name	*Description*
`TRANSACTION_READ_COMMITTED`	Dirty reads are prevented; non-repeatable and phantom reads can occur.
`TRANSACTION_READ_UNCOMMITTED`	Dirty reads, non-repeatable reads, and phantom reads can occur.
`TRANSACTION_REPEATABLE_READ`	Dirty and non-repeatable reads can occur; phantom reads are prevented.
`TRANSACTION_SERIALIZABLE`	Dirty, non-repeatable, and phantom reads are prevented.

One value is defined as a field of the `java.sql.Connection` interface: That value is `TRANSACTION_NONE`, but you cannot use it as a value to the `setTransactionIsolationLevel()` method. Some of the values in Table 23-10 may not be supported by the DBMS vendor you are using.

What are Dirty, Non-Repeatable, and Phantom Reads?

A *dirty read* is basically one in which you are reading data that may change in a subsequent read. The data are quite possibly in the midst of changing in a transaction, and these changes will not have been committed. A *non-repeatable* read is one in which one transaction reads a row, a second transaction modifies a row, and then the first transaction rereads the row and gets different values. This differs from a *dirty read* in that the read by the affected transaction is done in the same transaction as opposed to being done in a different transaction.

The last type of read, a *phantom read,* is one where a transaction reads a table and retrieves a set of rows that satisfy the WHERE clause of a SQL statement. Meanwhile, a second transaction inserts a row that would be shown as it satisfies the WHERE clause the first transaction executed. Then the first transaction rereads the row, and lo and behold!, a new "phantom" row has appeared.

Now that you've had a look at what JTS and JTA are, and seen the primary interfaces and how they affect the way you use container-managed and bean-managed transactions, take a look at an example of using both container-managed and bean-managed transactions.

Before continuing with the following examples, make sure you have installed the J2EE SDK. You can look at Appendix A for information about how to install, set up, and use the J2EE server that comes with the J2EE SDK.

ACME Widgets Inc. – A Shopping-Cart Demo

A shopping-cart application will serve as a means of demonstrating the use of container-managed and bean-managed transactions. You will construct three EJB session beans to be used for various functions of the application.

The ACME Widget Inc. is thinking of providing a way for customers to buy its products online, and has developed a prototype of some of the components (this demo) to see how things can fit together. This demo in no way attempts to illustrate comprehensive application architecture. Rather, it attempts to illustrate the use of the Java Transaction API in a pseudo-real-world application.

This application, as we noted briefly already, will illustrate the use of three EJB session beans that perform order taking, catalog inquiry, and inventory management, respectively. Each of the beans implements a minimal set of functionality. You will also see how to use transaction management in the application.

The Order and Inventory beans will use container-managed transactions, because they have the potential to do update operations. The Catalog bean will use JTA, bean-managed transactions. This way you can see the use of all three in the same application.

In this example, we will discuss only the relevant business methods of the EJB and not the EJB-specific methods and what they are for. The EJB-specific methods we're referring to are EJB lifecycle methods like `ejbCreate()`, `ejbActivate()`, and `ejbPassivate()`, just to name a few. You can learn more about these methods and what they are for by reading Chapter 16.

For a complete discussion on constructing EJB and associated interfaces, please refer to Chapter 16.

Before continuing, make sure that you have installed the J2EE SDK. These examples were tested and deployed against the J2EE server and EJB container that come with the J2EE SDK. You should also be somewhat familiar with the CloudView database utility, an application that enables you to manage Cloudscape database instances, create tables, insert data into those tables, and assign permissions. You can also execute SQL scripts directly in the CloudView database utility GUI, which is how you will create the tables for this example.

The CloudView utility can be downloaded from `http://www.cloudscape.com`.

Create the database and tables

Three tables will reside in a database called ACMEWIDGET. You can build the database and tables for this example using the SQL script in Listing 23-5.

Listing 23-5: SQL script to generate the ICATALOG, INVENTORY, and ORDERS tables

```
CREATE TABLE ICATALOG (
  NAME varchar(20),
  PRODUCTID INTEGER
);
CREATE TABLE INVENTORY (
  PRODUCTID INTEGER,
  NUMBERINSTOCK INTEGER
);
CREATE TABLE ORDERS (
  CUSTOMERID INTEGER,
  PRODUCTID INTEGER,
  NUMBERORDERED INTEGER
);
```

Continued

Listing 23-5 *(continued)*

```
INSERT INTO ICATALOG (NAME,PRODUCTID) VALUES('Simple
Widget',1000);
INSERT INTO ICATALOG (NAME,PRODUCTID) VALUES('Mega
Widget',1001);
INSERT INTO ICATALOG (NAME,PRODUCTID) VALUES('Ultra
Widget',1002);

INSERT INTO INVENTORY (PRODUCTID,NUMBERINSTOCK)
VALUES(1000,100);
INSERT INTO INVENTORY (PRODUCTID,NUMBERINSTOCK)
VALUES(1001,50);
INSERT INTO INVENTORY (PRODUCTID,NUMBERINSTOCK)
VALUES(1002,10);
```

You can run this script by starting the CloudView utility and pasting it into the SQL window and then clicking the lightning-bolt symbol. The tables will be created and the data inserted into them. You can launch the CloudView utility using this command:

```
java COM.cloudscape.tools.cview
```

You can create the ACMEWIDGET database by selecting Files ➪ New ➪ Database. You will be prompted for the name of the database. This will create a database in the system home directory of Cloudscape: Usually this means the same working directory from which you started CloudView.

The Order session bean

The Order session bean represents the business logic necessary for placing an order for an item. Listing 23-6 shows the source for the `Order` interface.

Listing 23-6: The order

```
/*
 *
 * The interface representing an Order
 *
 */

import javax.ejb.EJBObject;
import java.rmi.RemoteException;
```

```
public interface Order extends EJBObject {

    public void placeOrder(int productId,
                           int numberOfItems,
                           int customerId)
        throws RemoteException;

}
```

The Order interface represents the interface to the Order bean. Listing 23-7 shows the source of the home interface for the Order bean.

Listing 23-7: The Order home interface

```
/*
 *
 * Interface representing the home interface of the Order
 *
 */

import java.rmi.RemoteException;
import javax.ejb.*;

public interface OrderHome extends EJBHome {

    public Order create(int id)
        throws RemoteException, CreateException;
}
```

Next, take a look at the source for the Order session bean itself. This bean is responsible for placing an order into the ORDER table. Listing 23-8 shows the source of the Order session bean.

Listing 23-8: The OrderBean session-bean class

```
/*
 *
 * OrderBean to illustrate the use of SessionSynchronization
 * interface.
 *
 */
```

Continued

Listing 23-8 (continued)

```
import java.util.*;
import javax.ejb.*;
import java.sql.*;
import javax.sql.*;
import javax.naming.*;

public class OrderBean implements SessionBean,
SessionSynchronization {

   private int productId = 0;
   private int numberOfItems = 0;
   private int customerId = 0;
   private SessionContext context;
   private Connection con;
   private String dbName = "java:comp/env/jdbc/ACMEWidgetDB";

   public void placeOrder(int productId,
                          int numberOfItems,
                          int customerId) {

     try {

      String insertStatement =
            "insert INTO ORDER values " +
            "( ? , ?, ? )";


      PreparedStatement prepStmt =
            con.prepareStatement(insertStatement);

      prepStmt.setInt(1, productId);
      prepStmt.setInt(2, numberOfItems);
      prepStmt.setInt(3, customerId);
      prepStmt.executeUpdate();
      prepStmt.close();

     } catch (Exception ex) {
        System.out.println(ex);
     }

   }

   public void ejbCreate(int customer) throws CreateException {

      customerId = customer;

      try {
         makeConnection();
      } catch (Exception ex) {
```

```
            throw new CreateException(ex.getMessage());
        }

    }

    public void ejbRemove() {

        try {
            con.close();
        } catch (Exception ex) {
            throw new EJBException("ejbRemove SQLException: " +
ex.getMessage());
        }
    }

    public void ejbActivate() {

        try {
          makeConnection();
        } catch (Exception ex) {
            throw new EJBException("ejbActivate Exception: " +
ex.getMessage());
        }
    }

    public void ejbPassivate() {

        try {
          con.close();
        } catch (Exception ex) {
            throw new EJBException("ejbPassivate Exception: " +
ex.getMessage());
        }
    }


    public void setSessionContext(SessionContext context) {
        this.context = context;
    }

    public void afterBegin() {

        System.out.println("afterBegin()");
    }

    public void beforeCompletion() {

        System.out.println("beforeCompletion()");
    }

    public void afterCompletion(boolean committed) {
```

Continued

Listing 23-8 *(continued)*

```
        System.out.println("afterCompletion: " + committed);
        if (committed == false) {
           try {
              productId = 0;
               customerId = 0;
                numberOfItems = 0;
           } catch (Exception ex) {
               throw new EJBException("afterCompletion
SQLException: " +
                  ex.getMessage());
           }
        }
     }

     public OrderBean() {}


     private void makeConnection()
        throws NamingException, SQLException {

        InitialContext ic = new InitialContext();
        DataSource ds = (DataSource) ic.lookup(dbName);
        con =  ds.getConnection();
     }

  }
```

The `placeOrder()` method takes three integer arguments, representing the product ID of the product you are ordering, the number of that product, and a customer ID, respectively.

You perform the updates using a `java.sql.PreparedStatement` object.

The Inventory session bean

The Inventory session bean is responsible for making sure an item is available in the quantity requested. It also enables you to remove a certain number of items from the inventory. Listing 23-9 shows the source for the `Inventory` interface for the session-bean class.

Listing 23-9: The Inventory interface

```
/*
 *
 * The interface representing an Order
 *
 */

import javax.ejb.EJBObject;
import java.rmi.RemoteException;

public interface Inventory extends EJBObject {

    public boolean checkInventory(int productId,
                                  int numberOfItems)
        throws RemoteException;

}
```

The `Inventory` interface represents the interface to the Inventory bean. Listing 23-10 shows the source for the `Inventory` home interface.

Listing 23-10: The Inventory home interface

```
/*
 *
 * Interface representing the home interface of the Order
 *
 */

import java.rmi.RemoteException;
import javax.ejb.*;

public interface InventoryHome extends EJBHome {

    public Inventory create()
        throws RemoteException, CreateException;
}
```

The `InventoryHome` interface represents the `Home` interface of the EJB.

The InventoryBean session bean is the class responsible for implementing the actual business logic. With the InventoryBean, you can remove items from the INVENTORY database table. Listing 23-11 shows the source for the Inventory session-bean class.

Listing 23-11: The Inventory session-bean class

```
/*
 *
 * InventoryBean to illustrate the use of
SessionSynchronization
 * interface.
 *
 */

import java.util.*;
import javax.ejb.*;
import java.sql.*;
import javax.sql.*;
import javax.naming.*;

public class InventoryBean implements SessionBean,
SessionSynchronization {


   private SessionContext context;
   private Connection con;
   private String dbName = "java:comp/env/jdbc/ACMEWidgetDB";

   public boolean checkInventory(int productId,
                                 int numberOfItems) {

      boolean itemsAvailable = false;

      String selectStatement =
           "select * " +
           "from INVENTORY WHERE PRODUCTID = ? AND
NUMBERINSTOCK > ?";

      try {

        PreparedStatement prepStmt =
             con.prepareStatement(selectStatement);

        prepStmt.setInt(1, productId);
        prepStmt.setInt(2, numberOfItems);
```

```
            ResultSet rs = prepStmt.executeQuery();

            if (rs.next())
                itemsAvailable = true;

            rs.close();
            prepStmt.close();

        } catch (Exception ex) {
                System.out.println("Exception: " + ex);
        }

        return itemsAvailable;

    }

    public void ejbCreate() throws CreateException {

        try {
            makeConnection();
        } catch (Exception ex) {
            throw new CreateException(ex.getMessage());
        }

    }

    public void ejbRemove() {

        try {
            con.close();
        } catch (Exception ex) {
            throw new EJBException("ejbRemove SQLException: " +
ex.getMessage());
        }
    }

    public void ejbActivate() {

        try {
            makeConnection();
        } catch (Exception ex) {
            throw new EJBException("ejbActivate Exception: " +
ex.getMessage());
        }
    }

    public void ejbPassivate() {
```

Continued

Listing 23-11 *(continued)*

```
         try {
            con.close();
         } catch (Exception ex) {
              throw new EJBException("ejbPassivate Exception: " +
ex.getMessage());
         }
      }


      public void setSessionContext(SessionContext context) {
         this.context = context;
      }

      public void afterBegin() {

         System.out.println("afterBegin()");
      }

      public void beforeCompletion() {

         System.out.println("beforeCompletion()");
      }

      public void afterCompletion(boolean committed) {

         System.out.println("afterCompletion: " + committed);
   }

      public InventoryBean() {}


      private void makeConnection()
          throws NamingException, SQLException {

          InitialContext ic = new InitialContext();
          DataSource ds = (DataSource) ic.lookup(dbName);
          con =  ds.getConnection();
       }

   }
```

The `checkInventory()` method takes two integer arguments: The first represents the product ID, and the second the number of items desired. The method uses a `java.sql.PreparedStatement` to execute the query. If the result set that comes back has at least one record, the method sets the value of the `itemsAvailable` to `true` and returns it. Otherwise it returns `false`, indicating that the inventory contained no items with that product ID in the specified quantity.

The Catalog session bean

The Catalog session bean is responsible for accessing the catalog and returning a list of items that ACME sells. Listing 23-12 shows the source for the `Catalog` interface.

Listing 23-12: The Catalog interface

```
/*
 *
 * The interface representing an Order
 *
 */

import javax.ejb.EJBObject;
import java.rmi.RemoteException;
import java.util.*;

public interface Catalog extends EJBObject {

    public List listItems()
        throws RemoteException;

}
```

The `Catalog` interface represents the interface to the Catalog bean. Listing 23-13 shows the source for the Catalog home interface.

Listing 23-13: The Catalog home interface

```
/*
 *
 * Interface representing the home interface of the Order
 *
 */

import java.rmi.RemoteException;
import javax.ejb.*;

public interface CatalogHome extends EJBHome {

    public Catalog create()
        throws RemoteException, CreateException;
}
```

Next is the CatalogBean itself, which provides all the business logic for interacting with the ICATALOG table you created earlier. Listing 23-14 shows the source for this class.

Listing 23-14: The CatalogBean session-bean class

```
/*
 *
 * OrderBean to illustrate the use of SessionSynchronization
 * interface.
 *
 */

import java.util.*;
import javax.ejb.*;
import java.sql.*;
import javax.sql.*;
import javax.naming.*;
import javax.transaction.*;

public class CatalogBean implements SessionBean,
SessionSynchronization {

   private List catalogItems = new LinkedList();
   private SessionContext context;
   private Connection con;
   private String dbName = "java:comp/env/jdbc/ACMEWidgetDB";

   public List listItems() {

      List items = new LinkedList();

      UserTransaction ut = context.getUserTransaction();

      String selectStatement =
           "select NAME " +
           "from ICATALOG";
      try {

        ut.begin();

        PreparedStatement prepStmt =
             con.prepareStatement(selectStatement);
        ResultSet rs = prepStmt.executeQuery();
        while (rs.next()){
           String item = rs.getString(1);
           catalogItems.add(item);
        }
        rs.close();
        s.close();
```

```
            ut.commit();

         } catch (Exception ex) {
              System.out.println("Exception: " + ex);
         }
         return catalogItems;

      }

      public void ejbCreate() throws CreateException {

         try {
            makeConnection();
         } catch (Exception ex) {
            throw new CreateException(ex.getMessage());
         }

      }

      public void ejbRemove() {
         try {
            con.close();
         } catch (Exception ex) {
            throw new EJBException("ejbRemove SQLException: " +
   ex.getMessage());
         }
      }
      public void ejbActivate() {
         try {
            makeConnection();
         } catch (Exception ex) {
            throw new EJBException("ejbActivate Exception: " +
   ex.getMessage());
         }
      }
      public void ejbPassivate() {
         try {
            con.close();
         } catch (Exception ex) {
            throw new EJBException("ejbPassivate Exception: " +
   ex.getMessage());
         }
      }
      public void setSessionContext(SessionContext context) {
         this.context = context;
      }
      public void afterBegin() {
         System.out.println("afterBegin()");
      }
      public void beforeCompletion() {
         System.out.println("beforeCompletion()");
```

Continued

Listing 23-14 *(continued)*

```
    }
    public void afterCompletion(boolean committed) {
       System.out.println("afterCompletion: " + committed);
       //catalogItems.clear();
    }
    public CatalogBean() {}


    private void makeConnection()
       throws NamingException, SQLException {
       InitialContext ic = new InitialContext();
       DataSource ds = (DataSource) ic.lookup(dbName);
       con =  ds.getConnection();
    }
}
```

The `listItems()` method takes no arguments and simply reads all the items out of the INVENTORY table of the ACMEWIDGET database. When the result set comes back, it is looped through, and you retrieve each product NAME using the `getString()` method of the `java.sql.ResultSet` interface. The NAME is added to an instance of the `java.util.List` interface that you return at the end of the method.

The shopping-cart client application

Now that you've created the two session beans that you will use in the application, you need to write a client that will make use of them. The client you will write for this example will be a simple, GUI-less, command-line application that exercises each of the session beans. Listing 23-15 shows the source for the command-line application called `ShoppingCartClient`.

Listing 23-15: The ShoppingCartClient application

```
/*
 *
 * The shopping cart client.
 *
 */

import java.util.*;
import javax.naming.Context;
import javax.naming.InitialContext;
import javax.rmi.PortableRemoteObject;

public class ShoppingCartClient {
```

```
    public static void main(String[] args) {

        try {
            Context initial = new InitialContext();
            Object objref1 =
initial.lookup("java:comp/env/ejb/CatalogEJB");
            Object objref2 =
initial.lookup("java:comp/env/ejb/InventoryEJB");
            Object objref3 =
initial.lookup("java:comp/env/ejb/OrderEJB");

            CatalogHome catHome =

(CatalogHome)PortableRemoteObject.narrow(objref1,
                                             CatalogHome.class);
            InventoryHome invHome =

(InventoryHome)PortableRemoteObject.narrow(objref2,

InventoryHome.class);
            OrderHome ordHome =
                (OrderHome)PortableRemoteObject.narrow(objref3,
                                             OrderHome.class);

            System.out.println("Getting reading to call
create...");

            Catalog catalog = catHome.create();
            Inventory inventory = invHome.create();
            Order order = ordHome.create(1000);

            // Retrieve list of items in catalog //
            List items = catalog.listItems();
            System.out.println("There are " + items.size() + "
items in the catalog ");
            Iterator iter = items.iterator();
            while (iter.hasNext()) {
                String item = (String)iter.next();
                System.out.println("Catalog Item: " + item);
            }
            // Check the inventory of Simple Widgets //
            boolean hasItems =
inventory.checkInventory(1000,10);
            if (hasItems)
                System.out.println("Inventory has 10 Simple
Widgets");

            // Place an order for 100 Simple Widgets //
            order.placeOrder(1000,10,1000);
```

Continued

Listing 23-15 *(continued)*

```
            catalog.remove();
            inventory.remove();
            order.remove();

            System.exit(0);

        } catch (Exception ex) {
            System.err.println("Caught an exception." );
            ex.printStackTrace();
        }
    }
}
```

The ShoppingCartClient application begins by obtaining a reference to each session bean using the lookup() method of the InitialContext() class. Next, it gets a reference to each bean's home interface. With the home interface, it can then create an instance of each bean, using this code from the application:

```
Catalog catalog = catHome.create();
Inventory inventory = invHome.create();
Order order = ordHome.create(1000);
```

The next line of code is where you begin using the beans. The first way you do this is by using the listItems() method of the Catalog bean. This returns a list of all the items in the catalog as an instance of the java.util.List interface. You print the number of items in the list using the size() method and then attempt to iterate over the items in the list. Each time through the loop you print out the name of the item. You add the items in the listItems() method of the CatalogBean session-bean class.

Next, attempt to check the inventory level using the checkInventory() method of the InventoryBean session-bean class. Pass in an integer representing the product ID and another representing the number of items you want, in order to make sure that the product exists in sufficient quantity.

Next, attempt to place an order using the OrderBean session bean. Call the placeOrder() method and pass in three arguments: the first argument an integer representing the product ID, the second argument representing the number of items for which you wish to place an order, and the last the customer ID.

Packaging and deploying

To package and deploy the Shopping Cart demo, you will use the J2EE deploytool utility. The deploytool utility is in the bin sub-directory of the J2EE installation directory and, once invoked, will display a GUI for packaging and deploying the application.

You need to create a new application and add an Enterprise JavaBean and application client to it. The application should be called shoppingcart, which will result in the creation of an Enterprise Application Resource (EAR) file called shoppingcart.ear.

In the EAR, you will need to add the `ShoppingCartClient` application as well as add three Enterprise Java Beans to the application. With a few subtle differences, each EJB session bean can be deployed in the same way; I will go over deploying the `CatalogBean` session bean for reference. Follow these steps:

1. Click the shoppingcart application node in the tree.
2. Next, select File ➪ New ➪ Enterprise Bean.
3. The first dialog that comes up is purely informational; click Next.
4. The radio button Create new EJB File in Application should already be selected, and the Shopping Cart application should be the current selection.
5. In the EJB Display Name text field, type **Catalog**.
6. In the Contents window, click Edit. This will produce a dialog from which you must select the classes that comprise the bean. From the top part of the dialog in the Available Files section, select `Catalog.class`, `CatalogHome.class` and `CatalogBean.class`. After selecting each one, click the Add button in the lower right-hand corner. This will add the classes to the bean jar. When you are ready to proceed, click Next.
7. In the next dialog, you specify the type of bean. The radio button for session bean should already be selected. In the Enterprise Bean Class drop-down, select the value Catalog. Then, in the Enterprise Bean Name text box, type in **CatalogEJB**. At the lower right of the dialog is a section called Remote Interfaces. In the Remote Home Interface drop-down, select CatalogHome and in the Remote Interface drop-down below it, select Catalog. Click Next when you are ready to proceed.
8. In the next dialog, you specify the type of transaction management you want. Since the Catalog bean is using bean-managed persistence, you can leave the Bean Managed radio button selected and click Next.
9. You can click through the next couple of dialogs until you come to the one titled Resource References. It is in this dialog that you indicate the resource that this bean will be using. In the Coded Name field, type **jdbc/ACMEWidgetDB**. (Later in this chapter, you set up this resource to point to the Cloudscape database used in this example.)
10. You can now click through the last few dialogs until you come to the end, at which point you can click Finish.

At this point the enterprise bean has been added to the application. The process for the remaining two beans is nearly identical, except that they use container-managed transactions. When you come to this dialog you will select the radio button marked Container Managed. You can also leave all the default values as they are for the purposes of this example. This includes leaving the value of Required for the methods in each bean.

Once you have added each Enterprise bean and the application client to the application, you can deploy it. Before deploying, you need to make sure that the J2EE server is running. You can start the J2EE server from the J2EE SDK using this command:

```
j2ee -verbose
```

This executes a batch file and passes the `-verbose` argument to the J2EE server, which causes lots of diagnostic and informational messages to be printed to the console while the server starts. After the server is started, you can access it by selecting File ➪ Add Server. A small dialog will pop up, prompting you for the name of the host that the J2EE server is running on. By default, the value of localhost will be in the dialog, you can select this and click OK.

Next, select Tools ➪ Deploy. You will be prompted for the name of the application you are deploying: Select shoppingcart from the Object to Deploy drop-down, and select localhost from the Target Server drop-down. You will also need to select the checkbox next to Return client jar. This creates a JAR containing all the classes and stubs necessary to use the EJBs from a client application.

If you did not fill out a JNDI name for the enterprise bean, simply type **ejb\Catalog** in the JNDI name field of the dialog in the Application section. There should also be an entry in the References field to the ACMEWIDGET database. Click Next when you are ready to proceed. The last screen only confirms your choices; click Finish to deploy the application and the Catalog bean.

Setting up the data source

Before you attempt to run the Shopping Cart demo, you need to make sure that the Cloudscape database is available. When the J2EE server is started, it simply binds the JNDI names of the database so that they may be found by the naming service. When an actual connection is attempted by one of the session beans, it will attempt to connect to the Cloudscape database you created earlier: ACMEWIDGET.

You first need to configure a JNDI name for the data source using the deploytool utility that comes with the J2EE SDK. To set up the data source, follow these steps:

1. Select Tools ➪ Server Configuration.
2. From the Data Sources node in the tree, select Standard.
3. In the Data Sources section of the dialog, click Add.
4. Enter **jdbc/ACMEWidgetDB** for the JNDI name, and **jdbc:cloudscape:rmi:CloudscapeDB** for the JDBC URL property.
5. Click OK.

If the J2EE server is started, you will need to restart it for the changes to take effect. Once you have done this, you need to make sure the Cloudscape database is available. You will do this by using the RMI JDBC driver framework that ships with the Cloudscape database product. This will allow your session beans to connect to the database to perform their operations.

To start the Cloudscape RMI JDBC framework, you first need to make sure that the RmiJdbc.jar file in the frameworks/RmiJdbc/classes sub-directory of the CloudScape install directory is in your `CLASSPATH`. Next, start the framework by executing the following command:

```
java -ms16m -mx32m RmiJdbc.RmJJdbcServer
COM.cloudscape.core.JDBCDriver
```

When this command executes, you should see messages similar to the following printed to the console window from which you launched the RMI JDBC framework.

```
Thu Nov 29 23:36:52 EST 2001: [RmiJdbc]
COM.cloudscape.core.JDBCDriver registere
d in DriverManager
Thu Nov 29 23:36:52 EST 2001: [RmiJdbc] Binding
RmiJdbcServer...
Thu Nov 29 23:36:52 EST 2001: [RmiJdbc] No installation of RMI
Security Manager.
..
Thu Nov 29 23:36:52 EST 2001: [RmiJdbc] RmiJdbcServer bound in
rmi registry
```

Running the Shopping Cart demo

Once you have deployed the application, you can run the application using the following command:

```
runclient -client shoppingcart.ear -name ShoppingCartClient
```

When the client is started, you will be presented with a dialog that asks you for a user name and a password. You can enter guest for the user name and guest123 for the password. Once you have clicked OK, the application will run, and you should see the output below:

```
There are 3 items in the catalog
Inventory has 10 Simple Widgets
```

While the application runs, you can also view the messages being printed to the J2EE console window as the EJB container calls the different methods, such as the `afterBegin()`, `beforeCompletion()`, and `afterCompletion()` methods of the `javax.transaction.SessionSynchronization` interface.

Summary

In this chapter, you looked at transaction processing and how it is used in Enterprise Java applications that use EJBs. We started by presenting some of the background behind transaction basics and behind the components involved with transaction processing. You also saw how these different components can affect transactions, and when and how you should use transactions.

Transaction processing is a big part of the Enterprise Java equation, and using it does not have to be a burden. Fortunately, JTS and JTA make your life easier by providing container-managed persistence as well as the option of using bean-managed persistence. JTA also enables your Enterprise Java components to work in other J2EE and JTA/JTS environments with little or no changes.

✦ ✦ ✦

CHAPTER 24

System Architecture Issues

✦ ✦ ✦ ✦

In This Chapter

Looking at system-design issues for applications beyond the simple example

Examining the requirements of an enterprise-system design

Discuss ways of dividing application workload among the tiers

Choosing the right type of API to use

✦ ✦ ✦ ✦

Previous chapters have concentrated on introducing you to the various APIs of the J2EE environment. While these are very important, in order to be an effective developer, you must also understand how these fit into the larger picture. How do you bring all of those technologies into a single, coherent, easy to maintain, application? In this chapter and the next, we place the Java tools down and consider all the issues that are important when you come to put all of the techniques you have learnt in the rest of this book into practice. This chapter is mainly focused on the design process and hardware issues surrounding the implementation of large-scale systems, while the next looks at the architecture issues for the code.

As part of the introduction to J2EE, the first two chapters of this book looked at various issues such as application architectures. Now that you are familiar with all the capabilities that J2EE can provide, it is time to go back through those architectures armed with this new knowledge. At the same time, you as an enterprise-application manager must consider many other architectural issues. Building real-world systems to handle from tens of dollars to hundreds of millions of dollars requires the same sorts of processes. Just sitting down and hacking out a bit of code is not going to be acceptable.

Designing Real-World Systems

Moving from the small examples that we've been using in this book to large, and often complex, real-world systems can seem like quite a jump. So often these simple examples look like what you need to implement in a real application, and yet when you attempt to make them fit, everything falls apart at the seams. How do you move beyond the examples and on to building a customer's Web site?

It is an often-heard complaint — but those examples don't bear any resemblance to what my application needs to do! More often than not, the reason for this is the programmer's need to understand the greater system rather than the details of a particular example. Moving beyond examples to making a real application is not about the little pieces of code, but about understanding how those little pieces fit into the larger whole.

You have probably heard these points before, but we really must stress their importance. Building enterprise applications follows the same sets of rules and guidelines as does building any other form of application. It's all about software engineering, not code hacking.

Understanding the customer

The first step to building an application is to work out what the user actually wants. Naturally, the customer will always ask for everything. You must distill fantasy from reality as well as keeping the customer happy! This is the process of requirements-gathering and analysis. Even though the customer may give you a piece of paper or spreadsheet with the list of requirements, the requirements typically bear no resemblance to reality.

Requirements analysis can be broken down into a number of smaller parts. Each of these parts is designed to make your life easier. At some point you are going to have to sit down with the customer and explain why Requirement X cannot be met. Technical issues may not be the main reason (and usually aren't!).

Making sure you build the right system

In come the system requirements. Usually the first reaction is a huge groan and an expression that says "No way, that can't be done. . . ." Some time later you get to the end of the project, and it looks nothing like what the customer originally asked for. Is the customer happy with the results?

Managing expectations and delivering a system start with you taking the customer's requirements, reading them, and then sitting down with the customer to work out what he or she really wants. Sometimes you'll strike it lucky, and those requirements really will match reality, but that is rare. What may be a one-line item on paper could be four months' work involving hundreds of classes and thousands of lines of code. Where you find big items like this, try to break them down into simpler pieces. At all times, think about what they might mean in terms of the system design. Can you match that item to a specific set of functionality, a set of beans for example?

Before you start wondering what we're saying here, we are not advocating designing the system before you even understand what is required! What we are trying to get you to do is critically examine what the customer requires and make sure that you can think of at least one solution to the problem before you get yourself too involved. Very rarely will an enterprise system be creating groundbreaking technology; therefore, you should never find yourself in a position where you have no real idea how a solution may be implemented. Enterprise applications are more about assembling a list of known components than about inventing the Holodeck.

Starting small

Every story must have a beginning, every tale an end. You have 30 pages of requirements and six months to implement them. What do you do?

Our first piece of advice is that you should not try to implement the system all at once. Deciding on a starting point for a large project can sometimes be tricky. Throw in the customer changing his or her mind halfway through the project and a bunch of technology bugs (for example, the app server not behaving as you expected), and the risk of failure is very high. Your job is to make sure this risk is as low as possible.

The best place to start is with the smallest possible part that you can break off. It is much easier when you can swallow the piece that you've bitten off. This small item allows you to try a taste-test , both with the third-party software that you've acquired (usually some form of J2EE application server), and with your customer.

When choosing this small piece, you should also try to grab a good chunk of the core functionality. As you grow more accustomed to the requirements (by talking to the customer, of course!), it will become obvious what the core part of the application is. It might be user management, inventory management, or something else. No matter what the task, there will always be something that almost every other part of the application depends on. Find this part and start there. For testing this first piece of design and implementation, find the smallest possible piece of client code, and you are set to go.

Using the appropriate tools for the job

Often application development is driven more by buzzwords than by technical motivations. EJB this, XML that, intranet here, extranet there. Often, these buzzwords are not applicable to the problem you need to solve. Resisting that push, particularly from management, can be terribly difficult at times.

Although you may be pressured to use particular technologies, there are times where you don't have much of a choice. As we shall discuss shortly in the section on dealing with your neighbors, the solutions you need to implement are often driven by those systems around you. For example, you can't implement an EJB system when the other applications use IBM 3270 terminal interfaces.

As you are now aware, the J2EE specification offers a huge range of possible implementations. For almost every task, there's at least two different sets of APIs you can use. When presenting a Web page, should you use a JSP or a servlet? Subtle differences among these APIs mean you should be careful with the tools you chose.

In the same vein, you should also critically evaluate just what technologies you need to use. Do you really need to use middleware when a servlet directly interacting with a database will be sufficient? Although its buzzword compliance is high, using middleware may be massive overkill for your project requirements. Following the KISS principle, the smaller the number of pieces involved, the lower the odds of problems and the greater the chance of a happy customer.

Still having problems?

Sometimes, no matter what you do, things just don't work out right. Maybe you are having difficulties understanding exactly what the customer wants. Perhaps the requirements are difficult to meet. Or, as you unfortunately might come across, the customer is just difficult to get along with.

While we can't offer a panacea, the remedy that we have found works best is to follow the process we've outlined in the Starting Small section. By doing a small piece at a time and presenting it to the customer as soon as possible, you can help alleviate any problems. If you can't work out the requirements, then a small pilot with an "Is this what you mean?" piece of *working* code for the customer can help you quickly sort out what is going on both in your mind and in the customer's. The *working* part is critical. We've found that if all you do is show a demonstration and not let the customer touch the application, you won't get any benefit. Maximum benefit is obtained when the customer can sit down and play with it, to see how it feels. When a solution is not obvious, a couple of small projects can help you sort out problem areas without having to throw out months of work, which means less stress on the developers and a quicker path to the right solution. And when dealing with that difficult customer, you can use this method to show your progress as well as getting him to give you feedback about what he really wants.

Many different approaches to software engineering exist—from the classic waterfall model to the latest fad: eXtreme Programming (XP). While we don't advocate any of these approaches over any other, the reasoning tends toward the XP end of the scale. In our experience, building many different systems that lie along this "Problem Child" path, this approach to software development seems to be the most reliable at keeping the customer happy *and* keeping your programmers happy.

Being nice to the neighbors

After sorting out the requirements of the customer, you need to know still more. Enterprise applications will need to work in an environment in which there are many other applications. Your customer will not be happy if your application decides to run riot over everything else in the system. Even the most trivial application must learn to share.

Formal Design Methodologies

The process of designing software can vary hugely. You can spend years just learning about the different styles. Instead, we'll present you with a 30-second introduction.

Although many themes and variations exist, if you ignore the code-hacking-with-no-design proponents you are left with three main forms: waterfall, iterative, and the latest trend, called XP or eXtreme Programming.

Waterfall design is the original software-engineering methodology. With waterfall design you pass through a set of fixed stages. At each stage you have one task to perform. Once you have completed that stage, you move to the next, and the next, until you have a complete, delivered piece of software. The first stage is the requirements-gathering stage, followed by the requirements-analysis stage, and so forth until you come to the delivery and of course the maintenance stage afterwards. You can move back to a previous stage once it is finished. If you represent requirements-gathering as a box at the top of the page, and then represent the subsequent stages as a series of boxes going down the page, you get a nice waterfall-type picture—hence the name.

With the iterative style of design, you take all the steps of the waterfall process and do the whole system many times over. Now, instead of doing the whole project in one hit, you apply a mini-waterfall to a number of component pieces. If you come to a problem in one component and need to re-evaluate earlier decisions, then you start at the top again. The result is a lot of passes through the waterfall.

Take the iterative approach and hit the fast-forward button, and you get XP. Within XP you do a lot of very small mini-projects and perform many tasks in parallel. The core premise is to work on a 20-percent solution and put that in front of the customer for feedback while you work on the next piece. The customer gives you ticks and crosses on what you have so far, and you go back and revisit that code. In the end, you have a process where the whole project takes shape from a lot of swirling masses of code that are gradually refined according to the needs of the project. Unlike the other methods, XP also incorporates many disciplines other than code. For example, it takes into account how programmers work together.

Determining whom else you must play with

Rare is the case when you get to design an enterprise application that does not need to co-exist with other applications. Thus, your next order of business is to determine what other applications exist—not only applications that you have to directly interact with, but also those that you should *not* be interacting with. Side effects of your application can often have nasty, hidden consequences that you don't know about until it is too late.

Some aspects of systems analysis are pretty easy: The customer comes to you and says, "I need to add a Web interface to my XYZ system." That part is simple. However, what if the customer asks you to completely replace an existing system? Many behaviors of the old system may not be immediately noticeable. For example, the act of adding a new user in one system may have an effect on some apparently unrelated one. Make sure that you really do understand who else is involved in the application.

What technologies do you need?

At this point, you know what the customer says she needs and also what sort of systems you are going to have to integrate with. Each of those systems is going to require some sort of communication mechanism. If you are lucky, this mechanism may be nothing more than a database interface using JDBC. On the more complex end of the spectrum are older technologies such as the message-based interfaces that JMS is so good at dealing with. If you are dealing with IBM mainframes, it is likely that you will need to use their CICS interface — which requires proprietary libraries.

Remember that although J2EE is a great collection of functionalities, it won't solve every problem in the world; quite frequently you will need to use proprietary systems. One of the more common you are likely to come across is BEA's Tuxedo application-server software. Tuxedo is a precursor to the J2EE systems and has many things in common with them.

Deploying the system

With the application completed, you need to start deploying it into the real world. Following the line of thought we have been presenting so far, the hardest way for you to deploy an application is to rock up right at the end of the project and dump it into the customer's lap.

No matter how heavily you test the application in your development, the real world will always produce more problems. Why not try to get bits of the application onto the customer's site as early as possible? In this way, you can fight the small bugs right at the front before they compound into impossible-to-deal-with monsters hidden in a huge collection of code. Each time you add a new piece to the customer's version of the code, new bugs can only come from that small area. Tracking them down should be much more manageable with a small chunk of code than with one monolithic lump.

Dividing up the Workload

By its very nature, J2EE encourages you to build highly modular systems. Of course, the word "enterprise" in its name also suggests that the main focus is on large application areas. When you put these two thoughts — modularity and large systems (read: scalability) — together, it should become immediately apparent that you are going to need more than one box to put all this code on.

When you have to deal with the multiple computers containing your code, you must consider many other issues. Do you have many small computers serving up your business functionality or a couple of big ones? If you have many small computers, how do you divide the code among them? These are all issues that you may have to deal with as a J2EE programmer and architect.

Assigning work to the various tiers of your application

One of the eternal dilemmas of enterprise programmers is deciding where to place various parts of the application's functionality. Some code works equally well as a database trigger, as a middleware object, or on the client. Where should it all go?

Taking stock of your code

During your analysis of the requirements, you've worked out what the customer wants to see on the desktop (Web browser or standalone application), what sort of functionality he needs (business logic), and the data that must be stored (structures and relationships). During this process, the customer has probably indicated the type of computing systems that all of this is to run on. That is, the customer will tell you that he has a couple of big Sun/HP/IBM boxes that he doesn't want to throw away just yet, and it would be really good if you could make use of them. Wink, wink, nudge, nudge, say no more! Now that you have to apply your code to that hardware, how should you divide up the functionality?

Well, the easiest way to approach the situation is to look at exactly what you have to do. Some tasks are much more suited to a particular tier of the application. In order to refresh your memory, Figure 24-1 represents a "typical" enterprise application and the tiers that you might encounter.

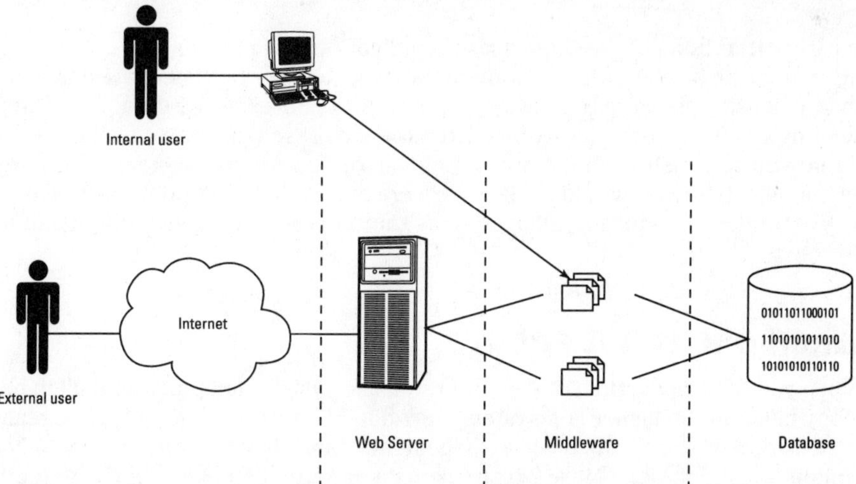

Figure 24-1: The layout of the tiers of a typical enterprise application

Client versus Web server versus middleware versus database

Now let's look at how you might divide your application among these various tiers. Please note that these should only be considered rules of thumb, not hard and fast rules. We've derived them from years of experience in developing all sorts of applications, and so we feel that they should aid you in building a well-balanced application right from the start.

- *Client code should present the user interface.* No application logic should exist here. What client code should concentrate on is providing basic input verification (did the user type a floating point number where only an integer is allowed?). The main job of the client is to make sure that navigation among the various screens presented to the user is consistent.
- *Web servers, if present, should provide verification services* and translate between the user's data and interface with the application logic presented by the middleware. For example, secure connections retrieve credit-card data, verify that the credit-card number is roughly valid (this can be done without needing to contact an outside provider) and then pass the data on to the bank and merchant. Basically, this server is a formatter — it takes the low-level data and formats it in a way suitable for the client to use (HTML, XML, raw binary and so on).
- *Middleware is where all the good work is done.* Here is where you find all the business logic (can I add this part to that product?). Because you need the logic to act on data, it will also act as the abstraction of the data you're applying the logic to.
- *Databases store data and retrieve it on request.* Ideally, you keep all logic out of them (no stored procedures, for example), as you might want to change the logic depending on the viewer (which is the role of the middleware). All databases should be concerned about is maintaining the integrity of the data.

In earlier iterations of the "enterprise" application, the middleware tier was usually either missing or combined with the database. Most of the time, data correctness and business logic were built around stored procedures in the database. The movement now is to remove all the logic from the database wherever possible. The idea is that you can customize the business logic for a particular system user more easily that way than you would if the logic were embedded in the database. This new way of thinking is typically referred to as the separation of presentation and data layers.

When one is not enough

When you have more than one computer in the system, keeping them all in harmony becomes an issue. The system shown in Figure 24-1 is not a typical realistic system. Sure it shows the basic arrangements, but it is very rare to have only one computer at each tier. Figure 24-2 presents a more realistic view of the potential situation, in which you can expect to find multiple computers at each level.

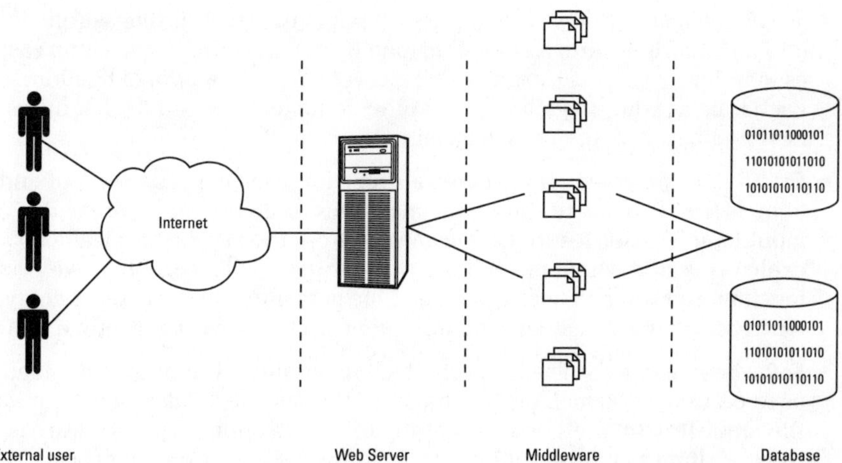

Figure 24-2: When you look at real systems, multiple computers exist at each tier.

You might be wondering just how to keep everything working. The answer lies in a number of different, but similar, terms. The typical approach is called *load balancing* or *distributed server management*. In reality you, as a programmer, should not need to know about the complex arrangements that typically come with these setups. That should be the job of the system administrator. However, as we mentioned a number of times in the EJB chapters, these systems also influence the way you need to design your code, and so you should at least be aware of the basic principles.

What is load balancing?

Depending on who you talk to, the term *load balancing* can have many different meanings. In real terms, what we are discussing is how to manage a number of servers at a single-tier. These servers should provide the "same" service regardless of which machine does the actual code-crunching. (We'll explain why "same" is in quotes in the next section.)

On the simplest level, load balancing is about making sure each physical box is running at the same amount of load — CPU and memory usage, I/O to the database, services handled, and so on. So when it comes to that server farm for Web servers, each Web server will contain exactly the same information. Regardless of which server your request gets handed off to, you should always see the same result, and everyone making requests should have the same response time.

Load balancing solutions vary in complexity. The following list is a simplistic summary of how these different types are implemented, starting from the simplest:

- *Round-robin DNS* — This type uses the simple query of turning a domain name into an IP address into a simplistic load balancer. For any given address, such as `www.hungryminds.com`, the DNS server will have a pool of IP addresses. Each time a request is made to turn the domain name into the IP address, the next number from the pool is given out.
- *External balancer* — In this model, a single machine acts as the input and then funnels the requests to the server machines to do the real processing. The input handler uses feedback information from the servers, typically by serial cable, to decide where to send the next request. This method provides a much more even balance: If one machine gets hung up processing an overly long request, more requests do not queue up for it in the meantime.
- *Software managed* — The software itself maintains a watch over the load being used on each system. If one machine finds itself overloaded, it will forward the request onto another, more lightly loaded machine. This software is above the operating system — typically only in the J2EE environment (or its equivalent, for other systems like CORBA) does this work.

The J2EE approach

For the environment, you are mostly dealing with — J2EE — the typical approach is for the J2EE environment implementer to take care of all the load balancing issues for you. There are many good reasons for this, mostly having to do with the EJB specification.

When you are managing an EJB, the server is responsible for the bean's lifecycle management. It may create and destroy individual bean instances as needed. Naturally, if many machines exist at the same tier, the server has many choices in terms of where to create that bean. It would be a waste if every machine had a new bean instance created when you only need one extra instance. Because the J2EE server has to create just that one extra instance, it must choose which machine to put it on. The result is a load-management system, because the server will choose to put the new bean instance on the machine with the lightest load.

Deciding on the appropriate machine to send the next request to or start the new bean instance on is something that is not specified by J2EE. However, most vendors offer similar approaches. You will typically see two features: partitioning of services to specific machines and partitioning services on one machine.

In real life, it is unlikely that every bean you write will do exactly the same amount of work. One entity bean might do very little while a session bean is doing hundreds of calculations. Obviously, in this situation you might want to allocate more resources to the hard-working bean so that the overall service remains balanced. Here the J2EE environment enables you to partition the workload by machine. Although all machines are kept at the same tier, they will be grouped according to the beans deployed on them, as shown in Figure 24-3.

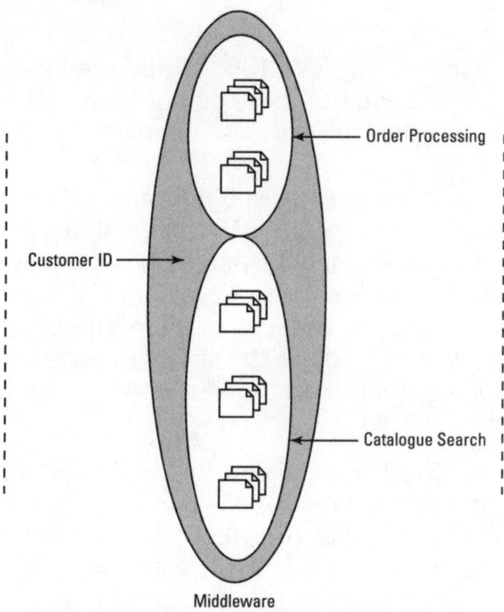

Figure 24-3: Grouping several servers within a single tier enables better load management when your system is providing many different services.

Choosing a Design

With so many different options to choose from, making the right choice of APIs for your project can sometimes feel like a bit of a lottery. After all, you've just finished a few hundred pages of information detailing lots of different options. The head can be quite muddled after all this if you don't have much experience. So this section is about putting together a quick summary of the pros and cons of the major decision areas.

Large-scale technology options

As you go through the design process, you need to keep in mind the technology options that are available. Often the technology requirements of the system you are incorporating your project with will drive the overall design and architecture. That is, if you have to integrate with an existing CORBA system then that is the Java technology that is going to be the centerpiece of your application's architecture. Before visiting some architecture options, let's firstly recap on the various technology options that we have presented to you in this book.

The middleware options

In the middleware tier, you have four basic options: RMI, EJB, CORBA, and proprietary code. Other options, such as JINI, also exist, but these do not seem to be in widespread use, so we'll ignore them for the purposes of this summary.

- *RMI*—The original Java option for providing remote-object capabilities. Although it forms the basis of the EJB specification, RMI's capabilities are relatively simplistic. You can provide a remote-object instance to clients, but no scalability exists in the system: One instance means one instance. If you have 100 or more clients, that single instance must serve all of them. On the other hand, RMI has a number of useful features, such as the ability to register remote listeners to an object and a distributed garbage-collection system to maintain that Java-centric view of the world.
- *EJB*—The technology with the most hype. Built to be a better CORBA, EJB has many of its useful features, but restricts you to a Java-only design solution. This is great if you have a new system that you can write entirely in Java, but not particularly useful if you have to interface mainly with a lot of pre-existing code. Designed to provide small functional components that are glued together to service a single application or applications.
- *CORBA*—A language-neutral set of technologies that provide remote-object capabilities. CORBA is the original attempt at building a large-scale, distributed computing framework. It hasn't been spectacularly successful (at least in marketing-hype terms), but CORBA is a solid system that offers a far wider variety of services than its pure-Java relatives. The difference lies in the fact that CORBA seems to be mainly a service-abstraction system, whereas EJBs try to concentrate on providing data abstractions. That is, a CORBA interface will provide a single "class" with a lot of methods for doing one thing—displaying or analyzing map data, for example—while EJBs will provide a class that does nothing but represent a single customer within a huge database.
- *Proprietary*—Before the network and open standards was proprietary code. That is, the programmers wrote their own interfaces over the top of some very low-level connections—IP sockets or UNIX-domain sockets. This choice is best when you want a tightly bound system that offers the highest performance. The trade-off is longer development time, as you must write all the basic systems—such as load balancing, transaction support, and high-level abstractions—yourself.

The client-access options

You also have a range of options when presenting data to the end user. Sometimes you have no choice over the presentation mechanism—when the client must be a Web browser, for example. When you do, there are a variety of ways for you to take the data presented by the middleware tier and format it into something that the client might use: servlets, JSPs, JMS, and Web services such as SOAP and XML-RPC all can be used for this task.

For the purposes of this summary, we are ignoring situations in which you have client applications directly interacting with the middleware – in the case of a POS terminal, for example.

✦ *JSP*—This option is best when the output must be HTML, as it doesn't give you much of an ability to present any other form of data. JSPs enable you to customize the output somewhat by interacting with Java code, which can then communicate with middleware systems. JSP is great for building simple interactive sites, such as the front end to an online shop, but it falls down when you're trying to build heavily customized interactions that completely change the output each time a service is called.

✦ *Servlet*—The latest incarnation of the method of adding dynamic code to a Web server. The original systems started with CGI calls and native code, followed by Perl and ASP. Servlets take the best parts of these systems (such as the module-extension mechanism available in the Apache Web server to provide mod_perl), and put a Java spin on them. They are capable of providing output in any format, although the most common interaction that they process is to deal with HTTP requests and replies. Servlets are the most flexible of the options.

✦ *Web services*—Many different technologies can be classified as "Web services," which is the latest marketing spin on the ability to provide remote procedure–call capabilities without requiring the programmer to build a complete middleware system. Web services typically use HTTP as the basic communication mechanism and then build another layer in which the body of the message is encoded in XML structures. Sometimes servlets are used as the implementation of the server side of Web-services systems. Remote procedure–call systems have existed for decades—the most notable being the RPC system on UNIX machines. Web services are just the latest fad associated with this very old idea. Two technologies to watch for: SOAP and XML-RPC.

✦ *JMS*—When dealing with large, pre-existing enterprise systems, you will almost certainly come across many interesting challenges. The most prominent of these will be the fact that, owing to the mainframe legacy, the communications mechanisms will not be designed around real-time, interactive capabilities. That is, you send the request off, and at some later time, maybe after several minutes or more, you *might* get an answer back; even if you do it won't go directly to the "user" that sent the request in the first place. What these systems lack in interactive capabilities they make up for in robustness. Those messages are stored and processed. If the receiver goes down, not to worry: When it comes back up again, the messages will still be waiting to be processed. From the Java perspective, your view into this world, as either a sender or receiver, is through JMS.

Design options

After you've formulated a rough idea about the technologies that will be needed to implement your application, you need to come up with an architecture. This architecture needs to accommodate both the hardware and the software you will use in your application: How many tiers should there be, what sort of scalability is required, and just how many computers are needed to get it all done? All of these questions and more need to be answered as part of your architecture — and you haven't even started on the software part yet!

Deciding on a software design is a personal decision based on your years of experience as a programmer. You know what works and what doesn't work. Moving to designing products using the J2EE environment is not a gigantic leap. A J2EE design process should take the same approach as designing any other application: Understand your basic technology building blocks and then apply standard design principles to come up with the overall design and architecture.

Just because you are now designing an enterprise application rather than a desktop or an applet, you should not forget everything that you've learned in the past. Modeling tools should be used to create Use Cases and UML designs. Your architecture should be influenced by standard designs such as using design patterns. Of course, some design patterns work better in the enterprise environment than others. Basically, just keep calm and do what you have always done.

Various options for design patterns in the J2EE environment are covered in depth in Chapter 25.

Implementing Security

Lastly we cover the most important topic of all in enterprise applications: security. There's no point in having the world's best business model if you don't have any customers because they've all been scared off by someone breaking into your system.

Providing a secure system means thinking about the consequences right from the beginning. Simply tacking on some security at the end will guarantee that holes are waiting to be exploited. Don't ever be fooled into thinking that you don't need to worry about security because everyone can be trusted. They can't. Although you know who is using the system now, what about in a year's time? What if a user decides to turn vindictive toward a colleague? While you can't protect against every circumstance, building levels of access into the system and taking simple security measures will eliminate all but the most dedicated attackers.

While the intricacies of designing and implementing proper securing your application are something that only you will know about, the following is a short cookbook dealing with areas you should pay attention to. In short, these are minimal steps that must be undertaken for every enterprise application.

Securing the connections

The typical first method of attack is sniffing the network traffic. Brain-dead protocols like POP3, IMAP, and SMB allow any user on the network to watch user names and passwords go past without the watcher ever needing to directly attack a system. Once the attacker has a user name and password, your application is history, as this can be used as a beachhead for more sophisticated attacks.

At a minimum, all external connections should use a secure connection mechanism whenever sensitive information is being sent. For example, if a password or access key is required to access your system, you must use encryption on the connection to pass the data. For Web-based data, use HTTPS rather than HTTP connections. If your application uses sockets, make use of JSSE, the secure-sockets extension for Java. It will provide you with SSL-based connections for secure communications.

You should use secure connections wherever your application must interact with external applications — such as through an extranet to other suppliers or customers. While it is pointless to secure your basic homepage, shopping-cart checkouts definitely require security. Similarly, within your middleware network, using secure connections so the beans can communicate from the server to the client is not necessary, but using secure connections for messages sent through JMS dealing with customer-account information is.

Securing the data

In an enterprise, your most important asset is the data — information about your clients, products, sales, and almost anything else that can be stored in computerized form. Just imagine what can happen when someone decides to change the sale price of one of your most popular items. You could very quickly be looking at some large debts, possibly sending your company into bankruptcy.

Note You think that outside users can't play with your pricing information? One very well-known attack against Web-based commerce has been to order one product, save the confirmation HTML page, make some modifications to it, and then submit the confirmation using a much cheaper price on the goods being purchased. Although these attacks were first seen more than two years ago, they are still being used effectively against e-commerce Web sites that don't implement any form of data protection.

Securing your raw data means making sure that every access to it is authorized. Never accept anonymous connections to a database. Make sure that you know that those who do connect are the correct users, and restrict their access to the system. Finally, once they have connected, validate every transaction. Make sure that pricing information is correct, and if it is not, get the authorization details of the user making the approval. Most importantly — log everything. If something does happen, you can always do some forensic analysis to catch the malicious person.

Securing the system

Data security also involves some level of physical security. Is the company's vital e-commerce server a box sitting on the programmer's desk, where the cleaner can come in and accidentally turn it off?

There's really no point having a secure application if any Joe Random User has direct access to the server machine. These machines are the life of your company: Do you want the accounts staff firing up a game of Quake Arena on your server? Probably not!

If any user can gain access to the server machines, then any user has a way of directly attacking your application. Many sabotage attempts are made by disgruntled employees who want to leave a parting message after being given the pink slip. If you use a firewall to keep the outsiders out, why should you let everyone on your staff have a better level of access to the machine? Surely your accountant doesn't need direct access to the server. Besides, if external attackers make it through the first line of defense, do you really want to open up your entire network to them?

At each critical point in your system, you should firewall the communications. In a minimal system, this would mean installing a firewall between each of the tier levels. Middleware machines have no need to contact a database server on any port other than the SQL socket connection. Web servers need only to access the beans and so only need the IIOP ports. Not only that, but your firewall should limit connections to those established between known IP addresses. Don't put a firewall between the middleware and the database and then allow any random machine to make a connection to the database. That still allows a malicious internal machine to directly access the database and make unauthorized changes.

Securing the users

Finally, there are the users themselves. Do you really want the marketing manager to be allowed to delete the entire database of products? No, we didn't think so. Even if everything else is protected, you still have the problem of the user not knowing what he or she is doing, or just being really tired and making a stupid, catastrophic mistake. There's an old cliché that is worth remembering—don't attribute to malice that which can be attributed to stupidity. In most cases, this is applicable to end users. When someone is tired at the end of the day's work, a mouse click that's off by a few pixels can be the difference between success and disaster.

When you are in the requirements-gathering stage, work out just who needs to access the system and what tasks those users must perform. In the design phase, craft access levels to the system that follow those requirements. As you have seen in the EJB specification, each bean, and even each method within a bean, can have an individual user assigned to it. Make use of the ability to prevent the users from making that dumb mistake. If one person needs to occupy a number of different roles, make her assume those roles as necessary. Don't just give users open carte blanche to the full application. By forcing them to change, you not only protect against inappropriate use of the system, but you also help them remember which roles they are currently playing (not to mention the appropriate visual cues on the user interface).

Summary

Building enterprise applications requires much more than just slapping a bunch of code together. Even at its most fundamental level, you need to consider many different issues in both design and the final deployment of the system.

During this chapter, we have walked you through, and given you pointers about, areas you should keep in mind when designing an enterprise application:

- Design issues for building enterprise applications
- How to build applications that work across more than one machine
- Tips on which API is the most appropriate in a given situation
- Securing the system to prevent unauthorized interference with your most vital assets

✦ ✦ ✦

CHAPTER 25

J2EE Design Patterns

✦ ✦ ✦ ✦

In This Chapter

Introducing design patterns

Examining existing patterns in the core J2SE APIs

Implementing enterprise design patterns in J2EE

✦ ✦ ✦ ✦

As IT technology evolves, new ideas are created and added to the programmer's toolkit. Each level is more complex than the last, making the simpler things seem so trivial that you barely think about them. First came assembly language, and then higher-level languages like ALGOL and FORTRAN. Complex projects brought forth object-oriented programming and structured design (the classic waterfall model). As programmers got used to describing more and more complex structures, CASE design tools made an appearance. While at that time programmers tended to reuse their own structures, the light-bulb moment came with the release of a small book called *Design Patterns*. Programmers the world over exclaimed "Yes!" and since then the term design patterns has taken off. Now we even have patterns specific to J2EE applications, and these are what we are going to introduce you to in this chapter.

Design-Pattern Basics

Design patterns are more than just the latest fad in software development. The whole concept is based on years of knowledge being accumulated, sorted, and presented in easy-to-digest and easy-to-implement packages. Before diving into design patterns specific to J2EE development, take a step back and go through the basics of design patterns.

What is a design pattern?

As we just stated, design patterns come from years of programming experience. The programmers responsible for design patterns have taken their knowledge and come up with a collection of reusable chunks of knowledge that can be applied to any design. Each chunk of knowledge contains one idea, a small piece of an application design. Think of using these chunks as knowledge re-use, much like the code re-use provided by object-oriented development languages.

Design patterns in the design process

Not surprisingly, design patterns are used at design time. As you are analyzing the requirements specification and attempting to come up with an architecture, you can apply one or more design patterns to create the whole application. Compare using design patterns to code re-use. In your code, you create a class that does one thing — say representing a circular list. As you are coding another part of the application, you find that you need a buffer. Looking up your documentation, you discover that you have this circular-list code that would perfectly suit the buffer. In order to use the list, you import the class, create an instance of it, and then call the various methods. Design patterns act in a similar way at design time.

When designing an application, you will rarely have to create something completely original. Although you may be inventing The Next Big Thing, when you look at the nuts-and-bolts level, really all you are doing is arranging a collection of existing small ideas into a new form. Your design consists of lots of smaller designs. Each of these pieces has been used many times before — in fact, most of them will occur to you because you remember having used them in previous practice. This process of reusing knowledge is the beginning of a design pattern.

The best definition of a pattern is provided by Jim Coplien on his Patterns Definitions page (`http://hillside.net/patterns/definition.html`). According to this definition, a pattern has the following characteristics:

- *It solves a problem* — Patterns capture solutions, not just abstract principles or strategies.
- *The solution is a proven concept* — Patterns capture solutions with track records, not theories or speculation.
- *The solution isn't obvious* — Many problem-solving techniques (such as software-design paradigms or methods) try to derive solutions from first principles. The best patterns generate solutions to problems indirectly — a necessary approach for the most difficult problems of design.
- *It describes a relationship* — Patterns don't just describe modules, but describe deeper system structures and mechanisms.
- *The pattern has a significant human component* — All software serves human comfort or quality of life; the best patterns explicitly appeal to aesthetics and utility.

Standard patterns

Design patterns as a standard tool of the software architect came into being in 1994, with the release the book appropriately named *Design Patterns*. The book had four authors: Erich Gamma, Richard Helm, Ralph Johnson, and John Vlissides. Together they have affectionately become known as The Gang of Four or GoF. This book has formed the reference point for all the patterns that can be considered standard. The revelation of the GoF approach was not that they defined something completely new, but that they took all the existing knowledge, classified it, and gave each idea an identifiable name.

You are probably familiar with the four main design patterns, but you may not know their names: model-view-controller (MVC), command, observer, and factory.

Design patterns in the core Java libraries

Now that you are familiar with some of the basic design patterns, you should be starting to notice them appearing in all sorts of places — especially in the core Java libraries. To cement your knowledge about some of the standard patterns and how they end up being translated to real-world code, we will now cover an example of each of the main patterns and how it appears in the core APIs.

The observer pattern

An *observer pattern* is defined as a class watching and listening for state changes in the target class. If you think about any event listener in the Java APIs, you have seen the observer pattern at work. For example, the `ActionListener` that you register with a button or menu item, whether Swing or AWT, is an observer. Another reasonably well-known class is the `ImageObserver` interface that passes you state information as an `Image` object is constructed.

An observer needs only to observe the state of another object. An observer is different from a callback system, in which the callback returns information to the calling class. In the observer pattern, your methods do not return any state information; that is, they return `void`. That is why your event-listener methods never have to return values — they observe the state of the button.

The factory pattern

After the observer, the next best-known pattern is the *factory pattern*. You are probably already familiar with it, as you have seen several examples of it in the book so far: For example, the `DriverManager` class used to fetch JDBC database connections. The factory pattern describes a system in which one class (the factory) is used to create other classes based on some parameter information. All the generated classes implement a single basic interface or base class.

Within the core Java APIs, you can find factory classes all over the place. For example, `java.net.SocketFactory` generates instances of `java.net.Socket` classes. A less noticeable factory is any of the Swing editor or cell renderer interface implementations. Why? Well, have a look at how the interfaces work. A cell renderer, such as `TreeCellRenderer`, has a single method, `getTreeCellRendererComponent()`. A number of arguments are provided, and the return type is `Component`. The `getTreeCellRendererComponent()` method has the hallmarks of a factory — a number of arguments and a single return type. You are the one providing the implementation of the factory, as you must provide an instance of `Component` that will render the information provided in the parameter.

Now, before you start considering that just any method that takes parameters and returns a value can be considered a factory, there are certain other requirements that need to be met.

✦ A factory is a complete class. All it does is produce instances of other classes. Those EJBs you saw earlier in the book would not be classified as an implementation of the Factory pattern.

✦ A factory only produces new instances of a common base class, with the idea that the calling code only ever uses the base class (in other words, does not cast up to the individual class types produced by the factory). For example, a method that returned `ArrayList` instances all the time would not be considered a factory, but one that produced instances of `Collection` could be so long as that method did not return only `ArrayLists` in disguise.

✦ Factories also tend to implement the Singleton pattern as well. This is not a hard and fast requirement, but you will generally find this to be the case.

For an example of the Factory pattern in code, here is an example of a factory that produces shape objects:

```
public class ShapeFactory {
    ...

    public Shape createShape(int type) {
        Shape ret_val = null;
        switch(type) {
          case BOX:
              ret_val = new Box();
              break;
          case CIRCLE:
              ret_val = new Circle();
              break;

          ...
        }

        return ret_val;
    }
}
```

The command pattern

The command pattern uses object-oriented techniques to hide the working code from the method call. In this pattern, you create a base class or interface, and the working code is called through the common methods defined in the base class/interface. An example of using the command pattern would be building a state machine, like a parser. In the traditional implementation, you would have a variable that tracks the current state. Then, each time something needed to be done, you would enter a big switch statement and execute the code for the current state. Using the command pattern, however, you lose the switch statement and replace it with a base interface that contains the methods to be executed. Each option of the switch statement is replaced with a class that implements the base interface.

How does the command pattern transfer to code? Here is an example snippet:

```
public SomeValue parseStream(Reader input) {

    StreamTokenizer strtok = new StreamTokenizer(input);

    ...

    while(strtok.nextToken() != strtok.TT_EOF) {

        int cmd = tokenMap.get(strtok.sval);

        switch(cmd) {
           case TOKEN_1:  // do stuff
               break;
           case TOKEN_2:  // do stuff
               break;
           case TOKEN_3:  // do stuff
               break;
           ...
        }
    }

    ...
}
```

To replace this traditional code with a command pattern, you change the switch statement so that it uses a set of derived classes like this:

```
public SomeValue parseStream(Reader input) {

    StreamTokenizer strtok = new StreamTokenizer(input);

    ...

    while(strtok.nextToken() != strtok.TT_EOF) {

       Command cmd =
           commandCreator.getCommand(strtok.sval);
       cmd.execute();
    }

    ...
}
```

From the preceding code, you will also notice that you still need to generate instances of the command implementation class. The simplest way to remove the switch statement completely is to combine the command pattern with the factory pattern. The factory then becomes responsible for generating the command instance in response to the command type (in this case the string that was parsed from the input stream).

The MVC pattern

The last of the standard patterns that we will present is the *Model-View-Controller* pattern. As the name suggests, this pattern has three parts; this makes it much more complex than the other patterns. In essence the MVC pattern describes a way of separating your program code into parts that are individually responsible for either holding the data (M), rendering the data (V), or providing logic to manipulate the data (C).

Swing is the most obvious user of the MVC pattern (and unfortunately, some of this shows through in the complexity of the interfaces). All the user-interface components provided by Swing use the MVC architecture, and so, to illustrate the pattern, we will take just one class — `JTree`. The model part of the pattern provides information about the underlying data. You don't present the data in the raw form as they come from the data source, but in a form that the patterned item wants — in the `JTree` case, `TreeModel`. View information is the rendering part of the pattern. Rendering is provided by you, but the patterned item requests the information through a factory class that you must implement — `TreeCellRenderer`. You can view the item in several different ways, and so `TreeCellEditor` is also a view component to this pattern. Finally you have the controller part of the pattern. The controller is responsible for management tasks and any logic. Control actions are provided by the `JTree` class, because it must hook the listeners of the data model and make the appropriate requests for rendering components, and then arrange for all the right bits to appear on screen.

Jumping ahead just a little here — the MVC pattern can be applied to enterprise applications just as much as a GUI API. Now, you are looking at a much larger scale. The model is the underlying data system, such as the database and the entity beans. On the other end of the application are the JSPs and servlets that make up the pages — the View portion of the pattern. In between you need the control logic to assemble a user's shopping basket, which is the control part of the pattern. Almost every enterprise application that has been developed can be broken into these three components, and hence conforms to the MVC pattern.

Introducing Enterprise Design Patterns

Using design patterns in the enterprise application means following the same basic process as when using design patterns in any other form of application. Factories, commands, and most of the other patterns still make sense. Just because there is no fancy GUI does not mean that a pattern is not applicable. Patterns are applicable to all areas of design and architecture, and you will find yourself using most of the forthcoming patterns every day.

The role of enterprise design patterns

Within the enterprise environment, a number of patterns have emerged as standard and particularly suited to enterprise-application development. These enterprise patterns take the most common tasks that you need and turn them into a pattern. Enterprise patterns are typically more concerned with the large-scale aspects of implementation than the individual bean level.

In addition to the new patterns for enterprise development, some of the standard patterns are very useful in the enterprise space, too. For example, the Pet Store example (`http://java.sun.com/`) that Sun uses to show off J2EE uses the MVC pattern as its basic architecture. The model is the store data, the view is JSPs, and the controller is a series of EJBs — both session and entity.

To bolster the use of design patterns within J2EE-based development, Sun has released a book and a series of tutorials on its Java Developer Connection Web site (`http://java.sun.com/blueprints/patterns/j2ee_patterns/`). There you can find a complete range of patterns specifically aimed at the J2EE developer.

Standard enterprise design patterns for J2EE

When you consider what goes into a typical J2EE application, you will find that the core set of functionality is implemented by EJBs. For this reason, most of the design patterns developed for use in J2EE applications center around EJB design and implementation. Several of these patterns you will already be familiar with, as we have introduced them in earlier chapters. In this chapter, we will formally introduce you to the four most commonly used patterns: value object, data access object, session façade and the fast reader.

Value objects

One of the main performance problems associated with EJBs is the amount of network traffic needed to access attributes of the bean. For each method call, there is a relatively long delay between the time when you make the method call and the time when the return value finally makes its way back to the client. When you need to retrieve many attributes, this delay can be quite significant. As we introduced in Chapter 17, the standard pattern for alleviating the network delays is to return all the attributes in one method call, using a simple data-holder class. This approach has a formal pattern name — *value objects.*

To see how you would apply a value object design pattern to a standard bean, consider the following example bean's remote interface:

```
public interface Address extends EJBObject {
  public String getStreet() throws RemoteException;
  public String getSuburb() throws RemoteException;
  public String getAreaCode() throws RemoteException;
  public String getState() throws RemoteException;
  public String getCountry() throws RemoteException;
}
```

A typical usage of this address bean will take all the attributes shown and present them on a Web page or in a collection of textfield GUI components of an application. This is an example of a bean that uses an all-or-nothing approach — a typical client user of the code will either use all of the information or none of it. If a network query takes 100 ms to execute, half a second is lost before your application can begin to display a response. For most users, that sort of delay is unacceptable.

Because of the nature of the underlying network connections used by EJBs, that 100-ms time cannot be reduced by much. Most of the time is taken in marshalling the arguments, sending the request, and unpacking the message at the other end. However, packing more items into a single query will not change the total processing time by much, as most of the overhead is in the processing at either end, not the transmission time over the network. The value object pattern takes advantage of this to pack more information into a single query without dramatically changing the total response time. Now, instead of a single string, you get five strings.

To refactor the preceding example to make use of the value object pattern, you must change all the method calls into a single method. All the values that were previously returned one at a time are now stored together in a separate class that is returned from the new method. Your new remote-interface implementation looks like this:

```
public interface Address extends EJBObject {
  public AddressValue getAddressDetails()
      throws RemoteException;
}
```

Of course, now you also need to define the `AddressValue` class to hold the attributes:

```
public class AddressValue implements Serializable {
  public String street;
  public String suburb;
  public String areaCode;
  public String state;
  public String country;
}
```

Notice that the class that represents the value object is serializable. That is a requirement of the EJB specification. In this case, all the values are declared as simple public variables. Remember that remote beans always pass classes by value, which means that you receive a copy of the data, not the original. There is no real point to having data hiding with getter methods. Even if you somehow changed that data, the bean would not know; this arrangement saves you from having to write a lot of pointless code.

Data access objects

If you have ever had to develop portable code that will operate with more than one database vendor, you will appreciate the implementation difficulties that arise. Despite the existence of the various SQL standards, each vendor appears to have its own take on what exactly should be supported. For example, Oracle does not support column types such as `INTEGER` and `BIGINT`, which DB2 and PostgreSQL handle, and instead has a single numerical type, `DECIMAL`. From your point of view, as someone writing the code for the bean, this can become quite frustrating as you have to add yet another piece of code to handle the vagaries of the next database vendor's product. Obviously this is not an isolated problem and has resulted in the data access object (DAO) design pattern.

The DAO design pattern has nothing to do with the old Microsoft specific Data Access Objects technology for database programmers.

The core tenet of the DAO pattern is the abstraction of the database queries away from the bean-implementation code and into a separate set of classes. In this pattern, you start with a factory pattern to produce an implementation of the basic interface to the underlying database. That interface provides standard methods for accessing the raw data, while each implementation of it deals with the particular nuances of each database product.

In order to illustrate the use of a DAO pattern in an EJB, consider a typical database-access call in an entity-bean implementation class for the `ejbLoad()` method:

Although the following example is for an entity bean, you can use the DAO pattern with any of the three bean types: session, entity, and message-driven.

```
public void ejbLoad() throws EJBException {
  Connection conn = null;
  Statement stmt = null;
  ResultSet rs = null;

  try {
    conn = dataSource.getConnection();
    stmt = conn.createStatement();

    UserIdPk pk =
      (UserIdPk)entityContext.getPrimaryKey();

    StringBuffer sql =
      new StringBuffer("SELECT * FROM ADDRESS WHERE user_id=");
    sql.append(pk);

    rs = stmt.executeQuery(sql.toString());

    addressValueObject = new AddressValueObject();
```

```
        if(rs.next()) {
          addressValueObject.street =
            rs.getString("street");
          addressValueObject.suburb =
            rs.getString("suburb");
          addressValueObject.areaCode =
            rs.getString("areaCode");
          addressValueObject.state = rs.getString("state");
          addressValueObject.country =
            rs.getString("country");
          addressValueObject.lastUpdated =
            rs.getTimestamp("last_update");
        }
      } catch(SQLException se) {
      } finally {
        try {
          rs.close();
        }catch(SQLException se) {
        }
        try {
          stmt.close();
        }catch(SQLException se) {
        }
        try {
          conn.close();
        }catch(SQLException se) {
        }
      }
    }
```

Now, most of this code is fairly straightforward, as strings can be carted between databases. However, the one issue is the `TIMESTAMP` datatype. Each database likes to support different things here. Where you might have `DATE` available in DB2, you will only have `TIMESTAMP` in Oracle. These two will require different method calls on the `ResultSet` to get the appropriate information. Now you start getting complicated code, because in a simple implementation, such as the preceding snippet, you will need to access the database metadata to work out which types are supported. That probably adds another 20 lines of code — just for one attribute value. Imagine what happens when more complicated modifications are needed — say when the database does not support join operations.

Good object-oriented design principles aim to reduce code complexity by breaking code into many component parts. The role of the DAO pattern is to separate the entity-bean implementation code from the low-level database-access code. Modifying the `ejbLoad()` method to make use of the DAO pattern starts with defining your database access–code interface:

```
public interface AddressDAO {
  public AddressValue loadAddress(Connection conn,
                                  int user);
}
```

Your interface defines only one method here—that which loads the address value object class. In a real situation, you would have methods for each operation inside the bean, for example for storing (`ejbStore()`) and creating new instances (`ejbCreate()`) of the bean.

The `loadAddress` method takes all the information you need in order to load values from any database, and returns the generic information. You may be wondering why we supply the JDBC `Connection` instance to the method call. Why not have the implementation code deal with that internally? It would limit a lot of your scalability to handle the request internally, as that would make the implementation code dependent on knowing everything about your bean implementation code, such as the value of the environment entry that defines which database you want to use. Remember, all you want to do is have the DAO deal with the database query, not the entire management of the database.

Assuming that you have some implementations of the DAO interface, you will need some way to access those implementations without hard-coding the classes into your code. Remember, your intention is to keep the code as simple as possible. Even your bean implementation code should not know which database is in use. You provide that information as a deployment option through an environment entry. For example:

```
public AddressEntityBean implements EntityBean {
  private DataSource datasource;
  private AddressDAO addressDao;
  ....

  public void setEntityContext(EntityContext ctx) {
    try {
      InitialContext i_ctx = new InitialContext();
      String database = i_ctx.lookup("database_type");

      ???

      dataSource = i_ctx.lookup("jdbc/pooledSource");

    } catch(Exception e) {
    }
  }
}
```

Missing from this code is the means by which you obtain that implementation of the DAO. You have specified the type of database and you have a `DataSource` to create a `Connection` from, but missing is the fetching of the correct `AddressDAO` implementation for the database type. If you are thinking about needing a `Factory` pattern to handle this, you're absolutely correct. In this DAO pattern, you fetch the appropriate implementation from a factory by providing the generator method with the name of the implementation type you require:

```
public class AddressDAOFactory {
  public static AddressDAO getAddressDAO(String dbType);
}
```

Now you can finish the missing bits of the `setEntityContext()` method like this:

```
String database = i_ctx.lookup("database_type");

addressDao = AddressDAOFactory.getAddressDAO(database);

dataSource = i_ctx.lookup("jdbc/pooledSource");
```

One final piece of code remains — the trimmed-down version of `ejbLoad()`. With the DAO instance obtained, you can eliminate a large amount of code:

```
public void ejbLoad() throws EJBException {
  Connection conn = null;
  Statement stmt = null;
  ResultSet rs = null;

  try {
    conn = dataSource.getConnection();

    UserIdPk pk = (UserIdPk)entityContext.getPrimaryKey();

    addressValueObject =
      addressDao.loadAddress(conn, pk.getRawId());

  } catch(SQLException se) {
  } finally {
    try {
      conn.close();
    }catch(SQLException se) {
    }
  }
}
```

Notice how much simpler your code becomes. Each piece of functionality is compartmentalized. To add a new database product, all you need to do is provide another implementation of the DAO interface. You do not need to edit and re-deploy your bean.

Session façade

In most typical applications, the user works within a given framework to accomplish a specific task. For example, creating an order at an e-commerce Web site involves not just a single page view, but many pages and the need to track what the user has placed in a shopping basket.

Entity beans are just an abstraction of an underlying data source. That does not really make them useful for tracking the movement of a user through the data. What you really need is something higher-level that represents the path the user may take in the application, and that simplifies the process for them. This is the job of the session façade: to provide a high-level abstraction of the tasks using session beans, and to hide the details of the entity beans and possibly other lower-level session beans.

The EJB chapters, 16 and 17, presented a number of beans that represented a small e-commerce–style set of data. Missing from that example was a concrete means of building a complete order system. While you could code a system directly as part of a collection of JSPs or servlets, that would mean reproducing a lot of code over many different pages. It would be much nicer if you could put all that functionality in a single place and leave the servlet/JSP to do its job of just providing the rendering—a perfect task for a session façade pattern.

Another reason for using a session façade is that it enables you to place all the important data manipulation as entity beans that have only local interfaces. This reduces network traffic and also prevents incorrect usage of the underlying data structures, because the only way to manipulate them is through the façade.

The design of a typical session-façade bean mimics that of the task being performed. With the shopping basket, you have a collection of methods that allow you to create a new basket, add items to and remove items from it, list the current contents, and finally check out.

Creating a session façade starts with the usual question for designing an EJB—What are you going to be doing? As the bean is going to represent a single user's interaction with the system, it will need to be a stateful session bean. Starting with the home interface, you need the `create()` method to generate the original session. A session needs to be created for a specific user or task, and so, for this task, you start with a user's login name and password with which to create the session:

```
public interface PurchaseSessionHome extends EJBHome {
  public PurchaseSession create(String name,
                                String passwd)
    throws RemoteException;
}
```

Calling the `create()` method on the home interface establishes a session to be used: From now on, you call methods on the session. These method calls now become a listing of the tasks we mentioned a short time ago:

```
public interface PurchaseSession extends EJBObject {
  public void addItemToCart(ProductId product,
                            int quantity)
    throws RemoteException;

  public void modifyItemInCart(ProductId product,
                               int quantity)
    throws RemoteException, InvalidItemException;

  public float tallyOrder() throws RemoteException;

  public void checkOut(int cardType,
                       String cardNum,
                       String expiryDate,
                       String cardOwnerName)
       throws RemoteException, InvalidCardException;
}
```

Notice that this code does not provide methods to list the products. We leave that to the product bean because it is more worthwhile to leave it there than to cover it up in a session. Your Web site will need to list products for many reasons, so leaving that information exposed is a good design decision, because it will be used in many different places.

Making use of the session façade in client-side code is now a relatively straightforward affair. Whereas previously you had to keep track of a number of different bean types, you now only need to use a single bean and have the back-end system do all the hard work for you.

Fast-lane reader

When you develop an enterprise application, one of the reasons for going with an enterprise architecture provided by J2EE is that it will enable you to handle large amounts of data. Besides giving you this ability, another common trait of these applications is that most of the data are used for read-only display purposes rather than for creating or modifying data. It is more important that these applications be able to grab a large chunk of data fast, than that the information always be up to date. Another common use for this style of approach is to let the database do some of the heavy work, such as sorting a very large list of objects, to avoid clogging up the middleware server. The fast-lane reader pattern circumvents all these slow operations and replaces them with a single, highly optimized, fast operation.

Optimizing code to use a fast-lane reader involves throwing out some of the other lessons in this book. As with almost every optimization, you start by doing things the proper way and then find ways to circumvent them so that your code performs better (or more correctly — in line with expectations of the customer).

You have two ways of implementing this design pattern: via direct access to the data access objects that you normally use in the bean implementation, or via a session bean that does direct database queries. In either case, you are throwing away the entity-bean middleware layer and returning raw data. For this reason, there's no real example code to show you for this pattern: You are just using existing code in a different way.

Summary

Design patterns are an extremely important part of any programmer's toolkit. Not only do they help you to design code quickly using standard architectures, but they also provide a common language for communicating your design to other programmers. During this chapter you have

- Recapped what design patterns are
- Looked at the use of standard design patterns in the Java APIs
- Learned about the most common standard patterns used in J2EE programming

✦ ✦ ✦

Installing the J2EE Reference Implementation

If you are one of the many people using this book to take your first look at the J2EE specification, you might be wondering how on earth you can test all the code we've presented. Well, Sun has made life easy for you by providing a reference implementation of the complete Java 2 Enterprise Edition environment. You can use the reference environment to get a fast start on J2EE development without needing to spend large amounts of money on a fully fledged commercial environment.

A reference implementation of the specification is used as a measure for all of the other commercial and free implementations. When an implementer wants to check what the correct behavior should be, he can test his implementation against the reference. If it varies from the reference, then the reference is the yardstick. A reference implementation is not the same as the specification. The specification is just a document that all implementations must conform to.

In this appendix, we will run through the processes that will enable you to use the reference implementation for the code in this book. We'll cover the following:

- ✦ Downloading and installing the reference implementation
- ✦ Configuring the basic environment to run the reference implementation and to enable you to compile code
- ✦ Using the reference environment to install, run, and test your J2EE applications

Tip: If you are not interested in trying the reference implementation, or would like to compare it to other J2EE environments, take a look at `http://java.sun.com/j2ee/developer/`, which lists companies that offer free trial downloads.

Installing the Reference Implementation

The first step in using the reference environment is obviously obtaining a copy and installing it. Unless you have obtained it on CD at a conference, this means that you need to download it. In this section, we'll run through everything you need to do to get an environment up and running.

Required software

Naturally, the first requirement for the reference environment is a copy of it. (The next section will show you where to download everything.) Unlike the standard Java development environment, the reference environment does not contain everything you need to get running; it depends on a number of other environments.

Tip: Sun calls the reference implementation the J2EE SDK. However, most of the time you will see it referred to as the reference implementation, and it can be a bit confusing trying to sort out the difference between the two. When you download the SDK, you also get the reference implementation (the server and deployment tools and so on), so it can all get a bit muddled. For simplicity's sake, and because we are concerned more about the runtime-testing and deployment issues than about the code-compilation issues, we will refer to everything here as the reference implementation.

Java Development Kit

At the simplest level, the J2EE specification requires the existence of the J2SE specification. It is a superset. While this dependency does not imply the same requirements for the development environment, in the case of the reference implementation, that is exactly the case. Now, determining which J2SE development environment you require is tricky, and your choice really depends on the version of the J2EE environment you are using.

Caution: The J2EE v1.2.1 reference implementation does not recognize the J2SE v1.4 environment. It is not possible to run the two together.

So let's start with the simple things — you are going to need to download and install both the standard J2SE development environment (the JRE alone is not sufficient) and the reference implementation (you can find the reference implementation from `http://java.sun.com/j2ee/`). Easy, wasn't it? Oh, we forgot to tell you something else — the J2SE environment you have will probably conflict with the J2EE code for most versions (of both!). It seems that good coordination between the two teams does not exist, and that the IIOP implementation of RMI as well as JAXP (for XML processing) conflict between the two SDKs.

The suggested workaround for the conflicts is to use "a fresh installation without the standard extensions." Unfortunately, this is not all that easy to do. While JAXP is a separate download, and you can simply remove the items from the CLASSPATH or extensions directory, RMI-IIOP is a part of the core JAR file. Fortunately, after a fair amount of personal testing, we can assure you that the RMI-IIOP issue has not yet raised its head. JAXP will certainly cause a problem, but not RMI-IIOP. If you do have conflicts, it appears that removing the jaxp.properties file from the JAXP installation directory (or at least make it not-findable in the CLASSPATH), should fix most problems.

Using the J2EE environment does not require that you install Sun's J2EE SDK implementation. We have successfully used the enterprise applications in combination with IBM's Java runtime environment on both Win32 and Linux.

Optional packages and drivers

Apart from the issues you just saw, you may want to download additional libraries for some of the other standard extensions. For example, if you are interested in working with JavaMail, you may need to download the service providers for IMAP and POP handling. Another popular download will be JDBC drivers. By default, the reference implementation comes with drivers for Oracle, Cloudscape (the built-in database), and Microsoft SQLServer.

If you are interested, or require drivers not included in the standard set, you should take a look at the page that lists Optional Packages (`http://java.sun.com/products/OV_stdExt.html`) and then follow the appropriate links for drivers/service providers for each API.

Extra applications

With the reference environment, you get a limited set of applications. For example, while a small database (Cloudscape, a form of Ingress) is included with it, no directory-service software is included. This means that you need to use something else, like ActiveDirectory or OpenLDAP (`http://www.openldap.org/`). Whatever the case, you will need to locate extra applications to install to take care of all the missing items.

For applications that need to use JavaMail, you are going to need a mail server of some description. According to what you intend to write, that mail server will have to either accept incoming SMTP requests or enable you to access e-mail through IMAP or POP.

Apart from the CORBA implementation that ships by default, JNDI will require service-provider implementation(s) for your system. This may be LDAP, DNS or even the Windows Registry.

Downloading the software

For most of your downloading needs, the best place to start is Sun's Java site. Keep in mind that because most of the APIs are pluggable with driver implementations, once you have downloaded drivers to use with the J2EE reference implementation, these drivers will be usable with any commercial environment that you may purchase at a later date.

Implementations of the reference environment for Solaris, Linux, and Win32 are available from Sun at `http://java.sun.com/j2ee/download.html`. If you also need a copy of the J2SE environment, head to `http://java.sun.com/j2se/1.3/` for the latest copy of v1.3. (1.4 is in beta at the time of writing).

Tip The reference implementation does not contain any native code. If you are confident playing with shell scripts, it will not be very difficult to grab the installation bundle and copy it onto any other UNIX-based platform, including Apple's Mac OS X.

If you don't have either the JDK or J2EE reference implementation downloaded, then we suggest looking at obtaining a CD copy, which is also available from `http://java.sun.com/j2se/1.3/`. When you combine the two development kits and the documentation you are looking at around 150 MB of downloads. That's a lot of download time if you are only on a 56K modem!

Running the installation program

When you have all the software that you require, start by installing the J2SE environment. The J2EE environment checks for the presence of a J2SE full installation and will not install unless it finds one. Next, install all the optional packages and drivers you want to use.

To install the reference implementation, run the installation program that you downloaded. If you are a Win32 user, double-click the installation program (for example, j2sdkee-1_2_1-win.exe). UNIX users can run the installation script from the command line as follows:

```
./j2sdkee-1-2-1.bin
```

From this point, answer the appropriate questions about installation directory and that's it. Nothing else to do.

Configuring the Reference Implementation

After installing the reference implementation and any supporting software, you must now configure the environment so that it can find all the extra libraries, such as JDBC drivers. The other part of the configuration routine is making sure the reference implementation has the right settings for your needs.

If you have very simple requirements for your J2EE test applications, you don't need to perform any further setup. For example, if you can use the provided JDBC drivers to talk to your database, there is nothing more for you to do. The default setup is ready for you to go. You can ignore this section.

The settings we describe here and in the rest of this appendix are those defined by the J2EE SDK v1.3.

Environment settings

Environment settings are used for both compiling code and running it. Settings are also used to control the runtime action of the reference implementation — such as where it will write log files.

User environment settings

User settings consist of three environment variables. You should already be familiar with `CLASSPATH` and `JAVA_HOME`; J2EE adds an extra environment variable called `J2EE_HOME`.

Where `JAVA_HOME` describes the root directory of your J2SE installation (for example, c:\jdk1.3), `J2EE_HOME` describes the installation directory of your J2EE environment. The reference implementation uses this description to locate many different parts of its runtime information, such as configuration files.

When compiling code, you may want to set the `CLASSPATH` to contain the J2EE JAR file for all the extra APIs. The `CLASSPATH` does not need to be set for the running of code, but for compiling it will make life much easier. All the classes defined by the J2EE environment can be found in the file $`J2EE_HOME`/lib/j2ee.jar. If you are using command-line compiling, then adding the j2ee.jar file to the `CLASSPATH` will make life simpler for you. Of course, the other option is to use the `-classpath` option on the Java compiler, but typing it out can get annoying. If you are running an IDE, consult the documentation to learn how to add the extra libraries to your compilation settings.

A collection of scripts takes care of running the reference implementation. These scripts can be found in the directory `J2EE_HOME`/bin: It is worth adding this directory to your `PATH` environment variable so you will be able to run the reference-environment applications with no extra work.

Reference implementation internal settings

Internally the reference implementation contains a collection of settings that specify the ports to listen on, user-authentication information, and much more. The `J2EE_HOME`/config directory contains a collection of configuration files you can edit.

The auth.properties file handles the process of changing the default user name and password of the reference environment. Although this environment is meant to be a reference implementation, changing the default settings is a good idea anyway. The two properties that control the default settings are as follows:

```
default.principal.name
default.principal.password
```

You can set these values to something more appropriate for your system.

To change the setup of the built-in Web server, edit the web.properties file. Here you will find the port numbers for the server to answer on (defaults to 8000 rather than the standard 80) and the directory in which you'll find the HTML files. Here you'll also find another password that you should change: It is the password for the key information used in the secure HTTPS connection.

If you are running CORBA services, such as the default JNDI service provider, then editing the orb.properties file will modify that setup. You can change two port settings as well as the name of the server on which you want to look up names. The default server is the local machine, but if you want to test the reference environment in a networked setup, then you can set this value to the name of the machine that will provide naming services for the entire network (typically the server rather than one of the clients).

Finally, you have the default.properties file, which controls the behavior of the server and resource.properties. We'll go into most of the details of this file shortly when we talk about adding new JDBC drivers.

Setting the log-file information

An important part of the setup is keeping log files of everything that happens. Logging information ranges from capturing the `System.out` calls to tracking low-level user access and errors.

The log files write to a default area of `J2EE_HOME`/logs. However, you can modify the way that logs are stored in this directory. To change the default directory, change the value of the property `log.directory` in the default.properties file. If you want to change the name of a log file for a particular activity, properties exist for that, too. For example, if you want to change the name of the file to which the `System.err` information is written, you can edit the `log.error.file` property and specify a new name.

Beyond changing the basic directory and file names, you can customize the log files according to how you intend to use the system. A default setup assumes that your machine will run all the J2EE servers in a single JVM instance. All log files are written in the log directory and then in a subdirectory based on your machine name. Under the machine-name directory you have a single subdirectory structure based on `ejb`.

When running the reference implementation with a JVM for each service, the machine-name directory contains a set of subdirectories — one for each service. So, instead of just the `ejb` directory, you will find directories named `ejb` and `httpd`, and then one directory for each EJB application. You will still, however, have the log files with the same names as in the single JVM version.

Configuring drivers and service providers

For most users, the most important part of configuring the reference implementation will be managing the various drivers and service providers. To set these up, you need to edit the resources.properties file.

Tip If you are running the reference implementation server on your local machine, the GUI Deploytool application provides a nice graphical tool to perform the following configuration.

JDBC drivers

Defining drivers to use with the reference implementation depends on which type of drivers you want to use. Is the driver a JDBC 1.0 `Driver` instance or the 2.0 `DataSource`- or `XADataSource`-derived driver? As JDBC 1.0 driver implementations are required to register themselves, you do not need to define a property for them. However, as `DataSource`-based implementations are accessed through JNDI, you need to provide a collection of registration details for them so that the reference implementation can make sure they are loaded for your use.

The first step in defining a data source is to tell it the name of the classes that implement the `DataSource` interface. Each driver for a database comes with its own set of properties. These properties start with `jdbcDriver`. Following the prefix is a number. The first driver has the number 0, the second driver uses 1 and so on for each additional driver you want to use. The numbers must be sequential. You cannot leave gaps, otherwise any drivers after the gap in the sequence will not be loaded. To complete the specification of the driver, you end the property name with `.name` and then assign the fully-qualified class name to that driver. Say you have two drivers, one for Oracle and one for DB2 — the property setup would look like this:

```
jdbcDriver.0.name=oracle.jdbc.driver.OracleDriver
jdbcDriver.1.name=COM.ibm.jdbc.net.DB2Driver
```

Tip The default property value in the file includes the Cloudscape driver. You should not remove the Cloudscape information from here if you are using other databases, as the reference implementation uses the database internally and relies on the existence of this driver.

To complete the data source setup, you need to provide the JNDI reference information so you can relate the drivers to the JNDI access name you use. Inside your various EJBs, servlets and JSPs, you define a JNDI name that is your driver. As part of your standard security, the application needs to know a user name, a password, and which virtual database the JDNI name refers to. All of this information is supplied through the properties that start with `jdbcDataSource`. The syntax of this property follows the same styles as for the basic driver setup. After the first part of the property name, you need to supply a number. This number should match the number you used for the driver. So, based on the preceding example, `jdbcDataSource.0` supplies all the information for the Oracle driver, and `jdbcDataSource.1` is used by the DB2 driver. This time you need to specify the name that the driver is registered as for JNDI name and also the JDBC URL for connecting to the database. This is what an Oracle driver definition looks like:

```
jdbcDataSource.0.name=jdbc/Oracle
jdbcDataSource.0.url=jdbc:oracle:thin:@127.0.0.1:1571:acct
```

If you are unsure about the necessary URL or how to write one, consult the section "Requesting a connection instance" in Chapter 7.

Loading transaction-aware data sources

The process of loading drivers for data sources that are transaction-aware (implements the `XADataSource` interface) does not involve the properties that you have just looked . Instead, you must use a different system. Because a transaction-aware data source needs a lot of configuration information, you need a list of properties rather than just a pair.

Describing transaction-aware data sources follows the same pattern established for the other drivers; this time with the prefix of `jdbcXADataSource`. Again, a sequentially numbered list is used.

Properties for each data source define extra information passed through during the construction phase. This mostly usurps the role of the basic properties in other drivers. You must define two properties for each driver you want to register: `.name` and `.classname`. In addition to these two mandatory properties, you can define a collection of other property names:

```
jdbcXAxaDataSource.<n>.name
jdbcXAxaDataSource.<n>.classname
jdbcXAxaDataSource.<n>.dbuser
jdbcXAxaDataSource.<n>.dbpassword
jdbcXAxaDataSource.<n>.prop.<property name>
```

The `name` property is the basic JNDI name you have registered this driver under, and the `classname` property should be the fully qualified name of the class to be loaded. As with the other JDBC drivers, you may need to provide a user name and password to access the database, so there are properties that enable you to do that. The last item is a means of allowing you to specify arbitrary properties for the driver. A given driver may request that you provide extra items for definition: You can use this item to do it.

Other service providers

You can set other service providers through the resources.properties file. Most importantly, if you are using JMS or message-driven beans, you will need to set up the topic areas and message queues.

If you need to define properties used by other APIs, you can provide them in the default.properties file. When this file is loaded, it is used to set the system properties for the application. (Effectively it replaces the `-D` option for the Java runtime.) The default properties file is loaded, and the system runs through all the items and calls `System.setProperty()` with them.

As an alternative, each of the APIs will also define its own default properties file. For example, JDNI will look for the file jndi.properties for its default setup.

Deploying and Running Applications

At last you have the J2EE reference environment installed and configured to taste. Now you can get on with the good stuff — running the system and deploying your enterprise software.

Running the tools

Tools form the basis of deploying our application. These tools provide the underlying infrastructure, doing things like loading JDBC drivers, managing our EJBs, and deploying the EJBs to the server.

In total, the reference implementation contains 12 tools — most of which you won't use under normal circumstances. We are going to cover the four most commonly used tools — the server, a tool to package and deploy EJB, the included database, and also a tool to reset the other tools when you make a mistake. As the reference implementation is very simple, all these tools are run from a command line — so fire up a new shell or DOS prompt and let's get going!

All the tools are run by batch files. You can find these in the `bin` directory underneath the installation directory. If you have set up the `PATH` correctly (as we demonstrated in the previous section), you will have access to all these tools with no further effort.

Using the J2EE server

At the heart of every J2EE environment is the server. This server is responsible for managing the EJBs that you've created. Unlike the commercial servers, the reference implementation is pretty simple. You only have a few options.

The server is represented by the `j2ee` command. By running this command without any arguments, you will start the server. As the server starts, you will see the output shown in Figure A-1. Note, though, that we have used the `-verbose` option to print out a little extra information. If you want to know what the options are, you can use the command `j2ee -help` to print them out, as you can see at the top of Figure A-1. Note that very few commands exist, and that only one or two of them are actually any use.

```
Projects - j2ee -verbose
Microsoft Windows 2000 [Version 5.00.2195]
(C) Copyright 1985-2000 Microsoft Corp.

C:\justin>ebible

C:\justin\books\ebible>j2ee -verbose
Warning: This J2EE SDK release is designed to run on J2SE 1.3
J2EE server listen port: 1050
Naming service started:1050
Binding DataSource, name = jdbc/DB1, url = jdbc:cloudscape:rmi:CloudscapeDB;crea
te=true
Binding DataSource, name = jdbc/DB2, url = jdbc:cloudscape:rmi:CloudscapeDB;crea
te=true
Binding DataSource, name = jdbc/InventoryDB, url = jdbc:cloudscape:rmi:Cloudscap
eDB;create=true
Binding DataSource, name = jdbc/Cloudscape, url = jdbc:cloudscape:rmi:Cloudscape
DB;create=true
Binding DataSource, name = jdbc/EstoreDB, url = jdbc:cloudscape:rmi:CloudscapeDB
;create=true
Binding DataSource, name = jdbc/XACloudscape, url = jdbc/XACloudscape__xa
Binding DataSource, name = jdbc/XACloudscape__xa, dataSource = COM.cloudscape.co
re.RemoteXaDataSource@14b82b
Starting JMS service...
Initialization complete - waiting for client requests
Binding: < JMS Destination : jms/Queue , javax.jms.Queue >
Binding: < JMS Destination : jms/Topic , javax.jms.Topic >
Binding: < JMS Cnx Factory : TopicConnectionFactory , Topic , No properties >
Binding: < JMS Cnx Factory : QueueConnectionFactory , Queue , No properties >
Binding: < JMS Cnx Factory : jms/TopicConnectionFactory , Topic , No properties
>
Binding: < JMS Cnx Factory : jms/QueueConnectionFactory , Queue , No properties
>
Starting web service at port: 8000
Starting secure web service at port: 7000
J2EE SDK/1.3
Starting web service at port: 9191
J2EE SDK/1.3
Loading jar:/c:/j2sdkee1.3/repository/GOLEM/applications/Simple Demo for Appendi
x A1008539898970Server.jar
/c:/j2sdkee1.3/repository/GOLEM/applications/Simple Demo for Appendix A100853989
8970Server.jar
Binding name:`java:comp/env/jdbc/cloudscape`
Warning: Reference reference java:comp/env/jdbc/cloudscape is using a JNDI name
that is not bound: jdbc/cloudscape
J2EE server startup complete.
```

Figure A-1: Output from running the J2EE reference implementation server

When the server is run, you do not get your prompt back. The application effectively stops you from using that window. In order to stop the server, you need to start another prompt and type the command `j2ee -stop`, which will result in the server stopping (and you getting that prompt back!). Stopping the server may take a few seconds, so please be patient!

If you are running in a Unix environment, you can run everything in one shell session by backgrounding the tasks with the & operator.

Using the deployment tool

After starting the server, you can now use other tools. The deployment tool enables you to create, package, and deploy EJBs. Unlike the server, this tool can be run as a command-line driven application or as a graphical tool. To start the deployment tool, you run the `deploytool` command. When you run the tool, you get the output shown in Figure A-2. The first command shown in the figure is accessing the help information and options available to the user, while the second command shows the output when running the tool.

In order for the deployment tool to be useful, you need to have the server running first. Without the server, you can create and package EJBs, but you cannot deploy them for use by client applications.

```
Projects
Microsoft Windows 2000 [Version 5.00.2195]
(C) Copyright 1985-2000 Microsoft Corp.

C:\justin>ebible

C:\justin\books\ebible>deploytool -help
Warning: This J2EE SDK release is designed to run on J2SE 1.3
The deployment tool version is 1.3
Options
     -ui     Runs the tool with a UI (default mode)
     -help     Display this help message
     -deploy <ear file> <server name> [<client jar>]
     -uninstall <application name> <server name>
     -listApps <server name>
     -deployConnector <rar filename> <server name>
     -undeployConnector <rar filename> <server name>
     -listConnectors <server name>
C:\justin\books\ebible>_
```

Figure A-2: Output on the command line when running the deployment tool

From the options, you can see that there are ways of running the tool without the GUI if necessary. Running without the graphical interface is useful if you just need to tweak the current EJBs.

Using he standalone Cloudscape database

For some applications you will need a standalone relational database. If you have not used another database, you will need to run the provided database, Cloudscape. You have no options when running the database—only start and stop commands. For example, to run the database, type

```
cloudscape -start
```

To stop it, in another prompt, type

```
cloudscape -stop
```

Cleaning up after a mistake

No matter how hard you try, you always end up making mistakes. Sometimes you need to make a clean start for testing purposes. In these situations you need to strip the server clean and start again. The reference implementation provides the `cleanup` tool to enable you to do this. This tool has no options and will remove all the configuration information from the server, so use it with caution. Once you have run the tool, the server does not contain any deployed applications. In order to use your applications, you will need to re-deploy them again using the deployment tool.

Deploying an Enterprise JavaBean

Your next step in using the reference environment is to deploy all the EJBs that you have previously coded and compiled. This environment has all of the normal features of a J2EE environment. All bean types may be deployed, and you can have complex bean arrangements that allow beans to reference other beans.

For demonstration purposes, we have used a simple set of home, remote, and EJB code to illustrate the process of deploying an Enterprise JavaBean. You can work with these items or with your own examples, or even with those in earlier chapters.

Deploying an EJB takes three basic steps (assuming you've coded and compiled them already): packaging the bean, giving the bean an identity, and uploading the bean to the server.

Packaging the bean

To package a bean, follow these steps:

Although we describe using menu items, most of the tasks described in the rest of this chapter can also be activated using the buttons on the toolbar too.

1. Start the server and deployment tool as illustrated earlier. For the purpose of this example, we'll assume that you want to create a completely new application (you haven't pre-packaged the bean using the manual steps shown back in Chapter 17). Your raw materials for this stage are the classes that describe and implement the home interface, the remote interface, and the bean itself.

   Creating a new bean starts with selecting the New Application option from the File menu. This will show the dialog box that you see in Figure A-3. In this dialog, you need to provide a name of the file that you will package the application into (remember, the file name must end in .ear) and a simple text string to describe the application.

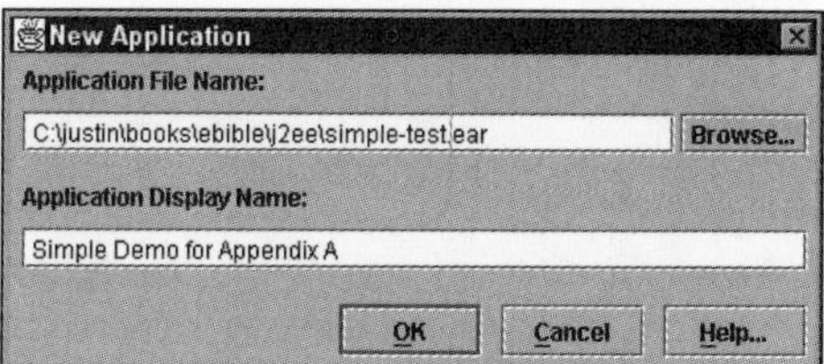

Figure A-3: The first dialog needed to create a new enterprise application

2. After entering all the required information, click OK. This closes the dialog and leaves you back at the first window. Now you need to create a new bean for the application.
3. Select the New Enterprise Bean option from the File menu. This brings up the next dialog, shown in Figure A-4. You cannot provide anything useful here as it is just introductory text. If these sorts of dialogs annoy you, there is a checkbox in the bottom left corner to hide the dialog. However, we have included it so that you can read the information on it, as this information is pertinent to the next few steps.

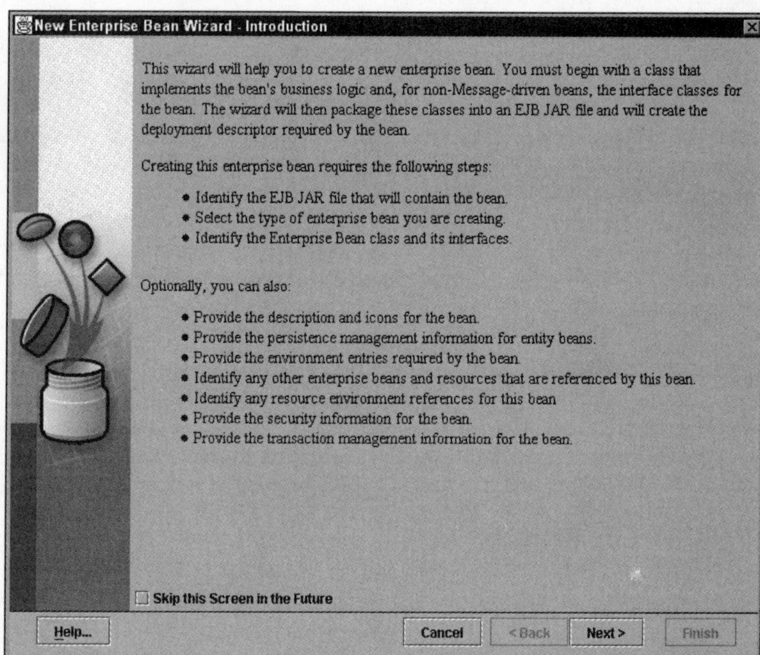

Figure A-4: The introductory information dialog when creating a new EJB

Now you need to provide the information necessary to creating the JAR file that will contain the class files of your EJB. The complex dialog is shown in Figure A-5.

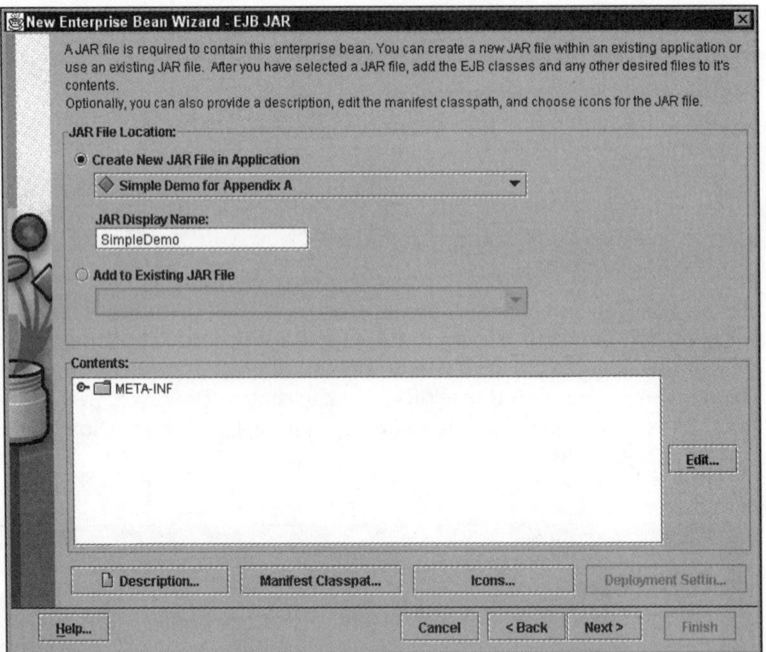

Figure A-5: The dialog that allows you to specify all the information needed for the EJB JAR file

Filling in the dialog is simply a case of starting at the top and working your way to the bottom.

4. From the drop-down menu, select the file that the EJB will go in. As this is your first EJB, this menu will only contain a single option.

5. Type in the display name you want to see for the JAR. Remember this name, as you will be using it throughout the rest of these steps.

   At the bottom of the dialog are the contents of the JAR file. As you can see, there is currently no content in the JAR file. To add your bean classes to the JAR file, click the Edit button on the right.

   Before we show you how to add classes, we will finish the rest of the dialog. Along the bottom you will see a row of buttons. The Manifest Classpath button allows you to specify any library JAR files that you may have previously registered (which we haven't done in this application). You can also supply an icon that can be used with the JAR. This icon makes it easy to pick your EJB when it is deployed to a server, it is also used by the deployment tool's tree view on the left-hand side.

6. After clicking the Edit button to add files to the EJB JAR file, you will see the dialog shown in Figure A-6. The top section of the dialog provides a view of your file system. Navigate this tree as you would any other graphical file system explorer. Once you have found the directory where you have developed your beans, select the .class files. Here, for our demonstration code, we select the three .class files to be packaged into the bean and then click the Add button. The selected files appear in the bottom window. If you accidentally added files that should not be there, select them in the bottom window and click the Remove button. When you are finished, click the OK button, and you will be brought back to the main window shown in Figure A-5. You should now see that the classes are located in the bottom window.

Note that you should not select any `.java` files, only the compiled bytecode. Having the source files in the JAR file will cause problems later on.

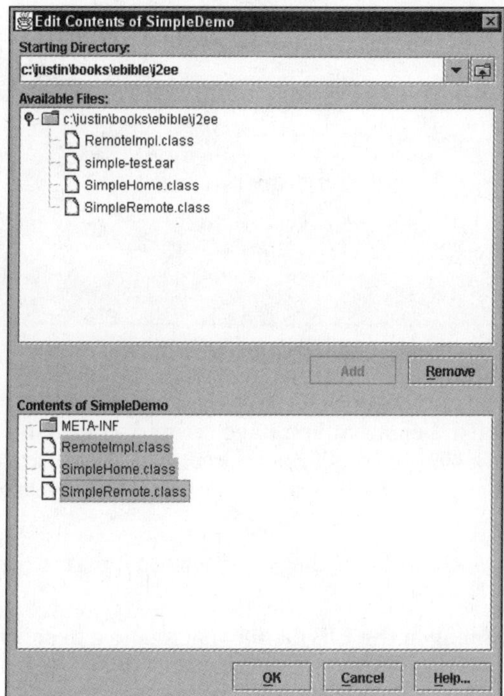

Figure A-6: Selecting the class files to be part of the EJB

Once you are happy with the setup for the bean, you can move to the next stage by clicking the Next button. If everything is fine, then this will not cause any problems. If there is a problem, then you will be warned with a dialog.

So everything passes the first check. This will bring you to the dialog shown in Figure A-7. This time you specify the nature of the EJB you are deploying and which of the files belongs to which part of the EJB.

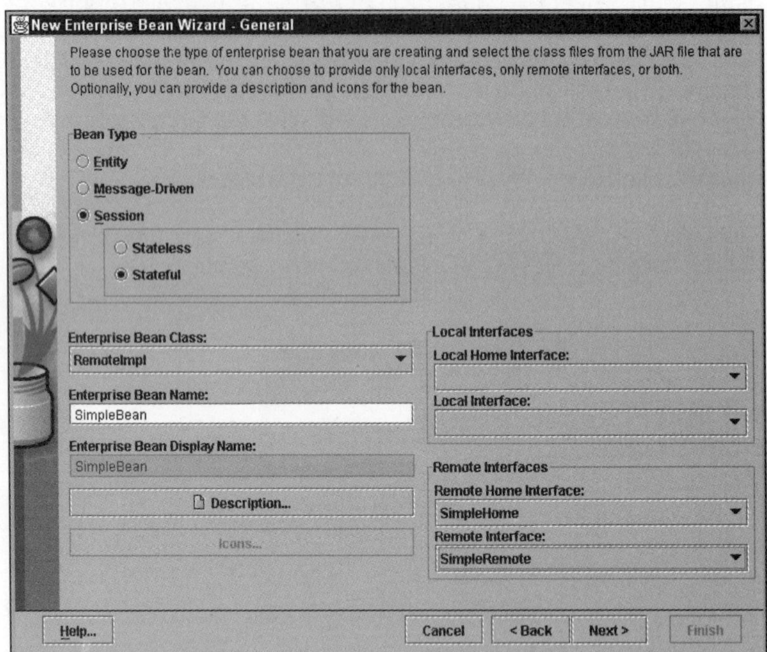

Figure A-7: Nominating the EJB internal relationships and bean type

7. Firstly, nominate the type of bean that you have created. (Again, for demo purposes we just have a very simple stateless session bean.) If you are deploying a session bean, remember to define it as stateful or stateless by selecting the appropriate sub-option.

   For each part of the bean, choose the appropriate class file from the pull-down menus.

8. Complete the dialog by filling in the EJB display name and a description.

9. Your next dialog (Figure A-8) provides information about how the transactions are handled. Select whether the container or your bean code will be managing them. If you selected the Container-managed option, the large table on the right will fill with the list of methods and their current attribute setting. By default, the attribute is set to Required. If you want to change this, click the appropriate cell and select the new attribute value from the pull-down menu.

There is a bug in the wizard code that sometimes "forgets" to set the transaction attribute. Even though it appears to be set in the UI, when you run the verification tool over the bean, errors will be generated.

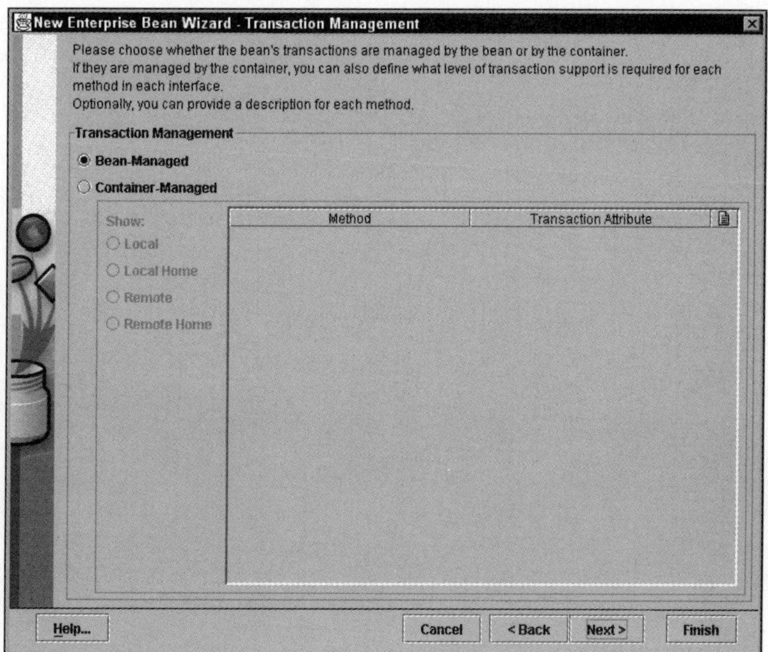

Figure A-8: Selecting transaction attributes for the methods of your EJB

10. If your enterprise bean requires that you set any environment variables, then the next dialog, shown in Figure A-9, will allow you to do that. To add a new environment entry, click Add and then fill in the appropriate values into the table. The first column is the name that you have used in the JNDI lookup. The second column contains a pull-down menu to allow you to select the type of the, for example Integer, String etc. Finally, the third column is the value to be used for that entry.

If you do not need to provide any more information, you can exit the process at any time from now on simply by clicking the Finish button.

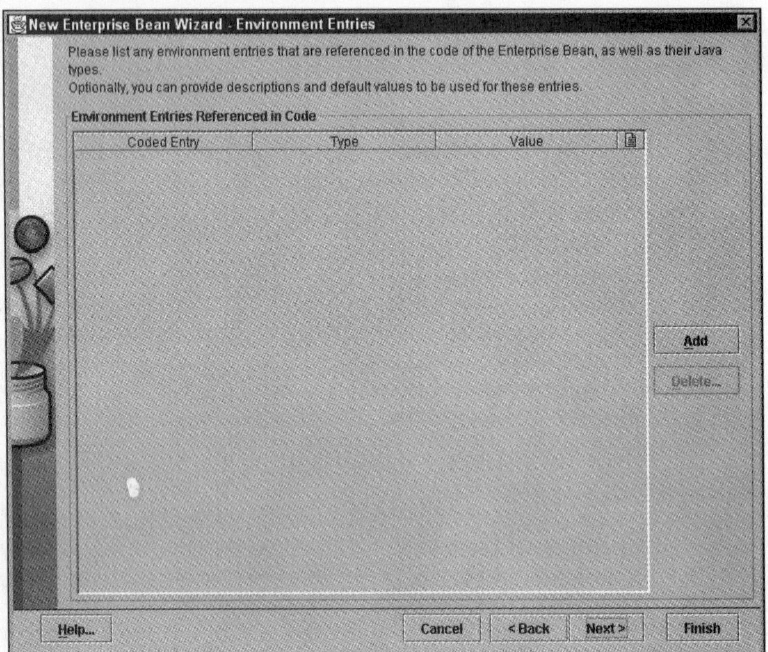

Figure A-9: Setting environment variables needed by the EJB

11. After setting the environment properties, you may want to nominate the other beans this bean will reference through the dialog shown in Figure A-10. In this demo application, you don't have any, but in more complex cases, such as the example beans you developed in Chapters 17 and 18, you will need to select them by clicking the Add button. A new row will appear in the table, which you are required to fill in. Going from left to right, the columns define the JNDI name that this bean uses to reference the other bean, the type of bean (session, entity or message-driven), the access type (local or remote), and the fully qualified class names for home and remote/local interface. For each bean that this bean references, you will need to add one entry to this table.

The deployment environment does not require that the JNDI name used by this bean actually correspond to the name that you deployed the referenced bean as. A later step in the deployment process allows you to provide mappings between the two names. For example, you could deploy this example bean using the name `ejb/SimpleBean`, and then you could deploy a second bean that references this example bean that uses the name `ejb/appendix_a/DemoBean`.

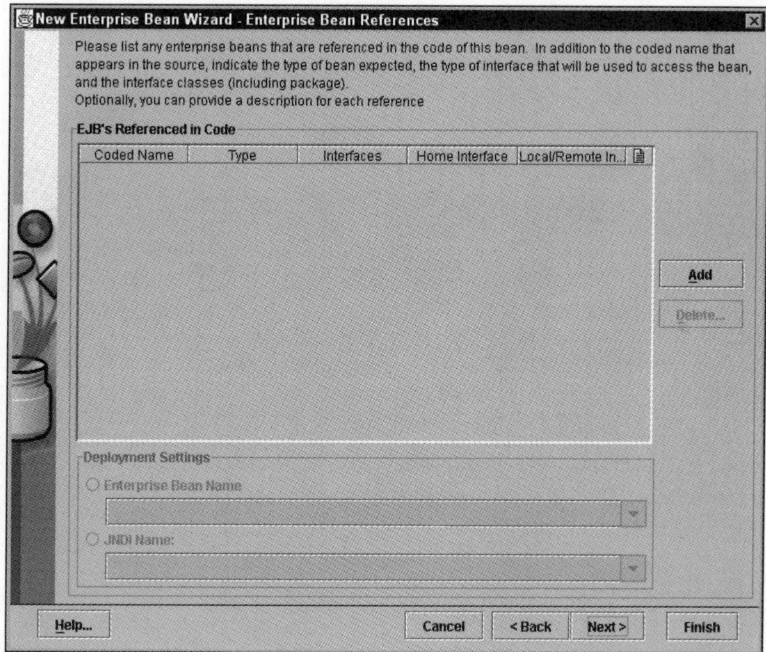

Figure A-10: Selecting a list of EJBs that you want this bean to reference

12. If your code requires any resource factories, then the dialog shown in Figure A-11 allows you to enter the information. A resource factory is any factory. If you have a bean using JDBC, then the `DataSource` you use to create connection instances is considered a resource factory. To add the new item, click the Add button: A new row will appear in the table on the left. Enter the JNDI name used (for example, jdbc/Cloudscape) in the first column. Click the mouse in the second and third columns and select the appropriate items (the default resource factory is the JDBC `DataSource`). At the bottom of the dialog is the area for you to specify any access information that the factory will require. Enter the JNDI name that you expect to use and, if appropriate, a user name and password.

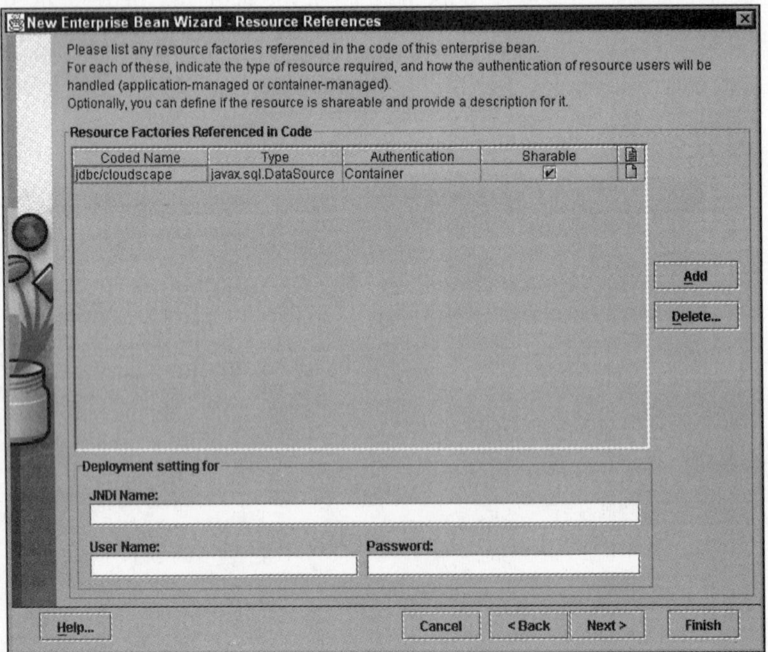

Figure A-11: Dialog allowing you to set any resource factories used by the EJB

13. Now you start getting into the more esoteric items. Figure A-12 shows you the dialog used to defined environment entries required by the resource factories. Most of the time this will not be needed. Figure A-13 is the dialog that allows you to define how users will access your beans.

    If you have defined role information for your methods on the bean, you specify this in the dialog shown in Figure A-13. Add new roles using the Add button on the right and provide the name and password information requested. For each role name you add, a column will appear in the table on the bottom. Once you have completed the roles, move to this table and select the roles that can access each method by selecting the appropriate checkbox(es).

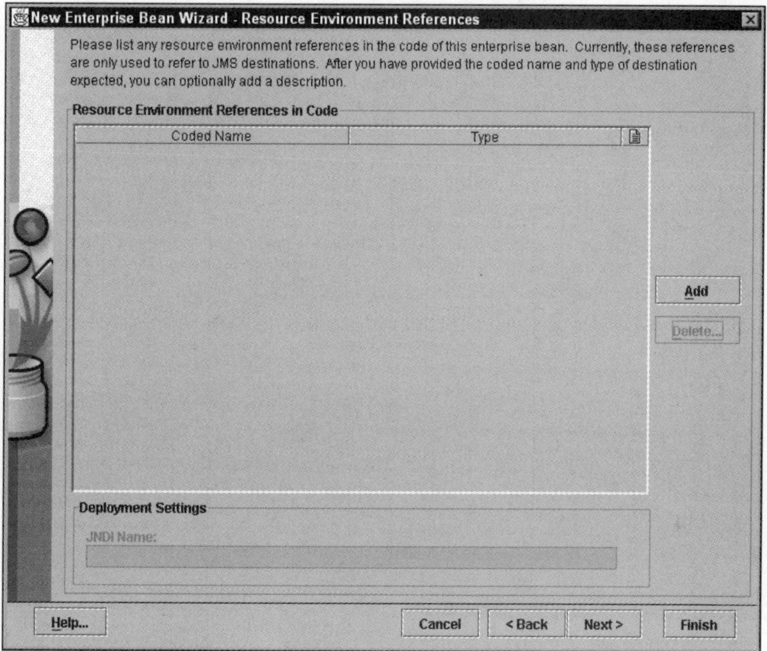

Figure A-12: Dialog for specifying any environment entries required by the resource factories

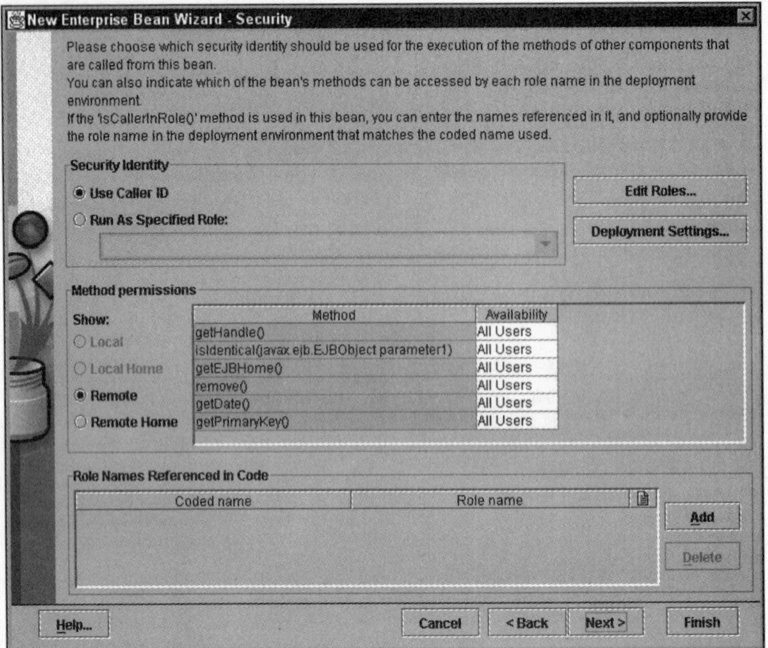

Figure A-13: Dialog specifying security-role information for each method in the bean

14. The final dialog, shown in Figure A-14, offers you a last chance to look over the deployment descriptor information generated by the previous choices. Clicking the Finish button here completes the process and returns you to the main window once more. Figure A-15 shows the main window with the completed bean information showing.

Setting up name information

With a bean created, you are now ready to set up the naming information so that the client applications can find it. In the Local Applications tree on the left, make sure that your application ("Simple Demo for Appendix A" in this case) has been selected. On the right you should see a set of tabbed windows, which should look something like what is shown in Figure A-15.

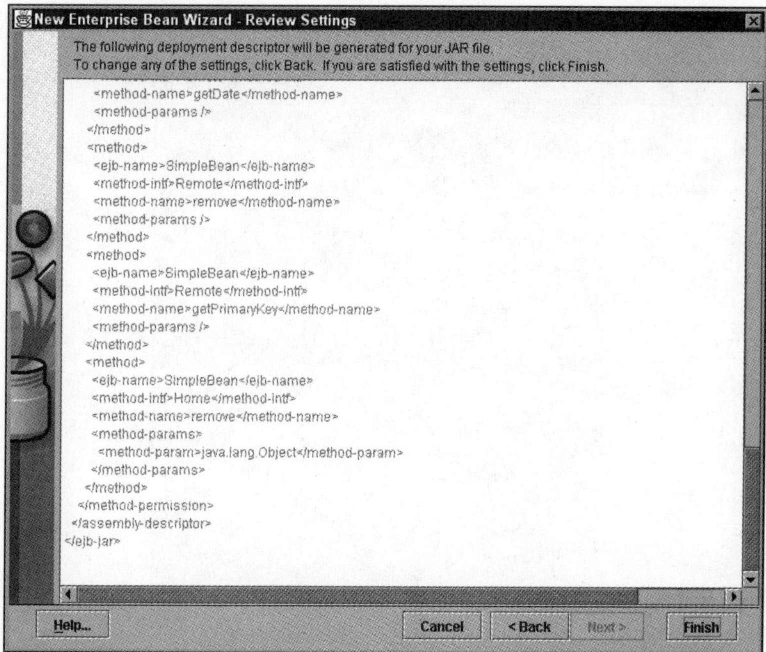
New Enterprise Bean Wizard - Review Settings
The following deployment descriptor will be generated for your JAR file.
To change any of the settings, click Back. If you are satisfied with the settings, click Finish.
<method-name>getDate</method-name>
<method-params />
</method>
<method>
<ejb-name>SimpleBean</ejb-name>
<method-intf>Remote</method-intf>
<method-name>remove</method-name>
<method-params />
</method>
<method>
<ejb-name>SimpleBean</ejb-name>
<method-intf>Remote</method-intf>
<method-name>getPrimaryKey</method-name>
<method-params />
</method>
<method>
<ejb-name>SimpleBean</ejb-name>
<method-intf>Home</method-intf>
<method-name>remove</method-name>
<method-params>
<method-param>java.lang.Object</method-param>
</method-params>
</method>
</method-permission>
</assembly-descriptor>
</ejb-jar>
Help...
Cancel
< Back
Next >
Finish

Figure A-14: Your final chance to check the deployment descriptor before committing the results

The next step is to associate a name with the EJB so that client applications can find the EJB. Name information is defined in the JNDI Names tab, so select this tab, and you will see something resembling what is shown in Figure A-16. To set the name, simply click the cell of the right-most column and type in the JNDI name that you want to associate with this bean.

In addition to supplying a name for the bean, you will need to provide a name for the JDBC driver. Remember how back in Figure A-11 you provided the JNDI name of the JDBC data source that your code needed. Now you need to map that name to the name that you previously defined in when you originally configured the server (see the section "Configuring drivers and service providers" earlier in this chapter). Again, click the right-most cell of the lower table and enter the appropriate name.

This completes the naming section, and now we can move on to the final step—deploying the bean to the server.

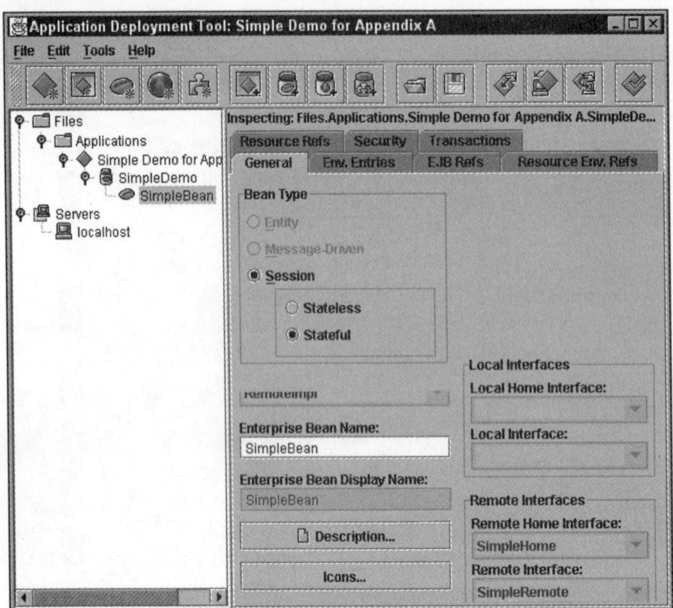

Figure A-15: The main window showing the complete, packaged bean

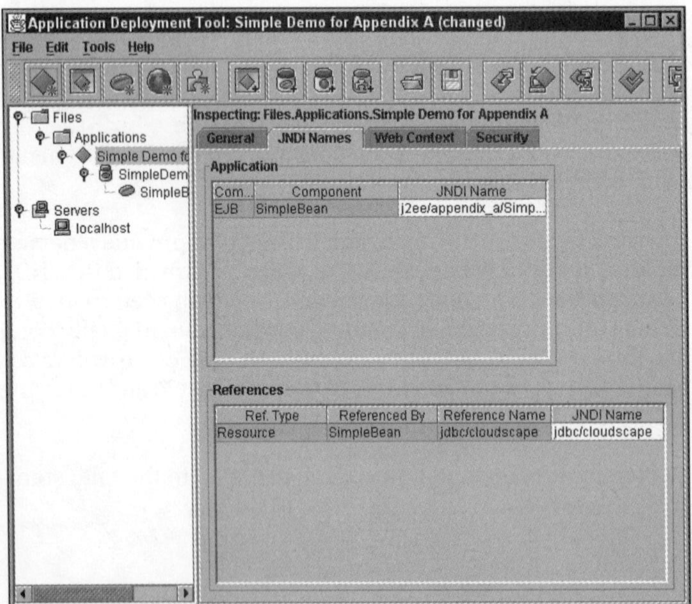

Figure A-16: The JNDI Names tab, showing the entering of a name for the example bean

Verifying your bean before deployment

Before you move on to deploying your bean, one more sanity check needs to be performed. In this step, you run a verification tool over the bean to make sure that all the information is supplied, and that the supplied information is correct. For example, this step will make sure that you have the right methods in the home interface and that the bean implementation class provides an implementation of those methods.

To run the verifier tool, first select the part of the application you want to verify in the tree-view window. The verifier tool will run on whatever you selected, so if you choose just one bean, then the verifier will only work with that bean. However, if you select the application, then the verifier will check all the beans, JSPs and servlets you have packaged.

After selecting the verification target, start the verifier by selecting the Tools ➪ Verifier menu option. You should now see the dialog that is shown in Figure A-17, although without all the output in the bottom window. From the option list on the right side, select what output you want to see, and then click OK. The tool will now go away and run a large collection of tests over your chosen code. (If you selected the whole application for verification this could take quite a few minutes, so go grab a coffee if you do this!)

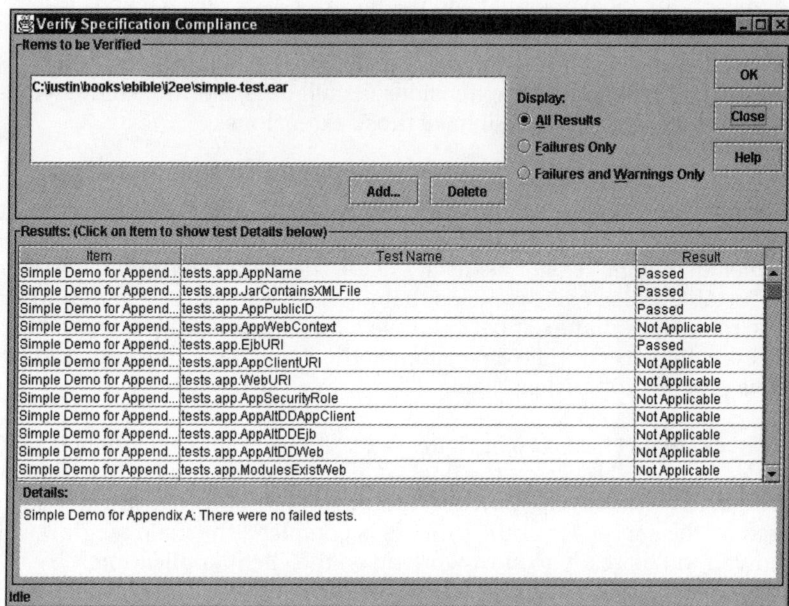

Figure A-17: The verifier tool dialog showing the output after a verification run

In the bottom of the window, you will see the output from the tool. Generally, look for the items that failed (much easier if you selected the Failures Only display option). Unfortunately, some of the error messages are quite cryptic, although mostly they are well explained. For example, if you have a method name mismatch between the remote interface and the implementation, it will tell you which files to look at.

There is a really odd bug in the verifier tool. We've found that if you specify when one bean references another in the deployment tool the verifier tool will generate an error. Typically that error will describe a `NullPointerException` inside one of the tests. If you get this, you can ignore the verification error and continue as though all your beans are fine. The deployment step you are about to go through does not require your bean/application to pass the verification step.

Deploying your bean to the server

Packaged, named and verified for correctness, beans are now ready to be deployed to the server. The next step is to run the deployment wizard from your applications. You start this wizard by selecting the Deploy Application option under the Tools menu.

After selecting the menu item, you end up with the dialog shown in Figure A-18. For most users, you will just use the default values provided — the server you are deploying to is on the local machine and the Return Client Jar checkbox is left unchecked. This checkbox is useful if you don't know the state of the client machine's Java implementation. If the client machine has an old Java 2 implementation, it may not have the RMI-IIOP extensions installed: This option allows you to make sure that the end machine will have those extensions.

Clicking the Next button reveals the dialog shown in Figure A-19. This dialog is a last chance to make sure that you have all the name mappings supplied correctly. If you forgot this step in the earlier processes (which we've done on more than one occasion when deploying tens of beans at once!), then you can provide the information now. The table will list all the beans that have been registered in this application and the references that exist between the various beans. This is more of a check that everything is OK than a real step in the deployment process, and all you need to do is proceed to the next dialog.

The "final check" dialog is shown in Figure A-20. At this point everything is ready to go, and the dialog just shows you the final summary. Clicking the Finish button will cause the bean to be deployed. A progress dialog will be shown as the application is registered on the server. Once the process is complete, the main window will return, and you will be ready to start working on the client application.

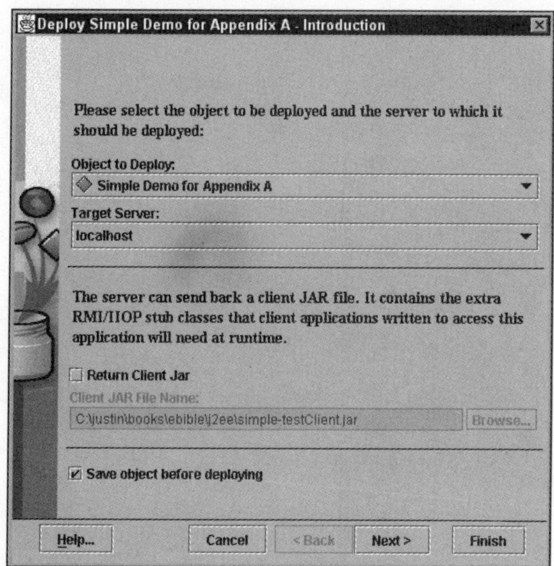

Figure A-18: The first dialog you encounter when deploying an application to the server

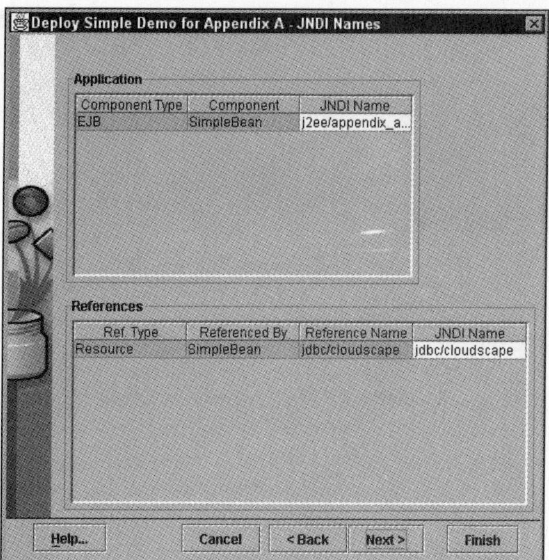

Figure A-19: A final check of the contents of the application before deployment

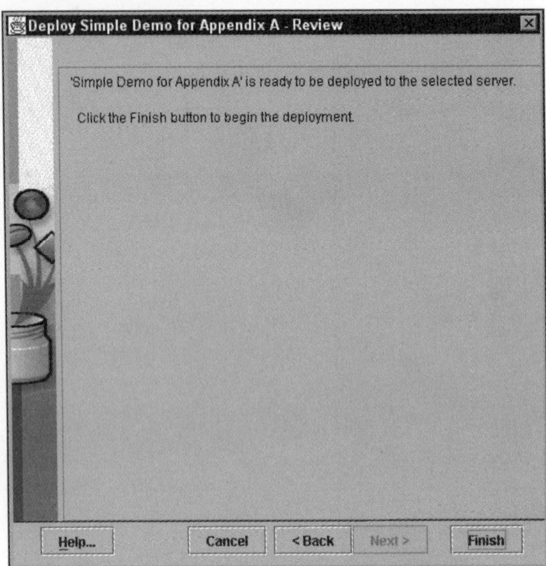

Figure A-20: The "final check" dialog you see before committing to the deployment

Now you will see a progress dialog like that shown in Figure A-21. This dialog gives you feedback about what is happening in the deployment process. The two columns on the left show progress information while the text area on the right shows the current step being performed. If there is any error during this process, you will see the error message in this text area.

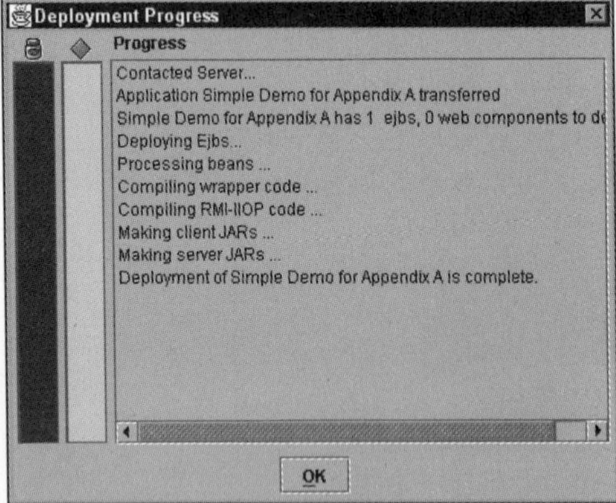

Figure A-21: Progress dialog showing the output of a successfully completed deployment

Updating beans after you have deployed them

It is inevitable that you will need to update beans after that initial deployment. For example, there is no way to debug the bean implementations without deploying them first. If you had to go through the full deployment process each time you changed the bean code, it would quickly send you insane! Luckily the deployment tool provides a shortcut to redeploying existing beans.

After you have made your changes to the code, recompile it. In order for the deployment tool to update the code, you need to inform it that you have changed something. Select the Update Files option from the Tools menu. The deployment tool will now go away and check which files have been changed and present you with a dialog that names all the changed files. Click OK to continue. Now, you must save the application again. This is an extremely important step. If you do not explicitly save the application after the update step, the tool will redeploy the old code, not the new files. We believe this is a bug as it appears the tool is fetching the update from the file on disk, but does not do an implicit save of the changed file before reading the file off disk to do the deployment with. If you wish to re-verify the application/bean before redeploying, you will also need to save the file.

Updating the application on the server is now just a matter of selecting the Update and Redeploy option from the Tools menu. You should now see the same dialog as you saw back in Figure A-21 as the deployment process proceeds.

Running a client application

Client applications for a J2EE server and EJB can come in one of two forms — a standalone client, or a client that is also part of the J2EE environment (for example a servlet or JSP).

Running standalone clients

A standalone client is an application that will run on the command line. These applications do not require the use of a full environment. However, in order to access the EJB, you will still need to do a small amount of work to allow the application to function correctly.

Running a standalone application still needs access to the client stubs of the EJB. While you might be tempted to solve this by just including the path to the client JAR file in your CLASSPATH setting, that is the wrong way to solve the problem. The big issue here is that your application makes use of JNDI to find beans, so how do you get the JNDI system correctly configured in the first place? To get the environment going, you will need to create an application that resides as part of the EJB/J2EE environment — that means using the deployment tool, even for standalone applications.

To create an deploy a standalone client, in the deployment tool, you use the New Application Client option under the File menu. The steps look reasonably similar to the EJB deployment steps. Select the collection of classes and JAR files you need, and any beans you are going to reference. Once that is complete, save and deploy the client application.

The deployed application client will still use the local CLASSPATH setting. That means you only need to provide a simple boostrap class in the application client and then leave the rest of your client code on the local disk. Only registering the stub file will save you needing to re-deploy the entire application every time that a file changes.

While you could do everything yourself, the reference implementation provides a convenient tool for making sure that all of the setup and environment variables are correctly set. The command to run this tool is `runclient`. Say you created a standalone application called TestApp and deployed it with the bean. You can use the runclient command with the following syntax:

```
runclient -client MyAppClient.jar -name TestApp
```

To make sure that all client applications run correctly, make sure you check the Return Client Jar checkbox (shown in Figure A-18) when deploying the bean.

Before explaining this syntax, there are a few more environment settings you need to get right. Firstly, you need to tell the application where to locate the J2EE information — so make sure you include the J2EE JAR file (typically $J2EE_HOME/lib/j2ee.jar) in your ordinary CLASSPATH. You will also need to define a new property that is used by the `runclient` command to locate where your EAR file is. To do this, you need to define a new variable APPCPATH that points to the `.ear` file (this is the file that you specified in the dialog box shown back in Figure A-3).

Back to the `runclient` command syntax. The first option, -client, provides the name of the client JAR file. When you asked the deployment wizard to return the client JAR file, this option specifies the path to that JAR file. The second option, -name, is the name of the application that you provided when you added the application in the deployment tool. This is an optional parameter and really only needed if you have registered more than one client application to be deployed.

When the command runs, you will be presented with a dialog box asking for a name and password. The name and password you need to supply are the settings you configured in the auth.properties file earlier in the chapter. If you didn't change these settings, then the default user name is `guest`, and the default password is `guest123`. Having a (slow) Swing dialog start up each time is annoying so you can use the `-textauth` option for `runclient` to instead use the command line to enter the name and password instead of the dialog box.

If you are running the client application on a different machine from the server, don't forget to set the property `org.omg.CORBA.ORBInitialHost` to the name of the machine running the server as part of the command line too.

Packaging a Web client

If, like many enterprise applications, your front end is a servlet or JSP, then you need to provide a Web server to run them in. If you don't have Apache and Tomcat installed, then the reference environment also provides a minimal Web server environment.

More information on the Apache and Tomcat projects can be found in Appendix C.

Packaging and deploying the Web-client code is the next step in the process of making all your system available to the users. The end result of this next series of steps is a WAR file that contains the starting HTML page and the servlet code that can then be deployed to the server.

As with the EJB, packaging a Web client takes the form of a wizard. To start the packager, select the New Web Component option under the File menu. The first screen you see is shown in Figure A-22, and it asks you to provide the setup information for the file (note that here we've skipped the introductory dialog that you might see if you did not check the "Skip this Screen in the Future" option when shown the introductory screen for EJBs).

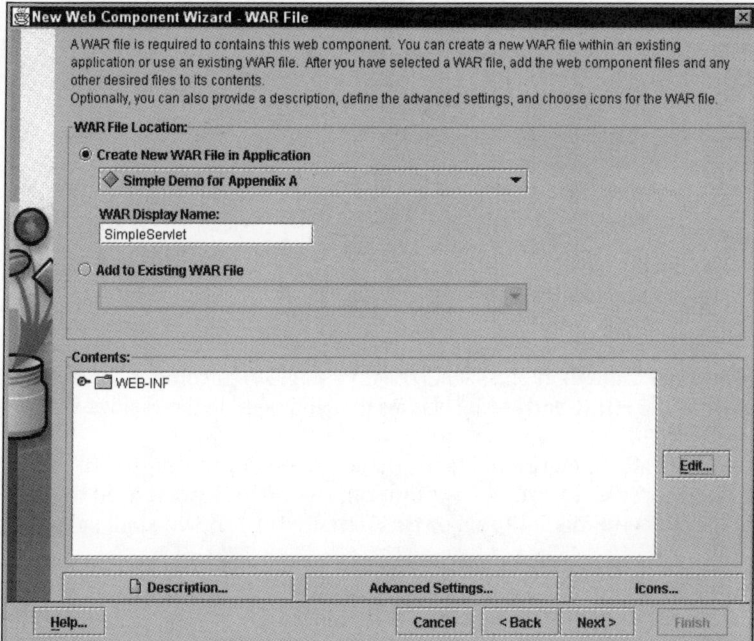

Figure A-22: The first screen of the Web-component–packaging process

Creating a new Web client is very similar to the process used for creating a new EJB. If you compare Figures A-22 and A-5, you will notice the similarity. Note here that your content of the WAR file is empty — it does not use the content of the EJB JAR file. Your content of a WAR file should be the servlet classes, JSPs and any HTML files. As you did with the EJB JAR file, click the Add button, and you will see the dialog presented in Figure A-23. Again, use the top tree to select the files and then click the Add button to place those files into the WAR file. When you are finished, click the OK button.

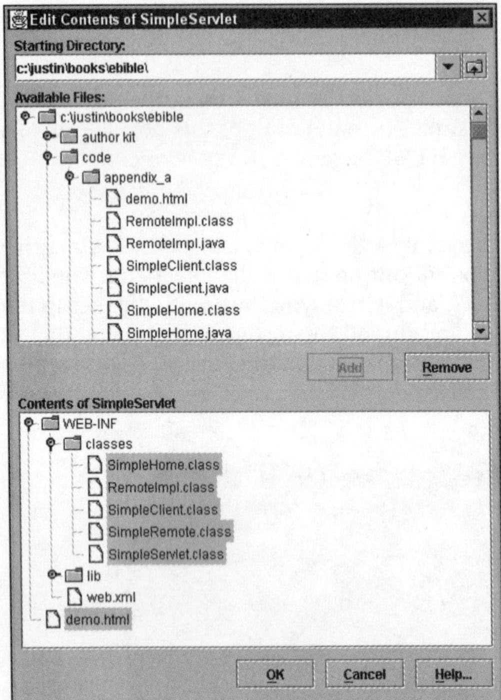

Figure A-23: The dialog allowing you to specify the contents of the WAR archive file

Tip You can include more than one servlet/JSP in a single Web component if you wish. Just select all the HTML and servlet classes that you need in the dialogs all at once.

The next dialog, shown in Figure A-24, allows you to select the type of Web client you are going to be creating. From this point on, the dialogs presented diverge based on the choice you made here. For this demonstration, we shall select a servlet.

Figure A-25 shows the dialog used to select the class that is a servlet and how it is loaded by the servlet engine. Select the class file that extends the class that extends `Servlet` (or `HTTPServlet`) and give it a name.

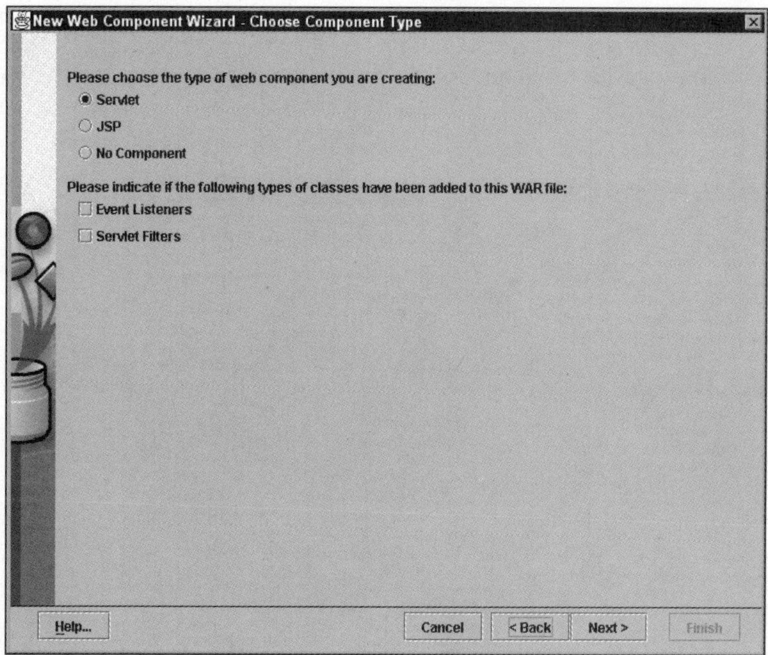

Figure A-24: Selecting the type of Web client

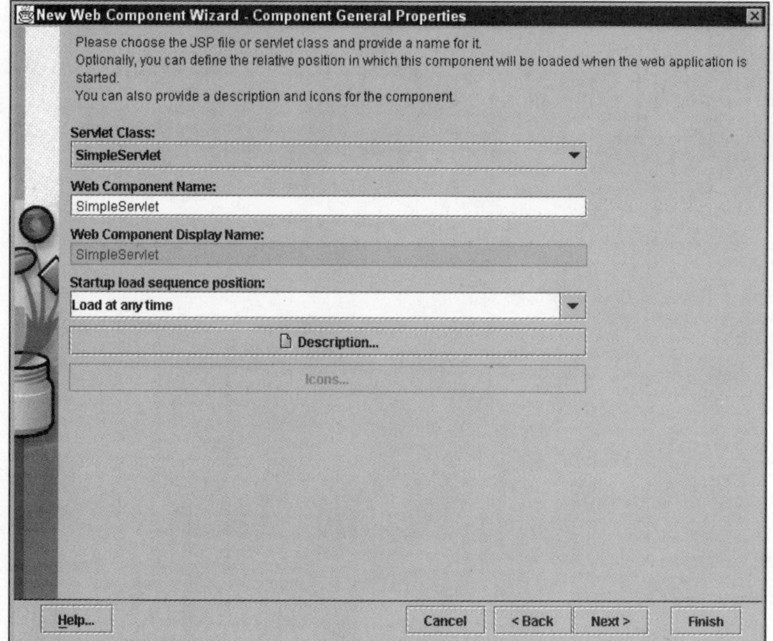

Figure A-25: Selecting the class files for the servlet

Servlets usually require some sort of initialization parameters, so you use the next dialog, shown in Figure A-26. To add a parameter, click the Add button and then fill in the new row in the table. The name of the parameter is on the left and the value is on the right.

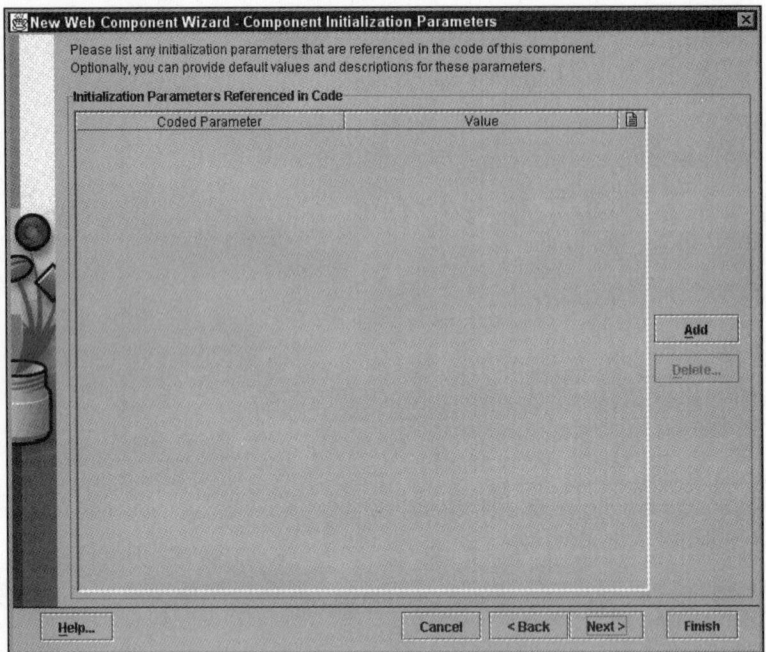

Figure A-26: Editing the initialization parameters for the servlet

For the next dialog, shown in Figure A-27, this provides the ability to describe one or more aliases for the servlet class — the name that will appear in the HTML file's `action` attribute of the `form` tag. Multiple aliases can be provided for a single servlet class, so just click Add and type in the alias name for each one.

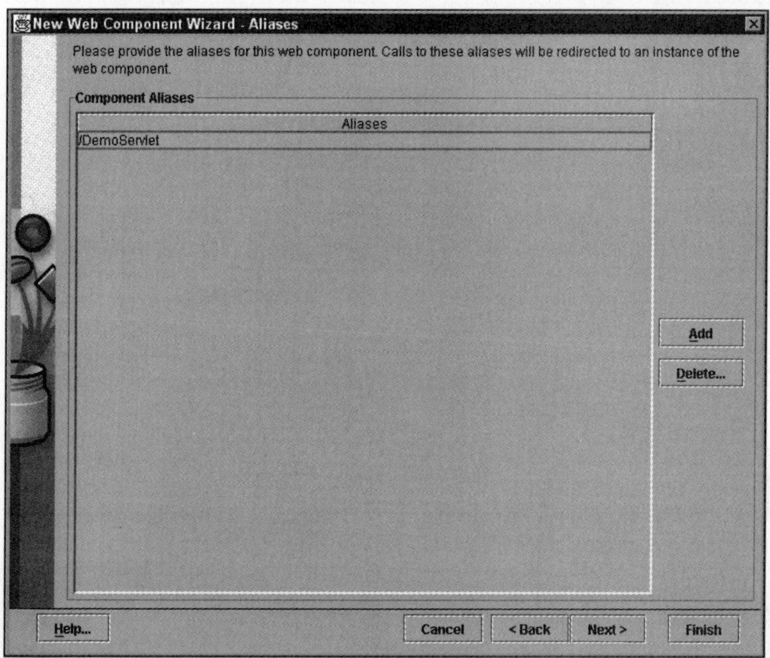

Figure A-27: Dialog in which you configure the aliases for the servlet class

From this point, you enter a series of dialogs that are almost identical to those used in EJB creation. The dialog shown in Figure A-28 is where you specify the roles and names that your servlet wishes to assume or provide for security purposes. This is exactly the same dialog as the one shown in Figure A-13, and so the process of adding new roles is the same for the servlet as for the EJB. For the EJB, where you specified a role name that was required to access a method, the role name here is the identity that the servlet will assume in order to call that EJB method. Naturally, the two should be the same.

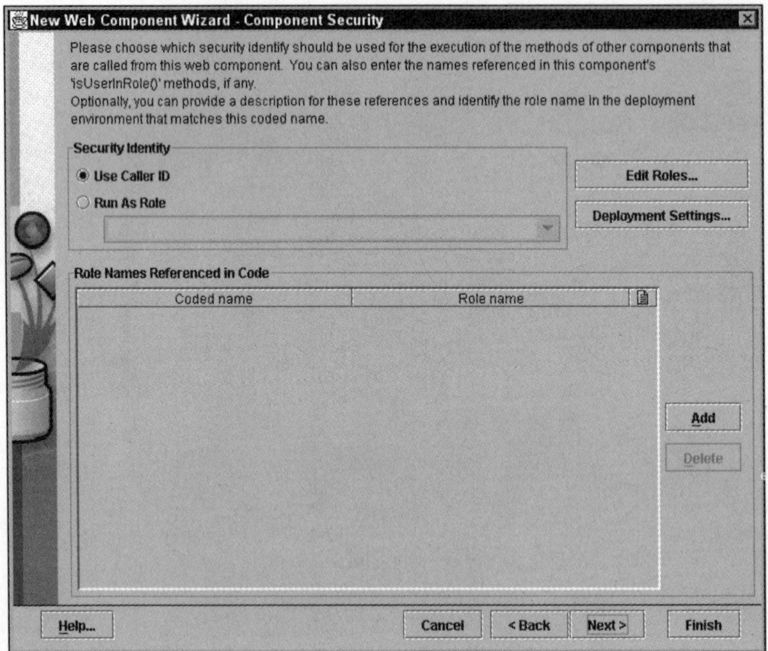

Figure A-28: Dialog in which you specify security-role information for each method in the servlet

In the bean, you had the ability to set environment properties, and so that is what the next dialog, shown in Figure A-29, enables you to do. To add a new property, click the Add button and then select the new row in the table. Move along each cell and specify the property name, the primitive type (`float`, `int`, `boolean`, and so on), and then the value.

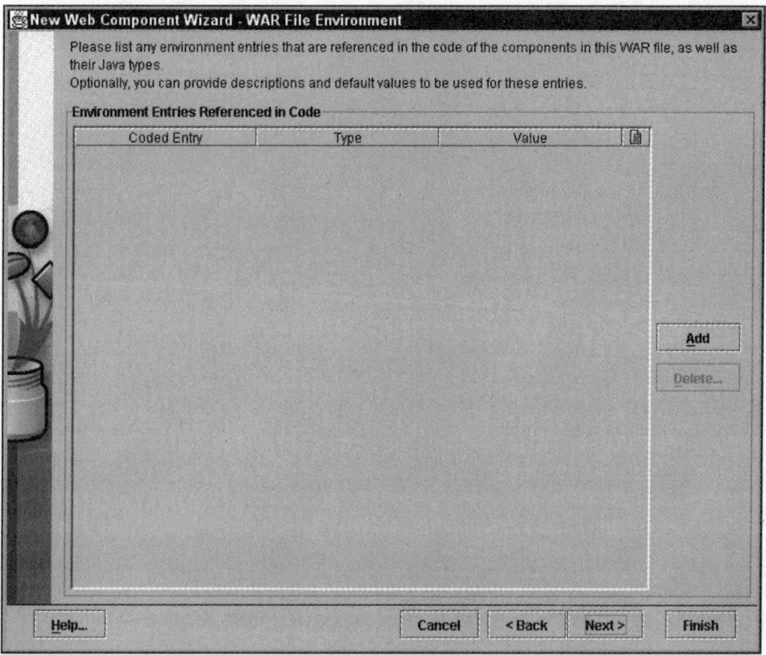

Figure A-29: Dialog in which you specify any environment properties that may be needed

After the environment entries, you need to provide context parameters (Figure A-30). These follow the same process as adding the initialization parameters that you saw previously in Figure A-26. Click Add and then provide a JNDI name and the value.

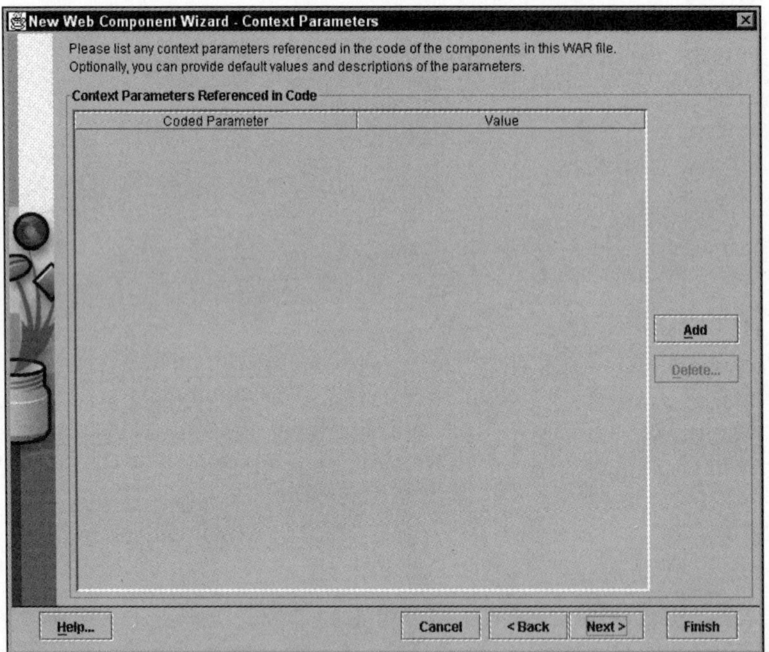

Figure A-30: The dialog where you provide context parameters for the Web client

At last you get to the dialog, shown in Figure A-31, that enables you to specify the beans in use. As with most of the other dialogs, you start by clicking the Add button and selecting the newly created row of the table. Using the same process that you used when defining one EJB referencing another bean, provide the JNDI name, bean type, access type and the home and remote interface classes.

After specifying the beans, you will be presented with another familiar dialog — the dialog to specify resource factories (as shown in Figure A-32). This time, as you are defining a Web client, you may not need to define any information here. If you have written a two-tier application where the servlet or JSP interacts directly with the database using JDBC, then the data source information needs to be defined. If your resource factory needs any environment entries provided, then use the dialog shown in Figure A-33, which follows immediately after the resource factory dialog. Even if you have a three-tier application, another time where you might want to provide a resource factory is if you want to have custom error handlers for JSPs or servlets.

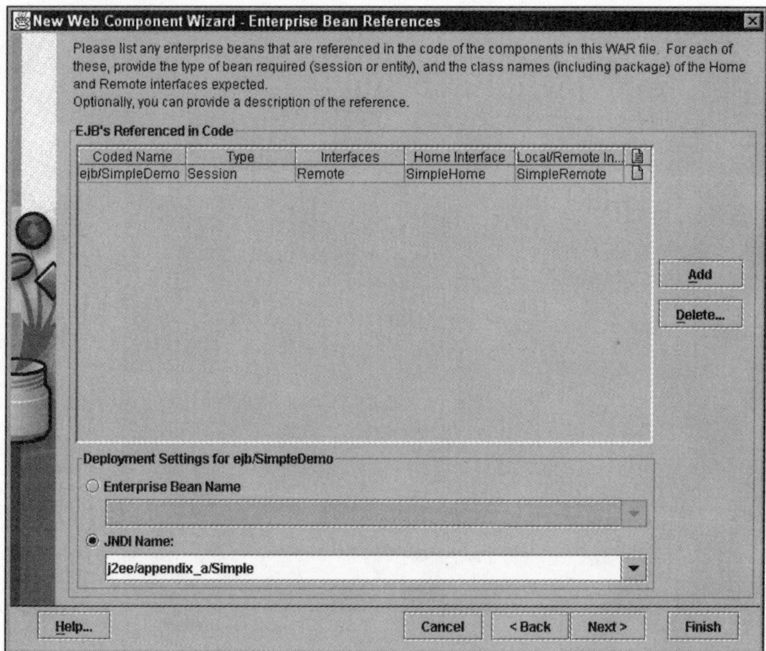

Figure A-31: Specification of the EJBs being referenced in the servlet code

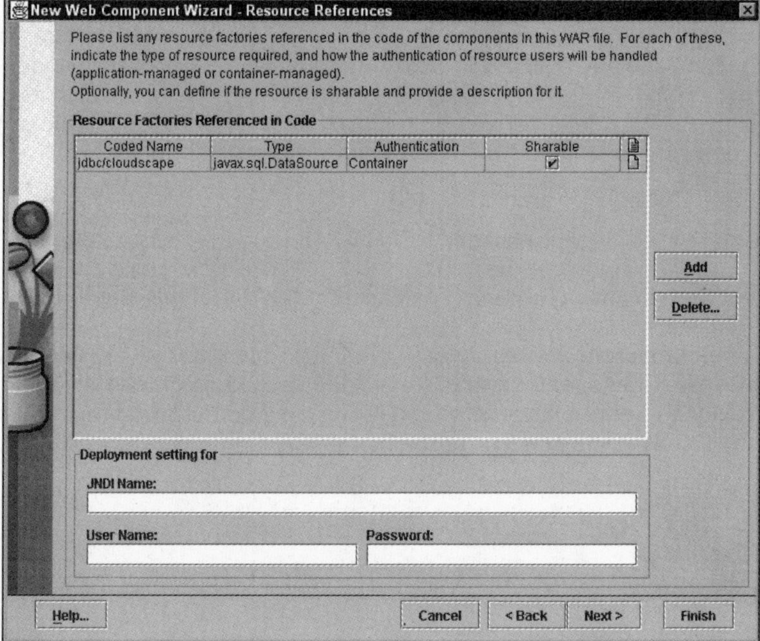

Figure A-32: Resource factory information is provided through this dialog.

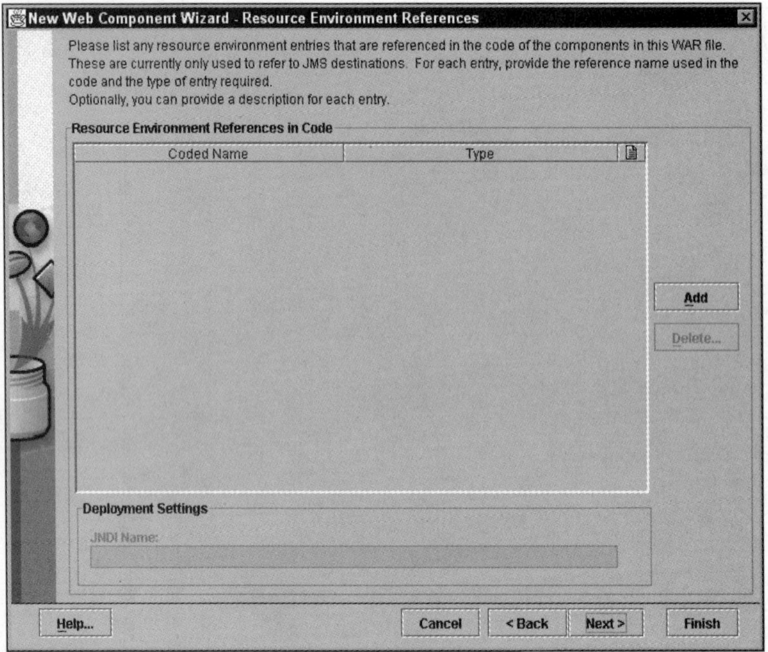

Figure A-33: If you need environment entries for the resource factories, use this dialog.

At last we come to something new! The dialog shown in Figure A-34 is where you provide Web client-specific configuration information. At the top of the window, you provide define any HTML files that are used by the Web server. Welcome files are those which are used by default if you do not provide a file. If you are familiar with standard Web page design, this is the equivalent of the index.html file. So, if a user requested the URL

```
http://www.mycompany.com/DemoServlet/
```

You would get the welcome file you have defined in the top of this window.

In the middle section of the window, you provide the definitions of any tag libraries that your JSPs use. Once again, a name is provided, and a mapping to the real library is provided. Create a new entry by clicking the Add button to the right and then enter the values in the new row of the table.

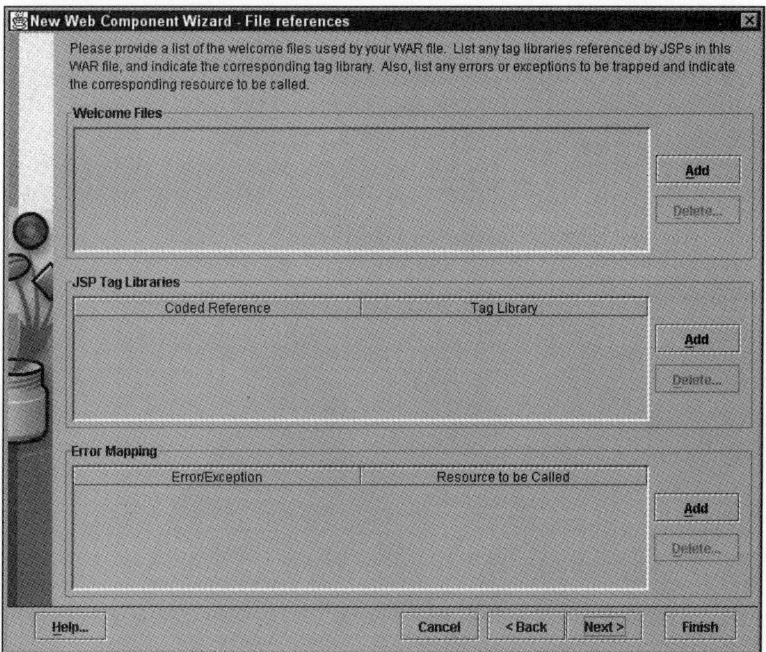

Figure A-34: Configure all of the startup and HTML files used by JSPs and servlets in this dialog.

On the bottom of the window you have the ability to control any error handling that the servlet engine may provide. As you can see, there are two values to be defined — the exception name and then the resource to be called. The name of the exception is the fully qualified class name. For example, you might have a default static HTML page for when the database connection fails; listing the exception here will cause the page to be shown. You can do the same thing for an HTTP error code. For example, if the HTML file is not shown, instead of generating a generic 404 error the servlet engine will automatically throw up an "Oops, we didn't find it"–type page that matches the rest of your site.

Security for most sites is a concern. The next dialog, shown in Figure A-35, allows you to control security on access to the WAR file. Note that this is a different action to defining the roles that you saw back with Figure A-28. Here you are controlling who is allowed to access the Web server and pages on the Web server. A public Web site may always be available, and hence not require security setups, but there may well be times where you want to restrict access to a certain site or part of a site (remember that each part of the site can be a separate JSP or servlet and hence reside in a different WAR file).

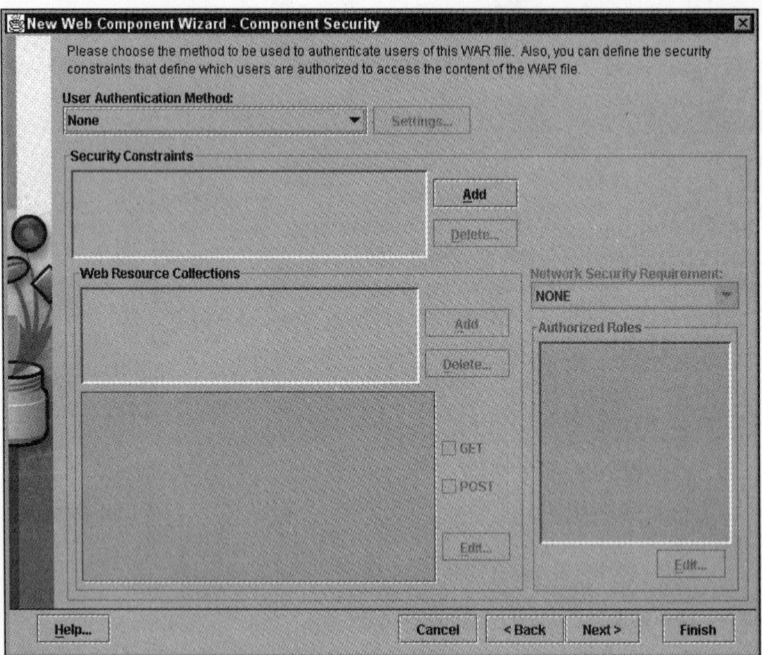

Figure A-35: Controlling who can access the Web site and how to authorize them are the functions of this dialog.

Authentication comes in many flavors. At the top of the dialog is the list of authentication methods, ranging from none to an SSL connection with a given certificate. For the purpose of this example, you need nothing more than basic security or no security. However, for a real Web site you may need to provide more complex information. There are two many options to go into detail with here, so please follow the suggestions provided by the tool.

And that's the end of the process. Your final dialog in the creation of a WAR file is shown in Figure A-36. Like the final dialog of the EJB and application deployment processes, this is a last-chance check over the content of the deployment descriptor information.

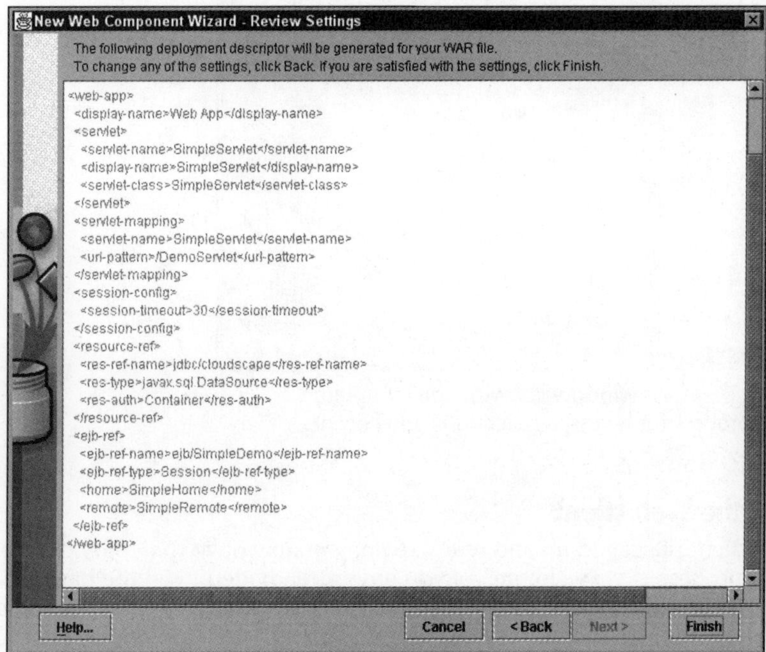

Figure A-36: One last check of the deployment descriptor information before committing it to the project

Clicking Finish here will return you to the main window. As Figure A-37 shows, your tree on the right now includes the new Web component (in addition to a bunch of the beans deployed from the examples developed in Chapter 16!).

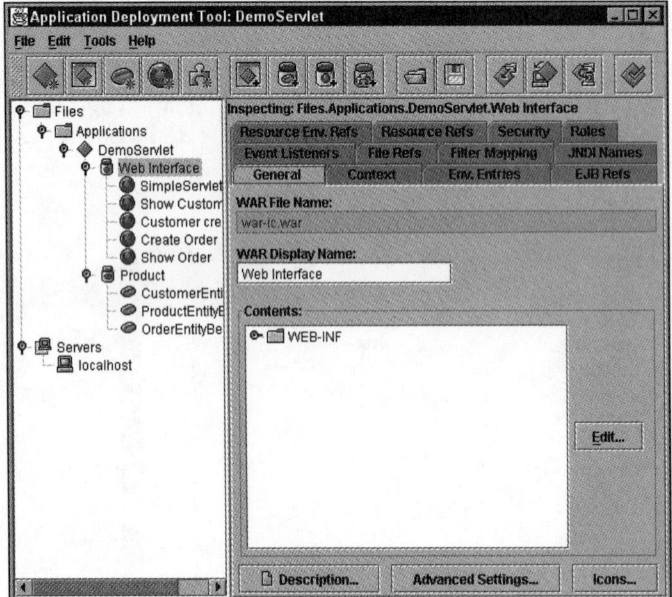

Figure A-37: The main window showing the completed deployment process for beans, applications and servlets

Deploying the Web client

With a new client packaged up and ready to go, you now have to deploy it to the server. This process is very simple. As you have already deployed the basic beans in earlier parts of this chapter, all you need to do to deploy the Web component is save the entire application and then use the Update and Redeploy option in the Tools menu. Everything is taken care of then.

Testing the application

Ah, now to sit back, relax, and play with your application. Fire up a Web browser so you can test the servlet. In that Web browser, type the URL for your introduction page as we did in Figure A-38. Note that the server here is localhost, and that it's running on port 8000 — the default port of the reference implementation. Shown in Figure A-37 is the demo application's introductory HTML page.

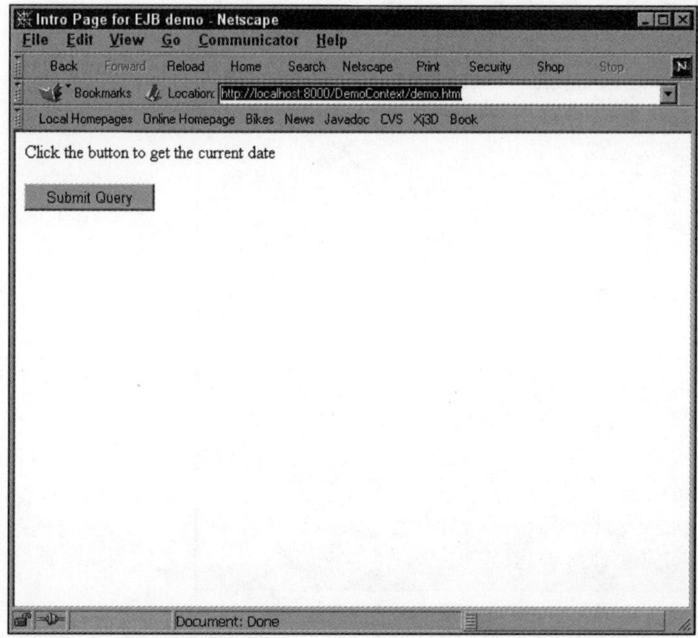

Figure A-38: A Web browser showing the basic HTML page to test the reference server

Testing that everything works is just a case of clicking the Submit button. If everything works correctly, you should see the output shown in Figure A-39. If errors occur, they will be displayed on the output (particularly if you set up exception and error-code redirection in the packaging step). Also, if an error occurs, don't forget to look in the log files!

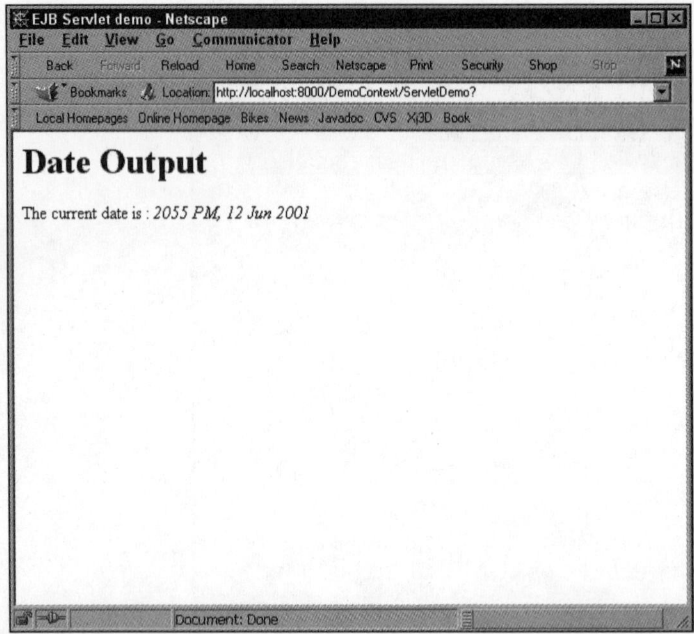

Figure A-39: Finally! A working J2EE application and its output

✦ ✦ ✦

J2EE API Version Requirements

The J2EE specification is built on a number of component technologies, each of which has its own specification, and therefore a separate development cycle outside the J2EE specification. With API names and version numbers being thrown about, it can be hard to keep track of what to expect as a minimum set of capabilities for a J2EE development and deployment environment.

In this appendix, we will outline the minimum requirements of the various APIs for the two most recent versions of J2EE—1.2.1 and 1.3. You can be assured of finding these versions of the component API in any compliant product. Also note that, although these are minimum specifications, each component API has its own life. As the component APIs have their specifications updated, vendors may choose to support later versions as well as those listed here. As always, make sure you read the vendor's documentation to find out what is supported.

J2EE v1.3

Version 1.3 is the latest version of the J2EE specification; it was released in September 2001. At its core is the requirement to provide J2SE v1.3 for basic Java-language capabilities. In addition to this, the specifications supplied in Table B-1 are required to be supported in any compliant product.

Table B-1
J2EE 1.3 required optional package versions

Optional Package	*Version*
JDBC Extensions	2.0
Enterprise JavaBeans	2.0
Servlets	2.3
Java Server Pages	1.2
Java Messaging Service	1.0
Java Transaction API	1.0
JavaMail	1.2
Java Application Framework	1.0
Java API for XML Processing	1.1
J2EE Connector Architecture	1.0
Java Authentication and Authorization Service	1.0

In addition to these basic requirements, J2EE includes a number of extra requirements for each API. For example, it requires the compliant product to support only a section of the JDBC Extensions API, not the full specification.

The full listing of requirements and restrictions for certain APIs can be found in the J2EE Specification v1.3, Section 6, Application Programming Interface. You can download the specification from the homepage of EJB at `http://java.sun.com/j2ee/`.

As far as the core J2SE specification is concerned, vendors are only required to provide 1.3. However, the 1.4 specification is nearing final release, so expect many vendors to support this specification as well. The reference implementation provided by Sun will run with J2SE 1.4 betas, but it does issue a warning (most of the code developed for this book was developed on the J2SE 1.4Beta and J2EE 1.3 reference implementation combination).

J2EE v1.2.1

The most recently superceded J2EE specification is version 1.2.1. At the time of this writing, most vendors had not yet completed an implementation of the 1.3 specification, and so Table B-2 outlines the required specifications for this earlier version of J2EE.

Table B-2
J2EE 1.2.1 required optional package versions

Optional Package	*Version*
JDBC Extensions	2.0
Enterprise JavaBeans	1.1
Servlets	2.2
Java Server Pages	1.1
Java Messaging Service	1.0
Java Transaction API	1.0
JavaMail	1.1
Java Application Framework	1.0
Java Naming and Directory Interface	1.2

J2EE v1.2.1 requires J2SE v1.2 to provide core language support. Although later versions of the J2SE specification can be used, it is unlikely that you will find support for any version later than 1.3. There are too many clashes between J2EE v1.2.1 and the J2SE 1.4 specification for the combination to work correctly. For example, the reference implementation from Sun just will not work with J2SE 1.4 betas and later.

Future Directions

The work of the enterprise API developers is never done. The market forces change, and new technologies are developed to help solve ever more complex business requirements. For example, one of the major directions in which the enterprise application is heading is toward the provision of Web Services. In this book, we tried to cover some of these future directions as well as the core J2EE-specification requirements.

Web services, although not a part of the core J2EE specification, is covered in Chapter 21.

Future additions to J2EE will rely on a lot of external work. Web Services and other systems are becoming heavily reliant on XML and technologies, such as XML-RPC, that use XML as the core. All of these new standards and technologies are being driven by organizations outside of Sun and the Java Community Process. The principal organization involved is the World Wide Web Consortium, more commonly known as W3C (`http://www.w3c.org/`).

In order to find potential future directions for J2EE, you need look no further than the specification itself. Section 11 provides an outline to the areas the spec authors are looking to expand the specification. The areas they think most likely to make it into the next revision are the following:

- *Web Services* — A number of APIs are in use here: JAXM (JSR 67), JAXR (JSR 93), and JAX-RPC (JSR 101).
- *XML Data Binding API (JSR 31)* — An API for building more complex XML document structures that rely on schema languages other than DTDs. It should support W3C Schemas, RELAX, and Schematron as document structure–definition languages.
- *Java Web Start (JWS)* — A means of deploying applications and any associated APIs from a server to a client computer. JWS is already in development for standard Java usage to replace the Java Plugin system. Both JWS and Java Plugin allow you to view applets and applications that have been downloaded from the Internet in a sandbox to stop them overrunning your system. JWS allows them to be run without the need to have a Web browser open — the applet is downloaded and saved to your computer so that you can run it whenever you want. Java Plugin must be embedded in a browser such as Netscape or Internet Explorer.
- *Greater focus on security APIs* — Although JAAS is part of the specification, dealing with user logins is still an application-specific process. Further work is being done on a more usable generic system, Java Authorization service provider Contract for Containers (JACC), that can be used across the entire J2EE environment.
- *SQLj integration* — SQLj started in 1998 as an effort by Oracle to replace its proprietary PL/SQL language for stored procedures. SQLj quickly caught on with many other database developers. It is a very popular means of providing database-independent stored procedures and access routines.

More information on SQLj can be found at `http://www.sqlj.org/`.

In addition to these basic updates, more detailed directions for the future specification are provided. One of the most outstanding issues is the need for an `ORDER BY` capability in the EJB QL language. Expect most of these issues to be addressed in revisions of the individual component specifications.

Information on the current specifications and tutorials can be found at `http://java.sun.com/j2ee/`.

✦ ✦ ✦

J2EE Vendors and Systems

Using the J2EE APIs is not really practical unless you have a system to run everything with. Although Sun Microsystems provides a reference implementation, it is by no means a good system on which to do anything other than prototyping or simple testing.

A variety of commercial vendors are available for you to choose from, and a small but increasing band of open-source projects that will provide parts or all of the J2EE environment. This appendix will outline a number of the more popular options for developing and deploying J2EE applications.

Commercial J2EE Products

Many commercial vendors provide complete J2EE environments for the development and/or deployment of your applications. Sun's licensee page (`http://java.sun.com/j2ee/licensees.html`) provides a complete list of companies that have licensed and been given the official branding. Table C-1 looks at some of the major players and what they provide.

Table C-1
Major commercial J2EE vendors and their products

Vendor	*Product*	*J2EE Version Supported*
BEA Systems	Weblogic Server 6.1	1.3
Borland Corp	JBuilder 5.0 AppServer 5.0	1.3 1.3
IBM	WebSphere Application Server 4.0 VisualAge for Java 3.5	1.2 1.2
IONA Technologies	iPortal Application Server 3.0	1.2
iPlanet	iPlanet Application Server 6.0	1.2
Oracle	Oracle9iAS	1.3
Silverstream	eXtend Workbench 1.0 eXtend Application Server 3.7.3	1.2 1.2
Sybase, Inc	PowerJ 4.0 IDE EAServer 4.0	1.3 1.3

Where we refer to IDE products, the version we list as being supported is the one generated by the wizards. Of course, where you can create text files, any version of J2EE is supported; however, for point-and-click interfaces, only a specific version may be targeted.

Of the commercial players, BEA's Weblogic and IBM's WebSphere products have the most users and are the best known. Many of the vendors come from proprietary-systems backgrounds, such as the BEA Tuxedo product. Similarly, a number of the vendors have their origins in the CORBA world and thus have extremely strong support for that part of the specification. For example, IONA was known for many years as *the* company for CORBA libraries and systems.

If you wish to know more about using BEA's Weblogic Server for J2EE development and deployment, we can recommend to you a sister book of this one – *BEA Weblogic Server Bible* by Joe Zuffoletto et al. (Hungry Minds, 2002).

Open-Source J2EE Projects

In addition to the large variety of commercial products, a couple of open-source projects are working on J2EE implementations. Though generally not as polished as the commercial products, some of these implementations — JBoss in particular — have huge followings among developers.

JBoss

JBoss is the premier open-source implementation of the J2EE specification. Apart from the Apache Project, most open-source developers are working on improving JBoss—particularly since the Enhydra product suite has turned proprietary. The project offers almost all of the capabilities of the commercial vendors, including:

- ✦ Hot-deployment of beans and Web services that enables you to quickly update any part of the functionality.
- ✦ Proxy-based EJBs to allow the system to be distributed across a number of servers.
- ✦ Configurable container whose resource usage you can adjust according to the needs of the application. For example, you can assign particular beans to a particular server or change the priority of the surrounding thread.
- ✦ Small footprint so that it can run on almost any sort of device. The commercial products tend to be oriented toward large server farms, whereas JBoss can run on small, obsolete PC hardware.
- ✦ JMX-based architecture to allow extensibility of the underlying system and enable you to add new/custom features as needed.
- ✦ Full clustering support works with either traditional fail-over computer support (considered "true clustering") or server-farms.

JMX is the Java Management eXtensions and is an API for controlling low-level services of hardware and software. If you are familiar with the SNMP management system, then JMX provides a similar capability. You can read more about JMX at `http://java.sun.com/products/JavaManagement/`.

JBoss is more than just a single project. In some respects it is like a meta-project—it uses many other open source projects to create a complete system. For example, the servlet and JSP engine are open to any system, but the default download uses the Apache Jakarta project or Jetty (which we don't cover here). JBoss uses JMX to manage each of the components so that you can replace any of the default implementation code with your own choice—even a proprietary application or library.

The license for the underlying application is the GNU LGPL. This means that you can package and sell it with your own application-specific code, and this seems to be quite a popular choice. Of course, if you are doing in-house projects, JBoss is a cheap and useful alternative to Sun's reference implementation. In particular, the ability to have to operate the server clusters means that you can perform useful large-scale testing and deployment.

At the time of this writing, JBoss is at v2.0, which supports the J2EE 1.2 specification. This means that you can't use the RMI-IIOP interoperability, but this is being worked on. As a form of compensation, JBoss 2.0 supports SOAP. Work has already begun on v3.0, which will support the full J2EE 1.3 specification. Already, the EJB 2.0 specification work is well advanced with 2.4.1 supporting some parts of the EJB specification.

Further information on JBoss can be found at `http://www.jboss.org/`.

Enhydra

Where JBoss sets out to be the best J2EE server, Enhydra heads in the opposite direction — its purpose is to cover as many different specifications as possible. The Enhydra core application server is all open source, and a commercial, packaged version is available from Lutris. One of this project's primary goals is to collect all the existing open-source projects and combine them into an application-server project. So in the code you will find a diverse range of licenses — from BSD to Apache to the GNU LGPL.

If you need the Swiss-army knife of application servers, Enhydra is the way to go. For example, miniature versions of the server can run on PDA-type devices, called EnhydraME, as well as WAP/WML front ends. Also, instead of providing their own deployment tools, plugins are available for most of the popular IDEs.

Further information on Enhydra can be found at `http://www.enhydra.org/`.

Apache Projects

Special mention must go to the projects run by the Apache Foundation (`http://www.apache.org`). Originally starting with the Open Source Apache Webserverproject, the group has taken on a huge number of projects, all of which deal with Web technologies. Of these, the Java projects are the most interesting to us.

XML projects

The Apache Foundation maintains two major Java-based XML projects — Xerces and Crimson. Both of these projects are XML parsers. So why have two projects doing the same thing? Well, Sun did a lot of early work with XML, providing a simple SAX-based parser called Project X. As Sun's focus moved to the broader XML requirements of Java and the JAXP API, the Project X code was donated to the Apache Foundation to become known as Crimson. Xerces, meanwhile, was started as another internal project, prior to the Sun donation, for some of the other projects to use. Despite the head-start that Crimson had, Xerces is now the main development project for parsing XML.

Crimson

Crimson is the original Sun parser for XML files, and it is still in use in today's J2SE and J2EE implementations if you download them from Sun as part of JAXP. All the code can be found in the package `org.apache.crimson` and the packaged below it.

Crimson is a fairly basic parser as far as XML support goes. It will generate SAX2 events and handle namespaces, but not much else. For example, it does not support any of the schema languages available for validation.

Further information on Crimson can be found at `http://xml.apache.org/crimson/`.

Xerces

Xerces is the more modern of the two XML parsers available from the Apache group. The aim of this parser is to be as lightweight and as fast as possible. Xerces is the heart of all XML projects in the Apache Java world. For example, it is the Xerces parser that reads and writes configuration files for the servlet engine and Jakarta.

Xerces, as one of the more advanced XML processors, can handle W3C Schemas as well as DTDs for document validation. Xerces is also compliant with the JAXP specification, so you can substitute it for Sun's standard parser if you need the greater capabilities of schema support.

Further information on Xerces can be found at `http://xml.apache.org/xerces2-j/`.

Xalan

Xalan is a processor of XSLT stylesheets; it supports the W3C XSLT and XPath specifications. If you need separate XPath processing without the XSLT, it can give you that, too. Xalan uses the Bean Scripting Framework (BSF) to implement Java or script extensions, and it features multiple document-output extensions. Some work is being done on data-binding extensions for SQL/JDBC.

Java is the main language, but an alpha form in C++ is also available. Further information can be found at `http://xml.apache.org/xalan-j/`.

Web services

Web services are gaining a lot of momentum in the business-software industry. Standards are still relatively young, but gaining wide acceptance, as we indicated in Chapter 21, "Implementing Web Services." As Web services fundamentally lie over the basic Web structure of HTTP and Web servers like Apache, the Apache group has tackled this task of providing Web services as well.

SOAP

The Apache SOAP project was kick-started by IBM's donation of its SOAP4J project. This implementation, now almost fully compliant, is available and supports SOAP v1.1. The code requires most of the J2EE standard APIs, such as a servlet engine and JAXP, as well as a few other parts of the J2EE specification, such as JavaMail. The latest stable release is v2.2 but 2.3 should offer complete compliance.

Further information on Apache SOAP can be found at `http://xml.apache.org/soap/`.

Slide

Slide is the Apache Foundation's project for maintaining site content such as Web pages and other documentation. The core of the Slide project is a WebDAV library. WebDAV is another of the Web services, originally started by Microsoft to allow client applications to update Web-site content. Like that of many of the other projects in this appendix, the core implementation of Slide is written in Java, so if you need to write an application that updates Web content with the WebDAV protocol, this is the project for you.

Further information on Slide can be found at `http://jakarta.apache.org/slide/`.

Jakarta

Jakarta is the name of the umbrella project of the Apache Foundation, designed to collect all of the group's Java-related projects into a single, consistent development. This project was started by, and is maintained with, a lot of help and financing from Sun Microsystems and a number of other commercial vendors. Within Jakarta are a number of sub-projects, of which Tomcat (which we'll describe in the next section) is probably the best known. Each of these projects may stand alone or be combined with others into a larger system. Although part of the Apache group, Jakarta is intended to provide functionality without needing the Apache Web Server.

Tomcat

Arguably the best known of the Jakarta projects, Tomcat is designed to provide a fully conformant servlet engine. (It is Sun's official reference implementation of the servlet and JSP specifications.) The engine may run as a standalone server, or, as is often the case, as a module within the Apache Web Server. It is one of the projects currently being actively developed by Sun engineers and others.

The current version of Tomcat is 4.0, which supports the Servlet 2.3 and JSP 1.2 specifications. Fast and robust, this code is excellent for use in both commercial and prototyping environments. As this code is fully spec-conformant, you can do many things with Tomcat that other engines won't enable you to do. Our development experience in migrating code developed for Tomcat and then moved to other servlet engines demonstrated to us many of the deficiencies in the others (for example the ability to dynamically re-configure servlets without needing to restart the server). If you need to use all the corners of the Servlet and JSP specifications, we recommend Tomcat extremely highly.

Further information on the Tomcat project can be found at `http://jakarta.apache.org/tomcat/`.

Log4j

Log4j is the best-known logging API. It is in use in many different projects outside of the Apache group. It is so successful that Sun decided to replicate it in J2SE 1.4, and in the process threw out many of the lessons it had learnt in developing it. There has been a lot of community anger about this. Most developers who have used Log4j in the past are refusing to support or use the Sun-sanctioned API.

Log4j is a hierarchical, flexible system for providing logging capabilities in any application. Part of this system allows you to control filtering (messages from source classes or error levels) to different logs, formatting of log messages, and many different output devices. One crucial benefit of Log4j is that you can use it within enterprise-bean implementations in order to log everything that is going on (remember that EJBs are prohibited from reading and writing files directly).

Log4j might seem like a rather familiar name. The code has gone through a number of owners, including life as a former IBM research project on Alphaworks (`http://www.alphaworks.ibm.com/`), and is now maintained by the Apache group.

Further information on Log4j can be found at `http://jakarta.apache.org/log4j/`.

Ant

In any project of reasonable size, maintaining and building the codebase will just not be possible with nothing but the plain old `javac` command line. Hundreds of class files and tens of packages make keeping track of the whole thing quite a job. And then you need to generate the Javadoc. . . .

If you are not using an IDE, the UNIX world has provided many tools for you to use. Typically these tools rely on the makefiles, a fact that can be both good and bad. The Ant project was started to provide an alternative to make both for platform independence and to clean up many of the other problems that developers had with make.

Ant is based on a combination of Java and XML. The files that describe the build information are written in XML, and the processing, such as the compilation of Java source code or the generation of javadocs, takes place in Java. The Ant system is very Java-oriented, and does not appear to work well with other languages, such as C and C++ (a very important requirement if you are working with CORBA projects). However, the future versions of Ant, are looking to address these issues.

Further information on Ant can be found at `http://jakarta.apache.org/ant/`.

Alexandria

In enterprise projects (and really anything other than a trivial bit of hacking), maintaining a good repository of all the versions of your code is absolutely essential. The software that maintains this information is typically known as version-control systems or configuration-management systems, according to the complexity of the information they store. Many different programs fulfill this need, but the most popular in the open-source world is called CVS.

CVS as a basic system is fairly crude, although it does its job extremely well. Most users access it through a command-line interface; however, this interface doesn't give you all the features that managers like to have — such as lots of fuzzy, feel-good pictures and reports. A number of projects have been running to provide these features as a layer over CVS. Of these, Bugzilla from the Mozilla project and Alexandria are the best known.

More information on the Bugzilla project can be found at `http://www.mozilla.org/projects/bugzilla/`.

Alexandria is the CVS system from the Apache Foundation and is written in Java. Its main purpose is to combine the documentation from many projects into a single source for all documentation. For example, although you might have developed a set of beans for a specific project, your company might have 10 different projects. Each of these projects might share a set of common components: beans, custom user-interface components, and so on. Alexandria can enable you to jump from project to project all within a single interface and Web site.

Further information on Alexandria can be found at `http://jakarta.apache.org/alexandria/`.

Glossary

ASP 1. (Active Server Pages): A Microsoft-specific technology for generating dynamic Web pages. Usually associated with Microsoft's IIS Web server, but becoming available for other servers such as Apache. 2. (Application Service Provider): A business model in which a single company provides the same service (probably customized) to a number of different companies. For example, a single e-commerce system for all local bookstores.

B2B (business to business): Usually, a type of application or business model for electronic commerce; two companies exchanging information for mutual benefit.

B2C (business to commerce): Usually, a type of application or business model in which a business offers services to unknown consumers (such as the public at large).

BMP (Bean Managed Persistence): A type of EJB persistence where an entity bean decides to do all the data management, such as opening connections to the database, reading and writing the raw data, itself.

CMP (Container Managed Persistence): A type of EJB persistence where an entity bean decides to let the EJB container do all the management of the internal data structures.

COM (Component Object Model): A Microsoft-specific object model that allows applications on the same machine to work together and share common elements, as when the Internet Explorer HTML-rendering engine is embedded inside MS Word applications.

CORBA (Common Object Request Broker Architecture): A language- and platform-neutral standard for sharing distributed objects.

DCOM (Distributed Component Object Model): The distributed form of COM that allows parts working on different machines to work together.

DOM (Document Object Model): A standard language-independent API for representing the content and structure of an XML document after it has been parsed.

DTD (Document Type Definition): A language that is part of the XML specification and that defines a structure that an XML document is to conform to. DTDs were also a part of the older SGML specification and are gradually being replaced by the various schema languages.

EJB (Enterprise Java Beans): A Java-specific technology for defining and distributing shared objects among a number of machines.

IDL (Interface Definition Language): A language defined as part of the CORBA specification. Allows the definition of objects to be shared and then run through a pre-processor to generate a programming language–specific skeleton.

IETF (Internet Engineering Task Force): The standards body responsible for the technical implementation of the Internet. Everything from Ethernet cables to networking protocols is handled through this purely volunteer organization. Standards are produced in documents called RFCs.

IMAP (Internet Message Access Protocol): A protocol and system for providing remote access to e-mail. The particular feature of interest is the ability to leave the mail on the server yet have it sorted and stored for each user as though it were being kept on the user's local computer.

IVR (Interactive Voice Response (System)): A dedicated piece of programmable specialty hardware designed to interact with phones. Provides a menu-driven system to enable users to phone up and request information without needing to speak with a human assistant. Responsible for that well-known phrase: "Press 1 to get a list of products. Press 2 to speak to an operator. . . . "

JAXB (Java API for XML Binding): The Java APIs for mapping between XML files and Java classes.

JAXP (Java API for XML Processing): The core Java-specific API for loading and managing the various XML APIs available to a Java programmer. Later versions move beyond the simple parsing systems to include complex transformation capabilities for changing one XML structure to another.

JDBC (Java DataBase Connectivity): A Java-specific API to allow vendor-independent querying of relational databases such as Oracle and SQL Server The JDBC spec was originally derived from Microsoft's ODBC APIs. Uses SQL as its primary query language.

JMS (Java Messaging Service): A Java store-and-forward API allowing you to send a selection of requests and possibly get answers back at some later time. Typically used with big-iron systems like mainframes.

JNDI (Java Naming and Directory Interface): A Java-specific abstracted interface to many different technologies. Anything that may look like a directory service, or that provides the ability to look up information like in a telephone directory style, is represented by this API. The most commonly used underlying data store that JNDI accesses is LDAP, but JNDI can also access normal file systems, DNS services, and JINI objects.

JNI (Java Native Interface): The standardized API that enables the mixing of Java code and native code like C and C++ into a consistent environment. This allows you to incorporate platform-specific implementations of code or integrate existing third-party libraries that you don't have Java bindings for.

JRE (Java Runtime Environment): The standalone Java application that allows end users to run a Java application but not to develop any new code.

JTA (Java Transaction API): A Java-specific API for harnessing the capabilities of the X/Open Group's transaction-management system. This system allows multiple vendors and applications to operate together in an enterprise setting to provide the ability to manage a transaction.

JTAPI (Java Telephony API): A Java-specific API for accessing telephony devices such as modems and fax machines. Can be used to create both server and client applications. Useful if your enterprise application needs to send faxed confirmation messages, for example.

JSP (Java Server Pages): A Java-specific technology for generating dynamic Web pages. Usually combined with other Java-specific technologies such as EJBs.

JWS (Java WebStart): A technology from Sun that allows Java applets and applications to be downloaded and run in a standalone sandbox, without the need to be connected to the internet. The application code is downloaded and stored on the local machine before being run.

LDAP (Lightweight Directory Access Protocol): A protocol that originated from the ISO X.500 series of protocols and has now become a standard in its own right. Typically used to store information in hierarchical structures that could be thought of as large address books. Forms the core of Novell's NDS and Microsoft's ActiveDirectory services.

MIME (Multipurpose Internet Mail Extensions): More widely known as MIME types, such as `text/plain` or `image/jpeg`. MIME allows you to put different content types into a standard mail message, and can now be used in the Web-browser/-server area as well.

***n*-tier:** A type of enterprise-application architecture that has more than three layers of computers and functionality. These systems may contain many different layers of code and hardware that connect many different organizations.

ORB (Object Request Broker): Technology that is part of the CORBA standard and that acts as the server offering objects to remote client applications.

POP3 (Post Office Protocol version 3): A simple protocol for fetching email from a server on which it has been stored.

RDBMS (Relational DataBase Management System): A style of database that stores common data in a series of tables and links the data with relationship information. The most widely used form of database.

RFC (Request For Comment): A standards document generated by the IETF to define a particular element of the Internet. Originally a real request, once published as a formal RFC, it has become a working standard that all parties adhere to. There is nothing to require strict adherence to RFCs, except the weight of opinion of the people running the Internet.

RMI (Remote Method Invocation): A Java-specific technology for offering remote objects to client applications. The original technology that now forms the heart of other Java-specific technologies such as JINI and EJB.

RPC (Remote Procedure Call): There are many different types of "RPC" standards, but the basic framework is a system that allows one application to call a set of functionality on another machine. In its earliest incarnation (early 1980's) it provided the first real chance to start building distributed applications. In the most recent incarnation, the XML-RPC specification uses XML as the message format to make the method calls.

Schema: A means of describing the structure that an XML document should conform to. Similar in many respects to a DTD but able to be more stringent in what it can enforce. Many different types of schema languages exist — W3C Schema, RELAX, and TREX are the three most popular choices currently.

SGML (Standard Generalized Markup Language): A text-based structured meta-language for describing structured documentation. Originally built for the U.S. defense market in the late 1970s and early 1980s, it has been re-birthed through a reduced subset called XML.

SMS (Short Messaging Service): A technology that allows you to send text messages up of to 120 characters between mobile phones. Related to the GSM digital mobile-phone technology of which it is a sub-protocol.

SMTP (Simple Mail Transport Protocol): The routing protocol used to deliver mail around the Internet. All mail servers on the Internet must be capable of supporting this standard.

SQL (Structured Query Language): The standardized language for making queries of and updates to relational databases such as Oracle and DB/2. The language has gone through a number of versions — the most commonly implemented is SQL92 and the most recent is SQL99.

Unicode: An ISO standard that defines how to define non-English characters as computer readable and renderable information. A widely used subset of this specification is UTF8 and UTF16 and can be found in XML documents.

W3C (World Wide Web Consortium): The industry group responsible for defining standards for Web documentation. Responsible for HTML and XML standards. Works with the IETF on subjects of common interest, such as HTTP.

WAP (Wireless Access Protocol): A low-level communications protocol specifically designed for wireless devices, such as mobile phones and pagers, that have low bandwidth capabilities.

Web Service: A form of remote procedure calling that uses standard web technology such as HTTP and XML as the backbone technology. Differs from RMI, EJB and CORBA in that web services uses commodity protocols to get the job done rather than custom systems.

WML (Wireless Markup Language): A cut-down form of HTML that is specifically designed for the low-bandwidth communications and small display areas of such devices as mobile phones.

Xlink: A W3C specification for allowing one XML document to reference a part of another XML document. The equivalent in the HTML world is the `<A>` tag to load another document (`<A HREF=...>`) or describe an internal point (`<A NAME=...>`).

XML (eXtensible Markup Language). A text-driven meta-language for defining structured information. Derived from SGML, it is finding use in a lot of Web-based technologies.

Xpointer: A W3C specification that enables you to describe a particular location in a source document.

XSL (XML Stylesheet Language): A means of describing how to render particular tags from XML in a particular viewer. For example, one stylesheet might define how to render an XML document to a HTML Web page, and a different stylesheet might define how to render it to a WML page.

✦ ✦ ✦

Index

Symbols & Numbers

A

B

C

D

E

G

H

Continued

Continued

P

Q

R

T

Continued

U

V